CIMA

STUDY TEXT

STRATEGIC

PAPER P3

PERFORMANCE STRATEGY

Our text is designed to help you study **effectively** and **efficiently**.

In this edition we:

- **Highlight** the **most important elements** in the syllabus and the **key skills** you will need

- **Signpost** how each chapter links to the syllabus and the learning outcomes

- **Provide** lots of **exam alerts** explaining how what you're learning may be tested

- **Include examples** and **questions** to help you apply what you've learnt

- **Emphasise key points** in **section summaries**

- **Test your knowledge** of what you've studied in **quick quizzes**

- **Examine your understanding** in our **exam question bank**

- **Reference all the important topics** in the **full index**

FOR EXAMS IN NOVEMBER 2010 AND MAY 2011

LEARNING MEDIA

First edition 2009
Second edition June 2010

ISBN 9780 7517 8465 7
(Previous ISBN 9780 7517 7508 2)

e-ISBN 9780 7517 8648 4

British Library Cataloguing-in-Publication Data
A catalogue record for this book
is available from the British Library

Published by

BPP Learning Media Ltd
BPP House, Aldine Place
London W12 8AA

www.bpp.com/learningmedia

Printed in the United Kingdom

Your learning materials, published by BPP
Learning Media Ltd, are printed on paper sourced
from sustainable, managed forests.

We are grateful to the Chartered Institute of
Management Accountants for permission to
reproduce past examination questions. The
suggested solutions in the exam answer bank have
been prepared by BPP Learning Media Ltd.

Contents

		Page
Introduction		
How our Study Text can help you pass		iv
Features in our Study Text		v
Streamlined studying		vi
Syllabus and learning outcomes		vii
Old and new syllabuses		xiv
Studying P3		xv
The exam paper		xix
Part A Risks		
1	Introduction to risk	3
2	Risk management	23
Part B Management and internal control systems		
3	Corporate governance	57
4	Ethics	97
5	Control systems I	119
6	Control systems II	157
7	Management accounting control systems	205
Part C Management of financial risk		
8	Financial risk management	233
9	Interest rate risk	263
10	International risks	291
11	Transaction risk I	309
12	Transaction risk II	337
Part D Risk and control in information systems		
13	Information strategy and systems	361
14	Information operations	399
Part E Audit and review		
15	Internal audit	435
16	Internal audit review and reporting	455
Appendix: Mathematical tables and exam formulae		487
Exam question bank		493
Exam answer bank		513
Specimen exam paper		581
Specimen exam paper: answers		591
Index		607
Review form and free prize draw		

How our Study Text can help you pass

Streamlined studying	• We show you the best ways to study efficiently
	• Our Text has been designed to ensure you can easily and quickly navigate through it
	• The different features in our Text emphasise important knowledge and techniques
Exam expertise	• **Studying P3** on page vii introduces the key themes of the syllabus and summarises how to pass
	• We highlight throughout our Text how topics may be tested and what you'll have to do in the exam
	• We help you see the complete picture of the syllabus, so that you can answer questions that range across the whole syllabus
	• Our Text covers the syllabus content – no more, no less
Regular review	• We frequently summarise the key knowledge you need
	• We test what you've learnt by providing questions and quizzes throughout our Text

Our other products

BPP Learning Media also offers these products for the P3 exam:

Practice and Revision Kit	Providing lots more question practice and helpful guidance on how to pass the exam
Passcards	Summarising what you should know in visual, easy to remember, form
Success CDs	Covering the vital elements of the P3 syllabus in less than 90 minutes and also containing exam hints to help you fine tune your strategy
i-Pass	Providing computer-based testing in a variety of formats, ideal for self-assessment
Interactive Passcards	Allowing you to learn actively with a clear visual format summarising what you must know
Strategic case study kit	Providing question practice with specially written questions, based on the preseen issued by CIMA

You can purchase these products by visiting http://www.bpp.com/mybpp

CIMA Distance Learning

BPP's distance learning packages provide flexibility and convenience, allowing you to study effectively, at a pace that suits you, where and when you choose. There are four great distance learning packages available.

Online classroom	Bringing the classroom experience to you via the web and offering you great flexibility, with the quality for which BPP classroom courses are renowned
Basics Plus	Combining the paper-based and e-learning approaches of our Basics and Basics Online distance learning packages
Basics	Consisting of high quality BPP Learning Media study materials and access to BPP Professional Education subject experts
Basics Online	Including the best online learning and practice

You can find out more about these packages by visiting http://www.bpp.com/courses/examination-courses/accounting--finance/cima/study-options/distance-learning.aspx

Features in our Study Text

 Section Introductions explain how the section fits into the chapter

 Key Terms are the core vocabulary you need to learn

KEY TERM

 Key Points are points that you have to know, ideas or calculations that will be the foundations of your answers

KEY POINT

 Exam Alerts show you how subjects are likely to be tested

 Exam Skills are the key skills you will need to demonstrate in the exam, linked to question requirements

 Formulae To Learn are formulae you must remember in the exam

LEARN

 Exam Formulae are formulae you will be given in the exam

EXAM

 Examples show how theory is put into practice

 Questions give you the practice you need to test your understanding of what you've learnt

 Case Studies link what you've learnt with the real-world business environment

CASE STUDY

 Links show how the syllabus overlaps with other parts of the qualification, including Knowledge Brought Forward that you need to remember from previous exams

 Website References link to material that will enhance your understanding of what you're studying

 Further Reading will give you a wider perspective on the subjects you're covering

 Section Summaries allow you to review each section

Streamlined studying

What you should do	In order to
Read the Chapter and Section Introductions	See why topics need to be studied and map your way through the chapter
Go quickly through the explanations	Gain the depth of knowledge and understanding that you'll need
Highlight the Key Points, Key Terms and Formulae To Learn	Make sure you know the basics that you can't do without in the exam
Focus on the Exam Skills and Exam Alerts	Know how you'll be tested and what you'll have to do
Work through the Examples and Case Studies	See how what you've learnt applies in practice
Prepare Answers to the Questions	See if you can apply what you've learnt in practice
Revisit the Section Summaries in the Chapter Roundup	Remind you of, and reinforce, what you've learnt
Answer the Quick Quiz	Find out if there are any gaps in your knowledge
Answer the Question(s) in the Exam Question Bank	Practise what you've learnt in depth

Should I take notes?

Brief notes may help you remember what you're learning. You should use the notes format that's most helpful to you (lists, diagrams, mindmaps).

Further help

BPP Learning Media's *Learning to Learn Accountancy* provides lots more helpful guidance on studying. It is designed to be used both at the outset of your CIMA studies and throughout the process of learning accountancy. It can help you **focus your studies on the subject and exam**, enabling you to **acquire knowledge, practise and revise efficiently and effectively**.

Syllabus and learning outcomes

Paper P3 Performance Strategy

The syllabus comprises:

Topic and Study Weighting

A	Management Control Systems	10%
B	Risk and Internal Control	25%
C	Review and Audit of Control Systems	15%
D	Management of Financial Risk	35%
E	Risk and Control in Information Systems	15%

Learning Outcomes

Lead		Component		Syllabus content
A	**Management control systems**			
1	Evaluate control systems for organisational activities and resources	(a)	Evaluate appropriate control systems for the management of an organisation	(i) The ways in which systems are used to achieve control within the framework of an organisation (eg contracts of employment, policies and procedures, discipline and reward, reporting structures, performance appraisal and feedback)
		(b)	Evaluate the appropriateness of an organisation's management accounting control systems	(ii) The application of control systems and related theory to the design of management accounting control systems and information systems in general (ie control system components, primary and secondary feedback, positive and negative feedback, open- and closed-loop control)
		(c)	Evaluate the control of activities and resources within an organisation	
		(d)	Recommend ways in which identified weaknesses or problems associated with control systems can be avoided or solved	(iii) Structure and operation of management accounting control systems (eg identification of appropriate responsibility and control centres within the organisation, performance target setting, avoiding unintended behavioural consequences of using management accounting controls)
				(iv) Variation in control needs and systems dependent on organisational structure (eg extent of centralisation versus divisionalisation, management through strategic business units)

				(v)	Assessing how lean the management accounting system is (eg extent of the need for detailed costing, overhead allocation and budgeting, identification of non-value adding activities in the accounting function)
				(vi)	Cost of quality applied to the management accounting function and 'getting things right first time'

B	Risk and internal control				
1	Evaluate types of risk facing a organisation	(a)	Discuss ways of identifying, measuring and assessing the types of risk facing an organisation, including the organisation's ability to bear such risks	(i)	Types and sources of risk for business organisations: financial, commodity price, business (eg fraud, employee malfeasance, litigation, contractual inadequacy, loss of product reputation), technological, external (eg economic and political), and corporate reputation (eg from environmental and social performance or health and safety) risks
		(b)	Evaluate risks facing an organisation		
				(ii)	Fraud related to sources of finance (eg advance fee fraud and pyramid schemes)
				(iii)	Risks associated with international operations (eg from cultural variations and litigation risk, to loss of goods in transit and enhanced credit risk). (Note no specific real country will be tested)
				(iv)	Quantification of risk exposures (impact if an adverse event occurs) and their expected values, taking account of likelihood
				(v)	Information required to report fully on risk exposures
				(vi)	Risk map representation of risk exposures as a basis of reporting and analysing risks
2	Evaluate risk management strategies and internal controls	(a)	Discuss the purposes and importance of internal control and risk management for an organisation	(i)	Purposes and importance of internal control and risk management for an organisation
				(ii)	Issues to be addressed in defining management's risk policy
		(b)	Evaluate risk management strategies	(iii)	The principle of diversifying risk (Note. Numerical questions will not be set)

		(c)	Evaluate the essential features of internal control systems for identifying, assessing and managing risks	(iv)	Minimising the risk of fraud (eg fraud policy statements, effective recruitment policies and good internal controls, such as approval procedures and separation of functions, especially over procurement and cash)
		(d)	Evaluate the costs and benefits of a particular internal control system	(v)	The risk manager role (including as part of a set of roles) as distinct from that of the internal auditor
				(vi)	Purposes of internal control (eg safeguarding of shareholders' investment and company assets, facilitation of operational effectiveness and efficiency, contribution to the reliability of reporting)
				(vii)	Operational features of internal control systems (eg embedding in company's operations, responsiveness to evolving risks, timely reporting to management)
				(viii)	The pervasive nature of internal control and the need for employee training
				(ix)	Costs and benefits of maintaining the internal control system
3	Evaluate governance and ethical issues facing an organisation	(a)	Discuss the principles of good corporate governance, particularly as regards the need for internal controls	(i)	The principles of good corporate governance based on those for listed companies (the Combined Code) (eg separation of Chairman and CEO roles, appointment of non-executive directors, transparency of directors' remuneration policy, relations with shareholders, the audit committee). Other examples of recommended good practice may include the King Report on Corporate Governance for South Africa, Sarbanes-Oxley Act in the USA, the Smith and Higgs Reports in the UK, etc)
		(b)	Evaluate ethical issues as a source of risk to the organisation and control mechanisms for their detection and resolution		
				(ii)	Recommendations for internal control (eg the Turnbull Report)
				(iii)	Ethical issues identified in the CIMA Code of Ethics for Professional Accountants, mechanisms for detection in practice and supporting compliance

C	Review and audit of control systems				
1	Discuss the importance of management review of controls	(a)	Discuss the importance of management review of controls	(i)	The process of review (eg regular reporting to management on the effectiveness of internal controls over significant risks) and audit of internal controls
				(ii)	Major tools available to assist with a review and audit process (eg audit planning, documenting systems, internal control questionnaires, sampling and testing)
2	Evaluate the process and purposes of audit in the context of internal control systems	(a)	Evaluate the process of internal audit and its relationship to other forms of audit	(i)	Role of the internal auditor and relationship of the internal audit to the external audit
		(b)	Produce a plan for the audit of various organisational activities including management, accounting and information systems	(ii)	Relationship of internal audit to other forms of audit (eg value-for-money audit, management audit, social and environmental audit)
		(c)	Recommend action to avoid or solve problems associated with the audit of activities and systems	(iii)	Operation of internal audit, the assessment of audit risk and the process of analytical review including different types of benchmarking, their use and limitations
		(d)	Recommend action to improve the efficiency, effectiveness and control of activities	(iv)	Particular relevance of the fundamental principles in CIMA's Ethical Guidelines to the conduct of an impartial and effective review of internal controls
		(e)	Discuss the relationship between internal and external audit work	(v)	Detection and investigation of fraud
				(vi)	The nature of the external audit and its process, including the implications of internal audit findings for external audit procedures
3	Discuss corporate governance and ethical issues facing an organisation	(a)	Discuss the principles of good corporate governance for listed companies, for conducting reviews of internal controls and reporting on compliance	(i)	The principles of good corporate governance for listed companies, for the review of the internal control system and reporting on compliance
		(b)	Discuss the importance of exercising ethical principles in conducting and reporting on internal reviews	(ii)	Application of CIMA's Ethical Guidelines on the resolution of ethical conflicts in the context of discoveries made in the course of internal review, especially Section 210

D	Management of financial risk				
1	Evaluate financial risks facing an organisation	(a)	Evaluate financial risks facing an organisation	(i)	Sources of financial risk, including those associated with international operations (eg hedging of foreign investment value) and trading (eg purchase prices and sales values)
				(ii)	Transaction, translation, economic and political risk
				(iii)	Quantification of risk exposures, their sensitivities to changes in external conditions and their expected values
2	Evaluate alternative risk management tools	(a)	Evaluate appropriate methods for managing financial risks	(i)	Minimising political risk (eg gaining government funding, joint ventures, obtaining local finance)
		(b)	Evaluate the effects of alternative methods of risk management	(ii)	Operation and features of the more common instruments for managing interest rate risk: swaps, forward rate agreements, futures and options. (Note. Numerical questions will not be set involving FRAs, futures or options. See the note below relating to the Black Scholes model)
		(c)	Discuss exchange rate theory and the impact of differential inflation rates on forecast exchange rates		
		(d)	Recommend risk management strategies and discuss their accounting implications	(iii)	Operation and features of the more common instruments for managing currency risk: swaps, forward contracts, money market hedges, futures and options. (Note. The Black Scholes option pricing model will not be tested numerically, however, an understanding of the variables which will influence the value of an option should be appreciated)
				(iv)	Simple graphs depicting cap, collar and floor interest rate options
				(v)	Theory and forecasting of exchange rates (eg interest rate parity, purchasing power parity and the Fisher effect)
				(vi)	Principles of valuation of financial instruments for management and financial reporting purposes (IAS 39), and controls to ensure that the appropriate accounting method is applied to a given instrument
				(vii)	Quantification and disclosure of the sensitivity of financial instrument values to changes in external conditions
				(viii)	Internal hedging techniques (eg netting and matching)

E	Risk and control in information systems				
1	Evaluate the benefits and risks associated with information-related systems	(a)	Advise managers on the development of IM, IS and IT strategies that support management and internal control requirements	(i)	The importance and characteristics of information for organisations and the use of cost-benefit analysis to assess its value
		(b)	Evaluate IS/IT systems appropriate to an organisation's need for operational and control information	(ii)	The purpose and content of IM, IS and IT strategies, and their role in performance management and internal control
		(c)	Evaluate benefits and risks in the structuring and organisation of the IS/IT function and its integration with the rest of the business	(iii)	Data collection and IT systems that deliver information to different levels in the organisation (eg transaction processing, decision support and executive information systems)
		(d)	Recommend improvements to the control of information systems	(iv)	The potential ways of organising the IT function (eg the use of steering committees, support centres for advice and help desk facilities, end user participation)
		(e)	Evaluate specific problems and opportunities associated with the audit and control of systems which use information technology	(v)	The arguments for and against outsourcing
				(vi)	Methods for securing systems and data back-up in case of systems failure and/or data loss
				(vii)	Minimising the risk of computer-based fraud (eg access restriction, password protection, access logging and automatic generation of audit trail)
				(viii)	Risks in IS/IT systems: erroneous input, unauthorised usage, imported virus infection, unlicensed use of software, theft, corruption of software etc.
				(ix)	Risks and benefits of Internet and Intranet use by an organisation
				(x)	The criteria for selecting outsourcing/Facilities Management partners and for managing ongoing relationships, service level agreements, discontinuation/ change of supplier, hand-over considerations
				(xi)	Controls which can be designed into an information system, particularly one using information technology (eg security, integrity and contingency controls)

(xii) Control and audit of systems development and implementation

(xiii) Techniques available to assist audit in a computerised environment (computer-assisted audit techniques eg audit interrogation software)

Old and new syllabuses

The syllabus for the P3 *Performance Strategy* paper is very similar to the syllabus for the old syllabus paper P3 *Risk and Control Strategy*. The five main areas are the same for both the old and new syllabus exams, and there have only been minor changes in study weightings. Some topics that have been added into the new syllabus were examined under the old syllabus, and their inclusion in the new syllabus just clarifies their status.

The following topics have been added into the syllabus, with references to the chapter in which they are covered:

- Information requirements to report fully on risk exposures (2)

- Risk map representation (2)

- Role of the risk manager (2)

- Mechanisms for detecting ethical issues in practice and supporting compliance (4)

- Sensitivities of financial risk exposures to changes in external conditions (8)

- Quantification and disclosure of the sensitivity of financial instrument values to changes in external conditions (8)

- Nature of external audit and its process, including the implications of internal audit findings for external audit procedures (15)

Studying P3

1 What's P3 about

1.1 Risks

P3 covers risks, and how businesses and not-for-profit entities **respond** to risks through controls. In Chapter 1 we introduce the main risks organisations face and emphasise that these are wide-ranging:

- Covering not just financial risks
- But also other kinds of **strategic**, **business and operational risks**.

In Chapter 2 we take an overview of how organisations analyse and manage risks. We'll see that the appetite that managers and shareholders have for taking risks influences the risks taken, and also how the risks link in with the returns from business activities. However all organisations should have procedures in place for analysing risks, and need to have a coherent framework of **enterprise risk management**.

1.2 Corporate governance and ethics

Corporate governance and ethics are bound up together. In Chapter 3 we examine what boards need to do function effectively and promote accountability to shareholders. Good governance needs to be founded on ethical principles, and boards must take the lead in promoting ethical behaviour. In Chapter 4 therefore we look at CIMA's ethical requirements and how businesses should manage ethics.

1.3 Control systems

The next three chapters focus on the control systems that boards oversee. Having discussed the basics of control systems in the first part of Chapter 5, we look at the aspects of control that influence the **inputs** that businesses use, in particular business structures, culture and human resources. Chapter 6 concentrates on internal controls over business **processes**. Chapter 7 looks at the role of management accounting control systems, such as costing and budgeting, in measuring business **outputs**.

1.4 Financial and international risks

Financial and international risks are a major part of the syllabus because they have a **major impact on strategic decisions** and because of the **potential for large losses** due to adverse foreign exchange or interest rate movements. The financing risks stressed by the examiner are those relating to foreign currency, financing strategies and overseas investment. Chapters 8 to 12 therefore discuss evaluation of these risks and the best methods for managing them. Most of the calculations you encounter in P3 will relate to risks in these areas, although the examiner has stated that calculations won't carry many marks.

1.5 Information technology risks

In Chapters 13 and 14 we focus on **information systems**. As well as looking at risks and controls the syllabus also requires you to consider how **information strategies** and the **IT function** support control requirements. This links in with coverage earlier in the Text about the information managers need to exercise control effectively, and the significance of organisational structure.

1.6 Internal audit

The syllabus emphasises that **review** of control systems is vital if they are to operate successfully. The **internal audit function** is therefore one of the most important parts of many internal control systems. Internal audit's work can provide much insight into the way the organisation is managing its risks. Chapters 15 and 16 deal with the role of internal audit, the main types of audit, audit procedures, and the main stages of the audit process, ending up in Chapter 16 with audit committee and board review of internal controls.

2 What's required

2.1 Risks and controls

The most common question type on this paper will be:

(a)   Identify/Analyse the risks
(b)   Recommend controls that will manage them effectively

Some questions will ask you to evaluate existing controls and recommend improvements (Question 2 on the Specimen exam paper is a good example of this type of question).

You should read the question requirements carefully as they will determine the risks you discuss. A question may ask you to identify significant risks, risks that are controllable or risks that arise from marketing strategy.

The risks you discuss in your answer must follow from the **content** of the scenario. You may have to use appropriate numerical techniques to quantify risk levels.

The controls you recommend must not only be **relevant** to counter the risks, but be **appropriate** for the organisation. It's no use for example suggesting that internal audit carries out a lot of work when the organisation is not large enough to be able to maintain a large internal audit function.

Your recommendations must also be **specific**. It will never be enough just to say improve information technology access controls. Instead you should specify what **new controls** should be **introduced** and which **existing controls** should be **enhanced** (for example compelling staff to change passwords regularly).

3 How to pass

3.1 Study the whole syllabus

You need to be comfortable with **all areas of the syllabus**, as questions, particularly compulsory Question 1, will often span a number of syllabus areas. Question 1 on the Specimen exam paper is a good illustration of the breadth questions can cover. **Wider reading** will help you understand the main risks businesses face.

3.2 Lots of question practice

You can **develop application skills** by attempting questions in the Exam Question Bank and later on questions in the BPP Practice and Revision Kit.

The kit contains a lot of questions that were set under the 2005 syllabus, and the examiner has stated that these questions are still indicative of P3's broad approach.

3.3 Analysing questions

For P3 it's particularly important to **consider the question requirements carefully** to:

- Make sure you understand exactly what the question is asking

- See whether each question part has to be answered in the context of the scenario or is more general.

When reading through the scenario you need to think widely about the risks the organisation faces and the controls it is operating and needs to operate.

3.4 Answering questions

Well-judged, clear recommendations grounded in the scenario will always score well as markers for this paper have a wide remit to reward good answers. You need to be **selective**. The examiner has stated that lists of points memorised from texts and reproduced without any thought won't score well. Similarly scenario details should only be used if they support the points you're making.

The examiner has also commented that marks will be given for well-structured, clear and concise scripts that demonstrate a clear and logical thought process.

3.5 Exam technique

The following points of exam technique are particularly relevant to this paper.

- Answers with **answer plans** attached tend to score better and don't repeat the same material in different question parts.

- There may be up to 5 marks allocated in certain questions for **style, coherence and presentation of a report**; you should aim to achieve all of these.

- **Time pressure** seems to be less of an issue if Question 1 is done first.

- You should consider in advance how you are going to use the **20 minute reading time**. Our advice is firstly to choose which Section B questions you attempt and then analyse the Section A question.

- **Read the question carefully**; a question that may appear on a hasty read to be about the risk management cycle may not require you to state the main stages of the cycle, but discuss how the model is used or the principles behind it.

- Leave time to **check your answers** at the end to identify and correct any silly mistakes.

4 Brought forward knowledge

The examiner may test knowledge or techniques you've learnt at lower levels. As P3 is part of the Performance pillar, the content of Papers P1 and P2 will be significant.

However material from other papers is relevant as well, including

- Risks and risk management
- Information systems
- Human resources
- Organisational structure
- Corporate governance
- Ethics

The examiner has explained that P3 draws on aspects of earlier papers that develop a sense of commercial awareness.

Your knowledge of IASs 32 and 39 and IFRS 7 from Paper F2 (formerly Paper P8) will help you when you come to study financial risks.

Remember however that brought forward knowledge will only be useful if it is **linked to risk analysis and control responses**. Hence for example you would not be asked to prepare a budget, but you may have to discuss how effective budgets are as control mechanisms. The numerical techniques you've studied previously that are most likely to be tested in P3 are those that are used to quantify risks or predict outcomes, for example standard deviations or expected values.

5 Links with other Strategic level papers

CIMA expects you to make links between the various papers and not see the three subjects in isolation.

- **Enterprise strategy decisions** will **impact** upon the financial objectives, sources of finance chosen, the investment decisions, the risks the organisation faces and the controls necessary to counter those risks.

- **Financial and performance strategies** must therefore fulfil the same criteria as enterprise strategy; for example they should be **acceptable, suitable and feasible.**

- At the same time **enterprise strategy** will be **constrained** by the finance available and the level of risks the organisation is prepared to bear.

- **Financial strategy decisions** will **impact** upon the **risks** the organisation bears and perhaps impose limitations on the controls the organisation can implement. Financial strategy will also be determined by the **financial risks** (some sources of finance may be thought too risky, the benefits of investment decisions too uncertain, risk may impact upon investment appraisal calculations).

- **Performance measurement** techniques such as ratio analysis may be useful in any paper. The **effectiveness of management accounting systems**, particularly the information provided and how useful they are as control mechanisms, could impact upon any of the papers.

The exam paper

Format of the paper

		Number of marks
Section A:	A maximum of 4 compulsory questions, totalling 50 marks, all relating to a pre-seen study and further new un-seen case material	50
Section B:	2 out of 3 questions, 25 marks each. These questions will tend to be scenario-based and will typically have two to three requirements with the possibility that each requirement will be sub-divided.	50
		100

Time allowed: 3 hours, plus 20 minutes reading time

The examiner has stated that some questions will be drawn from more than one area.

CIMA guidance

CIMA has stated that credit will be given for focusing on the right principles and making practical evaluations and recommendations in a variety of different business scenarios, including manufacturing, retailing and financial services. Some questions may require discussion of concepts, but most of the marks will be awarded for applying concepts to a scenario.

A likely weakness of answers is excessive focus on details. Plausible alternative answers could be given to many questions, so model answers should not be regarded as all-inclusive. Valid, relevant points will always be rewarded.

Breadth of question coverage

Questions in *both* sections of the paper may cover more than one syllabus area.

Knowledge from other syllabuses

Candidates should also use their knowledge from other Strategic level papers. One aim of this paper is to prepare candidates for the TOPCIMA exam.

May 2010

Section A

1   International investment risks; management information systems; foreign exchange risk management; ethics systems

Section B

2   Directors' remuneration; risk management strategy

3   Forward contracts; economic risks

4   IT risks; fraud

Specimen exam paper

Section A

1   Information strategy; financial risks; environmental audit; internal audit; reporting risk

Section B

2   Control systems; risk mapping

3   Product launch risks; interest rate swaps

4   Internal control systems and control environment; internal control and risk management procedures; analytical procedures

RISKS

Part A

INTRODUCTION TO RISK

 This chapter introduces themes that will be developed not only in Part A, but throughout the rest of this text. We start by considering the significant risks organisations face, and we shall look at these in more detail later in this text.

You need to understand straightaway that the risks organisations face aren't just those that relate to the financial statements – organisational risks cover the whole range of activities. A common complaint of examiners is that students often don't consider a sufficiently wide range of risks. One important distinctions is between **strategic risks** (integral, long-term risks that the board is likely to be most concerned with) and **operational risks** (largely the concern of line management).

Chapters 1 and 2 are vital for your exam. The essentials to remember are not just a list of the major risks, but also:

- What determines organisations' risk responses

- The fact that risk responses will only be effective if set within a coherent risk management framework

- The stages of assessing risks

- How risks can be managed

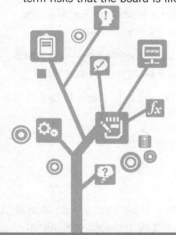

topic list	learning outcomes	syllabus references	ability required
1 The nature of risks	B1(b)	B1(i)	evaluation
2 Strategic and operational risks	B1(b)	B1(i), (ii), (iii)	evaluation
3 Types of risk faced by organisations	B1(b)	B1(i), (ii), (iii)	evaluation

1 The nature of risks

Introduction

In this section we introduce some basic definitions of risk, explain the difference between risk and uncertainty and emphasise the important links between risk and return.

KEY TERM

RISK is a condition in which there exists a quantifiable dispersion in the possible outcomes from any activity. Risk can be classified in a number of ways.   *(CIMA Official Terminology)*

In other words, risk is the possibility that actual results will turn out differently from what is expected.

Question 1.1	Risks

Learning outcome B1(b)

What sort of risks might an organisation face?

1.1 Categories of risk

KEY TERMS

FUNDAMENTAL RISKS are those that affect society in general, or broad groups of people, and are beyond the control of any one individual. For example there is the risk of atmospheric pollution which can affect the health of a whole community but which may be quite beyond the power of an individual within it to control.

PARTICULAR RISKS are risks over which an individual may have some measure of control. For example there is a risk attaching to smoking and we can control that risk by refraining from smoking.

SPECULATIVE RISKS are those from which either good (upside risks) or harm (downside risks) may result. A business venture, for example, presents a speculative risk because either a profit or loss can result.

PURE RISKS are those whose only possible outcome is harmful. The risk of damage to property by fire is a pure risk because no gain can result from it.

There are various types of risk that exist in business and in life generally.

1.2 Negative risks

A simple view of risk would see it in negative terms, as **downside risk**. Risk management would involve minimising the chances that adverse events will happen. However, it may **not be possible to eliminate negative risks** without undermining the whole basis on which the business operates or without incurring excessive costs and insurance premiums. Therefore there is likely to be a level of residual or remaining risk which it is simply not worth eliminating.

1.3 Benefits of risk management

However there are some benefits to be derived from the management of risk, possibly at the expense of profits such as:

- **Predictability** of **cash flows**
- **Well-run systems**
- **Limitation of the impact** of potentially **bankrupting events**
- **Increased confidence** of shareholders and other investors

1.4 Risk and uncertainty

A complication in dealing with risks is the level of uncertainty involved. Ultimately risk assessment may be able to tell you the **possible outcomes**, and the **chances** that each outcome will occur. All that is unknown is the actual outcome. Uncertainty however means that you do not know the possible outcomes and/or the chances of each outcome occurring. It may arise from a lack of information about input/output relationships or the environment within which the business operates.

1.5 Risk and return

As you may remember from your Financial Strategy studies, businesses may be willing to **tolerate a higher level of risk** provided they receive **a higher level of return**. Indeed a willingness to take certain risks in order to seize new opportunities may be **essential for business success.** Shareholders who themselves ultimately bear the risk of a business may welcome some risk-taking.

Under this view a business should:

- **Reduce risk** where possible and necessary, but not eliminate all risks
- **Maximise the returns** that are possible given the levels of risk

1.6 Risk taking and reduction

Boards therefore should not just focus on managing negative risks, they should also seek to **limit uncertainty** and to **manage speculative risks and opportunities** in order to **maximise positive outcomes and hence shareholder value**.

Exam alert

The examiner has stressed the importance of decision-makers being seen to manage upside and downside risks.

Boards should consider the factors that determine **shareholder valuations** of the company, the **risks** associated with these and the ways in which shareholders would like the **risks to be managed**.

Most risks must be managed to some extent, and some should be sought to be eliminated as being outside the scope of the remit of the management of a business. For example, a business in a high-tech industry, such as computing, which evolves rapidly within ever-changing markets and technologies, has to accept high risks in its research and development activities; but should it also be speculating on interest and exchange rates within its treasury activities?

Risk management under this view is an integral part of strategy, and involves analysing what the key value drivers are in the organisation's activities, and the risks tied up with those value drivers. In its Risk Management Standard, the Institute of Risk Management linked in key value drivers with major risk categories.

CASE STUDY

Since risk and return are linked, one consequence of focusing on achieving or maintaining high profit levels may mean that the organisation bears a large amount of risk. The decision to bear these risk levels may not be conscious, and may go well beyond what is considered desirable by shareholders and other stakeholders.

This is illustrated by the experience of the National Bank of Australia, which announced it had lost hundreds of millions of pounds on foreign exchange trading, resulting in share price instability and the resignation of both the Chairman and Chief Executive. In the end the ultimate loss of A$360 million was 110 times its official foreign exchange trading cap of A$ 3.25 million.

The bank had become increasingly reliant on speculation and high-risk investment activity to maintain profitability. Traders had breached trading limits on 800 occasions, and at one stage had unhedged foreign exchange exposures of more than \$A2 billion. These breaches were reported internally, as were unusual patterns in trading (very large daily gains) but senior managers took no action. For 3 years, the currency options team had been the most profitable team in Australia, and had been rewarded by bonuses greater than their annual salaries. Eventually however the team made large losses, and entered false transactions to hide their deficits.

The stock market however was unimpressed by the efforts of the bank to make members of the team scapegoats, and market pressure forced changes at the top of the organisation, a general restructuring and a more prudent attitude to risk. Observers, however, questioned whether this change in attitude would survive the economic pressures that the bank was under in the long term.

Section summary

Risks can be classified according to **whom** they affect, whether their outcomes will be **beneficial** or **adverse**, and the **area** of an organisation's **affairs affected**.

2 Strategic and operational risks

Introduction

There are many different types of risks faced by commercial organisations, particularly those with international activities.

CASE STUDY

You only need to glance at the business pages of a newspaper on any day to find out why risk management is a key issue in today's business world. For example, look at some of the main stories in the UK Daily Telegraph on a single day.

(a)   A former head of regulatory risk of the bank HBOS alleged in written evidence to a UK select Treasury committee that he had informed the board of his concerns that management were taking excessive risks, but was subsequently sacked. (We shall return to this story in later chapters.)

(b)   JJB Sports was planning to call in administrators for its fashion business after it had failed to find a buyer. JJB was in talks with banks to see it through the retail slump.

(c)   Figures produced by BAA showed a sharp drop in the tonnes of air cargo transported. The air freight industry was in competition with the marine ship industry, and the cost of sending cargo by ship had fallen to almost zero.

(d)   Scotland's ski industry was under threat from global warming leading to a decline in the number of snowy days.

(e)   The UK Office of Fair Trading (OFT) launched a scam awareness month, as in the UK an estimated three million people a year are taken in by scams.

Exam alert

Remember in your exam questions will cover a range of risks, not just financial risks.

2.1 Strategic risks

KEY TERM

STRATEGIC RISK is the potential volatility of profits caused by the nature and type of the business operations.

The most significant risks are focused on the **strategy** the organisation adopts including concentration of resources, mergers and acquisitions and exit strategies. These will have major impacts on **costs, prices, products and sales,** also the **sources of finance** used. Organisations also need to guard against the risks that **business processes and operations** are **not aligned** to **strategic goals**, or are disrupted by events that are not generated by business activities.

2.1.1 Business and non-business strategic risks

A useful classification of strategic risks is the division between business and non-business risks.

KEY TERMS

BUSINESS RISKS are threats to profits, the magnitude of which depends on the decisions the organisation makes about the products and services it supplies. (You will encounter other ways of defining business risks.)

NON-BUSINESS RISKS are threats to profits that are not influenced by the products or services the organisation supplies.

(a)   Examples of **business risks** include:

    (i)   Threats of long-term **product** obsolescence

    (ii)   **Changes in technology** changing the production process

    (iii)   Long-term **macroeconomic changes**, for example a worsening of a country's exchange rate

(b)   Examples of **non-business risks** include:

    (i)   Risks arising from the long-term **sources of finance** chosen

    (ii)   Risks from a collapse in trade because of an **adverse event**, an accident or natural disaster

CASE STUDY

The global credit crunch

A credit crunch is a crisis caused by banks being too nervous to lend money to customers or to each other. When they do lend, they will charge higher rates of interest to cover their risk.

One of the first obvious high-profile casualties of the recent global credit crisis was New Century Financial – the second largest sub-prime lender in the United States – which filed for Chapter 11 bankruptcy in early 2007. By August 2007, credit turmoil had hit financial markets across the world.

In September 2007 in the UK, Northern Rock applied to the Bank of England for emergency funding after struggling to raise cash. This led to Northern Rock savers rushing to empty their accounts as shares in the bank plummeted. In February 2008 the UK Chancellor of the Exchequer, Alistair Darling, announced that Northern Rock was to be nationalised.

Years of lax lending on the part of the financial institutions inflated a huge debt bubble as people borrowed cheap money and ploughed it into property. Lenders were quite free with their funds – particularly in the US where billions of dollars of 'Ninja' mortgages (no income, no job or assets) were sold to people with weak credit ratings (sub-prime borrowers). The idea was that if these sub-prime borrowers had trouble with repayments, rising house prices would allow them to remortgage their property. This was a good idea when US Central Bank interest rates were low – but such a situation could not last. In June 2004, following an interest rate low of 1%, rates in the US started to climb and house prices fell in response. Borrowers began to default on mortgage payments and the seeds of a global financial crisis were sown.

The global crisis stemmed from the way in which **debt was sold onto investors**. The US banking sector packaged sub-prime home loans into mortgage-backed securities known as **collateralised debt obligations** (CDOs). These were sold onto hedge funds and investment banks that saw them as a good way of generating high returns. However when borrowers started to default on their loans, the value of these investments plummeted, leading to huge losses by banks on a global scale.

In the UK, many banks had invested large sums of money in sub-prime backed investments and have had to write off billions of pounds in losses. On 22 April 2008, the day after the Bank of England unveiled a £50 billion bailout scheme to aid banks and ease the mortgage market, Royal Bank of Scotland (RBS) admitted that loan losses hit £1.25 billion in just six weeks. In August 2008, RBS reported a pre-tax loss of £691 million (after writing down £5.9 billion on investments hit by the credit crunch) – one of the biggest losses in UK corporate history. At the beginning of 2009, RBS announced that it expected to suffer a loss of up to £28 billion as a result of the credit crunch. On 3 March 2008, it was reported that HSBC was writing off sub-prime loans at the rate of $51 million per day.

2.1.2 Factors influencing strategic risks

Factors that determine the level of strategic risks will include:

- The types of industries/markets within which the business operates
- The state of the economy
- The actions of competitors and the possibility of mergers and acquisitions
- The stage in a product's life cycle, higher risks in the introductory and declining stages
- The dependence upon inputs with fluctuating prices, eg wheat, oil etc
- The level of operating gearing – the proportion of fixed costs to total costs
- The flexibility of production processes to adapt to different specifications or products
- The organisation's research and development capacity and ability to innovate
- The significance of new technology

There may be little management can do about some of these risks, they are inherent in business activity. However, strategies such as **diversification** can contribute substantially to the reduction of many business risks.

Exam alert

Strategic risks may be particularly important in Question 1 of the *Performance Strategy* exam; you may for example have to evaluate risks connected with branding and marketing strategy.

They may also be an important element in optional questions. Question 3 of the specimen paper asked about the risks associated with product launch opportunities in different countries.

2.2 Operational risks

KEY TERM

OPERATIONAL OR PROCESS RISK is the risk of loss from a failure of internal business and control processes.

Operational risks include:

- Losses from internal control system or audit inadequacies
- Non-compliance with regulations or internal procedures
- Information technology failures
- Human error
- Loss of key-person risk
- Fraud
- Business interruptions

2.3 Strategic and operational risks

KEY POINT

The main difference between strategic and operational risks is that

(a) **Strategic risks** relate to the organisation's **longer-term** place in, and relations with, the **outside environment**. Although some of them relate to internal functions, they are internal functions or aspects of internal functions that have a **key bearing** on the organisation's situation in relation to its environment.

(b) **Operational risks** are what could go wrong on a **day-to-day basis**, and are not generally very relevant to the key strategic decisions that affect a business.

As strategic risks relate primarily to an outside environment that is not under the organisation's control, it is more difficult to mitigate these risks than it is to deal with the risks that relate to the internal environment that is under the organisation's control.

Many of the risks discussed in Section 3 may be strategic or operational.

(a) For example the **legal risk of breaching laws** in day-to-day activities (for example an organisation's drivers exceeding the speed limit) would be classed as an **operational risk**. However the legal risk of **stricter health and safety legislation** forcing an organisation to make changes to its production processes would be classed as a **strategic risk**, as it is a **long-term risk** impacting seriously on the way the business produces its goods.

(b) The same is true of **information technology risks**. The risks of a **system failure resulting in a loss of a day's data** would clearly be an **operational risk**. However the risks from using **obsolete technology** would be a **strategic risk**, as it would affect the organisation's ability to compete with its rivals.

Many of these risks will also be significant in the *Enterprise Strategy* exam.

Section summary

Strategic risks are risks that relate to the fundamental and key decisions that the directors take about the future of the organisation.

Operational risks relate to matters that can go wrong on a day-to-day basis while the organisation is carrying out its business.

3   Types of risks faced by organisations

Introduction

Having categorised risks in broad terms, we now look in more detail at the major risks that organisations face.

3.1 Competitor risks

Competitor risks are the threats to cash flows arising from the action of competitors. Obvious examples are competitors **introducing a new product** that is better than your product, or **reducing the price of their product** so that it is cheaper than yours.

3.2 Product risks

Product risks are risks that revenues from products will fall. These can arise from a variety of sources. A **change in customer tastes** could mean that products become less fashionable.

Product risks will include the risks of financial loss due to producing a poor quality product. These include the need to **compensate dissatisfied customers**, possible **loss of sales** if the product has to be withdrawn from the market or because of loss of reputation (see below) and the need for **expenditure on improved quality control procedures**.

Other risks connected with products would be **poor branding and marketing strategies.**

3.3 Commodity risks

3.3.1 Supply risks

Supply risks include the **risks of disruption to operations** due to a **shortage of necessary supplies**. These may only be temporary. However longer-term shortages, for example a worldwide shortage of a particular raw material may be classified as strategic since they force a change in business strategy into producing different products, or changing the mix of raw materials in the products. Another example of supply risks would be **substandard supplies** disrupting the production process or affecting demand.

3.3.2 Commodity price risks

Large or unexpected fluctuations in the price of a commodity can cause significant problems for businesses that provide that commodity or for which the commodity is a key resource. An example is the risk to road haulage companies of changes in the price of fuel.

3.4 Stakeholder risks

A poor relationship with stakeholders is also a significant strategic risk because of the consequences of non-cooperation, for example investors not contributing new funds, suppliers not delivering on time, employees disrupting production and ultimately of course customers not buying goods and services. Organisations must be aware of the key factors that may lead to problems in relations with stakeholders:

- **Investors** will be concerned with financial returns, accuracy and timeliness of information and quality of leadership

- Relations with **suppliers** and **employees** will be influenced by the terms and conditions of business. With employees, the organisation also needs to consider whether they have the appropriate knowledge and attitudes

- Customers will obviously be influenced by the **level** of **customer service,** also product safety issues and perhaps whether the organisation is 'ethical' in matters such as marketing practice

Exam skills

You would also classify competitor, product, supply, and stakeholder risks as threats in a SWOT analysis.

3.5 Environmental and social risks

Environmental risk is a term used in different senses. It can be defined as the risk to cashflows arising from changes in the business environment within which the organisation trades. This includes the PEST factors – a variety of political, economic, social and technological issues (many of which are discussed in detail below).

Alternatively environmental risk can mean the risks arising from the impact of the organisation on the **natural environment**.

Much business activity takes place at some cost to the environment. A 1998 IFAC report identified several examples of impacts on the environment

- Depletion of natural resources
- Noise and aesthetic impacts
- Residual air and water emissions
- Long-term waste disposal (exacerbated by excessive product packaging)
- Uncompensated health effects
- Change in the local quality of life (through for example the impact of tourism)

Question 1.2	Environmental costs

Learning outcome B1(b)

List examples of costs that are related to businesses' impact on the natural environment.

3.6 Financial risks

You may have come across financial risks in your earlier studies and we shall examine many of them in detail in Chapters 8 to 12. The ultimate financial risk is that the organisation will not be able to continue to function as a going concern.

Exam alert

Don't forget that other risks directly impact upon the financial statements. Remember with cash flows that impacts on the timing and predictability of cash flows may be as important as impacts on the magnitude of cash flows.

Financial risks include the risks relating to the **structure of finance** the organisation has. In particular the risks include those relating to the mix of equity and debt capital, the risk of not being able to access funding, also whether the organisation has an insufficient long-term capital base for the amount of trading it is doing (overtrading).

Finance structure risk is covered in detail in BPP's F3 *Financial Strategy* **text.**

Organisations also must consider the risks of **fraud and misuse** of financial resources.

Other shorter-term financial risks include:

- **Credit risk** – the possibility of payment default by the customer

- **Liquidity risk** – the risk of being unable to finance the credit, arising from cash restrictions or the need for more cash

- **Cash management risk** – risks relating to the security of cash, risks arising from unpredictable cash flows

Longer-term risks include currency and interest rate risks, and risks arising from other changes in the **macroeconomic environment**.

3.6.1 Currency risks

KEY TERM

CURRENCY RISK is the possibility of loss or gain due to future changes in exchange rates.

When a firm trades with an overseas supplier or customer, and the invoice is in the overseas currency, it will expose itself to exchange rate or currency risk. The final amount payable/receivable in the home currency will be uncertain at the time of entering into the transaction and the exchange rates may change between the date of the transaction and the date of settlement. Investment in a foreign country or borrowing in a foreign currency will also carry this risk.

Currency risks	
Transaction risk	Changes in transaction settlement values arising from exchange rate movements
Translation risk	Changes to values of foreign assets and liabilities arising from retranslation at different exchange rates at the year-end in the statement of financial position
Economic risk	Effect of exchange rate movements on the international competitiveness of the organisation

Of these three, transaction risk has the greatest immediate impact on day to day cash flows of an organisation, and there are many ways of reducing or eliminating this risk, for example by the use of **hedging** techniques. These and other currency risk management strategies are discussed in detail in Chapters 11 and 12.

3.6.2 Interest rate risks

Future interest rates cannot be easily predicted. If a firm has a significant amount of variable (floating) rate debt, interest rate movements will give rise to uncertainty about the cost of servicing this debt. Conversely, if a company uses a lot of fixed rate debt, it will lose out if interest rates begin to fall.

There are many arrangements and financial products that a firm's treasury department can use to reduce its exposure to interest rate risk for example, involving **hedging** techniques similar to those used for the management of currency risk. The topic of interest rate risk is covered in greater depth in Chapter 9.

3.6.3 Market risks

KEY TERM

MARKET RISK is a risk of loss due to an adverse move in the market value of an asset – a stock, a bond, a loan, foreign exchange or a commodity – or a derivative contract linked to these assets.

Market risk is thus connected to interest rate or exchange rate risk when derivatives are used to hedge these risks. Market risk can be analysed into various other risks that cover **movements in the reference asset**, the **risk of small price movements** that change the **value of the holder's position**, and the risks of losses relating to a change in the **maturity structure** of an asset, the **passage of time** or **market volatility**. Market risk can also apply to **making a major investment**, for example a recently-floated company, where the market price has not yet reached a 'true level', or if there are other uncertainties about the price.

Calculation of fair value can be **particularly uncertain. Significant assumptions** may have to be made, and **judgements** exercised as to what techniques should be used to calculate fair value. The value calculated may be as good an estimate as possible, but it cannot reflect the **risk levels** and variations associated with the investment. This is true not only of direct investments, but of investments in companies who themselves hold investments of uncertain value.

Question 1.3	Significant risks

Learning outcome B1(b)

Try listing as many significant risk areas that you think might be of relevance to major international banks. Try to list at least ten risks.

3.6.4 Financial records and reporting risks

Financial risks can also be said to include **misstatement risks** relating to published financial information. This in turn may arise from **breakdown in the accounting systems**, **uncertainty in measurement**, **unrecorded liabilities** and **unreliable accounting records**.

3.6.5 Finance providers' risks

There are also risks to the organisation if it provides finance for others. If it lends money, there is the **risk of default** on debt payments, and ultimately the risk that the borrower will become insolvent. If it invests in shares, there is a risk that it will receive **low or no dividends**, and share price volatility will mean that it does not receive any **capital gains** on the value of the shares.

3.7 Investment risks

You will remember from earlier the risks and uncertainties associated with investment appraisal, particularly net present value calculations.

The fundamental risk relating to investment appraisal is that incorrect decisions are made, that:

- **Investments** are **made** when they **should not have been**, or are **not made** when they **should have been**

- When choosing between two investments, the **wrong investment** is **chosen**

A number of factors affect the decision to invest.

3.7.1 Choice of cost of capital

Using an **historic cost of capital** may not reflect the risks the organisation currently faces nor the **attitude to risk** of its finance suppliers. Choice of an **excessively large cost of capital** may affect the investment decision, as it can lead to a bias towards investments with high short-term returns, against investments with returns further in the future.

3.7.2 Use of total NPV

Total NPV may be used as the criteria when capital is rationed, but this fails to take into account the **levels of investment** involved and the **life of the investment**.

3.7.3 Inappropriate time horizon

The time horizon used for the investment appraisal may be **fairly arbitrary**. The investment decision might have a different outcome if the time horizon is different.

3.7.4 Data problems

There could be various problems with the data used in the appraisal. These include **use of historic data** that may not reflect what will happen in the future and **inconsistencies** between data from different sources.

3.7.5 Consideration of alternative scenarios

If only one projection is used for the investment appraisal, this implies **only one set of assumptions** has been used. There may be other, perhaps more likely, assumptions that could have been used.

3.7.6 Consideration of strategic issues and risk

In addition the decision may be taken largely on financial grounds, **ignoring other strategic criteria** that may be relevant.

3.8 Legal, political and cultural risks

3.8.1 Legal risks

Breaches of legislation, regulations or codes of conduct can have very serious consequences for organisations. Risks include **financial or other penalties** (including ultimately closedown), having to **spend money and resources** in fighting litigation and loss of reputation. Key areas include health and safety, environmental legislation, trade descriptions, consumer protection, data protection and employment issues.

Governance codes are a particularly important example of best practice, and organisations must consider the risks of breaching provisions relating to integrity and objectivity, and also control over the organisation. We shall look at corporate governance in detail in Chapter 3.

3.8.2 Contractual inadequacy risks

Businesses may also face problems arising out of **inadequately drafted or ambiguous contracts**. Contracts may be difficult to enforce or leave loopholes that render the business liable to legal action.

3.8.3 Political risks

Political risk is the risk that political action will affect the position and value of a company. It is connected with **country risk**, the risk associated with undertaking transactions with, or holding assets in, a particular country.

3.8.4 Cultural risks

Cultural risks are also linked with country risks. They relate to the businesses trading in environments that are different from its home country, and facing differences in customs, laws and languages. These may result in differences in the ways of doing business which are difficult to manage and problems in communication.

3.9 Information and technology risks

Risks relating to information and technology systems are covered in detail in Part D of this text. Information risks include taking decisions based on inadequate information and the threats of losing information.

Important technology risks relate to the **accuracy and continuing operation** of information systems. Organisations will be particularly concerned with the risk of unauthorised access and consequent disruption to computer systems.

In addition, as technology evolves and develops, organisations will face strategic risks from using out of date equipment and marketing methods, which may leave them at a **competitive disadvantage**. Products in a high-tech industry have a very short life-cycle. An organisation must recognise and plan for continual replacement and upgrading of products and systems if it is not to lose market share. However upgrading and developing systems carries the risks that the choices made will be **inappropriate for users' needs**, the new system will **operate less well** and the changeover will **cause disruption to operations**.

3.10 Knowledge management risks

Knowledge management risk concerns the effective management and control of knowledge resources. Threats might include unauthorised use or abuse of intellectual property, area or system power failures, competitor's technology or loss of key staff.

3.11 Property risks

Property risks are the risks from **damage**, **destruction** or **taking of property.** Perils to property include fire, windstorms, water leakage and vandalism.

If the organisation suffers damage, it may be liable for repairs or ultimately the building of an entirely new property. There may also be a risk of **loss of rent**. If a building is accidentally damaged or destroyed, and the tenant is not responsible for the payment of rent during the period the property cannot be occupied, the landlord will lose the rent.

If there is damage to the property, the organisation could suffer from having to **suspend or reduce** its **operations**.

3.12 Health and safety risks

Health and safety risks include loss of employees' time because of injury and the risks of having to pay compensation or legal costs because of breaches. Health and safety risks can arise from:

- **Lack of health and safety policy** – due to increased legislation in this area this is becoming less likely

- **Lack of emergency procedures** – again less likely

- **Failure to deal with hazards** – often due to a failure to implement policies such as inspection of electrical equipment, labelling of hazards and training

- **Poor employee welfare** – not just threats to health such as poor working conditions or excessive exposure to VDUs, but also risks to quality from tired staff making mistakes

- Generally **poor health and safety culture**

| Question 1.4 | Health and safety |

Learning outcome B1(b)

Can you think of some signs of a poor health and safety culture in an organisation?

3.13 Trading risks

Both domestic and international traders will face trading risks, although those faced by the latter will generally be greater due to the increased distances and times involved. The types of trading risk include:

3.13.1 Physical risk

Physical risk is the risk of goods being lost or stolen in transit, or the documents accompanying the goods going astray.

3.13.2 Trade risk

Trade risk is the risk of the customer refusing to accept the goods on delivery (due to sub-standard/inappropriate goods), or the cancellation of the order in transit

3.13.3 Credit risk

KEY TERM

CREDIT RISK is the possibility that a loss may occur from the failure of another party to perform according to the terms of a contract (*CIMA Official Terminology*).

CREDIT RISK can also be defined as the risk to a company from the failure of its debtors to meet their obligations on time.

Management of **credit risk** is of particular importance to exporters. You may remember from earlier studies that various arrangements are available to assist in this, such as **documentary credits**, **bills of exchange**, **export credit insurance**, **export factoring** and **forfeiting**.

3.13.4 Liquidity risk

Liquidity risk is the inability to meet day-to-day cash obligations, often caused by delays in expected cash inflows.

3.14 Event risks

The most important disruptions include failure of information technology or extreme weather, but operations may be delayed or prevented for other reasons as well. These include employee error, product problems, health and safety issues, losses of employees or suppliers, or legal action.

3.15 Cost and resource wastage risks

Important operational risks for most organisations are incurring excessive costs (through poor procurement procedures, lack of control over expenditure) or waste of employees' time and resources (employees being unproductive or their efforts being misapplied).

3.16 Organisational risks

Organisational risks relate to the behaviour of groups or individuals within the organisation. These are particularly important to organisations that are going through **significant change**, as failure by people or teams to adapt may jeopardise change.

3.17 Inadequate systems risks

As we shall see in later chapters, businesses may suffer losses through having management, accounting, risk analysis or internal control systems that are inadequate for their current needs.

3.18 Fraud and employee malfeasance risks

All businesses run the risk of loss through the fraudulent activities of employees including management. This is perhaps one of the risk areas over which the company can exert the greatest control, through a coherent corporate strategy set out in a **fraud policy statement** and the setting up of strict **internal controls**.

Employee malfeasance risk is the risk of employees carrying out an unethical or illegal act. These include misleading customers about products being sold or negligently.

3.19 Probity risks

KEY TERM

PROBITY RISK is the risk of unethical behaviour by one or more participants in a particular process.

Probity risk is commonly discussed in the context of procurement, the process of acquiring property or services. Guidance issued by the Australian government's Department of Finance and Administration Financial Management Group comments that:

'Procurement must be conducted with probity in mind to enable purchasers and suppliers to deal with each other on the basis of mutual trust and respect. Adopting an ethical, transparent approach enables business to be conducted fairly, reasonably and with integrity. Ethical behaviour also enables procurement to be conducted in a manner that allows all participating suppliers to compete as equally as possible. The procurement process rules must be clear, open, well understood and applied equally to all parties to the process.'

In this context probity risk would not only be the risk that the 'wrong' supplier was chosen as a result of improper behaviour, but it relates to other issues as well, for example **failing to treat private information** given by another party as **confidential**. It would also relate to the **risks of lack of trust** making business **dealings between certain parties** impossible, or time and **cost having to be spent resolving disputes arising** from the process. Probity risk is clearly linked with reputation risk, discussed below.

3.20 Reputation risks

KEY TERM

REPUTATION RISK is a loss of reputation caused as a result of the adverse consequences of another risk.

The loss of reputation will be usually perceived by external stakeholders, and may have serious consequences, depending on the **strength of the organisation's relationship** with them.

Consumers who wish to ensure that they do not have dealings with companies tainted by poor ethical records can refer to an A-Z list of current boycotts. http://www.ethicalconsumer.org/boycotts

The site recommends boycotts of a number of companies and also certain countries. Unethical behaviour highlighted includes animal testing, dealings with oppressive regimes (Burma being the most commonly quoted example), human rights abuses (for example suppression of trade union activity) destruction of forests and dumping of toxic waste.

3.20.1 Poor customer service

This risk is likely to arise because of failure to understand **why** the customers buy from the business, how they view the business and what they expect from the business in terms of product quality, speed of delivery and value for money. Early indications of potential reputation risks include **increasing levels of returns** and **customer complaints** followed inevitably by loss of business.

3.20.2 Failure to innovate

We have discussed this under strategic risks.

3.20.3 Poor ethics

A poor ethical reputation can have the following consequences:

- Suppliers and customers unwillingness to deal with the organisation for fear of being victims of sharp practice

- Inability to recruit high-quality staff

- Fall in demand because of consumer boycotts

- Increased public relations costs because of adverse stories in the media
- Increased compliance cost because of close attentions from regulatory bodies or external auditors
- Loss of market value because of a fall in investor confidence

3.20.4 Poor environmental and social performance

Pressures on organisations to widen the scope of their accountability for environmental and social issues come from **increasing expectations of stakeholders** and knowledge about the **consequences of ignoring such pressures**.

Stakeholders in this respect include communities (particularly where operations are based), customers (product safety issues), suppliers and supply chain participants and competitors. Issues such as plant closures, pollution, job creation, sourcing, etc can have powerful **social effects** for good or ill on these stakeholders.

Increasingly a business must have the reputation of being a **responsible business** that enhances long-term shareholder value by addressing the needs of its **stakeholders** – employees, customers, suppliers, the community and the environment.

CASE STUDY

Charity Oxfam suffered a public relations crisis when it was revealed that the overseas manufacturer of its 'Make Poverty History' wristband was, in fact, exploiting its labour force in appalling conditions. With the increase in outsourcing to developing nations, a number of key brands have either positively positioned themselves as ethical sources (eg The Body Shop) or taken steps to counter allegations of unethical employment practices (eg Nike).

3.21 Risk categorisation

As well as identifying individual risks, businesses find it helpful to categorise or classify risks in a way that is relevant to the needs of the business. Risk categorisation serves the following purposes:

- Identifying **risks that are inter-related**
- Encouraging a **systematic approach** that is integral to an enterprise risk management system
- Making it easier to assign responsibility for **managing risks and to design controls to combat them**
- Assisting **management review and reporting of risk**

Question 1.5	Risk management techniques

Learning outcome B1(b)

If you were involved in the management of a secondary school (a school for children between the ages of 11–18), what might be some of the risks that you would need to consider and adopt a policy for managing?

The UK Institute of internal Auditors provides useful analysis on risks, emphasising they come from inside and outside the organisation. www.iia.org.uk

Section summary

Risks can be **classified** in various other ways, including financial, legal, IT, fraud and reputation.

Chapter Roundup

✓ Risks can be classified according to **whom** they affect, whether their outcomes will be **beneficial** or **adverse**, and the **area** of an organisation's **affairs affected**.

✓ **Strategic risks** are risks that relate to the fundamental and key decisions that the directors take about the future of the organisation.

✓ **Operational risks** relate to matters that can go wrong on a day-to-day basis while the organisation is carrying out its business.

✓ Risks can be **classified** in various other ways, including financial, legal, IT, fraud and reputation.

Quick Quiz

1   What is the difference between pure risks and speculative risks?

2   Fill in the blank

.... risks are risks from which good or harm may result.

3   Risk-averse businesses always seek to minimise the levels of risk that they face.

True   ☐

False   ☐

4   Which of the following would normally be classified as an operational risk?

A   The risk that a new product will fail to find a large enough market
B   The risk of competitors moving their production to a different country and being able to cut costs
C   The risk that a senior manager with lots of experience will be recruited by a competitor
D   The risk of resource depletion meaning that new sources of raw materials will have to be found

5   What are the major property risks that organisations face?

6   List three business risks that are associated with the Internet.

7   Give three examples of short-term financial risks.

8   The level of reputation risk depends significantly on the level of other risks.

True   ☐

False   ☐

9   Fill in the blank

.... risks arise from the effect of exchange rate movements on the international competitiveness of the organisation.

Answers to Quick Quiz

1   Pure risks relate to harmful outcomes; speculative risks relate to positive and harmful outcomes.

2   **Speculative** risks are risks from which good or harm may result.

3   False. Risk-averse businesses may be prepared to tolerate risks provided they receive appropriate returns.

4   C. Loss of a senior manager would be an operational risk. The other risks are strategic risks.

5   Damage, destruction or taking of property

6   Hackers accessing the internal network; staff downloading viruses; staff downloading inaccurate information; information being intercepted; the communication link breaking down or distorting data

7   Credit, liquidity and cash management risks

8   True, although the threat to reputation also depends on how likely it is that the organisation will suffer bad publicity if risks in other areas materialise.

9   **Economic** risks arise from the effect of exchange rate movements on the international competitiveness of the organisation.

 ## Answers to Questions

1.1 Risks

Make your own list, specific to the organisations that you are familiar with. Here is a list extracted from an article by Tom Jones 'Risk Management' (Administrator, April 1993).

- Fire, flood, storm, impact, explosion, subsidence and other hazards

- Accidents and the use of faulty products

- Error: loss through damage or malfunction caused by mistaken operation of equipment or wrong operation of an industrial programme

- Theft and fraud

- Breaking social or environmental regulations

- Political risks (the appropriation of foreign assets by local governments, or of barriers to the repatriation of overseas profit)

- Computers: fraud, viruses, and espionage

- Product tamper

- Malicious damage

1.2 Environmental costs

Direct or indirect environmental costs

- Waste management
- Remediation costs or expenses
- Compliance costs
- Permit fees
- Environmental training

- Environmentally driven research and development
- Environmentally related maintenance
- Legal costs and fines
- Environmental assurance bonds
- Environmental certification and labelling
- Natural resource inputs
- Record keeping and reporting

Contingent or intangible environmental costs

- Uncertain future remediation or compensation costs
- Risk posed by future regulatory changes
- Product quality
- Employee health and safety
- Environmental knowledge assets
- Sustainability of raw material inputs
- Risk of impaired assets
- Public/customer perception

1.3 Significant risks

There isn't a 'correct' answer to this question, but shown below are the top 18 risks mentioned by senior bankers in a survey of risks in the banking industry, and published by the Centre for the Study of Financial Innovation in March 2005 (*Banana Skins 2005*). This list is not comprehensive, and you might have thought of others.

- Too much regulation
- Credit risk
- Corporate governance
- Complex financial instruments
- Hedge funds
- Fraud
- Currencies
- High dependence on technology
- Risk management techniques

- Macro-economic trends
- Insurance sector problems
- Interest rates
- Money laundering
- Commodities
- Emerging markets
- Grasp of new technology
- Legal risk
- Equity markets

A notable extra was environmental risk which, while positioned low in the overall ranking (28th), was seen to be gaining strongly because of fears about the impact of pollution claims and climate change on bank assets and earnings.

1.4 Health and safety

Glynis Morris in the book *An Accountant's Guide to Risk Management* lists a number of signs:

- Trailing wires and overloaded electricity sockets
- Poor lighting
- Poor ventilation
- Uneven floor surfaces
- Sharp edges
- Cupboards and drawers that are regularly left open
- Poorly stacked shelves or other poor storage arrangements
- Excessive noise and dust levels
- Poor furniture design, workstation or office layout

Morris points out that all these problems can be solved with thought.

1.5 Risk management techniques

Of course there is no definitive solution to this question. In no particular order a list of risks to be assessed might include:

- The risk of failing to attract sufficient numbers of students

- The risk of poor examination results

- The risk of inadequate numbers of students going on to higher education

- The risk of focusing too much on academic subjects, and ignoring broader aspects of education

- Physical security: risks to students, teachers and school property

- The risk of theft of individuals' property

- Inability to recruit sufficient teachers

- Not having enough money to spend on essential or desirable items

- The risk of an adverse report from school inspectors

- The risk of an adverse report on the quality of school meals! (This is a little tongue in cheek, but a serious point could be made, given the recent adverse publicity given to school dinners in the UK and the impact on pupils' concentration and behaviour.)

Now try this question from the Exam Question Bank

Number	Level	Marks	Time
Q1	Introductory	N/A	30 mins

RISK MANAGEMENT

Given the risks organisations face it is vital that they adopt a coherent framework for dealing with risks. The **risk management** models, which we discuss in Section 1, have evolved over the last few years. Section 2 deals with some of the key organisational factors that determine what risks are taken and how these are managed.

In Section 3 we deal with how organisations **identify and analyse risk.** One important aspect of this process is to try to quantify risk exposure, and we shall examine financial risk quantification in more detail in Chapter 8.

The last three sections of this chapter deals with how organisations **manage risks**. They can take certain steps to deal with all risks, including appointing specialists to deal with the risks. However organisations have also to consider how to deal with each significant risk, and we shall look at the choices that they have.

We emphasise once more that this chapter is very important in your studies of P3.

topic list	learning outcomes	syllabus references	ability required
1 Risk management models	B2(a), (b)	B2(i)	evaluation
2 Risk appetite and culture	B2(a)	B2(ii)	evaluation
3 Risk assessment	B1(a), (b)	B1(iv), (vi)	evaluation
4 Risk response	B2(a), (b)	B2(i)	evaluation
5 Risk responsibilities	B2(a), (b)	B2(v)	evaluation
6 Risk monitoring	B2(a), (b)	B1(v), B2(vii)	evaluation

1 Risk management models

Introduction

We start the chapter by taking an overview of risk management, looking at risk management models and observing what they have in common.

1.1 Risk management models

Risk management models are designed to show that **risk management** is continuous and that it is a logical process. They aim to demonstrate the **interaction and comparison** of risks, as well as the **assessment of individual risks**.

1.2 COSO's risk management model

KEY TERM

ENTERPRISE RISK MANAGEMENT is a process, effected by an entity's board of directors, management and other personnel, applied in strategy setting and across the enterprise, designed to identify potential events that may affect the entity and manage risks to be within its risk appetite, to provide reasonable assurance regarding the achievement of entity objectives.

COSO

The Committee of Sponsoring Organisations of the Treadway Commission (COSO) goes on to expand its definition. It states that enterprise risk management has the following characteristics.

Process	Should tie up with existing operations and exist for fundamental business reasons
Operated at every level	Provides a mechanism helping people to understand risk, their responsibilities and level of authority
Applied in strategy setting	Management considering the risks in alternative strategies
Applied across the enterprise	Takes into account activities at all levels of business, from strategic planning and resource allocation, to business unit activities and business planning
Identifies key events and manage their risks	Events that affect the organisation and manage risk within risk appetite, amount of risk accepted in pursuit of value, aligned with desired return from strategy
Provides reasonable reassurance	Assurance can at best be reasonable, as risk relates to uncertain future
Geared to achievement of objectives	Objectives including supporting organisation's mission, making effective and efficient use of organisation's resources, ensuring reporting is reliable and complying with applicable laws and regulations

In applying the process, managers will take a **portfolio view** of risk. Each unit manager assesses the risks for his unit and senior managers consider these risks and also interrelated risks. They will ultimately assess whether the overall risk portfolio is consistent with the organisation's **risk appetite**.

Because these characteristics are broadly defined, they can be applied across different types of organisations, industries and sectors. Whatever the organisation, the framework focuses on **achievement of objectives.**

An approach based on **objectives** contrasts with a **procedural approach** based on rules, codes or procedures. A procedural approach aims to eliminate or control risk by requiring conformity with the rules.

However a procedural approach cannot eliminate the possibility of risks arising because of poor management decisions, human error, fraud or unforeseen circumstances arising.

1.3 Framework of enterprise risk management

The COSO framework consists of eight interrelated components.

They are covered in this text as follows:

- **Internal environment** or control environment – see Chapter 6
- **Objective setting** – covered in this section below
- **Event identification** – see Section 3 of this chapter
- **Risk assessment** – see Section 3 of this chapter
- **Risk response** – see Section 4 of this chapter
- **Control activities** – see Chapter 6
- **Information and communication** – see Sections 6.2 and 6.3 of this chapter
- **Monitoring** – see Section 6 of this chapter

Diagrammatically all of the above may be summarised as follows.

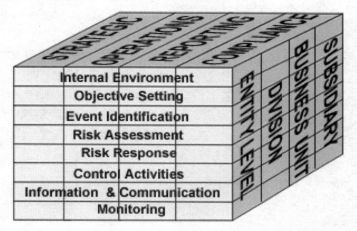

1.3.1 Objective setting

You will have discussed objective setting in a number of other papers. Enterprise risk management emphasises the importance of **setting objectives** at entity and activity levels and **identifying critical success factors**.

Objectives need to exist before management can recognise potential evens affecting their achievement. Enterprise risk management emphasises the importance of having an objective-setting process, and ensuring that objectives **support and align with the organisation's mission**, and are **consistent with its risk appetite**.

COSO categorises objective into four categories, illustrated on another face of the cube:

- **Strategic** – high level goals, aligned with, and supporting, the organisation's mission
- **Operational** – effective and efficient use of resources
- **Reporting** – reliability of reporting
- **Compliance** – compliance with applicable laws and regulations

Initially the organisation establishes strategic objectives and sets aligned objectives throughout the organisation.

COSO states that this categorisation allows entities to focus on separate aspects of risk management. The categories have some overlaps, but they address different needs and may be the direct responsibility of different managers.

1.3.2 Components of entity

The third dimension of the cube reflects the different ways in which the entity can be analysed. It shows that the business can focus on objectives and risk management at the entity level, also at the division, subsidiary or business unit level.

1.4 Benefits of enterprise risk management

COSO highlights a number of advantages of adopting the process of enterprise risk management.

Alignment of risk appetite and strategy	The framework demonstrates to managers the need to consider risk toleration. They then set objectives aligned with business strategy and develop mechanisms to manage the accompanying risks and to ensure risk management becomes part of the culture of the organisation, embedded into all its processes and activities.
Link growth, risk and return	Risk is part of value creation, and organisations will seek a given level of return for the level of risk tolerated.
Choose best risk response	Enterprise risk management helps the organisation select whether to reduce, eliminate or transfer risk.
Minimise surprises and losses	By identifying potential loss-inducing events, the organisation can reduce the occurrence of unexpected problems.
Identify and manage risks across the organisation	As indicated above, the framework means that managers can understand and aggregate connected risks. It also means that risk management is seen as everyone's responsibility, experience and practice is shared across the business and a common set of tools and techniques is used.
Provide responses to multiple risks	For example risks associated with purchasing, over and under supply, prices and dubious supply sources might be reduced by an inventory control system that is integrated with suppliers.
Seize opportunities	By considering events as well as risks, managers can identify opportunities as well as losses.
Rationalise capital	Enterprise risk management allows management to allocate capital better and make a sounder assessment of capital needs.

1.5 CIMA's risk management cycle

CIMA's suggested approach to risk management is illustrated in the diagram below. It is based on the idea of continual feedback that is inherent in management control systems that we shall consider in later chapters.

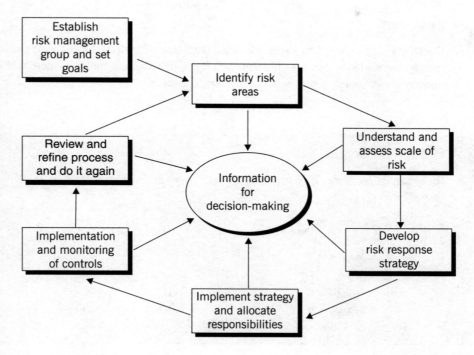

1.6 Risk architecture

In their 1999 report *Enhancing shareholder wealth by better managing business risk* the International Federation of Accountants argued for the development of a **risk architecture** within which risk management processes could be developed. The architecture involves designing and implementing **organisational structures**, **systems** and **processes to manage risk**. This is a slightly different framework to that of enterprise risk management.

IFAC argued that developing a risk architecture is not just a response to risk but marks an organisational shift, changing the way the organisation:

- Organises itself
- Assigns accountability
- Builds risk management as a core competency
- Implements continuous, real-time risk management

The risk architecture developed by IFAC has eight components:

- Acceptance of a risk management framework
- Commitment from executives
- Establishment of a risk response strategy
- Assignment of responsibility for risk management process
- Resourcing
- Communication and training
- Reinforcing risk cultures through human resources mechanisms
- Monitoring of the risk management process

IFAC identified four components of risk management:

- **Structure** to facilitate the identification and communication of risk
- **Resources** – sufficient to support implementation
- **Culture** – reinforcing decision-making processes
- **Tools and techniques** developed to enable organisation-wide management of risk

Exam alert

Questions may require you to discuss risk management strategy, basing your discussion on any risk management model. You should score well if you use any reasonable model, as it is unlikely that questions will specify which model you have to discuss.

Section summary

Risk management models provide a coherent framework for organisations to deal with risk, based on the following components:

- Risk appetite
- Risk identification
- Risk assessment
- Risk profiling
- Risk quantification
- Risk management
- Review and feedback

2 Risk appetite and culture

Introduction

If organisations manage risk systematically, that does not remove the human element from decision-making on dealing with risks. How organisations respond to risk will be determined by the views of directors or managers, and also the stakeholders to whom they are accountable.

2.1 Factors influencing risk appetites

Because risk management is bound up with strategy, how organisations deal with risk will not only be determined by events and the information available about events, but also **management perceptions or appetite** to take risk. These factors will also influence risk **culture**, the values and practices that influence how an organisation deals with risk in its day-to-day operations.

Because of its significance, the **board** should be responsible for **determining risk appetite** and **tolerance**.

A number of factors may influence risk appetite.

2.2 Personal views

Surveys suggest that managers acknowledge the **emotional satisfaction** from successful risk-taking, although this is unlikely to be the most important influence on appetite.

2.3 Response to shareholder demand

Shareholders demand a **level of return** that is consistent with taking a certain level of risk. Managers will respond to these expectations by viewing risk-taking as a key part of decision-making.

2.4 Organisational influences

Organisational influences may be important, and these are not necessarily just a response to shareholder concerns. Organisational attitudes may be influenced by **significant losses** in the past, **changes in regulation and best practice**, or even **changing views** of the benefits risk management can bring.

2.5 National influences

There is some evidence that national culture influences attitudes towards risk and uncertainty. Surveys suggest that attitudes to risk vary nationally according to how much people are shielded from the consequences of adverse events.

2.6 Cultural influences

Adams argued that there are four viewpoints that are key determinants in how risks is viewed.

Fatalists	Think they have no control over their own lives and hence risk management is pointless
Hierachists	Most likely to exist in a bureaucratic organisation, with formal structures and procedures. Will emphasise risk reduction through formal risk management procedures
Individualists	Seek to control their environment rather than let their environment control them. Often found in small, single-person dominated, organisations with less formal structures, and hence risk management too will be informal, if indeed it is considered at all
Egalitarians	Loyal to groups but have little respect for procedures. Often found in charities and public sector, non-profit making activities, prefer sharing risks as widely as possible, or transfer of risks to those best able to bear them

CASE STUDY

Consider a company such as **Virgin**. It has many stable and successful brands, and healthy cash flows and profits: little need, you would have thought, to consider risky new ventures.

Yet Virgin operates a subsidiary called **Virgin Galactic** to own and operate privately-built spaceships, and to offer 'affordable' sub-orbital **space tourism to everybody** – or everybody willing to pay US$200,000 for the pleasure. The risks are enormous: developing the project will involve investing very large amounts of money, there is no guarantee that the service is wanted by sufficient numbers of people to make it viable, and the risks of catastrophic accidents are self-evident.

There is little doubt that Virgin's risk appetite derives directly from the risk appetite of its chief executive, Richard Branson – a self-confessed adrenaline junkie – who also happens to own most parts of the Virgin Group privately, and so faces little pressure from shareholders.

2.7 Risk thermostat

Adams illustrated the links between perceptions of risk, influences on risk taking, and results of risk-taking by a risk thermostat.

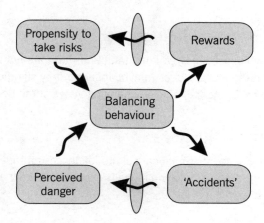

Source: J Adams Risk

2.8 Risk aversion and risk toleration

Aversion and **seeking** are two different attitudes towards risk.

- **Aversion** focuses on the risk level. An organisation should not undertake an activity if it results in **higher risk**, unless the higher level of return that compensates for the risk is acceptable.

- **Seeking** focuses on the return level. An activity should be undertaken if it results in **higher returns**, even if the resulting risk level is also higher.

2.9 Conformance and performance

IFAC has highlighted two aspects of risk management which can be seen as linking in with risk aversion and seeking.

(a) **Conformance** focuses on controlling pure (only downside) strategic risks. It highlights compliance with laws and regulations, best practice governance codes, fiduciary responsibilities, accountability and the provision of assurance to stakeholders in general. It also includes ensuring the effectiveness of the risk analysis, management and reporting processes and that the organisation is working effectively and efficiently to achieve its goals.

(b) **Performance** focuses on taking advantage of opportunities to increase overall returns within a business. It includes policies and procedures that focus on alignment of opportunities and risks, strategy, value creation and resource utilisation, and guides an organisation's decision-making.

IFAC guidance states that risk management should seek to **reconcile performance and conformance** – the two enhance each other. Case studies and surveys commissioned by IFAC have shown that many people believe that organisations focus too much on compliance, and not enough on strategy and building a business. IFAC's 2004 report *Enterprise Governance; Getting the balance right* showed that though compliance is necessary to avoid failure, it cannot ensure success.

CASE STUDY

Failing to take fresh strategic opportunities may be the most significant risk the business faces. Woolworths did not fail simply because of the impact of the credit crunch. It had already become **irrelevant** to its customers – people were no longer sure why they should go to Woolworths. The credit crunch simply speeded up the inevitable result of catastrophic strategic wear-out. Woolworths had continued to offer the same products to the same customers despite the changing customer and competitor landscape.

2.10 Deal and Kennedy: risk, feedback and reward

Deal and Kennedy (Corporate Cultures) consider cultures to be a function of the level of risks that employees need to take, and how quickly they get feedback on whether they got it right or wrong and/or rewards for doing so.

		Risk	
		Low	*High*
Feedback and reward	*Rapid*	Work hard, play hard culture	Tough guy macho culture
	Slow	Process culture	Bet your company culture

(a)   **Low risk cultures**

(i)   **Process culture**

The process culture occurs in organisations where there is low risk and little or no feedback. People become bogged down with how things are done, not with what is to be achieved. This is often associated with **bureaucracies**. Whilst it is easy to criticise these cultures for being over-cautious or bogged down in red tape, they do produce consistent results, which is ideal in, for example, public services, banking and insurance.

(ii)   **Work hard, play hard culture**

This culture is characterised by few risks being taken, all with rapid feedback. This is typical in large organisations such as retailers which strive for high quality customer service. They are often characterised by team meetings, jargon and buzzwords.

(b)   **High risk cultures**

(i)   **Bet your company culture**

In the bet your company culture big stakes decisions are taken, but it may be years before the results are known. Typically, these might involve development or exploration projects, which take years to come to fruition, such as could be expected with oil exploration, development of drugs or aircraft manufacturers.

(ii)   **Tough-guy macho culture**

Feedback is quick and the risks and rewards are high. This often applies to fast-moving financial activities such as brokerage, but could also apply to the police, athletes competing in team sports, advertising and certain types of construction. This can be a very stressful culture in which to operate.

CASE STUDY

In his evidence to the UK House of Commons Treasury select committee, Paul Moore, former head of Group Regulatory Risk at HBOS stated:

'There is no doubt that you can have the best governance processes in the world but if they are carried out in a culture of greed, unethical behaviour and indisposition to challenge they will fail.'

We shall come back to Paul Moore and HBOS later in this chapter.

Section summary

Management responses to risk are not automatic, but will be determined by their **own attitudes to risk**, which in turn may be influenced by **shareholder attitudes** and **cultural factors**.

3 Risk assessment

Introduction

This section covers all the stages that organisations go through to analyse the likelihood and impact of a risk materialising.

3.1 Assessment framework

A commonly used framework for analysing risk is made up as follows:

- Identification
- Analysis
- Mapping
- Consolidation

3.2 Risk and event identification

No-one can manage a risk without first being aware that it exists. Some knowledge of perils, what items they can affect and how, is helpful to improve awareness of whether **familiar risks** (potential sources and causes of loss) are present, and the extent to which they could harm a particular person or organisation. The risk manager should also keep an eye open for **unfamiliar risks** which may be present.

Actively identifying the risks before they crystallise makes it easier to think of methods that can be used to manage them.

Risk identification is a **continuous process**, so that new risks and changes affecting existing risks may be identified quickly and dealt with appropriately, before they can cause unacceptable losses.

3.2.1 Risk conditions

Means of identifying conditions leading to risks (potential sources of loss) include:

(a) **Physical inspection**, which will show up risks such as poor housekeeping (for example rubbish left on floors, for people to slip on and to sustain fires)

(b) **Enquiries**, from which the frequency and extent of product quality controls and checks on new employees' references, for example, can be ascertained

(c) **Checking** a copy of every letter and memo issued in the organisation for early indications of major changes and new projects

(d) **Brainstorming** with representatives of different departments

(e) **Checklists** ensuring risk areas are not missed

(f) **Benchmarking** against other sections within the organisation or external experiences

(g) **Human reliability analysis**, reviewing decision points within operational processes.

CASE STUDY

When Edscha, a German manufacturer of sun roofs, door hinges and other car parts, filed for insolvency, it presented BMW with a crisis. The luxury carmaker was about to introduce its new Z4 convertible – and Edscha supplied its roof. "We had no choice to go to another supplier, as that would have taken six months and we don't have that. We had to help Edscha and try and stabilise it," BMW said.

Today, Edscha is still trading, thanks to the support offered by its leading clients. Nevertheless, BMW remains so worried about disruption to its supply chain that it has increased staff numbers in its risk monitoring department looking only at component-makers.

Richard Milne, Financial Times, 24 March 2009

3.2.2 Event identification

A key aspect of risk identification, emphasised by the Committee of Sponsoring Organisations of the Treadaway Commission's report *Enterprise Risk Management Framework* is identification of events that could impact upon implementation of strategy or achievement of objectives.

External events	Economic changes, political developments, technological advances
Internal events	Equipment problems, human errors, difficulties with products
Leading event indicators	Identifying conditions that could give rise to an event, customers having balances outstanding beyond a certain time being likely to default
Trends and root causes	May be better to tackle the causes rather than respond to the events
Escalation triggers	Certain events happening or levels being reached that require immediate action
Event interdependencies	Identifying how one event can trigger another and how events can occur concurrently, for example failure to invest in new machinery may increase the number of production delays

Once events have been identified, they can be **classified** horizontally across the whole organisation and vertically within operating units. By doing this management can gain a better understanding of the interrelationships between events, gaining enhanced information as a basis for risk assessment.

3.3 Risk analysis

This means obtaining an idea of the **severity** of the consequences of the risk of materialising and how **frequently** (or how likely) it is that the risk will materialise.

It is not always simple to forecast the effects of a possible disaster, as it is not until *after* a loss that extra expenses, inconveniences and loss of time can be recognised. Even then it can be difficult to identify all of them. If your car is stolen, for example, and found converted to a heap of scrap metal, in addition to the cost of replacing it you can expect to pay for some quite **unexpected items**:

- Fares home, and to and from work until you have a replacement

- Telephone calls to the police, your family, your employer, and others affected

- Movement and disposal of the wrecked car

- Increased grocery bills from having to use corner shops instead of a distant supermarket

- Notifications to DVLA that you are no longer the owner

- Work you must turn down because you have no car

- Hire purchase charges on the new car because you have insufficient funds to buy one, when all this happens

- Your time (which is difficult to value)

Organisations will probably keep more detailed records of their activities and the unit costs involved. It is unlikely that any organisation can predict with certainty the full cost of every loss that might affect it.

3.3.1 Risk quantification

Risks that require more analysis can be quantified, where **possible results or losses** and **probabilities** are **calculated** and **distributions** or **confidence limits** added on. From this exercise is derived the following key data.

- **Average or expected result or loss**
- **Frequency of losses**
- **Chances of losses**
- **Largest predictable loss**

to which the organisation could be exposed by a particular risk. The risk manager must also be able to **estimate the effects** of each possible cause of loss, as some of the effects that he needs to consider may not be insured against.

The likely **frequency** of losses from any particular cause can be predicted with some degree of confidence, from studying available records. This confidence margin can be improved by including the likely effects of **changed circumstances** in the calculation, once they are identified and quantified. Risk managers must therefore be aware of the possibility of the **increase of an existing risk**, or the **introduction** of a **new risk**, affecting the probability and/or possible frequency of losses from another cause.

Ultimately the risk manager will need to know the **frequency** and **magnitude** of losses that could place the organisation in serious difficulty.

3.3.2 Exposure of physical assets

Exposures with physical assets may include:

- **Total value of the assets**, for example the value of items stolen from a safe

- **Costs of repair**, if for example an accident occurs

- **Change of value of an asset,** for example property depreciating in value because of a new airport development nearby

- **Decrease in revenues**, for example loss of rent through a rental property being unlettable for a period

- **Costs of unused capacity**, costs incurred by spare capacity that is taken as a precaution but does not end up being used

Managers need to be aware of indirect risks as well as direct risks. For example if assets are damaged, the direct costs are the costs of repairing the asset, whilst the indirect costs might be the costs of interruption of operations, the **loss of contribution** and the **extra expenses** incurred to keep the organisation operating.

3.3.3 Exposure of financial assets

We shall examine in detail the risks of financial assets in Part C of this text. For now it is worth noting that whilst the risk of trading shares and most forms of debt might be that their values fall to zero, this is not necessarily true of futures and options, where the loss depends on margin requirements. In addition anyone who is exposed to loss as a **result of price rises** is in theory exposed to the risk of **infinite loss**, since prices could rise indefinitely.

3.3.4 Exposure of human assets

(a) **Death or serious injury**

The most severe risk to employees is the risk of death or serious injury. The loss to the employee's family, for which the organisation may be liable, could be the **future value** of their **expected income stream.** This is mitigated by any benefits available but enhanced by other losses that arise as a result of death, for example loss of any available tax allowance.

(b) **Key persons**

Certain individuals may make a significant contribution to the office because of their knowledge, skills or business contacts. One measure of this loss will be the present value of the individual's contribution (attributable earnings less remuneration). Indirect costs may include the effect on other staff of the loss of the key person (decreased productivity or indeed the costs of their own departure).

(c) **Business discontinuation losses**

If a director, partner or senior employee dies or departs, there may be costs of having to cope with the disruption, including even the costs of dissolution if local law requires termination of a partnership on the departure of a single partner.

3.4 Risk mapping

This stage involves using the results of a risk assessment to group risks into risk families. One way of doing this severity/frequency matrix (also known as a likelihood/consequences matrix).

Severity

	Low	High
Low	Loss of small suppliers	Loss of senior or specialist staff Loss of sales to competitor Loss of sales due to macroeconomic factors
High	Loss of lower-level staff	Loss of key customers Failure of computer systems

(Frequency is shown on the vertical axis with Low at top and High at bottom)

This **profile** can then be used to set **priorities** for risk mitigation.

Exam alert

Mapping of risks in a scenario using the matrix is likely to come up frequently in your exam. It featured in Question 2 of the specimen paper.

CASE STUDY

CIMA's *Risk Management – A guide to good practice* provides a list of factors that can help determine in which section of the quadrant the risk is located:

- The importance of the strategic objective to which the risk relates
- The type of risk and whether it represents an opportunity or a threat
- The direct and indirect impact of the risk
- The likelihood of the risk

- The cost of different responses to the risk
- The organisation's environment
- Constraints within the organisation
- The organisation's ability to respond to events

It is worth reading the CIMA guidance *Risk Management – a guide to good practice* **in full.**

An alternative method of mapping risk is shown below.

A risk map can be drawn, as a chart or graph, and each risk family can be plotted on the graph. A typical risk map is a graph with one axis for severity of loss and the other axis for frequency of loss. The approach to managing the risks should vary according to their position on the risk map.

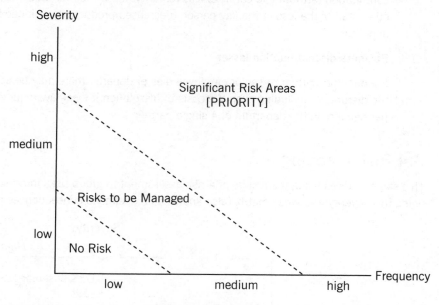

(a)   Risk cannot be eliminated, so it is unlikely that anything will exist in the 'no risk' area.

(b)   The next area is where **severity and frequency are between low and medium, and represents risks that can be managed in a variety of ways**, depending on where they sit on the graph.

The significant risk area shows those risks that should be **prioritised and dealt with first.** The lines between low, medium and high risk may be hard to define, so are likely to 'blur at the edges'. One of the factors that drives this 'blurring' is **risk appetite**, another is the **pace of change** in any organisation. A key part of this approach is therefore frequent review and re-evaluation of risk.

3.5 Risk consolidation

Risk that has been analysed and quantified at the divisional or subsidiary level needs to be aggregated to the corporate level and grouped into categories (categorisation or classification discussed in Chapter 1). This aggregation will be required as part of the overall review of risk that the board needs to undertake which we shall look at in more detail in later chapters. The process of risk categorisation also enables the risks categorised together to be managed by the use of **common control systems**.

Exam skills

A good way to approach exam questions on risk is to analyse

- What do we know or what can we infer from the scenario about the risks and their causes (consider events that result in risk and conditions that result in risk)
- What is the likelihood of the risk materialising and how severe will the consequences be

3.6 Risk register

Organisations should have formal methods of collecting together information on risk and response. A risk register **lists and prioritises the main risks** an organisation faces, and is used as the basis for decision-making on how to deal with risks. **Monetary value** should be allocated if possible, and **interdependencies** with other risks noted. The register also details **who is responsible for dealing** with risks and the **actions taken**. The register should show the risk levels **before** and **after** control action is taken, to facilitate a cost-benefit analysis of controls.

Section summary

Risk analysis involves **identifying, assessing, profiling** and **quantifying risks**.

4 Risk response 5/10

Introduction

We now move on to consider what organisations can do to deal with the risks they are facing.

4.1 Managing risk

In the rest of this chapter we shall consider **risk portfolio management**, the various ways in which organisations can try to mitigate risks or indeed consider whether it will be worthwhile for them to accept risks.

Risk response can be linked into the severity/frequency matrix, discussed earlier and also the organisation's **appetite** for risk-taking.

	Severity	
	Low	*High*
Low	**Accept** Risks are not significant. Keep under view, but costs of dealing with risks unlikely to be worth the benefits.	**Transfer** Insure risk or implement contingency plans. Reduction of severity of risk will minimise insurance premiums.
High	**Control or reduce** Take some action, eg enhanced control systems to detect problems or contingency plans to reduce impact.	**Abandon or avoid** Take immediate action, eg changing major suppliers or abandoning activities.

(Frequency — vertical axis label)

Exam alert

May 2010 Question 2 asked for an evaluation of a bank's risk management strategy.

4.2 Abandonment

A company may deal with risk by **abandoning** operations, for example operations in politically volatile countries where the risks of loss (including loss of life) are considered to be too great or the costs of security are considered to be too high.

4.3 Control of risk

Often risks can be controlled or reduced, but not avoided altogether. This is true of many business risks, where the risks of launching a new product can be reduced by market research, advertising and so on.

Methods of controlling risk over the whole organisation include **risk diversification** and **hedging** risks; both involve turning the multiple risks an organisation faces to its advantage by limiting or countering the impact of individual risks.

4.3.1 Contingency planning

Contingency planning involves identifying the **post-loss needs** of the business, **drawing up plans** in advance and **reviewing them regularly** to take account of changes in the business. The process has three basic constituents.

Information	How, for example, do you turn off the sprinklers once the fire is extinguished? All the information that will need to be available during and after the event should be gathered in advance.
Responsibilities	The plan should lay down what is to be done by whom.
Practice	A full-scale test may not always be possible; simulations, however, should be as realistic as possible and should be taken seriously by all involved. The results of any testing should be monitored so that amendments can be made to the plan as necessary.

4.3.2 Loss control

Control of losses also requires careful advance planning. There are two main aspects to good loss control, the physical and the psychological.

(a)   There are **many physical devices** that can be installed to minimise losses when harmful events actually occur. Sprinklers, fire extinguishers, escape stairways, burglar alarms and machine guards are obvious examples.

(b)   The key psychological factors are **awareness** and **commitment**. Every person in the business should be made aware that losses are possible and that they can be controlled. Commitment to loss control can be achieved by making individual managers **accountable for** the losses under their control. Staff should be encouraged to draw attention to any aspects of their job which makes losses possible.

4.3.3 Procedural approach to risk control

A procedural approach to risk control sees it as being built on adherence to regulations, codes and operating procedures:

• **Rules and regulations** include statute and corporate governance guidance, such as the Combined Code (discussed further in Chapter 3)

• **Other codes** include professional and organisation ethical codes (discussed further in Chapter 4)

• **Procedures** include detailed authorisation or operating procedures (examples for accounting areas are discussed in Chapter 6, operating procedures for computers in Chapter 14)

This approach is likely to be particularly characteristic of a bureaucratic organisation (discussed further in Chapter 5).

4.3.4 Risk pooling and diversification

Risk pooling and diversification involves using portfolio theory to reduce overall risk levels. You may well remember that portfolio theory is an important part of an organisation's financial strategy, but its principles can be applied to non-financial risks as well.

Risk pooling or diversification involves creating a **portfolio of different risks** based on a number of events, which, if some turn out well others will turn out badly, and the average outcome will be neutral. What an organisation has to do is to avoid having all its risks **positively correlated** which means that everything will turn out **extremely well** or **extremely badly**.

One means of diversification may be **geographical diversification** across countries at different stages of the trade cycle.

In addition, although diversification may sound good in theory, the company may have **insufficient expertise** in the product or geographical markets into which it diversifies and it may be vulnerable to competition from other companies who focus on a specific market or product type.

4.3.5 Risk hedging

We shall discuss hedging, taking action to offset one risk by incurring a new risk in the opposite direction, in the context of financial risk in Chapter 8.

| Question 2.1 | Controls |

Learning outcome B2(c)

To demonstrate how controls are an important part of managing risks, we list below a number of the important risks that a business may well face. See if you can suggest some appropriate controls.

Risks		Example controls
Business process	Business processes not aligned with strategic objectives	
Staff departure	Strategy and operations disrupted by key staff leaving	
Resource wastage	Employee time being wasted on unproductive activities	
Investor	Investors losing confidence in the way the company is run and selling their shares	
Staff behaviour	Staff behaving in a way that is not compatible with the ethos of the organisation	
Employee error	Employee error causing loss of key resources to the business	
Technology access	Unauthorised persons gaining access to computer systems	
Fraud	Monies or assets being stolen	
Investment	Loss-making investments being made	
Foreign exchange transaction	Having to pay more on a future transaction because of adverse exchange rate movements	

Risks		Example controls
Political	Operations or revenues being disrupted by political activity	
Information	Taking the wrong decisions due to inadequate information	
Information disruption	Disruption to operations caused by failures of information technology	
Systems development	Unreliable systems that are not in accordance with user needs being developed	

4.4 Risk acceptance

Risk acceptance or retention is where the organisation bears the risk itself. If an unfavourable outcome occurs, it will suffer the full loss. Risk retention is inevitable to some extent. However good the organisation's risk identification and assessment processes are, there will always be some unexpected risk. Other reasons for risk retention are that the risk is considered to be **insignificant** or the **cost of avoiding** the risk is considered to be too great set against the potential loss that could be incurred.

The decision of whether to retain or transfer risks depends first on whether there is anyone to transfer a risk to. The answer is more likely to be 'no' for an individual than for an organisation. In the last resort organisations usually have customers to pass their risks or losses to, up to a point, and individuals do not.

You must remember that risk acceptance is a **conscious decision** to take no action to counter the risk. Risk acceptance and ignoring risk are **not** the same. Risks accepted should generally be **low frequency**, **low severity risks**.

An organisation can ignore risks of any degree of seriousness. If it does so, it may suffer some nasty surprises.

4.5 Transfer of risk

Alternatively, risks can be transferred – to other internal departments or externally to suppliers, customers or **insurers**. Risk transfer can even be to the state.

Decisions to transfer should not be made without careful consideration. A decision not to rectify the design of a product, because rectification could be as expensive as paying any claims from disgruntled customers, is in fact a decision to transfer the risk to the customers without their knowledge. It may not take into account the possibility of courts awarding exemplary damages to someone injured by the product, to discourage people from taking similar decisions in the future.

4.5.1 Risk sharing

Risks can be partly held and partly transferred to someone else. An example is an insurance policy, where the insurer pays any losses incurred by the policyholder above a set amount.

Risk-sharing arrangements can be very significant in business strategy. For example in a **joint venture** arrangement each participant's risk can be limited to what it is prepared to bear.

Exam alert

The compulsory question in particular offers a lot of scope to test risk management techniques, as the unseen could well contain risks of differing natures that have to be managed in different ways.

Section summary

Methods of dealing with risk include **abandonment, control, acceptance** and **transfer**.

5   Risk responsibilities

Introduction

Organisations need to approach risk management in a systematic way. A risk policy statement sets out general guidelines, including responsibilities for risk management. Everyone in the organisation has some responsibility for risk management, but the organisation may employ specialists to oversee the risk management processes.

5.1 Risk policy statement

Organisations ought to have a statement of risk policy and strategy that is distributed to all managers and staff and covers the following areas:

- Definitions of risk and risk management
- Objectives of risk policy
- Regulatory requirements
- Benefits of risk management
- How risk management is linked into strategic decision-making and performance
- What areas of risk management (risk avoidance, risk reduction) are particularly important
- Risk classification
- Roles of board, managers, staff and audit and risk committees
- Internal control framework and important controls
- Other tools and techniques
- Assurance reporting
- Role of training
- How to obtain help

5.2 Responsibilities for risk management

Everyone who works for the organisation has accountability for risk management, not just risk specialists whose roles we shall discuss later in this chapter.

5.2.1 The board

As we shall see in Section 6 and in later chapters, the board's role in managing risk is one of its most important. The board is responsible for **determining risk management strategy** as part of its responsibility for the organisation's overall strategy and its responsibilities to shareholders and other stakeholders. It is also responsible for monitoring risks and internal controls and communicating the organisation's strategy to employees.

Exam alert

You may be asked to explain the concept of risk ownership at board level.

5.2.2 Risk management group

The board may be supported by a risk management group, which is responsible for building on the overall strategy and framework prescribed by the board. As well as representatives from risk managers and internal audit, the group should also include operational and information systems managers. This group will prescribe **methods of risk management** that operating units will employ. It will concentrate on **risk responses** and will also **monitor risk management** to see that the strategies and policies are operating effectively. The risk management group will report to the board and in turn will receive **reports from line managers and employees**.

CASE STUDY

Risk management groups

Strode's College

The key tasks of the Risk Management Group are to:

- Take overall responsibility for the administration and implementation of the risk management process

- Identify and evaluate the significant risks faced by the College and produce a Risk Management Action Plan for consideration by the Senior Management Team and the Board of Governors

- Provide adequate information in a timely manner to the Board of Governors and its committees on the status of risks and controls

- Report regularly on the Risk Management Action Plan implementation to the Senior Management Team and the Board of Governors and to undertake an annual review of effectiveness of the system of internal control to be presented to the Board of Governors

The membership of the Risk Management Group will reflect the full range of the College's activities and will include the Principal, Vice Principal, Finance Manager, Resources Manager, Estates Manager and a Director of Faculty.

The Risk Management Group will report on a regular basis to the Senior Management Team.

The Risk Management Group will prepare a report of its review of the effectiveness of the internal control system annually for consideration by the Senior Management Team, the Audit Committee and the Board of Governors.

5.2.3 Internal and external audit

Risk is integral to the work of internal and external audit, both in terms of influencing **how much work** they do (with more work being done on riskier areas) and also **what** work they actually do. The external auditors will be concerned with risks that impact most on the figures shown in the **financial accounts**. Internal auditors' role is **more flexible**, and their approach will depend on whether they focus on the controls that are being operated or the overall risk management process. Again we shall discuss this in more detail later on.

5.2.4 Line managers

Depending on whether specialist risk managers are involved, part of the role of line managers may be to carry out detailed risk management functions. The office manager may deal with fire precautions, and the managing director with buying insurances, for example, and each may call in experts to assist with these functions.

In any event line managers will be involved in communicating risk management policies to staff and will of course 'set a good example'. Line managers also are responsible for **preparing reports** that will be considered by the board and senior managers.

5.2.5 Staff

Staff will be responsible for following the **risk management procedures** the organisation has established, and should be alert for any conditions or events that may result in problems. Staff must be aware of how to **report** any concerns they have, particularly reports of risk, failures of existing control measures, variances in budgets and forecasts.

5.3 Risk management personnel

5.3.1 Risk specialists

Most individuals have little time for looking after their personal safety and security, still less for searching the market for the most suitable insurances; they frequently employ agents to help manage some of their risks.

A **specialist** advising on management of personal risks can work only as well as the client allows. A good specialist will ask for information and for co-operation with the expert surveys that enable him to provide a proper service; he will ensure that the client understands what safety measures are required and he will see that they are put into practice.

5.3.2 Risk manager

The risk manager will need technical skills in **credit, market**, and **operational risk**. Leadership and persuasive skills are likely to be necessary to overcome resistance from those who believe that risk management is an attempt to stifle initiative.

Lam (Enterprise Risk Management) includes a detailed description of this role, and the COSO framework also has a list of responsibilities. Combining these sources we can say that the risk manager is typically responsible for:

(a)   Providing the **overall leadership**, **vision** and **direction** for enterprise risk management.

(b)   Establishing an **integrated RM framework** for all aspects of risk across the organisation, integrating enterprise risk management with other business planning and management activities and framing authority and accountability for enterprise risk management in business units.

(c)   Promoting an **enterprise risk management competence** throughout the entity, including facilitating development of technical enterprise risk management expertise, helping managers align risk responses with the entity's risk tolerances and developing appropriate controls.

(d)   **Developing RM policies**, including the quantification of management's risk appetite through specific risk limits, defining roles and responsibilities and participating in setting goals for implementation.

(e)   **Establishing a common risk management language** that includes common measures around likelihood and impact, and common risk categories. Developing the analytical systems and data management capabilities to support the risk management programme.

(f)   **Implementing a set of risk indicators and reports** including losses and incidents, key risk exposures, and early warning indicators. Facilitating managers' development of reporting protocols, including quantitative and qualitative thresholds, and monitoring the reporting process.

(g)   **Dealing with insurance companies**; an important task because of increased premium costs, restrictions in the cover available (will the risks be excluded from cover) and the need for negotiations with insurance companies if claims arise. If insurers require it demonstrating that the organisation is taking steps actively to manage its risks. Arranging financing schemes such as self-insurance or captive insurance.

(h)   **Allocating economic capital to business activities** based on risk, and optimising the company's risk portfolio through business activities and risk transfer strategies.

(i)   **Reporting to the chief executive on progress** and recommending action as needed. Communicating the company's risk profile to key stakeholders such as the board of directors, regulators, stock analysts, rating agencies and business partners.

The risk manager's contribution will be judged by how much he **increases the value of the organisation**. The specialist knowledge a risk manager have should allow the risk manager to assess **long-term risk** and hazard outcomes and therefore decide what resources should be allocated to combating risk.

Clearly certain strategic risks are likely to have the biggest impact on corporate value. Therefore a risk manager's role may include management of these strategic risks. These may include those having a **fundamental effect on future operations** such as mergers and acquisitions or risks that have the potential to cause **large adverse impacts** such as currency hedging and major investments

CASE STUDY

The role of the risk manager was highlighted in February 2009 during the UK House of Commons's Treasury select committee enquiry into the banking system. The enquiry received evidence from Paul Moore, ex head of Group Regulatory Risk at HBOS. Moore had allegedly been sacked by Sir James Crosby, Chief Executive Officer at HBOS. As a result of Moore making the allegations, Sir James resigned as deputy chairman of London city watchdog, the Financial Services Authority.

Moore stated that in his role he 'felt a bit like being a man in a rowing boat trying to slow down an oil tanker'. He said that he had told the board that their sales culture was out of balance with their systems and controls; the bank was growing too fast, did not accept challenges to policy, and was a serious risk to financial stability and consumer protection. The reason why Moore was ignored and others were afraid to speak up was, he alleged, that the balance of power was weighted towards executive directors, not just in HBOS but in other banks as well.

'I believe that, had there been highly competent risk and compliance managers in all the banks, carrying rigorous oversight, properly protected and supported by a truly independent non-executive, the external auditor and the FSA, they would have felt comfortable and protected to challenge the practices of the executive without fear for their own positions. If this had been the case, I am also confident that we would not have got into the current crisis.'

Moore was replaced by a Group Risk Director who had never previously been a risk manager. The new head had been a sales manager and was appointed by the Chief Executive Officer, allegedly without involving other board members in the recruitment decision.

During the time that Paul Moore was head of Group Regulatory Risk, the Financial Services Authority had raised its own concerns about practices at HBOS and had kept a watching brief over the bank. In December 2004 the Authority noted that although the group 'had made good progress in addressing the risks highlighted in February 2004, the group risk functions still needed to enhance their ability to influence the business'. In June 2006 the authority stated that whilst the group had improved its framework, it still had concerns: 'The growth strategy of the group posed risks to the whole group and these risks must be managed and mitigated.'

At the end of the week in which Paul Moore's evidence was published, Lloyds, which had taken HBOS over, issued a profit warning in relation to HBOS for 2008 for losses of over £10 billion.

5.3.3 Risk management function

Larger companies may have a bigger risk management function whose responsibilities are wider than a single risk manager or risk specialists. The Institute of Risk Management's Risk Management standard lists the main responsibilities of the risk management function:

*   **Setting policy and strategy** for risk management

*   **Primary champion of risk management** at a strategic and operational level

*   Building a **risk aware culture** within the organisation including appropriate education

*   Establishing **internal risk policy** and structures for business units

- **Designing and reviewing processes** for risk management

- **Coordinating the various functional activities** which advise on risk management issues

- **Developing risk response processes**, including contingency and business continuity programmes

- Deciding **how frequently risks** should be **monitored and reported**

- **Preparing reports on risks** for the board and stakeholders

CASE STUDY

Writing in *Risk Management* magazine, Gayle Tollifson, chief risk officer at QBE Insurance Company, emphasises the importance of culture. She comments that in a number of corporate collapses, the tone or culture that boards set for their companies was flawed or ignored; in many instances boards were not aware of problems until too late.

Tollifson emphasises the board's responsibility to ensure the right culture exists at all levels of an organisation. At the board level selecting a chief executive who embraces the company's cultural values is vital, and board-approved policies and standards must lead the way in risk management practice. Communication is also important. This includes a risk management policy, ensuring the right mechanisms are in place for disclosing issues and that there is a culture of disclosure. This must mean sending a message to staff that the sooner bad news is identified and reported, the sooner the problem can be solved.

As well as embedding risk into the culture, Tollifson explains that companies need to ensure that risk management is an essential part of business operations, considered as part of doing business **every day**. Risk appetite needs to be considered when overall strategy and policy are set; risk analysis must form a key part of the business planning framework.

Tollifson also stresses that whilst a risk management team can make a significant contribution, the board must set the culture entrenching risk awareness, disclosure and transparency; the business managers who create risks must also take responsibility for managing them.

The Risk Management standard can be downloaded from www.theirm.org/publications/documents/Risk_Management_Standard

Section summary

General steps organisations can take to manage risks include issuing a **risk policy statement**, appointing a **risk manager** or **risk specialists** and **communicating risks** to staff and shareholders.

6 Risk monitoring

Introduction

A key responsibility of the board is to oversee and review the risk management process.

6.1 Board review

The 2010 UK Corporate Governance Code emphasises the importance of the board's responsibility for determining the **nature** and **extent** of the significant risks it is willing to take. Boards should also consider:

(a)   The **threat** of such **risks becoming a reality**

(b)   If that happened, the company's ability to **reduce** the **incidence** and **impact** on the business and to adapt to changing risks or operational deficiencies

(c)   The **costs and benefits** related to operating relevant controls

The board should focus on serious risks, whether they are long-term or short-term and strategic or operational. Although the board will spend a lot of time on risks associated with strategy, it must gain assurance that serious operational risks are being appropriately managed. That said, too great a focus on immediate issues, such as the consequences of the recession, may mean longer-term trends, such as technological developments associated with serious strategic risks, may be neglected.

6.2 Information and communication

Boards should review risks and internal control as a regular part of their agenda. A key aspect for the directors to consider is the **frequency of monitoring of risks**. Some risks may need to be monitored daily; others much less frequently.

The information directors need to be able to monitor controls effectively comes from a wide variety of sources. We shall discuss these further in Chapter 6.

6.3 Board monitoring

COSO has published guidance covering how board should monitor risks and controls. The guidance states that **ineffective** monitoring results in control breakdowns and material impacts on the organisation's ability to achieve its objectives. **Inefficient** monitoring leads to a lack of focus on the areas of greatest need. Three elements influence the effectiveness and efficiency of monitoring:

- **Control environment** in relation to monitoring
- The ability to **prioritise effective monitoring procedures**
- The **communication structure** and the ability to report the results of monitoring

6.3.1 Prioritising effective monitoring procedures

The COSO guidance stresses that the business's overall risk assessment process will influence the scope of monitoring. Key factors will include the **size and complexity of the organisation**, the **nature of the organisation's operations**, the **purpose for which monitoring is being conducted** and the **relative importance of the underlying controls.**

To ensure monitoring has an appropriate risk-based focus, the organisation should establish a structure that firstly ensures that internal control is effective in a given area and focuses monitoring attention on areas of change. This structure will have the following elements:

Control baseline	Heading
Change identification process	Identifying changes in processes or risks that indicate controls should have changed. Monitoring should focus on the ability of the risk assessment procedures to identify changes in processes or risks that should result in changes in controls. Monitoring should also assess whether indicators of change in control design and operation are effective
Change management process	Verifying that the internal control systems have managed changes in controls effectively

6.3.2 Communication structure for monitoring

The results of monitoring need to be reported to the right people and corrective action taken. Weaknesses in internal controls should be reported to the person **responsible for the control's operation** and **to at least one level higher.** The weaknesses need to be assessed in the same terms as risks, the **likelihood** that a control will fail to detect or prevent a risk's occurrence and the **significance** of the potential impact of the risk.

Where control weaknesses are potentially significant, additional monitoring procedures may be needed during the correction period to protect against errors.

6.3.3 Scale of monitoring

The **size of the organisation** and the **complexity of its operations and controls** will be key determinants.

CASE STUDY

The practical example given in the COSO guidance is a distinction between the purchase function in a large and small company. A company that has 20 people processing invoices, one of whom is not properly trained, may be able to operate for some time without material error. Senior management would not therefore be concerned. A company with only one person processing invoices cannot afford that person to be inadequately trained. Senior management monitoring on a day-to-day basis may be required.

6.3.4 Formality of monitoring

Increased formality will be required in larger organisations, where managers' knowledge of day-to-day operational control activities is less. If the results of monitoring are being reported outside the organisation, monitoring will also need to be more formal. In particular the organisation will need to be able to provide evidence that supports the reports made.

Increased formality may include:

- Processes to document and retain monitoring information

- Policies and processes regarding aggregation, evaluation and reporting of weaknesses to the board, or to the audit and risk committees.

CASE STUDY

BP's monitoring procedures include the work carried out by the safety, ethics and environment assurance committee. The committee's work encompasses all non-financial risks; the audit committee monitors all financial risks. The safety, ethics and environment assurance committee monitors risks identified in BP's business and annual plans, and also the review of risk conducted by the internal auditors.

6.4 Internal risk reporting

Risk reporting needs to cover all stages of the risk management system and be carried out on a **systematic**, **regular basis**. The system also needs to ensure that significant changes in the risk profile are notified quickly to **senior management**. Reporting of high impact-likelihood risks may occur daily, other risks may be reported **monthly or quarterly**. The **risk register** is a key document in risk reporting, not only in terms of identifying risks, but also allocating responsibility for **managing, monitoring and reporting**.

Reports should show the **risk levels before controls are implemented** and the **residual risk** after controls are taken into account.

Reporting also needs to include comparisons of actual risks against predicted risks, **feedback** on the **action taken** to manage and reduce risks that the system has identified.

- Have the actions taken **fulfilled their objectives**?
- What **further action** is needed?
- Have the **costs of taking action justified the benefits**?

If risks have not been managed effectively at lower levels of the organisation, senior management may need to take a **more active role**.

As it will not be worthwhile to eliminate all risks, the reporting system needs to highlight **residual risks**, the **remaining exposure to risk** after appropriate management action has been taken.

6.5 External risk reporting

This will be determined by the **local laws**, **regulations** and **governance requirements** of the country concerned. The Turnbull report in the UK requires the board to:

- **Acknowledge its responsibility** for ensuring the effectiveness of control systems
- State the existence of a **risk management process**
- Explain what the board has done to **review its effectiveness**

In 2010 the UK Corporate Governance Code introduced a requirement for the company's business model to be explained.

Various reports also require disclosing the full implications of problems. For example Sarbanes-Oxley requires boards to **disclose material weaknesses in internal controls over financial reporting**.

6.5.1 Other accounts disclosures

The risk and control report should **link in with other disclosures** in the accounts about business developments. UK 2008 regulations require disclosure in the directors' report of likely future developments in the business of the company, including presumably changes in risk exposure.

6.5.2 Interests of users

The directors must also take account of the views of shareholders, who will be interested in learning about the risks that could have most impact on the **value of their investment**, and how these risks are being controlled. These would include **principal strategic and financial risks**, and also **operational risks** that could have severe financial consequences. The views of other principal **stakeholders** will also be important.

6.5.3 Risks materialising or changing over the year

Disclosure of risks that have **significantly changed** will also be important, and how control systems have developed to meet these changes.

6.5.4 Reputation risks

Risks that could cause a significant fall in the organisation's reputation may well be risks about which the board wishes to reassure stakeholders. Disclosures may focus on threats to reputation that may have a large impact on the business, particularly **product safety**.

6.5.5 Limitations on risk disclosures

The board may be less willing to disclose some risks on the grounds of **commercial confidentiality**. Directors may also fear that **disclosures about certain risks** will be **misinterpreted** by readers of the accounts. However they may also be motivated to include matters included in the reports of competitors or those identified as **best practice** to evidence how they are managing the risks that are common in this industry.

Exam alert

The examiner has stressed that the success of a risk management strategy should be judged by what was known **at the time action was taken** to manage risk. If for example a company faces a serious risk, it may not be able to afford the consequences of that risk crystallising. If that risk appears likely to materialise, the company's management of the risk must be judged against the potentially serious consequences, even if in the end the risk does not materialise.

Section summary

Board review is an essential part of the risk management process.

Board review should be based on **information collected from various sources**.

Factors influencing the **extent of external reporting** of risk include **regulations**, **governance codes** and **attitudes of stakeholders**, particularly shareholders.

Chapter Roundup

✓ **Risk management model**s provide a coherent framework for organisations to deal with risk, based on the following components:

- Risk appetite
- Risk identification
- Risk assessment
- Risk profiling
- Risk quantification
- Risk management
- Review and feedback

✓ Management responses to risk are not automatic, but will be determined by their **own attitudes to risk**, which in turn will be influenced by **shareholder attitudes** and **cultural factors**.

✓ **Risk analysis** involves **identifying, assessing, profiling** and **quantifying risks**.

✓ Methods of dealing with risk include **abandonment**, **control**, **acceptance** and **transfer**.

✓ General steps organisations can take to manage risks include issuing a **risk policy statement**, appointing a **risk manager** or **risk specialists** and **communicating risks** to staff and shareholders.

✓ **Board review** is an essential part of the risk management process.

✓ **Board review** should be based on **information collected from various sources**.

✓ Factors influencing the **extent of external reporting** of risk include **regulations**, **governance codes** and **attitudes of stakeholders**, particularly shareholders.

Quick Quiz

1 Match the viewpoint to the attitude to risk.

(a) Fatalist

(c) Individualist

(b) Hierarchist

(d) Egalitarian

(i) Risk reduction through formal risk management procedures

(ii) Sharing or transfer of risk

(iii) Informal risk management systems

(iv) Risk management is pointless

2 Complete the severity/frequency matrix in relation to methods of dealing with risk.

Severity

	Low	High
Low		
High		

Frequency

3 What according to COSO are the key characteristics of enterprise risk management?

4 What does event identification aim to identify?

5 What key indicators should risk quantification provide?

6 What are the main elements that should be covered in a risk register?

7 Upon what theory is the process of risk diversification based?

A Contingency theory
B Portfolio theory
C Control theory
D Performance theory

8 Fill in the blank.

.... is taking an action that will offset an exposure to a risk by incurring a new risk in the opposite direction.

9 Insurance is an example of risk

A Acceptance
B Avoidance
C Transfer
D Reduction

10 What areas should formal reporting of risk management address?

Answers to Quick Quiz

1   (a)(iv); (b)(i); (c)(iii); (d)(ii)

2

Severity

	Low	High
Low	Accept	Transfer
High	Control	Abandon

(Frequency on vertical axis)

3
- Process
- Operated by people at every level
- Applied in strategy setting
- Applied across the organisation
- Identifies significant events
- Provides reasonable assurance
- Geared to the achievement of objectives

4
- External events
- Internal events
- Leading event indicators
- Trends and root causes

5
- Average or expected result
- The frequency of losses
- The chances of loss
- The largest predictable loss

6
- Lists and priorities of risks
- Monetary value
- Interdependencies
- Responsibilities for dealing with risks and action taken
- Risk levels before and after action taken

7   B   Portfolio theory

8   **Risk hedging** is taking an action that will offset an exposure to a risk by incurring a new risk in the opposite direction.

9   C   Transfer

10
- Control methods
- Processes for identifying risks
- Primary control systems
- Monitoring and review systems

Answers to Questions

2.1 Controls

The risks chosen in the question are designed to illustrate how different types of control can be used to counter different risks. Important points from the list below are that:

(a)   Some controls are meant to **match exactly with specific risks**; for example the risk of a transaction in foreign exchange causing losses can be mitigated by undertaking an equal and opposite transaction designed to match the first.

(b)   With other controls the matching is less obvious; these controls are designed to deal with the ways the **business is organised**, the way **decisions are taken** and the ways in which **employee performance** is **maximised**.

(c)   Some controls are designed to **prevent** problems occurring in the first place; others to **detect** problems if they arise and **minimise their impact**.

(d)   **Information** is key to control and decision-making. Effective risk management depends on having the right type and level of information, including, but not only, management accounting information.

Risks		Example controls	Chapter reference
Business process	Business processes not aligned with strategic objectives	The way the business is **structured**, particularly how much **central control** is exercised over operations	5
Staff departure	Strategy and operations disrupted by key staff leaving	**Human resource measures** such as incentives to encourage staff and appraisals to monitor views and dissatisfaction	5
Resource wastage	Employee time being wasted on unproductive activities	**Management accounting systems**, enabling assessment of employee contribution and highlighting problem areas	7
Investor	Investors losing confidence in the way the company is run and selling their shares	**Corporate governance** arrangements ensuring board exercises proper stewardship over the company and communicates effectively with shareholders	3
Staff behaviour	Staff behaving in a way that is not compatible with the ethos of the organisation	Strong **control environment** highlighting the need for ethical behaviour and integrity	6
Employee error	Employee error causing loss of key resources to the business	**Control procedures** to **detect** errors before they cause loss such as approval by senior staff, and **training** to improve staff's abilities and **prevent** errors occurring	5, 6
Technology access	Unauthorised persons gaining access to computer systems	**Internal audit detecting** unauthorised access and **failure** by the controls in place to stop unauthorised persons accessing systems	14, 16
Fraud	Monies or assets being stolen	**Fraud response plan** if fraud is detected or suspected	6
Investment	Loss-making investments being made	Use of **different financial measures** to provide extra perspectives on the investment	8
Foreign exchange transaction	Having to pay more on a future transaction because of adverse exchange rate movements	**Purchase an instrument** fixing the exchange rate used in the transaction	11–12

BPP
LEARNING MEDIA

Risks		Example controls	Chapter reference
Political	Operations or revenues being disrupted by political activity	**Monitor** political situation; **negotiate with key stakeholders** (political parties)	10
Information	Taking the wrong decisions due to inadequate information	**Information systems** the organisation chooses providing quality of information needed for decision-making	13
Information disruption	Disruption to operations caused by failures of information technology	Controls to **prevent** disruption occurring, such as **avoiding** placing IT in **vulnerable locations**, and **contingency plans** if disruption occurs	14
Systems development	Unreliable systems that are not in accordance with user needs being developed	A formal systems **development process** encompassing planning, testing and review	14

Now try this question from the Exam Question Bank

Number	Level	Marks	Time
Q2	Examination	25	45 mins

MANAGEMENT AND INTERNAL CONTROL SYSTEMS

Part B

CORPORATE GOVERNANCE

In Part B we move on to the control systems and internal controls that organisations operate. We start by looking at corporate governance arrangements, which provide **overall control** over the organisation and **monitor the specific controls** that it operates.

Corporate governance is a key area in this syllabus, and one in which you are expected to have a good knowledge of major worldwide developments. There have been a number of reports worldwide on corporate governance and to help you get your bearings, we have set out in an appendix to this chapter the main

provisions of the UK Corporate Governance Code, Sarbanes-Oxley legislation and the King report. However the examiners have stressed that the **principles of corporate governance** are most important, so in the main body of the chapter we cover the main areas of corporate governance, mixing in the recommendations of various reports.

The focus of this chapter is on the role of the **board**, its membership, its committees and how it communicates with shareholders. Other important elements of corporate governance include **risk management** which we have already covered, and the **audit committee** and **internal audit** which we will cover in Chapters 15 and 16.

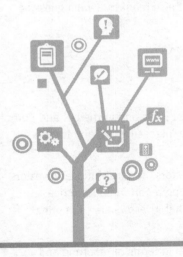

topic list	learning outcomes	syllabus references	ability required
1 Developments in corporate governance	B3(a)	B3(i)	analysis
2 Corporate governance principles and reports	B3(a)	B3(i)	analysis
3 The board of directors	B3(a)	B3(i)	analysis
4 Directors' remuneration	B3(a)	B3(i)	analysis
5 Accounts and audit	B3(a)	B3(i)	analysis
6 Shareholders	B3(a)	B3(i)	analysis
Appendix: Corporate governance reports			

1 Developments in corporate governance

Introduction

We start this chapter by looking at the forces that have generated the development of governance best practice over the last 20 years. These include, but are not confined to, the risks of poor governance that corporate scandals have highlighted. Increasing globalisation of investment has also been significant.

1.1 What is corporate governance?

KEY TERM

CORPORATE GOVERNANCE is the system by which organisations are directed and controlled.

Although mostly discussed in relation to large quoted companies, governance is an issue for all bodies corporate; commercial and not for profit.

There are a number of elements in corporate governance:

(a) The **management and reduction of risk** is fundamental in all definitions of good governance.

(b) The notion that **overall performance enhanced** by **good supervision** and **management** within **set best practice guidelines** underpins most definitions.

(c) Good governance provides a **framework** for an organisation to pursue its strategy in an **ethical and effective** way from the perspective of all stakeholder groups affected, and offers safeguards against misuse of resources, physical or intellectual.

(d) Good governance is not just about externally established codes, it also requires a willingness to **apply the spirit** as well as the letter of the law.

(e) **Accountability** is generally a major theme in all governance frameworks.

1.2 The driving forces of governance development

Corporate governance issues came to prominence in the USA during the 1970s and in the UK and Europe from late 1980s. The main, but not the only, drivers associated with the increasing demand for the development of governance were:

(a) **Increasing internationalisation and globalisation** meant that investors, and institutional investors in particular, began to invest outside their home countries. The King report in South Africa highlights the role of the free movement of capital, commenting that investors are promoting governance in their own self-interest.

(b) The **differential treatment of domestic and foreign investors**, both in terms of reporting and associated rights/dividends caused many investors to call for parity of treatment.

(c) Issues concerning **financial reporting** were raised by many investors and were the focus of much debate and litigation.

(d) The characteristics of individual countries may have a **significant influence** in the way corporate governance has developed. The King report emphasises the importance of qualities that are fundamental to the South African culture such as collectiveness, consensus, helpfulness, fairness, consultation and religious faith in the development of best practice.

(e) An increasing number of **high profile corporate scandals** and collapses including Polly Peck International, BCCI, and Maxwell Communications Corporation prompted the development of governance codes in the early 1990s. However the scandals since then have raised questions about further measures that may be necessary.

CASE STUDY

In the UK the Cadbury committee was set up in May 1991 because of the lack of confidence which was perceived in financial reporting and in the ability of external auditors to provide the assurances required by the users of financial statements. The main difficulties were considered to be in the relationship between external auditors and boards of directors. In particular, the commercial pressures on both directors and auditors caused pressure to be brought to bear on auditors by the board and the auditors often capitulated. Problems were also perceived in the ability of the board of directors to control their organisations. The lack of board accountability in many of these company collapses demonstrated the need for action.

1.3 Risks of poor corporate governance

The scandals over the last 25 years have highlighted the need for guidance to tackle the various risks and problems that can arise in organisations' systems of governance.

1.4 The board of directors

Boards that have failed to manage companies effectively have been a key aspect of governance scandals. Different scandals have highlighted certain key weaknesses.

1.4.1 Domination by a single individual

A feature of many corporate governance scandals has been boards dominated by a single senior executive with other board members merely acting as a rubber stamp. Sometimes the single individual may bypass the board to action his own interests. The report on the UK Guinness case suggested that the Chief Executive, Ernest Saunders paid himself a £3million reward without consulting the other directors.

Even if an organisation is not dominated by a single individual, there may be other weaknesses. The organisation may be run by a small group centred round the chief executive and chief financial officer, and appointments may be made by personal recommendation rather than a formal, objective process.

1.4.2 Lack of involvement of board

Boards that meet irregularly or fail to consider systematically the organisation's activities and risks are clearly weak. Sometimes the failure to carry out proper oversight is due to a **lack of information** being provided, or the directors lacking the knowledge or skills necessary to contribute effectively.

1.4.3 Lack of supervision

Employees who are not properly supervised by the board can create large losses for the organisation through their own incompetence, negligence or fraudulent activity. The behaviour of Nick Leeson, the employee who caused the collapse of Barings bank was not challenged because he appeared to be successful, whereas he was using unauthorised accounts to cover up his large trading losses. Leeson was able to do this because he was in charge of dealing and settlement, a systems weakness or **lack of segregation of key roles** that was featured in other financial frauds.

1.5 Directors' remuneration

Complaints over directors' remuneration levels have been a common feature of corporate governance debates. Complaints have not only focused on remuneration levels, but on the unwillingness of those who can challenge remuneration packages effectively (non-executive directors, institutional shareholders) to do so. Various problems have been highlighted:

(a)   **Remuneration levels** that are **excessive** per se, and are not justified by the contribution directors have made

(b) Directors being **rewarded for failure**, for example receiving bonuses when their companies have performed poorly and receiving **significant compensation payments** when they lose office

(c) **Remuneration arrangements** providing incentives for directors to allow risk-taking beyond levels that would be deemed acceptable by many shareholders

CASE STUDY

Paul Moore, in his evidence to the Treasury Select Committee on HBOS, highlighted examples of excessive risk-taking:

'There must have been a very high risk if you lend money to people who have no jobs, no provable income and no assets. If you lend that money to buy an asset which is worth the same or even less than the amount of the loan and secure that loan on the value of that asset purchased and, then, assume that asset will always to rise in value, you must be pretty much close to delusional.'

1.6 Accounts and audit

A lot of governance guidance has been concerned with defining effective internal control. Inevitably many companies involved in scandals have had glaring weaknesses in internal control, weaknesses that have not been picked up by those monitoring control.

1.6.1 Lack of adequate control function

An obvious weakness is a **lack of internal audit**. Another important control is **lack of adequate technical knowledge** in key roles, for example in the audit committee or in senior compliance positions. A rapid turnover of staff involved in accounting or control may suggest inadequate resourcing, and will make control more difficult because of lack of continuity.

1.6.2 Lack of independent scrutiny

External auditors may not carry out the necessary questioning of senior management because of fears of losing the audit. Often corporate collapses are followed by criticisms of external auditors, such as the Barlow Clowes affair where poorly planned and focused audit work failed to identify illegal use of client monies.

CASE STUDY

To quote Paul Moore again, on HBOS (and other banks):

'There has been a completely inadequate "separation" and "balance of powers" between the executive and all those accountable for overseeing their actions and "reining them in" i.e. internal control functions such as finance, risk, compliance and internal audit, non-executive Chairmen and Directors, external auditors, the FSA, shareholders and politicians.'

1.6.3 Misleading accounts and information

Often misleading figures are symptomatic of other problems but clearly poor quality accounting information is a major problem if markets are trying to make a fair assessment of the company's value. Giving out misleading information was a major issue in the UK's Equitable Life scandal where the company gave contradictory information to savers, independent advisers, media and regulators.

Clearly the ultimate risk is of the organisation **making such large losses** that **bankruptcy** becomes inevitable. The organisation may also be closed down as a result of **serious regulatory breaches,** for example misapplying investors' monies.

CASE STUDY

Worldcom was a good example of a company with aggressive earnings targets and fraudulent accounting practices being developed when it appeared that those earnings targets would not be met.

'In mid 2000, with the telecommunications industry in a severe slump. Worldcom announced that the company's results for the second half of the year might fall below expectations… thus began the process of managing earnings in order to hit the 2000 year-end profit target, reserves were used to cover line charges. The establishment of these reserves had been questionable at best, and the use of reserves to cover accounting expenses was in clear violation of accounting rules. When mid-level accounting personnel raised objections to this strategy, the CFO assured them that this was a one-time event that would help WorldCom over a rough place in the road.'

IFAC/CIMA report *Enterprise Governance Getting the Balance Right*

1.7 Shareholders

Often board members may have grown up with the company but lose touch with the interests and views of shareholders. One possible symptom of this is the payment of remuneration packages that do not appear to be warranted by results.

Section summary

Good corporate governance involves **risk management** and **internal control, accountability** to stakeholders and other shareholders and conducting business in an **ethical and effective way.**

2 Corporate governance principles and reports

Introduction

In this section we look at the principles underlying corporate governance best practice, and introduce the most significant worldwide codes. Fuller coverage of a number of these codes is included in the appendix to this chapter.

2.1 Perspectives on governance

Debates about the place of governance are founded on three differing views associated with the **ownership** and **management** of organisations.

2.1.1 Stewardship theory

Some approaches to good governance view the management of an organisation as the **stewards** of its assets, charged with their employment and deployment in ways consistent with the overall strategy of the organisation. Technically, shareholders or member/owners have the right to dismiss their stewards if they are dissatisfied by their stewardship, via a vote at an annual general meeting.

Fundamentally though governance is undermined if shareholders do **not take an active interest** in the organisation, and do not exercise their right to vote. Good governance can therefore be seen to require active participation on the part of owners.

2.1.2 Agency theory

Another approach to governance is enshrined in **agency theory**. This takes the stance that, rather than acting as stewards, management will act in an **agency capacity**, seeking to **service their own self-interest** and looking after the performance of the company only where its goals are co-incident with their own.

This approach takes a very negative, short term/tactical stance, but is one that has found a home in some elements of the frameworks. The development of **performance related remuneration** and **incentive schemes**, such as Long Term Incentive Plans (LTIPs) and executive share option schemes, are rooted in an agency theory approach, aiming to direct management towards achieving the long-term goals of the company.

Exam alert

The examiner has stated that students need to know how to ensure that agency problems are addressed.

2.1.3 Stakeholder theory

The stakeholder approach takes a much more **'organic' view** of the organisation, imbuing it with a 'life' of its own, in keeping with the notion of a separate legal personage. Effectively stakeholder theory is a development of the notion of stewardship, stating that management has a **duty of care, not just to the owners** of the company in terms of maximising shareholder value, but also to the **wider community** of interest, or stakeholders.

2.2 Governance principles

Most corporate governance codes are based on a set of principles founded upon ideas of what corporate governance is meant to achieve. This list is based on a number of reports.

(a)   To **ensure adherence** to and **satisfaction** of the **strategic objectives** of the organisation, thus aiding effective management.

(b)   To **minimise risk**, especially financial, legal and reputational risks, by ensuring appropriate systems of financial control are in place, systems for monitoring risk, financial control and compliance with the law.

(c)   To **promote integrity**, that is **straightforward dealing** and **completeness**.

(d)   To **fulfil responsibilities to all stakeholders** and to **minimise potential conflicts of interest** between the owners, managers and wider stakeholder community.

(e)   To **establish clear accountability** at senior levels within an organisation. However, one danger may be that boards become **too closely involved with day-to-day issues** and do not delegate responsibility to management.

(f)   To **maintain the independence** of those who scrutinise the behaviour of the organisation and its senior executive managers. Independence is particularly important for **non-executive directors,** and **internal and external auditors.**

(g)   To **provide accurate and timely reporting of trustworthy/independent financial and operational data** to both the management and owners/members of the organisation to give them a true and balanced picture of what is happening in the organisation.

(h)   To **encourage more proactive involvement** of owners/members in the effective management of the organisation through recognising their responsibilities of oversight and input to decision making processes via voting or other mechanisms.

Exam alert

The problems that resulted in governance reforms and the principles of good corporate governance are a likely exam topic.

CASE STUDY

Identification of the most important principles of corporate governance will often depend on the standpoint taken. In an article in CIMA Student, JA Williams identified the following broad aims of corporate governance at a **political** level.

•   **Creating a framework** for the **control of large, powerful companies** whose interests may not coincide with the national interest

•   **Controlling multinationals** which can dominate the local economy

- Ensuring that **companies** are **answerable** to all **stakeholders**, not just to shareholders
- Ensuring that **companies** are **run according** to the **laws and standards** of the country and are not in effect 'states within states'
- **Protecting investors** who buy shares in the same way as investors are protected who buy any other financial investment product, such as insurance or a pension.

2.3 Principles vs rules

A continuing debate on corporate governance is whether the guidance should predominantly be in the form of principles, or whether there is a need for detailed laws or regulations.

CASE STUDY

A principles-based approach to regulating the behaviour of motorists might say that motorists should drive safely having regard to traffic and road conditions whereas a rules-based approach might specify that motorists should not drive at speeds in excess of 100 km per hour.

This example of motoring regulation indicates a basic weakness with both types of regime. Using a principles-based approach, what criteria can be used to determine when a motorist is not driving safely? The motorist being involved in an accident perhaps, but the accident may have been due to other factors. A problem with a rules-based approach is that attention is focused on whether the rules have been broken, and not perhaps on more relevant factors. For example a motorist driving on a motorway at 100 km per hour on a day where the motorway was seriously affected by snow might be driving within the speed limit, but would clearly be driving at an undesirably fast speed.

The Hampel report in the UK came out very firmly in favour of a principles-based approach. The committee preferred relaxing the regulatory burden on companies and were against treating the corporate governance codes as sets of prescriptive rules, and judging companies by whether they have complied ('box-ticking'). The report stated that there may be **guidelines** which will normally be appropriate but the differing circumstances of companies meant that sometimes there are valid reasons for exceptions.

However a number of commentators criticised the Hampel report for this approach. Some critics have commented that the principles set out in the Hampel report are so **broad** that they are of very little use as a guide to best corporate governance practice.

Critics have also suggested that the Hampel comments about **box-ticking** are incorrect for two reasons.

(a)   Shareholders do not apply that approach when assessing accounts.

(b)   It is far less likely that disasters will strike companies with a 100% compliance record since they are unlikely to be content with token compliance, but will have set up procedures that contribute significantly to their being governed well.

CASE STUDY

Before the Combined Code (as was) underwent a limited revision in 2006, the UK Financial Reporting Council carried out a consultation exercise. The main comments that they received were that corporate governance had improved, particularly dialogue between boards and shareholders. However the Combined Code was perceived as a rigid set of rules. The Financial Reporting Council's response was to emphasise the comply or explain basis of the Code. If the Code was to work successfully in different company circumstances, companies needed to improve disclosure, particularly in areas where they had chosen not to comply with the Code.

2.4 Corporate governance and strategy

CIMA and IFAC published a joint report in 2004, *Enterprise Governance; Getting the Balance Right*, stressing the need for balance between:

- **Conformance** – basically corporate governance

- **Performance** – strategic decisions, use of resources, value adding activities; analysis of these will help the board develop strategy, consider what levels of risk it is prepared to tolerate and utilise appropriate performance measures

KEY POINT

The report highlights a number of key features of success.

- Choice and clarity of strategy
- Effective strategy execution
- Competency in mergers and acquisition
- Responsiveness to information flows
- Effective risk management

CASE STUDY

The UK Northern Rock Building Society has been identified as an example of an organisation where the performance aspect of enterprise governance did not match conformance. Northern Rock conformed to all regulatory requirements. It had a formal approach to risk management with sound management of exposure to interest rate and foreign exchanges rate changes.

However Northern Rock's strategy left it vulnerable. It raised 70% of its borrowings from banks and other financial institutions. It used monies it raised to finance mortgage lending and was therefore vulnerable to a tightening of global credit and no longer having the access to the funds it had assumed it would continue to have. As a result Northern Rock no longer had sufficient cash to cover its liabilities.

The Bank of England agreed to give emergency financial support to Northern Rock. Eventually emergency Parliamentary legislation was required to allow the bank to be taken into public ownership, the first major nationalisation for around 30 years in the UK.

2.5 Reports on corporate governance

A number of reports have been produced in various countries aiming to address the risk and problems posed by poor corporate governance.

2.5.1 United Kingdom

There were three significant corporate governance reports in the United Kingdom during the 1990s. The **Cadbury and Hampel reports** covered general corporate governance issues, whilst the **Greenbury report** concentrated on remuneration of directors.

The recommendations of these three reports were merged into a **Combined Code** in 1998, with which companies listed on the London Stock Exchange are required to comply.

Since the publication of the Combined Code a number of reports in the UK have been published about specific aspects of corporate governance.

- The **Turnbull report** focused on risk management and internal control
- The **Smith report** discussed the role of audit committees
- The **Higgs report** focused on the role of the non-executive director

The Combined Code was renamed as the UK Corporate Governance Code when a new version was published in 2010.

2.5.2 USA

Corporate scandals in the United States, particularly the Enron and Worldcom scandals, led to the Sarbanes-Oxley Act 2002 and consequent changes to the listing rules that companies quoted on Wall Street have to fulfil.

The following is a comparison of the main points of UK and US guidance. We shall examine them in more detail later in this chapter.

CASE STUDY

	UK guidance (UK Corporate Governance Code and Turnbull report except where indicated)	US guidance (Sarbanes-Oxley)
Scope	All types of internal control including financial, operational and compliance	Internal control over financial reporting
Audit committee	Smith report states should consist of independent non-executive directors, at least one having relevant and recent financial experience	Should consist of independent directors, one of whom should be a financial expert
Audit rotation	Ethical guidance states lead audit partner should be rotated at least every five years, other key audit partners at least every seven years	Rotation of lead partner required every five years
Non-audit services	Audit committee should review non-audit services provided by auditor to ensure auditor objectivity and independence is safeguarded. Accountancy bodies state that executing transactions or acting in a management role not compatible with being an objective auditor; other services (custody, preparing accounting records) cast doubts on objectivity	Auditors forbidden by law from carrying out a number of non-audit services including internal audit, bookkeeping, systems design/implementation, valuation, actuarial, management, expert services
Reports on internal control	Accounts include statement of responsibility of management for internal controls; also disclosure that there is a process for identifying, evaluating and managing risks and the process board has applied to review this	Accounts include statement of responsibility of management for internal controls and financial reporting; accounts should also include audited assessment of effectiveness of financial reporting controls
Code of ethics	No equivalent guidance	Companies should adopt a code of ethics for senior financial officers
Certification by directors	Under UK legislation directors required to state in directors' report that there is no relevant audit information that they know and that auditors are unaware of	Certification of appropriateness and fair presentation of accounts by chief executive and chief finance officer
Sanctions	No equivalent UK provision	If accounts have to be restated, chief executive and chief finance officer forfeit their bonuses

2.5.3 South Africa

South Africa's major contribution to the corporate governance debate has been the **King report**, first published in 1994 and updated in 2002 to take account of developments in South Africa and elsewhere in the world.

The King report differs in emphasis from other guidance by advocating an integrated approach to corporate governance in the interest of a wide range of stakeholders – embracing the social, environmental and economic activities of a company's activities. The report encourages activism by shareholders, business and the financial press and relies heavily on disclosure as a regulatory measure.

2.5.4 OECD guidance

The Organisation for Economic Co-operation and Development (OECD) has developed a **set of principles of corporate governance** that countries and companies should work towards achieving. The OECD has stated that its interest in corporate governance arises from its concern for **global investment**. Corporate governance arrangements should be credible and should be understood across national borders. Having a common set of accepted principles is a step towards achieving this aim.

The OECD developed its Principles of Corporate Governance in 1998 and issued a revised version in April 2004. They are non-binding principles, intended to assist governments in their efforts to evaluate and improve the legal, institutional and regulatory framework for corporate governance in their countries. They are also intended to provide guidance to stock exchanges, investors and companies.

The OECD principles deal mainly with governance problems that result from the **separation of ownership and management** of a company. Issues of ethical concern and environmental issues are also relevant, although not central, to the problems of governance.

The OECD principles are grouped into five broad areas:

(a) **The rights of shareholders**

Shareholders should have the right to **participate and vote in general meetings** of the company, **elect** and **remove members of the board** and **obtain relevant and material information** on a timely basis. Capital markets for corporate control should function in an **efficient and timely manner**.

(b) **The equitable treatment of shareholders**

All shareholders of the same class of shares should be treated equally, including **minority shareholders** and **overseas shareholders**. **Impediments** to **cross-border shareholdings** should be **eliminated**.

(c) **The role of stakeholders**

Rights of stakeholders should be **protected**. All stakeholders should have **access to relevant information** on a regular and timely basis. **Performance-enhancing mechanisms** for employee participation should be **permitted to develop**. Stakeholders, including employees, should be able to **freely communicate their concerns** about illegal or unethical relationships to the board.

(d) **Disclosure and transparency**

Timely and accurate disclosure must be made of all material matters regarding the company, including the financial situation, foreseeable risk factors, issues regarding employees and other stakeholders and governance structures and policies. The company's approach to disclosure should promote the provision of analysis or advice that is relevant to decisions by investors.

(e) **The responsibilities of the board**

The board is responsible for the **strategic guidance** of the company and for the **effective monitoring** of management. Board members should act on a fully informed basis, in good faith, with due diligence and care and in the **best interests of the company and its shareholders**. They should treat **all shareholders fairly**. The board should be able to exercise **independent judgement**; this includes assigning independent non-executive directors to appropriate tasks.

Section summary

Most corporate governance reports are based around the principles of **integrity**, **accountability**, **independence** and **good management** but there is disagreement on how much these principles need to be supplemented by detailed rules.

3 The board of directors

Introduction

In this section we begin to consider governance in more detail by examining the role of the board. An effective, balanced board is at the heart of good governance. A common problem in corporate scandals has been boards dominated by the chief executives or by a small group of executive directors.

3.1 Scope of role

The King report provides a good summary of the role of the board.

> 'To define the purpose of the company and the values by which the company will perform its daily existence and to identify the stakeholders relevant to the business of the company. The board must then develop a strategy combining all three factors and ensure management implements that strategy.'

3.1.1 Formal schedule of matters

If the board is to act effectively, its role must be defined carefully. The Cadbury report suggests that the board should have a **formal schedule of matters** specifically reserved to it for decision. Some would be decisions such as **mergers and takeovers** that are **fundamental** to the business and hence should not be taken just by executive managers. Other decisions would include **acquisitions and disposals of assets of the company** or its subsidiaries that are material to the company and **investments, capital projects, bank borrowing** facilities, **loans** and their repayment, foreign currency transactions, all above a certain size (to be determined by the board). The board should also be responsible for determining the **nature** and **extent** of the significant risks that it is prepared to take.

3.1.2 Performance and conformance

The IFAC/CIMA report *Enterprise Governance: Getting the balance right* and the IFAC Good Practice Guideline *Evaluating and Improving Governance in Organisations* stress the importance of boards fulfilling their performance role as well as their conformance role. The IFAC/CIMA report recommends the establishment of a strategic committee to undertake regular reviews of strategy and have the right to access external advice if necessary. The IFAC good practice guideline stresses:

- **Establishment of a robust decision-making process** including determination of risk appetite, oversight of strategic implementation and evaluation of strategy's ongoing relevance and success

- **Alignment of business operations and resource utilisation** with strategic direction and risk appetite

- **Identification of critical points** at which an organisation needs to make decisions in response to changing conditions

3.1.3 Other tasks

Other tasks the board should perform include:

- Monitoring the chief executive officer

- Monitoring risks and control systems

- Monitoring the human capital aspects of the company in regard to succession, morale, training, remuneration etc.

- Ensuring that there is effective communication of its strategic plans, both internally and externally

CASE STUDY

For the voluntary sector, the UK's *Good Governance, A Code for the Voluntary and Community Sector* stresses the board of trustees' role in ensuring compliance with the objects, purposes and values of the organisation and with its governing document. The Code stresses that the Board must ensure that the organisation's vision, mission, values and activities remain true to its objects.

The Code also lays more stress than the governance codes targeted at listed companies on trustees focusing on the strategic direction of their organisation and not becoming involved in day-to-day activities. The Chief Executive Officer should provide the link between the board and the staff team, and the means by which board members hold staff to account. Where in smaller organisations trustees need to become involved in operational matters, they should separate their strategic and operational roles.

3.2 Attributes of directors

In order to carry out effective scrutiny, directors need to have **relevant skills and expertise** in industry, company, functional area and governance. The board as a whole needs to contain a **mix of experience** and show a **balance** between **executive management** and **independent non-executive directors**. The King report stresses the importance also of having a good **demographic balance.**

All directors should receive induction on joining the board. New and existing directors should also have **appropriate training** to develop the knowledge and skills required.

All directors (including non-executive directors) must be able to **allocate sufficient time** to the company to carry out their responsibilities effectively.

CASE STUDY

It is very important also for charities to ensure that trustees have a suitable range of skills. The *Good Governance: A Code for the Voluntary and Community Sector* stresses the importance of trustees having the diverse range of skills, experience and knowledge necessary to run the organisation effectively. It states that the collective experience of trustees should ideally cover the following areas:

- Providing effective strategic leadership and working as a team
- Direct knowledge of the organisation's beneficiaries and users, and of their needs and aspirations
- Governance, general finance, business and management
- Human resources and diversity
- The operating environment and the risks that exist for the organisation
- Other specific knowledge such as fundraising, health, social services, property or legal

3.2.1 Nomination committee

In order to ensure that balance of the board is maintained, the board should set up a **nomination committee,** to oversee the process for board appointments and make recommendations to the board. The UK Corporate Governance Code recommends that a majority of the committee members should be independent non-executive directors.

The nomination committee needs to consider the balance between executives and independent non-executives, the **skills and knowledge** possessed by the board, the need for continuity and succession planning and the desirable **size** of the board. Recent corporate governance guidance has laid more stress on the need to attract board members from a **diversity** of backgrounds.

The nomination committee should ensure that appointments to the board are made on merit, using **objective criteria**. However the criteria should not be so restrictive that it limits too greatly the number of candidates.

The nomination committee should also be responsible for **reviewing the time required** from non-executive directors, as a basis for deciding whether the non-executive directors are spending enough time on the company's activities. The nomination committee should also brief newly-appointed non-executive directors about what is expected of them in terms of **time commitments**, **committee service** and **involvement outside board meetings**.

In 2004 the UK Department of Trade and Industry published 'Building better boards', demonstrating to companies how to improve board recruitment and development
http://www.berr.gov.uk/files/file19615.pdf

3.3 Possession of necessary information

As we have seen above, in many corporate scandals, the board were not given full information. The UK's Higgs report stresses that it is the responsibility both of the chairman to decide what information should be made available, and directors to satisfy themselves that they have **appropriate information** of **sufficient quality** to make sound judgements. The King report highlights the importance of the board receiving **relevant non-financial information**, going beyond assessing the financial and qualitative performance of the company, looking at **qualitative measures** that involve **broader stakeholder interests**.

3.3.1 Strategic scorecard

The IFAC/CIMA report *Enterprise Governance: Getting the balance right* recommends the establishment of a strategic scorecard to monitor performance, with the aim of helping the board ensure that all aspects of the strategic process have been completed thoroughly.

Strategic scorecard	
Position	Review of micro and macro-environments, threats, business position, capabilities, stakeholders
Options	Change of scope (geography, product, market sector) or change of direction (high/low growth, offering of price/quality)
Implementation	Detailed evaluation of specific options including attainable milestones and timelines
Risks	Linked in with enterprise risk management, impact and probability analysis, risks embedded in plans, action plans monitored against milestones

3.4 Performance of board

Appraisal of the board's performance is an important control over it. The Higgs report recommends that **performance of the board** should be **assessed** once a year. The UK Corporate Governance Code states that FTSE 350 companies should have externally facilitated board effectiveness reviews at least once every three years. **Separate appraisal** of the chairman and chief executive should also be carried out, with links to the remuneration process.

CASE STUDY

Corporate governance a practical guide, published by the London Stock Exchange and the accountants RSM Robson Rhodes, suggests that board evaluation needs to be in terms of clear objectives. Boards ought to be learning lessons from specific decisions they have taken (Did they receive adequate information? Did they address the main issues well?).

Considering how the board is working as a team is also important; this includes issues such as deterring criticism, existence of factions, whether dominant players are restricting the contribution of others. The guidance suggests involving an external facilitator to help discover key issues.

The guide also compares the working of an effective board with other types of board and suggests that boards should consider which unsuccessful elements they demonstrate.

Type of board	Strengths	Weaknesses
Effective board	• Clear strategy aligned to capabilities • Vigorous implementation of strategy • Key performance drivers monitored • Effective risk management • Focus on views of City and other stakeholders • Regular evaluation of board performance	
The rubber stamp	• Makes clear decisions • Listens to in-house expertise • Ensures decisions are implemented	• Fails to consider alternatives • Dominated by executives • Relies on fed information • Focuses on supporting evidence • Does not listen to criticism • Role of non-executives limited
The talking shop	• All opinions given equal weight • All options considered	• No effective decision-making process • Lack of direction from chairman • Failure to focus on critical issues • No evaluation of previous decisions
The number crunchers	• Short-term needs of investors considered • Prudent decision-making	• Excessive focus on financial impact • Lack of long-term, wider awareness • Lack of diversity of board members • Impact of social and environmental issues ignored • Risk averse
The dreamers	• Strong long-term focus • Long-term strategies • Consider social and environmental implications	• Insufficient current focus • Fail to identify or manage key risks • Excessively optimistic
The adrenalin junkies	• Clear decisions • Decisions implemented	• Lurch from crisis to crisis • Excessive focus on short-term • Lack of strategic direction • Internal focus • Tendency to micro-manage

Type of board	Strengths	Weaknesses
The semi-detached	<ul><li>Strong focus on external environment</li><li>Intellectually challenging</li></ul>	<ul><li>Out of touch with the company</li><li>Little attempt to implement decisions</li><li>Poor monitoring of decision-making</li></ul>

Exam alert

A question about the effectiveness of a governing body won't necessarily be about the board of a company. You may for example be asked about the governing body of a school, charity or local government body.

3.5 Chairman and chief executive

All reports acknowledge the importance of having a division of responsibilities at the head of an organisation. One way to do this is to require the roles of **chairman** and **chief executive** to be held by two different people.

This division has not been made compulsory by legislation in the UK, although the UK Corporate Governance Code states that the two roles should be held by different people.

CASE STUDY

A good illustration of how sensitive an issue the same person acting as chief executive and chairman can be is the recent experience of Marks and Spencer in the UK. Sir Stuart Rose had been group chief executive for a number of years, and was considered generally to have been successful in this role. In March 2008 the group proposed that Sir Stuart take on the role of executive chairman as well as being chief executive. This clearly breached the guidance that was then in the Combined Code that the same person should not be both chief executive and chairman, and that the chief executive should not go on to become chairman. Marks and Spencer's justification for non-compliance with the Combined Code was that it would allow the company extra time to find a new chief executive within the company

However a number of institutional investors objected to this arrangement. In spite of meeting with Marks and Spencer board representatives, Legal and General maintained its objections, stating that it did not support the dilution of corporate governance standards, particularly in leading UK companies. Peter Chambers, Chief Executive of Legal and General Investment Management, commented: 'We believe we have a moral responsibility to uphold corporate ethics in the UK and believe bellwether companies in the UK share this responsibility... We don't think they [M&S]should be explaining why they are not complying – they should be complying.' Richard Buxton of Schroders, another investor in Marks and Spencer, commented: 'For such a household name to do this sets an appalling precedent.'

Marks and Spencer proposed a number of concessions to alleviate investor concerns. These included:

- Sir Stuart standing for re-election every year at the company's annual general meeting, starting in July 2008

- His pay remaining unchanged

- Two new non-executive directors being appointed

- M&S reverting to having a separate chairman and chief executive once Sir Stuart's tenure as executive chairman ended. In early 2010, Marc Bolland took over from Stuart Rose as Chief Executive, but Stuart Rose planned to continue as non-executive Chairman until mid 2011.

3.5.1 Role of chairman

The UK Higgs report provides a thorough analysis of the role of the chairman. Higgs comments that the chairman is 'pivotal in creating the conditions for overall board and individual non-executive director effectiveness, both inside and outside the boardroom'. The chairman is responsible for:

(a) **Running the board and setting its agenda**

The chairman should **lead the board** and ensure its effectiveness in all aspects of its role. The chairman should ensure the board focuses on **strategic matters** and takes account of the key issues and the concerns of all board members. The chairman should ensure the contributions of executives and non-executives are co-ordinated and good relationships are maintained.

(b) **Ensuring the board receives accurate and timely information**

We shall discuss this further later in the Text, but good information will enable the board to take sound decisions and monitor the company effectively.

(c) **Ensuring effective communication with shareholders**

The chairman should take the lead in ensuring that the board develops an understanding of the views of major investors. The chairman is often the **public face** of the company as far as investors are concerned.

Financial statements in many jurisdictions include a **chairman's statement** that must be compatible with other information in the financial statements. The chairman may also be **responsible for signing off the financial statements.**

(d) **Ensuring that sufficient time is allowed for discussion of controversial issues**

All members should have enough time to **consider critical issues** and not be faced with unrealistic deadlines or decision-making.

(e) **Taking the lead in board development**

The chairman is responsible for **addressing the development needs** of the board as a whole and enhancing the effectiveness of the whole team, by also **meeting the development needs of individual directors**. The chairman should ensure that the induction programme for new directors is **comprehensive, formal and tailored**. The UK Corporate Governance Code requires the Chairman to hold regular development reviews with each director.

(f) **Facilitating board appraisal**

The chairman should ensure the performance of the whole board, board committees and individuals is evaluated at least once a year.

(g) **Encouraging active engagement by all the members of the board**

The chairman should promote a culture of **openness and debate**, by, in particular, ensuring that non-executive directors make an **effective contribution** to discussions.

(h) **Reporting in and signing off accounts**

Financial statements in many jurisdictions include a **chairman's statement** that must be compatible with other information in the financial statements. The chairman may also be responsible for signing off the financial statements.

CASE STUDY

Higgs goes on to provide a description of an effective chairman, as someone who:

- Upholds the highest standards of integrity and probity

- Leads board discussions to promote effective decision-making and constructive debate

- Promotes effective relationships and open communication between executive and non-executive directors

- Builds an effective and complementary board initiating change and planning succession

- Promotes the highest standards of corporate governance

- Ensures a clear structure for, and the effective running of, board committees

- Ensures effective implementation of board decisions

- Establishes a close relationship of trust with the CEO, providing support and advice whilst respecting executive responsibility

- Provides coherent leadership of the company

3.5.2 Role of CEO

The CEO is responsible for **running the organisation's business** and for **proposing and developing the group's strategy** and overall commercial objectives in consultation with the directors and the board. The CEO is also responsible for **implementing the decisions of the board** and its committees, **developing the main policy statements** and **reviewing** the business's **organisational structure and operational performance.**

The CEO is the senior executive in charge of the management team and is answerable to the board for its performance. He will have to formalise the roles and responsibilities of the management team, including determining the degree of delegation.

A guidance note suggests that the major responsibilities of the CEO will be as follows:

(a) **Business strategy and management**

The CEO will take the lead in **developing objectives and strategy** having regard to the organisation's stakeholders, and will be primarily responsible for ensuring that the organisation achieves its objectives, whilst optimising the use of resources.

(b) **Investment and financing**

The CEO will **examine major investments**, capital expenditure, acquisitions and disposals and be responsible for identifying new initiatives.

(c) **Risk management**

The CEO will be responsible for **managing the risk profile** in line with the risk appetite accepted by the board. He will also be responsible for ensuring that appropriate internal controls are in place.

(d) **Board committees**

The CEO will make **recommendations** to be discussed by the board committees on **remuneration policy**, **executive remuneration** and **terms of employment**, also on the role and capabilities relating to future director employments.

3.5.3 Division of responsibilities

All governance reports acknowledge the importance of having a division of responsibilities at the head of an organisation to avoid the situation where one individual has **unfettered control** of the decision-making process.

As mentioned above, the simplest way to do this is to require the roles of **chairman** and **CEO** to be held by two different people, for the following reasons.

(a)   It reflects the reality that both jobs are **demanding roles** and ultimately the idea that no one person would be able to do both jobs well. The CEO can then run the company. The chairman can run the board and take the lead in liaising with shareholders.

(b)   There is an important difference between the authority of the chairman and the authority of the chief executive, which having the roles taken by different people will clarify. The chairman **carries the authority of the board** whereas the chief executive has the authority that is **delegated by the board.** Separating the roles emphasises that the chairman is acting on behalf of the board, whereas the chief executive has the authority given in his **terms of appointment.** Having the same person in both roles means that **unfettered power** is concentrated into one pair of hands; the board may be ineffective in controlling the chief executive if it is led by the chief executive.

(c)   The separation of roles avoids the risk of **conflicts of interest**.

(d)   The board cannot make the CEO **truly accountable** for management if it is led by the CEO.

(e)   Separation of the roles means that the board is more able to **express its concerns effectively** by providing a point of reporting (the chairman) for the non-executive directors.

(f)   The chairman is responsible for obtaining the information that other directors require to **exercise proper oversight and monitor the organisation effectively**. If the chairman is also chief executive, then directors may not be sure that the information they are getting is sufficient and objective enough to support their work. The chairman should ensure that the board is receiving sufficient information to make **informed decisions**, and should put pressure on the chief executive if the chairman believes that the chief executive is not providing adequate information.

The UK Corporate Governance Code also suggests that the CEO should not go on to become Chairman of the same company. If a CEO did become chairman, the main risk is that the old CEO will interfere in matters that are the responsibility of the new CEO and thus exercise undue influence over the new CEO.

3.6 Non-executive directors

KEY TERM

NON-EXECUTIVE DIRECTORS have no executive (managerial) responsibilities.

Non-executive directors should provide a **balancing influence**, and play a key role in **reducing conflicts of interest** between management (including executive directors) and shareholders. They should provide reassurance to shareholders, particularly institutional shareholders, that management is acting in the interests of the organisation.

One method of enhancing the contribution of non-executive directors is to appoint one of the **independent non-executive directors** as **senior independent director** to provide a sounding board for the chairman and to serve as an **intermediary** for the other directors and shareholders if they have concerns they cannot resolve through other channels.

CASE STUDY

The UK Higgs report made a number of suggestions about possible sources of non-executive directors:

•   Companies operating in international markets could benefit from having at least one non-executive director with international experience

•   Lawyers, accountants and consultants can bring skills that are useful to the board

•   Listed companies should consider appointing directors of private companies as non-executive directors

- Including individuals with charitable or public sector experience but strong commercial awareness can increase the breadth of diversity and experience on the board

3.6.1 Role of non-executive directors

The UK's Higgs report provides a useful summary of the role of non-executive directors:

(a) **Strategy**: non-executive directors should contribute to, and challenge the direction of, strategy.

(b) **Performance**: non-executive directors should scrutinise the performance of management in meeting goals and objectives, and monitor the reporting of performance.

(c) **Risk**: non-executive directors should satisfy themselves that financial information is accurate and that financial controls and systems of risk management are robust. They should also consider whether the directors' approach to risk-taking is reasonable. Are the directors excessively risk-averse because of worries about job security, or do they take excessive risks to increase their bonuses?

(d) **Directors and managers**: non-executive directors are responsible for determining appropriate levels of remuneration for executives, and are key figures in the appointment and removal of senior managers and in succession planning. The UK Corporate Governance Code suggests that the Chairman should hold meetings with the non-executive directors without the executive directors being present. The non-executive directors should meet annually without the Chairman being present to assess the Chairman's performance.

3.6.2 Advantages of non-executive directors

Non-executive directors can bring a number of advantages to a board of directors.

(a) They may have **external experience and knowledge which executive directors do not possess.** The experience they bring can be in many different fields. They may be executive directors of other companies, and thus have experience of different ways of approaching corporate governance, internal controls or performance assessment. They can also bring knowledge of markets within which the company operates.

(b) Non-executive directors can provide a **wider perspective** than executive directors who may be more involved in detailed operations.

(c) Good non-executive directors are often a **comfort factor** for third parties such as investors or creditors.

(d) The English businessman Sir John Harvey-Jones has pointed out that there are **certain roles** non-executive directors are well-suited to play. These include 'father-confessor' (being a confidant for the chairman and other directors), 'oil-can' (intervening to make the board run more effectively) and acting as 'high sheriff' (if necessary taking steps to remove the chairman or chief executive).

(e) The most important advantage perhaps lies in the dual nature of the non-executive director's role. Non-executive directors are **full board members** who are expected to have the level of knowledge that full board membership implies. At the same time they are meant to provide the so-called **strong, independent element** on the board. This should imply that they have the knowledge and detachment to be able to assess fairly the remuneration of executive directors when serving on the remuneration committee, and to be able to discuss knowledgeably with auditors the affairs of the company on the audit committee.

3.6.3 Problems with non-executive directors

Nevertheless there are a number of difficulties connected with the role of non-executive director.

(a) In many organisations, non-executive directors may **lack independence**. There are in practice a number of ways in which non-executive directors can be linked to a company, as suppliers or customers for example.

(b) There may be a **prejudice in certain companies** against widening the recruitment of non-executive directors to include people proposed other than by the board or to include stakeholder representatives.

(c) High-calibre non-executive directors may gravitate towards the **best-run companies**, rather than companies which are more in need of input from good non-executives.

(d) Non-executive directors may have **difficulty imposing** their views upon the board. It may be easy to dismiss the views of non-executive directors as irrelevant to the company's needs. If executive directors are determined to push through a controversial policy, it may prove difficult for the more disparate group of non-executive directors to oppose them effectively.

(e) Sir John Harvey-Jones suggested that not enough emphasis is given to the role of non-executive directors in **preventing trouble**, in warning early on of potential problems. Contrawise, when trouble does arise, non-executive directors may be expected to play a major role in rescuing the situation, which they may not be able to do.

(f) Perhaps the biggest problem which non-executive directors face is the **limited time** they can devote to the role. If they are to contribute valuably, they are likely to have time-consuming other commitments. However, governance guidance emphasises that all directors need to be able to **allocate sufficient time** to the company to perform their responsibilities effectively.

3.6.4 Number of non–executive directors

Most corporate governance reports acknowledge the importance of having a significant presence of non-executive directors on the board. The question has been whether organisations should follow the broad principles expressed in the Cadbury report:

> 'The board should include non-executive directors of sufficient character and number for their views to carry significant weight.'

or whether they should follow prescriptive guidelines. New York Stock Exchange rules now require listed companies to have a majority of non-executive directors. The UK Corporate Governance Code states that at least half the board should be independent non-executive directors.

3.6.5 Independence of non-executive directors

Various safeguards can be put in place to ensure that non-executive directors remain independent. Those suggested by the corporate governance reports include:

(a) Non-executive directors should have **no business**, **financial** or other **connection** with the company or its directors, apart from fees and shareholdings. Recent reports such as the UK's Higgs report have widened the scope of business connections to include anyone who has been an employee or had a material business relationship over the last few years, or served on the board for more than ten years.

(b) They should **not take part in share option or performance-related pay schemes** and their service should not be pensionable, to maintain their independent status.

(c) **Appointments** should be for a **specified term** and reappointment should not be automatic. The board as a whole should decide on their nomination and selection.

(d)   Procedures should exist whereby non-executive directors may take **independent advice**, at the company's expense if necessary.

Exam skills

Whenever a question scenario features non-executive directors, watch out for threats to, or questions over, their independence.

3.6.6 Multi-tier boards

Some jurisdictions take the split between executive and other directors to its furthest extent. Institutional arrangements in German companies are based on a **two-tiered board**. A **supervisory board** has workers' representatives, and perhaps shareholders' representatives including banks' representatives, in equal numbers. The board has no executive function, although it does review the company's direction and strategy and is responsible for safeguarding **stakeholders'** interests. An **executive board**, composed entirely of managers, will be responsible for the **running** of the business.

Proposals to introduce two (or more) tier boards have been particularly criticised in the UK and USA as leading to confusion and a lack of accountability. This has affected the debate on enhancing the role of non-executive directors, with critics claiming that moves to increase the involvement of non-executive directors are a step on the slippery slope towards two-tier boards.

Section summary

The board should be responsible for taking major **policy** and **strategic** decisions.

Directors should have a **mix of skills** and their **performance** should be assessed regularly.

Appointments should be conducted by formal procedures administered by a **nomination committee**.

Division of responsibilities at the head of an organisation is most simply achieved by separating the roles of chairman and chief executive.

Independent non-executive directors have a key role in governance. Their number and status should mean that their views carry significant weight.

4   Directors' remuneration   5/10

Introduction

Directors' remuneration is likely to remain a topical issue throughout the life of this edition of this text. Look out for news stories in the business press.

4.1 Need for guidance

Directors being paid excessive salaries and bonuses has been seen as one of the major corporate abuses for a large number of years. It is thus inevitable that the corporate governance provisions have targeted it.

The **Greenbury committee** in the UK set out principles which are a good summary of what remuneration policy should involve.

- Directors' remuneration should be set by **independent members** of the board
- Any form of bonus should be related to **measurable performance** or enhanced shareholder value

- There should be **full transparency of directors' remuneration** including pension rights in the annual accounts

In November 2008 Peter Wuffli, former chief executive of the Swiss bank UBS, revealed that he had handed back SFr 12 million (£6.7 million) in bonus entitlements in sympathy with its plight. The decision contributed to pressure on other UBS directors and directors of other banks to renounce incentive payments gained through past performance.

Exam alert

May 2010 Question 2 covered controversial proposals for remunerating directors.

4.2 Remuneration committee

The remuneration committee plays the key role in establishing remuneration arrangements. In order to be effective, the committee needs both to **determine** the organisation's **general policy** on the **remuneration of executive directors** and **specific remuneration packages** for each director.

Measures to ensure that the committee is **independent** include not just requiring that the committee is staffed by non-executive directors, but also placing limits on the members' connection with the organisation. Measures to ensure independence include stating that the committee should have no personal interests other than as shareholders, no conflicts of interest and no day-to-day involvement in running the business.

4.3 Establishing remuneration arrangements

Packages will need to **attract, retain and motivate directors** of sufficient quality, whilst at the same time taking into account shareholders' interests as well. However assessing executive remuneration in an imperfect market for executive skills may prove problematic.

The link between remuneration and company performance is particularly important. Recent UK guidance has stressed the need for the performance-related elements of executive directors' remuneration to be **stretching, designed to align their interests with those of shareholders** and **promote the long-term success of the company.** Remuneration incentives should be **compatible with risk policies and systems** and **criteria for paying bonuses** should be **risk-adjusted.**

However non-executive directors should **not** be remunerated by shares or other performance-related elements, to preserve their independence.

The committee needs to be mindful of the **implications** of **all aspects** of the package. Particularly sensitive areas include terms of **share option schemes**, the phasing of rewards, and the pension consequences of various elements of the remuneration package.

Share options can be used to **align management and shareholder interests**, particularly options held for a long time when value is dependent on long-term performance.

Length of service contracts can be a particular problem. If service contracts are too long, and then have to be terminated prematurely, the perception often arises that the amounts paying off directors for the remainder of the contract are essentially rewards of failure. Corporate governance guidance has indicated that service contracts greater than 12 months need to be carefully considered.

Other issues the remuneration committee have to consider include:

(a) The **differentials at management/director level** (difficult with many layers of management)

(b) The **ability of managers to leave**, taking clients and knowledge to a competitor or their own new business

(c) **Individual performance** and additional work/effort

(d) The company's **overall performance**

4.4 Disclosures

In order for readers of the accounts to achieve a fair picture of remuneration arrangements, the accounts would need to disclose:

* Remuneration policy
* Arrangements for individual directors

4.5 Voting on remuneration

Along with disclosure, the directors also need to consider whether members need to signify their approval of remuneration policy by voting on the **remuneration statement** and elements of the remuneration packages of individual directors, for example long-term incentive schemes.

4.6 Re-election of directors

In 2010 the UK Corporate Governance Code introduced the controversial requirement that directors of FTSE 350 companies should put themselves forward for re-election every year. Directors of other listed companies should stand for re-election at least once every three years.

Section summary

Directors' remuneration should be set by a **remuneration committee** consisting of independent non-executive directors.

Remuneration should be dependent upon **organisation** and **individual performance**.

Accounts should disclose **remuneration policy** and (in detail) the **packages of individual directors**.

5 Accounts and audit

Introduction

Accountability and audit are important topics in all major governance codes. This means that organisations not only need sound systems of internal control; they also need to ensure these systems are monitored and audited, and reported to shareholders.

5.1 Internal control

We shall discuss internal control in detail later in this text, but in this section we shall focus on the role of the board in maintaining internal control.

The USA's Sarbanes-Oxley regulations have forced American boards to look carefully at internal controls and in particular:

(a) **Disclose to the auditors** and **audit committee deficiencies** in the operation of internal controls

(b) In the accounts **acknowledge their responsibility** for **internal control**, and assess its effectiveness based on an evaluation within 30 days prior to the report

5.1.1 Review of internal controls

The UK's **Turnbull committee** suggested that review of internal controls should be an **integral part** of the **company's operations**; the board, or board committees, should actively consider reports on control issues from others operating internal controls. We shall look in detail at this review in Chapter 16.

5.2 Audit committee

We discuss the role of the audit committee, and the relationships between the audit committee and internal and external audit in Chapters 15 and 16.

5.3 Reporting on corporate governance

The London Stock Exchange requires the following general disclosures:

(a)   A **narrative statement** of how companies have **applied the principles** set out in the UK Corporate Governance Code, providing explanations which enable their shareholders to assess how the principles have been applied

(b)   A **statement** as to whether or not they **complied** throughout the accounting period with the **provisions** set out in the UK Corporate Governance Code. Listed companies that did not comply throughout the accounting period with all the provisions must specify the provisions with which they did not comply, and give reasons for non-compliance

CASE STUDY

BP's 2009 accounts contain an example of non-compliance in a couple of areas.

'Letters of appointment do not set out fixed time commitments, since the schedule of board and committee meetings is subject to change according to the exigencies of the business. All directors are expected to demonstrate their commitment to the work of the board on an ongoing basis. This is reviewed by the nomination committee in recommending candidates for annual re-election.

The remuneration of the chairman is not set by the remuneration committee. Instead the chairman's remuneration is reviewed by the remuneration committee which makes a recommendation to the board as a whole for final approval, within the limits set by shareholders.'

The corporate governance reports also suggest that the directors should **explain** their **responsibility for preparing accounts**. They should **report that the business is a going concern**, with supporting assumptions and qualifications as necessary.

In addition further statements may be required depending on the jurisdiction such as:

(a)   Information about the **board of directors**: the composition of the board in the year, the role and effectiveness of the board, information about the independence of the non-executives, frequency of, and attendance at, board meetings, how the board's performance has been evaluated. The King report suggests a charter of responsibilities should be disclosed

(b)   Brief report on the **remuneration, audit and nomination committees** covering terms of reference, composition and frequency of meetings

(c)   Information about **relations with auditors** including reasons for change and steps taken to ensure auditor objectivity and independence when non-audit services have been provided

(d)   A statement that the directors have reviewed the **effectiveness** of **internal controls**, including risk management, also sufficient disclosures for shareholders to understand the main features of the risk management and internal control processes. Boards should also give details of, or at any rate confirm, action taken to remedy significant failings or weaknesses.

(e)   A statement on relations and **dialogue with shareholders**

(f)   A statement that the company is a **going concern**

(g)   **Sustainability reporting**, defined by the King report as including the nature and extent of social, transformation, ethical, safety, health and environmental management policies and practices

(h)   A **business review**. The UK's Accounting Standards Board summarised the purpose of such a review:

'The (review) should set out the directors' analysis of the business, in order to provide to investors a historical and prospective analysis of the reporting entity 'through the eyes of management'. It should include discussion and interpretation of the performance of the business and the structure of its financing, in the context of known or reasonably expected changes in the environment in which it operates.'

The UK Corporate Governance Code states that the annual report should include an explanation of the basis on which the company generates or preserves value over the longer term (the business model) and the strategy for delivering the objectives of the company.

Section summary

Boards should regularly review **risk management** and **internal control**, and carry out a wider review annually, the results of which should be disclosed in the accounts.

Audit committees of **independent non-executive directors** should liaise with **external audit, supervise internal audit**, and **review** the **annual accounts** and **internal controls**.

Annual reports must **convey** a **fair and balanced view** of the organisation. They should state whether the organisation has complied with governance regulations and codes, and give specific disclosures about the board, internal control reviews, going concern status and relations with stakeholders.

6 Shareholders

Introduction

Listed companies need to take active steps to keep shareholders (particularly institutional shareholders) informed. To work well, the relationship between listed companies and their major institutional shareholders has to be two-way.

6.1 Relationships with shareholders

A key aspect of the relationship is the accountability of directors to shareholders. This can ultimately be ensured by requiring all directors to submit themselves for **regular re-election**.

The need for regular communication with shareholders is emphasised in most reports. Particularly important is communication with **institutional shareholders** such as pension funds who may hold a significant proportion of shares. A number of the reports stress how institutional shareholders can be an important force for good corporate governance, and that they have a responsibility to use their votes wisely.

The annual general meeting is the most important formal means of communication, and the governance guidance suggests that boards should **actively encourage** shareholders to attend annual general meetings. The UK's Hampel report contained some useful recommendations on how the annual general meeting could be used to **enhance communications** with shareholders.

(a) Notice of the AGM and related papers should be **sent** to shareholders **at least 20 working days** before the meeting.

(b) Companies should consider providing a **business presentation** at the **AGM**, with a question and answer session. The chairmen of the key sub-committees (audit, remuneration) should be available to answer questions.

(c) Shareholders should be able to **vote separately** on each substantially separate issue; the practice of 'bundling' unrelated proposals in a single resolution should cease.

(d) Companies should propose a resolution at the AGM relating to the **report and accounts**.

The most important document for communication with shareholders is the annual report and accounts.

6.2 Relationships with stakeholders

How much the board are responsible for the interests of stakeholders other than shareholders is a matter of debate. The Hampel committee claimed that although relationships with other stakeholders were important, making the directors responsible to other stakeholders would mean there was no clear yardstick for judging directors' performance.

However the OECD guidelines see a rather wider importance for stakeholders in corporate governance, concentrating on employees, creditors and the government. Creditors supply external capital to the firm and employees human capital.

The OECD guidelines stress that the corporate governance framework should therefore ensure that respect is given to the **rights of stakeholders** that are protected by law. These rights include rights under labour law, business law, contract law and insolvency law.

The corporate governance framework should also permit '**performance-enhancing mechanisms** for stakeholder participation'. Examples of this are employee representation on the board of directors, employee share ownership, profit-sharing arrangements and the right of creditors to be involved in any insolvency proceedings.

Exam alert

The examiner has stressed the importance of organisations ensuring that there are effective mechanisms for reassuring stakeholders.

Question 3.1	Codes and corporate governance

Learning outcome B3(a)

Briefly explain what is meant by corporate governance and discuss how the main measures recommended by the corporate governance codes should contribute towards better corporate governance.

Section summary

The board should maintain a **regular dialogue with shareholders**, particularly **institutional shareholders**. **The annual general meeting** is the most significant forum for communication.

How much organisations consider the interests of other stakeholders will depend on their **legal responsibilities** and their **view of stakeholders as partners**.

Chapter Roundup

- ✓ Good corporate governance involves **risk management** and **internal control, accountability** to stakeholders and other shareholders and conducting business in an **ethical and effective way.**

- ✓ Most corporate governance reports are based around the principles of **integrity**, **accountability**, **independence** and **good management** but there is disagreement on how much these principles need to be supplemented by detailed rules.

- ✓ The board should be responsible for taking major **policy** and **strategic** decisions.

- ✓ Directors should have a **mix of skills** and their **performance** should be assessed regularly.

- ✓ Appointments should be conducted by formal procedures administered by a **nomination committee**.

- ✓ **Division of responsibilities** at the head of an organisation is most simply achieved by separating the roles of chairman and chief executive.

- ✓ **Independent non-executive directors** have a key role in governance. Their number and status should mean that their views carry significant weight.

- ✓ Directors' remuneration should be set by a **remuneration committee** consisting of independent non-executive directors.

- ✓ Remuneration should be dependent upon **organisation** and **individual performance**.

- ✓ Accounts should disclose **remuneration policy** and (in detail) the **packages of individual directors.**

- ✓ Boards should regularly review **risk management** and **internal control**, and carry out a wider review annually, the results of which should be disclosed in the accounts.

- ✓ Audit committees of **independent non-executive directors** should liaise with **external audit**, **supervise internal audit**, and **review** the **annual accounts** and **internal controls.**

- ✓ Annual reports must **convey** a **fair and balanced view** of the organisation. They should state whether the organisation has complied with governance regulations and codes, and give specific disclosures about the board, internal control reviews, going concern status and relations with stakeholders.

- ✓ The board should maintain a **regular dialogue with shareholders**, particularly **institutional shareholders**. **The annual general meeting** is the most significant forum for communication.

- ✓ How much organisations consider the interests of other stakeholders will depend on their **legal responsibilities** and their **view of stakeholders as partners**.

Quick Quiz

1   Fill in the blanks.

Corporate governance is the system by which organisations are .... and .... controlled.

2   Give four examples of symptoms of poor corporate governance.

3   How did the Cadbury report suggest that the board's responsibilities should be defined?

4   Audit committees are generally staffed by executive directors.

True   ☐

False   ☐

5   What, according to the Greenbury report, should be the key principles in establishing a remuneration policy?

6   How can an organisation ensure that there is a division of responsibilities at its highest level?

7   Fill in the blank.

A .... sets out the directors' analysis of the business, in order to provide to investors a historical and prospective analysis of the reporting entity 'through the eyes of management'.

8   Which of the following is not a recommendation of the UK Hampel report in relation to annual general meetings?

A   Notice of the AGM should be sent to shareholders at least 20 working days before the meeting.
B   To simplify voting, the key proposals made at the AGM should be combined in one resolution.
C   Companies should propose a resolution at the AGM relating to their report and accounts.
D   Institutional shareholders should provide their clients with details of how they've voted at AGMs.

Answers to Quick Quiz

1   Corporate governance is the system by which organisations are **directed** and **controlled**.

2   • Domination by a single individual
     • Lack of board involvement
     • Inadequate control function
     • Inadequate supervision
     • Lack of independent scrutiny
     • Lack of contact with shareholders
     • Excessive emphasis on short-term profitability
     • Misleading accounts

3   Boards should have a formal schedule of matters reserved for their decisions including decisions such as approval of mergers and acquisitions, major acquisitions and disposals of assets and investments, capital projects, bank borrowing facilities, major loans and their repayment, foreign currency transactions above a certain limit.

4   False. They should be staffed by non-executive directors.

5   • Directors' remuneration should be set by independent members of the board

     • Any form of bonus should be related to measurable performance or enhanced shareholder value

     • There should be full transparency of directors' remuneration, including pension rights, in the annual accounts

6   • Splitting the roles of chairman and chief executive
     • Appointing a senior independent non-executive director
     • Having a strong independent element on the board with a recognised leader

7   A **business review** sets out the directors' analysis of the business, in order to provide to investors a historical and prospective analysis of the reporting entity 'through the eyes of management'.

8   B   The Hampel report recommends that shareholders should be able to vote separately on each substantially separate issue.

Answers to Questions

3.1 Codes and corporate governance

Definition of corporate governance

Corporate governance can be defined broadly as the **system** by which an **organisation** is **directed and controlled**. It is concerned with systems, processes, controls, accountability and decision making at the heart of and at the highest level of an organisation. It is therefore concerned with the way in which top managers **execute their responsibilities** and authority and how they **account** for that authority to those who have entrusted them with assets and resources. In particular it is concerned with the potential abuse of power and the need for openness, integrity and accountability in corporate decision making.

Recommendations of corporate governance codes

Clearly, a company must have senior executives. The problem is how to ensure as far as possible that the actions and decisions of the executives will be for the benefit of shareholders. Measures that have been recommended by various corporate governance codes include the following.

Directors

(a) A listed company is required by the 'voluntary' UK Corporate Governance Code to appoint **non-executive directors**, most of whom should be **independent.** The non-executives are intended to provide a check or balance against the power of the chairman and chief executive.

(b) The posts of **chairman and chief executive** should not be held by the same person, to prevent excessive executive power being held by one individual.

(c) Non-executive directors should **make up** the **membership** of the remuneration committee of the board, and should determine the remuneration of executive directors. This is partly to prevent the executives deciding their own pay, and rewarding themselves excessively. Another purpose is to try to devise incentive schemes for executives that will motivate them to **achieve results** for the company that will also be in the best interests of the shareholders.

Risk assessment

The requirement in many codes for a risk audit should ensure that the board of directors is **aware** of the **risks** facing the company, and have **systems** in place for managing them. In theory, this should provide some protection against risk for the company's shareholders.

Dialogue with shareholders

The UK Corporate Governance Code encourages **greater dialogue** between a **company** and its **shareholders**. Institutional investor organisations are also encouraging greater participation by shareholders, for example in voting.

Audits

The **audit committee** of the board is seen as having a **major role** to play, in promoting dialogue between the external auditors and the board. Corporate governance should be improved if the views of the **external auditors** are given greater consideration.

Now try these questions from the Exam Question Bank	Number	Level	Marks	Time
	Q3	Examination	25	45 mins
	Q4	Examination	25	45 mins
	Q5	Examination	25	45 mins

1 UK Corporate Governance Code

A Leadership

A1 Role of the board

All listed companies should be led by an **effective board**, responsible for providing **entrepreneurial leadership**, within a **framework of prudent** and **effective controls**, enabling **risk to be assessed** and **managed**. The board is responsible for setting strategic aims, ensuring sufficient resources are available, setting values and standards and ensuring obligations to shareholders. The board should **meet regularly**, with a **formal schedule of matters** reserved for it. The annual report should explain how the board operates, and give details of members and attendance.

A2 Division of responsibilities

A **clear division of responsibilities** should exist so that there is a balance of power, and no one person has unfettered powers of decision. The roles of **chairman** and **chief executive** should not be exercised by one person.

A3 The chairman

The chairman is responsible for leading the board and ensuring its effectiveness. The chairman should establish the board's agenda, and ensure there is **adequate time for discussion**, particularly of strategic matters. The chairman should promote **openness and debate**, help non-executive directors contribute effectively and promote constructive relations between executives and non-executives. The chairman should ensure that the board receives **accurate, timely and clear information** and should ensure communication with shareholders is effective. The chairman should meet the independence criteria for non-executive directors. A chief executive should not go on to become chairman.

A4 Non-executive directors

Non-executive directors should scrutinise management's performance and constructively challenge strategy. They should obtain assurance about the integrity of financial information and that financial controls and risk management systems are **robust** and **defensible**. Other important tasks include **determining executive remuneration** and playing a significant role in decisions about **board changes**. One of the independent non-executives should be appointed as senior independent director, to act as an intermediary with other directors and shareholders. The chairman should hold meetings with the non-executives without the executives being there, and the non-executives should meet without the chairman to appraise the chairman's performance. Directors should ensure that concerns they have that cannot be resolved are formally recorded.

B Effectiveness

B1 Composition of the board

The board and its committees should have a balance of **skills, experience, independence and knowledge** of the company. The board should be of sufficient size to **operate effectively**, but not so large as to be **unwieldy.** The board should have a **balance** of **executive and non-executive directors** so that no individual or small group is dominant. Decisions on committee membership should take into account the need to avoid undue reliance on particular individuals. At least half the board of FTSE 350 companies should be **independent non-executive directors**. Smaller listed companies should have at least **two independent non-executive directors.**

B2 Appointments to the board

There should be a **clear, formal procedure** for appointing new directors. A nomination committee should make recommendations about all new board appointments. The majority of members of this committee should be independent non-executives. Directors should be appointed **on merit,** against objective criteria, and considering the value of diversity, including gender diversity. There should be an **orderly succession process** in place.

B3 Commitment

Directors should allocate sufficient time to the company to **discharge their duties effectively**. In particular the nomination committee should assess the **time commitment expected** of the chairman, and the chairman's other commitments should be disclosed to the board and shareholders. Non-executives' letters of appointment should set out the expected time commitment and non-executives should undertake to have sufficient time to fulfil their responsibilities. Their other significant commitments should be disclosed to the board. A full time executive director should not take on more than one non-executive directorship of a FTSE 100 company, nor the chairmanship of a FTSE 100 company.

B4 Development

All directors should be properly inducted when they join the board and regularly update their skills and knowledge. The chairman should **agree training and development needs** with each director.

B5 Information and support

The board should be **promptly supplied** with **enough information** to enable it to carry out its duties. Information volunteered by management will sometimes need to be supplemented by information from other sources. The chairman and secretary should ensure good information flows. Directors should be able to obtain independent professional advice and have access to the services of the company secretary. The company secretary is responsible for **advising the chairman** on **all governance matters.** The whole board should be responsible for appointing and removing the company secretary.

B6 Evaluation

There should be a **vigorous annual performance evaluation** of the board as a whole, individual directors (effective contribution and commitment) and board committees. Evaluation of the board of FTSE 350 companies should be externally facilitated at **least once every three years.** The chairman should take action as a result of the review, if necessary proposing new board members or seeking the **resignation of directors.**

B7 Re-election

All directors should submit themselves for **re-election regularly**, and at least once every three years. Directors of FTSE 350 companies should be subject to **annual election by shareholders.**

C Accountability

C1 Financial and business reporting

The board should present a **balanced and understandable assessment** of the **company's position and prospects** in the annual accounts and other reports such as interim reports and reports to regulators. The directors should explain their responsibility for the accounts, and the auditors should state their reporting responsibilities. The directors should explain the basis on which the company **generates or preserves value** and the s**trategy for delivering the company's longer-term objectives**. The directors should also report on the going concern status of the business.

C2 Risk management and internal control

The board is responsible for determining the **nature and extent of the significant risks** it is willing to take to achieve objectives. Good systems of **risk management and control** should be maintained. The directors should **review effectiveness** annually and report to shareholders that they have done so. The review should cover all controls including financial, operational and compliance controls and risk management.

C3 Audit committee and auditors

There should be **formal and clear arrangements** with the **company's auditors**, and for applying the financial reporting and internal control principles. Companies should have an **audit committee** consisting of independent non-executive directors. One member should have **recent and relevant financial experience**. The committee should **monitor the accounts**, review **internal financial controls** and also other **internal controls and risk management systems** if there is no risk committee. The audit committee should make recommendations for the **appointment and remuneration of the external auditor**, and consider the auditor's **independence and objectivity,** the **effectiveness of the audit process** and whether the external auditor should **provide non-audit services.** The audit committee should also **review internal audit's work.** If there is no internal audit function, the audit committee should consider annually whether it is needed. The audit committee should also review 'whistleblowing' arrangements for staff who have **concerns about improprieties.**

D Directors' remuneration

D1 Level and components of remuneration

Remuneration levels should be sufficient to attract directors of **sufficient calibre** to run the company effectively, but companies should not pay more than is necessary. A proportion of remuneration should be based on **corporate and individual performance.** Comparisons with other companies should be used with caution. When designing performance-related elements of remuneration, the remuneration committee should consider annual bonuses and different kinds of long-term incentive schemes. Targets should be stretching. Levels of remuneration for non-executive directors should reflect **time commitment and responsibilities**, and should not include share options or performance-related options.

Boards' ultimate objectives should be to set **notice periods at one year or less**. The remuneration committee should consider the appropriateness of compensation commitments included in the contracts of service.

D2 Procedure

Companies should establish a formal and clear procedure for **developing policy** on **executive remuneration** and for fixing the remuneration package of individual directors. **Directors should not be involved** in **setting their own remuneration**. A **remuneration committee**, staffed by independent non-executive directors, should make **recommendations** about the framework of executive remuneration, and should determine remuneration packages of executive directors and the chairman. The board or shareholders should determine the remuneration of non-executive directors.

E Relations with shareholders

E1 Dialogue with shareholders

The board should keep up a dialogue with shareholders, particularly **major (institutional) shareholders**. The board should try to understand issues and concerns, and discuss governance and strategy with major shareholders.

E2 Constructive use of the AGM

The AGM should be a **means of communication** with **investors.** Companies should count all proxies and announce proxy votes for and against on all votes on a show of hands, except when a poll is taken. Companies should propose a **separate resolution** on each substantially separate issue, and there should be a resolution covering the **report and accounts**. The chairmen of the audit, nomination and remuneration committees should be available to answer questions at the AGM. Papers should be sent to members at least 20 working days before the AGM.

Compliance with the Code

The UK Corporate Governance Code requires listed companies to include in their accounts:

(a) A narrative statement of how they **applied** the **principles** set out in the UK Corporate Governance Code. This should provide explanations which enable their shareholders to assess how the principles have been applied.

(b) A statement as to whether or not they **complied throughout** the **accounting period** with the provisions set out in the UK Corporate Governance Code. Listed companies that did not comply throughout the accounting period with all the provisions must specify the provisions with which they did not comply, and give **reasons** for **non-compliance**.

2 Revised guidance for directors on the Combined Code (Turnbull report)

Note: The Turnbull report was published before the Combined Code became the UK Corporate Governance Code. Hence references below are to the Combined Code that was in place when Turnbull was published.

2.1 Introduction

The importance of internal control and risk management

The internal control systems have a key role in **managing the risks linked with a company's business objectives, helping to safeguard assets and the shareholders' investment**. The control system also aids the **efficiency and effectiveness of operations**, the **reliability of reporting and compliance with laws** and **regulations**. Effective financial records, including proper accounting records, are an important element of internal control.

A company's environment is constantly evolving and the risks it faces are constantly changing. To maintain an effective system of internal control, the company should regularly carry out a **thorough review of the risks** it faces.

As profits are partly the reward for risk-taking in business, the purpose of internal control is to help **manage risk** rather than eliminate it.

Objectives of guidance

The guidance is designed to reflect good business practice by **embedding internal control in a company's business processes**, remaining relevant in the evolving business environment and enabling each company to apply it to its own circumstances. Directors must exercise judgement in determining how the Combined Code has been implemented. The guidance is based on a **risk-based approach**, which should be incorporated within the normal management and governance processes, and not be treated as a separate exercise.

Internal control requirements of the Combined Code

This guidance aims to provide guidance for the directors on the requirements of the Combined Code relating to:

- Maintaining a sound system of internal control
- Conducting an annual review of internal control
- Reporting on this review in the annual report

2.2 Maintaining a sound system of internal control

Responsibilities

The board is responsible for the system of internal control, for setting policies and seeking assurance that will enable it to satisfy itself that the system is functioning effectively, in particular managing risks.

In determining what the system of controls should be, the board should take account of the following:

- The nature and extent of risks facing the company
- The extent and categories of acceptable risks
- The likelihood of the risks materialising
- The company's ability to reduce the impact of risks
- The costs versus the benefits of internal controls

Management is responsible for implementing board policies on risk and control. Management should **identify and evaluate the risks faced** by the company for board consideration, and **design**, **implement** and **monitor a suitable internal control system**. All employees have some responsibility for internal control as part of their accountability for achieving business objectives. They should have the knowledge, skills, information and authority to operate the system of internal control effectively.

Elements of internal control systems

The control system should **facilitate a company's effective and efficient operation** by enabling it to respond to risks effectively. It should help ensure the quality of reporting by ensuring the company maintains proper accounting records and processes that generate the necessary information. The system should also help **ensure compliance with laws and regulations**, and internal policies.

Control systems reflect the **control environment and organisational structure**. They include control activities, information and control processes and monitoring the continuing effectiveness of internal control systems. The systems should be **embedded in the company's operations** and form part of its **culture**, be able to **respond quickly to evolving risks** and include procedures for **reporting immediately to management**.

Control systems reduce rather than eliminate the possibility of poor judgement in decision-making, human error, control processes being circumvented, management override of controls and unforeseeable circumstances. They provide reasonable but not absolute assurance against risks failing to materialise.

2.3 Reviewing the effectiveness of internal controls

Reviewing control effectiveness is an essential part of the board's responsibilities. Management is responsible for **monitoring the system of internal control and providing assurance to the board that it has done so**. Board committees may have a significant role in the review process. The board has responsibility for disclosures on internal control in the annual report accounts.

A reliable system of internal control requires **effective monitoring**, but the board cannot just rely on monitoring taking place automatically. The board should regularly **review and receive reports on internal control** and should undertake **an annual assessment for** the purposes of making its report on internal controls.

The reports from management should provide a balanced assessment of the **significant risks and the effectiveness of the internal controls in managing those risks**. Reports should include details of control failings and weaknesses, including their impact and the action taken to rectify them.

When reviewing reports during the year, the board should consider what the risks are and how they have been identified, evaluated and managed. It should **assess the effectiveness of the internal controls**, consider whether any actions are being taken to remedy weaknesses and consider whether more effective monitoring is required.

The board should also carry out an **annual assessment**, considering what has been reported during the year plus any other relevant information. The annual assessment should consider the **changes in the significant risks** and the company's **ability to respond to changes in its environment**. It should also cover the monitoring of risks, the internal control and audit systems, the reports regularly given to the board, the significance of control failings and weaknesses, and the effectiveness of reporting.

2.4 The board's statement on internal control

The annual report and accounts should include **appropriate high-level information** to aid shareholders' understanding of the main features of the company's risk management and internal control processes. The minimum disclosure should be that a process of risk management exists, it has been in place for the whole period, the board has reviewed it and it accords with the provisions in the Turnbull report. The board should acknowledge its responsibility for internal controls and that the system is designed to manage rather than eliminate the risk of failure. It should disclose details of its review process and what actions have been taken to deal with weaknesses and related internal control aspects.

3 Sarbanes-Oxley Act 2002

3.1 Public Oversight Board

A **Public Oversight Board** has been established to register and regulate accounting firms.

3.2 Auditing standards

Audit firms should **retain working papers** for several years, have **quality control standards** in place, and as part of the audit review internal control systems to ensure that they **reflect the transactions** of the client and provide **reasonable assurance** that the transactions are recorded in a manner that will **permit preparation** of the **financial statements.**

3.3 Non-audit services

Auditors are expressly prohibited from carrying out a number of services including internal audit, bookkeeping, systems design and implementation, appraisal or valuation services, actuarial services, management functions and human resources, investment management, legal and expert services. **Provision of other non-audit services** is only allowed with the **prior approval** of the **audit committee**.

3.4 Partner rotation

There should be **rotation** of lead or reviewing audit partners every five years.

3.5 Auditors and audit committee

Auditors should discuss **critical accounting policies** and **alternative treatments** with the audit committee.

3.6 Audit committees

All members of audit committees should be **independent.** At least one member should be a financial expert. Audit committees should be responsible for the **appointment, compensation** and **oversight** of auditors. Audit committees should establish mechanisms for dealing with complaints about accounting, internal controls and audit.

3.7 Corporate responsibility

The **chief executive officer** and **chief finance officer** should certify the **appropriateness** of the **financial statements** and that those **financial statements fairly present** the **operations and financial condition** of the issuer. If the company has to prepare a restatement of accounts due to material non-compliance with standards, the **chief finance officer** and **chief executive officer** should **forfeit their bonuses.**

3.8 Transactions not included in accounts

There should be **appropriate disclosure** of **material transactions** and other relationships.

3.9 Internal control reporting

Annual reports should contain **internal control reports** that state the responsibility of management for establishing and maintaining an **adequate internal control structure** and **procedures for financial reporting.** Annual reports should also contain an **assessment** of the **effectiveness** of the **internal control structure** and **procedures** for **financial reporting**. Auditors should report on this assessment.

Companies should also report whether they have adopted a **code of conduct** for senior financial officers and the content of that code.

3.10 Whistleblowing provisions

Employees of **listed companies** and **auditors** will be granted whistleblower protection against their employers if they **disclose private employer information** to parties involved in a fraud claim.

4 The King report

4.1 The seven characteristics of good corporate governance

(a) **Discipline**, adherence to correct and proper behaviour including the underlying principles of good corporate governance

(b) **Transparency**, ease with which analysis can be made of actions, economic fundamentals, and non-financial matters. This reflects how good management is at making necessary information available

(c) **Independence**, reflecting mechanisms to minimise or avoid conflicts of interest such as composition of board, appointments to board committees and relations with auditors

(d) **Accountability,** mechanisms allowing investors to query and assess actions of board

(e) **Responsibility,** including responsibility to stakeholders. Governance should permit corrective action and penalising of mismanagement

(f) **Fairness,** balanced systems that take into account everyone having an interest in the company

(g) **Social responsibility**, in particular ethical standards, but also laying stress on being non-discriminatory and non-exploitative

4.2 Boards and directors

4.2.1 The board

A **unitary board** ensures positive interaction and diversity of views. The board must give **strategic direction**, retain **full and effective control** over the company, **monitor management, ensure** that the company **complies** with all relevant laws, regulations and codes of practice and **communicate** with shareholders and relevant stakeholders openly and promptly. The board should consider whether its **size, diversity** and **demographics** make it effective. The board should consider developing a **code of conduct**, covering conflicts of interest of management. The board should **identify key risk areas** and **key performance indicators**, and **identify and monitor non-financial aspects** of these.

4.2.2 Board composition

The board should comprise a mix of executive and non-executive directors, particularly **independent non-executives**, to protect shareholder interests. **Formal appointment procedures**, including a nomination committee, should be in place. **Board continuity** should be ensured by a director rotation programme.

4.2.3 Chairperson and chief executive

There should be a clear **division of responsibilities**, with preferably **separation of the roles of chairperson and chief executive** and the **chairperson** being an **independent non-executive director.** The chairperson's performance should be **appraised** regularly, the chief executive's at least annually.

4.2.4 Directors

No one individual or **block of individuals** should dominate the board's decision-taking.

Non-executive directors should have **calibre** and **credibility** and have the necessary skill and experience to assess all strategic, operational and conduct issues.

4.2.5 Remuneration

Remuneration should be sufficient to **attract**, **retain** and **motivate** executives of the required quality. A **remuneration policy** should be established and a remuneration committee should make **recommendations**; the **chief executive** can be **consulted** but should not fix his own remuneration. Full disclosure should be made in the accounts. **Performance-related elements** should constitute a substantial part of **executives' total remuneration packages.** Executive directors' **fixed term service contracts** should **not exceed three years**.

4.2.6 Board meetings

Boards should meet at **least once a quarter. Non-executive directors** should have **access to management**. Boards should regularly review **processes** and **procedures** to ensure the **effectiveness** of the company's **system of internal controls**. The board should receive **relevant non-financial information**, going beyond assessing the financial and quantitative performance of the company, looking at **qualitative measures** that involve **broader stakeholder interests**.

4.2.7 Board committees

Boards should not shelter behind board committees, but there should be a **formal procedure** for **certain functions** of the board to be **delegated.** At a minimum boards should have **audit** and **remuneration committees.** All board committees should preferably be chaired by an independent non-executive director.

4.2.8 Company secretary

The company secretary has a pivotal role in corporate governance, in providing detailed guidance on responsibilities, inducting new directors and assisting the chairperson.

4.3 Risk management

The board is responsible for the total process of **risk management** and for forming its opinion on the **effectiveness** of the process. Management is responsible for integrating the **risk management process** into the activities of the company. **Risk strategy policies** should be **communicated** to **all employees.**

The board should make use of **generally accepted models** to assess whether **organisational objectives** are being **achieved.** The board should **at a minimum** assess the following risks:

- Physical and operational
- Human resource
- Technology

- Business continuity
- Credit and markets
- Compliance

A board committee should aid the board in risk assessment. Boards should consider the need for a **whistle-blowing** process.

A comprehensive system of control should be established to **ensure risks are mitigated and objectives obtained. Risks** should be assessed on an on-going basis and control activities respond to risks, with relevant information about risks being **identified**, **captured** and **communicated.** Management should report on significant risks, system effectiveness and weaknesses found.

Boards should acknowledge their accountability for risk management and state that there is an **ongoing process** for **identifying, evaluating and managing risks** and there is an **adequate system of internal control** in place to mitigate risks.

4.4 Internal audit

Companies should have an **effective internal audit function,** with **access** to the **chief executive**, **chairman** and **audit committee.** There should be **adequate segregation of duties** if internal and external audit are carried out by the same firm.

Internal audit should **seek assurance** that **management processes** are **adequate** to **identify and monitor significant risks**, **confirm the effective operation** of **control systems**, **review processes** for **feedback** on **risk management** and **assurance,** and **confirm** that the board **receives** the **right quality of information**. The audit plan should be risk-based and **linked** to the **board's risk assessment**.

4.5 Sustainability reporting

Companies should report at least annually on the nature and extent of its **social, transformation, ethical, safety, health** and **environmental management policies** and practices. These include concerns such as workplace accidents, impact of HIV/AIDS, environmental concerns, black economic empowerment, human capital development and equal opportunities policies.

Each company should introduce a **code of ethics** and **disclose adherence** to it.

4.6 Accounting and auditing

The audit committee should recommend the **appointment of external auditors** and should **encourage consultation** between external and internal auditors. The audit committee should set out principles for whether non-audit services should also be supplied by auditors.

The majority of members of the audit committee should be independent non-executive directors and should be **financially literate**. It should be chaired by an independent non-executive director who is not the chairperson of the board. The committee should have formal terms of reference.

4.7 Relations with shareowners

Companies should maintain a **dialogue** with **institutional shareholders.** They should explain each item of special business and consider using **polls** to approve special business.

4.8 Accounts

Boards should present a **balanced and understandable assessment** of the company's position and a **comprehensive and objective assessment** of the activities of the company. Reports must be made in the context of society demanding **greater transparency and accountability** from companies regarding their non-financial matters.

ETHICS

This chapter emphasises the importance of ethics in business decisions. We cover ethics early on as ethics, like corporate governance, underpins organisational behaviour and control.

We start off by considering what ethics are, and highlighting the most important aspects of CIMA's Ethical Code. You need to remember that the key elements of ethical codes are fundamental principles, threats and safeguards. In Section 2 we go on to see how organisations promote and enforce ethical behaviour. Despite these efforts, accountants may face serious dilemmas in their working lives, and Section 3 deals with some of the dilemmas accountants may need to resolve.

Lastly we examine how you should approach the kind of situation that you will encounter in your exam.

The examiner has stressed the need for students to be aware of the ethical implications of practising as a management accountant and managing an entity. Questions will incorporate political and cultural sensitivities.

4

topic list	learning outcomes	syllabus references	ability required
1 Ethics	B3(b), C3(b)	B3(iii), C2(iv), C3(ii)	evaluation
2 Ethics and control systems	B3(b), C3(b)	B3(iii), C2(iv), C3(ii)	evaluation
3 Problems facing accountants in business	B3(b), C3(b)	B3(iii), C2(iv), C3(ii)	evaluation
4 Practical situations	B3(b), C3(b)	B3(iii), C2(iv), C3(ii)	evaluation
5 Examination questions: an approach	B3(b), C3(b)	B3(iii), C2(iv), C3(ii)	evaluation

1 Ethics

Introduction

We begin this chapter by defining ethics and summarising the key points in CIMA's ethical code.

1.1 What do ethics mean?

KEY TERM

ETHICS are a set of moral principles to guide behaviour.

1.2 CIMA's Code of ethics

CIMA's Code of ethics give the **basic principles** which members should follow in their professional lives. There are **serious consequences for failing to do so**, quite apart from the unacceptability of failure. Whenever a complaint is made against a member, failure to follow the contents of the ethical guide will be taken into account when a decision is made as to whether a *prima facie* case exists of professional misconduct.

'Members' include registered students, and this means you. If you are doing anything unethical it might help your understanding of this chapter, but we suggest you stop it at once!

1.3 Definitions

The introduction to the guide concentrates on defining the **general characteristics** and **skills** of the professional, the most important being: skills acquired by training and education; acceptance of duties to society as a whole; an objective outlook; high standards of conduct and performance.

1.3.1 Public interest

KEY TERM

PUBLIC INTEREST is 'the collective well-being of the community of people and institutions the professional accountant serves'.

The professional accountant's duty is **not** just that given to an individual client or employer, but extends to the public as a whole.

1.3.2 Objectives

The objectives of the profession can only be achieved if four basic needs are met.

- Credibility (of information and information systems)
- Professionalism
- Quality of services
- Confidence (in a framework of professional ethics)

1.4 Fundamental principles

The fundamental principles which must be observed by all members are as follows.

1.4.1 Professional behaviour

Professional behaviour means, in essence, not doing anything that might bring discredit to the profession.

1.4.2 Integrity

Integrity is the important principle of honesty and requires that you are not to be party to the supply of false or misleading information.

1.4.3 Professional competence and due care

Professional competence and due care means you should refrain from performing any services that you cannot perform with reasonable care, competence and diligence. You have a duty to remain technically up-to-date. This includes conforming to standards of bodies such as IFAC, IASC, national professional bodies, national regulatory bodies and relevant international and national legislation.

1.4.4 Confidentiality

You have a duty to respect an employer's or client's confidentiality unless there is a **legal or professional right or duty to disclose**. It also means not using information obtained in the course of work for personal advantage.

1.4.5 Objectivity

Objectivity is a combination of impartiality, intellectual honesty and a freedom from conflicts of interest. Members should act fairly and not allow prejudice or bias or the influence of others to override objectivity.

1.5 Ethical conflicts

There are many situations which could cause ethical conflicts, threatening compliance with the fundamental principles. These range from the trivial to the very serious (such as fraud or illegal acts). The situations mentioned in the guide affecting members in business include.

Threat	Examples
Advocacy	Furthering the employer's cause aggressively without regard to reasonableness of statements made. (Furthering legitimate goals of employer organisation would not generally create an advocacy threat)
Self-interest	Financial interests, loans and guarantees, incentive compensation arrangements, personal use of corporate assets, external commercial pressures
Intimidation	Threats of dismissal from employment, influence of a dominant personality
Familiarity	Making a business decision that will benefit a close family member, long association of a business contact, acceptance of a gift
Self-review	Business decisions being subject to review and justification by the same accountant responsible for making those decisions or preparing the data supporting them

CIMA accountants who work in practice, particularly in audit roles, face similar threats.

Threat	Examples
Advocacy	Advocating the client's case in a lawsuit
Self-interest	Having a financial interest in a client
Intimidation	Threats of replacement due to disagreement
Familiarity	Audit team member having family at the client
Self-review	Auditing financial statements prepared by the firm

The conceptual framework underlying CIMA's code of ethics requires CIMA members to risk manage these ethical risks.

1.6 Professional safeguards

There are various safeguards available to CIMA members to counter the ethical threats. These include:

- Entry requirements into CIMA
- Continuing professional development
- Professional standards
- Laws and corporate governance codes
- Professional monitoring, complaints and disciplinary procedures
- Reporting requirements
- Resolutions of ethical conflicts

1.7 Safeguards in the work environment   5/10

CIMA suggests that the following safeguards in the workplace should help reduce ethical threats along with their other purposes:

- The system of corporate oversight
- Ethics and conduct programs
- Recruitment procedures
- Strong internal controls
- Appropriate disciplinary procedures
- Leadership that stresses the importance of ethical behaviour
- Standards over, and monitoring of, employee performance
- Timely communication of, and training in, the organisation's policies and procedures
- Procedures enabling employees to communicate ethical issues to senior management without fear of retribution
- Consultation with another appropriate professional accountant

Exam alert

Question 1 in May 2010 asked about systems to prevent unethical behaviour in relation to transactions.

1.8 Safeguards for accountants working in practice

If CIMA members work for an accountancy practice, the firm should have the following safeguards in place in relation to the firm.

- The firm's leadership stressing **compliance with fundamental principles**
- Leadership of the firm establishing the expectation that **employees will act in the public interest**
- **Quality control policies and procedures**
- Documented policies on **identification and evaluation of threats** and **identification and application of safeguards**
- Documented policies covering **independence threats and safeguards** in relation to assurance engagements
- Documented internal procedures requiring **compliance with fundamental principles**
- Policies and procedures enabling **identification of interests and relationships between firm's team and clients**

- Policies and procedures to **manage reliance on revenue from single client**
- Using **different teams for non-assurance work**
- Prohibiting individuals who are not team members from **influencing outcome of engagement**
- **Timely communication of policies and procedures** and appropriate training and education
- Designating a senior manager to be **responsible for overseeing quality control**
- Advising staff of **independence requirements** in relation to specific clients
- **Disciplinary measures**
- **Promotion of communication** by staff to senior management of any ethical compliance issue that concerns them

There should also be safeguards relating to specific assignments:

- **Involving an additional professional accountant** to review the work done or otherwise advise
- **Consulting an independent third party**, such as a committee of independent directors, a professional regulatory body or another professional accountant
- **Rotating senior personnel**
- **Discussing ethical issues** with those in charge of client governance
- **Disclosing to those charged with governance the nature of services** provided and extent of fees
- **Involving another firm** to perform or reperform part of the engagement

1.9 Resolution of ethical conflicts

CIMA's guide suggests the following route to resolving ethical conflicts:

- **Gather all the relevant information** to make sure of the facts and decide whether an ethical problem exists
- **Raise the concern internally** with manager, colleague, senior management; use internal grievance or whistleblowing procedures
- **Raise the concern externally** with CIMA's whistleblowing advice line, auditors, regulators. Remember that confidentiality still applies. You may need to obtain legal advice
- **Remove yourself from the situation**. Stop working with a particular team, refuse to be associated with a particular report, or ultimately resign

Exam alert

The examiner has stressed that questions on ethics won't test a rote-learned knowledge of CIMA's ethical code. However you need to be aware of its principles and apply them if required.

Section summary

Ethics, a set of moral principles, are manifest in various ways, for example CIMA's code.

CIMA's Code of ethics is founded on a number of **objectives and fundamental principles**.

2 Ethics and control systems

Introduction

This section gives more detail about some of the ways organisations promote ethical behaviour.

2.1 Corporate codes and corporate culture

Look at just a few of the 'news stories' for a few days in May 2009.

CASE STUDIES

(a) **4th May Financial Times – Mafia links to Sicilian wind farms**

Anti-Mafia magistrates in Sicily have opened a sweeping investigation into the wind power sector. Local officials, entrepreneurs and crime gangs are suspected of collusion in the construction of lucrative wind farms before their eventual sale to multinational companies. Italian and EU subsidies for the building of wind farms (at highest guaranteed rates, £160 per kwh), for the electricity they produce have turned southern Italy into a highly attractive market exploited by organised crime.

http://www.ft.com/cms/s/0/b69fdf3a-38d1-11de-8cfe-00144feabdc0.html

(b) **5th May Personnel Today.com – HR must be on watch for directors' fraud**

HR must be extra-vigilant against a rise in fraud by company directors during the recession, a lawyer has warned. Statistics published by the government's UK Insolvency Service at the weekend revealed that the number of directors banned for criminal malpractice jumped by almost one third (31%), to 1,852 directors who were charged in the 12 months to March. Disqualification proceedings launched against directors for crimes such as fraud or theft rose by 72%, while cases of misappropriation of assets grew by almost 20%.

http://www.personneltoday.com/articles/2009/05/05/50531/hr-must-be-on-watch-for-directors-fraud.html

(c) **5th May Financial Times – FSA threatens City with higher fines**

Financial wrongdoers could face significantly higher fines from the City watchdog under proposals it is due to put forward this summer. Hector Sants, chief executive of the Financial Services Authority, on Tuesday told City lawyers that the regulator was considering a "new framework" for the penalties it imposed, which would include higher fines.

"The rationale for this is a perception that financial penalties have not been sufficiently large to deter wrongdoing in large institutions," he told the Financial Services Lawyers Association. The lawyers, many of whom follow the FSA's deliberations closely, expressed surprise at the announcement.

http://www.ft.com/cms/s/0/d053ba60-39bb-11deb82d-00144feabdc0.html

(d) **6th May Financial Times – Windows release sparks complaints**

Microsoft has stirred up fresh complaints of anti-competitive behaviour with its release this week of a late-stage trial version of the next Windows PC operating system. The complaints, from some of the leading makers of web browsers, look set to intensify the software company's regulatory headaches just as it is seeking to head off swingeing anti-trust action from the European Commission over a related issue. The latest row has been stirred up by provisions in the next version of the operating system, known as Windows 7, which rivals say give an unfair advantage to Microsoft's own browser.

http://www.ft.com/cms/s/0/4621afa2-3a6d-11de-8a2d-00144feabdc0.html

Exam alert

An examination question may include an extract from a set of corporate guidelines on which you will be expected to comment. Even if you are not given specific information about a company's policy, though, remember that all organisations have ethical standards. There will almost certainly be something in the information that you are given that will enable you to infer at least some of the values held by the people or departments involved.

You may also be asked to criticise or evaluate a code of ethics, to interpret actions in a case scenario in the light of a code or to argue the pros and cons of adopting corporate codes of ethics.

Question 4.1	Code of ethics

Learning outcome B3(b)

Here are some extracts from an article that appeared in the UK *Financial Times*:

'Each company needs its own type of code: to reflect the national culture, the sector culture, and the exact nature of its own structure.

The nature of the codes is changing. NatWest's code, for example, tries to do much more than simply set out a list of virtues. Its programme involves not only the production of a code, but a dedicated effort to teach ethics, and a system by which the code can be audited and monitored.

For example, it has installed a 'hot-line' and its operation is monitored by internal auditors. The board of NatWest wanted it to be confidential – within the confines of legal and regulatory requirements – and the anonymity of 'whistle-blowers' has been strictly maintained.

The code contains relevant and straightforward advice. For example: 'In recognising that we are a competitive business, we believe in fair and open competition and, therefore, obtaining information about competitors by deception is unacceptable. Similarly, making disparaging comments about competitors invariably invites disrespect from customers and should be avoided.' Or: 'Employment with NatWest must never be used in an attempt to influence public officials or customers for personal gain or benefit.'

How would you suggest that the effectiveness of a company's policy on ethics could be measured?

2.2 Compliance vs integrity based approaches

Lynne Paine (Harvard Business Review, March-April 1994) suggests that there are two approaches to the management of ethics in organisations.

- **Compliance**-based
- **Integrity**-based

2.2.1 Compliance-based approach

A compliance-based approach is primarily designed to ensure that the company **acts within the letter of the law,** and that violations are prevented, detected and punished. Some organisations, faced with the legal consequences of unethical behaviours, take legal precautions such as those below.

- Compliance procedures to detect misconduct
- Audits of contracts
- Systems for employees to report criminal misconduct without fear of retribution
- Disciplinary procedures to deal with transgressions

Corporate compliance is limited in that it relates only to the law, but legal compliance is 'not an adequate means for addressing the full range of ethical issues that arise every day'. Furthermore, mere compliance with the law is no guide to **exemplary** behaviour.

2.2.2 Integrity-based programmes

'An integrity-based approach combines a concern for the law with an **emphasis on managerial responsibility** for ethical behaviour. Integrity strategies strive to define companies' guiding values, aspirations and patterns of thought and conduct. When integrated into the day-to-day operations of an organisation, such strategies can help prevent damaging ethical lapses, while tapping into powerful human impulses for moral thought and action.'

An integrity-based approach to ethics treats ethics as an issue of organisational culture.

The table below indicates some of the differences between the two main approaches.

	Compliance	Integrity
Ethos	Knuckle under to external standards	Choose ethical standards
Objective	Keep to the law	Enable legal and responsible conduct
Originators	Lawyers	Management, with lawyers, HR specialists etc
Methods (both include education, audits, controls, penalties)	Reduced employee discretion	Leadership, organisation systems
Behavioural assumptions	People are solitary self-interested beings	People are social beings with values
Standards	The law	Company values, aspirations (including law)
Staffing	Lawyers	Managers and lawyers
Education	The law, compliance system	Values, the law, compliance systems
Activities	Develop standards, train and communicate, handle reports of misconduct, investigate, enforce, oversee compliance	Integrate values into company systems, provide guidance and consultation, identify and resolve problems, oversee compliance

In other words, an integrity-based approach incorporates ethics into corporate culture and systems.

 In the marking grid for TOPCIMA, there is a separate criterion covering ethics, so ethical concerns will be an issue in every TOPCIMA exam.

2.3 Company code of conduct

An **ethical code** typically contains a **series of statements setting out the organisation's values and explaining how it sees its responsibilities towards stakeholders.**

Codes of corporate ethics normally have the following features.

- They **focus on regulating individual employee behaviour**.
- They are **formal documents**.
- They **cover specific areas** such as gifts, anti-competitive behaviour and so on.

- Employees may be **asked to sign** that they will comply.
- They may be **developed from third party codes** (eg regulators) or use third parties for monitoring.
- They tend to **mix moral with technical imperatives**.
- Sometimes they do **little more than describe current practices**.
- They can be used to **shift responsibility** (from senior managers to operational staff).

2.3.1 Example of code of conduct

Typical statements in a corporate code

- The company conducts all of its business on **ethical principles** and expects staff to do likewise.

- **Employees** are seen as the most important component of the company and are expected to work on a basis of trust, respect, honesty, fairness, decency and equality. The company will only employ people who follow its ethical ideals.

- **Customers** should be treated courteously and politely at all times, and the company should always respond promptly to customer needs by listening, understanding and then performing to the customer requirements.

- The company is dedicated to complying **with legal or regulatory standards** of the industry, and employees are expected to do likewise.

- The company's relationship with **suppliers and subcontractors** must be based on mutual respect. The company therefore has responsibilities including ensuring fairness and truthfulness in all of its dealings with suppliers, including pricing and licensing, fostering long-term stability in the supplier relationship, paying suppliers on time and in accordance with agreed terms of trade and preferring suppliers and subcontractors whose employment practices respect human dignity.

- The company has a responsibility to: foster open markets for trade and investment; promote **competitive behaviour** that is socially and environmentally beneficial and demonstrates mutual respect among competitors; and refrain from either seeking or participating in questionable payments or favours to secure competitive advantages.

- A business should protect and, where possible, improve **the environment**, promote sustainable development, and prevent the wasteful use of natural resources.

- The company has a responsibility in **the community** to: respect human rights and democratic institutions, and promote them wherever practicable; recognise government's legitimate obligation to the society at large and support public policies and practices that promote human development through harmonious relations between business and other segments of society; collaborate with those forces in the community dedicated to raising standards of health, education, workplace safety and economic well-being; respect the integrity of local cultures; and be a good corporate citizen through charitable donations, educational and cultural contributions and employee participation in community and civic affairs.

Question 4.2   Employee behaviour

Learning outcome B3(b)

How can an organisation influence employee behaviour towards ethical issues?

CASE STUDY

A Bangladeshi teenager who died in a factory that supplies cheap jeans for the European market, was "overworked to death", a rights group said. Fatema Akter, 18, died during her shift in December 2008, the US-based National Labor Committee said.

"Forced to work 13 to 15 hours a day, seven days a week, Fatema was sick and exhausted, with pains in her chest and arms", the report said. Her job was to clean 90 to 100 pairs of finished jeans an hour.

The committee said an investigation showed that 14-hour shifts with few breaks were common at the factory, overtime was compulsory and workers were regularly beaten by their superiors. The report, released this week, said 80 per cent of garments produced at the factory were supplied to German-based retail giant Metro Group.

A statement issued by Metro Group said the company was "deeply saddened" by the death and had immediately terminated its contract with the Bangladeshi supplier that used the factory.

Rights groups have long questioned the working conditions in Bangladesh's thousands of garment "sweatshops", which provide some of the cheapest labour in the world. Last year Spanish fashion firm Zara forced the closure of a supplier's factory in the capital Dhaka after workers said they were being abused.

2.4 The impact of codes of conduct

A code of conduct can set out the company's expectations, and in principle a code such as that outlined above addresses many of the problems that the organisations may experience. However, **merely issuing a code is not enough**.

(a)   The **commitment of senior management** to the code needs to be real, and it needs to be very clearly communicated to all staff. Staff need to be persuaded that expectations really have changed.

(b)   Measures need to be taken to **discourage previous behaviours** that conflict with the code.

(c)   **Staff need to understand** that it is in the **organisation's best interests** to change behaviour, and become committed to the same ideals.

(d)   Some employees – including very able ones – may find it very difficult to buy into a code that they **perceive may limit their own earnings** and/or restrict their freedom to do their job.

(e)   In addition to a general statement of ethical conduct, **more detailed statements** (codes of practice) will be needed to set out formal procedures that must be followed.

2.5 Problems with codes of conduct

2.5.1 Inflexibility

Inflexible rules may not be practical. One example would be a **prohibition on accepting gifts from customers**. A simple prohibition that would be quite acceptable in a Western context would not work in other cultures, where non-acceptance might be seen as insulting.

2.5.2 Clarity

It is difficult to achieve **completely unambiguous wording**.

2.5.3 Irrelevancy

Surveys suggest that ethical codes are often perceived as irrelevant, for the following reasons:

(a)   They fail to say anything about the sort of **ethical problems that employees encounter**.

(b)   Other people in the organisation **pay no attention** to them.

(c)   They are **inconsistent with the prevailing organisational culture**.

(d)   Senior managers' behaviour is **not seen as promoting ethical codes**. Senior managers rarely blatantly fail to comply, rather they appear out-of-touch on ethics because they are too busy or unwilling to take responsibility.

2.6 Identity and values guidance

Corporate ethical codes are often **rather legalistic documents**, consisting largely of prohibitions on specific undesirable actions such as the acceptance of gifts from suppliers. More general guidance with an emphasis on principles may be more appropriate.

Identity and values programmes describe corporate values without specifying in detail what they mean. Rather than highlighting compliance with negatives they **promote positive values** about the company and form part of its culture. (Compliance programmes are about limiting legal and public relations disasters.) Even so, they need to be integrated with a company's values and leadership.

2.7 Other measures

To be effective, ethical guidance needs to be accompanied by **positive attempts to foster guiding values, aspirations and patterns of thinking that support ethically sound behaviour** – in short a **change of culture**.

Increasingly organisations are responding to this challenge by devising **ethics training programmes** for the entire workforce, instituting comprehensive **procedures for reporting and investigating ethical concerns** within the company, or even setting up an **ethics office** or department to supervise the new measures.

CASE STUDY

'The view from the trenches'

Badaracco and Webb (1995) carried out in-depth interviews with 30 recent Harvard MBA graduates. They found that unethical behaviour appeared to be widespread in the middle layers of business organisations.

'...in many cases, young managers received explicit instructions from their middle-manager bosses or felt strong organisational pressures to do things that they believed were sleazy, unethical, or sometimes illegal.'

However, these young managers categorised only a few of their superiors as fundamentally unethical; most were basically decent, but themselves pushed into requiring unethical behaviour by four strong organisational pressures.

(a)   Performance outcomes are what really count.
(b)   Loyalty is very important.
(c)   Don't break the law.
(d)   '...don't over-invest in ethical behaviour'.

The outcome of these pressures was a firm impression that ethical conduct was a handicap and a willingness to evade ethical imperatives an advantage in career progression.

Exam skills

You may need to discuss corporate ethical behaviour as part of a wider discussion on the control environment.

Section summary

Organisations have responded to pressures to be seen to act ethically by publishing **ethical codes**, setting out their **values and responsibilities** towards stakeholders.

3 Problems facing accountants in business

Introduction

In this section we go into more detail about some of the ethical dilemmas facing accountants in business.

3.1 Conflicts between professional and employment obligations

Ethical guidance stresses that a professional accountant should normally support the **legitimate and ethical obligations** established by the employer. However he may be pressurised to act in ways that threaten compliance with the fundamental principles. These include:

- Acting contrary to law, regulation, technical or professional standards
- Aiding unethical or illegal earnings management strategies
- Misleading auditors or regulators
- Issuing or being associated with a report that misrepresents the facts

If the accountant faces these problems he should obtain advice from inside the employer, CIMA or lawyers, or use the formal procedures within the organisation.

3.2 Preparation and reporting of information

As well as complying with financial reporting standards, the professional accountant in business should aim to prepare information that **describes clearly the nature of the business transactions**, **classifies and records information in a timely and proper manner** and **represents the facts accurately.** If the accountant faces pressures to produce misleading information, he should consult with superiors. The accountant should not be associated with misleading information, and may need to seek legal advice or report to the appropriate authorities.

3.3 Acting with sufficient expertise

Guidance stresses that the professional accountant should only undertake tasks for which he has **sufficient specific training or experience**. Certain pressures may threaten the ability of the professional accountant to perform duties with appropriate competence and due care:

- Lack of time
- Lack of information
- Insufficient training, experience or education
- Inadequate resources

Whether this is a significant threat will depend on the other people the accountant is working with, his seniority and the level of supervision over his work. If the problem is serious, the accountant should take steps to remedy the situation including obtaining training, ensuring time is available and consulting. Refusal to perform duties is the last resort.

3.4 Financial interests

Ethical guidance highlights financial interests as a self-interest threat to objectivity and confidentiality. In particular the temptation to **manipulate price-sensitive information** in order to gain financially is stressed. Financial interests may include shares, profit-related bonuses or share options.

This threat can be countered by the individual consulting with superiors and **disclosing all relevant information.** Having a remuneration committee composed of **independent non-executive directors** determining the remuneration packages of executive directors can help resolve the problems at senior levels.

3.5 Inducements

Ethical guidance highlights the possibility that accountants may be offered inducements to influence actions or decisions, encourage illegal behaviour or obtain confidential information.

The guidance points out that threats to compliance may appear to arise not only from the accountant **making or accepting the inducement**, but from the offer **having being made in the first place**. It recommends that directors or senior managers be informed, and disclosure may be made to third parties. The accountant should also disclose to senior management whether any close relatives work for competitors or suppliers.

Section summary

The accountant in business may face a variety of difficulties including **conflicts between professional and employment obligations, pressure to prepare misleading information, lack of sufficient expertise, financial interests** and **inducements**.

4 Practical situations

Introduction

In this section we start to generate an approach for dealing with ethical situations that you can use in your exam.

4.1 Examination questions

Examination questions will expect you to be able to apply your understanding of ethical issues to practical problems arising in organisations. Later in this chapter we are going to suggest an approach that you may find helpful in dealing with such questions, but first we are going to take the bare bones of a situation and see how it might be built up into the kind of scenario you will have to face.

4.2 The problem

The exam will present you with a scenario, typically containing an array of detail much of which is potentially relevant. The problem, however, will be one or other of two basic types.

(a)   **A wishes B to do C which is in breach of D**

where A = a situation, person, group of people, institution or the like
          B = you/a management accountant, the person with the ethical dilemma
          C = acting, or refraining from acting, in a certain way
          D = an ethical principle, quite possibly one of the CIMA's fundamental principles

(b)   Alternatively, the problem may be that A has done C, B has become aware of it and D requires some kind of response from B.

Exam alert

In an internal company role, ethical problems could be in the following forms.

- Conflict of duties to different staff superiors

- Discovering an illegal act or fraud perpetrated by the company (ie its directors)

- Discovering a fraud or illegal act perpetrated by another employee

- Pressure from superiors to take certain viewpoints, for example towards budgets (pessimistic/optimistic etc) or not to report unfavourable findings

Example: The problem

A management accountant joined a manufacturing company as its Finance Director. The company had acquired land on which it built industrial units. The Finance Director discovered that, before he had started at the company, one of the units had been sold and the selling price was significantly larger than the amount which appeared in the company's records. The difference had been siphoned off to another company – one in which his boss, the Managing Director, was a major shareholder. Furthermore, the Managing Director had kept his relationship with the second company a secret from the rest of the board.

The Finance Director confronted the Managing Director and asked him to reveal his position to the board. However, the Managing Director refused to disclose his position to anyone else. The secret profits on the sale of the unit had been used, he said, to reward the people who had secured the sale. Without their help, he added, the company would be in a worse position financially.

The Finance Director then told the Managing Director that unless he reported to the board he would have to inform the board members himself. The Managing Director still refused. The Finance Director disclosed the full position to the board.

The problem is of the **second basic type. B** is of course the easiest party to identify. Here it is the **Finance Director. A** is clear, as well: it is the **Managing Director. C** is the **MD's breach of his directorial duties** regarding related party transactions not to obtain any personal advantage from his position of director without the consent of the company for whatever gain or profit he has obtained. **D** is the **principle that requires B not to be a party to an illegal act.** (Note that we distinguish between ethical and legal obligations. B has legal obligations as a director of the company. He has ethical obligations not to ignore his legal obligations. In **this** case the two amount to the same thing.)

4.3 Relationships

You may have a feeling that the resolution of the problem described above is just too easy, and you would be right. This is because A, B, C and D are either people, or else situations involving people, who stand in certain relationships to each other.

- A may be B's boss, B's subordinate, B's equal in the organisational hierarchy, B's husband, B's friend.

- B may be new to the organisation, or well-established and waiting for promotion, or ignorant of some knowledge relevant to the situation that A possesses or that the people affected by C possess.

- C or D, as already indicated, may involve some person(s) with whom B or A have a relationship – for example the action may be to misrepresent something to a senior manager who controls the fate of B or A (or both) in the organisation.

Question 4.3   Relationships

Learning outcome B3(b)

Identify the relationships in the scenario above. What are the possible problems arising from these relationships?

Relationships should never be permitted to affect ethical judgement. If you knew that your best friend at work had committed a major fraud, for example, **integrity** would demand that **in the last resort** you would have to bring it to the attention of somebody in authority. But note that this is only in the last resort. Try to imagine what you would do in practice in this situation.

Surely your **first course** would be to try to **persuade your friend** that what they had done was wrong, and that they themselves had an ethical responsibility to own up. Your **second option**, if this failed, might be to try to get **somebody** (perhaps somebody outside the organisation) that you knew could **exert pressure** on your friend to persuade him or her to own up.

There is obviously a limit to how far you can take this. The important point is that just because you are dealing with a situation that involves ethical issues, this **does not mean that all the normal principles of good human relations and good management have to be suspended**. In fact this is the time when such business principles are most important.

4.4 Consequences

Actions have consequences and the consequences themselves are quite likely to have their own ethical implications.

In the example given above, we can identify the following further issues.

(a)   The MD's secret transaction appears to have been made in order to secure the sale of an asset the proceeds of which are helping to prop up the company financially. Disclosure of the truth behind the sale may mean that the company is pursued for compensation by the buyer of the site. The **survival of the company** as a whole may be jeopardised.

(b)   If the truth behind the transaction becomes public knowledge this could be highly damaging for the company's **reputation**, even if it can show that only one black sheep was involved.

(c)   The board may simply rubber stamp the MD's actions and so the Finance Director may still find that he is expected to be party to dishonesty. (This assumes that the **company as a whole is amoral** in its approach to ethical issues. In fact the MD's refusal to disclose the matter to the board suggests otherwise.)

In the last case we are back to square one. In the first two cases, the Finance Director has to consider the ethicality or otherwise of taking action that could lead to the collapse of the company, extensive redundancies, unpaid creditors and shareholders and so on.

4.5 Actions

In spite of the difficulties, your aim will usually be to reach a satisfactory resolution to the problem. **The actions that you recommend** will often include the following.

•   **Informal discussions** with the parties involved.

•   **Further investigation** to establish the full facts of the matter. What extra information is needed?

•   The **tightening up of controls or the introduction of new ones,** if the situation arose due to laxity in this area. This will often be the case and the principles of professional competence and due care and of technical standards will usually be relevant.

•   **Attention to organisational matters** such as changes in the management structure, improving communication channels, attempting to change attitudes.

Section summary

Exam questions are often founded on what should be done if breaches of laws, regulations or Code of ethics occur. **Close relationships** between the parties or other **conflicts of interest** are often a complication.

5 Examination questions: an approach

Introduction

We finish this chapter by demonstrating a step-by-step approach that you can use to approach exam questions.

5.1 Dealing with questions

An article in *CIMA Student* ('Learning and thinking about ethics') contained the following advice for candidates who wish to achieve good marks in ethics questions. (The emphasis is BPP's.)

'The precise question requirements will vary, but in general marks will be awarded for:

*   **Analysis of the situation**

*   **A recognition of ethical issues**

*   **Explanation if appropriate of relevant part of the Code of ethics**, and **interpretation** of its relevance to the question

*   Making clear, logical, and appropriate **recommendations** for action. Making inconsistent recommendations does not impress examiners

*   **Justifying recommendations** in practical business terms and in ethical terms

As with all case study based questions there is likely to be **more than one acceptable answer**, and marks will depend on how well the case is argued, rather than for getting the 'right' answer.

However, questions based on ethical issues tend to produce a range of possible solutions which are, on the one hand, consistent with the Code of ethics and acceptable, and on the other hand, a range of clearly inadmissible answers which are clearly in breach of the Code of ethics and possibly the law.'

5.2 Step-by-step approach

We suggest, instead, that:

(a) **You use the question format to structure your answer**
(b) **You bear in mind what marks are being awarded for** (see above)
(c) **You adhere to the following list of do's and don'ts**. Be sure to read the notes following.

DO	Note	DON'T
Identify the key facts as briefly as possible (one sentence?)	1	Merely paraphrase the question
Identify the ethical issues and fundamental principles	2	Regurgitate the entire contents of the Code of ethics
Consider alternative actions and their consequences	3	List every single possible action and then explain how all the unsuitable ones can be eliminated

DO	Note	DON'T
Make a decision and recommend action as appropriate	4	Fail to make a decision or recommend action. Propose actions in breach of the Code of ethics or the law
Justify your decision	5	Be feeble. 'This should be done because it is ethical' is not terribly convincing

Notes

1   **One sentence** is an ideal to aim for.

2   (a)   **Use the terminology of the Code of ethics, but not** *ad nauseam*. 'Integrity' is often more clearly described as 'honesty' (although the two words are not synonymous). Don't forget the words 'fairness', 'bias', and 'influence' when discussing 'objectivity'.

      (b)   **Don't torture the case study to make it fit a fundamental principle**: if, say, 'justice' is the most persuasive word for a situation don't be afraid of using it.

      (c)   If the law is involved, don't get carried away – this is **not a law exam**. 'The director has a statutory duty to ...' is sufficient: there is no need to go into legal detail.

3   Useful ways of generating alternatives are:

      (a)   To consider the problem from the other side of the fence: imagine you are the guilty party

      (b)   To consider the problem from the point of view of the organisation and its culture and environment

4   Making a decision is often very hard, but if you cannot do this you are simply not ready to take on the responsibilities of a qualified accountant. There are usually a number of decisions that could be justified, so **don't be afraid of choosing the 'wrong' answer.**

5   This is not actually as hard as you might think, as we shall show you in a moment.

5.3 Regurgitating the question

Possibly the most **common fault** in students' answers to questions on ethics is that they include large **amounts of unanalysed detail copied out from the question** scenarios in their answers. This earns no marks.

You can very easily avoid the temptation to merely paraphrase the question. Simply **begin your answer by stating that you are referring to 'issues'** (by which you mean all the details contained in the question) **discussed at a previous meeting, or set out in full in 'appended documents'.** If you do this you will be writing your report to someone already in possession of the same facts as you have.

5.4 Justifying your decision

The *CIMA Student* article quoted above says that **marks will be awarded for 'justifying recommendations in practical business terms and in ethical terms'.** We shall conclude by examining a passage from a CIMA model solution to a question on ethics to see how this can be done.

'Perhaps the first thing to do is to **report** the whole matter, **in confidence** and **informally**, to the chief internal auditor with suggestions that a **tactful investigation** is undertaken to **verify as many of the facts** as possible. The fact that the sales manager has already been tackled (informally) about the matter may be a positive advantage as **he/she may be recruited** to assist in the investigation. It could however be a problem as the information needed for further **investigation** may have already been removed. **Tact** is crucial as handling the matter the wrong way could adversely influence the whole situation. An understanding of who participants are and how they are implicated can be used positively to bring about change with the **minimum of disruption**.'

The key to this approach is **using the right language**, and to a large extent you cannot help doing so if you have sensible suggestions to make. The real problem that many students experience with questions of this type is lack of confidence in their own judgement. If you have sound business and managerial sense and you know your Code of ethics there is every reason to suppose that an answer that you propose will be acceptable, so don't be shy of expressing an opinion.

Section summary

In a situation involving ethical issues, there are **practical steps** which should be taken.

- Establish the facts of the situation by further investigation and work
- Consider the alternative options available for action
- Consider whether any professional guidelines have been breached
- State the best course of action based on the steps above

Chapter Roundup

✓ **Ethics**, a set of moral principles, are manifest in various ways, for example CIMA's code.

✓ **CIMA's Code of ethics** are founded on a number of **objectives and fundamental principles**.

✓ Organisations have responded to pressures to be seen to act ethically by publishing **ethical codes**, setting out their **values and responsibilities** towards stakeholders.

✓ The accountant in business may face a variety of difficulties including **conflicts between professional and employment obligations, pressure to prepare misleading information, lack of sufficient expertise, financial interests** and **inducements**.

✓ Exam questions are often founded on what should be done if breaches of laws, regulations or Code of ethics occur. **Close relationships** between the parties or other **conflicts of interest** are often a complication.

✓ In a situation involving ethical issues, there are **practical steps** which should be taken.

– Establish the facts of the situation by further investigation and work
– Consider the alternative options available for action
– Consider whether any professional guidelines have been breached
– State the best course of action based on the steps above

Quick Quiz

1   What does an organisation's ethical code usually contain?

2   Which of the following is not a category of threat identified in CIMA's guidance?

    A   Advocacy
    B   Confidentiality
    C   Familiarity
    D   Self-review

3   Fill in the blank. The temptation to manipulate .... information when preparing accounts is potentially a very serious ethical threat.

4   Give three examples of factors that may prevent a professional accountant from acting with sufficient expertise.

5   What fundamental principles should be observed by all CIMA members?

6   Fill in the blank.

    .... is the promotion of a particular viewpoint to the extent that objectivity becomes compromised.

7   Give three examples of situations that could cause ethical conflicts.

8   List five tips for exam questions on ethics.

9   Fill in the blanks.

    Recommendations for dealing with ethical situations should be.. , ... and ....

10   An integrity-based ethics approach emphasises values, aspirations and thought patterns.

    True   ☐

    False   ☐

Answers to Quick Quiz

1   A statement of the organisation's values and an explanation of its responsibilities towards its stakeholders

2   B   Confidentiality

3   The temptation to manipulate **price-sensitive** information when preparing accounts is potentially a very serious ethical threat.

4   • Lack of time
    • Lack of information
    • Insufficient training
    • Insufficient experience
    • Insufficient education
    • Inadequate resources

5   • Integrity
    • Objectivity
    • Professional competence and due care
    • Confidentiality
    • Professional behaviour

6   **Advocacy** is the promotion of a particular viewpoint to the extent that objectivity becomes compromised.

7   • Pressure from an overbearing colleague or from family or friends
    • Members being asked to act contrary to technical and/or professional standards
    • Divided loyalties between colleagues and professional standards
    • Publication of misleading information
    • Having to do work beyond one's degree of experience or expertise

8   • Identify key facts as briefly as possible
    • Identify major principles at issue
    • Consider alternative actions and their consequences
    • Make a decision and recommend action
    • Justify your decision

9   Recommendations for dealing with ethical situations should be **clear**, **logical** and **appropriate**.

10 True

Answers to Questions

4.1 Code of ethics

Some ideas that you might think through are: **training effectiveness measures; breaches of the code dealt with; activity in the ethics office; public perceptions of the company**. Try to flesh them out and think of some other ideas. The extract above should suggest some.

4.2 Employee behaviour

Here are some suggestions.

- Recruitment and selection policies and procedures
- Induction and training
- Objectives and reward schemes
- Ethical codes
- Threat of ethical audit

4.3 Relationships

The MD is the Finance Director's boss. He is also a member of the board and is longer established as such than B the Finance Director.

In outline the problems arising are that **by acting ethically the Finance Director will alienate the MD**. Even if the problem were to be resolved the episode would sour all future dealings between these two parties. Also, **the board may not be sympathetic to the accusations of a newcomer**. The Finance Director may find that he is ignored or even dismissed.

You should attempt this question from the Exam Question Bank after you have completed Chapter 6	Number	Level	Marks	Time
	Q7	Examination	25	45 mins

CONTROL SYSTEMS I

 We now move onto the role of control systems in managing organisations effectively. We start off by providing an overview of systems and control theory, in order to show how control is exercised at all levels of the organisation, and the many types of control system that exist.

You will see in Section 2 that the three component parts of a system are Input, Processes and Output. In this chapter we shall deal with the **input** elements in systems, what the system needs to be able to operate. Chapter 6 will mainly deal with the internal control systems that operate over a business's **processes** and Chapter 7 will deal with the management accounting control systems that measure **output**.

A key element of control over inputs is how the organisation is structured. In Section 4 we look at different types of structure and how they are used as mechanisms of control. Whatever the structure, different people involved in a system may have different views as to what an organisation is for and what it is. A strong organisational culture mean that managers share a common view, and thus cultural control is also an important aspect of organisational life. We therefore look at how control can be imposed through **culture** in Section 5.

In the last section of this chapter we look in more detail at **human resource controls** and measures for improving performance.

topic list	learning outcomes	syllabus references	ability required
1 The context of control	A1(a),(c),(d)	A1(i)	evaluation
2 Elements of systems	A1(a),(c),(d)	A1(i), (ii)	evaluation
3 Elements of control systems	A1(a),(c),(d)	A1(i),(ii)	evaluation
4 Structure of organisations	A1(a),(c),(d)	A1(iv)	evaluation
5 Organisational culture	A1(a),(c),(d)	A1(i)	evaluation
6 Human resources	A1(a),(c),(d)	A1(i)	evaluation

1 The context of control

Introduction

We start this chapter by giving a well-known example of where controls and systems spectacularly failed to work.

1.1 The context of governance: macro level

You are expected to evaluate and recommend appropriate control systems to the management of an organisation. We start with a case study to give you some idea as to context and **links with risk management**.

CASE STUDY

Enron Corporation

A major corporate scandal of recent years has been Enron, the American energy supplier, which had promised to revolutionise energy businesses. Enron was a US-based energy supply company, with global activities. For example, it owned power plants in India, but the terms of the ownership were controversial.

As well as operating physical power plants, Enron also supported the liberalisation of energy trading markets and the introduction of competition. Many countries saw the injection of competition into the power supply industry as a means of reducing prices for consumers (in the developed world), or providing additional capacity to support economic growth (in the developing world).

At the heart of Enron's business strategy was the belief that it could be a big energy company without owning all the power plants, ships, pipelines and other facilities. Instead, it could use contracts to control the facilities in which other companies had invested. Deregulation had destroyed the integrated production and distribution operations, and users could buy energy from different sources. In this free market, Enron acted as an intermediary, buying and selling energy (and other assets such as Internet bandwidth).

This business model is not valueless or fraudulent in itself. UBS Warburg, the merchant bank, has acquired Enron's energy trading operations, including 635 employees. UBS Warburg believed that, scandals aside, the trading operations were profitable (The Economist, 20 April 2002).

However, Enron's business practices and accounting methods raise a number of issues.

1 **Non-consolidated affiliates**

   Enron set up about 3,500 affiliates, which effectively removed assets and liabilities from Enron's balance sheet (effectively additional debt of $1.2bn). Some of these affiliated partnerships were run by Enron's directors and managers who are alleged to have profited from this, including the Chief Financial Officer, Andrew Fastow. (As accountants, you are doubtless aware of what this means in terms of 'off balance sheet finance' or even 'related party transactions'.)

   Many small investors did not know of the extent of off balance sheet financing although it is estimated that $27 billion of $60 billion assets were treated in this way. It is suggested that Enron's directors and advisers were well aware of the position. Enron did not have to report them and chose not to.

   The share price rose from $30 to $90 between 1998 and 2000, as sales increased from $31 billion to more than $100 billion. In 2001, Enron had to restate its profits. The share price fell by 90 percent in 2001. In October 2001, Enron reported a third-quarter loss of $618 million. The company's massive debt was downgraded to near junk-bond status, and the CEO and CFO left the company. Shareholders sued and the (US) Securities and Exchange Commission (SEC) launched an investigation.

   Enron capitalised these affiliates not with cash but with its own shares: if the shares were rising these investments appeared well-capitalised, but once Enron's shares began to fall, the company had to inject more shares to keep its side of the agreement with the affiliates. These affiliates were used to draw in money from outside investors.

These arrangements were justified on the basis that the investments offered little in the short term. By taking them off balance sheet, Enron could raise more money for other investments and enhance its corporate earnings.

2   **Accounting**

It is possible that such ventures were perfectly legal under US GAAP (Generally Accepted Accounting Principles) which is more rule-bound than the approach adopted in the UK and elsewhere. (There is a wider issue about ethics here: rules or principles and how these apply to corporate codes of practice.)

There is little doubt however that many shareholders were seriously misled about the financial position of the company. Enron's profits had to be restated.

Enron's accountants, Arthur Andersen, and its lawyers endorsed the accounting treatment. Arthur Andersen is alleged to have destroyed large numbers of documents relating to its dealings with Enron when these matters were finally investigated.

An internal management report revealed the following accounting treatments (Financial Times, 4 February 2002).

(a)   **Inflate profits and revenues**. Book income immediately on contracts that could take years to complete, and count trades made through online subsidiaries as revenues

(b)   **Offload debt**. Transfer it to 'off-balance-sheet' partnerships, some managed by Enron officers.

(c)   **Massage quarterly figures**. Transactions were timed for the end of accounting periods to flatter earnings and balance sheet.

(d)   **Avoid taxes**. Use offshore vehicles and other methods to minimise tax bill.

(e)   **Do deals**. Mask poor performance by buying, selling and trading assets rapidly.

(f)   **Use derivatives**. Hide speculative losses, bury debts and inflate asset values with complex financial instruments.

3   **Enron's directors and employees**

As mentioned above, many of Enron's employees had their personal wealth tied up in Enron shares, now worthless. They were actively discouraged from selling them. Many of Enron's directors, however, sold the shares when they began to fall, potentially profiting from them. It is alleged that the Chief Financial Officer, Andrew Fastow, concealed the gains he made from his involvement with affiliated companies.

4   **Enron's political influence**

Like many firms, Enron actively lobbied legislators and government agencies for government contracts or for legislation favourable to its commercial interests. Indeed, Enron's directors advised the new Republican administration on energy policy. Such lobbying is hardly rare. Enron paid money to support the re-election campaigns of many American legislators of both main parties. So Enron's activities fed into a far wider debate on campaign finance reform in the US.

Enron and Arthur Andersen also had contacts with the Labour government in the UK. The extent to which Enron benefited from these arrangements is debatable, however, and is subject to much speculation.

5   **Enron's customers and market behaviour**

In 2001, California faced an energy crisis. Power supply was open to competition, but prices were fixed, and capacity was limited. Unable to cope with increasing prices which they could not pass on to consumers, a number of local power companies faced financial ruin.

Eventually, a political solution was found, and Enron became a significant beneficiary by selling power to California. It has been alleged that Enron overcharged California for the energy supplied by systematically manipulating the power trading system.

It might have been difficult to criticise the company's actions at the time on grounds that they were actually harmful to individuals. Indeed, Enron was highly praised by external experts for its innovative approach to financial strategy, and the shareholders were very happy. However, the firm's alleged exploitation of the letter of the accounting rules, in defiance of their spirit, suggests that legality, rather than ethicality, was the only yardstick of behaviour.

The point about introducing this example at the start of our coverage of control systems is to introduce some of the wider issues covered, and it is worth drawing out some lessons.

Who 'controlled' Enron?	Clearly, something went wrong with Enron's corporate governance, in other words the overall guidance mechanism of the company. There was a **failure of oversight**. The audit committee did not have enough information on which to make judgments: the management system interfered with the running of the formal 'control' system.
Financial performance	In this case, accounting standards were followed to the letter, most of the time, but the overall effect was to inflate Enron's apparent performance. Performance measurement systems – as we shall see an important part of control – were clearly measuring something, but not everything. After all, 'off balance sheet finance' exists **precisely** because it does not have to be reported as a liability.
Incentive schemes	Everyone benefited from the rocketing share price: employees, managers and shareholders. So few had an interest in telling the truth.
Performance appraisal and **reward systems**	Enron was notorious for **aggressive human resource management**, with the bottom 'performers', as defined by management being sacked regularly.
Culture, ethics and targets	The culture of the company encouraged **aggressive accounting** and **over booking of revenues**. It was more important to report meeting targets than to meet them in fact.

Many of the structures that are supposed to manage and control corporate behaviour failed. Enron was a sophisticated business operation, with talented people, innovative business models, and the whole panoply of board committees. Yet the rot set in from the top. A lot of the controls that are supposed to protect shareholders from potentially rapacious management failed in this instance. Enron is, unlike some other companies, not simply a case of simple fraud, as a lot of what it did was technically legal.

Section summary

Control matters at all levels of an organisation, from its **overall governance**, to the **details of its operating practices**. The purpose and types of control at each level will differ and even the best intentioned controls can be undermined by human action.

2 Elements of systems

Introduction

Having seen what happens when systems fail to operate, in this section we go back to basics and define the key elements of systems.

Exam alert

The syllabus content identifies 'the application of control systems and related theory' and identifies components such as 'primary and secondary feedback, positive and negative feedback, open and closed loop control). The syllabus also explicitly brings in control within the framework of the organisation.

2.1 What are systems?

KEY TERMS

A SYSTEM is a set of interacting components that operate together to accomplish a purpose.

A BUSINESS SYSTEM is a collection of people, machines and methods organised to accomplish a set of specific functions.

An understanding of the concepts of systems theory is relevant to the design of **financial and management accounting systems.** The application of systems theory may:

- Create an awareness of **subsystems** (the different parts of an organisation)
- Help in the design and development of **information systems**
- Help identify the effect of the **environment** on systems
- Highlight the **dynamic aspects** of the business organisation
- Gain an understanding of the **risks** that may impact on a system.
- Identify areas of **control** to make sure the system achieves its objectives

2.2 System objectives and targets

2.2.1 Objectives

An organisation generally exists for a purpose, to which its activities are directed. **Hospitals exist** to cure the **sick** for example.

Objectives of systems will often be **conflicting**, so that some form of compromise or **trade-off** between them must be reached.

2.2.2 Targets

Targets will also be set in the light of objectives and goals. These will include **financial targets** such as return on **investment and profits**, and **non-financial targets** such as **product quality.**

Question 5.1	System objectives

Learning outcome A1(a)

You work in a credit control department of a large organisation which runs a number of different accounts for business clients. Sales people are encouraged to maximise sales, and your job is to maximise debt recovery. Sales people are paid on commission and there is an increasing problem with bad debts. What might be the problems with the objectives to the systems and how would you correct them?

2.3 The component parts of a system

A system has three component parts: inputs, processes and outputs. Other key characteristics of a system are the environment and the system boundary – as shown in the following diagram.

The diagram below shows that, in order to make profits businesses obtain **inputs** (resources from the environment), and transform them in some way into **outputs** to the environment.

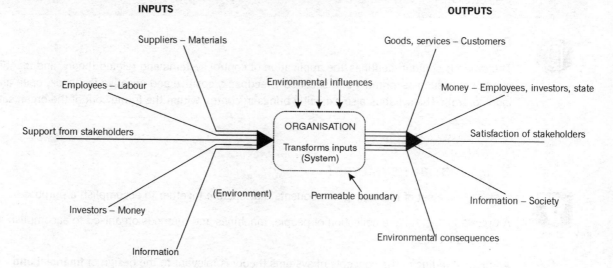

2.3.1 Inputs

Inputs **provide the system with what it needs** to be able to operate. Input may vary from matter, energy or human actions, to information.

2.3.2 Processes

A process **transforms an input into an output**. Processes may involve tasks performed by humans, plant, computers, chemicals and a wide range of other actions.

Processes may consist of **assembly**, for example where electronic consumer goods are being manufactured, or **disassembly**, for example where oil is refined.

2.3.3 Outputs

Outputs are the **results of the processing**. They could be said to represent the **purpose** for which the system exists. For example, a product is output at the end of a manufacturing process. In service terms, an output might be a completed medical procedure resulting in a well patient.

There is **not necessarily a clear relationship** between the number of inputs to a process and the number of outputs.

| Question 5.2 | Which outputs? |

Learning outcome A1(c)

A problem faced by public sector organisations is that outputs are harder to measure. Identify the problems in measuring the outputs of a publicly funded, or charitable, hospital.

2.4 The system boundary

Every system has a boundary that **separates it from its environment**. For example, a cost accounting department's boundary can be expressed in terms of who works in it and what work it does. This boundary will separate it from other departments, such as the financial accounts department.

2.5 The environment

Anything which is outside the system boundary belongs to the system's environment and not to the system itself. A system **accepts inputs** from the environment and **provides outputs** into the environment. The parts of the environment from which the system receives inputs may not be the same as those to which it delivers outputs. The environment exerts a considerable influence on the behaviour of a system; at the same time the system can do little to **control** the behaviour of the environment.

Question 5.3	Environmental impact

Learning outcome A1(a)

The environment affects the performance of a system. Using a business organisation as an example of a system, give examples of environmental factors which might affect it.

2.5.1 Adapting to the environment

Social systems have to adapt to survive. Businesses, in particular, have to adapt to changes in the legal, political, economic, social and competitive environment.

As the environment changes, a system may **react in one of two ways**.

(a) It may respond to external changes by making adjustments to its own operations. These changes are **short-term**, functional adaptations.

(b) It may also adopt a **long-term** approach, making structural alterations.

These are similar to the difference between changing performance and changing the plan.

2.6 Subsystems

A system itself may contain a number of systems, called **subsystems**. The goals of subsystems must be consistent with the goal of the overall system.

Subsystems may be **differentiated** from each other by six different factors:

- Function
- Space
- Time
- Formality
- People
- Automation

CASE STUDY

A nuclear power station contains many technical systems, but there are underlying social systems determining what is good practice.

2.7 Open and closed systems

Organisations have many relationships with the environment, and we can use systems theory to explore this point. In systems theory a distinction is made between open and closed systems.

2.7.1 Closed systems

A **closed system** is a system which is isolated from its environment and independent of it, so that no environmental influences affect the behaviour of the system, nor does the system exert any influence on its environment.

> Shut off from its
> environment

Closed system

2.7.2 Open systems

An **open system** is a system interacting with its environment. It takes in influences from its environment and also influences this environment by its behaviour. An open system is a stable system which is nevertheless continually changing or evolving.

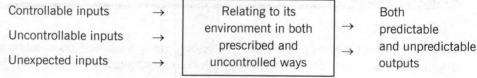

Controllable inputs	$\rightarrow$	Relating to its environment in both prescribed and uncontrolled ways	$\rightarrow$	Both predictable and unpredictable outputs
Uncontrollable inputs	$\rightarrow$			
Unexpected inputs	$\rightarrow$			

Open system

The open systems concept provides a tool for understanding the relationship between:

- The technical and the social aspects of an organisation.

- The parts and the whole organisation (eg the individual and the group, the individual and the organisation).

- The whole organisation and the environment.

A fundamental aspect of this approach is the way that **human interaction** affects the system and its subsystems.

2.8 The open systems approach

Social organisations, for example businesses and government departments, are by definition open systems. Why? All social organisations are comprised of human beings.

(a) Human beings participate in any number of social systems (eg family), of which the work organisation is only one, although it is important.

(b) In most societies, human beings are exposed to a variety of influences from the social environment, for example: advertising messages; family attitudes and pressures; government demands (eg for tax revenue).

Section summary

Control is often discussed in the **context of systems theory**. An organisation is a type of system, and a control system is a type of system.

Most systems have **inputs, processes and outputs** and are separated from the environment by a **boundary** that can be physical, social, legal, or all three.

---

3 Elements of control systems

Introduction

In this section we move on to look at the basics of control systems, including how they link in with different elements of management accounting systems.

KEY TERMS

CONTROL means ensuring that activities planned and undertaken lead to desired outcomes.

(CIMA Official Terminology)

A CYBERNETIC CONTROL SYSTEM describes the process of control within a system, with normally six key stages:

- Identification of system objectives
- Setting targets for system objectives
- Measuring achievements/outputs of the system
- Comparing achievements with targets
- Identifying what corrective action might be necessary
- Implementing corrective action

The key feature of a cybernetic system is that **feedback** is used as the basis of control.

3.1 What does a control system contain?

Basic concepts in talking about control include the following.

Plan, target, standard, objective	What the system is designed to achieve, eg budgeted revenues?
	Objectives for the process being controlled must exist, for without an aim or purpose control has no meaning. Objectives and targets are set in response to environmental pressures such as customer demand
Sensor	Detects the actual system behaviour, and gathers information about it – eg sales force and output from sales order processing system
	The **output of** the process must be **measurable** in terms of the dimensions defined by the objectives
Operations, inputs, processes and outputs	The main stages of operations, discussed earlier
Comparator	Compares actual system behaviour with the plan above, eg management accounts with variances
	A **predictive model** of the process being controlled is required so that causes for the non-attainment of objectives can be determined and proposed corrective actions evaluated
Effector	Enacts control action to change the actual system behaviour, eg the instructions of a manager
	There must be a **capability of taking action** so that deviations of attainment from objectives can be reduced. Action could involve changing objectives, inputs, process, modelling of system, or the whole system (systemic learning)

This concept of control involves more than just measuring results and taking corrective action. Control in the broad sense also embraces the formulation of objectives – deciding what are the 'right things' that need to be done – as well as monitoring their attainment by way of feedback.

3.2 Loop systems

In loop systems part of the output is fed back to the system. This is called feedback. **Feedback** is part of the output generated by a system, but is used to control the behaviour of the system.

3.2.1 Introducing single loop control to a system

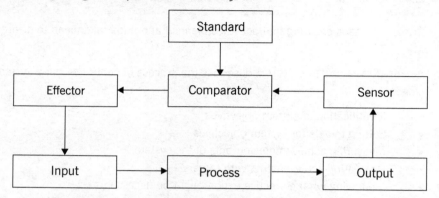

In this example, there is one loop of control. The actual output is compared to the standard or plan (a comparison known as **primary feedback**), and the effector controls the input to the system.

Simple example: a kettle is switched off by a thermostat once the water has boiled; no external intervention is needed. For a business example, see the case study below.

CASE STUDY

Booking airline tickets for low-cost airlines

An airline's system keep records of seats booked. As the plane fills up, the airline maximises revenue by increasing the price of the remaining, and scarcer seats, so that those who book late pay more. The output of the system – filled seats – automatically adjusts one of the inputs, the price of the remaining tickets.

Not all airlines have priced seats in this way. Some airlines would charge the maximum possible price early on, only to offer discounts to 'bucket' shops to fill up seats near to take off. This is a fundamentally different approach to pricing.

3.2.2 The need for double loop control

Notice that the control loop is a single loop control system; control is exercised once and there is no control over the plan. Sometimes the plan or standard is at fault, and so feedback has to be exercised twice.

Double loop or **secondary feedback** indicates that the plan is wrong, and requires adjustment.

Environmental influence

High Level Controller

Standard

Effector ← Comparator ← Sensor

Input → Process → Output

3.3 Feedback

FEEDBACK CONTROL is 'The measurement of differences between planned outputs and actual outputs achieved, and the modification of subsequent action and/or plans to achieve future required results'.

(*CIMA Official Terminology*)

A feature of **feedback** is that it is information that is at least partly gathered by **measuring the outputs** of the system itself. It has an **'internal' source**, as distinct from 'environmental' information, which comes from outside the system. For **some control systems**, notably for control by senior management at a strategic planning level, **control information** will be **gathered** from both **environmental sources and internal sources**.

The most common types of control system in businesses, such as **budgetary control, inventory control and production control systems,** are all based on **feedback cycles**.

3.4 Negative feedback

NEGATIVE FEEDBACK is information which indicates that the system is deviating from its planned or prescribed course (the performance gap between outputs and targets), and that corrective action is necessary to bring it back on to course. This feedback is called 'negative' because control action would seek to reverse the direction or movement of the system back towards its planned course.

Thus, if the budgeted sales for June and July were £100,000 in each month, whereas the report of actual sales in June showed that only £90,000 had been reached, this negative feedback would indicate that control action was necessary to raise sales in July to £110,000 in order to get back on to the planned course.

Corrective action could be a change in the **system**, a change in **objectives/targets**, a change in **inputs** or a change in **predictions of controls.**

3.5 Positive feedback

POSITIVE FEEDBACK results in control action which causes actual results to maintain (or increase) their path of deviation from planned results. This contrasts with negative feedback, which attempts to reverse the deviation and bring actual results back on to the prescribed course.

Suppose, for example, that a company budgets to produce and sell 100 units of product each month, maintaining an average inventory level of 40 units. Now if actual sales exceed the budget, and show signs of sustained growth, it will obviously be in the company's interests to produce and sell as much as possible (provided additional output earns extra contribution to profit).

Enron misreported its results, and the share price rose. Shareholders wanted even more.

CASE STUDY

3.6 Feedforward control and planning

KEY TERM

FEEDFORWARD CONTROL is 'The forecasting of differences between actual and planned outcomes, and the implementation of action, before the event, to avoid such differences'.   (*CIMA Official Terminology*)

Deviations in the system are **anticipated**, so that 'corrective action' can be taken in advance of them actually happening. (With feedback control, in contrast, actual errors have happened before they are reported and corrective action is taken.)

An example of feedforward control is a **cash budget**, prepared regularly. Future cash flows and cash balances are checked to make sure that the organisation will have available the cash resources that it needs, without overstepping its borrowing facility limits.

Exam alert

The principles of feedback and feedforward are integral to the risk management systems described in Chapter 2.

3.7 Problems with control systems

There are a number of **problems to overcome** in applying theory to practice.

(a) **Environmental change**. An **organisation is an open system** which is connected to and interacts with its environment. That environment is the world at large and it is chiefly characterised by **change**. Attempts have to be made to forecast what will happen in the future, but in most situations **uncertainty** exists: there are too many variables involved and too few of them are under the direct control of the organisation.

(b) **Organisations are made up of individuals**. People **cannot be relied upon to react predictably** in response to efforts to direct their behaviour towards a particular end (discussed further below).

(c) **Preparing a standard or plan** in the first place, which is reliable and acceptable to the managers who will be responsible for the achievement of the standard or plan.

(d) **Measuring actual results with sufficient accuracy**.

(e) **Measuring actual results with suitable feedback periods**. The reporting cycle time must be kept sufficiently short to give managers a chance to take prompt control action when serious deviations from plan occur.

(f) **Providing non-accounting** as **well as accounting information** to help with the assessment of plans and results.

(g) **Identifying the causes of variations** between actual results and the standard or plan, and distinguishing controllable from uncontrollable causes.

(h) **Drawing the attention of managers to a deviation** between actual results and plan, and persuading them to do something about it.

(i) **Coordinating the plans and activities** of different departments in the organisation.

(j) **Informing everybody** who needs to be informed about how results are going.

3.8 Contingency theory

KEY TERM

CONTINGENCY THEORY relates to the design of accounting systems and presupposes that systems can be effectively designed to suit the circumstances of the firm including its technology, entity structure and its competitive environment.

(CIMA Official Terminology)

Contingency theory developed as a reaction to prescriptive ideas that claimed to offer a universal 'best way' to design organisations. Research indicated that **different forms of organisational structure could be equally successful**, that there was no inevitable correlation between organisational structures and effectiveness, and that there were a number of variables to be considered in the design of organisations. Essentially, **'it all depends'**.

KEY POINT

What is most appropriate for an organisation is dependent in part on the following variable (**contingent**) factors. (SECRET mnemonic)

- **S**tructure of the organisation
- **E**nvironmental conditions (eg competition, economy, markets)
- **C**ulture present within the organisation
- **R**ole of centre in terms of decision making
- **E**stablished strategy being pursued
- **T**echnology usage and dependency

Section summary

A **cybernetic control system** is one whose behaviour is coupled to feedback from its own performance. Most control systems in organisations fit this model.

Feedback occurs at several levels: single loop, in which **performance is changed**, and double loop in which **the plan itself is adjusted**.

Contingency theory states that what is most appropriate for an organisation depends upon its **structure, environmental conditions, culture, role of centre, established strategy and technology**.

4 Structure of organisations

Introduction

In this section we examine how different types of organisational structure shape the organisational environment in which a business operates.

4.1 Components of organisational structures

According to Mintzberg (1979), organisations contain five main components.

- **Strategic apex** (eg board of directors) directs strategy.
- **Operating core** contains those people directly involved in the process of adding value.
- **Middle line** converts the wishes of the strategic apex into the work of the operating core. Middle managers at this level exert a pull to make autonomous decisions, for example the establishment of separate business units.

- **Technostructure** standardises the work of others, by designing procedures they must follow, and can include finance department personnel, HRM specialists, work study analysts, and all people who 'design' jobs and who design control mechanisms.

- **Support staff** provide ancillary services such as public relations or legal counsel.

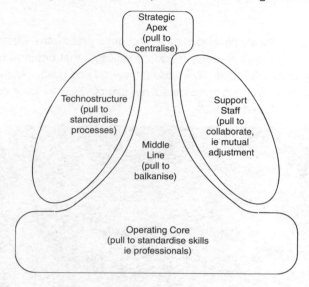

4.1.1 Hierarchy

Within the organisation's hierarchy there are lines of authority or **chains of command**, running from senior management vertically downwards through the organisation connecting the various levels of managers.

The chain of command not only represents the **decision making hierarchy**, it also provides a **defined channel for formal communication up and down the organisation**.

Decisions on chains of command must also take into account the following issues.

(a)   Communications can become **distorted** as more layers are added to the chain of command.

(b)   Long chains of command will increase the amount of time taken for **information to reach the relevant decision makers**.

(c)   Long chains of command **distance junior managers** from thinking and decision making at the top, and limit development into a general management role. Managers may therefore become **frustrated** and **de-motivated**, and may leave the organisation in search of flatter organisations and greater opportunities for responsibility.

4.1.2 Tall and flat organisations

A **tall organisation** is one which, in relation to its size, has a large number of management levels, whereas a **flat organisation** is one which, in relation to its size, has a smaller number of hierarchical levels.

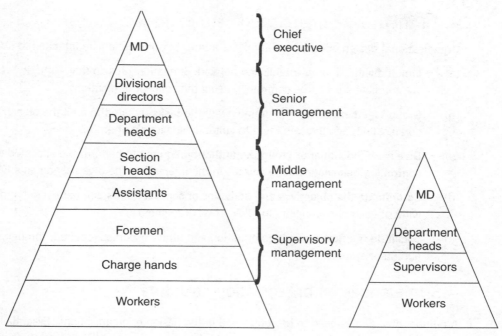

Tall and flat organisations

A tall organisation structure might be inefficient, despite the advantages of a narrow span of control and the possibility of graduated promotions. Tall structures can impose rigid supervision and control and therefore block initiative and ruin the motivation of subordinates.

Flat organisations have become more common as a result of the current fashion for **delayering and empowerment**.

CASE STUDY

CIMA's *Risk management – a guide to good practice* links organisational structure with the risk identification process. A hierarchical organisation is likely to look at risk from a corporate perspective, involving senior managers who will consider risk in the context of business strategy and be alert for external influences.

By contrast flatter organisations are likely to identify risks at local or departmental levels and then aggregate them. This has the advantages of helping to establish risk awareness throughout the organisation, identifying department-specific risks and providing a perspective from those responsible for dealing with risks on a day-to-day basis.

4.1.3 Empowerment

Empowerment is the term for making workers (and particularly work teams) responsible for achieving, and even setting, work targets, with the freedom to make decisions about how they are to be achieved.

Empowerment goes hand in hand with the following developments.

(a)   **Delayering** or a cut in the number of levels (and managers) in the chain of command.

(b)   **Flexibility**, since giving responsibility to the people closest to the products and customer encourages responsiveness.

(c)   **New technology**, since there are more 'knowledge workers'. Such people need less supervision, being better able to identify and control the means to clearly understood ends.

Establishing control in an empowered culture can be achieved perhaps through:

•   **Standardisation of processes**, with clear guidelines (eg bank lending)

•   **Cultural control**, so that everyone accepts the responsibilities that come with empowerment

•   **Team working**

4.2 Purposes of organisation structure

Organisational design or structure implies a framework or mechanism intended to do the following.

(a) **Link individuals** in an established network of relationships so that authority, responsibility and communications can be controlled, using the concept of hierarchy.

(b) **Group together** (in any appropriate way) the **tasks** required to fulfil the objectives of the organisation, and allocate them to suitable individuals or groups.

(c) **Give each individual or group the authority** required to perform the allocated functions, while **controlling behaviour and resources** in the interests of the organisation as a whole.

(d) **Co-ordinate the objectives and activities of separate units**, so that overall aims are achieved without gaps or overlaps in the flow of work required.

(e) **Facilitate the flow** of work, information and other resources required, through planning, control and other systems.

4.3 Influences on organisation structure

A number of variables need to be considered in the design of organisations. Essentially, it depends on the internal factors and external environment of each organisation and the design of organisational structure is a best fit between the tasks, people and environment **in the particular situation**. Here are some generalisations about the influences on an organisation's structure.

1	The **older** the organisation, the **more formalised** its behaviour. Work is repeated, so is more easily formalised, and so is more easily measured and controlled.
2	Organisation structure reflects the age of the **industry's** foundation.
3	The **larger** the organisation, the more **elaborate** its structure. This is because there are more activities that need to be measured.
4	The **larger** the organisation, the larger the **average size of the units** within it.
5	The **larger** the organisation, the more **formalised** its behaviour (for consistency).
6	The more **sophisticated** the technology, the more **elaborate and professional** the administrative structure will be.
7	The automation of the work transforms a controlled **bureaucratic** administrative structure into an organic one. An **organic organisation** is characterised by fluid hierarchies and communications, and is the opposite of the rigid rule-bound bureaucracy. This is because procedures are incorporated into equipment routines or software. It requires specialists to manage the process, and such people tend to communicate informally.
8	The more **dynamic the environment**, the more **organic the structure** (see point 7 above).
9	The more **complex the environment**, the more **decentralised the structure**.
10	The more **diversified the markets**, the greater the propensity to split into **market based departments**.
11	Extreme environmental hostility is a force for centralisation, since central control permits rapid action.
12	Environmental disparities encourage selective decentralisation for some activities, centralisation for others.
13	The more an organisation is subject to **external control** (eg by government, holding company) the more **centralised and formalised its structure**.

14	The **power needs** of organisational members (to control others, or at least to control their own working conditions) lead to centralisation.
15	**Fashion** is a poor guide. For example, while bureaucracies are deeply unfashionable, they are often the best at doing certain kinds of work.

4.4 Centralisation and decentralisation

Centralisation and decentralisation refer to the degree to which authority is delegated in an organisation – and therefore the level at which decisions are taken in the management hierarchy. There are several issues.

(a) In some businesses, authority is **centralised** and **decisions are taken at the top**. In a small business, the owner-manager may take all the decisions. However, in a hospital environment, 'life or death' decisions are taken at 'operations level'.

(b) Some businesses have **regional offices** with **decision autonomy**. In other businesses, decisions of any significance have to be referred back to head office.

(c) **Operations** might be **decentralised**, but standards might be set centrally and distributed throughout the organisation.

Arguments in favour of centralisation and decentralisation	
Pro centralisation	**Pro decentralisation/delegation**
1 Decisions are made at **one point** and so easier to co-ordinate.	1 **Avoids overburdening top managers**, in terms of workload and stress.
2 Senior managers in an organisation can take a **wider view of problems** and **consequences**.	2 **Improves motivation** of more junior managers who are given responsibility – since job challenge and entrepreneurial skills are highly valued in today's work environment.
3 Senior management can keep a **proper balance** between different departments or functions – eg by deciding on the resources to allocate to each.	3 **Greater awareness of local problems** by decision makers. Geographically dispersed organisations should often be decentralised on a regional/area basis.
4 **Quality of decisions is (theoretically) higher** due to senior managers' skills and experience.	4 **Greater speed of decision making**, and response to changing events, since no need to refer decisions upwards. This is particularly important in rapidly changing markets.
5 **Possibly cheaper**, by reducing number of managers needed and so lower costs of overheads.	5 **Helps junior managers to develop** and helps the process of transition from functional to general management.
6 **Crisis decisions are taken more quickly** at the centre, without need to refer back, get authority etc.	6 **Separate spheres of responsibility** can be identified: controls, performance measurement and accountability are better.
7 **Policies, procedures and documentation** can be standardised organisation-wide.	7 **Communication technology** allows decisions to be **made locally**, with information and input from head office if required.

Whatever system is set up, it is of paramount importance that all managers at all levels should clearly know where they fit into the organisation.

4.4.1 Centralisation and strategic management

Goold and Campbell conducted a study of a large number of high profile diversified companies to examine **how different companies cope with the problem of managing diversity**. They discovered three main philosophies and three corresponding styles of strategic management.

Philosophy	Example	Style of management
Core businesses	Cadbury's. 'The company commits itself to a few industries and sets out to win big in those industries.'	Strategic planning style
Manageable businesses	'The emphasis is on selecting businesses for the portfolio which can be effectively managed using short-term financial controls...' The businesses have few linkages with each other, should be in relatively stable competitive environments and should not involve large or long-term investment decisions.	Financial control style
Diverse businesses	Samsung, perhaps. 'The centre seeks to build a portfolio that spreads risk across industries and geographic areas as well as ensuring that the portfolio is balanced in terms of growth, profitability and cash flow.'	Strategic control style

Goold and Campbell describe the features of the different styles of central management in terms of the management structure that we have already seen under contingency theory.

Style of central management	Features
Strategic planning	Entails the centre **participating in** and **influencing the strategies** of the **core businesses**. The centre establishes a planning process and contributes to strategic thinking. Rather less emphasis is placed on financial controls and performance targets are set flexibly and reviewed within the context of long-term progress.
Strategic control	Concerned with the plans of its business units but believes in **autonomy for business unit managers**. Plans are therefore made locally but reviewed in a formal planning process to upgrade the quality of the thinking. The centre does not advocate strategies or interfere with major decisions but maintains control through financial targets and strategic objectives.
Financial control	As the name suggests, **focuses on annual profit targets**. There are no long-term planning documents and no strategy documents. The role of the centre is limited to approving budgets and monitoring performance.

4.5 Functional structure

In a functional organisation structure, departments are defined by their **functions,** that is, the work that they do. It is a traditional approach and many organisations are structured like this. Primary functions in a manufacturing company might be production, marketing, finance, and general administration. Sub departments of marketing might be selling, advertising, distribution and warehousing.

A functional structure is based on work specialism and is therefore logical. The organisation can benefit from economies of scale.

However a functional structure does not reflect the actual business processes by which **value is created**. Staff may not have an understanding of how the *whole* business works. There are problems of co-ordinating the work of different specialisms.

4.6 Matrix organisation

Matrix organisation is a structure which provides for the **formalisation** of management control between different functions, whilst at the same time maintaining functional departmentation. It can be a mixture of functional, product, and territorial organisation. Matrix organisation means that **subordinates have two (or more) superiors**, in the sense that they must report to both a functional manager and a project manager. However, a subordinate cannot easily take *orders* from two or more bosses. The authority of each would have to be **carefully defined**.

Advantages	Disadvantages
• **It is flexible**. Members of project teams adapt quickly to a new challenge or new task, and develop an attitude which is geared to accepting change.	• **Dual or triple authority** threatens a conflict between functional managers, product/project managers and nation/country managers.
• It should **improve communication** within the organisation.	• **One individual with two or more bosses** is **more likely** to **suffer role stress** at work.
• Dual authority gives the **organisation multiple orientation**.	• It is **complex and thus more costly** – eg product managers are additional jobs which would not be required in a simple structure of functional departmentation. There may be other ways of improving communication or obtaining the benefits than a complex structure.
• It provides a **structure for allocating responsibility** to managers for end-results, rather than merely fulfilling processes.	
• It provides for **inter-disciplinary co-operation** and a mixing of skills and expertise.	

4.7 Divisionalisation

The m-form, or **divisionalised** form has been adopted to reduce the level of complexity in large organisations. Responsibility is devolved to divisions which have a clear business focus. The classic model is a conglomerate with a number of strategic business units, each occupying a different niche in the industry and market, or working in different markets. Strategic business units are run as separate businesses, with local autonomy.

A division can be constructed on the bases below.

Geography	Not all multinational firms operate as genuinely global or boundaryless companies. Instead, they have regional or national operating units. The challenge is to avoid duplication of effort and to enable both sides to learn from each other.
Product-market	Big car manufacturers have divisions for cars and trucks.
Customer	For example, divisions for business customers and for personal customers.
Technology	Different divisions may use different information systems.

Divisionalisation is a solution to the problem of too much complexity, by driving down responsibility to a lower level.

Advantages	Disadvantages
• Divisionalisation makes **diversification easier**, as the organisational structure can reflect how the company is organised.	• Divisions are **funded by the holding company** and thus are **not directly answerable to markets** which ultimately reward performance.
• Divisionalisation **facilitates the allocation of management responsibility**.	• Central management tends to usurp **divisional profit** through management charges.
• Central planning can be retained, but implementation of plans can be **devolved to local divisions** which should have a better understanding of local conditions.	• Divisions may **not be independent**: is it fair to measure a division's performance in terms of profit, if the division has to pay a centrally imposed transfer price?
	• Divisionalisation assumes that head office can **allocate resources better** than the market.
	• Divisionalisation can make the **investment hard to value**.

4.7.1 Divisionalisation and information flows

For **central management**, there will be a **reduction in the amount of information** that they receive about each unit's operations. Reports to them from unit managers will be selected and edited. With this information, central management must try to apply overall strategic planning and control measures. There could be some danger that head office managers will **lose touch** with what is happening at an operational level.

For **unit managers**, information about their own unit's performance should be readily accessible, but the **flow of information about the organisation** as a whole, or about other units within the organisation, will be **restricted**. Some information will come from head office, and inter-divisional information flows might be established, but it might nevertheless be difficult for unit managers to **assess the contribution of their own unit to the organisation as a whole**.

Question 5.4	Divisionalisation

Learning outcome A1(a)

Company Y began manufacturing a single product. As the company grew, it adopted a typical functional structure. More recently, as a result of both internal development and a series of acquisitions, it has become a multi-product company serving diverse markets.

What are the limitations of Company Y's functional structure, given its recent development into a multi-product company? What type of organisation structure might be more appropriate?

Exam alert

You may be asked to consider the impact of structure on risks. This also ties in with the management accounting systems and output measures; whatever systems are chosen will lead to different results and hence different risk indicators.

4.8 Evolution of organisational structures

Organisation structures are responding to the problems of control, as follows.

Growth of knowledge work	'Today's economy runs on knowledge and most companies work assiduously to capitalise on that fact. They use cross-functional teams, customer– or product-focused business units, and workgroups.' (Wenger and Snyder, 2000).
Delayering	A reduction in the number of levels in the management hierarchy.
Communications technology	Organisational life has been revolutionised by email and network technology.
Core/periphery	Some firms have been changing the structure of their workforces for the sake of greater flexibility, eg a core of full-time permanent staff and periphery part-timers and temporary or contract workers.

4.8.1 Business Process Re-engineering (BPR)

KEY TERM

BUSINESS PROCESS RE-ENGINEERING **(BPR)** means selection of areas of business activity in which repeatable and repeated sets of activities are undertaken, and the development of improved understanding of how they operate and of the scope for radical redesign with a view to creating and delivering better customer value. *(CIMA Official Terminology)*

There are three common themes.

(a) The **need to make radical changes to the entire organisation**. Changing conditions 'impact all functions of the company and lead to a radically different way of doing business.'

(b) The **need to change functional hierarchies.**

(c) The **need to address the problem of fragmented staff roles**: 'roles have become specialised with the result that staff are only responsible for a small part of an overall task. This can result in loss of accountability for a finished task, de-skilling of work and the need for highly complex scheduling systems.'

Properly implemented BPR may help an organisation to **reduce costs, improve customer services, cut down on the complexity of the business and improve internal communication**.

(a) At best it may bring about new insights into the objectives of the organisation and how best to achieve them.

(b) At worst, BPR is simply a **synonym for squeezing costs** (usually through redundancies). Many organisations have taken it too far and become so 'lean' that they cannot respond when demand begins to rise.

4.8.2 The horizontal organisation

Based on business process re-engineering, the horizontal organisation is a technique which breaks down 'vertical' departmental boundaries, and claims to eliminate the hierarchies of command and control. Instead management is based on processes.

Characteristic	Comment
Structure	Organisation structure is based on cross-functional processes rather than tasks or geography.
Team	Teams, not individuals, are the basis of this approach.
Ownership	A process owner is responsible for the whole process.
Customers	Customers drive the process: the process owner puts customer-performance first.

The process does focus the organisation on the customer. However, the customer may be at the receiving end of several 'core' processes. Also the process owner should be the person or group that controls the process. Where, however, a horizontal structure is in place, the responsibility for taking control action is not always clear.

4.9 Outsourcing

KEY TERM

OUTSOURCING is the use of external suppliers as a source of finished products, components or services.

(CIMA Official Terminology)

You will have encountered outsourcing in your earlier studies. We shall look at outsourcing in detail in the context of internal auditing in Chapter 15 and information technology in Chapter 13. For now, we include a brief reminder of key considerations that relate to outsourcing.

4.9.1 Advantages of outsourcing

These include:

- Outsourcing can **free up internal time and resources** for more important value-earning activities

- The suppliers of the outsourced activity can provide **specialist expertise** which is not available in-house or would not be worth maintaining in-house

- **Less administration** is involved dealing with an outsourced service

- Outsourcing is the **most cost-effective way** of providing a service, particularly for smaller organisations

4.9.2 Disadvantages of outsourcing

However outsourcing has some possible drawbacks:

- It may be more difficult to **monitor** the standard of service provided than if the activity was retained in-house

- Outsourcing the activity may mean that **skills are lost** as staff who previously provided the service transfer to the outsource supplier or leave

- Staff may be **unhappy** because of the departure of colleagues and the feeling that their own jobs are insecure

- Transferring a service may result in the **transfer of sensitive information** to the supplier with a possibly increased threat to the confidentiality of that information

4.9.3 Selection of outsourced function

The potential advantages and disadvantages described above will be important. Other significant factors will include:

- Whether the activity is **core**; if it is, it may be too risky to transfer

- The extent to which outsourcing results in a **transfer of risk** to the supplier

- The consequences of making the wrong decision and maybe having to take the activity back **in-house**

- Ultimately, of course, the **costs versus benefits**

Section summary

Organisation structure determines how **work is carried out**, and is the result of the **environment, technology** and the **organisation's** and **industry's development**.

Centralisation gives more central control at the expense of rigidity and inflexibility, perhaps reducing the long term adaptive power of the organisation.

Decentralisation reduces the benefits from standardisation: complexity imposes its own costs.

Attacks on hierarchy have developed out of **technology** and a **changed perception** of the relative cost of hierarchy compared to market and process mechanisms. **Horizontal organisations** require that control is exercised over the process as a whole. Similarly, there is a growth in **business networks** and **outsourcing relationships**.

5　Organisational culture

Introduction

In this section we look at the role of organisational culture in determining how the organisation operates.

5.1 What is culture?

KEY TERM

CULTURE is the sum total of the beliefs, knowledge, attitudes of mind and customs to which people are exposed. It is 'the pattern of basic assumptions that a given group has invented, discovered, or developed, in learning to cope with its problems, and that have worked well enough to be considered valid and therefore to be taught to new members.'

5.2 Handy: power, role, task and person cultures

Handy recognises that while an organisation might reflect a single culture, it may also have elements of different culture.

Type of culture	Description
Power	Found mainly in **smaller organisations**, this is where power and influence stem from a **central source**. Organisation is capable of **adapting quickly** to meet change; however, success in adapting will depend on the luck or judgement of the key individuals who make the decisions. Political competition for power is rife, and emotional behaviour is encouraged by the **personality cult surrounding the leader**.
Role/bureaucracy	**Formal structure**, operating well-established **rules and procedures. Job descriptions** establish definite tasks for each person's job. **Procedures** are established for many work routines, for communication between individuals and departments, and for the settlement of disputes and appeals
Task	Reflected in a **matrix organisation**, in **project teams** and **task forces**. Principal concern is to **get the job done**; therefore the important individuals are the experts with the ability to accomplish a particular aspect of the task.
Person	Purpose is to **serve the interests** of individuals within it. Some individuals may use any organisation to suit their own purposes; to gain experience, further their careers or express themselves.

5.3 Culture and the environment

Denison maps the strategic orientation of organisation culture on a grid, to assess the **relationship of culture with the environment**. There are two dimensions.

(a)   **How orientated** is the firm to the environment rather than to its internal workings?

(b)   To what extent does the environment **offer stability or change**?

		Orientation	
		Internal	*External*
Environmental responses required	*Stability*	Consistency	Mission
	Change/flexibility	Involvement	Adaptability

Type of culture	Description
Consistency culture	This exists in a **stable environment**, and its structure is well integrated. Management are preoccupied with **efficiency**. Such cultures are characterised by **formal** ways of behaviour. Predictability and reliability are valued.
Mission culture	The environment is relatively stable, but the organisation is **orientated** towards its **key elements** (eg 'customers'). A **mission culture**, whereby members' work activities are given meaning and value, is appropriate (eg, hospitals).
Involvement culture	The **satisfaction of employees' needs** is necessary for them to provide optimum performance. An example might be an orchestra, whose performance depends on each individual. Involvement and participation create a greater sense of commitment and hence performance.
Adaptability culture	The company's **strategic focus** is on the **external environment**, which is in a state of change. Corporate values encourage inquisitiveness and interest in the external environment. Fashion companies are an example: ideas come from a variety of sources. Customer needs are fickle and change rapidly.

5.4 Cultural control

This means **applying control** (through firm central direction, and shared values and beliefs) but also **allowing maximum individual autonomy and even competition between individuals or groups within the organisation**. Culture, peer pressure, a focus on action, customer-orientation and so on are ways of exercising control over employees. Individuals should be given at least the **'illusion of (personal) control'** over their destinies, while still being given a **sense of belonging and a secure, perceived meaningful framework in which to act**.

CASE STUDY

Sexism in the City

Culture as a risk factor

Financial dealing firms in New York and in the City of London have been sued by their women employees. These stories have hit the media, as the sums involved have been large.

Sometimes the cause has related to issues of pay equality and sex discrimination legislation. At other times, the concern has been the culture of sexism and sexual harassment. The point is that this culture is not something that is 'inevitable' or even natural. This culture is not present in all organisations and is actively discouraged in some (eg the public sector).

Similarly, a culture of shoddy workmanship and carelessness, or lack of attention to quality, can damage a firm's reputation.

Question 5.5   Types of control

Learning outcome A1(c)

Sally Keene works for a large department store, as a manager.

- At the beginning of each year she is given a yearly plan, subdivided into twelve months. This is based on the previous year's performance and some allowance is made for anticipated economic conditions. Every three months she sends her views on the next quarter to senior management, who give her a new plan in the light of changing conditions.

- She monitors sales revenue per square foot, and sales per employee. Employees who do not meet the necessary sales targets are at first counselled and then if performance does not improve they are dismissed. Sally is not unreasonable. She sets what she believes are realistic targets.

- She believes there is a good team spirit in the sales force, however, and that employees, whose commission is partly based on the sales revenue earned by the store as a *whole*, discourage slackers in their ranks.

What kind of control, control system or control information can you identify in the three cases above?

Question 5.6   Risk culture

Learning outcomes A1(d)

Johnson and Scholes have identified various change management strategies that could be used to embed a new risk culture.

Method	Techniques	Benefits	Drawbacks
Education and communication	<ul><li>Small group briefings</li><li>Newsletters</li><li>Management development</li><li>Training</li></ul>		
Participation and involvement	<ul><li>Small groups</li><li>Delegates and representatives</li></ul>		
Facilitation and support	<ul><li>One on one counselling</li><li>Personal development</li><li>Provision of organisational resources</li></ul>		
Negotiation and agreement	<ul><li>Provision of rewards</li><li>Collective bargaining</li></ul>		
Manipulation and co-optation	<ul><li>Influence staff that are positively disposed</li><li>Buy-off informal leaders</li><li>Provide biased information</li></ul>		
Explicit and implicit coercion	<ul><li>Threaten staff with penalties</li><li>Create sense of fear</li><li>Victimise individuals to send message to the rest</li></ul>		

Required

Complete the table by identifying the benefits and drawbacks of each strategy.

Section summary

Culture is the **shared pattern** of **behaving and thinking**. As part of a control system, it identifies what is 'unacceptable' behaviour, and shows common responses. It is therefore a source of control. As it involves shared attitudes, it is also manifested in different attitudes to risk.

6　Human resources

Introduction

In this last section we examine how organisations exercise control over the managers and staff they employ, in order to ensure that their work contributes to achievement of the organisation's goals.

Exam alert

Human resource issues may be an issue for organisations of all types and sizes. They are perhaps more likely to be a significant issue in organisations, particularly smaller organisations, where controls are more informal. Look out also for human resource weaknesses in organisations that are dominated by a single individual.

6.1 Role of HRM

KEY TERM

HUMAN RESOURCES MANAGEMENT (HRM) is 'a **strategic and coherent approach** to the management of an organisation's most valued assets: the people working there who individually and collectively contribute to the achievement of its objectives for sustainable competitive advantage.' (Armstrong).

Control is so fundamentally involved with the management of people, that the systems and techniques of human resources management are part of the organisation's control system.

6.2 Motivation

Motivation is not strictly speaking part of control theory as such, although it is an important tool for managers in driving the business.

Motivation, however, is relevant for control systems for a number of reasons.

(a)　Managers **cannot control everything employees do** – it is a fantasy that employees are robots, although robots have replaced humans in some processes.

(b)　Motivation is **not simply a matter for employees** in the system. The managers who carry out the planning have to be motivated too.

6.3 Influences on HRM

The overall emphasis of HRM will be dependent on how tightly the organisation wishes to control its employees, and also whether it wishes to focus on controlling behaviour or output.

6.3.1 Compliance and commitment

The distinction between tight and loose HRM may be characterised as the difference between a system based on compliance and a system based on commitment.

COMPLIANCE means performing according to set rules and standards, according to what you are expected and asked to do. Competence-based systems of control reflect a low level of trust and challenge: performance is expected to be no less than the set standard – but also no more, since there is little room for creative or exceptional input or effort, which may militate against tight managerial control.

COMMITMENT has been defined as 'the relative strength of an individual's identification with and involvement in a particular organisation'.

Commitment depends on:

- A **strong belief** in and **acceptance** of an **organisation's goals and values**
- A **willingness to exert considerable effort** on behalf of the organisation
- A **strong desire to maintain membership** of the organisation

Commitment based systems of control reflect a high level of trust, based on assumptions that the work relationship can offer employees opportunities to meet their needs and aspirations as well as the organisation's needs.

6.3.2 Behaviour or output

Behaviour control deals with how the work is performed, the **precise sequencing of tasks and procedures**. Behaviour control is exercised when outcomes cannot be assessed easily, or where procedure is everything. This can link with a bureaucracy culture.

Output control is based on specifying **key outputs** that individuals must achieve. This can be applied at various levels in the organisation.

- A **specified level of sales or profitability** for a division: managers might be left to meet the actual targets

- **Specified targets for service delivery** (eg waiting lists for hospital appointments)

- **Operational matters** such as quantity of products made, for example the number of cars per hour made in a factory (very different in different manufacturers, showing major differences in efficiency)

- **Performance targets** for individuals, for example deadlines, productivity, accuracy

Which is better, output or behaviour control? Two possible criteria are:

- How easy it is to **measure output**? For example, a pieceworker's output is easier to measure, but it is harder to measure the output of, say, someone in the service industry who must smile all day.

- How easy it is to **programme** what employees do to routine instructions?

Exam skills

Watch out in questions for intersections between problems with human resources and problems with other areas of the control systems such as corporate governance and organisational structure.

6.4 Control techniques over human resources

6.4.1 Job evaluation

Job evaluation is a systematic method of arriving at a wage or salary structure, so that the rate of pay for a job is felt to be **fair** in comparison with other jobs in the organisation.

6.4.2 Recruitment and selection

Recruitment and selection have several roles in organisational control.

(a) In the cybernetic model, recruitment is one of the ways of obtaining **resource inputs**.

(b) Recruitment can be a way by which the system adapts to the environment or maintains itself in a **steady state**.

(c) Recruitment and selection can be **feedforward control actions**, in terms of obtaining more resources to that capacity can match demand.

(d) The ability to recruit can, in fact, be a **measure of performance**. For academic institutions, the ability to recruit good staff is a statement that people want to study there.

(e) Recruitment and selection can be a way of bringing a greater possibility for **agency** into the system, if a different type of person is recruited.

(f) Recruitment and selection may be necessary to ensure the **quality of the output**.

(g) Recruitment and selection are important in **maintaining cultural control** if people with the 'right' attitudes and outlook are recruited.

The process of control over recruitment and selection is outlined briefly below. Some recruitment arises out of strategic needs; in other cases, the recruitment might only be replacement.

 Plan for personnel requirements

The overall requirements of the organisation are determined by the business strategy. The organisation needs to determine the skills and competences in requires.

You could argue that this is a type of feedforward control.

 Identify how the skills and personnel requirements can be met

Recruitment is not the only solution to lack of staff. Alternatives might include:
– Outsourcing to low-cost countries
– Temporary staff
– Investment in technology

 Assess the actual/required content of jobs

A job analysis is a review of the current content of the job.

This can be converted into a job specification, which describes in detail the tasks of the job. This can be based on the job analysis or, alternatively, the job can be designed in a different way.

 Person specification

The 'type of person' and the skills required are then outlined. This can be a fairly simple exercise ('We need a qualified CIMA accountant with three years post qualification experience.') In practice this can be:
– Based on the skills
– Based on the person

Many organisations look for potential, rather than actual achievement if they want to develop staff.

 Advertisement

Internal vs external recruitment.

Choice of media is important here: the internet is becoming more important.

 Interview

Selection for interview is only of candidates who possess required skills – readvertise or widen the search if choice insufficient.

Approach to interviewing candidates is consistent between interviews.

Checking of employment histories, references and qualifications.

Selection   Candidates are chosen for the job.

Selection is when the choice is made – obviously, a control system needs to exist to ensure the right person is selected.

The important control objectives over recruitment and selection are as follows:

- The right candidates are recruited
- Good candidates are not passed over
- The organisation taps the right labour markets, or those most appropriate for its needs
- The selection process is timely

6.4.3 Contracts of employment

Employment contracts are a tool used to achieve control within an organisation. An actual **written contract stating clearly what is expected** of employer and employee (including a job description) provides a visible control tool.

6.4.4 Definition of roles

Lack of definition of roles can lead to confusion over responsibilities and a **lack of segregation of duties** (different key tasks being performed by different members of staff). It also can lead to problems in performance management, with a lack of **accountability for errors**, or **failing to give credit** when jobs have been done well.

The following controls should help ensure that jobs are allocated properly

(a)   Detailed role and task analysis

(b)   Allocation of more significant responsibilities to full-time or more experienced staff

(c)   Confining some roles or tasks to staff who have had appropriate training in, for example, health and safety risks

6.4.5 Training and learning

Training and learning are one aspect of performance management, and hence the control system, but they are, potentially, more than that. The roles of training and development are as follows:

(a)   **Improve the performance** of individuals in carrying out their roles, as control action

(b)   **Provide the skills and competences** that the **organisation needs** – effectively, an input to the production system

(c)   **Maintain existing performance** levels (eg by keeping people up to date with new developments, for example, training in how to use simple IT applications)

(d)   **Develop people** for **new roles in future**

(e)   As a **form of reward**, if the training is useful and valued

(f)   As a form of **cultural indoctrination** and team building, training programmes in big organisations can encourage a sense of team building, teach the company jargon

6.4.6 Performance management

Performance management is that aspect of HRM that appears to reflect control systems thinking.

There are four key performance management activities.

(a) **Preparation of performance agreements** (also known as performance contracts). These set out the individual's or team's **objectives**, how performance will be measured (ie the performance measures to be used), the knowledge, skills and behaviour needed to achieve the objectives and the organisation's core values

(b) **Preparation of performance and development plans**. These set out performance and personal development needs.

(c) **Management of performance throughout the year**. This involves the **continuous process** of providing feedback on performance, conducting informal progress reviews and dealing with performance problems as necessary.

(d) **Provision of performance reviews and appraisals**. These involve both taking a view of an individual's progress to date *and* reaching an agreement about what should be done in the future.

6.5 Managerial performance and responsibility accounting

It is difficult to devise performance measures that relate specifically to a manager to judge his or her performance as a manager. It is possible to calculate statistics to assess the manager as an employee like any other employee (days absent, professional qualifications obtained, personability and so on), but this is not the point. As soon as the issue of **ability as a manager** arises it is necessary to **consider him in relation to his area of responsibility**.

It may be unreasonable to assess managers' performance in relation to matters that are beyond their control. Therefore **management performance measures** should perhaps **only include those items that are directly controllable by the manager** in question. However, a wider view may be appropriate:

- Motivating them to **pay attention** to cost and revenue **factors that are relevant** even if they are not controllable, such as interest expenses.

- Encouraging them to **respond to economic and competitive conditions** such as a rival's lower prices or higher quality.

- 'Helping them' (in Ezzamel's words) to **minimise the one-time damage** caused by events such as accidents and earthquakes.

6.5.1 Possible management performance measures

In the light of the above the following can be suggested.

(a) **Subjective measures** may be used, for example ranking performance on a scale of 1 to 5.

(b) **The judgement of outsiders** can be regarded as a measure of managerial performance. This may be difficult to implement for many companies but the method is used.

(c) **Upward appraisal** is used by some businesses. This involves staff giving their opinions on the performance of their managers. To be effective this requires very healthy working relationships, however.

(d) **Accounting measures** can be used, but must be tailored according to what or whom is being judged.

(e) **Non-financial measures** may include market share measurements or a variety of other qualitative criteria.

We shall examine responsibility accounting and budgeting in Chapter 7.

Exam alert

Your exam may ask about the validity of using **accounting measures**. In essence, this means **profitability**, whether it is calculated in terms of sales volume, or as profits or as return on investment, or residual income, or something else. You may be asked to consider this from the point of view of the manager, or of the organisation, or of both.

6.5.2 Performance-related rewards

Rewarding managers for their performance is a method of control in the sense that it is assumed that attempts will be made to achieve the organisation's objectives in return for rewards. This, in turn, derives from **motivation theory,** which suggests that people have wants or desired outcomes and modify their behaviour accordingly.

Exam skills

As well as being part of the overall control systems, it's always worth considering whether human resource controls will be relevant when you're asked about the controls that counter specific risks. They will certainly be relevant if the likelihood of the risk crystallizing and the magnitude of losses is dependent upon the action (or lack of it) of employees.

Section summary

The organisational subsystem for **human resources management** is an attempt to control the behaviour of people.

HRM uses many techniques to motivate and control employees such as **contracts of employment, reward schemes and appraisals. Recruitment and selection** and **training** are also key processes.

Chapter Roundup

✓   **Control** matters at all levels of an organisation, from its **overall governance**, to the **details of its operating practices**. The purpose and types of control at each level will differ and even the best intentioned controls can be undermined by human action.

✓   Control is often discussed in the **context of systems theory**. An organisation is a type of system, and a control system is a type of system.

✓   Most systems have **inputs, processes and outputs** and are separated from the environment by a **boundary**.

✓   A **cybernetic control system** is one whose behaviour is coupled to feedback from its own performance. Most control systems in organisations fit this model.

✓   Feedback occurs at several levels: single loop, in which **performance is changed**, and double loop in which the **plan itself is adjusted**.

✓   **Contingency theory** states that what is most appropriate for an organisation depends upon its **structure, environmental conditions, culture, role of centre, established strategy and technology**.

✓   Organisation structure determines how **work is carried out**, and is the result of the **environment, technology** and the **organisation's and industry's development**.

✓   **Centralisation** gives more central control at the expense of rigidity and inflexibility, perhaps reducing the long term adaptive power of the organisation.

✓   **Decentralisation** reduces the benefits from standardisation: complexity imposes its own costs.

✓   Attacks on hierarchy have developed out of **technology** and a **changed perception** of the relative cost of hierarchy compared to market and process mechanisms. **Horizontal organisations** require that control is exercised over the process as a whole. Similarly, there is a growth in **business networks** and **outsourcing** relationships.

✓   **Culture** is the **shared pattern** of **behaving and thinking**. As part of a control system, it identifies what is 'unacceptable' behaviour, and shows common responses. It is therefore a source of control. As it involves shared attitudes, it is also manifested in different attitudes to risk.

✓   The organisational subsystem for **human resources management** is an attempt to control the behaviour of people.

✓   HRM uses many techniques to motivate and control employees, such as **contracts of employment, reward schemes** and **appraisals**. **Recruitment and selection** and **training** are also key processes.

Quick Quiz

1   Fill in the blank.

    A system is.......................................

2   What is special about a cybernetic system?

3   Organisations are closed systems.

    True   ☐

    False   ☐

4   Fill in the blanks.

    Positive feedback leads a system to....................................... its current course. Negative feedback encourages a system to....................................... its current course in the light of the plan.

5   What issues might be taken into account when designing a 'chain of command'?

6   According to Mintzberg, divisionalisation results from a split into self-managed units. What are the main problems for control at the centre?

7   Fill in the blanks.

    In a horizontal organisation, organisational structure is based around.................... .... as opposed to tasks or geography. Control is likely to be exercised, if at all, by a ....

8   Fill in the blank.

    .... is the use of external suppliers as a source of finished products, components or services.

9   Identify two key aspects of a reward system.

Answers to Quick Quiz

1   A system is **a set of interacting components that operate together to accomplish a purpose**.

2   A cybernetic system is special because the output of a system is used to control it.

3   False. Organisations are open as they depend on the environment. They still have boundaries, however (physical, legal, social).

4   Positive feedback leads a system to **continue** its current course. Negative feedback encourages a system to **change** its current course in the light of the plan.

5   • Communication effectiveness
    • Decision making effectiveness
    • Management development and motivation

6   The main control problems are that head office at the top may be less aware of what is going on, and the flow of information may be filtered on the way up. Divisions are not directly exposed to capital markets.

7   In a horizontal organisation, organisational structure is based around **cross-functional processes** as opposed to tasks or geography. Control is likely to be exercised, if at all, by a **process owner**.

8   **Outsourcing** is the use of external suppliers as a source of finished products, components or services.

9   Equity, or fairness; incentive

Answers to Questions

5.1 System objectives

Clearly, all sales have to be profitable sales in which the debt is fully recovered, as soon as possible. There are a number of different solutions.

(a)   You can introduce new controls over credit accounts, so that any credit sale must be approved.

(b)   You can, more radically, change the salespersons' objectives and reward: instead of focusing on sales, the objective can be set on cash recovery, for example so that a sales person's commission is not paid until the cash is received. Of course, this has the effect of making sales people into credit controllers, and the ultimate conflict, between maximising headline sales turnover and recovering cash is resolved, uncomfortably, in the sales person's head.

5.2 Which outputs?

UK governments set targets for hospitals, but the UK is unusual in having a health service provided largely by the state.

Is an output a 'finished consultant episode' – a course of treatment? Is this how productivity would be measured? Increasing the number of operations, and increasing the productivity of surgeons, may be something to be applauded – however, looking at the wider social system, preventative medicine may 'save' man lives, but these are difficult to measure.

5.3 Environmental impact

(a)   **Policies** adopted by the government or ruling political body.

(b)   The **strength of the domestic currency** of the organisation's country of operation.

(c)   **Social attitudes**: concern for the natural environment.

(d)   The **regulatory and legislative framework** within which the company operates.

(e)   The **number of competitors** in the marketplace and the strategies they adopt.

(f)   The **products of competitors**; their price and quality.

5.4 Divisionalisation

Problems of functional structure

A functional structure organises staff and work by professional speciality, all the accountants working for the finance director and all the sales people working for the sales director, for example. This is a logical approach and suitable for a small– to medium-sized company, since it enhances work standards by expert planning and supervision.

However, it tends to **preclude a multidisciplinary approach** to the management of complex projects; it can lead to poor interfunctional co-operation in simple matters; and it can even be a major cause of conflict within the organisation. A further problem is that it complicates the allocation of costs, hampering the identification of profitable and unprofitable products.

These problems are likely to be **particularly relevant** to the **situation Company Y** finds itself in.

Company Y's situation

The directors of Company Y may find that the **product/brand division** is more appropriate for its needs. The company would be organised into a number of divisions, each with responsibility for a coherent group of products and markets.

Advantages of divisionalisation

The overall aim would be to achieve **specialised expertise** and **economy of effort**. Each division would resemble a complete business, with its own management and functional specialists, and significant responsibility for its operations and financial success. Some element of central service may be retained: purchasing is often controlled centrally in order to achieve bulk buying economies, for example.

From the strategic point of view, such an organisation has several other advantages. It **enables costs** and **revenues to be analysed easily**. The overall business can, in fact, be treated as a portfolio of assets, with resources being directed to the ones with the best prospects.

The management of each division can keep a **very close eye on its own markets** and respond rapidly to problems and opportunities. The autonomy given to the people at the top of each division can be highly motivating.

An important HRM consideration is the **expanded opportunity** for practical experience at the strategic level within a division. Being in charge of a division is excellent training for a manager with high potential.

Problems with divisionalisation

There are several problems with the idea of divisionalisation that may be relevant here.

First, it may be **difficult**, if not impossible, to **identify clearly discrete product/market** areas suitable for exploitation by independent divisions. There are likely to be loose ends that have to be disposed of or swept up in a poor fit.

Also, as Company Y has grown partly by acquisition, there may be **major dislocation of premises** and staff if it seems necessary to form divisions from elements of more than one original company. There is clear potential for internal conflict here.

Divisions will **require able managers**, initially to set them up and later to run them. It may be that Company Y has plenty of such people, but, equally, it may not. Even the managers it thinks it can rely on may respond poorly to their isolation and responsibility.

The control of divisionalised companies raises two important problem areas. First, each division must have its own **functionally organised bureaucracy**, both to operate its own internal controls and to prepare the control reports the corporate headquarters will require. This can represent a significant duplication and reduplication of effort. Second, there will be a tendency towards short-termism in the divisions unless those control reports give due weight to the long-term view.

A final point is that the **divisions will be in competition for scarce resources**, including promotion for their heads. This can lead to undesirable political activity such as lobbying and a general lack of co-operation between divisions.

5.5 Types of control

- This shows the operation of **double loop feedback**. The plan has to be altered.

- This is a **standard**, in other words, a measure of expected performance. Counselling is control action to improve the individual's performance. Dismissal is control action too, if the employee is replaced by someone who performs better, thus raising the performance of the department as a whole.

- This is an example of **cultural or clan control**, perhaps.

5.6 Risk culture

Method	Techniques	Benefits	Drawbacks
Education and communication	• Small group briefings • Newsletters • Management development • Training	• Overcomes lack of information	• Time consuming • Direction of change may be unclear • Can't cope with change that opposes vested interests
Participation and involvement	• Small groups • Delegates and representatives	• Increases ownership of decisions and change • May improve quality of decisions	• Time consuming • Changes are limited to existing paradigm
Facilitation and support	• One on one counselling • Personal development • Provision of organisational resources	• Creates learning • Minimises feelings of being left out	• No guarantee of valuable outcome • Very slow
Negotiation and agreement	• Provision of rewards • Collective bargaining	• Retains goodwill • Deals with powerful interests	• May sacrifice change to need for agreement • Agreements may not be adhered to

Method	Techniques	Benefits	Drawbacks
Manipulation and co-optation	• Influence staff that are positively disposed • Buy-off informal leaders • Provide biased information	• Can remove powerful obstacles • Creates ambassadors for change • Swift	• Ethically questionable • Becomes like blackmail • May eliminate trust
Explicit and implicit coercion	• Threaten staff with penalties • Create sense of fear • Victimise individuals to send message to the rest	• Swift • Management control direction of change	• Ethically questionable • May eliminate trust • May rebound in future when management is weak

You may be able to draw on some of your own experiences when answering this question.

Now try this question from the Exam Question Bank	**Number**	**Level**	**Marks**	**Time**
	Q6	Examination	25	45 mins

CONTROL SYSTEMS II

In this chapter we move to the main elements of internal control systems that organisations operate. Controls must be linked to organisational objectives and the main risks faced by organisations. Internal control systems do not just consist of the controls themselves but also the control environment within which controls operate.

In this chapter we also examine how the risk of fraud is minimised through the use of appropriate controls and we consider briefly how it is detected and investigated.

It is important that the costs of controls are not excessive in relation to the benefits they bring. Later in this chapter we shall examine how organisations weigh up costs and benefits.

In the Appendix to this chapter we give details of the risks and controls in major accounting areas. You should study these in detail if you have not had experience in these areas. We also mention briefly how these are audited. You may want to delay going through the sections dealing with audit procedures until after you have read Chapters 15 and 16.

topic list	learning outcomes	syllabus references	ability required
1 Purposes of internal control systems	B2(a), B3(a)	B2(i), B3(ii)	evaluation
2 Internal control frameworks	B2(b)	B2(vi), (vii), (viii)	evaluation
3 Control environment	B2(c)	B2(vi), (vii), (viii)	evaluation
4 Control procedures	B2(c)	B2(vi), (vii)	evaluation
5 Internal controls and risk management	B2(c)	B2(vi), (vii)	evaluation
6 The risk of fraud	B2(c), C2(d)	B2(iv), C2(v)	evaluation
7 Communication with employees	B2(c)	B2(viii)	evaluation
8 Information requirements of directors	B2(c)	B2(vi), (vii)	evaluation
9 Control Self Assessment (CSA)	B2(c)	B2(vi), (vii)	evaluation
10 Costs and benefits of internal controls	B2(d)	B2(ix)	evaluation
Appendix: Systems risks and controls			

1 Purposes of internal control systems

Introduction

In the first section of this chapter we consider the purpose of internal control systems and spend time looking at the very important Turnbull report on internal control.

KEY TERM

An **INTERNAL CONTROL** is any action taken by management to enhance the likelihood that established objectives and goals will be achieved. Management plans, organises and directs the performance of sufficient actions to provide reasonable assurance that objectives and goals will be achieved. Thus, control is the result of proper planning, organising and directing by management.

(Institute of Internal Auditors)

1.1 Direction of control systems

In order for internal controls to function properly, they have to be well-directed. Managers and staff will be more able (and willing) to implement controls successfully if it can be demonstrated to them what the objectives of the control systems are, whilst objectives provide a yardstick for the board when they come to monitor and assess how controls have been operating.

1.2 Turnbull guidelines

The Turnbull guidance in the UK has been a very big influence on the way worldwide governance on control has developed. The UK's Turnbull report provides a helpful summary of the main purposes of an internal control system.

Turnbull comments that internal control consists of 'the **policies**, **processes**, **tasks**, **behaviours** and other aspects of a company that, taken together:

(a)   Facilitate its **effective** and **efficient operation** by enabling it to respond appropriately to significant **business**, **operational**, **financial**, **compliance** and other risks to achieving the company's objectives. This includes the **safeguarding of assets** from inappropriate use or from loss and fraud and ensuring that **liabilities** are **identified** and **managed**.

(b)   Help ensure the **quality** of **internal** and **external reporting**. This requires the **maintenance** of **proper records and processes** that generate a flow of **timely, relevant and reliable information** from within and without the organisation.

(c)   Help ensure **compliance with applicable laws and regulations,** and also with internal policies with respect to the conduct of business'

The Turnbull report goes on to say that a sound system of internal control reduces, but does not eliminate, the possibilities of **poorly-judged decisions**, **human error**, **deliberate circumvention of controls**, **management override of controls** and **unforeseeable circumstances.** Systems will provide **reasonable** assurance that the company will not be hindered in achieving its business objectives and in the orderly conduct of its business, but won't provide certain protection against all possible problems. The main provisions of Turnbull are summarised in the Appendix to Chapter 16.

Exam alert

Areas particularly highlighted in your syllabus are safeguarding of shareholders' investment and company assets, facilitation of operational effectiveness and efficiency, and contribution to the reliability of reporting. These areas need to be borne in mind in any question on internal control systems, although questions will doubtless cover other aims as well.

2 Internal control frameworks

Introduction

In this section we look at internal control frameworks, including the COSO and COCO frameworks.

2.1 Need for a control framework

Organisations need to consider the overall framework of controls since controls are unlikely to be very effective if they are developed sporadically around the organisation, and their effectiveness will be very difficult to measure by senior management.

2.2 Control environment and control procedures

Perhaps the simplest framework for internal control draws a distinction between

- **Control environment** – the overall context of control, in particular the attitude of directors and managers towards control

- **Control procedures** – the detailed controls in place

We shall examine both these elements in detail in the next two sections.

The Turnbull report also highlights the importance of

- **Information** and **communication processes**
- **Processes** for **monitoring** the **continuing effectiveness** of the system of internal control

2.3 The COSO framework

We saw earlier the control framework that the Committee of Sponsoring Organisations of the Treadway Commission has developed linking objectives with risk management. All elements of this framework affect what COSO call the objectives categories:

- Strategic development
- Operations
- Reporting
- Compliance

A significant advantage of the COSO framework is that it focuses on a wide concept of internal control and is not just limited to financial control.

COSO highlights monitoring the need for change as a particularly important element of internal control. The structure in place could include the following elements:

Control baseline	The belief that internal controls are operating effectively
Change identification process	Changes in: Process or risks The operation of controls that affect their ability to meet their objectives
Change management process	Establishing a new control baseline by changing existing controls or implementing new controls
Control reconfirmation	Periodic re-evaluation of controls

2.4 The COCO framework

A slightly different framework is the **criteria of control** or **COCO framework** developed by the Canadian Institute of Chartered Accountants (CICA).

2.4.1 Purpose

The COCO framework stresses the need for all aspects of activities to be clearly directed with a sense of purposes. This includes overall objectives, mission and strategy; management of risk and opportunities; policies; plans and performance measures. The corporate purpose should drive control activities and ensure controls achieve objectives.

2.4.2 Commitment

The framework stresses the importance of managers and staff making an active commitment to identify themselves with the organisation and its values, including ethical values, authority, responsibility and trust.

2.4.3 Capability

Managers and staff must be equipped with the resources and competence necessary to operate the control systems effectively. This includes not just knowledge and resources but also communication processes and co-ordination.

2.4.4 Action

If employees are sure of the purpose, are committed to do their best for the organisation and have the ability to deal with problems and opportunities then the actions they take are more likely to be successful.

2.4.5 Monitoring and learning

An essential part of commitment to the organisation is a commitment to its evolution. This includes

- Monitoring external environments
- Monitoring performance
- Reassessing the effectiveness of internal controls
- Reappraising information systems
- Challenging assumptions

Above all each activity should be seen as part of a **learning process** that lifts the organisation to a higher dimension.

2.5 Limitations of internal controls

However, any internal control system can only provide the directors with **reasonable assurance** that their objectives are reached, because of **inherent limitations** which include:

- The **costs** of control **not outweighing** their **benefits**. It would be inefficient, for example, for directors of large companies to spend time authorising petty cash expenditure

- The **potential** for **human error** or **fraud**

- **Collusion** between employees

- The possibility of controls being **by-passed** or **overridden by management**

- Controls being designed to cope with routine and **not non-routine transactions**

- Controls depending on the method of data processing – they should be **independent** of the method of data processing

Section summary

Internal control frameworks include the **control environment** within which **internal controls** operate. Other important elements are the **risk assessment and response processes,** the **sharing of information** and **monitoring** the environment and operation of the control system.

3 Control environment

Introduction

Here we will briefly look at the control environment and consider the elements of a strong control environment as set out in the UK's Turnbull report on internal control.

3.1 Nature of control environment

KEY TERM

The CONTROL ENVIRONMENT is the overall attitude, awareness and actions of directors and management regarding internal controls and their importance in the entity. The control environment encompasses the management style, and corporate culture and values shared by all employees. It provides the background against which the various other controls are operated.

The following factors are reflected in the control environment.

- The **philosophy** and **operating style** of the directors and management

- The organisation's **culture**, whether control is seen as an integral part of the organisational framework, or something that is imposed on the rest of the system

- The entity's **organisational structure** and methods of assigning authority and responsibility (including segregation of duties and supervisory controls)

- The directors' **methods of imposing control**, including the internal audit function, the functions of the board of directors and personnel policies and procedures

- The **integrity, ethical values** and **competence** of directors and staff

The Turnbull report highlighted a number of elements of a strong control environment.

- **Clear strategies** for dealing with the significant risks that have been identified

- The company's **culture, code of conduct, human resource policies** and **performance reward systems** supporting the business objectives and risk management and internal control systems

- Senior management demonstrating through its actions and policies commitment to **competence, integrity** and **fostering a climate of trust** within the company

- **Clear definition** of **authority, responsibility** and **accountability** so that decisions are made and actions are taken by the appropriate people

- **Communication** to employees what is expected of them and scope of their freedom to act

- People in the company having the **knowledge, skills** and **tools** to support the achievements of the organisation's objectives and to manage effectively its risks

However, a strong control environment does not, by itself, ensure the effectiveness of the overall internal control system, although it will have a major influence upon it.

The control environment will have a major impact on the establishment of business objectives, the structuring of business activities, and dealing with risks.

Section summary

The **control environment** is influenced by **management's attitude** towards control, the **organisational structure** and the **values** and **abilities** of employees.

4 Control procedures

Introduction

In this important section, we examine control procedures. Controls can be financial and non-financial, or classified as prevent, detect, correct and direct.

KEY TERM

CONTROL PROCEDURES are those policies and procedures in addition to the control environment which are established to achieve the entity's specific objectives.

(Auditing Practices Board)

4.1 Classification of control procedures

You may find internal controls classified in different ways, and these are considered below. Classification of controls can be important because different classifications of control are tested in different ways.

4.1.1 Financial and non-financial controls

Financial controls focus on the key transaction areas, with the emphasis being on the **safeguarding of assets** and the **maintenance of proper accounting records** and **reliable financial information**.

Non-financial controls tend to concentrate on wider performance issues. Some commentators, for example Johnson and Kaplan, have argued that non-financial controls are better predictors of profitability. They also focus on the accountant understanding operations well and using this understanding to design effective controls and targets.

Financial	Quantitative non-financial	Qualitative non-financial
• Budgets	• Performance indicators	• Organisational structures
• Standard costs	• Error measurement	• Social cultures
• Variance analysis	• Project tracking	• Rules and guidelines
• Ratio analysis	• Balanced scorecard	• Documentation requirements
• Transfer pricing policy	• Activity-based management measures	• Physical access controls
• Investment appraisal	• Total quality management measures	• Strategic plans
		• Rewards/incentives
		• Human resource policies
		• Corporate governance
		• Project management
		• Post-completion audits

Exam alert

This is an important method of classifying controls that will often come up in the P3 exam.

4.1.2 Prevent, detect, correct and direct controls

Prevent controls are controls that are designed to prevent errors from happening in the first place. Examples of **prevent controls** are as follows.

- Checking invoices from suppliers against goods received notes before paying the invoices

- Regular checking of delivery notes against invoices, to ensure that all deliveries have been invoiced

- Signing of goods received notes, credit notes, overtime records and so forth, to confirm that goods have actually been received, credit notes properly issued, overtime actually authorised and worked

- Denying access to sensitive areas of the business to unauthorised people

Detect controls are controls that are designed to detect errors once they have happened. Examples of detect controls in an accounting system are bank reconciliations and regular checks of physical inventory against book records of inventory.

Correct controls are controls that are designed to minimise or negate the effect of errors. An example of a **correct control** would be back-up of computer input at the end of each day, or the storing of additional copies of software at a remote location.

Direct controls direct activities or staff towards a desired outcome. Examples include operational manuals or training in dealing with customers.

4.1.3 Input, processing and output controls

These focus on the different elements of systems that we discussed in Chapter 5 Section 2.

Input controls focus on the resources that are used in the organisation's processes. They include controls over the materials supplied, the quality of the staff used and the information used.

Processing controls focus on what the organisation does as part of its operations. They can include controls over manufacturing, service delivery, information processing, distribution and storage. They include controls at different stages of operational processes, as well as controls that should be operated before a process is started or finished. Procedures and rules are examples of processing controls.

Output controls focus on the products or services that are produced as part of operations. As discussed in Chapter 5, a key element of controls here is comparing what is **actually produced** with what was **expected to be produced** and taking appropriate action if there are differences (as a result of feedback).

Exam alert

The input-processes-output classification was a good way to classify the relevant controls in Question 2 of the specimen paper.

Question 6.1	Prevent controls

Learning outcome B2(c)

How can prevent controls be used to measure performance and efficiency?

4.2 Types of procedure

The main procedures can be remembered as a mnemonic.

Segregation of duties
Physical
Authorisation and approval
Management
Supervision
Organisation
Arithmetical and accounting
Personnel
Information systems
Internal audit
Audit committee

Examples of these controls include the following.

(a)   **Segregation of duties**. For example, the chairman/Chief Executive roles should be split.

(b)   **Physical**. These are measures to secure the custody of assets, eg only authorised personnel are allowed to move funds on to the money market.

(c)   **Authorisation and approval**. All transactions should require authorisation or approval by an appropriate responsible person; limits for the authorisations should be specified, eg a remuneration committee is staffed by non-executive directors (NEDs) to decide directors' pay.

(d)   **Management** should provide control through analysis and review of accounts, eg variance analysis, provision of internal audit services.

(e)   **Supervision** of the recording and operations of day-to-day transactions. This ensures that all individuals are aware that their work will be checked, reducing the risk of falsification or errors, eg budgets, managers' review, exception or variance reports.

(f)   **Organisation**: identify reporting lines, levels of authority and responsibility. This ensures everyone is aware of their control (and other) responsibilities, especially in ensuring adherence to management policies, eg avoid staff reporting to more than one manager. Procedures manuals will be helpful here.

(g)   **Arithmetical and accounting**: to check the correct and accurate recording and processing of transactions, eg reconciliations, trial balances.

(h)   **Personnel**. Attention should be given to selection, training and qualifications of personnel, as well as personal qualities; the quality of any system is dependent upon the competence and integrity of those who carry out control operations, eg use only qualified staff as internal auditors.

(i)   **Information systems.** Using systems that fulfil the organisation's strategic needs and deliver appropriate information (discussed further in Chapter 13).

(j)   **Internal audit.** Reviewing the operation of risk management and internal control systems and other roles, depending on business needs (discussed in Chapters 15 and 16).

(k)   **Audit committee.** Overseeing the accounting systems and the work of internal and external audit (see Chapter 16).

4.3 Financial accounting system controls

In the Appendix to this chapter we examine how the controls listed above would apply to the main areas of accounting systems. We look at the risks, the aims of controls, the controls, and the audit procedures. You may wish to read the risk and control elements of the appendix when you've completed this chapter, and come back to the audit elements when you've read Chapters 15 and 16, or you may wish to put off reading the appendix until you've gone through Chapters 15 and 16.

We **do not** recommend that you learn list after list after list of controls; rather you see the lists as examples of what management and internal auditors will regard as important.

To help you, we've listed below the main risks, aims of controls and controls that are common across accounting systems below:

4.3.1 Risks

Risks that affect many areas of the accounting systems include the following:

- **Failure to receive income that is due** to the organisation
- **Misappropriation of assets**
- **Deterioration in the value of assets** due to poor maintenance
- Transactions being completed **without adequate authorisation**
- **Inadequate value** being received in exchange for payments made
- **Deterioration in relationships** with customers and suppliers
- **Failure to record assets, liabilities and transactions correctly**

4.3.2 Aims of controls

Clearly controls will be designed with the aims of combating the main risks. Significant aims are likely to include:

- Income is **received fully and promptly**
- Assets are **safeguarded against loss in value, pilferage, damage or deterioration**
- Transactions are **properly authorised**
- Transactions are **completed successfully**
- **Sufficient value is received** in return for payments made
- **No errors** are made in dealings with customers and suppliers
- **Dealings with customers and suppliers** are on the **terms laid down**
- **Assets, liabilities and transactions** are **recorded correctly**

4.3.3 Controls

Adequate controls and risk management processes should exist, and managers should be able to assure themselves that their risk assessments and controls are adequate, including of course the control of having an internal audit.

Important controls in many areas will include:

- **Segregation of duties** to reduce fraud and increase checks
- **Full documentation** of assets, liabilities and transactions
- **Matching of source documents** and accounting records
- **Reconciliation of information** from different source documents and other sources
- **Completeness checks** over **documents and accounting entries**
- **Physical security controls** over assets
- **Authorisation of payments and customer and supplier terms** by senior staff
- **Regular reviews of assets held**
- **Reperformance** of accounting calculations
- **Confirmation** of information by suppliers, customers and bank

4.4 Operational controls

In Section 7 of the appendix we list risks, controls and audit work that would be done on other operational areas. As you work through this section you will see that the operational risks and controls are very similar in most areas and the similarities are summarised below.

4.4.1 Risks

Risks that affect many areas of operations include the following:

- Assets, resources and facilities are **not available** when required
- Assets, resources and staff are **not** utilized efficiently
- **Sales** are **lost** because of operational difficulties or weaknesses
- **Assets** are **damaged** or **misappropriated**
- **Business** is **interrupted**
- The organisation fails to **comply with internal guidelines** or **external legislation**

4.4.2 Aims of controls

Aims are likely to include:

- **Internal procedures** are **sufficient** to meet risks and are complied with
- **Operational functions** are **properly resourced**
- **Customer requirements** are **identified** and taken into account
- **Assets and facilities** are **available** when required
- **Assets** and staff are **managed effectively**
- **Back-up resources** and **facilities** are **available** in the event of disruption

4.4.3 Controls

Significant controls in many areas will include:

- **Regular review of resources** and **assets** to ensure they are available, adequate and have not been misappropriated

- **Quality checks** on resources and products

- **Monitoring** of staff **performance** and **time spent**

- Procedures such as competitive tendering and review of alternative supply sources to ensure **resources** are **obtained** at a **reasonable price**

- **Planning and forecasting procedures**

- **Comparison of actual results** with **plans**

- **Regular reports** to senior management

- **Security procedures** for safeguarding assets

- **Contingency plans** and resources being available if the organisation suffers serious disruption

Exam alert

Don't just think of controls as being designed to combat error and dishonesty. Efficient utilisation of resources may be as important. In Question 4 on the specimen paper, poor usage of sales representatives' time was as important an issue as problems with their expense claims.

Section summary

Controls can be classified in various ways including **financial** and **non-financial; prevent, detect, correct** and **direct**.

5   Internal controls and risk management

Introduction

In this section we examine how risk assessment and internal controls are linked.

5.1 Links between controls and risks

We have looked in earlier chapters about how organisations deal with the risks they face. In this section we examine the links between risk assessment and internal controls.

COSO points out that an organisation needs to establish **clear and coherent objectives** in order to be able to tackle risks effectively. The risks that are important are those that are **linked with achievement of the organisation's objectives**. In addition there should be control mechanisms that identify and adjust for the risks that arise out of changes in economic, industry, regulatory and operating conditions.

Question 6.2   Responses to risk

Learning outcome B2(c)

A new employee in the marketing department has asked you about the business objective of meeting or exceeding sales targets.

Required

(a)   What are the main risks associated with the business objective to meet or exceed sales targets?

(b)   How can management reduce the likelihood of occurrence and impact of the risk?

(c)   What controls should be associated with reducing the likelihood of occurrence and impact of the risk?

COSO also suggests that the links between risks and controls may be complex. Some controls, for example calculation of staff turnover, may indicate how successful management has been in responding to several risks, for example competitor recruiting and lack of effectiveness of staff training and development programmes. On the other hand some risks may require a significant number of internal controls to deal with them.

The UK's Turnbull report stresses the link between the **costs of operating particular controls** with the **benefits obtained in managing the related risks.**

Section summary

An organisation's internal controls should be designed to counter the **risks** that are relevant to the objectives it pursues.

6 The risk of fraud

Introduction

In this section we pay special attention to the risk of fraud in an organisation, looking at examples of common types of fraud, the risks of fraud, and how it may be prevented and detected.

6.1 Types of fraud

KEY TERM

In a famous court case, FRAUD was defined as:

'a false representation of fact made with the knowledge of its falsity, or without belief in its truth, or recklessly careless, whether it be true or false.'

While the vast majority of employees are honest, some employees may decide to **act dishonestly**. The incidence of financial fraud, particularly in a computer environment, is increasing. This presents a challenge to management and to auditors. The following are all examples of fraud:

Types of fraud	
Ghost employees	Imaginary employees set up and wages paid and distributed amongst the fraudsters.
Miscasting of the payroll	Skimming a very small amount off each genuine wage or salary payment.
Stealing unclaimed wages	Confined to wages paid in cash.
Collusion with external parties	Involving suppliers, customers or their staff.
Altering cheques and inflating expense claims	Including claiming expenses more than once, paying personal expenses by company credit card and claiming, inflated car mileage claims and claiming private entertaining.
Stealing assets	Using the organisation's assets for personal gain, stealing inventory or fully depreciated assets.

Types of fraud	
Identity fraud	Taking details such as means of identification of someone else and using them to obtain financial services and goods.
Issuing false credit notes	Issuing credit notes that are not sent to the customer.
Sales fraud	Opportunity when there are poor controls over sales recording and minimal segregation of duties.

6.2 Fraud risks

The following table sets out examples of conditions or events that could increase the risk of fraud, error or both.

Fraud and error	
Previous experience or incidents which call into question the integrity or competence of management	Management dominated by one person (or a small group) and no effective oversight board or committee
	Complex corporate structure where complexity does not seem to be warranted
	High turnover rate of key accounting and financial personnel
	Personnel (key or otherwise) not taking holidays
	Personnel lifestyles that appear to be beyond their known income
	Significant and prolonged under-staffing of the accounting department
	Poor relations between executive management and internal auditors
	Lack of attention given to, or review of, key internal accounting data such as cost estimates
	Frequent changes of legal advisors or auditors
	History of legal and regulatory violations
Particular financial reporting pressures within an entity	Industry volatility
	Inadequate working capital due to declining profits or too rapid expansion
	Deteriorating quality of earnings, for example increased risk taking with respect to credit sales, changes in business practice or selection of accounting policy alternatives that improve income
	The entity needs a rising profit trend to support the market price of its shares due to a contemplated public offering, a takeover or other reason
	Significant investment in an industry or product line noted for rapid change
	Pressure on accounting personnel to complete financial statements in an unreasonably short period of time
	Dominant owner-management
	Performance-based remuneration

Fraud and error	
Weaknesses in the design and operation of the accounting and internal controls system	A weak control environment within the entity
	Systems that, in their design, are inadequate to give reasonable assurance of preventing or detecting error or fraud
	Inadequate segregation of responsibilities in relation to functions involving the handling, recording or controlling of the entity's assets
	Poor security of assets
	Lack of access controls over IT systems
	Indications that internal financial information is unreliable
	Evidence that internal controls have been overridden by management
	Ineffective monitoring of the operation of system which allows control overrides, breakdown or weakness to continue without proper corrective action
	Continuing failure to correct major weakness in internal control where such corrections are practicable and cost effective
Unusual transactions or trends	Unusual transactions, especially near the year end, that have a significant effect on earnings
	Complex transactions or accounting treatments
	Unusual transactions with related parties
	Payments for services (for example to lawyers, consultants or agents) that appear excessive in relation to the services provided
	Large cash transactions
	Transactions dealt with outside the normal systems
	Investments in products that appear too good to be true, for example low risk, high return products
	Large changes in significant revenues or expenses
Problems in obtaining sufficient appropriate audit evidence	Inadequate records, for example incomplete files, excessive adjustments to accounting records, transactions not recorded in accordance with normal procedures and out-of-balance control accounts
	Inadequate documentation of transactions, such as lack of proper authorisation, supporting documents not available and alteration to documents (any of these documentation problems assume greater significance when they relate to large or unusual transactions)
	An excessive number of differences between accounting records and third party confirmations, conflicting audit evidence and unexplainable changes in operating ratios
	Evasive, delayed or unreasonable responses by management to audit enquiries
	Inappropriate attitude of management to the conduct of the audit, eg time pressure, scope limitation and other constraints
Some factors unique to an information systems environment which relate to the conditions and events described above	Inability to extract information from computer files due to lack of, or non-current, documentation of record contents or programs
	Large numbers of program changes that are not documented, approved and tested
	Inadequate overall balancing of computer transactions and data bases to the financial accounts

6.3 Prevention of fraud

6.3.1 Prioritising prevention

Prevention of fraud must be an **integral** part of **corporate strategy**. Managing the risk of fraud is a key part of managing business risks in general, and if the company's risk management procedures are poor, management of fraud risk is also likely to be unsuccessful.

Certain recent developments, notably downsizing, have however meant that certain controls that are designed to prevent fraud, for example segregation of duties, may not be possible. Hence it is equally important the control system is designed so as to **detect and investigate** fraud.

KEY POINT

Bear in mind three conditions necessary for fraud to occur:

- **Dishonesty** – if all employees are honest, staff fraud will not be an issue
- **Opportunity** – caused by lack of control/controls failing to operate properly
- **Motive** – greed, feelings of being underpaid/not appreciated

6.3.2 Reasons for fraud

Management must have an understanding of how and why frauds might arise. Examples include:

(a)   The risk of fraud may be increased by factors that are specific to the **industry**. Lower profit margins due to increased competition may be a temptation to manipulate results.

(b)   Factors specific to the **business** may also increase the risk of fraud, such as extensive authority given to dominant managers.

(c)   **Changes in circumstances** may also increase the risk of fraud. Often a control system may become inadequate as a result of changes in the business, particularly changes in technology or internal organisation.

(d)   Certain areas, for example cash sales are **normally high risk**.

6.3.3 Reasons for poor controls

Management also need to understand factors that may prevent controls from operating properly.

(a)   Controls will not function well if there is a **lack of emphasis** on compliance or a **lack of understanding** of why the controls are required, how they should operate and who should be operating them.

(b)   **Staff problems** such as understaffing, poor quality or poorly motivated staff can impede the operation of controls.

(c)   **Changes in senior personnel** can lead to a lack of supervision during the transition period.

(d)   **Emphasis on the autonomy of operational management** may lead to controls being bypassed.

6.3.4 General prevention policies

Management can implement certain general controls that are designed to prevent fraud.

(a)   **Emphasising ethics** can decrease the chances of fraud. Several businesses have formal codes of ethics which employees are required to sign covering areas such as gifts from customers. Management can also ensure that they set 'a good example'.

(b)   **Personnel controls** are a very important means of preventing fraud. Thorough **interviewing** and **recruitment procedures** including obtaining references can be an effective screening for dishonest employees. **Appraisal** and grievance systems can prevent staff demotivation. Strong **disciplinary procedures** may deter fraud.

(c)   **Training and raising awareness** can be important. There are many examples of frauds taking place where people who were unwittingly close were shocked that they had no idea what was happening. **Fraud awareness education** should therefore be an integral part of the training programme, particularly for managers and staff in **high risk areas** such as procurement, and staff with key roles in fraud prevention and detection, for example human resources.

6.3.5 Prevention of fraud in specific business areas

Controls will also be needed in specific areas of the business where a high risk of fraud has been identified.

(a)   **Segregation of duties** is a key control in fraud prevention. Ultimately operational pressures may mean that segregation is incomplete. Management should nevertheless identify certain functions that must be kept separate, for example separating the cheque signing function from the authorisation of payments.

(b)   **Appropriate documentation** should be required for all transactions.

(c)   **Limitation controls** such as only allowing staff to choose suppliers from an approved list, or limiting access to the computer network by means of passwords can reduce the opportunities for fraud.

(d)   Certain actions should be **prohibited** such as leaving a computer terminal without logging off.

(e)   **Internal audit** work should **concentrate** on these areas.

6.4 Detection of fraud

6.4.1 Manager and staff responsibilities

If fraud is to be detected, it is important that everyone involved in detection should be aware of their responsibilities.

(a)   **Operational managers** should be **alert for signs** of petty fraud, as well as checking the work staff have done and also being aware of what staff are doing.

(b)   **Finance staff** should be alert for **unusual items** or **trends** in accounting data, also incomplete financial information.

(c)   **Personnel staff** should be alert for **signs of discontent** or **low morale**, and also should (if possible) be aware of close personal relationships between staff who work together.

(d)   **Internal audit staff** have responsibility for ensuring **systems** and controls are thoroughly **reviewed**. One off exercises such as surprise visits may be undertaken alongside annual audit work.

(e)   **External audit staff** are required to **assess** the **risk** that fraud may have a **material impact** on a company's accounts when planning their audit work. They are required to **report** all instances of fraud found to management, unless they suspect management of being involved in the fraud. The external auditors should also report to management any material weaknesses in the accounting and internal control systems.

(f)   **Non-executive directors** should **act** on **signs** of **dishonesty** by senior executive management. The **audit committee** should **review the organisation's performance** in fraud prevention and report any suspicious matters to the board.

6.4.2 Availability of information

It is of course important that information should be available to enable management to identify signs of actual fraud, or of an environment where fraud may occur.

(a) **Cost and management accounting systems** should **provide** promptly **information** with sufficient detail to enable management to identify parts of the business whose performance is out of line with expectations. Actual results should be compared with budgeted results and explanations sought for significant variances.

(b) **Personnel procedures** such as **staff meetings**, **appraisals** and **exit interviews** may indicate low morale or staff who are under undue pressure.

(c) **Lines of reporting** should be **clear**. Staff should know to whom they should report any suspicions of fraud.

6.4.3 Whistleblowing

The likelihood of fraud detection may have been increased by recent legislation in a number of countries that provides **employment protection rights** to 'whistleblowers', employees who reveal fraud or malpractice in a workplace. The legislation covers disclosure of certain 'relevant failures', including committal of a criminal offence, failure to comply with legislation, endangering health and safety or damaging the environment.

Some employers are introducing a formal concerns procedure, which sets out how potential whistleblowers should communicate their concerns.

6.4.4 Investigation of fraud

If the worst does happen there should be a **fraud response plan**, a strategy for **investigating** and **dealing with the consequences** of frauds that have occurred.

Certain actions might have to be taken as soon as the fraud comes to light. These may include **ensuring the security of the records** that will be used to investigate what has happened, and also the **securing of assets** that may be vulnerable to theft. Procedures may have to include suspending staff, changing passwords and so on.

Investigation procedures should be designed with the following aims in mind:

(a) **Establishing** the **extent** of the loss, ascertain on whom it fell and assess how it may be recovered

(b) **Establishing how** the fraud **occurred**, reviewing evidence of the activities of the fraudster

(c) Considering **who else** may have been **implicated** in the fraud

(d) Assessing whether the **fraud** was not detected because **existing controls** were not operating properly, or whether existing controls would have been unlikely to prevent or identify the fraud

Section summary

Common frauds include **payroll frauds**, **conspiracy with other parties** and **stealing assets**.

Signs of high fraud risk include indications of **lack of integrity**, **excessive pressures**, **poor control systems** and **unusual transactions**.

In order to prevent fraud, managers must be aware of the **risks** and **signs** of fraud.

Prevention policies include emphasis on **ethics** and **personnel and training procedures**. Controls within particular business areas such as **segregation of duties** are also significant.

Managers and staff should be aware of their **responsibilities** in detecting fraud, which is also helped by having **information readily available** and allowing **whistleblowing**.

7 Communication with employees

Introduction

This section of the chapter looks at how management communicates with employees so that controls can be implemented effectively.

7.1 Importance of human element

It is very easy to design a control system that appears good on paper but is unworkable, because it is **not geared** to the **user's practicality and usefulness.** A detailed technical manual covering information technology controls may be of little use if staff lack sufficient knowledge of information technology. Controls may not work very well if staff lack motivation or the basic skills for the job in the first place. On the other hand, if good staff are taken on, they may well develop the necessary controls as part of their day-to-day work.

7.2 Important human resource issues

The UK's Turnbull report stresses that all employees have some responsibility for internal control and need to have the necessary skills, knowledge and understanding in particular of the risks the organisation faces.

A briefing supporting the Turnbull report lists a number of human issues that management need to consider:

- Whether the **remuneration policies and working practices** encourage risk management and discourage taking unnecessary risks

- **Installing** an **attitude** of 'getting things right first time'

- Ensuring that responsibility for **fulfilling business objectives** and **managing related risk** is clear

- Creating an environment where problems are **reported** rather than unresolved

- **Co-ordinating** the activities of different parts of the organisation

- Ensuring that people in the company and in outsource providers have **sufficient knowledge, skills** and **resources** to support the achievement of the organisation's objectives and to manage risks

- Introducing a **common risk management vocabulary** across the organisation

- Adoption of **work practices** and **training** that result in **improved performance**

7.3 Improving staff awareness and attitudes

Turnbull stresses that it is important that all staff understand that risk management is an **integral, embedded part** of the **organisation's operations**. Elaborate risk management innovations may not be the best way to improve performance; it may be better to build warning mechanisms into existing information systems rather than develop separate risk reporting systems.

Turnbull suggests that it is vital to communicate policies in the following areas in particular:

- Customer relations
- Service levels for both internal and outsourced activities
- Health, safety and environmental protection
- Security of assets and business continuity
- Expenditure
- Accounting, financial and other reporting

The briefing suggests that the following steps can be taken:

- **Initial guidance** from the Chief Executive
- **Dissemination of the risk management policy** and codes of conduct, also key business objectives and internal control
- **Workshops** on risk management and internal control
- A **greater proportion of the training budget** being spent on internal control
- Involvement of staff in **identifying and responding** to change and in operating warning mechanisms
- **Clear channels of communication** for reporting breaches and other improprieties

7.4 Training staff

Training days can be particularly useful in emphasising to staff the importance of different types of control (preventative, detective etc) and also the need for some controls to assist staff development, but others to enforce sanctions particularly in cases of dishonesty or negligence.

Section summary

Procedures improving staff abilities and attitudes should be built into the control framework. **Communication** of control and risk management issues and strong **human resource procedures** reinforce the control systems.

8   Information requirements of directors

Introduction

This section considers the information needs of directors in order that control systems are efficient and effective.

8.1 Needs of directors

We have emphasised above that board and senior manager involvement is a critical element of internal control systems and the control environment. There are various ways in which management can obtain the information they need to play the necessary active part in control systems.

In order to be able to carry out an effective review, the Turnbull Report suggests boards should regularly receive and review reports and information on internal control, concentrating on:

(a) What the **risks** are and strategies for **identifying**, **evaluating** and **managing** them

(b) The **effectiveness** of the management and internal control systems in the management of risk, in particular how risks are **monitored** and **how** any **weaknesses** have been dealt with

(c) Whether **actions** are being taken to **reduce** the risks found

(d) Whether the results indicate that **internal control** should be **monitored more extensively**

8.2 Information sources

The information directors need to be able to monitor controls effectively comes from a wide variety of sources.

8.2.1 The directors' own efforts

Directors will receive reports from the audit committee and also the director nominated as compliance officer. Management by **walking about**, regular visits by the directors to operations, may yield valuable insights and should help the directors understand the context in which controls are currently operating.

8.2.2 Reports from subordinates

There should be systems in place for all staff with supervisory responsibilities to report on a regular basis to senior managers, and senior managers in turn to report regularly to directors.

8.2.3 Lines of communication

Very importantly directors must ensure that staff have lines of communication that can be used to **address concerns**. There should be normal communication channels through which most concerns are addressed, but there should also be failsafe mechanisms for reporting or **whistleblowing**, particularly serious problems and perhaps active seeking of feedback through **staff attitude surveys.**

8.2.4 Reports from control functions

Organisational functions that have a key role to play in internal control systems must report on a regular basis to the board and senior management. One example that we shall examine further later on is the need for a close relationship between **internal audit** and the **audit committee**. The **human resources function** should also report regularly to the board about personnel practices in operational units. Poor human resource management can often be an indicator of future problems with controls, since it may create dissatisfied staff or staff who believe that laxness will be tolerated.

8.2.5 Reports on activities

The board should receive regular reports on **certain activities**. A good example is major developments in computerised systems, which we shall look at in Part D of this text. As well as board approval before the start of key stages of the development process, the board need to be informed of progress and any problems during the course of the project, so that any difficulties with potentially serious consequences can be rapidly addressed.

8.2.6 Reports on resolution of weaknesses

Similarly the board should obtain evidence to confirm that control weaknesses that have previously **been identified** have been **resolved**. When it has been agreed that action should be taken to deal with problems, this should include timescale for action and also reporting that the actions have been implemented.

8.2.7 Results of checks

The board should receive confirmation as a matter of course that necessary **checks** on the operation of the controls have been **carried out** satisfactorily and that the results have been clearly reported. This includes gaining assurance that the **right sort** of check has been **performed**. For example **random checks** may be required on high risk areas such as unauthorised access to computer systems. Sufficient **independent** evidence from external or internal audit should be obtained to reinforce the evidence supplied by operational units.

8.2.8 Exception reporting

Exception reports highlighting variances in **budgeting systems**, **performance measures**, **quality targets** and **planning systems** are an important part of the information that management receives.

8.2.9 Feedback from customers

Customer responses, particularly complaints, are important evidence for the board to consider, particularly as regards how controls ensure the **quality of output**.

8.3 Making best use of information

8.3.1 Comparison of different sources of information

The pictures gleaned from different sources must be compared and discrepancies followed up and addressed. Not only do the board need to have a true picture of what is happening but discrepancies might highlight problems with existing sources of information that need to be addressed. In particular if random or special checks identify problems that should have been picked up and reported through regular channels, then the **adequacy** of these channels needs to be considered carefully.

8.3.2 Feedback to others

Directors need to ensure that as well as their obtaining the information they need to review internal control systems, that relevant information on controls is also passed to all those within the organisation who need it directly. For example sales staff who obtain customer feedback on product shortcomings need to be aware of the channels for communicating with staff responsible for product quality and also staff responsible for product design.

8.3.3 Review procedures

As well as investigating and resolving problems with the information they receive, the board ought to undertake a **regular review** of the **information sources** they need and indeed the whole system of supervision and review to assess its adequacy and also to assess whether any layers of supervision or review can be reduced.

8.3.4 Control and learning

Simons argued that managers have limited time to consider available information that relates to strategic uncertainties. Managers therefore use certain controls to **monitor and intervene in organisational activities.** Staff respond to this by the monitoring activities they undertake themselves, and by testing new ideas in certain ways. This testing influences organisational learning, and as a result of organisational learning, new strategies are formulated.

Section summary

Directors need **information** from a **large variety of sources** to be able to supervise and review the operation of the internal control systems. Information sources should include normal reporting procedures, but staff should also have channels available to report problems or doubtful practices of others.

9   Control Self Assessment (CSA)

Introduction

Here we consider how directors and senior management can assess the strength of the internal control system using control self assessment.

KEY TERM

CONTROL SELF ASSESSMENT (CSA) or CONTROL AND RISK SELF ASSESSMENT (CRSA) is a method by which senior management can obtain a view on the adequacy of internal control throughout the organisation in a consistent format.

9.1 Elements of CSA

CSA has been adopted by managers as a means of responding to reporting requirements on internal controls. However, it has many other benefits, the main one being that it helps management to control the business. CSA is described in a CIMA document *Control Self-Assessment (CSA) – a brief introduction.*

CSA consists of four elements or procedures.

(a)   **Risk analysis** is carried out, with agreement to, and documentation of the consequent control objectives.

(b)   The existing controls are **documented**.

(c)   The **adequacy** of **existing controls** is **evaluated**. This may include 'benchmarking' against known best practice. The evaluation will consider how well the controls are operating and identify an improvement plan (if required).

(d)   A **reporting** and **review structure** is **set up** which covers the whole organisation.

Every organisation's CSA process will be different, according to its needs. There is no set formula: some organisations will impose controls whereas others will integrate CSA as part of a continuous improvement process.

9.2 Limitations of CSA

CSA does *not*:

(a)   **Provide absolute assurance** that control requirements are being complied with (it only gives reasonable assurance)

(b)   **Necessarily identify**:

   (i)   **Issues** which would **not** be **identified** by a **traditional** audit (although it may)
   (ii)   **One-off errors** and omissions associated with individual transactions
   (iii)   **Loss of assets**
   (iv)   **Fraud**

There are costs involved in implementing CSA, mainly in staff time for **setting up**. As long as the procedures are accepted organisation-wide, however, the ongoing costs should be fairly moderate. Areas identified for improvement should be evaluated on a cost-benefit basis and cost savings might be made if duplicated or redundant controls are identified. Cost-benefit analysis of internal control systems is considered further in the next section.

CASE STUDY

The UK Turnbull committee provides a slightly different framework for assessing the effectiveness of internal controls.

Risk assessment	
	• Does the organisation have clear objectives and have they been communicated to provide direction to employees (examples include performance targets)?
	• Are significant risks identified and assessed on an ongoing basis?
	• Do managers and employees have a clear understanding of what risks are acceptable?

Control environment and control activities	• Does the board have a risk management policy and strategies for dealing with significant risks? • Do the company's culture, code of conduct, human resource policies and performance reward systems support the business objectives and risk management and control systems? • Does senior management demonstrate commitment to competence, integrity and fostering a climate of trust? • Are authority, responsibility and accountability defined clearly? • Are decisions and actions of different parts of the company appropriately coordinated? • Does the company communicate to its employees what is expected of them and the scope of their freedom to act? • Do company employees have the knowledge, skills and tools necessary to support the company's objectives and manage risks effectively? • How are processes and controls adjusted to reflect new or changing risks or operational deficiencies?
Information and communication	• Do managers receive timely, relevant and reliable reports on progress against business objectives and risks to provide the information needed for decision-making and review processes? • Are information needs and systems reassessed as objectives and related risks change or reporting deficiencies are identified? • Do reporting procedures communicate a balanced and understandable account of the company's position and prospects? • Are there communication channels for individuals to report suspected breaches of law or regulations or other improprieties?
Monitoring	• Are there ongoing embedded processes for monitoring the effective application of the policies, processes and activities relating to internal control and risk management? • Do these processes monitor the company's ability to re-evaluate risks and adjust controls effectively in response to changes in objectives, business and environment? • Are there effective follow-up procedures to ensure action is taken in response to changes in risk and control assessments? • Are there specific arrangements for management monitoring and reporting to the board matters of particular importance (including fraud or illegal acts)?

Section summary

Control self-assessment is the assessment by senior management of the strength of the internal control system involving risk analysis and review of the adequacy of controls.

10 Costs and benefits of internal controls

Introduction

In this final section we consider the benefits of internal controls and the costs required to implement and cover them.

10.1 Benefits of internal controls

The benefits of internal control, even well-directed ones, are not limitless. Controls can provide reasonable, not absolute, assurance that the organisation is progressing towards its objectives, safeguarding its assets and complying with laws and regulations. Internal controls cannot guarantee success as there are plenty of **environmental factors** (economic indicators, competitor actions) beyond the organisation's control.

In addition there are various inherent limitations in control systems including faulty decision-making and breakdowns occurring because of human error. The control system may also be vulnerable to **employee collusion** and **management override** of controls **undermining** the **systems** of **controls.**

However the benefits of internal control are not always measurable in financial terms; they may include improvements in **efficiency and effectiveness**. There may also be indirect benefits; improved control systems resulting in external audit being able to place more reliance on the organisation's systems, hence needing to do less work and (hopefully) charging a lower audit fee.

10.2 Costs of internal controls

As well as realising the limitations of the benefits of controls, it is also important to realise their costs. Some costs are obvious, for example the salary of a night security officer to keep watch over the premises. There will be costs involved in **establishing internal controls,** for example setting up **sources of information**. There are also **opportunity costs** through for example increased manager time being spent on review rather than dealing with customers for example.

More general costs include reduced **flexibility**, **responsiveness** and **creativity** within the organisation.

One common complaint is the controls stifle initiative, although this is not always well-founded, particularly if the initiative involves too casual an approach to risk management.

10.3 Benefits vs Costs

The principle that the costs of controls need to be compared with benefits is reasonable. We mentioned in a previous chapter that organisations will sometimes decide to accept risks and not insure them, and similarly the internal controls may not be felt to be worth the reduction in risk that they achieve.

However the comparison of benefits and costs may be difficult in practice:

- It can be difficult to **estimate the potential monetary loss or gain** that could occur as a result of exposure to risk if no measures are taken to combat the risk.

- It can be difficult to assess by how much the **possible loss or gain** is affected by a control measure, particularly if the benefit of control is to reduce, but not eliminate the risk (something which will be true for many controls).

- Many benefits of controls are **non-monetary,** for example improvements in employee attitudes or the reputation of the organisation.

- Certain drawbacks of controls are also difficult to factor into decisions including adherence to controls meaning an **inability to cope with the unexpected** and controls giving the **illusion** that **all risks are being reduced.**

Exam skills

The examiner has stressed the importance of risks being controlled effectively and at a realistic cost. Marks won't be awarded for recommendations that cost more to implement than it would to accept the risk.

Section summary

Sometimes the benefits of controls will be outweighed by their costs, and organisations should compare them. However it is difficult to put a monetary value on many **benefits** and **costs** of controls, and also the potential losses if controls are not in place.

Chapter Roundup

- ✓ **Internal controls** should help organisations counter risks, maintain the quality of reporting and comply with laws and regulations. They provide reasonable assurance that organisations will fulfil their objectives.

- ✓ Internal control frameworks include the **control environment** within which **internal controls** operate. Other important elements are the **risk assessment and response processes,** the **sharing of information** and **monitoring** the environment and operation of the control system.

- ✓ The **control environment** is influenced by **management's attitude** towards control, the **organisational structure** and the **values** and **abilities** of employees.

- ✓ Controls can be classified in various ways including **financial** and **non-financial; prevent, detect, correct** and **direct**.

- ✓ An organisation's internal controls should be designed to counter the **risks** that are relevant to the objectives it pursues.

- ✓ Common frauds include **payroll frauds, conspiracy with other parties** and **stealing assets**.

- ✓ Signs of high fraud risk include indications of **lack of integrity, excessive pressures, poor control systems** and **unusual transactions**.

- ✓ In order to prevent fraud, managers must be aware of the **risks** and **signs** of fraud.

- ✓ Prevention policies include emphasis on **ethics** and **personnel and training procedures**. Controls within particular business areas such as **segregation of duties** are also significant.

- ✓ Managers and staff should be aware of their **responsibilities** in detecting fraud, which is also helped by having **information readily available** and allowing **whistleblowing**.

- ✓ Procedures improving staff abilities and attitudes should be built into the control framework. **Communication** of control and risk management issues and strong **human resource procedures** reinforce the control systems.

- ✓ Directors need **information** from a **large variety of sources** to be able to supervise and review the operation of the internal control systems. Information sources should include normal reporting procedures, but staff should also have channels available to report problems or doubtful practices of others.

- ✓ **Control self-assessment** is the assessment by senior management of the strength of the internal control system involving risk analysis and review of the adequacy of controls.

- ✓ Sometimes the benefits of controls will be outweighed by their costs, and organisations should compare them. However it is difficult to put a monetary value on many **benefits** and **costs** of controls, and also the potential losses if controls are not in place.

Quick Quiz

1   What, according to Turnbull, should a good system of internal control achieve?

2   What are the main components of the criteria of control framework?

3   What are the main factors that will be reflected in the organisation's control environment?

4   Match the control and control type

    (a)   Checking of delivery notes against invoices   (i)   Prevent

    (b)   Back-up of computer input   (ii)   Detect

    (c)   Bank reconciliation   (iii)   Correct

5   According to the Turnbull report, in which areas do internal controls particularly need to be communicated?

6   Fill in the blank. .... can be used by managers to obtain a consistent view on the adequacy of control procedures throughout the organisation?

7   Which of the following is not a benefit of control self-assessment?

    A   Supporting concepts such as TQM and benchmarking

    B   Providing comprehensive control documentation

    C   Providing absolute assurance of compliance with control requirements

    D   Highlighting areas of potential weakness

8   Which of the following controls will help prevent fraud in an organisation?

    A   Obtaining references when recruiting

    B   Code of ethics

    C   Whistleblowing channels

    D   Segregation of duties

Answers to Quick Quiz

1 • Facilitate effective and efficient operation by enabling it to respond to significant risks
   • Help ensure the quality of internal and external reporting
   • Help ensure compliance with applicable laws and regulations

2 • Purpose   • Action
   • Commitment   • Monitoring and learning
   • Capability

3 • The philosophy and operating style of the directors and management

   • The entity's organisational structure and methods of assigning authority and responsibility
     (including segregation of duties and supervisory controls)

   • The directors' methods of imposing control, including the internal audit function, the functions of
     the board of directors and personnel policies and procedures

   • The integrity, ethical values and competence of directors and staff

4 (a) (i)
   (b) (iii)
   (c) (ii)

5 • Customer relations
   • Service levels for both internal and outsourced activities
   • Health, safety and environmental protection
   • Security of assets and business continuity
   • Expenditure
   • Accounting, financial and other reporting

6 **Control self-assessment** can be used by managers to obtain a consistent view on the adequacy of control
   procedures throughout the organisation.

7 C   Control self-assessment only provides reasonable assurance, not absolute assurance.

8 A   Obtaining references when recruiting
   B   Code of ethics
   D   Segregation of duties

   Whistleblowing channels (C) are primarily a way of **detecting** fraud

Answers to Questions

6.1 Prevent controls

In the above examples the system outputs could include information, say, about the time lag between delivery of goods and invoicing:

(a) As a measure of the **efficiency of the invoicing section**

(b) As an **indicator of the speed and effectiveness** of **communications** between the despatch department and the invoicing department

(c) As **relevant background information** in assessing the effectiveness of cash management

You should be able to think of plenty of other examples. Credit notes reflect customer dissatisfaction, for example: how quickly are they issued?

6.2 Responses to risk

This question is based on an example in the COSO guidance.

(a) One very important risk would be having insufficient knowledge of customers' needs.

(b) Managers can compile buying histories of existing customers and undertake market research into new customers.

(c) Controls might include checking progress of the development of customer histories against the timetable for those histories and taking steps to ensure that the data is accurate.

Now try these questions from the Exam Question Bank	Number	Level	Marks	Time
	Q7	Examination	25	45 mins
	Q8	Introductory	N/A	45 mins
	Q9	Examination	25	45 mins

Appendix: Systems risks and controls

In this Appendix we shall look at **how tests of controls** might be **applied in practice** in the context of accounting and operational systems.

For each area we shall look at the risks and the aims of the control system. We give examples of common controls. We shall then go on to look at a 'standard' programme of tests of controls.

As we have already discussed, the way to approach questions is not to learn list after list of controls, but

(a)   **Identify** the **risks** in the situation described

(b)   Think how the business will aim to combat those risks and what controls it can use to **prevent** problems or **identify** problems and minimise their effects.

(c)   Think how the internal auditors can **confirm** that these controls are operating effectively

1   The sales system

Introduction

This section looks at the risks over the sales system, the controls in place and how these could be tested.

1.1 Features of sales system

For **sales**, businesses want to give credit only to customers who will **pay their debts**. In addition there are various stages of the selling process – **ordering, dispatch and charging**, all of which should be **documented** and **matched** so that customers receive what they ordered and are appropriately billed. In order to keep track of who owes what and to be able to identify slow-paying customers, a **sales ledger** should be maintained.

1.2 Risks

- Customers being allowed **credits** that are **not bona fide**
- **Goods being supplied** to a **poor credit risk**
- Customers being **invoiced** for the **wrong amounts**
- **Failure to record sales** completely in accounting records

1.3 Ordering and granting of credit

1.3.1 Aims of control

- **Goods** and **services** are **only supplied** to **customers** with **good credit ratings**
- **Customers** are encouraged to **pay promptly**
- **Orders** are **recorded correctly**
- **Orders** are **fulfilled**

1.3.2 Controls

Key controls include **segregation of duties** between the granting of credit and ordering functions. Procedures for authorising credit terms should include **obtaining references and credit checks, authorisation** of terms by senior staff and **regular review. Controls over orders can** be maintained by **pre-numbered order forms** and **matching** of **order and dispatch notes.**

1.3.3 Audit procedures

Auditors will carry out reviews of customer files to ensure that **credit control procedures** are being **followed.** As well as reviewing order forms to see that they are complete, auditors will wish to see evidence that orders are only **accepted** from customers who have been granted. credit terms.

1.4 Dispatch and invoicing

1.4.1 Aims of control

- All **dispatches** of goods are **recorded**
- All **goods and services** sold are **correctly invoiced**
- All **invoices** raised **relate to goods and services supplied** by the business
- Credit notes are only given for **valid reasons**

1.4.2 Controls

Controls over dispatches such as dispatch only on a sale order and examination and recording of goods outwards are key controls. Customers should **sign for deliveries** on **delivery notes;** this, along with **checks on goods returned**, should minimise the credits that have to be given. As well as being matched to sales orders, dispatch notes should also be **matched** to invoices. This check is an important check on invoicing; other significant checks include use of **price lists**, checks of **pricing on individual invoices** and **sequential numbering** of blank invoices to ensure completeness.

1.4.3 Audit procedures

Auditors will check whether there is **full sequencing** of dispatch documentation and will **compare details** on dispatch documentation with orders, sales invoices and entries in inventory records. Checks on details on sales invoices should include quantities, prices, calculations, additions and discounts, also posting to the sales ledger and sales tax. Auditors will also be concerned with whether **credit notes** and **dispatches** on **special terms have been authorised.**

1.5 Recording, accounting and credit control

1.5.1 Aims of control

- All sales that have been **invoiced** are **recorded** in the general and sales ledgers
- All **credit notes** that have been **issued** are **recorded** in the general and sales ledgers
- All **entries** in the sales ledger are **made** to the **correct** sales ledger **accounts**
- **Cut-off** is applied correctly to the sales ledger
- Potentially **doubtful debts** are **identified**

1.5.2 Controls

Ideally different staff should be responsible for **recording sales** and dealing with the issue of customer statements. To complete the documentation process **cash receipts** and **remittance advices** should be matched with sales invoices.

From the accounting viewpoint, it is important that review of dates of sales takes place around the year-end, to ensure that **cut-off** is maintained and that **sales are recorded in the correct period.**

Credit control is also **important** here; regular procedures must include **sending statements to customers** and **reconciliation of the sales ledger control account. Regular review** and **follow-up** of overdue accounts is also important; if bad debts have to be written off, **write-offs** should be **authorised** by senior managers.

1.5.3 Audit procedures

Auditors will wish to compare the various sales accounting records to ensure that they have been **reconciled** and there is consistency between them. They will check whether **reconciliations** have been carried out, that **debtor accounts** are **regularly scrutinised** and statements are **dispatched to debtors.**

Section summary

Tests of controls of the **sales system** will be based around:

- **Selling** (authorisation)
- **Goods outwards** (custody)
- **Accounting** (recording)

2 The purchases and expenses system

Introduction

This section looks at the risks over the purchases systems, the controls in place and how these could be tested.

2.1 Features of purchases and expenses system

Businesses should ensure that only **properly authorised purchases** which are necessary for the business are made. Again all stages of the purchase process, ordering, receiving goods and being charged for them should be **documented and matched** so that the business gets what it ordered and only pays for what it ordered and received. Businesses also need to keep track of what they owe to each supplier by maintaining a purchase ledger.

2.2 Risks

- Payments being made **without being properly authorised**
- Payments being made for goods and services that are **not received** or are **wrongly valued**
- Goods and services being received **without liabilities being recorded** in the accounting records
- Suppliers' accounts being **improperly debited** and **credited**
- Goods being returned to suppliers or credit being **claimed** and **not being recorded**

2.3 Ordering

2.3.1 Aims of controls

- All **orders for goods and services** are properly **authorised**, and are for **goods and services** that are actually **received** and are for the company

- Orders are only made to **authorised suppliers**

- Orders are made at **competitive prices**

2.3.2 Controls

Ideally there should be **segregation of duties** between the key purchasing functions of **requisitions** and **ordering.** Choice of suppliers should be determined by a central purchasing policy. Controls over ordering itself should include requiring **evidence of requirements for purchase** before the purchase is authorised, orders only being made on receipt of a blank order form, and **prenumbering** and **safeguarding** of order forms. Orders not received should be followed up in case they have been 'diverted'.

2.3.3 Audit procedures

Auditors should concentrate on **testing the numerical sequence** of the various **internal documents**, including purchase orders, and should confirm that security arrangements over purchase orders are satisfactory. They should also carry out their **own enquiries on purchase orders** and other documentation that have been **outstanding for a long time** and cannot be matched with other documentation.

2.4 Receipts and invoices

2.4.1 Aims of controls

- All goods and services received are used for the **organisation's purposes**, and not private purposes
- Goods and services are **only accepted if** they have been **ordered**, and the **order** has been **authorised**
- All **goods** and **services received** are accurately **recorded**
- **Liabilities** are **recognised** for all **goods and services** that have been **received**
- All **credits** to which business is due are **claimed** and **received**
- **Receipt** of **goods** and **services** is **necessary** to establish a **liability to be recorded**

2.4.2 Controls

Goods received should be checked for **quantity, quality and condition.** They should be recorded on **prenumbered goods received notes**, and these should be **compared with purchase orders. Suppliers' invoices** when **received** should be checked to the earlier documentation. There should also be procedures for **returning goods to suppliers** and **obtaining credit notes.**

2.4.3 Audit procedures

A most important test of controls is for auditors to check that all **invoices** are **supported** by authorised **purchase invoices** and **purchase orders**. The officials who approve the invoices should be operating within laid-down **authority limits**. The auditors should also check that invoices are **supported** by **goods received notes** and have been **entered in inventory records**. They should themselves check the **pricing and calculations** on invoices, and **trace invoices** through to the purchase ledger, as well as checking that **calculations have been checked as required** by staff responsible and invoices cross-referenced.

2.5 Accounting

2.5.1 Aims of controls

- All **expenditure** is for goods that are **received**
- All **expenditure** is **authorised**
- All **expenditure** that is made is **recorded** correctly in the general and purchase ledger
- All **credit notes** that are received are **recorded** in the general and purchase ledger
- All **entries** in the **purchase ledger** are **made** to the **correct purchase ledger accounts**
- **Cut-off** is **applied correctly** to the purchase ledger

2.5.2 Controls

As in other areas, there should be **segregation of duties** between the accounting and other functions. Maintenance of a purchase ledger is a key control, and **statements received from suppliers** should be **reconciled with purchase ledger balances**. The purchase ledger balances should also be reconciled with the purchase ledger account, and there should be cut-off procedures to ensure purchases are recorded in the right year.

2.5.3 Audit procedures

Auditors should check the reconciliations have been carried out regularly, and **review the purchase ledger and purchase ledger control account** for unusual items. Entries in the purchase ledger should be traced back through to the originating documentation.

Section summary

Purchases systems tests will be based around:

- **Buying** (authorisation)
- **Goods** inwards (custody)
- **Accounting** (recording)

3 The wages system

Introduction

This section looks at the risks over the wages system, the controls in place and how these could be tested.

3.1 Features of wages system

For **wages and salaries** businesses are trying to ensure that they only pay for **hours worked** and that they pay the **right staff** the **right amount**. Controls should also be in place to ensure **tax liabilities** are calculated correctly otherwise penalties may be imposed by the tax authorities. While in practice separate arrangements are generally made for dealing with wages and salaries, the considerations involved are broadly similar and for convenience the two aspects are here treated together.

3.2 Risks

- Payroll **including invalid entries**

- **Payments being made to individuals** which differ from the names or amounts shown on the payroll

- Failure to account for **statutory tax deductions** correctly

3.3 Setting of wages and salaries

3.3.1 Aims of control

- **Employees** are **only paid** for **work** that they have **done**
- **Gross pay** has been **calculated correctly** and **authorised**

3.3.2 Controls

Maintenance of personnel records independent of the payroll system is an important control; wages and salaries should be regularly reconciled to personnel records. Records of hours worked also need to be **regularly reviewed**. Controls over changes and special arrangements are particularly important; these should be fully recorded and changes authorised. They will include engagement and discharge of employees, amendments to pay rates, overtime, non-statutory deductions and advances of pay.

3.3.3 Audit procedures

Auditors need to confirm that the **authorisation** procedures are being operated effectively.

A particular concern will be joiners and leavers. Auditors will need to obtain evidence that staff only start being paid when they join the company, and are removed from the payroll when they leave the company. They should check that the **engagement** of **new employees** and **discharges** have been **confirmed in writing**.

Auditors will also wish to check calculations of wages and salaries. This test should be designed to check that the client is carrying out **checks** on **calculations** and also to provide substantive assurance that **wages** and **salaries** are being **calculated correctly**.

For wages, this will involve checking **calculation** of **gross pay** with:

- Authorised rates of pay

- Production records. See that production bonuses have been authorised and properly calculated

- Clock cards, time sheets or other evidence of hours worked. Verify that overtime has been authorised

For salaries, auditors should **verify that gross salaries and bonuses are in accordance with personnel records, letters of engagement** etc and that increases in pay have been properly authorised.

3.4 Payment of wages and salaries and deductions

3.4.1 Aims of control

- The **correct employees** are **paid**
- All **deductions** have been **calculated correctly** and are **authorised**
- The **correct amounts** are **paid** to the **taxation authorities**

3.4.2 Controls

(a) **Cash wages**

There need to be **security arrangements** over wage packets, covering **custody of pay packets and arrangements** for their **safe transit** to the place of distribution. Security is also needed over unclaimed wage packets; the cash in these should be promptly banked. When distributed, employees should only be **allowed to collect their own wages** and must bring **verification of identity.** Separate arrangements should be made by payroll staff to distribute wages to staff who cannot attend the normal distribution.

(b) **Salaries**

Risks over payment of salaries are probably lower, although authorisation controls over salary payments need to be as rigorous as for any other significant payment. It is important that cheques and bank transfers are compared with payroll, and also that there **are comparisons** between the payroll and the wages and salaries ledger account, additionally between actual wages and budgeted wages. Even small discrepancies may need to be investigated as they may form part of a pattern; there are legends of fraud carried out by means of siphoning off a penny from each employee's salary and paying these into a separate account.

(c) **Deductions**

Appropriate arrangements should be made for dealing with statutory and other authorised deductions from pay, such as taxation, pension fund contributions, and savings held in trust. A primary consideration is the establishment of adequate controls over the calculations (records used must be up-to-date) and authorising **deductions**. There should also be **reconciliations** of **deductions** between one payday and the next.

3.4.3 Audit procedures

(a) **Cash wages**

Before the wages are paid auditors should **compare payroll** with **wage packets** to ensure all employees have a wage packet. Because of the importance of this area, internal auditors should attend the **pay-out of wages and salaries** on a regular basis, checking that identity is confirmed and **no employee receives more than one wage packet**. They should confirm documentation is maintained, that employees sign for wages received and that **unclaimed wages** are recorded in the unclaimed wages book, which should show reasons why wages are unclaimed. Any **pattern** of **unclaimed wages** in the unclaimed wages book should be investigated.

(b) **Salaries**

For salaries, auditors should check that comparisons are being made between payment records and they should themselves **examine paid cheques** or a **certified copy** of the **bank list** for employees paid by cheque or bank transfer.

(c) **Deductions**

Auditors should check the calculations of taxation and non-statutory deductions, and:

(i) Scrutinise the control accounts maintained to see appropriate deductions have been made
(ii) Check that the payments to the taxation bodies are correct

They should check **other deductions to appropriate records**. For voluntary deductions, they should see the authority completed by the relevant employees.

3.5 Recording of wages and salaries

3.5.1 Aims of control

- **Gross** and **net pay** and **deductions** are **accurately recorded** on the payroll
- **Wages and salaries paid** are **recorded correctly** in the **bank** and **cash records**
- **Wages and salaries** are **correctly recorded** in the **general ledger**

3.5.2 Controls

Responsibility for the preparation of pay sheets should be **delegated to a suitable person**, and adequate staff appointed to assist him. The extent to which the staff responsible for preparing wages and salaries may perform other duties should be clearly defined. In this connection full advantage should be taken where possible of the division of duties, and checks available where automatic wage-accounting systems are in use.

For wages, there should have been reconciliations with:

- The **previous week's payroll**
- **Clock cards/time sheets/job cards**
- **Costing analyses, production budgets**

The total of salaries should be reconciled with the previous week/month or the standard payroll.

3.5.3 Audit procedures

A key control auditors will be concerned with will be the **reconciliation of wages and salaries**. In addition auditors should confirm that **important calculations** have been **checked** and re-perform those calculations, and check postings of payroll summaries to the general ledger.

Section summary

Key controls over **wages** cover:

* **Documentation** and **authorisation** of staff changes
* **Calculation** of wages and salaries
* **Payment** of wages
* **Authorisation** of **deductions**

4 The cash system and loans

Introduction

This section looks at the risks over the cash receipts and payments systems, the controls in place and how these could be tested.

4.1 Features of cash system

Controls over **cash and bank balances** cannot be seen in complete isolation from controls over the sales, purchases and wages cycle. In this Appendix we concentrate on controls over, and testing of, the safe **custody and prompt recording** of cash. Bear in mind also when you work through the section on bank and cash that controlling cheque receipts and payments is significantly easier than controlling cash receipts and payments.

4.2 Risks

* **Misappropriation** of cash receipts
* **Failure to record** cash receipts and payments
* Payments being made **without authorisation or supporting documentation**

4.3 Aims of controls

* **All monies received** are **recorded**
* **All monies received** are **banked**
* **Cash and cheques** are **safeguarded** against loss or theft
* **All payments** are **authorised**, **made** to the **correct payees** and **recorded**
* **Payments** are **not made twice** for the same liability

4.4 Cash at bank and in hand – receipts

4.4.1 Controls

Controls over the **completeness** of **recording** of cash receipts are particularly important. If these controls are inadequate, there may be insufficient audit evidence available when the external auditor carries out substantive procedures.

Segregation of duties is also important. The person responsible for receiving and recording cash when it arrives in the post should not be the same as the person responsible for banking it. Ideally the cash book should be written up by a further staff member, and a fourth staff member should reconcile the various records of amounts received.

Controls over **recording of receipts by post** should ensure security by listing amounts received when the post is opened and **protection** of **cash and cheques** (restrictive crossing).

Key controls over cash sales and collections include **restrictions** on **receipt of cash** (by cashiers only, or by salesmen etc), **evidencing** of **receipt of cash** (serially numbered receipt forms, cash registers incorporating sealed till rolls). As in other areas, reconciliations are a very important control, including **agreement of cash collections with till rolls and receipts,** agreement of cash collections with bankings and cash and sales records. Any **cash shortages** and **surpluses** should be investigated.

Receipts should be banked daily and the **make-up** and **comparison** of **paying-in slips** checked against initial receipt records and cash book.

Retail businesses such as restaurants need to be aware of the high risks involved in only taking cash, in particular poor record-keeping and vulnerability to theft. Investment in an **EFTPOS** (Electronic Funds Transfer Point of Sale technology) would mean that customers could pay by **credit or debit card**, decreasing the volume of cash and providing a permanent record of sales.

4.4.2 Audit procedures

The auditors should observe that receipts are immediately recorded when the **post is opened.** The auditors should inspect the **security of tills** and compare cash with till rolls and, for collections, with collectors' cash sheets. They should confirm by looking at dates or sequential numbering that **documentation supporting receipts is complete.** The auditors should also track receipts through the banking and accounting documentation to check that they are **banked intact** and **completely recorded** in the cash book. Auditors should also **review the bank accounts and cash book** and investigate any unusual receipts.

4.5 Safeguarding of bank accounts

4.5.1 Controls

Generally the most significant controls will be over cheques and should cover their **supply and issue,** **restricting** the **staff allowed to prepare cheques, safeguards** over **mechanically signed cheques/cheques carrying printed signatures** and **restrictions** on issue of **blank** or **bearer** cheques. **Signed cheques** should be **dispatched promptly.**

4.5.2 Audit procedures

Auditors should inspect the procedures and **investigate anything** that appears to be wrong, for example blank cheques already signed or missing cheques. If the risks of fraud appear to be high, it will be worth paying to **obtain paid cheques from the bank** and scrutinising payees and signatories. As with receipts auditors should **scrutinise cash books** and bank accounts, and investigate unusual payments or transfers to other accounts. The auditors should check that **balances on bank accounts** are regularly **reconciled** with **cash book balances**, and **reperform** a **sample of reconciliations.**

4.6 Safeguarding of cash accounts

4.6.1 Controls

If the business has large amounts of cash, these controls will be significant, as cash can easily 'disappear.' Controls should include **limitations** on **cash floats** held, **restrictions** on **access** to cash registers and offices, and appropriate controls on custody of cash **outside office hours.** If the pattern of review is predictable, it is easy for cash to be removed and balances to be reimbursed when checks are due to take place. Hence **surprise cash counts** and **independent checks** on cash floats are very important.

4.6.2 Audit procedures

The auditors may themselves carry out the **surprise independent counts**, and should certainly **check the petty cash records** to see whether **guidelines are being followed.**

4.7 Cash at bank and in hand – payments

4.7.1 Controls

The arrangements for controlling payments will depend to a great extent on the **nature of business transacted**, the **volume of payments** involved and the **size of the company**.

Segregation of duties is again a key control. The cashier should generally not be concerned **with keeping or writing-up books of account** other than those recording disbursements nor should he have access to, or be responsible for the custody of, securities, title deeds or negotiable instruments belonging to the company. The person responsible for preparing cheques or traders' credit lists should not himself be a cheque signatory. Cheque signatories in turn should not be responsible for authorising requisitions or recording payments.

Documentation is also significant. **Cheque requisitions** should be raised, supported by **appropriate documentation**, and approved by senior staff. **Documentation** should be **cancelled** by crossing/recording cheque number on requisition. Signatories should **have limitations on authority to specific amounts** and should be prohibited from signing of blank cheques. Payments should be **recorded promptly** in the **cash book** and **general** and **purchase ledgers.**

Cash expenditure controls should cover **authorisation** of **expenditure, cancellation** of **vouchers** to ensure they cannot be paid twice and **limits** on cash **disbursements.** There should be strict controls over **cash advances** to employees, IOUs and cheque cashing.

4.7.2 Audit procedures

The most important audit procedures will be **checking details** to **suppliers' invoices and statements** for goods and services, also **other documentary evidence**, as appropriate (agreements, authorised expense vouchers, wages/salaries records, petty cash books etc). Auditors should verify that supporting documents are signed as having been **checked** and **passed for payment** and have been stamped 'paid'. Similar tests should be performed on **petty cash expenditure.**

Section summary

Key controls over **receipts** include:

- Proper **post-opening** arrangements
- **Prompt recording**
- **Prompt banking**
- **Reconciliation** of records of cash received and banked

Key controls over **payments** include:

- **Restriction of access** to cash and cheques
- Procedures for **preparation and authorisation** of payments

A further important control is **regular independent bank reconciliations**.

5 The inventory system

Introduction

This section looks at the risks over the inventory system, the controls in place and how these could be tested.

5.1 Features of inventory system

For **inventory**, there should be **proper security arrangements** and **prompt recording**. You should note however the other aspects of control of inventory, particularly reviews of the condition of inventory, and inventory holding policies designed to ensure that the business is not holding too much or too little inventory. These controls interest auditors since they may impact upon how inventory is valued.

5.2 Risks

Important risks include the following:

- **Misappropriation of inventory**
- **Failure** to record **inventory movements**
- **Deterioration in condition** and **value of inventory** due to age, obsolescence, or poor inventory holding conditions

5.3 Recording

5.3.1 Aims of controls

- All **inventory movements** are **authorised** and **recorded**
- **Inventory records** only **include items** that **belong** to the organisation
- **Inventory records include inventory** that **exists** and is **held** by the organisation
- **Inventory quantities** have been **recorded correctly**
- **Cut-off procedures** are **properly applied** to inventory

5.3.2 Controls

Segregation of duties is important in this area, with ideally separation of responsibilities between those responsible for **recording** of inventory and those responsible for its **custody.** There should be detailed records of inventory held, and inventory receipts and issues.

5.3.3 Audit procedures

Auditors will be particularly concerned with making sure that the organisation keeps tracks of inventory and should **compare** the various **inventory records,** and test the sequence of inventory records, to make sure it is complete.

5.4 Protection of inventory

5.4.1 Aims of controls

Inventory is **safeguarded** against loss, pilferage or damage.

5.4.2 Controls

Precautions against theft, misuse and deterioration include restriction of access to stores and controls over the temperature etc in which inventory is held.

Regular counts of inventory are a key control, not only to confirm how much inventory is there, but also its condition. All inventory should be counted at least once a year, counts should be carried out by persons other than the stores function, and there should be reconciliation of inventory count records to book records and control accounts.

5.4.3 Audit procedures

Internal audit may carry out the inventory count themselves, or they will attend and observe to see that the **count** is **carried out** in accordance with **prescribed procedures and fully recorded.** They should carry out test counts if they are not doing the full count themselves, and should investigate whether all **discrepancies between book value** and **actual value** have been resolved. Auditors should also observe the **security arrangements over inventory,** the **condition** of inventory and the environment in which it is held.

5.5 Valuation of inventory

5.5.1 Aims of controls

The **costing system values inventory correctly**.

Allowance is **made** for **slow-moving**, **obsolete** or **damaged inventory**.

5.5.2 Controls

There should be checks that calculations are correct and procedures to deal with **writing down the value** of slow-moving, damaged and obsolete inventory identified during the inventory count.

5.5.3 Audit procedures

Auditors should follow up their work at the inventory count, and confirm that inventory has, if necessary, been **written down** to **net realisable value.** They should also check that **inventory calculations** appear **reasonable** and have been checked.

5.6 Inventory holding

5.6.1 Aims of controls

Levels of **inventory held** are **reasonable**.

5.6.2 Controls

The main controls over inventory levels should be the system of **maximum and minimum inventory levels**, also **reorder quantities and levels** which you will remember from your earlier studies.

5.6.3 Audit procedures

Auditors should **review records of inventory** and query any **apparent excessive or under holdings**.

Section summary

Inventory controls are designed to ensure safe custody. These include:

- **Restriction of access** to inventory
- **Documentation** and **authorisation** of movements

Other important controls over inventory include regular **independent inventory counting** and **review of inventory condition**.

6 Revenue and capital expenditure

Introduction

This section looks at the risks of revenue and capital expenditure, the controls in place and how these could be tested.

6.1 Controlling non-current assets

As with inventory, organisations have to make sure that they maintain **safe custody** over non-current assets; the financial consequences of loss or pilferage could be much more serious than the loss of the odd item of inventory. Similarly assets must be guarded against the risk of **excessive loss of value** or their not being fully utilised.

The aims of controls and audit tests will be the same over non-current asset purchases as over other sorts of purchases, which we discussed earlier. However the auditor may test a higher proportion of non-current asset purchases, and may indeed look at all the purchases in a year if they are few in number but for large amounts individually.

6.2 Risks

- **Asset acquisitions** and **disposals not** being **authorised**
- **Asset acquisitions** and **disposals not** being **recorded**
- Asset records including items which have been **disposed** of, are of **negligible value** or **do not exist**
- **Misappropriation** of assets
- Assets being used for **private benefit**
- **Deterioration in condition** or obsolescence of assets
- **Depreciation** being **charged** at too high or too low a rate
- **Depreciation** being **calculated** incorrectly
- **Income from assets** not being **received** or recorded
- **Revenue and capital expenditure** are being accounted for **incorrectly**

6.3 Authorisation

6.3.1 Aims of control

- All **acquisitions** are **authorised**.
- All **disposals and scrappings** are **authorised**.

6.3.2 Controls

All the **controls over purchases** discussed above will be **relevant**. Including authorisation of orders and checking of condition when goods are received. As non-current assets are generally much more expensive than purchases of inventory, the decision to acquire significant assets should be taken by the board (a recommendation of corporate governance reports.

6.3.3 Audit procedures

Auditors will inspect evidence that **purchases have been authorised** and that their condition has been checked when they are purchased. Because non-current assets may be very costly, auditors may not sample, but check every purchase, or at any rate **every purchase over a certain amount** or **every purchase of particular asset types**, for example major computer equipment.

6.4 Security

6.4.1 Aims of control

Non-current assets are **safeguarded** against loss, pilferage or damage.

6.4.2 Controls

The organisation should also have similar controls over **asset security** as it does over inventory security, such as **restriction of access** and **controls over environmental conditions.** (We consider controls over information technology assets separately later in this text). In addition, the organisation should consider ways of marking ownership on the assets (for example on computer equipment), and should maintain a **non-current asset register**. All capital items should be written up in this register, including identification details. The non-current asset register should be regularly reconciled to the general ledger.

6.4.3 Audit procedures

Auditors will wish to inspect **security procedures** to confirm that they are **operating**. They will **inspect assets** to see that they are in **good condition** and that there are no environmental factors that are likely to cause excessive loss of value. They will also **compare the assets** that they have seen with the **non-current assets register.**

6.5 Valuation

6.5.1 Aims of control

- **Non-current assets** are **valued correctly**.
- **Depreciation** is **calculated correctly**.
- **Adjustments** are made for write-downs in the value of assets.

6.5.2 Controls

The calculation of depreciation should just involve mechanical controls, although senior, qualified staff should judge what **appropriate depreciation rates** are. As accounting standards are emphasising revaluations more, organisations should have appropriate controls over these including **specification of the qualifications of the valuer** and the **scope and objective** of the valuation. Similarly the need for **write-downs of assets** should be supported by evidence of loss of value, and the **write-downs authorised** by managers.

6.5.3 Audit procedures

Auditors will wish to confirm that **valuers are qualified,** and that the valuation appear reasonable on the **basis of the valuer's report** and the valuer has followed the **instructions given,** Auditors will also be concerned with the wider issues of whether **asset revaluations** are taking place **sufficiently regularly and cover all relevant assets**. Their inspection of assets may identify assets which need to be written down, and auditors should also be alert when reviewing repairs expenditure for excessive expenditure on certain assets.

6.6 Recording

6.6.1 Aims of control

- All **asset movements** are **recorded**
- **Asset records** only **include items** that belong to the organisation
- **Asset records** include **assets that exist** and are held by the client
- **All expenditure** is **classified correctly** in the accounts as capital or revenue expenditure

6.6.2 Controls

The asset register is obviously a **key recording control** and the general ledger should be regularly reconciled to it. Staff with **appropriate knowledge** should be involved in the **maintenance of sensitive codes** in the general ledger, such as non-current assets and repairs and maintenance, to confirm revenue and capital expenditure is being **allocated correctly.** As well as financial accounting records, **capital budgets** should be **prepared**, **actual expenditure compared** with **budgets** and **differences investigated**.

6.6.3 Audit procedures

As with other areas, auditors will compare documentation. They will pay particular attention to the **recording of the most valuable assets,** and will seek evidence that the judgements made about the allocation of capital and revenue expenditure are appropriate. They will also wish to see that the non-current register has properly maintained and check that discrepancies between the **non-current asset register** and **general ledger** have been investigated and cleared

Section summary

Most of the key controls over **capital and revenue expenditure** are the general purchase controls.

It is also important that **non-current assets** are **recorded correctly**, so that profit/loss and assets are not misstated.

7 Operational risks and controls

Introduction

This section looks at operational risks and controls in the following areas: logistics, procurement, marketing, human resources and research and development.

7.1 Logistics

KEY TERM

LOGISTICS are the processes by which materials or goods are brought into the business, transferred between locations and delivered to customers.

7.1.1 Risks

- **Inventory** is **not delivered** at the right time to the right place in the right condition
- **Inventory** is **stolen**
- Poor quality products result in **lost sales** or **damage** or **injury**
- Business is **interrupted**

7.1.2 Controls and audit

Logistics controls will include controls over the **safeguarding of inventory**, but they must also include controls ensuring that inventory is available when needed to meet **business requirements.** Hence businesses also need adequate **planning and forecasting systems, detailed analysis of volume requirements** and availability of **alternative facilities** at short notice. Having **sufficient vehicles** to **transport inventory** is also important.

Auditors should extend their work on inventory to **review logistics records** for accuracy and relevance and should **confirm** that managers are monitoring forecasts. They should also **review the adequacy of contingency plans** and **arrangements for vehicle maintenance.**

7.2 Procurement

KEY TERM

PROCUREMENT is the process of **purchasing** for the business.

A procurement audit will concentrate on the systems of the purchasing department(s). The internal auditor will be checking that the system achieves key objectives and that it operates according to the organisation's guidelines.

7.2.1 Risks

- Goods and services are **not available** when required
- The organisation **pays too much** for goods and services
- Employees or suppliers **defraud** the organisation

7.2.2 Controls and audit

Many of the controls over **procurement** will be the same as in the **purchases cycle.** In addition procurement processes aims to ensure that **goods and services** are **available** when required, and that the organisation pays **reasonable prices for goods and services.** This implies a rigorous **tendering process,** with research being carried out on potential suppliers before they are invited for tender. **Requirements for goods and services** should be put in **writing** and full use made of discount and long-term supply arrangements.

A procurement system is likely to have many systems within it (for example, tendering, placing orders, checking goods inwards), which the internal auditor would probably approach separately. The auditor should review the **adequacy of tendering arrangements,** and check that invoice details can be traced back to written requisitions.

7.3 Marketing

KEY TERM

MARKETING is the **process of assessing and enhancing demand for the company's products**.

Marketing and its link with sales is very important for the business. An audit may be especially critical for a marketing department that may be complex with several different teams, for example:

- Research
- Advertising
- Promotions
- After sales

7.3.1 Risks

- **Customer requirements** are not taken into account
- Customers **do not know about products**
- Prices are **not competitive**
- Goods are **priced** at **too low a level**, promotion considerations resulting in excessive discounts

7.3.2 Controls and audit

Controls and audit need to ensure:

- The process is **managed efficiently**
- **Information is freely available** on manager demand
- **Risks** are being **managed** correctly

There should be rigorous requirements for market research to be carried out before products are launched, so that **advertising and promotions** can be carefully targeted. The organisation should also monitor **competitor prices** and **activity,** as well as its own **actual sales against budget.**

Auditors should assess **whether adequate research appears to have been carried out,** and look at the **adequacy** of the **decision-making processes** on major decisions, for example timing of promotions. They should also **review terms and conditions** to ensure that they comply with company policy.

7.4 Human resources

KEY TERM

The HUMAN RESOURCES department on one hand procures human resources (employees) for the operation of the business and on the other supports those employees in developing the organisation.

The processes need to ensure that people are available to work as the business requires them and that the overall development of the business is planned and controlled.

7.4.1 Risks

- **Inadequate staffing**, either in terms of staff numbers or in terms of expertise
- **Over-reliance** on certain key personnel
- Excessive staff **turnover**
- **Staff** are paid the **wrong amounts**
- The **correct deductions** are not made for taxes
- Staff expenses are **not properly documented**
- Staff expenses are **unauthorised** or are **excessive**
- The organisation **reimburses** staff for **private expenditure**
- **Industrial action** disrupts the organisation
- The organisation is subject to **actions for wrongful dismissal**
- Failure to comply with **employment laws**

7.4.2 Controls and audit

The business has a **long-term human requirement plan, with long-term succession planning** is undertaken. There need to be various measures to ensure staff are content, including **benchmarking salary** against the market, **appraising staff performance,** and giving staff **adequate training.** Human resources managers should receive **training in employment law.**

Again, **ensuring company policies are maintained and information is freely available** are key factors for internal auditors to assess. They need also to review all the relevant internal records including appraisal and training records and long-term human resource plans.

As well as carrying out specific human resource audits, internal auditors should also consider human resource issues on a range of other operational audits, for example considering whether the treasury function is staffed by employees with sufficient experience of the financial markets.

7.5 Research and development

There are a number of elements in research and development processes; they need to be consistent with **business marketing strategy** and procedures are needed over both research projects and development.

7.5.1 Risks

- **Research and development effort** is **wasted** on projects that will provide no benefits for the company in terms of sales or are not in line with corporate strategy

- **Resources are wasted** on duplicated projects

- Projects do **not deliver** the **planned benefits**, are late or over budget

- **Loss of data** interrupts research and development

7.5.2 Controls and audit

Controls must ensure that **research and development is properly planned, budgeted, monitored and reported**. It must comply with **internal standards** and **with all relevant legislation**. **Research and development strategy** must be **decided** and **reviewed** by the board, and research and development activities **co-ordinated centrally**. Research and development activities follow a **common project methodology**, and **progress on projects** should be **reported regularly** against plans and forecasts. **Post implementation reviews** are important.

Because of the importance of research and development, auditors need to consider carefully the adequacy of **organisational guidelines** for research and development projects and **test projects** to see whether they have been following guidelines. They should **check** that **results** of research and development have been regularly **communicated** to management. Auditors should also **review results** of **post implementation reviews** and confirm that points arising have been actioned.

7.6 Post-completion audits

Post-completion audits are covered in detail in the BPP text for Paper F3 *Financial Strategy* in the context of investment and project appraisal. In this text we include a brief summary to introduce the topic or to refresh your memory.

KEY TERM

A POST-COMPLETION AUDIT is an **objective, independent assessment** of the success of a project in relation to plan. It covers the whole life of the project and provides feedback to managers to aid the implementation and control of future projects.

(CIMA Official Terminology)

7.6.1 Risks

- Capital expenditure on a project is **greater than anticipated**
- The project has failed to deliver the **anticipated benefits**
- **Excessive resources** have been utilised on developing the project

7.6.2 Controls and audit

The controls relate to the organisation's system for **approving and developing new investments**. These are discussed in the context of information technology developments in Chapter 14. The organisation's systems of budgeting and variance/progress reporting are also significant.

Post-completion auditing is partly an audit of controls, including weaknesses in the **budgeting and forecasting system**. It also examines the performance of management, using principles of **responsibility accounting**. As such it is an example of a management audit which we shall discuss in Chapter 15.

Section summary

Controls over operations are designed to ensure that **customer requirements** are taken into account, **assets and resources** are **made available when required**, assets are **safeguarded**, **legislation** and **internal guidelines** are **followed**, and **operations** are **monitored and reviewed** by management.

MANAGEMENT ACCOUNTING CONTROL SYSTEMS

The previous chapters covered control systems generally, and recognised that the wider context of control involves people management and organisation structure. In this chapter we narrow the focus to control systems and management accounting.

We start by introducing the key theme of this chapter, the response of the **management accounting systems** to **changing environments**. We examine in more detail the **impact of strategy on systems**.

In the second half of the chapter we discuss specific management accounting tools. Our discussion on

budgets brings in the organisational and motivational issues that we covered in Chapter 5. We also discuss the attention to the limitations of some of the traditional methods that you've covered in previous studies, and see how **recent developments in management accounting** attempt to overcome the problems of older methods.

We finish by looking at the role of the **management accounting function**, which has the prime responsibility for ensuring systems operate successfully. Remember that **all** organisations have some form of accounting function, from the multinational finance department to the football club's cash book.

7

topic list	learning outcomes	syllabus references	ability required
1 Management accounting systems	A1(b)	A1(ii)	evaluation
2 Design of management accounting systems	A1(b)	A1(ii)	evaluation
3 Budgeting	A1(b)	A1(ii)	evaluation
4 Management accounting techniques	A1(b)	A1(ii)	evaluation
5 Developments in management accounting	A1(b)	A1(v)	evaluation
6 The management accounting function	A1(b)	A1(vi)	evaluation

1 Management accounting systems

Introduction

We start this section by briefly looking at how management accounting systems have developed, and considering the implications of systems not developing quickly enough to keep pace with changes in the business world.

1.1 The development of management accounting

In the 1950s Simons identified **three attributes** of what could by now be called **management accounting information** as follows.

- It should be useful for **scorekeeping** – seeing how well the organisation is doing overall.

- It should be **attention-directing** – indicating problem areas that need to be investigated.

- It should be useful for **problem-solving** – providing a means of evaluating alternative responses to the situations in which the organisation finds itself.

Management accounting information is therefore used by managers for a number of purposes:

(a) To **make decisions**.

(b) To **plan** for the future. Managers have to plan and they need information to do this, much of it management accounting information.

(c) To **monitor the performance** of the business. Managers need to know what they **want the business to achieve** (targets or standards) and what the business is **actually achieving**.

(d) To **measure profits** and **put a value on inventory**.

1.2 Management accounting systems and risk management

As we shall see in this chapter management accounting systems have a role beyond identifying the risks associated with lax cost control. They need to assist management in **strategic decision-making** and thus provide **measures of performance** related to the business environment and **comparisons with competitor activity**.

Obviously also a key aspect of strategy should be **keeping the customer satisfied**. Traditional techniques do not always provide sufficient information about customer views and the attainment of the quality and timeliness levels needed to keep the customer satisfied. At the end of this chapter we shall look at measures such as the balanced scorecard and total quality management that are designed to address these issues.

1.3 Risks of management accounting systems

1.3.1 Excessive emphasis on financial measures

Managers' attention may be **unduly focused on financial costs** that can easily be measured. This will be a significant drawback if non-financial qualitative objectives are important to the organisation.

1.3.2 Internal orientation

Again this may due to the easy availability of data about internal targets. The business should instead be more **externally-orientated**, with a focus on customers and competitors, suppliers and perhaps other stakeholders.

1.3.3 Lack of goal congruence

Employees may **pursue targets that are not in the best interests of the organisation**. Often this may reflect poor overall design of the system, with **potential conflicts between short and long-term objectives** being ignored and incompatible targets being set for different parts of the organisation.

1.3.4 Lack of future perspective

The management accounting system may **highlight historic financial costs**. Future decision-making uses relevant costs (incremental and opportunity costs).

1.3.5 Failure to adapt performance measures to changing circumstances

This is a particular problem with the traditional methods that we discuss below and in Section 4 of this Chapter. It may also be a problem with budgeting (see Section 3).

1.4 Risks of traditional management accounting methods

A report by Scapen *The future direction of UK management accounting practice* highlighted a number of recent changes in the management accounting environment. These included:

- Globalisation and increased competition
- Information technology changes resulting in changes in production and information flows
- Changes in organisations including internal reorganisations and external mergers

Traditional management accounting systems may be inadequate for a modern business environment that focuses on marketing, customer service, employee involvement and total quality, and for modern industry using advanced manufacturing technology.

Section summary

Management accounting developed from cost accounting, for **scorekeeping**, **directing management attention** and **problem solving**. It has since branched out into behavioural aspects.

2 Design of management accounting systems

Introduction

In this section we focus on the factors determining the design of management accounting systems. The most important factor is the output they provide, with different output being used for various management purposes.

2.1 What is a management accounting system (MAS)?

The components of a MAS include the following.

(a) **People** with accounting knowledge

(b) **Equipment** they use

(c) Paper or computer **records of financial transactions**

(d) **Codes** or **titles** describing the purpose of the financial transaction ('Rent') and who it was incurred on behalf of ('Factory A')

(e) **Records of the usage of resources** other than money, such as time, physical materials, energy and so forth

(f) **Mathematical techniques** for arranging and analysing (c) in terms of (d) and (e).

(g) **Reports** that are produced by the people in (a), using (b) to (f). Also, prescribed formats for reports, at least in larger, more bureaucratic organisations

(h) **More people**, to whom the reports are given

> This is a **system because it has inputs** (items (a) to (e)), **processes** (item (f)) and **outputs** (item (g)). The list is not meant to be comprehensive.

2.2 Designing a management accounting system

The following factors should be considered when designing a management accounting system.

Factor	Detail
Sources of input information	Decisions are needed on **sources** of data, and the **methods** used to record that data.
Processing involved	This will depend on the method of accounting used. This is **generally a cost/benefit calculation**: some of the information that could be provided would cost more to produce than the benefit obtained from having it.
Output required	The management accountant must **identify the information needs of managers** making planning and control decisions, and monitoring progress. Levels of **detail and accuracy** of output must be determined in each case.
Response required	A further, vitally important issue is how managers are **likely to behave**, depending on what factors or figures are stressed in the information they are given. Ultimately the information is meant to result in making decisions.
When the output is required	If **information is needed** within the hour the system should be **capable of producing it at this speed**.

Question 7.1 Good management accounting information

Learning outcome A1(b)

What are the features of good management accounting information?

2.3 Strategic planning, management control and operational control

Robert Anthony suggested that there are **three levels or tiers within an organisation's decision-making hierarchy**.

KEY TERMS

STRATEGIC PLANNING is 'the process of deciding on objectives of the organisation, on changes in these objectives, on the resources used to attain these objectives, and on the policies that are to govern the acquisition, use and disposition of these resources'.

MANAGEMENT CONTROL is 'the process by which managers assure that resources are obtained and used effectively and efficiently in the accomplishment of the organisation's objectives'.

OPERATIONAL CONTROL is 'the process of assuring that specific tasks are carried out effectively and efficiently'.

Management control is sometimes called TACTICS or TACTICAL PLANNING. Operational control is sometimes called OPERATIONAL PLANNING.

We can look at the information that a MAS may be required to produce under Anthony's three headings, strategic planning, management control and operational control.

2.3.1 Strategic planning information

KEY TERM

STRATEGIC MANAGEMENT ACCOUNTING is a form of management accounting in which emphasis is placed on information which relates to factors external to the entity, as well as to non-financial information and internally-generated information.

(CIMA Official Terminology)

Some **examples** of strategic management accounting are provided below.

Item	Comment
Competitors' costs	What are they? How do they compare with ours? Can we beat them? Are competitors vulnerable because of their cost structure?
Financial effect of competitor response	Have sales fallen?
Product profitability	A firm should want to know not just what profits or losses are being made by each of its products, but why one product should be making good profits whereas another equally good product might be making a loss
Customer profitability	Some customers or groups of customers are worth more than others
Pricing decisions	Accounting information can help to analyse how profits and cash flows will vary according to price and prospective demand
Value of market share	A firm ought to be aware of what it is worth to increase the market share of one of its products
Capacity expansion	Should the firm expand its capacity, and if so by how much? Should the firm diversify into a new area of operations, or a new market?
Brand values	How much is it worth investing in a 'brand' which customers will choose over competitors' brands?
Shareholder wealth	Future profitability determines the value of a business
Cash flow	A loss-making company can survive if it has adequate cash resources, but a profitable company cannot survive unless it has sufficient liquidity

2.3.2 Management control information

The information required for management control **embraces the entire organisation** and **provides a comparison between actual results and the plan**. The information is often **quantitative** (labour hours, quantities of materials consumed, volumes of sales and production) and is commonly **expressed in money terms**.

Such information includes productivity measurements, budgetary control or variance analysis reports, cash flow forecasts, profit results within a particular department of the organisation, labour turnover statistics within a department and so on. Tactical information is usually **prepared regularly**, perhaps weekly, or monthly.

2.3.3 Operational control information

Operational information is information which is **needed for the conduct of day-to-day implementation of plans**. It will include much **'transaction data'** such as data about customer orders, purchase orders, cash receipts and payments.

The amount of **detail** provided in information is likely to vary with the purpose for which it is needed, and operational information is likely to go into much more detail than management control information, which in turn will be more detailed than strategic information. Operational information, although quantitative, is more often **expressed in terms of units, hours, quantities of material and so on.**

2.4 Performance measurement in different sectors

As well as taking into account the various levels at which information is required, the management accountant must have regard to the sector in which the organisation is located. A range of measures will be significant in each sector, similar to the balanced scorecard approach that you will have covered in your earlier studies.

2.4.1 Performance measurement in the manufacturing sector

Performance will not just be measured by traditional cost measures. Other non-financial measures will be important including:

- Quality
- Delivery
- Process time
- Flexibility

2.4.2 Performance measurement in the service sector

The management accountant must take into account the characteristics of the service sector, including the production and consumption occurring at the same time, the problems of ensuring consistently high-quality service and the problems of assessing which parts of the service the customer values most.

Ideally in the service sector performance evaluation should take place over six dimensions:

- Flexibility
- Innovation
- Resource utilisation
- Excellence
- Financial performance
- Competitiveness

2.4.3 Performance measurement in the not-for-profit sector

Performance is usually judged in terms of inputs and outputs, which tie into the idea of 'value for money', based on:

- **Economy** – obtaining suitable inputs at the lowest cost
- **Efficiency** – the process working as expected
- **Effectiveness** – achieving your goals

Section summary

A management accounting system comprises **people**, **accounting knowledge**, **records**, **processes**, **mathematical techniques**, and **reports**: inputs, processes and outputs. It is used for strategic decision making, performance measurement, operational control and costing.

3 Budgeting

Introduction

In this section we examine the role of budgets in management accounting systems. In particular we focus on the control problems that may arise.

KEY TERM

3.1 Responsibility accounting and budgeting

RESPONSIBILITY ACCOUNTING is a system of accounting that segregates revenue and costs into areas of personal responsibility in order to monitor and assess the performance of each part of an organisation.

A well-organised system of responsibility accounting should have the following features.

Feature	Explanation
A hierarchy of budget centres	If the organisation is quite large a hierarchy is needed. Subsidiary companies, departments and work sections might be budget centres.
Clearly identified responsibilities for achieving budget targets	Individual managers should be made responsible for achieving the budget targets of a particular budget centre.
Responsibilities for revenues, costs and capital employed	Budget centres should be organised so that all the revenues earned by an organisation, all the costs it incurs, and all the capital it employs are made the responsibility of someone within the organisation, at an appropriate level of authority in the management hierarchy.

Exam alert

Don't assume that budgets will always be tested in the context of large organisations with complex systems of budget centres.

Responsibility centres might be a mixture of cost centres, profit centres and investment centres.

Type of responsibility centre	Manager has control over . . .	Principal performance measure
Cost centre	Controllable costs	Variance analysis
Profit centre	Controllable costs Sales volumes Sales prices	Profit
Investment centre	Controllable costs Sales prices Output volumes Investment in fixed and current assets	Return on investment and residual income

Question 7.2   Responsibility accounting

Learning outcome A1(b)

Why might responsibility accounting be difficult to implement in a not-for-profit organisation?

3.1.1 Information needs of managers

If a manager is to bear responsibility for the performance of his area of the business he will need information about its performance. In essence, a manager needs to know three things.

Requirements	Examples of information
What are his **resources**?	Finance, stocks of raw materials, spare machine capacity, labour availability, the balance of expenditure remaining for a certain budget, target date for completion of a job.
At **what rate** are his resources being consumed?	How fast is his labour force working, how quickly are his raw materials being used up, how quickly are other expenses being incurred, how quickly is available finance being consumed?
How well are the resources being **used**?	How well are his objectives being met?

3.2 Budget centres

KEY TERM

A **BUDGET CENTRE** is 'A section of an entity for which control may be exercised through prepared budgets'.

(CIMA *Official Terminology*)

3.2.1 Budget centres and organisation structure

Possible **bases** for budget centres are **different activities** or **functions**, different **products**, different **geographical areas**, different **customers** and so on. Budget centres may overlap in the case of a matrix organisation.

Having budget centres down to a low level in the management hierarchy has a number of advantages.

- **Motivation and encouragement** of junior managers.

- **An awareness of management's authority** and responsibility is reinforced by a reporting system based on budget centres.

- **Perhaps, better budgeting** because of the better knowledge of detail that management will possess at budget centres lower down in the hierarchy of the organisation.

Establishing budget centres down to a low level in the management hierarchy also has **disadvantages**.

- **Greater decentralisation**, when head office might wish to retain greater control itself.

- The danger that junior managers will seek to **improve their own budget centre's** performance regardless of the consequences for other budget centres (sub-optimality in decision making).

- The **greater administrative problems** of having a reporting system with many budget centres.

- The **greater opportunities for building slack** into the organisation's budgets.

Exam skills

As well as considering budgets as part of the overall control system, you may need to show how budgetary targets, monitoring and reporting can be used specifically to counter the risks of wastage of resources.

Alternatively, you may need to consider the effectiveness of a budgeting system that is already in place.

3.3 Participation in budgeting

The idea that when individuals (employees or managers) **participate** in decision making, they will be **more satisfied** with their job and they will be more productive derives from **'human relations' thinking** about organisational behaviour, and is also in line with the **goal theory of motivation.**

3.4 Problems with participation

3.4.1 Lack of commitment

There are several reasons why managers **may not be committed** to producing a good budget.

- Managers who **dislike financial figures** will tend to minimise the amount of time they spend budgeting.

- Some managers may **dislike the formality** of a budget plan and wish to have more flexibility.

- Some may consider themselves to be **too busy** to 'waste' time on budgeting.

- **Job dissatisfaction** or an **imminent job change** will decrease the effectiveness of participation.

3.4.2 Lack of expertise

Particularly if they have **not received adequate training,** managers may not know how to produce a budget to reflect the business strategy of the company. Ideas may be based solely on past results **without considering alternative options**. In addition managers may not **understand how to co-ordinate** their plans with those of other budget centres.

3.4.3 Budget slack

KEY TERM

BUDGETARY SLACK is 'The intentional overestimation of expenses and/or underestimation of revenue during budget setting'.   (CIMA *Official Terminology*)

Participation in budgeting allows managers scope for overestimating costs (or underestimating income) in budgets, of introducing slack. There are several **reasons why** managers may do this.

- Managers will **'look good'** if actual costs are less than budgeted costs and their bonuses may even depend on it. And of course, they would not wish to be blamed for overspending.

- They may believe that budget padding is necessary so as to **cover unforeseen events** or they may fear that some expense has been forgotten in the budget.

- A **bigger budget** may be perceived as **indicating greater importance**.

Senior management can attempt to minimise slack by:

- Using a **range of performance measures** for assessment purposes (not just the achievement of budget targets)

- Imposing **pressure** on the budget holder by, for example, not allowing for any inflationary increase in the following year's budget

- Using a **balanced scorecard approach minimises opportunities for padding**

3.4.4 Undermining the implementation

Problems can also arise when a **budget is implemented.**

(a)   Managers might put in **only just enough effort** to achieve budget targets, without trying to beat targets.

(b)   A formal budget might **encourage rigidity and discourage flexibility** in operational decision making.

(c)   **Short-term planning** in a budget can **draw attention away from the longer term consequences of decisions.**

(d)   Managers might tolerate **slapdash and inaccurate methods of recording**, classifying and codifying actual costs.

(e)   **Co-operation and communication** between managers might be **minimal**. Managers may pursue their own objectives at the expense of wider organisational aims.

(f)   Managers will often try to make sure that they **spend up to their full budget allowance**, and do not overspend, so that they will not be accused of having asked for too much spending allowance in the first place.

(g)   Data is **filtered** so that the information system **reports good performance** and **suppresses evidence of poor performance**.

(h)   Managers collaborate to **flout organisational guidelines**.

(i)   Excessive emphasis is placed on **quantifiable data** and **not enough attention** is paid to **non-quantifiable data**.

3.5 Budgets as targets

Hopwood identified three different levels of significance for budgets as targets.

Supervisory style	Hopwood says...
Budget-constrained	'The manager's performance is primarily evaluated upon the basis of his ability to **continually meet the budget** on a short-term basis.'
Profit-conscious	'The manager's performance is evaluated on the basis of his ability to **increase the general effectiveness** of his unit's operations in relation to the long-term purposes of the organisation.'
Non-accounting	'The budgetary information plays a **relatively unimportant** part in the superior's evaluation of the manager's performance.'

In addition if budgets are to be treated as significant targets, how difficult should the targets be?

How might people react to targets of differing degrees of difficulty in achievement?

(a)   There is likely to be a **demotivating** effect where an **ideal** standard of performance is set, because **adverse efficiency variances** will always be reported.

(b)   A **low standard** of efficiency is also demotivating, because there is **no sense of achievement** in attaining the required standards: targets will be achieved easily, and there will be no impetus for employees to try harder to do better than this.

(c)   A budgeted level of attainment could be '**normal**': that is, the same as the level that has been achieved in the past. Arguably, this level will be **too low**. It might **encourage budget slack**.

Question 7.3   Style of evaluation

Learning outcome A1(b)

Hopwood summarised the effects of the three styles of evaluation in a table with the following headings and categories.

	Style of evaluation	
Non-accounting	*Profit-conscious*	*Budget-constrained*

Manipulation of accounting reports
Job-related tension
Involvement with costs

(a)   Which style or styles led to extensive manipulation of accounting reports?
(b)   Which style or styles created a medium level of job-related tension?
(c)   Which style or styles encouraged managers to be greatly concerned about costs?

Question 7.4   Budget comparisons

Learning outcome A1(b)

What is a possible solution to reconciling targets and forecasts?

3.6 Beyond budgeting

Beyond budgeting is designed to overcome the problems of budgeting discussed above. Managers prepare **rolling plans,** but for cash forecasting, not cost control. Beyond budgeting requires managerial authority to be devolved and gives managers goals linked to benchmarks based on ideal performance, peers, rivals and earlier periods. These forces managers to consider current and future opportunities and threats, particularly where monthly forecasts operate with performance measures based on non-financial 'value drivers". This should bring the following **benefits**.

- Beyond budgeting results in **performance targets based on competitive success**. Goals are agreed via reference to external benchmarks as opposed to internally-negotiated fixed targets.

- It **motivates** people by giving them challenges, responsibilities and clear values as guidelines. **Rewards are team-based**.

- It **devolves performance responsibilities to operational management** who are closer to the external situation, leading to a more rapid response to changing market needs.

- The **measures** used are **more flexible,** key ratios rather than detailed line-by-line budgets.

- It assists in developing a **customer orientation**, **faster response times** and **greater innovation**.

- It creates **transparent and open information systems** throughout the organisation, which should provide fast, open and distributed information to facilitate control at all levels.

CASE STUDY

The CIMA/ICAEW report *Better Budgeting* suggested that budgeting still adds value in most organisations. Most importantly it provides an overall framework of control without which it would be impossible to manage, although budgeting needs to be seen in the context of keeping an eye on the potential risks and changes in the environment. Budgets are seen as contributing significantly to strategy implementation, risk management and resource allocation.

Other important uses of budgets include providing the opportunity to discuss the factors influencing the performance of the business with staff in other departments of the organisation.

The report found that a significant problem that many managers have is linking financial data with non-financial data in a cause and effect relationship. Although technology has a number of very significant benefits, it is not without drawbacks; it encourages centralisation and produces excessive detail.

Section summary

Organisational structure determines responsibility and hence **budget centres**. If managers are to be held accountable for expenditure, they have to be able to **control it**.

Participation is sometimes seen as the way to **better budgeting** and **motivation**. However the effectiveness depends on management commitment and expertise, and there is always the temptation to introduce budgetary slack.

4 Management accounting techniques

Introduction

In this section we see how the criticisms made of traditional management accounting methods have meant that they have become less significant as means of maintaining effective management control. The balanced scorecard has been one response to these criticisms.

4.1 Cost accounting methods

Traditional cost accounting traces raw materials to various production stages via WIP, to the next stage and finally to finished goods, resulting in thousands of transaction entries. With just-in-time systems, production flows through the factory on a continual basis with near-zero inventories and very low batch sizes and so such transaction entries become **needlessly complicated and uninformative**. Cost accounting and recording systems can therefore be **greatly simplified in the modern environment**. **Backflush costing** is one possible approach.

4.1.1 Timing

As we will see later in this chapter, the **cost of a product is substantially determined when it is being designed**, not when it is in production. The materials that will be used, the machines and labour required, are largely determined at the design stage. In the car industry, 85% of all future product costs are determined by the end of the testing stage. **Management accountants**, however, **continue to direct their efforts to the production stage**.

4.1.2 Controllability

Only a small proportion of 'direct costs' are genuinely controllable in the short term. Controllable direct costs are about 10% of total costs, whereas controllable overhead costs represent about 27%. The reason why, in spite of this, accountants do not devote nearly three times as much effort to analysing overhead costs as they devote to direct costs may be because overheads are more difficult to measure.

4.1.3 Different assets

Traditional measures cannot always deal with assets other than tangible assets, such as knowledge-based assets. Systems need to be able to decide which **resources drive value**, determine how **knowledge-based assets help the organisation** determine its **strategic value** and develop **performance indicators** that will help determine **resource allocation** and **further strategic development**. This should link with risk management of those assets, designed to minimise the risk of **knowledge loss** by, for example, spreading knowledge more widely over the organisation.

4.1.4 Customers

Many costs are driven by customers (delivery costs, discounts, after-sales service and so on), but **conventional cost accounting does not recognise this**. Companies may be trading with certain customers at a loss but not realise it because costs are not analysed in a way that would reveal it.

4.2 Cost reporting

Costs are generally reported in a way that reflects organisational structure, notably on a **functional basis** ('production costs', 'administration overheads'). The **things that businesses** do, however, are '**processes**' that **cut across functional boundaries**. Traditional management accounting systems do not recognise this.

4.3 Absorption costing

The traditional methods of costing products have been largely based on **absorption costing** with direct labour hour recovery rates. These methods are often inappropriate in the modern environment when many processes are not labour intensive, but others are technology-based or use lots of space or consume significant working capital. Traditional absorption costing can also encourage businesses to produce more output to reduce unit costs and/or over recover overhead. This can lead to excess inventory being held, also the possibility of unwanted products. **Activity-based costing** provides a better method of allocating costs, based on cause and effect relationships, but may be expensive to implement.

4.4 Standard costing

Doubts about the suitability in the modern business environment of both the general philosophy and the detailed operation of standard costing have arisen. Standard costing is most appropriate in a large-scale production manufacturing environment with an emphasis on per unit costs. It is less appropriate when flexibility and customisation are key features, or often where labour service is the key element.

Scrap can also be a problem. If a scrap factor is included in standard costs, then the supervisor may aim to achieve an actual scrap level equal to the standard level, rather than concentrating reducing scrap to zero.

4.5 Performance measures

Much of the output of traditional management accounting consists of **short-term financial performance measures such as costs**, variances and so on. Many of these are **produced too long after the event** and are **too narrowly focused**. Expenditure cannot just **be evaluated on purely financial grounds**. The **non-financial benefits** can be extremely important (for example better product quality) and not all of the financial benefits are easily quantified (for example shorter set-up times, improved capacity utilisation).

Traditional management accounting performance measures can **produce the wrong type of response.**

Measurement	Response	Consequence of action
Purchase price variance	Buy in greater bulk to reduce unit price	Excess inventory Higher holding costs Quality and reliability of delivery times ignored
Labour efficiency variance	Encourage greater output	Possibly excess inventory of the wrong products
Machine utilisation	Encourage more running time	Possibly excess inventory of the wrong products

Measurement	Response	Consequence of action
Cost of scrap	Rework items to reduce scrap	Production flow held up by re-working
Cost centre reporting	Management focus is on cost centre activities, not overheads	Lack of attention to activities where cost reduction possibilities might exist

4.6 Investment appraisal

You will have studied investment appraisal at managerial level. BPP's F3 *Financial Strategy* **text covers these methods in detail.**

Here we are interested in investment appraisal as a control technique designed to ensure that an organisation with finite resources is investing them in the **best project**.

Judged as a financial control, investment appraisal has the limitations that many of the figures used are **estimates** of an uncertain future. Investment appraisal techniques often do not cope well with **multistage decisions or unusual patterns of cash flows** (eg multi-stage investment payments).

In addition, the decision may be influenced by the **availability of finance** or the need for the project to be profitable within a **certain timeframe**. Decisions need to be compatible with **strategic considerations** such as the **need to diversify**. Investment appraisal methods thus need to be supplemented by measures reflecting strategic considerations such as **value chain analysis** or **competitive advantage analysis**.

4.7 Transfer pricing

You will also have covered transfer pricing before, and again the subject is covered in detail in *Financial Strategy*.

As a means of control, the main concern is reconciling the need for transfer prices to be set at an **appropriate level to assess performance**, with the need for **goal congruence** within the organisation. Ideally, pricing levels should be set at a level to avoid the complications and loss of resources of departments dealing unnecessarily with external sources rather than with internal 'suppliers'.

Transfer pricing may also be a significant issue if one division of a company makes an **investment** that benefits all the other divisions.

A **transactions cost approach**, taking into account costs associated with setting and administering the transfer price, and also time commitments and obligations, is an appropriate way of determining which transactions should take place within an organisation, and which transactions should be with the outside world.

4.8 Balanced scorecard

The **balanced scorecard**, which you encountered in your earlier studies, is a way of integrating the traditional financial indicators with non-financial measures such as operational performance quality, customer satisfaction and staff potential. It is balanced in the sense that managers are required to think in terms of all four perspectives, to prevent improvements being made in one area at the expense of another.

They can be as effective as **financial measures as indicators of long-term profitability**, control mechanisms, business trends or benchmarks against other organisations. They can act as **targets** for employees, and will be more effective if linked to the organisation's reward schemes. The range of perspectives they provide can be a **better link** with strategy than a few financial measures.

Perspective	Addresses	Examples
Customer	Measures relating to what actually matters to customers (time, quality, performance of product)	• Customer complaints • On-time deliveries
Internal business	Measures relating to the business processes that have the greatest impact on customer satisfaction (quality, employee skills)	• Average set-up time • Quality control rejects
Innovation and learning	Measures to assess the organisation's capacity to maintain its competitive position through the acquisition of new skills/development of new products	• Labour turnover rate • % of revenue generated by new products
Financial	Measures that consider the organisation from the shareholders' viewpoint	• Return on capital employed • Earnings per share

4.8.1 Problems of balanced scorecard

However as a control measure, the balanced scorecard has certain limitations:

(a) Managers may have **difficulty understanding** some of the measures used. Non-finance specialists may have difficulty understanding the financial measures and vice-versa.

(b) It may be **difficult to gain an overall impression** of the results provided and hence be able to initiate control action based on those results. There may simply be too many measures; some measures (investment expenditure and cost control) may conflict; it may be difficult to integrate the results of the financial and non-financial measure

(c) Research suggests that in many companies non-financial measures are seen as from **separate from**, **not integrated with**, financial measures. External stakeholders place most emphasis on financial indicators, and therefore these have most impact upon on internal decisions. Non-financial indicators are used by many companies as a subsidiary internal indicator.

Exam alert

Nevertheless the balanced scorecard does provide a variety of performance measures that can be used as suggested controls in different scenarios.

CASE STUDY

An alternative model to the Balanced Scorecard is the Business Excellence model developed by the European Foundation for Quality Management.

The EFQM Excellence Model is a framework for assessing organisations for the European Quality Award. It can also be used practically in the following ways:

• As a tool for **self-assessment**
• As a way to **benchmark** with other organisations
• As a guide to identify areas for **improvement**
• As the basis for a common **vocabulary** and a way of thinking
• As a **structure** for the organisation's management system

The Model is based on nine criteria. Five of these are 'enablers' and four are 'results'. The 'enabler' criteria cover what an organisation does. The 'results' criteria cover what an organisation achieves. 'Results' are caused by 'enablers' and 'enablers' are improved using feedback from 'results'. In other words:

'Excellent results with respect to Performance, Customers, People and Society are achieved through Leadership driving Policy and Strategy, that is delivered through People, Partnerships and Resources, and Processes.'

The model has been summarised in a diagram:

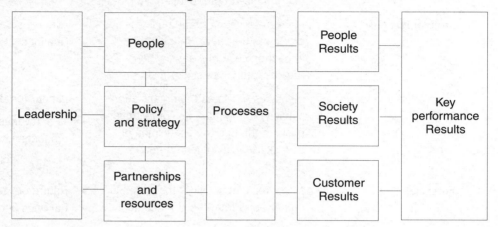

Exam skills

In the exam you may be asked to criticise various traditional measures that the organisation is using, and suggest as improvements the techniques we shall cover in the next section.

4.9 Environmental reporting

Environmental reporting focuses on the costs connected with the environmental impact of an organisation's activities, such as taking action to **reduce emissions, improving energy efficiency**, and using more **environmentally-friendly packaging**.

4.9.1 Full cost accounting

KEY TERM

FULL COST ACCOUNTING (FCA) is at its simplest a system that allows current accounting and economic numbers to incorporate all potential/actual costs and benefits into the equation including environmental (and perhaps social) externalities to get the prices right. Bebbington, Gray, Hibbitt and Kirk – FCA: An Agenda for Action (published by ACCA).

Full cost accounting is a method of classifying different kinds of environmental costs.

The Bebbington et al report recommends organisations report costs increasingly fully by using a number of tiers.

Tier 0	Usual costs	Basic capital and revenue costs
Tier 1	Hidden costs	Costs usually included as overheads eg costs of safety, costs of measurement and costs of prevention such as equipment and employee training
Tier 2	Liability costs	Contingent liability costs eg fines or remedial action such as cleanup costs
Tier 3	Less tangible costs	Costs of poor environmental management eg loss of goodwill of customers and suppliers, reputation risk
Tier 4	Environment focused costs	Costs that ensure that project has zero environmental effect

Section summary

Traditional management accounting methods have been seen as inadequate for a modern business environment that focuses on marketing, customer service, employee involvement and total quality, and for modern industry using AMT.

5 Developments in management accounting

Introduction

In this section we shall look at changes in the business environment and how management accounting techniques have been developed in response to them. Many are grouped around the concept of World-Class Manufacturing (WCM), attempting to sustain competitive advantage in an atmosphere of strategic cost reduction. Control systems are modified in line with this aim.

5.1 Just in time (JIT)

JIT encompasses a **commitment to continuous improvement** and the **search for excellence** in the design and operation of the production management system.

KEY TERMS

JUST-IN-TIME **(JIT)** is 'A system whose objective is to produce or to procure products or components as they are required by a customer or for use, rather than for stock. A JIT system is a 'pull' system, which responds to demand, in contrast to a 'push' system, in which stocks act as buffers between the different elements of the system, such as purchasing, production and sales.'

JUST-IN-TIME PRODUCTION is 'A system which is driven by demand for finished products whereby each component on a production line is produced only when needed for the next stage'.

JUST-IN-TIME PURCHASING is 'A system in which material purchases are contracted so that the receipt and usage of material, to the maximum extent possible, coincide'.

(CIMA *Official Terminology*)

The implications of JIT for the management accounting systems is that they have to reorganised to **include or highlight** items that are seen as **costs** under JIT but are not included in traditional systems. Systems must highlight **excessive inventory levels, machinery setups and long lead times.** The changes in organisation resulting from JIT such as the regroupings of workings will also result in changes in accounting systems to adjust to new demands and changed sources of information.

5.2 Total quality management

KEY TERM

TOTAL QUALITY MANAGEMENT (TQM) is the process of applying a zero defects philosophy to the management of all resources and relationships within an organisation as a means of developing and sustaining a culture of continuous improvement which focuses on meeting customers' expectations.

Mark Lee Inman listed 'eight requirements of quality', which could be seen as the **characteristics of total quality management programmes**.

(a)   Organisation wide there must be acceptance that the only thing that matters is the **customer**.

(b)   There should be recognition of the **all-pervasive nature of the customer-supplier relationship**, including internal customers; passing sub-standard material to another division is not satisfactory

(c)   Instead of relying on inspection to a predefined level of quality, the **cause of the defect** in the first place should be prevented.

(d)   Each employee or group of employees must be **personally responsible** for defect-free production or service in their domain.

(e)   There should be a move away from 'acceptable' quality levels. **Any level of defects** must be **unacceptable**.

(f)   All departments should **try obsessively to get things right first time**; this applies to misdirected phone calls and typing errors as much as to production.

(g)   **Quality certification programmes** should be introduced.

(h)   The **cost of poor quality** should be **emphasised**; good quality generates savings.

Key costs in a TQM system include:

(a)   **Conformance costs**, those costs incurred to **prevent** problems and to **appraise** quality.

(b)   **Non-conformance costs, internal failures** such as waste, and **external failures** selling faulty goods to customers and as a result suffering claims from customers because products or services supplied have been faulty. The emphasis will be on minimising or (preferably) eliminating non-conformance costs as these tend to be much larger than conformance costs.

Total quality management and continuous improvement very much tie in with ideas in risk management, the idea of a **continual review** of what went wrong and the organisations responding to this review.

5.3 Lean management accounting

Lean management accounting has a lot in common with the other techniques outlined above. Its emphasis is on the **elimination of waste** and **continuous improvement**. Customer demand determines the flow of products or services, and emphasis is on processes and value streams rather than departments.

In a lean system, management accounting systems need to be refocused to provide the information necessary to drive improvement, and **highlight waste**. Distortions such as reduced unit costs arising from producing large batches at a time need to be removed.

5.4 Life cycle costing

Life cycle costing tracks and accumulates actual costs and revenues attributable to each product or project over the entire product/project life cycle. The **total profitability** of any given product/project can therefore be determined.

Traditional management accounting systems usually total **all non-production costs** and record them as a **period expense. Using life cycle costing** such costs are **traced to individual products over complete life cycles**.

Some organisations find that approximately **90% of a product's life cycle cost is determined by decisions made early within the cycle** at the design stage. Life cycle costing is therefore particularly suited to such organisations and products, monitoring spending and commitments to spend during the early stages of a product's life cycle.

In order to compete effectively in today's competitive market, organisations need to **redesign continually their products** with the result that **product life cycles** have become much **shorter**. The **planning, design and development stages of a product's cycle** are therefore **critical to an organisation's cost management process**. Cost reduction at this stage of a product's life cycle, rather than during the production process, is one of the most important ways of reducing product cost.

5.4.1 Advantages of life cycle costing

The life cycle costing approach emphasises the **importance of development and design costs** by placing them in the context of the product's whole history. This may incline organisations away from under-expenditure **initially on design and development** that results in problems later. The approach deals well with other costs that may vary over a product's life cycle, notably advertising. The **life cycle approach** also highlights the importance of time to market; the success of a product may depend on whether it gets to market quicker than rivals.

5.4.2 Problems of life cycle costing

The biggest issue is **estimating product life costs** over a **number of years** and how realistic they will be in the light of the information available at the start of its life. When circumstances change, life cycle costs will have to change and management accounting systems may not be **flexible** enough to be able to cope with that. **Customer information**, though difficult to obtain, may also be important as customers may be prepared to pay a higher selling price for a product that has lower lifetime costs.

5.5 Target costing

Target costing requires managers to change the way they think about the relationship between cost, price and profit.

(a) The **traditional approach** is to **develop a product, determine the expected standard production cost** of that product and **then set a selling price** (probably based on cost) with a resulting profit or loss. Costs are controlled through variance analysis at monthly intervals.

(b) The **target costing approach** is to develop a **product concept** and the primary specifications for performance and design and then to **determine the price customers would be willing to pay** for that concept. The **desired profit margin is deducted from the price** leaving a figure that **represents total cost**. This is the target cost and the product must be capable of being produced for this amount otherwise the product will not be manufactured. **During the product's life the target cost** will **constantly be reduced** so that the **price can fall. Continuous cost reduction techniques** must therefore be employed.

5.5.1 Advantages of target costing

The **biggest advantage** of **target costing** is that it brings in market information into the management accounting system rather than the accounting system being internally focused. It also encourages **continual product** and **production improvements** and provides a **structured approach** for **dealing with those improvements**.

5.5.2 Problems of target costing

The most significant problem is **setting a target**, as it will be very difficult to forecast the market price. It will partly depend on **assumptions** made about the future market situation including **behaviour of competitors,** and **technological and customer preferences.**

A number of other problems may undermine the use of target costing as a means of control. These include whether to use one target cost or several target costs, what costs to include and on **what level of production** to base the target.

5.6 Kaizen

KEY TERM

KAIZEN is a Japanese term for continuous improvement in all aspects of an entity's performance at every level.

(CIMA Official Terminology)

The Kaizen method is applied during the **production process** when it is difficult to make really big changes. Kaizen focuses on the key elements of operations, **production**, **purchasing** and **distribution**. Kaizen aims to achieve a **specified cost reduction**, but to do so through **continuous improvements** rather than one-off changes.

Though managers may seek to establish the targets, **employees** working in the **production process** will ensure that those targets are met. The logic of this approach is that those involved in production will be best able to see how to achieve the necessary economies effectively but with minimum disruption. Often these targets will be achieved in **collaboration with suppliers**.

5.7 Transaction cost economics

Transaction cost economics is particularly relevant for determining transfer prices, the charging mechanism for inter-company transactions, which you will have covered in your *Financial Strategy* studies. It focuses on costs involved in the transaction such as negotiation, administration, time commitments and obligations.

5.8 Backflush costing

The pooling of costs can be done using backflush costing. Backflush costing can significantly reduce the detailed work carried out by the accounting department. Use of JIT means that all the costing entries are made at virtually the same moment. Therefore under backflush costing costs will be **calculated and charged when the product is sold,** or when it is **transferred to the finished goods store**. This eliminates the need for recording of materials used and work in progress. The data need not be reported in detail, and inaccuracies in inventory valuation will not be a big issue because inventory is being kept to a minimum.

Section summary

Management accountants have responded to developments such as **JIT, TQM and lean management accounting** by using techniques such as **target costing**, **lifecycle costing** and **Kaizen.**

---

6 The management accounting function

Introduction

We end this chapter by looking at what the management accounting function should seek to achieve and how its performance should be measured.

6.1 Role of the management accounting function

Clearly the information that the accounting function will provide covers all areas and includes information aiding **planning, control and decision-making, resource usage and asset security.** The management accounting function's role is seen more as providing **complex analysis and information to support** the business, since much routine work is now done on the computer. The computer has also meant that it is easier to pass accounting information to non-financial managers. In future management accountants will spend time **explaining links between various sources of information**, and providing information tailored to particular decisions, such as risk management.

6.2 Defining objectives of the accounting function

This may involve discussions with the function's customers. The overall objective is the provision of a quality service but it will be possible to break down this objective into a number of sub-objectives.

Sub-objective	Detail
The provision of good information	This requires supplying information that is **relevant** to the needs of the users (which involves identifying the user, getting the purpose right and getting the volume right), that is **accurate** within their needs, that **inspires their confidence** (so it should not be out-of-date, badly presented or taken from an unreliable source), that is **timely** (it must be in the right place by the right time) and that is **appropriately communicated** (since it will lose its value if it is not clearly communicated to the user in a suitable format and through a suitable medium).
The provision of a value-for-money service	User departments are likely to be charged in some way for the management accounting service and are therefore likely to require that the **charge incurred is reflected in the level of service and the quality of information provided.**
The availability of informed personnel	Users will require management accounting staff to be available to **answer queries and resolve problems** as and when required.
Flexibility	The management accounting function should be flexible **in its response to user requests** for information and reports.

6.3 Establishing activities

Once the objectives have been defined, the activities that the function should carry out to achieve its objectives must be established. The function must be sufficiently organised and staffed, for example, to ensure that reports are received on time and that queries can be answered promptly.

6.4 Identifying measures

Appropriate measures of output can then be established on the basis of the objectives and activities identified. There should be enough to provide **relevant indicators**, on a **timely** basis and in a **readily understood form**. Suitable **specific performance measures** might be as follows.

(a) **Relating to the provision of good information**, such as number of complaints from users about accuracy/timeliness and so on of reports and information

(b) **Relating to value for money**, such as cost of similar service provided by specialist contractor or cost of service provided by function in similar organisation

(c) **Relating to the availability of informed persons**, such as proportion of the time the staff mix and numbers are within required limits or proportion of telephone calls answered within, say, eight rings

(d) **Relating to flexibility**, such as number of ad-hoc reports/requests for information issued within pre-set time limit

(e) **Ratings provided from user satisfaction surveys** would provide extremely useful measures of performance

Exam alert

You may be asked in the exam to look critically at the work that the accounting department is doing, to see if it is operating at maximum efficiency.

Section summary

The management accounting function's role as an information provider has developed with increased computerisation. In order to measure its performance effectively, clear understanding is needed of its **objectives** and **activities**, and appropriate **measures** developed based on these.

Chapter Roundup

- ✓ Management accounting developed from cost accounting, for **scorekeeping**, **directing management attention** and **problem solving**. It has since branched out into behavioural aspects.

- ✓ A management accounting system comprises **people**, **accounting knowledge**, **records**, **processes**, **mathematical techniques**, and **reports**: inputs, processes and outputs. It is used for strategic decision making, performance measurement, operational control and costing.

- ✓ Organisational structure determines responsibility and hence **budget centres**. If managers are to be held accountable for expenditure they have to be able to **control** it.

- ✓ **Participation** is sometimes seen as the way to **better budgeting** and **motivation**. However the effectiveness depends on management commitment and expertise, and there is always the temptation to introduce budgetary slack.

- ✓ **Traditional management accounting methods** have been seen as inadequate for a modern business environment that focuses on marketing, customer service, employee involvement and total quality, and for modern industry using AMT.

- ✓ Management accountants have responded to developments such as **JIT**, **TQM** and **lean management accounting** by using techniques such as **target costing**, **lifecycle costing** and **Kaizen**.

- ✓ The management accounting function's role as an information provider has developed with increased computerisation. In order to measure its performance effectively, clear understanding is needed of its **objectives** and **activities**, and appropriate **measures** developed based on these.

Quick Quiz

1   What are the main uses of a management accounting control system?

2   Fill in the blank

.... is the process by which managers ensure that resources are obtained and used effectively and efficiently in the accomplishment of the organisation's objectives.

3   Over what six dimensions should performance evaluation take place in the service sector?

4   Fill in the blanks.

Managers should be held .... only for those costs they can ....

5   Why should user departments be charged for services?

6   Fill in the blank.

Where a manager's performance is primarily evaluated on the basis of his or her ability to continually meet the budget on a short term basis this is known as ....

What other styles are there?

7   What main steps are involved in measuring the performance of the accounts department?

8   Match the term with the description

A   Just-in-time
B   Total quality management
C   Target costing
D   Transaction cost economics

(i)   Sustaining a culture of continuous improvement

(ii)   Developing a product concept and determining the price customers would be willing to pay for that concept

(iii)   Aiming to produce goods when required by customer or for use

(iv)   Focusing on costs such as negotiation, administration, time commitments and obligation

Answers to Quick Quiz

1   • Score keeping
    • Problem-solving
    • Attention-directing

2   **Management control** is the process by which managers ensure that resources are obtained and used effectively and efficiently in the accomplishment of the organisation's objectives.

3   • Flexibility   • Excellence
    • Innovation   • Financial performance
    • Resource utilisation   • Competitiveness

4   Managers should be held **responsible** only for those costs they can **control**.

5   User departments should be charged for services to encourage them to work efficiently and to establish that the service department is itself operating efficiently.

6   Where a manager's performance is primarily evaluated on the basis of his or her ability to continually meet the budget on a short term basis this is known as **budgeted–constrained**.

    Other styles are profit-conscious and non-accounting.

7   (a)   Define role
    (b)   Define formal objectives
    (c)   Ascertain activities each section does
    (d)   Identify appropriate measures
    (e)   Select suitable basis of comparison

8   A(iii); B(i); C(ii); D(iv)

Answers to Questions

7.1 Good management accounting information

All good information should have the following features.

(a) It should be **relevant** to the user's needs.
(b) It should be **accurate** within the user's needs.
(c) It should inspire the user's **confidence**.
(d) It should be **timely**.
(e) It should be **appropriately communicated**.
(f) It should be **cost-effective**.

We may further identify features that pertain particularly to management accounting information.

(a) It is generally **forward-looking**.
(b) It can be **financial or non-financial, quantitative or qualitative**.
(c) It should be **free from bias**.
(d) It is often **comparative**.

7.2 Responsibility accounting

(a) Objectives are often unclear, so there is no obvious link between inputs and outputs. Responsibility is then hard to define.

(b) Budget holders may have to monitor costs rather than control them. For example, budget holders in a hospital are often not medical staff but medical decisions control the extent to which costs are incurred.

(c) The value for money objective of effectiveness may not be measurable in money terms.

7.3 Style of evaluation

(a) Budget-constrained
(b) Non-accounting and profit-conscious
(c) Profit-conscious and budget-constrained

7.4 Budget comparisons

The solution normally suggested is to have two budgets:

(a) A budget for planning and decision making based on reasonable **expectations**; and

(b) An '**aspirations budget**', for motivational purposes, with more difficult targets of performance (ie targets of an intermediate level of difficulty).

How satisfactory do you think this proposal is?

Now try these questions from the Exam Question Bank	Number	Level	Marks	Time
	Q10	Examination	25	45 mins
	Q11	Examination	25	45 mins

MANAGEMENT OF FINANCIAL RISK

Part C

FINANCIAL RISK MANAGEMENT

In this chapter we reintroduce financial risk that we looked at first in Chapter 1. We start off by reminding you of the main financial risks.

In Section 2 we examine the ways in which risks can be assessed. You will have covered many of the calculations and techniques in your earlier studies. Remember that everything you learnt before Strategic level is examinable; however where calculations do appear, the question will also contain a significant written element as well.

In Section 3 we introduce the various ways financial risks are managed, looking at the work of the treasury function and the important policies of diversification and hedging. In Section 4 we look at financial risk disclosures, focusing particularly on the requirements of IASs 32 and 39, and IFRS 7. As you will see, it is necessary to consider the risks linked with disclosures, and ensure that these too are effectively managed.

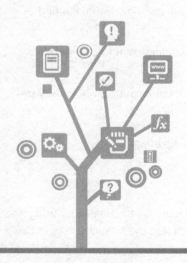

topic list	learning outcomes	syllabus references	ability required
1 Financial risks	D1(a)	D1(i),(ii)	evaluation
2 Financial risk analysis	D1(a)	D1(iii)	evaluation
3 Financial risk management	D2(a),(b),(d)	D2(ii),(iii),(viii)	evaluation
4 Financial risk disclosure	D2(a),(b),(d)	D2(vi),(vii)	evaluation

1 Financial risks

Introduction

In this section we review the main risks connected with sources of finance and international activity that businesses face.

1.1 Financing and liquidity risks

1.1.1 Financing risks

There are various risks associated with sources of finance:

- Long-term sources of finance **being unavailable or ceasing to be available**

- Taking on commitments **without proper authorisation**

- Taking on **excessive commitments to paying interest** that the company is unable to fulfil

- Having to **repay multiple sources of debt finance** around the same time

- Being **unable to fulfil other commitments** associated with a loan

- Being stuck with the wrong sort of debt (**floating rate debt** in a period when **interest rates are rising, fixed rate debt** in a period when **interest rates are falling**)

- **Excessive use of short-term finance** to support investments that will not yield returns until the long-term

- **Ceding of control to providers of finance** (for example banks demanding charges over assets or specifying gearing levels that the company must fulfil)

The **attitudes to risk** of the board and major finance providers will impact significantly on how risky the company's financial structure is.

These risks are obviously also at the heart of Paper F3 *Financial Strategy*.

Exam alert

Many companies have tried over time to reduce their cost of capital and increase their value by using debt as a larger part of their long-term finance. The credit crunch has demonstrated the financial risks of doing this.

1.1.2 Liquidity risks

You have covered liquidity risks in your earlier studies, and hopefully should remember the key indicators of liquidity problems (current and quick ratios and turnover periods for receivables, payables and inventory).

To recap briefly, if a business suddenly finds that it is **unable to cover or renew** its **short-term liabilities** (for example, if the bank suspends its overdraft facilities), there will be a **danger of insolvency** if it cannot convert enough of its current assets into cash quickly.

Current liabilities are often a cheap method of finance (trade payables do not usually carry an interest cost). Businesses may therefore consider that, in the interest of higher profits, it is worth accepting some risk of insolvency by increasing current liabilities, taking the maximum credit possible from suppliers.

1.1.3 Cash flow risks

Cashflow risks relate to the **volatility of a firm's day-to-day operating cash flows**. A key risk is having insufficient cash available because cash inflows have been unexpectedly low, perhaps due to delayed receipts from customers. If for example a firm has had a very large order, and the customer fails to pay promptly, the firm may not be able to delay payment to its supplier in the same way.

1.2 Credit risks

KEY TERM

CREDIT RISKS are financial risks associated with the possibility of default by a counterparty.

The most common type of credit risk is when customers fail to pay for goods that they have been supplied on credit.

A business can also be vulnerable to the credit risks of other firms with which it is heavily connected. A business may suffer losses as a result of a key supplier or partner in a joint venture having difficulty accessing credit to continue trading.

1.3 Market risks

KEY TERM

MARKET RISKS are the financial risks of possible losses due to changes in market prices or rates. They include:

- **Interest rate changes**

- **Exchange rate changes,** where the business has agreed to undertake a transaction in the future in a foreign currency

- **Commodity price changes**, particularly where the commodity is intrinsic to operations (such as oil for a transport company)

- **Equity price changes**, changes in the price of shares or financial instruments (especially for companies that use these as prime sources of finance, for example insurance and pension companies).

1.4 Foreign investment risks

Risks here are linked to the strategies of setting up presences overseas or deciding to participate in global markets.

1.4.1 Foreign exchange – economic risk

Economic risk refers to the effect of exchange rate movements on the **international competitiveness of a company**. For example, a UK company might use raw materials which are priced in US dollars, but export its products mainly within the European Union. A depreciation of sterling against the dollar or an appreciation of sterling against other EU currencies will both erode the competitiveness of the company.

1.4.2 Political risk

A multinational can face risks of **economic** or **political measures** being taken by governments, affecting the operations of its subsidiaries abroad. Risks include nationalisation, sanctions, civil war or political instability.

1.5 Fraud risks

1.5.1 Teeming and lading

This occurs when an employee, most probably a cashier has the chance to misappropriate payments from customers or to suppliers.

(a) Cash received by the company is '**borrowed**' by the **cashier** rather than being kept as petty cash or banked.

(b) When the cashier knows that a **reconciliation** is to be performed, or audit visit planned, the cashier **pays the money back** so that everything appears satisfactory at that point, but after the audit the teeming and lading starts again.

Surprise visits by auditors and **independent checking** of cash balances should discourage this fraud.

Another common fraud may arise when one employee has sole control of the sales ledger and recording customers' cheques.

(a) The employee **pays cheques** into a **separate bank account**, either by forged endorsement or by opening an account in a name similar to the employer's.

(b) The employee has to **allocate cheques** or **cash received** from other customers against the account of the customer whose payment was misappropriated. This prevents other staff from asking why the account is still overdue or from sending statements etc to the customers. However, the misallocation has to continue as long as the money is missing.

This fraud, therefore, never really stops. It can be detected by **independent verification** of receivables' balances (eg by circularisation) and by **looking at unallocated payments**, if the sales ledger is organised to show this. In addition, sending out **itemised monthly statements** to debtors should act as a deterrent.

1.5.2 Manipulation of accounts

While **employee fraud** is usually undertaken purely for the employee's financial gain, **management fraud** is often undertaken to **improve** the company's apparent **performance**, to **reduce tax liabilities** or to **improve managers' promotion prospects**. Managers are often in a position to override internal controls and to intimidate their subordinates into collusion or turning a blind eye. This makes such frauds difficult to detect.

This clash of interest between loyalty to an employer and professional integrity can be difficult to resolve. Management manipulation of results often comes to light after a takeover or on a change of internal audit staff or practices. Its consequences can be far reaching for the employing company in **damaging its reputation** or because it **results in legal action**. Because management usually has access to much larger sums of money than more lowly employees, the financial loss to the company can be immense.

1.5.3 Advance fee fraud

This type of fraud involves the fraudster taking a fee or deposit up-front, promising to **deliver in the future** goods and services that never materialise.

Many companies have been **exposed to such frauds** from international sources. In recent years, for example, the highest incidence of such fraud led to the Central Bank of Nigeria publishing warnings around the world. Hopefully, wide publicity about the details of such fraud schemes will mean that fewer such frauds will be perpetrated successfully.

CASE STUDY

Advance fee fraud in Nigeria

The advance fee fraud is normally perpetrated by sending a letter that promises to transfer million of US dollars to the addressee's bank account. In order to gain access to the funds, the addressee is requested to assist in paying various 'taxes' and 'fees' that will allow the funds to be processed. The fraudsters often make use of fake Government, Central Bank and Nigerian National Petroleum Corporation documents and go to considerable lengths to give the scam the appearance of a legitimate offer. They request confidentiality about the transaction.

The gathering of advance fees, made up of supposed legal fees, registration fees, VAT and so on, is the actual objective of the scam.

Two recent variants of the scam have been reported. The first, normally directed at religious and charitable organisations, is the request for fees to process bogus inheritances from a will. The second is an offer to use chemicals to transform paper into US dollar bills with the proceeds being shared by both parties.

1.5.4 Pyramid scheme frauds

Pyramid scheme frauds can take various forms. The schemes are based on the idea that the scope of the scheme **continually widens to involve more people**. People (or firms) newly recruited to the scheme may be **induced to invest money** that is not actually invested but goes towards paying returns to others already in the scheme. While the membership of the scheme multiplies, it appears that those in the scheme cannot lose.

1.6 Accounting risks

There are various risks associated with the requirements to produce accounts that **fairly reflect financial risks**. These risks are particularly significant if the business has financial instruments that are accounted for in accordance with the requirements of IASs 32 and 39 and IFRS 7. Section 4 discusses these standards in greater detail.

1.6.1 Accounts risks

The main risk is **loss of reputation or financial penalties** through being found to have produced accounts that are misleading. However accounts that **fully** and **fairly disclose risks** may also be problematic, if investors react badly. This doesn't just apply to misreporting financial risks, it also includes **misleading reporting** in other areas, either in accounts or in other reports, for example environmental reporting.

1.6.2 Income risks

Income may become **increasingly volatile** if fair value accounting for financial instruments is used. This may have an **adverse impact on the ability of companies to pay dividends** and on **companies' share price and cost of capital**, as accounts users find it difficult to determine what is causing the volatility. Investors may not be sure if **low market valuations of financial assets are temporary or permanent**.

1.6.3 Measurement risks

Measurement of financial risks and value of financial instruments may be problematic. There may well be **considerable uncertainty** affecting assets valued at market prices when **little** or **no market currently exists** for those assets. The problem is **enhanced for financial instruments** which are not **tradable** and therefore have **no market value**. Arguably also in slow markets use of market values underestimates long-term asset values.

1.6.4 Systems risks

Accounting fairly for risks may require investment in new systems, and there may be an **increased risk of systems problems** as systems have to cope with linking of assets with derivatives, accommodating changes in hedge allocations and measuring hedge effectiveness.

Section summary

The financial risks businesses include risks associated with **sources of finance, overseas investment** and **trading and financial fraud.** Businesses also face risks when **accounting for financial risks** and the **financial instruments** designed to manage financial risks.

2 Financial risk analysis

Introduction

In this section we look at some of the techniques designed to assess financial risks. Though you will have come across these techniques in the context of investment appraisal, they are also ways of assessing other financial risks.

2.1 Sensitivity analysis

KEY TERM

SENSITIVITY ANALYSIS is a modelling and risk assessment procedure in which changes are made to significant variables in order to determine the effect of these changes on the planned outcome. Particular attention is then paid to variables identified as being of special significance.

The basic approach of sensitivity analysis is to calculate under **alternative assumptions** how sensitive the outcome is to changing conditions. An indication is thus provided of those variables to which the calculation is most sensitive (**critical variables**) and the **extent** to which those variables **may change** before the decision based on the results of that calculation changes.

Management should review critical variables to assess whether or not there is a strong possibility of events occurring which will lead to a different decision. Management should also pay particular attention to controlling those variables to which the calculation is particularly sensitive, once the decision has been made.

Exam alert

Although sensitivity analysis can be used to analyse the impact on Net Present Value calculations, remember that sensitivity analysis has many other uses. Thinking sensitivity analysis is the same as internal rate of return is a common mistake in exams.

2.1.1 Weaknesses of sensitivity analysis

These are as follows.

(a) The method requires that **changes** in each key variable are **isolated.** However management is more interested in the combination of the effects of changes in two or more key variables.

(b) Looking at factors in isolation is unrealistic since they are often **interdependent**.

(c) Sensitivity analysis does not examine the **probability** that any particular variation in costs or revenues might occur.

(d)   **Critical factors** may be those over which managers have no control.

(e)   In itself it does not provide a decision rule. Parameters defining **acceptability** must be laid down by managers.

2.2 The certainty-equivalent approach

Another method is the **certainty-equivalent approach**. By this method, expected cash flows of the project are converted to riskless equivalent amounts. The greater the risk of an expected cash flow, the smaller the 'certainty-equivalent' value (for receipts) or the larger the certainty equivalent value (for payments).

Example: Certainty-equivalent approach

Dark Ages, whose cost of capital is 10%, is considering a project with the following expected cash flows.

Year	Cash flow £	Discount factor 10%	Present value £
0	(9,000)	1.000	(9,000)
1	7,000	0.909	6,363
2	5,000	0.826	4,130
3	5,000	0.751	3,755
			NPV +5,248

The project seems to be clearly worthwhile. However, because of the uncertainty about the future cash receipts, the management decides to reduce them to 'certainty-equivalents' by taking only 70%, 60% and 50% of the years 1, 2 and 3 cash flows respectively. (Note that this method of risk adjustment allows for different risk factors in each year of the project.)

On the basis of the information set out above, assess whether the project is worthwhile.

Solution

The risk-adjusted NPV of the project is as follows.

Year	Cash flow £	PV factor	PV £
0	(9,000)	1.000	(9,000)
1	4,900	0.909	4,454
2	3,000	0.826	2,478
3	2,500	0.751	1,878
			NPV = – 190

The project is too risky and should be rejected.

The disadvantage of the 'certainty-equivalent' approach is that the amount of the adjustment to each cash flow is decided **subjectively**.

2.3 Expected values

Where probabilities are assigned to different outcomes, it is common to evaluate the worth of a decision as the expected value, or weighted average, of these outcomes.

KEY TERM

EXPECTED VALUE is 'The financial forecast of the outcome of a course of action multiplied by the probability of achieving that outcome. The probability is expressed as a value ranging from 0 to 1.'

(*CIMA Official Terminology*)

If a decision maker is faced with a number of alternative decisions, each with a range of possible outcomes, the **optimum decision** will therefore be the **one which gives the highest expected value**.

The choice of the option with the highest EV is known as BAYES' STRATEGY.

2.3.1 EVs and risk analysis

Where some analysis of risk is required when probabilities have been assigned to various outcomes, an elementary, but extremely useful, form of risk analysis is the **worst possible/most likely/best possible technique**.

2.3.2 EVs and more complex risk analysis

EVs can be used to compare two or more mutually exclusive alternatives: the alternative with the most favourable EV of profit or cost would normally be preferred. However, **alternatives can also be compared** by looking at the **spread of possible outcomes**, and the **probabilities** that they will occur.

2.3.3 Linking EVs and risk

A **probability distribution** of 'expected cash flows' can often be estimated, and this may be used to do the following.

Calculate an expected value

Measure risk, for example in the following ways.

(a)   By calculating the worst possible outcome and its probability
(b)   By calculating the probability that the project will fail to achieve a positive result
(c)   By calculating the standard deviation of the result

2.3.4 Problems with expected values

There are the following problems with using expected values in making investment decisions.

*   An investment may be **one-off**, and 'expected' NPV may never actually occur.
*   **Assigning probabilities** to events is highly **subjective**.
*   Expected values **do not evaluate the range** of possible NPV outcomes.

2.4 The standard deviation of the calculation

The disadvantage of using the approach to assess the risk of the project is that the **construction** of the **probability distribution** can become **very complicated**. If we were considering a project over 4 years, each year having five different forecasted cash flows, there would be 625 (5^4) NPVs to calculate. To avoid all of these calculations, an indication of the risk may be obtained by calculating the **standard deviation** of the calculation.

2.5 Value at risk

Value at risk (VaR) is another method of assessing financial risk. The value at risk model measures the maximum loss possible due to normal market movements over a given period of time and a given level of probability. It can be used to measure **trading portfolio** and **financial price risks,** also market liquidity, cash flow, credit and default exposure. It is based on the normal distribution curve, that you should have studied in previous exams.

Knowledge brought forward from earlier studies

Normal distribution curve

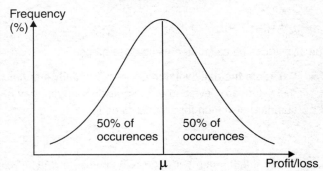

- Area under curve totals exactly 1
- It is symmetrical
- The mean $= \mu$, generally 0
- Area to the left of μ = area to the right of μ = 0.5

You can use the normal distribution curve to calculate at a given level of certainty what the maximum loss will be.

Say you were told that the mean was 0, standard deviation was £10,000 and you wanted to calculate the maximum loss,

(a)   With 95% certainty
(b)   With 99% certainty

(a)   **With 95% certainty**

The area of 95% certainty is the 50% > mean (all the profitable outcomes) + 45% < mean (the smallest loss outcomes) = 95%

Look for the figure of .4500 in the area under the normal curve table in appendix 2

The closest figure to .4500 is .4505

This represents a figure of 1.65 (1.6 (row) + 0.05 (column))

Multiply the standard deviation by 1.65

$1.65 \times 10,000 = £16,500$

You can thus say with 95% certainty that the maximum loss will not exceed £16,500.

(b)   **With 99% certainty**

The area of 99% certainty is the 50% > mean (all the profitable outcomes) + 49% < mean (the smallest loss outcomes) = 99%

Look for the figures of .4900 in the area under the normal curve table in Appendix 2.

The closest figure to .4900 is .4901

This represents a figure of 2.33 (2.3 (row) + 0.03 (column))

Multiply the standard deviation by 2.33

$2.33 \times 10,000 = £23,300$

You can thus say with 99% certainty that the maximum loss will not exceed £23,300.

Value at risk may be calculated over varying lengths of time, although you will often see it calculated daily. It depends on the **holding period** and the **confidence level**.

2.5.1 Calculating Value at risk

Daily Value at risk can be calculated using three steps:

 Calculate the daily volatility, that is the **daily standard deviation**. You may be given the daily standard deviation in the question, or you may have to calculate it if you are given the standard deviation for another period.

$$\sigma_D = \sigma_p \div \sqrt{P}$$

where P is the number of days in period covered

For example suppose you were given the weekly volatility. Assuming there are 5 working days in a week

$$\sigma_D = \sigma_p \div \sqrt{5}$$

 Using the normal curve table in Appendix 2, **determine the standard normal value** associated with the one tail confidence level X%

 Multiply Step 1 by Step 2 to determine the value at risk

Example: Value at risk

Fluffy Ted expects to receive £2 million from daily trading. The actual value in £ will depend on changes in market conditions which may result in gains or losses. Possible gains or losses are normally distributed around a mean of 0 and a daily standard deviation of £15,000. What is the daily value at risk at 5%, and what is the significance of this figure?

Solution

 Daily volatility is given as £15,000

 Normal value associated with 95% is 1.65

 1.65 × 15,000 = £24,750

There is a 5% chance that the daily loss will be greater than £24,750.

Of course the business then has to decide whether this loss and the probability of making this loss is acceptable or not.

Question 8.1   Value at risk

Learning outcome D1(a)

Tigger expects to receive $1 million from trading over the next week. The actual value in $ will depend on changes in foreign exchange market conditions which may result in gains or losses. Possible gains or losses are normally distributed around a mean of 0 and a weekly standard deviation of $5,000. What is the daily value at risk at 1%?

Value at risk limits can be used to **control the activities of traders**. A low limit will minimise the risks traders can take. Value at risk may also be used to determine risks **investors regard as excessive**. Changing the portfolio may **reduce the standard deviation** and hence the **value at risk** to an **acceptable level**.

However the statistical assumptions, and also the length of time over which Value at Risk is measured may limit its usefulness as a measure.

Value at risk does reflect normal market conditions and is less useful in fund markets that could be subject to **sudden shocks**. It does not indicate the **magnitude of maximum possible losses** if losses exceed the value at risk.

Exam skills

Questions on value at risk are likely to require you to define the term and carry out a calculation.

2.6 Regression analysis

Regression analysis, which you will have encountered in your earlier studies can be used to measure exposure to various risk factors. The analysis can result in an equation, such as:

X = a + B1i + B2fx + + B3rm

Where	X	=	changes in cash flows
	B1, B2, B3	=	measurements of the sensitivity of cash flows to the risk factors
	i, fx, rm	=	risk factors with
	i	=	change in interest rates
	fx	=	change in foreign exchange rates
	rm	=	change in raw materials prices

Regression analysis will produce a figure that is easy for the non-financial specialist to understand, though the processes used to arrive at this figure may be complicated.

Its main drawback is that it is based on **historical data**, and thus is dependent on what is available; also historical data may **not** be a good **guide to future risks**.

2.7 Simulation models and other methods

Simulation will overcome problems of having a very large number of possible outcomes, and allow for correlation of cash flows (a project which is successful in its early years is more likely to be successful in its later years).

2.8 Scenarios

KEY TERM

SCENARIO BUILDING is the process of identifying alternative futures, ie constructing a number of distinct possible futures permitting deductions to be made about future developments of markets, products and technology.

Scenarios are used in several situations.

2.8.1 Contingency planning

To develop contingency plans to cope with the arrival of threats or risks which, although they may arise at any time, are of indeterminable probability. For example, a chemicals company may develop a scenario of a major spillage at one of its plants and then set up emergency routines to cope with it. They cannot assess how likely the spillage is to occur in practice. Scenario analysis can also highlight **flaws in risk management or contingency planning**.

2.8.2 As a prediction technique

A series of alternative pictures of a future operating environment are developed which are consistent with current trends and consistent within themselves. The impact of each different scenario upon the business is assessed and specific risks highlighted. Contingency plans are drawn up to implement in the event of a given scenario becoming true, or to implement now to give protection against the scenario. However, it may not be easy to assess different scenarios and specification of scenarios is subjective.

2.9 Other methods of assessing risk

Other methods include the following:

(a) **Failure and effects analysis.** This involves breaking a system down into components, and analysing the effect of failure of each component, and the impact on the rest of the system.

(b) **Fault and event analysis.** Logic diagrams are used to analyse courses and consequences.

(c) **Root cause analysis.** This traces risks back to originating causes or events.

(d) **Delphi method.** This involves interaction between a number of experts, aiming to arrive at common ground.

2.10 Using the results of risk measurement

2.10.1 Investment appraisal

Only if management knows with certainty what is going to happen in the future can they appraise a decision in the knowledge that there is no risk. However the future is uncertain by nature. There are, nevertheless, steps that management can take to reduce the riskiness of a decision.

(a) A **maximum payback period** can be set to reflect the fact that risk increases the longer the time period under consideration.

(b) A **high discounting rate** can be used so that a cash flow which occurs quite some time in the future will have less effect on the decision.

(c) Decisions with **low standard deviations** and **acceptable average predicted outcomes** can be selected. If a business is making a range of decisions, it should ensure that some are **low-risk (diversification)**, and others are high-risk.

(d) As we have seen **sensitivity analysis** can be used to determine the critical factors within the decision-making process. Management effort can then be directed to those factors which are critical to the success of a particular decision.

(e)   To ensure that future events are no worse than predicted, **prudence**, **slack** and **overly pessimistic estimates** can be applied.

2.10.2 Risk and budgeting

Risk can impact on the budgeting process. How great an impact it will have will depend what **risks** have been **identified**, whether these risks have been thought to be **relevant** to the budgeting process and the estimates that have been made of the **financial consequences of risk**.

Section summary

Sensitivity analysis assesses how responsive a calculation is to changes in the variables used to in the calculation. One particular approach to sensitivity analysis, the **certainty-equivalent approach**, involves the conversion of the expected cash flows of the project to riskless equivalent amounts.

A probability analysis of expected cash flows can often be estimated and used both to calculate an expected result and to measure risk. The **standard deviation** can be calculated to assess risk when the construction of probability distributions is complicated.

Value at risk is based on normal loss theory, aiming to calculate the maximum financial loss at a given probability level.

Simulation models can be used to assess those projects that may have too many outcomes to allow the use of a decision tree or those projects that have correlated cash flows.

Scenario building, looking at an internally consistent view of the future, is a particularly useful technique of analysing the relative impact of lots of different types of risk.

Managers can make various **adjustments** and **allowances** to the calculations they have carried out in order to produce outcomes whose risk levels are satisfactory.

3   Financial risk management

Introduction

In this section we cover the important role of the treasury function in managing financial risks and also focus on the key controls of hedging and diversification.

3.1 Importance of financial risk management

Sound management of financial risks has a number of benefits. These were highlighted in the Management Accounting Guideline *Financial Risk Management for Management Accountants* by Margaret Woods and Kevin Dowd:

- Better reputation
- Reduction in earnings volatility meaning that published information is more reliable
- More stable earnings reducing average tax liabilities
- Protection of cash flows
- Reduction of cost of capital
- More opportunities to invest because of improved credit rating and more secure access to capital
- Stronger position in merger and acquisition negotiations
- Better managed supply chain and more secure customer base

3.2 Basel Committee

Since 1974 the Basel Committee on Banking Supervision has made important recommendations affecting risk management and internal controls operated by banks. The Basel II accords have been particularly important in establishing risk management and capital adequacy requirements. The committee's recommendations include recommendations about the **minimum capital** banks should hold and also how **credit**, **operational and market risk** should be measured and managed.

The Committee highlights the need for boards to treat the analysis of a **bank's current and future capital requirements** in relation to its strategic objectives as a vital element of the strategic planning process. Control systems should **relate risk** to the bank's **required capital levels**. The board or senior management should understand and approve control systems such as credit rating systems. Banks should use **value at risk models** that capture general market risks and specific risk exposures of portfolios.

The Committee stresses the importance of banks having an **operational risk management function** that develops strategies, codifies policies and procedures for the whole organisation and designs and implements assessment methodology and risk reporting systems. It is particularly important for banks to establish and maintain **adequate systems and controls** sufficient to give management and supervisors the confidence that their valuation estimates are prudent and reliable.

Banks' risk assessment systems (including the internal validation processes) must be subject to regular review by external auditors and/or supervisors. The regular review of the overall risk management process should cover:

- The adequacy of the documentation of the risk management system and process

- The organisation of the risk control unit

- The integration of market risk measures into daily risk management

- The approval process for risk pricing models and valuation systems

- The validation of any significant change in the risk measurement process

- The scope of market risks captured by the risk measurement model

- The integrity of the management information system

- The accuracy and completeness of position data

- The verification of the consistency, timeliness and reliability of data sources used to run internal models, including the independence of such data sources

- The accuracy and appropriateness of volatility and correlation assumptions

- The accuracy of valuation at risk calculations

- The verification of the model's accuracy through frequent testing and review of results

 Further details about the reports of the Basel committee are on the website of the Bank for International Settlements: http://www.bis.org/list/bcbs/index.htm

3.3 Role of the treasury function

KEY TERM

The Association of Corporate Treasurers' definition of TREASURY MANAGEMENT is 'the corporate handling of all financial matters, the generation of external and internal funds for business, the management of currencies and cash flows, and the complex strategies, policies and procedures of corporate finance'.

Larger companies have specialist treasury departments to handle financial risks.

 BPP's F3 text discusses the role of the treasury department; our discussion here concentrates on the risks connected with the treasury function.

The most important risks affecting the treasury function are as follows.

- **Business activities** have to be **curtailed** due to lack of funds
- Hedging results in **losses** over time
- **Exposures** are **not communicated** to the board

In addition there will be risks associated with the degree of **centralisation** of the treasury function:

(a) A **centralised department** may be able to reduce costs through undertaking **larger average transactions**. However it may offer greater potential for **speculative trading** in large contracts, and **better opportunities for fraud**. A central function may be less flexible in its responses to local needs.

(b) **Decentralising the treasury function** may mean that the local operations may not have the resources available to employ staff with the **expertise necessary** to handle complex treasury issues. There may be **inefficiencies** caused by duplication of staff and lack of centralisation of balances leading to unnecessary hedging. It may be **more difficult to exercise control** over geographically-dispersed activities.

3.3.1 Statement of treasury policy

All treasury departments should have a formal statement of treasury policy and detailed guidance on treasury procedures. A treasury policy should enable managers to **establish direction**, **specify parameters** and **exercise control**, and also **provide a clear framework and guidelines for decisions**.

The guidance needs to cover the **roles** and **responsibilities** of the **treasury function**, the **risks** requiring management, **authorisation** and **dealing** limits.

Guidance on **risks** should cover:

- **Identification** and **assessment** methodology
- **Criteria** including tolerable and unacceptable levels of risk
- **Management guidelines**, covering risk elimination, risk control, risk retention and risk transfer
- **Reporting guidelines**

The guidance must also include guidance on **measurement** of **treasury performance**. Measurement must cover both the **management of risk** and the **financial contribution** the department makes.

3.3.2 Other controls

As with other areas, there should be proper **forecasts** and **contingency arrangements,** with funds being made available by the bank when required. Because treasury activities have the potential to cost the organisation huge amounts of money, there ought to be a clear policy on **tolerated risk** and **regular review of investments.**

3.3.3 Audit of treasury function

Auditors must ensure that the **risk is managed in accordance with company procedures**. Again they need to **review forecasts** and **contingency arrangements** for adequacy and examine **investment reviews.** The auditors also need to see evidence that the board is fully aware of the treasury activities that are being carried out.

3.4 Risk diversification

Risk diversification involves creating a **portfolio of different risks** based on a number of events, which, if some turn out well others turn out badly, and the average outcome will be neutral. What an organisation has to do is to avoid having all its risks **positively correlated,** which means that everything will turn out **extremely well** or **extremely badly**.

Diversification can be used to manage the risks we discussed in Section 1 in a variety of ways:

- Having a **mix** of equity and debt finance, of short and long-term debt, and of fixed and variable interest debt

- Investing in a **variety of geographical locations and markets**

However except where restrictions apply to direct investment, investors can probably reduce investment risk more efficiently than companies as they may have a wider range of investment opportunities.

3.4.1 International diversification

Many financial risks bear particularly heavily on companies that trade or invest extensively overseas. We shall discuss specific ways of countering each of these risks in the next few chapters, but overall a business can reduce its exposure to risks internationally by **diversification** of its trading interests or portfolio of investments. **International portfolio diversification** can be very effective for the following reasons:

(a)   Different countries are often at **different stages of the trade cycle** at any one time.

(b)   **Monetary**, **fiscal and exchange rate policies** differ internationally.

(c)   Different countries have **different endowments of natural resources** and different industrial bases.

(d)   Potentially **risky political events** are likely to be localised within particular national or regional boundaries.

(e)   Securities markets in different countries differ considerably in the **combination of risk and return** that they offer.

However there are a number of factors that may limit the potential for international diversification.

(a)   **Legal restrictions** exist in some markets, limiting ownership of securities by foreign investors (discussed below under political risk).

(b)   **Foreign exchange regulations** may prohibit international investment or make it more expensive.

(c)   **Double taxation** of income from foreign investment may deter investors.

(d)   There are likely to be higher **information and transaction costs** associated with investing in foreign securities.

(e)   Some types of investor may have a parochial **home bias** for domestic investment.

3.5 Risk hedging

KEY TERM

HEDGING means taking an action that will **offset** an **exposure to a risk** by incurring a **new risk** in the **opposite direction**.

Hedging is perhaps most important in the area of currency or interest rate risk management, and we shall discuss in detail various hedging instruments. Generally speaking these involve an organisation making a commitment to offset the risk of a transaction that will take place in the future.

3.5.1 Advantages of hedging

Hedging can lead to a smoother flow of cash and lower risks of bankruptcy, and can result in a fall in the company's cost of capital.

3.5.2 Disadvantages of hedging

From the shareholders' viewpoint hedging will not affect their position if they hold a well-diversified portfolio. There will be possibly **significant transaction costs** from purchasing hedging products including brokerage fees and transaction costs. Because of lack of expertise, **senior management** may be unable to **monitor hedging activities effectively**. There may also be **tax and accounting complications**, particularly arising from IASs 32 and 39, and IFRS 7 (discussed in Section 4 of this chapter).

3.6 Methods of hedging

The business can take advantage of its own circumstances to **hedge naturally**. Some of its risk exposures may cancel out. **Internal netting**, the management of multiple internal exposures across a range of currencies so that receipts and payments cancel out is a form of natural hedging.

3.6.1 Forward contracts

A forward contract is a commitment to undertaking a future transaction at a set time and at a set price.

Example: Forward contract

1 January

On 1 January the price (the spot price) of a consignment of cocoa beans is $1,000.

You know you will need to buy a consignment of cocoa beans on 28 February, as they will be needed to fulfil a customer order. You are afraid that the price of cocoa beans will rise significantly between 1 January and 28 February.

You therefore contract with a cocoa beans supplier to buy a consignment of cocoa beans at $1,050 on 28 February.

28 February

The price of a consignment of cocoa beans is now $1,100.

You nevertheless can hold the supplier to the forward contract and can buy the cocoa beans at $1,050.

If however the market had not behaved as predicted and the price of cocoa beans was $980 on 28 February, you would still be obliged to buy the cocoa beans at the price of $1,050.

Similarly if the customer had pulled out of the transaction, you would still have to buy the consignment of cocoa beans and dispose of them as best you could.

3.6.2 Futures

A future represents a **commitment** to an **additional transaction** in the future that limits the risk of existing commitments.

Example: Futures 1

1 January

On 1 January the price (the spot price) of a consignment of cocoa beans is $1,000.

You have already agreed to buy a consignment of cocoa beans for $1,200 on 28 February, which means you appear to be at risk of paying too much for the cocoa beans.

You buy a three-month cocoa futures contract at $1,100 that expires on 31 March. This means you are committing to buying an additional consignment of cocoa beans, not at today's spot price, but at the futures price of $1,100. $1,100 represents what the market thinks the spot price will be on 31 March.

28 February

You buy the consignment of cocoa beans at $1,200.

You are still committed to buying the consignment at $1,100 on 31 March, but that will mean that you have two consignments of cocoa beans rather than just the one you need. You therefore sell the futures contract you bought on 1 January to eliminate this additional commitment. The futures contract is now priced at $1,233, as the market now believes that $1,233 will be the spot price on 31 March.

Because you have sold the contract for more than the purchase price, you have made a gain on the futures contract of 1,233 – 1,100 = $133. This can be set against the purchase you made.

Net cost = 1,200 – 133 = $1,067; the cost of paying more for the cocoa beans has been offset by the profit made on the futures contract.

One possible complication is a mismatch between the hedge transaction and the underlying transaction. This could occur for example if a contract to buy processed fuel is being hedged using crude oil futures.

Example: Futures 2

A road haulage company requires 250,000 barrels of processed fuel in the next three months. It can purchase the fuel for €120 per barrel. The treasury department believes that processed fuel prices may rise and wishes to hedge the exposure by purchasing crude oil futures. At present crude oil futures for delivery in three months' time are trading at €40 per barrel and the size of one futures contract is 1,000 barrels

Required

Calculate the number of futures contracts that the company should buy to hedge the exposure.

Solution

The calculation of the number of contracts has two elements here as a change in the price of the underlying asset, the processed fuel, won't match the change in the price of the crude oil futures.

$$\text{No of contracts required} = \frac{\text{Transaction quantity in barrels}}{\text{No of barrels in one futures contract}} \times \frac{\text{Price of barrel of processed fuel}}{\text{Price of futures contract}}$$

$$= \frac{250,000}{1,000} \times \frac{120}{40}$$

$$= 750 \text{ contracts}$$

3.6.3 Options

An option represents a commitment by a seller to undertake a future transaction, where the buyer has the option of not undertaking the transaction. With forwards and futures contracts, also swaps (see below) the risks are shared. However with options the risks are transferred to the seller (writer) of the option.

Example: Options

1 January

On 1 January the price (the spot price) of a consignment of cocoa beans is $1,000.

You know you will need to buy a consignment of cocoa beans on 28 February, as they will be needed to fulfil a customer order. You think it is likely that the price of cocoa beans will rise significantly between 1 January and 28 February, but you believe that with current market uncertainty, the price of cocoa beans could even fall.

You therefore take out an option to buy cocoa beans at $1,050 on 28 February. Because you are being given the privilege of choosing whether or not to fulfil the option contract, you have to pay a premium of $30.

28 February

Scenario 1

What if the price of the cocoa beans has now risen to $1,100?

You can hold the supplier to the option contract and buy the cocoa beans at $1,050.

Total cost = 1,050 + 30 = $1,080.

Secnario 2

What if the price of cocoa beans has fallen to $980. You could let the option contract lapse and buy cocoa beans at $980.

Total cost = 980 + 30 = $1,010.

Scenario 3

What if your customer pulls out of the contract? You would not have to buy the cocoa beans and the only cost to you will be the premium of $30.

3.6.4 Swaps

Strictly speaking a swap is a means of exploiting comparative advantage in the terms being offered to different customers.

Example: Swaps

You wish to buy a consignment of cocoa beans. Because you are considered a 'good customer', you could buy the cocoa beans for $1,000. You could also (if you wanted to) buy a consignment of groundnuts for $500.

Another business nearby wishes to purchase a consignment of groundnuts. Because it does not have your reputation, it will be charged $800 to buy the groundnuts. If it wished to purchase cocoa beans, it would be charged $1,200.

If therefore you buy the cocoa beans you need and the other business buys the groundnuts it needs, the total cost to both businesses will be 1,000 + 800 = $1,800.

If however you brought the groundnuts and the other business bought the cocoa beans, and you then swapped your purchases, the total cost to both businesses would be 500 + 1,200 = $1,700.

There is a net saving of $100 if the swap takes place.

The complication with this arrangement is that you have only paid $500 rather than the $1,000 you would have paid if there had been no swap. The other business has paid $1,200 rather than the $800 it would pay without a swap.

An adjustment is needed therefore to ensure both parties benefit from the swap. If you pay the other business $450, you will have paid in total 500 + 450 = $950, rather than $1,000 with no swap, so you will have gained $50. The other business will have paid net 1,200 – 450 = $750, rather than $800 with no swap, so it too will have gained $50.

Exam alert

The examiner has stated that students need an awareness of the implications of issuing or holding instruments, with questions focusing on the practical situations in which they could be used.

3.7 Hedging and speculation

As well as hedging, some types of derivative have also been used for speculation. The speculator is hoping to make a profit by prejudging how the price of the underlying asset will move. Indeed there would be no market for hedging unless counterparties were prepared to be involved in speculation. Because the derivatives market is **highly leveraged**, the speculator can for a small deposit invest in derivatives, whose movements in price are **proportionally much greater** than those of the underlying commodity. As a result the **profit or loss per pound invested is much greater** than speculating on the underlying commodity. Hence Warren Buffett and others view them as a potential time bomb.

3.8 Other risk management methods

3.8.1 Internal strategies

Internal strategies for managing financing and credit risks include working capital management and maintaining reserves of easily liquidated assets. Specific techniques businesses use include:

- **Vetting** prospective partners to assess credit limits
- **Position limits**, ceilings on limits granted to counterparties
- **Monitoring** credit risk exposure
- **Credit triggers** terminating an arrangement if one party's credit level becomes critical
- **Credit enhancement**, settling outstanding debts periodically, also margin and collateral payments

3.8.2 Risk sharing

There are various instruments that businesses can purchase in order to share credit risks. These include:

- **Credit guarantees** – the purchase from a third party of a guarantee of payment

- **Credit default swaps** – a swap in which one payment is conditional on a specific event such as a default

- **Total return swaps** – one part is the total return on a credit-related reference asset

- **Credit-linked notes** – a security that includes an embedded credit default swap

However credit derivatives are not a means of eliminating risk. Risks include counterparty defaulting and basis risk, the risk that derivative prices don't move in the same direction or to the same extent as the underlying asset.

3.8.3 Risk transfer

As you may remember from Chapter 2, **insurance** is an important way of transferring risk. Credit insurance can be used for a **specific transaction** or **all of the business**.

An alternative method of transferring risk is **securitisation**. This is the conversion of financial or physical assets into tradable financial instruments. This creates the potential to increase the scale of business operations by converting relatively illiquid assets into liquid ones.

However this may increase liquidity risk. Northern Rock's problems were initated by the US subprime crisis, which disrupted its trading and meant it could no longer cover its liabilities.

CASE STUDY

Section summary

Larger organisations may operate a **treasury function**. A treasury function can bring necessary expertise, but failure to control it properly could result in large losses.

Diversification limits financial risk by taking on a portfolio of different risks constructed so that, should they all crystallise, the outcome will be **neutral**.

Hedging is the main method used to control **interest rate and exchange rate risks**.

4   Financial risk disclosure   **5/10**

Introduction

In this section we look at the requirements affecting accounting for, and disclosures of, financial risks, and how control systems accommodate these requirements.

4.1 IASs 32 and 39 and IFRS 7

As you may remember from your studies at Managerial level, a number of standards affect how financial instruments are treated in the financial statements:

- IAS 32 Financial instruments: Presentation and disclosure
- IAS 39 Financial instruments: Recognition and measurement
- IFRS 7 Financial instruments: Disclosures

We summarise the main provisions of these standards below:

A FINANCIAL ASSET is:

KEY TERMS

- Cash, an equity instrument
- A contractual right to receive cash or other financial assets
- A contractual right to exchange financial instruments under potentially favourable conditions

A FINANCIAL LIABILITY is:

- A contractual obligation to deliver cash or other financial assets

- A contractual obligation to exchange financial instruments under potentially unfavourable conditions

An EQUITY INSTRUMENT is a contract that evidences a residual interest in the assets of an enterprise after deducting all its liabilities.

DERIVATIVES are defined as having the following components:

- An underlying index or variable
- Little or no initial net investment
- Future settlement

4.2 Financial instruments

The main provisions defining financial instruments are as follows:

- Financial instruments include **primary** instruments and **derivative** instruments

- A financial instrument must be classified as a **financial liability**, **financial asset** or **equity instrument**

- The **substance** of the financial instrument is more important than its **legal form**

- The **critical feature of a financial instrument** is incurring a contractual obligation to deliver cash or another financial instrument

- There are four categories of financial instrument:

  - **Financial asset** or **financial liability** held at **fair value through profit or loss** (designated at fair value or **held for trading**)

  - **Held-to-maturity investments** (non-derivative financial assets with fixed or determinable payments and fixed maturity)

  - **Loans and receivables** that are non-derivative financial assets with fixed or determinable payments that are not quoted in an active market

  - **Available for sale financial assets**

- **Compound instruments** are split into equity and liability parts and presented accordingly

- **Interest, dividends, losses and gains** are treated according to whether they relate to a financial liability or an equity instrument

4.3 Measurement of financial instruments

The main provisions are as follows:

- All financial assets and liabilities should be **recognised on the statement of financial position**, including derivatives

- On initial recognition, financial instruments are measured at **cost**

- Subsequent measurement depends on how a financial asset is **classified**

- Financial assets at **fair value through profit or loss** are measured at **fair value**; gains and losses are recognised in **profit or loss**

- **Available for sale** assets are measured at **fair value**; gains and losses are taken to **other comprehensive income**

- **Loans and receivables** and **held-to-maturity** investments are measured at **amortised cost**; gains and losses are recognised in **profit or loss**

- Financial **liabilities** are normally measured at **amortised cost**, unless they have been classified as at fair value through profit or loss

- **Fair value** is measured in the following ways in order of preference:

    – Quoted market price in an active market
    – Most recent transaction price
    – Current fair value of similar instruments
    – Discounted cash flow analysis
    – Option pricing models

4.4 Risks arising from financial instruments

In undertaking transactions in financial instruments, an entity may assume or transfer to another party one or more **different types of financial risk** as defined below. The disclosures required by the standard show the extent to which an entity is exposed to these different types of risk, relating to both recognised and unrecognised financial instruments.

Credit risk	The risk that one party to a financial instrument will cause a financial loss for the other party by failing to discharge an obligation.
Market risk	The risk that the fair value or future cash flows of a financial instrument will fluctuate because of changes in market prices. Market risk comprises three types of risk: **currency risk**, **interest rate risk** and **other price risk**.
Currency risk	The risk that the fair value or future cash flows of a financial instrument will fluctuate because of changes in foreign exchange rates.
Interest rate risk	The risk that the fair value or future cash flows of a financial instrument will fluctuate because of changes in market interest rates.
Other price risk	The risk that the fair value or future cash flows of a financial instrument will fluctuate because of changes in market prices (other than those arising from **interest rate risk** or **currency risk**), whether those changes are caused by factors specific to the individual financial instrument or its issuer, or factors affecting all similar financial instruments traded in the market.
Liquidity risk	The risk that an entity will encounter difficulty in meeting obligations associated with financial liabilities.

4.4.1 Qualitative disclosures

For each type of risk arising from financial instruments, an entity must disclose:

(a)   The **exposures to risk** and how they arise

(b)   Its **objectives, policies and processes** for managing the risk and the methods used to measure the risk

(c)   Any **changes** in (a) or (b) from the previous period

4.4.2 Quantitative disclosures

For each financial instrument risk, **summary quantitative data** about risk exposure must be disclosed. This should be based on the information provided internally to key management personnel. More information should be provided if this is unrepresentative.

Information about **credit risk** must be disclosed by class of financial instrument and includes maximum exposure at the year end and any collateral pledged as security.

For **liquidity risk** entities must disclose a maturity analysis of financial liabilities and a description of the way risk is managed.

Disclosures required in connection with **market risk** include sensitivity analysis, showing the effects on profit or loss of changes in each market risk.

4.5 Hedging

KEY TERMS

HEDGING, for accounting purposes, means designating one or more hedging instruments so that their change in fair value is an offset, in whole or in part, to the change in fair value or cash flows of a hedged item.

A HEDGED ITEM is an asset, liability, firm commitment, or forecasted future transaction that:

(a)   Exposes the entity to risk of changes in fair value or changes in future cash flows, and that

(b)   Is designated as being hedged

A HEDGING INSTRUMENT is a designated derivative or (in limited circumstances) another financial asset or liability whose fair value or cash flows are expected to offset changes in the fair value or cash flows of a designated hedged item.

HEDGE EFFECTIVENESS is the degree to which changes in the fair value or cash flows of the hedged item attributable to a hedged risk are offset by changes in the fair value or cash flows of the hedging instrument.

FAIR VALUE HEDGE: a hedge of the exposure to changes in the fair value of a recognised asset or liability, or an identified portion of such an asset or liability, that is attributable to a particular risk and could affect profit or loss.

CASH FLOW HEDGE: a hedge of the exposure to variability in cash flows that:

(a)   is attributable to a particular risk associated with a recognised asset or liability (such as all or some future interest payments on variable rate debt) or a highly probable forecast transaction (such as an anticipated purchase or sale), and that

(b)   could affect profit or loss.

4.5.1 Hedge accounting

Hedge accounting means designating one or more instruments so that their change in fair value is **offset** by the change in fair value or cash flows of another item.

Hedge accounting is permitted in certain circumstances, provided the hedging relationship is **clearly defined**, **measurable** and actually **effective**.

There are three types of hedge: **fair value** hedge; **cash flow** hedge; hedge of a **net investment in a foreign operation.**

The accounting treatment of a hedge **depends on its type**.

4.5.2 Fair value hedges

The **gain or loss** resulting from **re-measuring** the hedging instrument at fair value is **recognised in profit or loss**.

The gain or loss on the hedged item attributable to the **hedged risk** should **adjust the carrying amount** of the hedged item and be **recognised in profit or loss**.

4.5.3 Cash flow hedges

The portion of the gain or loss on the hedging instrument that is determined to be an **effective** hedge shall be **recognised directly** as other comprehensive income. To be eligible, the designated risk and cash flows must be separately identifiable. Changes in the cash flows or fair values arising from changes in the designated risks must be able to be measured reliably.

The **ineffective portion** of the gain or loss on the hedging instrument should be **recognised in profit or loss**.

When a hedging transaction results in the recognition of an asset or liability, changes in the value of the hedging instrument recognised in equity either:

(a)   Are adjusted against the carrying value of the asset or liability, or

(b)   Affect the profit or loss at the same time as the hedged item (for example, through depreciation or sale).

4.5.4 Hedge accounting disclosures

Disclosures must be made relating to **hedge accounting**, as follows:

(a)   **Description of hedge**

(b)   Description of financial instruments designated as **hedging instruments** and their fair value at the reporting date

(c)   The **nature of the risks** being hedged

(d)   For **cash flow hedges**, periods **when the cash flows will occur** and **when they will affect profit or loss**

(e)   For **fair value hedges**, **gains or losses on the hedging instrument** and **the hedged item**

(f)   The **ineffectiveness recognised in profit or loss** arising from cash flow hedges and net investments in foreign operations

4.6 IFRS 9

In November 2009 the International Accounting Standards Board published IFRS 9 *Financial Instruments* on the classification and measurement of financial assets. The publication represents the first part of a three part project to replace IAS 39. IFRS 9 uses a single approach to determine whether a financial asset should be measured at amortised cost or fair value. The approach is based on how the entity manages its financial instruments and contractual cash flows. The new standard also requires a single impairment method to be used. The aims are to improve comparability and make financial statements easier to understand.

The second and third parts of the project will deal with the impairment methodology and hedge accounting.

4.7 Impact of accounting standards

The significant requirements imposed by the accounting standards have placed major demands on the systems of many organisations. Organisations need to be able to:

- Value all financial assets, liabilities and derivatives
- Produce documentation of hedging strategies
- Provide testing of effectiveness
- Manage hedging relationships
- Generate the information necessary to fulfil accounting and disclosure requirements
- Accommodate modifications to new IAS requirements

4.8 Accounting issues

Correct accounting under IASs 32 and 39 is particularly important for companies who make lots of use of derivatives. The information published in the accounts may impact significantly on the **volatility of their share prices.** Changes in fair value year-on-year may cause **fluctuations in profits and earnings per share.** Investors may feel that this information is artificially volatile and does not help them manage the risks they face when deciding where to place their funds.

Organisations will have to pay particular attention to the following issues.

4.8.1 Classification of instruments

Correct classification of **hedges** will be particularly important. Other classifications will also require judgement. Whether an asset is **held for trading** will depend on the organisation's intentions when entering contracts and also whether it makes extensive use of credit techniques such as **leveraging** and **credit enhancement** and is mainly dealing with banks, traders and fund managers.

Similarly whether an asset is **held to maturity** will also depend on management intent. It is doubtful whether assets are held to maturity if the organisation's investment policy states that investments should be managed to meet short-term liquidity needs.

4.8.2 Measurement of fair value

The presumption in IAS 39 is that fair values can be reliably determined even for complex derivatives. In some cases valuation techniques may require complicated assumptions or large amounts of detail, and this may lead to the organisation incurring significant costs. The decision-making process will require informed judgement of which **methods, formulae and assumptions** to use and also **sensitivity analysis** on responsiveness to change in key variables.

4.8.3 Hedging

It may be difficult to determine the pattern of **income recognition** for hedged accounting adjustments.

4.8.4 Embedded derivatives

A very significant judgement will be how closely a derivative is **related to the host contract** and hence whether it is an **embedded derivative** that needs to be accounted for separately from the host contract.

4.8.5 Recognition and derecognition

It may be difficult to decide when precisely assets and liabilities should be derecognised. IAS 39 indicates that an organisation should consider both the **substance of control** and who bears the **risks and rewards,** and that the evaluation of the transfer of risks and rewards should precede the evaluation of the transfer of control.

4.9 Accounting systems

In order to deal effectively with the accounting issues, the accounting system should be able to produce **journal updates** and **accounting entries** for IAS 39 significant events such as hedge termination.

Organisations will also need to consider carefully how IAS 39 requirements impact upon the statements they have to produce for various regulatory bodies.

4.10 Business processes and systems

Organisations will need to make sure that their systems are robust enough to be able to **process** a trade or hedge from trading through risk management to accounting entry generation. The **market data** and **models** used must be consistent; inaccuracies may result in unnecessary income volatility.

The systems must also be able to **link assets and liabilities with derivatives**, **accommodate changes in hedge allocations** and **measure hedge effectiveness.**

Because of the requirements to measure instruments at fair value, **sources of fair value information** will need to be identified.

Organisations will also have to consider their **communication strategies.** Users will be examining a range of disclosures on fair value, hedging and gains and losses, and they need to receive a clear view of what is happening.

IAS 39 implementation may mean fair values and therefore **reported earnings fluctuate**; this could lead to significant share price fluctuations depending on how the organisation communicates with investors.

4.11 Risk monitoring

There are various ways in which companies can monitor the risks associated with financial instruments.

4.11.1 Monitoring of markets

Companies should **continually measure activity** on markets where assets with significant value are actively traded. Where assets are not actively traded, they should monitor activity on similar assets or take into account past price movements and quotations.

4.11.2 Financial techniques and models

Companies can base their valuation of risks on risk measurement techniques such as **sensitivity analysis**, or on financial models such as the **Black-Scholes model**.

4.11.3 Quotes from experts

Quotes from experts such as brokers may provide valuable assistance in measuring risk. However when markets are not active, brokers may rely on **models** rather than **actual market data**, and their opinions may be of less value unless the assumptions behind the models are made clear.

4.11.4 Trading limits

Companies can ensure risks are effectively monitored by **setting trading limits** such as maximum daily amounts or value at risk.

4.12 Risk management strategies

As well as needing to understand the new rules, treasury departments must also consider whether **risk management strategies** will need to be **modified**. **Monitoring procedures** may have to be **strengthened**. Risk officers may have to employ **different management techniques**, **limiting** the **hedging strategies used** or **specifying different effectiveness assessment methods for different structures**, so that the arrangements qualify as hedges under the standard.

Organisations may also provide means of allowing users to **select and test hedges** from a pre-approved set of hedge strategies.

The IAS may also impact upon **funding arrangements** with certain funding structures (debt factoring or securitisations) requiring review to ensure compliance with the IAS.

Section summary

IASs 32 and 39 and IFRS 7 have major impacts upon organisations using complex financial instruments. Such organisations may have to review their **accounting systems** and **risk management strategies**.

Chapter Roundup

✓ The financial risks businesses include risks associated with **sources of finance**, the **risks of overseas investment** and **trading and financial fraud.** Businesses also face risks when **accounting for financial risks** and the **financial instruments** designed to manage financial risks.

✓ **Sensitivity analysis** assesses how responsive a calculation is to changes in the variables used in the calculation. One particular approach to sensitivity analysis, the **certainty-equivalent approach**, involves the conversion of the expected cash flows of the project to riskless equivalent amounts.

✓ **A probability analysis** of expected cash flows can often be estimated and used both to calculate an expected result and to measure risk. The **standard deviation** can be calculated to assess risk when the construction of probability distributions is complicated.

✓ **Value at risk** is based on normal loss theory, aiming to calculate the maximum financial loss at a given probability level.

✓ **Simulation models** can be used to assess those projects that may have too many outcomes to allow the use of a decision tree or those projects that have correlated cash flows.

✓ **Scenario building**, looking at an internally consistent view of the future, is a particularly useful technique of analysing the relative impact of lots of different types of risk.

✓ Managers can make various **adjustments** and **allowances** to the calculations they have carried out in order to produce outcomes whose risk levels are satisfactory.

✓ Larger organisations may operate a **treasury function**. A treasury function can bring necessary expertise, but failure to control it properly could result in large losses.

✓ **Diversification** limits financial risk by taking on a portfolio of different risks constructed so that should they all crystallise, the outcome will be **neutral**.

✓ **Hedging** is the main method used to control **interest rate and exchange rate risks**.

✓ IASs 32 and 39 and IFRS 7 have major impacts upon organisations using complex financial instruments. Such organisations may have to review their **accounting systems** and **risk management strategies**.

Quick Quiz

1   Sensitivity analysis allows for uncertainty in project appraisal by assessing the probability of changes in the decision variables.

    True   ☐

    False   ☐

2   Fill in the blank.

    The .... is where expected cash flows are converted to riskless equivalent amounts.

3   Give three examples of ways that risk can be measured in probability analysis.

4   Expected values can help an accountant evaluate the range of possible Net Present Value outcomes.

    True   ☐

    False   ☐

5   What should treasury policy guidance on risks cover?

6   Fill in the blank.

    .... is reducing the impact of one risk by incurring a risk in the opposite direction.

7   Under IAS 39 at what values should financial assets and liabilities be recognised (with certain exceptions)?

8   Give three examples of the risks identified in the accounting standards on financial instruments.

9   Fill in the blank.

    .... is the degree to which changes in the fair value or cash flows of the hedged item attributable to a hedged risk are offset by changes in the fair value or cash flows of the hedging instrument.

Answers to Quick Quiz

1   False. Sensitivity analysis assesses the **effect** of changes in variables, not the probability of occurrence.

2   The **certainty equivalent approach** is where expected cash flows are converted to riskless equivalent amounts.

3
- Calculating the worst possible outcome and its probability
- Calculating the probability that the project will fail to achieve a positive outcome
- Calculating the standard deviation of the outcome

4   False

5
- Identification/assessment methodology
- Tolerable/unacceptable risks
- Management guidelines
- Reporting guidelines

6   **Risk hedging** is reducing the impact of one risk by incurring a risk in the opposite direction.

7   Fair values

8
- Credit
- Currency
- Interest rate
- Liquidity
- Market
- Other price

9   **Hedge effectiveness** is the degree to which changes in the fair value or cash flows of the hedged item attributable to a hedged risk are offset by changes in the fair value or cash flows of the hedging instrument.

Answers to Questions

8.1 Value at risk

      Daily standard deviation $= \dfrac{5,000}{\sqrt{5}} = \$2,236$

      Normal value associated with 99% is 2.33

      Daily value at risk $= 2,236 \times 2.33 = \$5,210$

Now try this question from the Exam Question Bank	Number	Level	Marks	Time
	Q12	Examination	20	36 mins

INTEREST RATE RISK

Here we consider **interest rate risk** and some of the financial instruments which are now available for managing financial risks, including '**derivatives**' such as **options**. The risk of interest rate changes is however less significant in most cases than the risk of currency fluctuations which, in some circumstances, can fairly easily wipe out profits entirely if not hedged.

The **Black-Scholes model** for valuing options is an increasingly important area; although you will not have to use the formula, you need an understanding of its components.

In the exam you will not be asked to carry out calculations on interest rate futures, options and forward rate agreements.

topic list	learning outcomes	syllabus references	ability required
1 Interest rate risk	D1(a)	D1(i), (iii)	evaluation
2 Forward rate agreements (FRAs)	D2(a), (b)	D2(ii)	evaluation
3 Interest rate futures	D2(a), (b)	D2(ii)	evaluation
4 Interest rate options	D2(a), (b)	D2(ii), (iv)	evaluation
5 Interest rate swaps	D2(a), (b)	D2(ii)	evaluation
6 Hedging strategy alternatives: example	D2(a), (b)	D2(ii)	evaluation

1 Interest rate risk

Introduction

In this section we cover the different interest rate risks companies face. These relate to specific loans and the company's whole debt portfolio.

KEY TERM

1.1 Managing a debt portfolio

The corporate treasurers will be responsible for managing the company's **debt portfolio**, that is, in deciding how a company should obtain its short-term funds so as to:

(a)   Be able to **repay debts** as they mature

(b)   **Minimise any inherent risks**, notably invested foreign exchange risk, in the debts the company owes and is owed

There are a number of situations in which a company might be exposed to risk from interest rate movements.

INTEREST RATE RISK is the risk to the profitability or value of a company resulting from changes in interest rates.

1.2 Risks from interest rate movements

(a)   **Fixed rate versus floating rate debt**

A company can get caught paying **higher interest rates** by having fixed rather than floating rate debt, or floating rather than fixed rate debt, as market interest rates change.

Expectations of interest rate movements will determine whether a company chooses to borrow at a fixed or floating rate. The term structure of interest rates – the rates available on loans of different length - should help businesses determine the market's view on how interest rates are likely to move in the future.

Fixed rate finance may be more expensive: however the business runs the risk of **adverse upward rate movements** if it chooses floating rate finance.

Other factors include:

(i)   **Finance term** (the longer the term the more difficult interest rates are to predict)

(ii)   The **differences between fixed and floating rates**, plus arrangement costs or new finance

(iii)   The **finance risk tolerance** of the directors

(iv)   **Existing debt mix** (greater finance diversification may be desirable to hedge all possibilities)

(v)   **Current pressures on liquidity** – if the business is stretched in the short-term, it may prefer to take the lower rate available on floating rate debt. In doing so, it is taking the risk that rates may rise and borrowing eventually become more expensive. However the directors are calculating that if that happens, the company will have accumulated sufficient cash to be able to bear the higher rates.

(b)   **Currency of debt**

A company can face higher costs if it borrows in a currency for which exchange rates move adversely against the company's domestic currency. The treasurer should seek to **match the currency of the loan** with the **currency of the underlying operations/assets** that generate revenue to pay interest/repay the loans.

(c)   **Term of loan**

A company can be exposed by having to **repay a loan earlier** than it can afford to, resulting in a need to re-borrow, perhaps at a higher rate of interest.

(d)   **Term loan or overdraft facility**

A company might prefer to **pay for borrowings only when it needs the money** as with an overdraft facility: the bank will charge a commitment fee for such a facility. Alternatively, a term loan might be preferred, but this will cost interest even if it is not needed in full for the whole term.

(e)   **Rises in interest rates**

A company may plan to take out borrowing at some time in the future, but face the possibility that **interest rates may rise before the term of borrowing commences**. This problem can be addressed by using financial instruments to fix or cap the rate of interest. This is described later in this chapter.

Exam skills

In the exam, watch out for information in the scenario about factors affecting the company's attitude to risk such as company size or risk appetite of directors. This may determine both the composition of the debt portfolio and the methods used to manage its risks.

1.3 Interest rate risk management

If the organisation faces interest rate risk, it can seek to **hedge the risk**. Alternatively where the magnitude of the risk is **immaterial** in comparison with the company's overall cash flows or appetite for risks, one option is to **do nothing**. The company then accepts the effects of any movement in interest rates which occur.

The company may also decide to do nothing if **risk management costs are excessive**, both in terms of the costs of using derivatives and the staff resources required to manage risk effectively. **Appropriate products** may not be available and of course the company may consider hedging unnecessary as it believes that the **chances of an adverse movement** are **remote**.

Exam alert

Bear in mind this possibility – the decision *not* to take action to reduce interest rate risk – when answering questions in the exam.

The company's **tax situation** may also be a significant determinant of its decision whether or not to hedge risk. If hedging is likely to **reduce variability of earnings**, this may have tax advantages if the company faces a higher rate of tax for higher earnings levels. The directors may also be unwilling to undertake hedging because of the need to **monitor the arrangements**, and the **requirements to fulfil the disclosure requirements** of IASs 32 and 39 and IFRS 7.

Question 9.1	Hedging

Learning outcomes D2(a), (b)

Explain what is meant by hedging in the context of interest rate risk.

CASE STUDY

In its 2009/10 annual report, **Kingfisher** discussed its management of financial and interest rate risk: 'Borrowings arranged at floating rates of interest expose the Group to cash flow interest rate risk, whereas those arranged at fixed rates of interest expose the Group to fair value interest rate risk. The Group manages its interest rate risk by entering into certain interest rate derivative contracts which modify the interest rate payable on the Group's underlying debt instruments ... The main types of financial instruments used are Medium Term Notes and other fixed term debt, bank loans and deposits, money market funds, interest rate swaps, commodity swaps and foreign exchange contrasts.'

Tate and Lyle noted in its 2008 annual report that: 'The Group has an exposure to interest rate risk arising principally from changes in US dollar, sterling and euro interest rates. This risk is managed by fixing or capping portions of debt using interest rate derivatives to achieve a target level of fixed/floating rate net debt, which aims to optimise net finance expense and reduce volatility in reported earnings. The Group's policy is that between 30% and 75% of Group net debt (excluding the Group's share of joint venture net debt) is fixed or capped (excluding out of-the-money caps) for more than one year and that no interest rate fixings are undertaken for more than 12 years. At 31 March 2008, the longest term of any fixed rate debt held by the Group was until June 2016.'

1.4 Interest rate risk management

Methods of reducing interest rate risk include:

- Netting – aggregating all positions, assets and liabilities, and hedging the net exposure
- Smoothing – maintaining a balance between fixed and floating rate borrowing
- Matching – matching assets and liabilities to have a common interest rate
- Pooling – (see below)
- Forward rate agreements (FRAs) (Section 2)
- Interest rate futures (Section 3)
- Interest rate options or interest rate guarantees (Section 4)
- Interest rate swaps (Section 5)

1.5 Pooling

Pooling means asking the bank to pool the amounts of all its subsidiaries when **considering interest levels and overdraft limits**. It should **reduce the interest payable, stop overdraft limits being breached** and **allow greater control by the treasury department**. It also gives the company the potential to take advantage of **better rates of interest** on **larger cash deposits**.

Section summary

Factors influencing **interest rate risk** include the following.

- Fixed rate versus floating rate debt
- The term of the loan

2 Forward rate agreements (FRAs)

Introduction

Forward rate agreements are a straightforward way of fixing the rate of interest that borrowers pay.

2.1 Forward rate agreements

KEY TERM

FORWARD RATE AGREEMENTS (FRAs) are agreements, typically between a company and a bank, about the interest rate on future borrowing or bank deposits.

A company can enter into an FRA with a bank that fixes the rate of interest for borrowing at a certain time in the future. If the actual interest rate proves to be higher than the rate agreed, the **bank pays the company the difference**. If the actual interest rate is lower than the rate agreed, the company pays the bank the difference. The **interest rates** which banks will be willing to set for FRAs will reflect their **current expectations** of **interest rate movements**.

A **3-9 forward rate agreement** starts in three months and lasts for six months (that is it is settled in nine months' time).

FRAs **protect the borrower** from adverse market interest rate movements to levels above the rate negotiated for the FRA. With a normal variable rate loan the **borrower is exposed to the risk of such adverse market movements**. On the other hand, the borrower will similarly not benefit from the effects of favourable market interest rate movements.

Example: Forward rate agreement

It is 30 June. Lynn will need a £10 million 6 month fixed rate loan from 1 October. Lynn wants to hedge using an FRA. The relevant FRA rate is 6% on 30 June.

What is the result of the FRA and the effective loan rate if the 6 month FRA benchmark rate has moved to

(a)   5%
(b)   9%

Solution

(a)   At 5% because interest rates have fallen, Lynn will pay the bank:

	£
FRA payment £10 million × (6% − 5%) × $^6/_{12}$	(50,000)
Payment on underlying loan 5% × £10 million × $^6/_{12}$	(250,000)
Net payment on loan	(300,000)

Effective interest rate on loan = 6%

(b)   At 9% because interest rates have risen, the bank will pay Lynn

	£
FRA receipt £10 million × (9% − 6%) × $^6/_{12}$	150,000
Payment on underlying loan at market rate 9% × £10 million × $^6/_{12}$	(450,000)
Net payment on loan	(300,000)

Effective interest rate on loan = 6%

Exam alert

This example is shown for illustration; in the exam you will not be expected to carry out such interest rate risk calculations.

2.2 Advantages of forward rate agreements

(a) **Protection provided**

An FRA would protect the borrower from **adverse interest rate movements** above the rate negotiated.

(b) **Flexibility**

FRAs are **flexible**; they can in theory be arranged for any amounts and any duration, although they are normally for amounts of over $1 million.

(c) **Cost**

Forward rate agreements may well be **free** and will in any case **cost little**.

2.3 Disadvantages of forward rate agreements

(a) **Rate available**

The rate the bank will set for the forward rate agreement will reflect **expectations of future interest rate movements**. If interest rates are expected to rise, the bank may set a **higher rate** than the rate currently available.

(b) **Falling interest rate**

The borrower will **not be able to take advantage** if interest rates fall unexpectedly.

(c) **Term of FRA**

The FRA will **terminate on a fixed date**.

(d) **Binding agreement**

FRAs are **binding agreements** so are less easy to sell to other parties.

Section summary

Forward rate agreements hedge risk by **fixing the interest rate** on future borrowing.

---

3 Interest rate futures

Introduction

Futures are a similar method of hedging to FRAs, but can be traded and are for standardised terms.

3.1 Futures contracts

Most futures contracts involve interest rates (**interest rate futures**). These offer a means of hedging against the risk of interest rate movements.

Interest rate futures are similar in effect to FRAs, except that the terms, amounts and periods are **standardised**. For example, a company can contract to buy (or sell) £100,000 of a notional 30-year Treasury bond bearing an 8% coupon, in say, 6 months time, at an agreed price. The basic principles behind such a decision are:

(a) The futures price is likely to vary with **changes in interest rates**. This acts as a **hedge** against adverse interest rate movements. We shall see how this works in a later example.

(b) The outlay to buy futures is much less than for buying the financial instrument itself.

3.1.1 Borrowing and lending

Borrowers will wish to hedge against an **interest rate rise** by:

*   **Selling futures now**
*   **Buying futures** on the day that the interest rate is fixed

Lenders will wish to hedge against the possibility of **falling interest rates** by:

*   **Buying futures now**
*   **Selling futures** on the date that the actual lending starts

3.2 Pricing futures contracts

The **pricing** of an interest rate futures contract is determined by prevailing interest rates

*   For short-term futures, if three month interest rates are 8%, a three month futures contract will be priced at 92 (100 − 8)

*   If interest rates are 11%, the contract price will be 89 (100 − 11)

This decrease in price, or value, of the contract, reflects the reduced attractiveness of a fixed rate deposit in a time of rising interest rates.

The price of long-term futures reflects market prices of the **underlying bonds**. A price of £100 equals par. The interest rate is implied in the price. If a long-term 10% futures contract has a price of £114.00, the implied interest rate on long-term bonds is approximately $^{100}/_{114} \times 10\% = 8.8\%$.

Example: Interest rate hedge using futures

Yew has taken a 3 month $1,000,000 eurodollar loan with interest payable of 8%, the loan being due for rollover on 31 March. At 1 January, the company treasurer considers that interest rates are likely to rise in the near future. The futures price is 91 representing a yield of 9%. Given a standard contract size of $1,000,000 the company **sells** a eurodollar three month contract to hedge against interest on the three month loan required at 31 March (to **sell** a contract is to commit the seller to take a deposit). At 31 March the spot interest rate is 11%.

What is the cost saving to Yew?

Solution

The company will **buy back** the future on 31 March at 89 (100 − 11). The cost saving is the **profit on the futures contract**.

$1,000,000 \times (91 − 89) \times ^{3}/_{12} = \$5,000$

The hedge has effectively reduced the net annual interest cost by 2%. Instead of a cost of 11% at 31 March ($27,500) for a three month loan, the net cost is $22,500 ($27,500 − $5,000), a 9% annual cost.

3.3 Use of interest rate futures

The seller of a futures contract does not have to own the underlying instrument. However, the seller may need to deliver it on the contract's delivery date if the buyer requires it. Many, but not all, interest rate contracts are **settled for cash** rather than by delivery of the underlying instrument.

Interest rate futures offer an attractive means of **speculation** for some investors, because there is no requirement that buyers and sellers should actually be lenders and borrowers (respectively) of the nominal amounts of the contracts.

3.4 Setting up a futures hedge

CIMA has stated that numerical questions will not be set on these, but knowing the step-by-step process of dealing with these will help you understand them.

Example: Setting up a futures hedge

Panda has taken a 6 month $10,000,000 dollar loan with interest payable of 8%, the loan being due for rollover on 31 March. At 1 January, the company treasurer considers that interest rates are likely to rise in the near future. The futures price is 91 representing a yield of 9%. Given a standard contract size of $1,000,000 the company sells a dollar three month contract to hedge against interest on the three month loan required at 31 March (to sell a contract is to commit the seller to take a deposit). At 31 March the interest rate is 11% and the futures price had fallen to 88.50.

Required

Demonstrate how futures can be used to hedge against interest rate movements.

Solution

The following steps should be taken.

Setup

(a)   What contract: 3 month contract

(b)   What type: sell (as borrowing and rates expected to rise)

(c)   How many contracts: $\dfrac{\text{Exposure}}{\text{Contract size}} \times \dfrac{\text{Loan period}}{\text{Length of contract}} = \dfrac{10m}{1m} \times {}^{6}/_{3} = 20$ contracts

Closing price

Closing futures price = 88.50

Outcome

(a)   **Futures outcome**

At opening rate:	0.91 sell
At closing rate:	0.8850 buy
	0.0250 receipt

Futures outcome:

$$\text{Receipt} \times \text{Size of contract} \times \text{Number of contracts} \times \dfrac{\text{Length of contract}}{\text{One year}}$$

$0.0250 \times 1,000,000 \times 20 \times {}^{3}/_{12} = \$125,000$

(b)   **Net outcome**

	$
Payment in spot market $10m × 11% × ${}^{6}/_{12}$	(550,000)
Receipt in futures market	125,000
Net payments	(425,000)

Effective interest rate $= \dfrac{425,000}{10,000,000} \times {}^{12}/_{6} = 8.5\%$

3.5 Advantages of interest rate futures

(a)   **Cost**

Costs of interest rate futures are reasonably **low**.

(b)   **Amount hedged**

A company can **hedge relatively large exposures of cash** with a **relatively small initial employment of cash**.

3.6 Disadvantages of interest rate futures

(a)   **Inflexibility of terms**

Traded interest rate futures are for **fixed periods** and **cover begins in March, June, September or December**. Contracts are for **fixed, large, amounts**, so may not entirely match the amount being hedged

(b)   **Basis risk**

The company may be liable to the risk that the **price of the futures contract** may not move in the expected direction.

(c)   **Daily settlement**

The company will have to settle **daily profits or losses** on the contract.

Section summary

Interest rate futures can be used to hedge against interest rate changes between the current date and the date at which the interest rate on the lending or borrowing is set. Borrowers **sell futures** to hedge against **interest rate rises;** lenders **buy futures** to hedge against **interest rate falls**.

4   Interest rate options

Introduction

Options limit the impact of adverse interest rates movements and allow the borrower or lender to take advantage of favourable interest rate movements.

4.1 Interest rate options (guarantees)

KEY TERM

An **INTEREST RATE OPTION** grants the buyer of it the right, but **not the obligation**, to deal at an agreed interest rate (strike rate) at a future maturity date. On the date of expiry of the option, the buyer must decide whether or not to exercise the right.

Clearly, a buyer of an **option to borrow** will not wish to exercise it if the market interest rate is now **below that specified in the option agreement**. Conversely, an **option to lend** will not be worth exercising if market rates have **risen above the rate specified** in the option by the time the option has expired.

Tailor-made **'over-the-counter' interest rate options** can be purchased from major banks, with specific values, periods of maturity, denominated currencies and rates of agreed interest. The cost of the option is the **'premium'**. Interest rate options offer more flexibility than and are more expensive than FRAs. Exchange **traded options** are also available.

4.2 Caps, floors and collars

KEY TERMS

An interest rate CAP is an option which sets an interest rate ceiling.

A FLOOR is an option which sets a lower limit to interest rates.

Using a 'COLLAR' arrangement, the borrower can buy an interest rate cap and at the same time sell an interest rate floor which reduces the cost for the company.

Various **cap** and **collar** agreements are possible.

The cost of a collar is lower than for a cap alone. However, the borrowing company forgoes the benefit of movements in interest rates below the floor limit in exchange for this cost reduction.

Example: Cap and collar

Suppose the prevailing interest rate for a company's borrowing is 10%. The company treasurer considers that a rise in rates above 12% will cause serious financial difficulties for the company. How can the treasurer make use of a 'cap and collar' arrangement?

Solution

The company can buy an interest rate cap from the bank. The bank will reimburse the company for the effects of a rise in rates above 12%. As part of the arrangements with the bank, the company can agree that it will pay at least 9%, say, as a 'floor' rate. The bank will pay the company for agreeing this. In other words, the company has sold the floor to the bank, which partly offsets the costs of the cap. The bank benefits if rates fall below the floor level.

4.3 A graphical approach to caps, collars and floors

Interest rate caps, collars and floors can be illustrated graphically, and this approach may help in understanding the effect of such arrangements.

This diagram illustrates a collar arrangement for a bank loan. The bank subsidises its client to the extent represented by shaded area A when the market interest rate exceeds the capped level, while the bank gains to the extent of area B when interest rates dip below the floor.

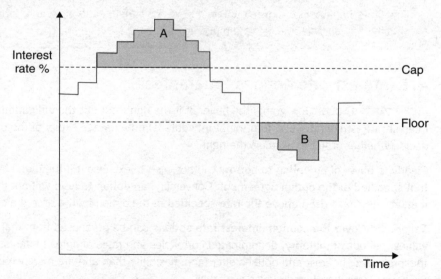

Interest rate collar through time

In the example shown below, a company has a loan at LIBOR (London Inter-Bank Offered Rate). Suppose that for an annual cost of 1% of principal, it can buy a cap at 8%. When LIBOR is between 6% and 8%, the vertical distance between the two lines on the graph represents the cost of the cap. The cap begins to pay off when LIBOR rises above 8%, with a break-even point where LIBOR is 9%.

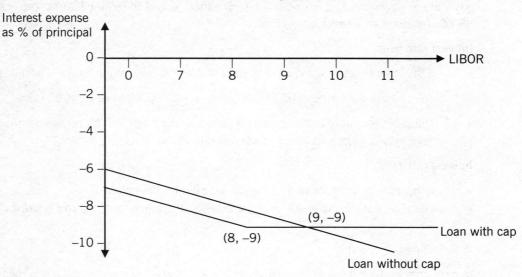

4.4 Traded interest rate options

Exchange-traded interest rate options are available as **options on interest rate futures,** which give the holder the right to buy (**call option**) or sell (**put option**) one futures contract on or before the expiry of the option at a specified price. The best way to understand the pricing of interest rate options is to look at a schedule of prices. The schedule below (from the *Financial Times*) is for 12 October.

UK long gilt futures options (LIFFE) £100,000 100ths of 1%

		Calls			Puts	
Strike price	Nov	Dec	Jan	Nov	Dec	Jan
£113.50	0.87	1.27	1.34	0.29	0.69	1.06
£114.00	0.58	0.99	1.10	0.50	0.91	1.32
£114.50	0.36	0.76	0.88	0.77	1.18	1.60

This schedule shows that an investor could pay $^{1.34}/_{100} \times £100,000 = £1,340$ to purchase the right to buy a sterling futures contract in January at a price of £113.50 per £100 stock.

If, say, in December, January futures are priced **below** £113.50 (reflecting an interest rate **rise**), the option will not be exercised. In calculating any gain from the call option, the premium cost must also be taken into account.

If the futures price moves **higher,** as it is likely to if interest rates **fall,** the option will be exercised. The profit for each contract will be current futures prices − 113.50 − 1.34.

4.5 Traded put and call options

To use traded interest rate options for hedging, follow exactly the same principles as for traded currency options.

(a)   If a company needs to hedge borrowing at some future date, it should **purchase put options** to **sell futures**.

(b)   Similarly, if a company needs to lend money, it should **purchase call options** to **buy futures**.

4.6 Traded caps, floors and collars

4.6.1 Traded caps

Say you are a borrower and have bought a put option (a right to sell the future). The exercise price is 93.00, reflecting an interest rate of 7%.

Interest rate rises

- If the interest rate you have to pay **rises to 8%**, the price of the future will fall to 92.00

- You will buy the future at 92.00 and exercise your option to sell it at 93.00

- The profit you make on buying and then selling the future can be set against the 8% interest you have to pay, to give an **effective interest rate of 7%**

Interest rate falls

- If the interest rate **falls to 6%**, you **do not exercise the option**
- Therefore don't worry about buying and selling the future, and just **pay interest at 6%**

4.6.2 Traded floors

In order to set a floor if you are investing/lending, you have to buy a call option – a right to buy a future. Say the exercise price is 95.00, corresponding to an interest rate of 5%.

Interest rate falls

- If the interest rate you receive **falls to 4%**, the price of the future will rise to 96.00

- However you will exercise your option to buy the future at 95.00 and then you will sell it on at 96.00

- The profit you make on the future will be added to the 4% interest you receive to give an **effective interest rate of 5%**

Interest rate rises

- If the interest rate **rises to 6%**, you will not exercise the option
- You will **receive interest at 6%**

4.6.3 Traded collars

With collars, if you're a borrower, you are buying a put and selling a call. Say the exercise price is 96.00, corresponding to an interest rate of 4%.

- Buying a put as above
- Selling a call means that you are selling someone else the right to buy a future from you

Interest rate falls

- If the interest rate **falls to 3%**, the price of the future will rise to 97.00

- You will **pay interest at 3%**

- However the holder of the call option will wish to exercise the option to buy the future at 96.00

- You therefore have to buy the future yourself at 97.00 and sell it to the option holder at 96.00, thus incurring a loss

- The loss you incur will be added to the 3% interest you have to pay to give an effective net interest rate of 4%

- If interest rates **fall further**, you will pay a lower interest rate but incur a larger loss on the option, netting out always at an **interest rate of 4%**

Interest rate rises

- If the interest rate rises above 4%, the option holder will not exercise the option .

- You will pay interest at more than 4%, but be able to offset against this a profit on selling the future, to give an **effective interest rate of 4%.**

4.7 Using interest rate options for hedging

CIMA has stated that numerical questions will not be set on these, but again knowing the step-by-step process of dealing with these will help you understand them.

Example: Using interest rate options for hedging

Panda wishes to borrow £4 million fixed rate in June for 9 months and wishes to protect itself against rates rising above 6.75%. It is 11 May and the spot rate is currently 6%. The data is as follows:

INTEREST RATE GUARANTEES

Short sterling options (LIFFE)

£1,000,000 points of 100%

Effective interest rate %	Calls June	Calls Sept	Calls Dec	Puts June	Puts Sept	Puts Dec
6.75	0.16	0.03	0.03	0.14	0.92	1.62
6.50	0.05	0.01	0.01	0.28	1.15	1.85
6.25	0.01	0.01	0.01	0.49	1.39	2.10

Panda negotiates the loan with the bank on 12 June (when the £4m loan rate is fixed for the full nine months) and closes out the hedge.

What will be the outcome of the hedge and the effective loan rate if prices on 12 June have moved to:

Closing prices

	Case 1 %	Case 2 %
Interest rate	7.4	5.1

Solution

The following method should be used.

 Setup

(a)   Which contract?   June

(b)   What type?   As paying interest put

(c)   Strike price   93.25 (1000 – 675)

(d)   How many? $\dfrac{£4m}{£1m} \times {}^{9}/_{3} = 12$ contracts

(e)   Premium   At 93.25 (6.75%) June Puts = 0.14p

$$\text{Contracts} \times \text{premium} \times \dfrac{\text{Size of contract}}{\left(\dfrac{12\,\text{months}}{\text{Length of contract}}\right)} = 12 \times 0.0014 \times \dfrac{1,000,000}{(12/3)} = £4,200$$

STEP 2   **Closing prices**

		Case 1 %	Case 2 %
	Interest rate	7.4	5.1

STEP 3   **Outcome**

(a)   Options market outcome

	Case 1	Case 2
Right to pay interest at	6.75	6.75
Closing rate	7.40	5.10
Exercise?	Yes	No

(b)   Net position

	Case 1 £	Case 2 £
Spot ($£4m \times {}^9/_{12} \times 5.1\%$)	–	153,000
Option ($£4m \times {}^9/_{12} \times 6.75\%$)	202,500	–
Option premium	4,200	4,200
Net outcome	206,700	157,200

(c)   Effective interest rate

$$\text{Case 1} \quad \frac{206,700}{4,000,000} \times {}^{12}/_9 = 6.89\%$$

$$\text{Case 2} \quad \frac{157,200}{4,000,000} \times {}^{12}/_9 = 5.24\%$$

4.8 Advantages of options

(a)   **Upside risk**

The company will have the choice **not to exercise the option**, and will be able **to take advantage of falling interest rates**.

(b)   **Over-the-counter options**

Over the counter options **tailored to the company's needs** can be obtained.

4.9 Disadvantages of options

(a)   **Premium**

The premium cost may be **relatively expensive** compared with the costs of other hedging opportunities. It will be payable whatever the movement in interest rates, and whether or not the option is exercised.

(b)   **Collar**

If the company has a **collar**, this will limit its ability to take advantage of lower interest rates to the lower limit set by the cap.

(c)   **Maturity**

The maturity of guarantees may be **limited to one year**.

(d)   **Traded options**

If the company purchases traded options, then the **large, fixed amounts of the contracts available** may not match the terms of the contract.

4.10 Valuation of options

The share option is a common form of option, giving the right but not the obligation to buy or to sell a quantity of a company's shares at a specified price within a specified period.

The value of a share option is made up of:

- 'Intrinsic value'
- 'Time value'

The **intrinsic value** of an option depends upon:

- Share price
- Exercise price

The **time value** of an option is affected by:

- Time period to expiry
- Volatility of the underlying security
- General level of interest rates

In this section we will use a share call option to illustrate how the factors listed affect an option's value. We will then describe in outline the Black-Scholes model for valuing options.

4.10.1 Time to expiry

The value of all options will **increase** with the **length of the expiry period**: in this period the underlying security has time to rise and create a gain for the option holder. If the underlying security falls in value, the option holder makes no loss other than the initial premium cost.

4.10.2 Volatility of the underlying security

Options on volatile securities will be **more valuable** than options on securities whose prices do not change much. This is because volatile securities will either show large increases or large decreases in value. The holder of a call option will gain a lot from a large increase in the value of the security but will lose nothing if it falls in value.

4.10.3 The general level of interest rates

The intrinsic value of an in-the-money call option is equal to the share price minus the exercise price. If the option has time to run before expiry, the exercise price will not have to be paid until the option is exercised.

(a) The option's value will therefore depend on the **current share price minus** the **present value of the exercise price**.

(b) If interest rates increase, this present value will decrease and **the value of the call option will increase**.

4.11 The Black-Scholes model

The **Black-Scholes** model for the valuation of **European call options** is based on the principle that the equivalent of an investment in a call option can be set up by **combining an investment in shares** with **borrowing the present value of the option exercise price**.. (**European options** are options that can only be exercised on the expiry date, as opposed to **American options**, which can be exercised on any date up till the expiry date.)

The model requires an estimate to be made of the variation in return on the shares. One way of making such an estimate is to measure the variation in the share price in the recent past and to make the assumption that this variability will apply during the life of the option.

4.11.1 Assumptions of Black-Scholes model

- **Returns** are **normally distributed**.
- **Share price changes** are **lognormally distributed**.
- Potential price changes follow a **random** model.
- **Volatility** is constant over the life of the option.
- Traders can trade **continuously**.
- **Financial markets** are perfectly **liquid**.
- **Borrowing** is possible at the **risk-free rate**.
- There are **no transaction costs**.
- Investors are **risk-neutral**.

4.11.2 Using the Black-Scholes model to value share options

The value of an option depends upon:

(a) **Current share price**

If the share price rises, the value of a call option will increase.

(b) **Exercise price of the option**

The higher the exercise price, the lower is the value of a call option.

(c) **Share price volatility or standard deviation of return on underlying share**

The higher the standard deviation of the return, the higher is the value of a call option, because there is more likelihood that the share price will rise above the option price.

(d) **Time to expiration of the option**

The longer the period to expiration, the higher is the value of a call option because there is more time for the share price to rise above the option price.

(e) **Risk-free rate of interest**

The higher the risk-free rate of interest, the higher is the value of a call option. As the exercise price will be paid in the future, its present value diminishes as interest rates rise. This reduces the cost of exercising and thus adds value to the option.

Within the model:

(a) The difference between the share price and the option exercise price is the **intrinsic value** of the option.

(b) A **time differential** factor, reflecting the fact that the option will be exercised in the future, is included.

(c) The model is very dependent upon the **share price volatility**. This is likely to be calculated on the basis of historical movements, and different conditions may apply in the future.

SUMMARY OF DETERMINANTS OF OPTION PRICES		
↑ in	*Call price*	*Put price*
Share price	↑	↓
Exercise price	↓	↑
Volatility	↑	↑
Time to expiry	↑	↑
Risk-free rate of return	↑	↓

Section summary

Interest rate options allow an organisation to limit its exposure to adverse interest rate movements, while allowing it to take advantage of favourable interest rate movements.

Borrowers can set a **maximum** on the interest they have to pay by buying **put** options.

Lenders can set a **minimum** on the interest they receive by buying **call** options.

Caps set a ceiling to the interest rate; a **floor** sets a lower limit. A **collar** is the simultaneous setting of a cap and floor.

The **value of an option** depends on the current price of the asset, the exercise price, the volatility (standard deviation) of the asset value, the time period to expiry and the risk-free rate of interest.

5 Interest rate swaps

Introduction

Interest rate swaps allow companies to take advantage of differences in the conditions connected with fixed and floating rate debt.

KEY TERM

INTEREST RATE SWAPS are transactions that exploit different interest rates in different markets for borrowing, to **reduce interest costs** for either **fixed or floating rate loans**.

5.1 Arranging a swap

An **interest rate swap** is an arrangement whereby two companies, or a company and a bank, swap interest rate commitments with each other. In a sense, each simulates the other's borrowings, with the following effects.

(a) A company which has **debt at a fixed rate of interest** can make a **swap** so that it ends up paying **interest at a variable rate**.

(b) A company which has **debt at a variable rate of interest** (floating rate debt) ends up paying a **fixed rate of interest**.

An example is illustrated below.

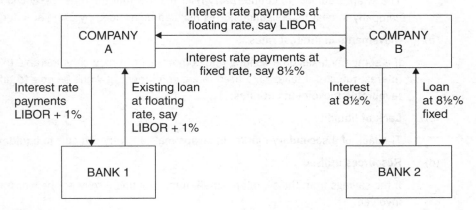

Interest rate swap

In this example, company A can use a swap to change from paying interest at a floating rate of LIBOR + 1% to one of paying fixed interest of (8½% + 1%) = 9½%.

A swap may be arranged with a bank, or a counterparty may be found through a bank or other financial intermediary. Fees will be payable if a bank is used. However a bank may be able to find a **counterparty more easily**, and may have **access to more counterparties** in **more markets** than if the company seeking the swap tried to find the counterparty itself.

Swaps are generally terminated by agreeing a **settlement interest rate**, generally the current market rate.

5.2 Advantages of interest rate swaps

(a) **Flexibility and costs**

Swaps are **flexible**, since they can be arranged in any size, and they can be **reversed** if necessary. **Transaction costs are low**, particularly if no intermediary is used, and are potentially much lower than the costs of terminating one loan and taking out another.

(b) **Credit ratings**

Companies **with different credit ratings** can **borrow in the market** that offers each the best deal and then swap this benefit to reduce the mutual borrowing costs. This is an example of the principle of **comparative advantage**.

(c) **Capital structure**

Swaps allow **capital restructuring** by changing the nature of interest commitments without renegotiating with lenders.

(d) **Risk management**

Swaps can be used to **manage interest rate risk** by swapping floating for fixed rate debt if rates are expected to rise. Swaps can also be used to swap a variable rate for a fixed rate investment if interest rates are expected to fall.

(e) **Convenience**

Swaps are relatively **easy to arrange**.

(f) **Predictability of cash flows**

If a company's future cash flows are uncertain, it can use a swap to ensure it has **predictable fixed rate commitments**.

5.3 Problems with interest rate swaps

(a) **Additional risk**

The swap is subject to **counterparty risk;** the risk that the other party will default leaving the first company to bear its obligations. This risk can be avoided by using an intermediary.

(b) **Movements in interest rates**

If a company takes on a floating rate commitment, it may be vulnerable to **adverse movements in interest rates**. If it takes on a fixed rate commitment, it won't be able to **take advantage of favourable movements in rates**.

(c) **Lack of liquidity**

The **lack of a secondary market in swaps** makes it **very difficult to liquidate a swap contract**.

(d) **Resources utilised**

If the savings from the swap are **small**, implementing it may not be worth the **time and effort involved**.

Exam alert

It is certainly worth learning the advantages and disadvantages of swaps, since they will normally give you some very easy marks in any question on swaps.

Example: Interest rate swaps

Goodcredit has been given a high credit rating. It can borrow at a fixed rate of 11%, or at a variable interest rate equal to LIBOR, which also happens to be 11% at the moment. It would like to borrow at a variable rate.

Secondtier is a company with a lower credit rating, which can borrow at a fixed rate of 12½% or at a variable rate of LIBOR plus ½%. It would like to borrow at a fixed rate.

Solution

	Goodcredit	Secondtier	Sum total
Company wants	Variable	Fixed	
Would pay (no swap)	(LIBOR)	(12.5%)	(LIBOR + 12.5%)
Could pay	(11%)	(LIBOR + 0.5%)	(LIBOR + 11.5%)
Potential gain			1%
Split evenly	0.5%	0.5%	
Expected outcome	(LIBOR – 0.5%)	(12%)	(LIBOR + 11.5%)
Swap terms			
Pay interest that could pay	(11%)	(LIBOR + 0.5%)	(LIBOR + 11.5%)
Swap floating	(LIBOR + 0.5%)	LIBOR + 0.5%	
Swap fixed (Working)	12%	(12%)	
Net paid	(LIBOR – 0.5%)	(12%)	(LIBOR + 11.5%)
Would pay	(LIBOR)	(12.5%)	(LIBOR + 12.5%)
Gain	0.5%	0.5%	1%

Working

The floating interest swapped is the amount paid by Secondtier.

Given that the gains are split equally, the fixed interest swap can be calculated as

$$12.5\% - \frac{12.5 - 11.5}{2} = 12\%$$

The starting point, the 12.5%, is what Secondtier would pay without the swap. The $\frac{12.5 - 11.5}{2}$ is half the gain, half the difference between what Secondtier would pay and could pay.

The results of the swap are that Goodcredit ends up paying variable rate interest, but at a lower cost than it could get from a bank, and Secondtier ends up paying fixed rate interest, also at a lower cost than it could get from investors or a bank.

5.4 Reason for gain

If both parties ended up paying interest at a lower rate than was obtainable from the bank, where did this gain come from? To answer this question, set out a table of the rates at which both companies could borrow from the bank.

	Goodcredit	*Secondtier*	*Difference* %
Can borrow at fixed rate	11%	12.5%	1.5
Can borrow at floating rate	LIBOR	LIBOR + 0.5%	0.5
Difference between differences			1.0

Goodcredit has a better credit rating than Secondtier in both types of loan market, but its advantage is comparatively higher in the fixed interest market. The 1% differential between Goodcredit's advantage in the two types of loan may represent a market imperfection or there may be a good reason for it. Whatever the reason, it represents a potential gain which can be made out of a swap arrangement. For a gain to happen:

(a) Each company must borrow in the loan market in which it has **comparative advantage**. Goodcredit has the greatest advantage when it borrows fixed interest. Secondtier has the least disadvantage when it borrows floating rate.

(b) The parties must actually **want** interest of the opposite type to that in which they have comparative advantage. Goodcredit wants floating and Secondtier wants fixed.

Once the target interest rate for each company has been established, there is an infinite number of swap arrangements which will produce the same net result. The example illustrated above is only one of them.

Question 9.2   Swap terms

Learning outcomes D2(a), (b)

We illustrated above one way in which the swap could work. (Swap fixed 12%, swap floating (LIBOR + 0.5%). Suggest an alternative arrangement for the swap, based on swapping fixed interest at 11%.

	Goodcredit	Secondtier
Could pay	(11%)	(LIBOR + 0.5%)
Swap floating		
Swap fixed		
Net interest cost	(LIBOR – 0.5%)	(12%)

Question 9.3   Swaps

Learning outcomes D2(a), (b)

Seeler Muller wishes to borrow 300 million euros for five years at a floating rate to finance an investment project in Germany. The cheapest rate at which it can raise such a loan is Euro LIBOR + 0.75%.

The company's bankers have suggested that one of their client companies, Overath Maier, would be interested in a swap arrangement. This company needs a fixed interest loan at €300 million. The cheapest rate at which it can arrange the loan is 10.5% per annum. It could, however, borrow in euros at the floating rate of euro LIBOR + 1.5%.

Seeler Muller can issue a fixed interest 5 year bond at 9% per annum interest. The banker would charge a swap arrangement fee of 0.15% per year to both parties. You are required to devise a swap by which both parties can benefit.

5.5 Speculation

As with all hedging methods, interest rate swaps can alternatively be used as a means of financial speculation. In cases receiving much publicity, local authority treasurers in the UK have engaged in such speculation with disastrous results.

Exam alert

Note that the financial advantages of a swap are not necessarily shared equally; it depends on the relative bargaining power of the two parties involved.

5.6 Swaptions

Swaptions are options on swaps, giving the holder the right but not the obligation to enter into a swap with the seller.

Payer swaptions give the holder the right to enter the swap as the fixed rate payer (and the floating rate receiver). **Receiver swaptions** give the holder the right to enter the swap as the fixed rate receiver (and the floating rate payer).

Swaptions generate a worst case scenario for buyers and sellers. For example an organisation that is going to issue floating rate debt can buy a payer swaption that offers the option to convert to being a fixed rate payer should interest rates increase.

They can also be used to counterbalance an existing arrangement and hence effectively terminate it.

Section summary

Interest rate swaps are where two parties agree to exchange interest rate payments.

Interest rate swaps can act as a means of **switching** from paying one type of interest to another, raising **less expensive loans** and **securing better deposit rates**.

6 Hedging strategy alternatives: example

Introduction

In this section we use a worked example to draw together what you've learnt in this chapter.

6.1 Hedging instruments

Different hedging instruments often offer alternative ways of managing risk in a specific situation. In this section, we consider the different ways in which a company can hedge interest rate risk.

Example: Hedging alternatives

It is 31 December. Octavo needs to borrow £6 million in three months' time for a period of six months. For the type of loan finance which Octavo would use, the rate of interest is currently 13% per year and the Corporate Treasurer is unwilling to pay a higher rate.

The treasurer is concerned about possible future fluctuations in interest rates, and is considering the following possibilities:

(a)   Forward rate agreements (FRAs)
(b)   Interest rate futures
(c)   Interest rate guarantees or short-term interest rate caps

Required

Explain briefly how each of these three alternatives might be useful to Octavo.

Solution

Forward rate agreements (FRAs)

Entering into an FRA with a bank will allow the treasurer of Octavo to **effectively lock in an interest rate** for the six months of the loan. This agreement is independent of the loan itself, upon which the prevailing rate will be paid. If the FRA were negotiated to be at a rate of 13%, and the actual interest rate paid on the loan were higher than this, the bank will pay the difference between the rate paid and 13% to Octavo. Conversely, if the interest paid by Octavo turned out to be lower than 13%, they would have to pay the difference to the bank. Thus the cost to Octavo will be 13% regardless of movements in actual interest rates.

Interest rate futures

Interest rate futures have the same effect as FRAs, in effectively **locking in an interest rate**, but they are standardised in terms of size, duration and terms. They can be **traded on an exchange** (such as LIFFE in London), and they will generally be **closed out before the maturity date**, yielding a profit or loss that is offset against the loss or profit on the money transaction that is being hedged. So, for example, as Octavo is concerned about rises in interest rates, the treasurer can sell future contracts now. If that rate does rise, their value will fall, and they can then be bought at a lower price, yielding a profit which will compensate for the increase in Octavo's loan interest cost. If interest rates fall, the lower interest cost of the loan will be offset by a loss on their futures contracts.

There may not be an **exact match** between the **loan and the future contract** (100% hedge), due to the standardised nature of the contracts, and margin payments may be required whilst the futures are still held.

Interest rate guarantees

Interest rate guarantees (or short term interest rate options) give Octavo the opportunity to **benefit from favourable interest rate movements** as well as protecting it from the effects of adverse movements. They give the holder the **right** but not the **obligation** to deal at an agreed interest rate at a future maturity date. This means that if interest rates rise, the treasurer would exercise the option, and 'lock in' to the predetermined borrowing rate. If, however, interest rates fall, then the option would simply lapse, and Octavo would feel the benefit of lower interest rates.

The main disadvantage of options is that a premium will be payable to the seller of the option, whether or not it is exercised. This will therefore add to the interest cost. The treasurer of Octavo will need to consider whether this cost, which can be quite expensive, is justified by the potential benefits to be gained from favourable interest rate movements.

Exam skills

When considering interest rate or currency risk hedging, don't discuss every possible technique that you can recall. Marks will only be awarded for techniques that are **appropriate** to the circumstances described in the question.

Section summary

If you have to discuss which instrument should be used to hedge interest rate risk, consider **cost**, **flexibility**, **expectations** and **ability to benefit** from favourable interest rate movements.

Chapter Roundup

✓ Factors influencing **interest rate risk** include the following.

  – Fixed rate versus floating rate debt
  – The term of the loan

✓ **Forward rate agreements** hedge risk by **fixing the interest rate** on future borrowing.

✓ **Interest rate futures** can be used to hedge against interest rate changes between the current date and the date at which the interest rate on the lending or borrowing is set. Borrowers **sell futures** to hedge against **interest rate rises;** lenders **buy futures** to hedge against **interest rate falls.**

✓ **Interest rate options** allow an organisation to limit its exposure to adverse interest rate movements, while allowing it to take advantage of favourable interest rate movements.

✓ **Borrowers** can set a **maximum** on the interest they have to pay by buying **put** options.

✓ **Lenders** can set a **minimum** on the interest they receive by buying **call** options.

✓ **Caps** set a ceiling to the interest rate; a **floor** sets a lower limit. A **collar** is the simultaneous selling of a cap and floor.

✓ The **value of an option** depends on the current price of the asset, the exercise price, the volatility (standard deviation) of the asset value, the time period to expiry and the risk-free rate of interest.

✓ **Interest rate swaps** are where two parties agree to exchange interest rate payments.

✓ Interest rate swaps can act as a means of **switching** from paying one type of interest to another, raising **less expensive loans** and **securing better deposit rates**.

✓ If you have to discuss which instrument should be used to hedge interest rate risk, consider **cost**, **flexibility**, **expectations** and **ability to benefit** from favourable interest rate movements.

Quick Quiz

1   Identify three aspects of a debt in which a company may be exposed to risk from interest rate movements.

2   What are 'FRAs'?

3   Fill in the blanks.

     If a company wishes to hedge borrowing at a future date, it should purchase

     .... options, if it wishes to hedge lending, it should purchase
     .... options

4   Fill in the blanks.

     With a **collar**, the borrower buys .... and at the same time sells ....

5   What aspect of the valuation of an option does the standard deviation measure?

     A   Asset price
     B   Exercise price
     C   Volatility of asset value
     D   Time to expiration

6   What happens if one party to a interest rate swap defaults on the arrangements to pay interest?

7   Give three uses of an interest rate swap.

8   Under the terms of a swap arrangement, Louie has paid interest at 10%, Dewie at LIBOR + 1%.

     The parties have swapped floating rate interest at LIBOR + 1%. What amount of fixed rate interest do they need to swap for Louie to end up paying net interest of LIBOR − 0.5%?

Answers to Quick Quiz

1   Any **three** of:

- Fixed rate *versus* floating rate debt
- Debt in different currencies
- Different terms of loan
- Term loan or overdraft facility

2   Forward interest rate agreements.

3   If a company wishes to hedge borrowing at a future date, it should purchase **put** options, if it wishes to hedge lending, it should purchase **call** options.

4   With a **collar** the borrower buys **an interest rate cap** and at the same time sells **an interest rate floor**.

5   C   Volatility of asset value

6   The original party is liable to the lender.

7   Any three of:

(a)   Switching from paying one type of interest to another
(b)   Raising less expensive loans
(c)   Securing better deposit rates
(d)   Acting as a cost-effective method of managing interest rate risk
(e)   Avoiding charges for early termination of loans
(f)   Accessing a type of finance that could not be accessed directly

8   Fixed interest swapped – Louie interest paid – Floating rate interest swapped = – (LIBOR – 0.5%)
Fixed interest swapped – 10% – (LIBOR + 1%) = – (LIBOR – 0.5%)
Fixed interest swapped = 10% + (LIBOR + 1%) – (LIBOR – 0.5%) = 11.5%

Answers to Questions

9.1 Hedging

Hedging is a means of reducing risk. Hedging involves coming to an **agreement with another party** who is prepared to take on the risk that you would **otherwise bear**. The other party may be willing to take on that risk because he would otherwise bear an opposing risk which may be 'matched' with your risk; alternatively, the other party may be a speculator who is willing to bear the risk in return for the prospect of making a profit. In the case of interest rates, a company with a variable rate loan clearly faces the risk that the rate of interest will increase in the future as the result of changing market conditions which cannot now be predicted.

Many financial instruments have been introduced in recent years to help corporate treasurers to hedge the risks of interest rate movements. These instruments include forward rate agreements, financial futures, interest rate swaps and options.

9.2 Swap terms

	Goodcredit	Secondtier
Could pay	(11%)	(LIBOR + 0.5%)
Swap floating (working)	(LIBOR – 0.5%)	LIBOR – 0.5%
Swap fixed	11%	(11%)
Net interest cost	(LIBOR – 0.5%)	(12%)

Working

Given that the gains are split equally, the floating interest swap can be calculated as:

$$\text{LIBOR} - \frac{12.5 - 11.5}{2} = \text{LIBOR} - 0.5\%$$

The starting point, the LIBOR, is what Goodcredit would pay without the swap.

The $\dfrac{12.5 - 11.5}{2}$ is half the gain, half the difference between what Goodcredit would pay and could pay.

9.3 Swaps

	Seeler Muller Floating	Overath Maier Fixed	Sum total
Company wants			
Would pay (no swap)	(LIBOR + 0.75%)	(10.5%)	(LIBOR + 11.25%)
Could pay	(9%)	(LIBOR + 1.5%)	(LIBOR + 10.5%)
Commission	(0.15%)	(0.15%)	(0.3%)
Potential gain (difference between would pay and could pay – commission)			0.45%
split evenly	0.225%	0.225%	
Expected outcome (would pay + potential gain)	(LIBOR + 0.525%)	(10.275%)	(LIBOR + 10.8%)
Swap terms			
Could pay	(9%)	(LIBOR + 1.5%)	(LIBOR + 10.5%)
Swap floating	(LIBOR + 1.5%)	LIBOR + 1.5%	
Swap fixed (W)	10.125%	(10.125%)	
Commission	(0.15%)	(0.15%)	(0.3%)
Net paid	(LIBOR + 0.525%)	(10.275%)	(LIBOR + 10.8%)
Would pay	(LIBOR + 0.75%)	(10.5%)	(LIBOR + 11.25%)
Gain	0.225%	0.225%	0.45%

Both companies make a net gain of 0.225%. The swap proceeds as follows.

 Seeler Muller raises a fixed interest 5 year loan for €300 million at 9% interest.

 Overath Maier raises a floating rate €300 million loan at LIBOR + 1.5%.

 The companies swap loan principals.

 Each year, each company pays its own loan interest and swaps the interest to the counterparty, and receives the interest swap from the counterparty. As shown above, the exact payments between the two companies will depend on how the gains are to be split.

Here the floating swap is the floating interest Overath Muller pays. The fixed interest swap can be calculated as:

$$10.5\% - \frac{11.25 - 10.5}{2} = 10.125\%$$

 At the end of 5 years, the loan principals are swapped back and the companies repay their original loans.

Now try this question from the Exam Question Bank	**Number**	**Level**	**Marks**	**Time**
	Q13	Examination	17	31 mins

INTERNATIONAL RISKS

In this chapter we shall concentrate on the risks facing businesses that have international involvements, particularly those that trade or invest overseas. They include, but are not confined to, risks from adverse movements in exchange rates. Other risks may well have a significant impact on an organisation's strategy; directors will be concerned for example if there is political risk that the company will not be able to repatriate funds from overseas operations.

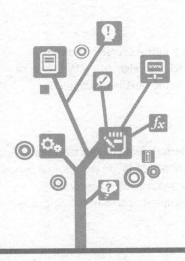

10

topic list	learning outcomes	syllabus references	ability required
1 International risks	D1(a)	D1(i),(ii)	evaluation
2 Economic and translation risks	D1(a), 2(a), (b), (d)	D1(i),(ii)	evaluation
3 Political risks	D1(a), 2(a), (b), (d)	D1(i),(ii), 2(i)	evaluation
4 Product and cultural risks	D1(a), 2(a), (b), (d)	D1(i),(ii)	evaluation
5 Trading and credit risks	D1(a), 2(a), (b), (d)	D1(i), (ii)	evaluation

1 International risks

Introduction

In this section we introduce the international risks that will be significant for many businesses. Some relate to **specific operational problems** such as slow payment by customers, others affect **strategic decisions** such as whether to invest in countries where the political situation is delicate.

1.1 International risks

Businesses face various significant risks relating to international trading, operations and investments.

1.2 Currency risks

Currency risk arises from unexpected movements in exchange rates. A company may become exposed to **currency risk** (or '**exchange rate risk**') in a number of ways, including the following.

- As an exporter of goods or services
- Through having an overseas subsidiary
- Through being the subsidiary of an overseas company
- Through transactions in overseas capital markets

The following different types of currency risk may be important.

1.2.1 Transaction risks

Transaction risk is the risk of adverse exchange rate movements occurring in the course of **normal international trading transactions**. This arises when export prices are fixed in foreign currency terms, or imports are invoiced in foreign currencies. Transaction risks are covered in the next two chapters.

1.2.2 Economic risks

Economic risk refers to the effect of exchange rate movements on the **international competitiveness** of a company. For example, a UK company might use raw materials which are priced in US dollars, but export its products mainly within the European Union. A depreciation of sterling against the dollar or an appreciation of sterling against other EU currencies will both erode the competitiveness of the company.

1.2.3 Translation risks

Translation risk arises from differences in the currencies in which **assets and liabilities** are denominated. If a company has different proportions of its assets and liabilities denominated in particular currencies, then exchange rate movements are likely to have varying effects on the value of these assets and liabilities.

1.2.4 Other risks

As well as the risks of adverse movements in the foreign exchange and interest markets, there are other risks if organisations become involved in dealings.

- **Dealer risk** – the risk of losses through poor performance or communication by dealers
- **Counterparty risk** – if dealing with another party (eg with swaps) the risk that the other party will default and leave you with losses or liabilities
- **Legal risk** – the risks of not being able to enforce contracts internationally
- **Control risk** – the adequacy of controls over treasury departments or over dealers

1.3 Political risks

When a multinational company invests in another country, by setting up a subsidiary for example, it may face a **political risk** of action by that country's government which **restricts the multinational's freedom**.

CASE STUDY

Mining companies in Canada are carrying out social risk assessments for major projects, assessing how the local social, economic and cultural conditions may affect the project. These assessments reflect the impact that mining projects often have on environmentally and socially sensitive areas such as wildlife habitats, biodiversity points and indigenous communities. Linked issues may include poverty, conflict, political instability and human rights violations. Failure to take account of these issues may result in serious opposition, cultural conflict, delays in granting of mining rights and rejections of mining licenses.

Social risk assessments aim to engage stakeholders and understand their concerns as well as assessing key social and political issues. They feed through not only into strategic and operational plans, but also community investment, stakeholder engagement and communications plans.

Exam alert

Question 1 in May 2010 asked about the risks of a new subsidiary, including political risks.

1.4 Product and culture risks

Businesses that trade abroad have to be sensitive to differences in the environment that affect the **products they sell** and the **ways they do business**.   Sometimes these differences are easy to see, for example legal requirements and restrictions affecting products. However other, vaguer, factors may also be significant, for example customs and tastes affecting how products are presented, relations with customers and the ways the business is **structured abroad**.

Exam alert

Question 3 on the specimen paper featured a discussion about the issues connected with launching a product in two different countries.

1.5 Trade and credit risks

Risks may arise during the course of trading activities, some related to the distances involved in product distribution. Credit control over overseas customers may prove more challenging than over **domestic customers**.

Exam alert

The Section A question in your exam may well feature a large international company.

Section summary

Many business risks have an **international** dimension.

2 Economic and translation risks

Introduction

In this section we look at the longer-term exchange risks that organisations face. Remember that the shorter-term exchange risks on transactions are covered in the next two chapters.

2.1 Economic risks

5/10

KEY TERM

ECONOMIC RISK is the risk that exchange rate movements might reduce the international competitiveness of a company. It is the risk that the present value of a company's future cash flows might be reduced by adverse exchange rate movements.

Economic exposure reveals itself in many different ways, as shown in the following examples.

Example: Economic exposure

Trends in exchange rates

Suppose a UK company invests in setting up a subsidiary in Eastern Europe. The currency of the Eastern European country depreciates continuously over a five year period. The cash flows remitted back to the UK are worth less in sterling terms each year, causing a reduction in the value of the investment project.

Another UK company buys raw materials which are priced in US dollars. It converts these materials into finished products which it exports mainly to Spain. Over a period of several years, the pound depreciates against the dollar but strengthens against the euro. The sterling value of the company's income declines while the sterling cost of its materials increases, resulting in a drop in the value of the company's cash flows.

The value of a company depends on the **present value** of its **expected future cash flows**. If there are fears that a company is exposed to the sort of exchange rate movements described above, this may reduce the company's value. Protecting against economic exposure is therefore necessary to protect the company's share price.

A company need not even engage in any foreign activities to be subject to economic exposure. For example if a company trades only in the UK but the pound strengthens appreciably against other world currencies, it may find that it loses UK sales to a foreign competitor who can now afford to charge cheaper sterling prices.

One-off events

As well as trends in exchange rates, one-off events such as a major stock market crash or disaster such as 9/11 may administer a 'shock' to exchange rate levels.

Assessing the impact of economic risks

None of these examples are as simple as they seem, however, because of the compensating actions of economic forces. For example, if the exchange rate of an Eastern European country depreciates significantly, it is probably because of its high inflation rate.

So if the Eastern European subsidiary of a UK company **increases its prices** in line with inflation, its cash flows in the local currency will increase each year. These will be converted at the depreciating exchange rate to produce a fairly constant sterling value of cash flows. Alternatively, if the subsidiary does not increase its prices, it may increase its sales volume by selling at more competitive prices.

2.2 Hedging economic risks

Various actions can reduce economic exposure, including the following.

(a)   **Matching assets and liabilities**

A foreign subsidiary can be financed, so far as possible, with a loan in the currency of the country in which the subsidiary operates. A depreciating currency results in reduced income but also reduced loan service costs. A multinational will try to match assets and liabilities in each currency so far as possible.

(b)   **Diversifying the supplier and customer base**

For example, if the currency of one of the supplier countries strengthens, purchasing can be switched to a cheaper source.

(c)   **Diversifying operations world-wide**

On the principle that countries which confine themselves to one country suffer from economic exposure, international diversification is a method of reducing economic exposure.

2.3 Translation risks

KEY TERM

TRANSLATION RISK is the risk that the organisation will make **exchange losses** when the **accounting results** of its foreign branches or subsidiaries are **translated** into the **home currency**.

Translation losses can result, for example, from restating the book value of a foreign subsidiary's assets at the exchange rate on the **date** of the **statement of financial position**. Such losses will not have an impact on the firm's cash flow unless the assets are sold. This could influence **investors' and lenders' attitudes** to the financial worth and creditworthiness of the company. Such risk can be reduced if assets and liabilities denominated in particular currencies can be **held in balanced amounts**.

Section summary

Economic exposure can be hedged by **matching assets and liabilities** and **diversification**.

Translation exposure, the risk of apparent losses appearing when accounting results are translated, probably does not need to be hedged.

3   **Political risks**   **5/10**

Introduction

Actions by overseas governments can very seriously affect businesses that trade and invest board. The risks may be so significant that the business abandons operations and pulls out of the overseas location; however there are a number of possible measures it can take to reduce risks.

3.1 Political risks for multinationals

KEY TERM

POLITICAL RISK is the risk that political action will affect the position and value of a company.

When a multinational company invests in another country, by setting up a subsidiary, it may face a **political risk** of action by that country's government which restricts the multinational's freedom. The government of a country will almost certainly want to encourage the development and growth of commerce and industry, but it might also be suspicious of the motives of multinationals which set up subsidiaries in their country, perhaps fearing exploitation.

3.2 Methods of government action

If a government tries to prevent the exploitation of its country by multinationals, it may take various measures.

(a) Import **quotas** could be used to limit the quantities of goods that a subsidiary can buy from its parent company and import for resale in its domestic markets.

(b) Import **tariffs** could make imports (such as from parent companies) more expensive and domestically produced goods therefore more competitive.

(c) Legal standards of safety or quality (**non-tariff barriers**) could be imposed on imported goods to prevent multinationals from selling goods through a subsidiary which have been banned as dangerous in other countries.

(d) **Restrictions** on the **use of local resources.**

(e) **Export and import controls** for political, environmental, or health and safety reasons. Such controls may not be overt but instead take the form of bureaucratic procedures designed to discourage international trade or protect home producers.

(f) **Favourable trade status** for particular countries, eg EU membership, former Commonwealth countries.

(g) **Monopolies and mergers legislation**, which may be interpreted not only within a country but also across nations. Thus the acquisition of a company in country A, by company B, which both sell in country C may be seen as a monopolistic restraint of trade.

(h) **Taxation law** may be used to encourage or discourage particular import/export activities. For example, freeports may be set up, or generous tax incentives for inward investment may be offered.

(i) A government could **restrict** the ability of foreign companies to buy domestic companies, especially those that operate in politically sensitive industries such as defence contracting, communications, energy supply and so on.

(j) A government could **nationalise** foreign-owned companies and their assets (with or without compensation to the parent company).

(k) A government could insist on a **minimum shareholding** or **majority shareholding** in companies by residents. This would force a multinational to offer some of the equity in a subsidiary to investors in the country where the subsidiary operates.

(l) **Exchange control regulations** could be applied (see below).

3.3 Assessment of political risk

There are a large number of factors that can be considered to assess political risk, for example government stability, remittance restrictions and assets seized. Measurement is often by **subjective weighting** of these factors. **Industry specific factors** are also important.

3.4 Dealing with political risk

There are various strategies that multinational companies can adopt to limit the effects of political risk.

3.4.1 Negotiations with host government

The aim of these negotiations is generally to obtain a **concession agreement**. This would cover matters such as the transfer of capital, remittances and products, access to local finance, government intervention and taxation, and transfer pricing. The main problem with concession agreements can be that the initial terms of the agreement may not prove to be satisfactory subsequently.

3.4.2 Insurance

In the UK the Export Credits Guarantee Department (ECGD) provides protection against various threats including **nationalisation, currency conversion problems**, war and revolution.

3.4.3 Production strategies

It may be necessary to strike a balance between **contracting out to local sources** (thus losing control) and **producing directly** (which increases the investment and hence increases the potential loss). Alternatively it may be better to locate key parts of the production process or the distribution channels abroad. Control of patents is another possibility, since these can be enforced internationally.

3.4.4 Contacts with markets

Multinationals may have **contacts with customers** that interventionist governments cannot obtain.

3.4.5 Financial management

If a multinational **obtains funds** in **local investment markets**, these may be on terms that are less favourable than on markets abroad, but would mean that local institutions suffered if the local government intervened. However governments often limit the ability of multinationals to obtain funds locally.

Alternatively guarantees can be obtained from the government for the investment that can be enforced by the multinational if the government takes action.

3.4.6 Management structure

If governments do intervene, multinationals may have to make use of the advantages they hold or **threaten withdrawal**. The threat of expropriation may be reduced by negotiation or legal threats.

Overseas investment risks can also be managed effectively by adopting the most appropriate **structure** for their operations. For example:

(a)   **Branches** are a simple way of expanding an existing legal entity but do not allow local tax initiatives to be exploited.

(b)   **Subsidiaries** will increase the local profile of a company and allow greater use of being a separate legal entity, but have far more administration to deal with (eg an external audit).

(c)   **Joint ventures** are a good way of **sharing risks** but require strategic fit and trust with the other partner.

(d)   **Licensing** allows for a quick and cheap way of supplying goods and services but is at the mercy of quality control of the local producer.

3.5 Blocked funds

Exchange controls restrict the flow of foreign exchange into and out of a country, usually to defend the local currency or to protect reserves of foreign currencies. Exchange controls are generally more restrictive in developing and less developed countries although some still exist in developed countries. Typically, a government might enforce regulations:

(a)   **Rationing the supply of foreign exchange**. Anyone wishing to make payments abroad in a foreign currency will be restricted by the limited supply, which stops them from buying as much as they want from abroad.

(b)   **Restricting the types of transaction** for which payments abroad are allowed, for example by suspending or banning the payment of dividends to foreign shareholders, such as parent companies in multinationals, who will then have the problem of **blocked funds**.

Exam alert

Discussion of methods of dealing with blocked funds is a likely exam topic.

3.5.1 Ways of overcoming blocked funds

(a) The parent company could **sell goods or services** to the subsidiary and obtain payment. The amount of this payment will depend on the volume of sales and also on the transfer price for the sales.

(b) A parent company that grants a subsidiary the right to make goods protected by patents can charge a **royalty** on any goods that the subsidiary sells. The size of any royalty can be adjusted to suit the wishes of the parent company's management.

(c) If the parent company makes a **loan** to a subsidiary, it can set the interest rate high or low, thereby affecting the profits of both companies. A high rate of interest on a loan, for example, would improve the parent company's profits to the detriment of the subsidiary's profits.

(d) **Management charges** may be levied by the parent company for costs incurred in the management of international operations.

| **Question 10.1** | Political risk |

Learning outcomes D2(a), (b)

Your company has purchased the following data which provide scores of the political risk for a number of countries in which the company is considering investing in a new subsidiary.

	Total	Economic performance	Debt in default	Credit ratings	Government stability	Remittance restrictions	Access capital
Weighting	100	25	10	10	25	15	15
Gmala	37	13	4	5	5	10	0
Forland	52	5	10	9	16	8	4
Amapore	36	12	2	3	9	5	5
Covia	30	9	3	2	15	1	0
Settia	39	15	4	3	11	4	2

Countries have been rated on a scale from 0 up to the maximum weighting for each factor (eg 0–15 for remittance restrictions). A high score for each factor, as well as overall, reflects low political risk.

A proposal has been put before the company's board of directors that investment should take place in Forland.

Required

Prepare a brief report for the company's board of directors discussing whether or not the above data should form the basis for:

(a) The measurement of political risk, and
(b) The decision about which country to invest in

Section summary

Multinationals can take various measures to combat the risks of **political interference** or **turbulence** including agreements with governments, insurance, and location elsewhere of key parts of the production process.

4 Product and cultural risks

Introduction

In this section we deal with the risks that relate to the products companies sell and the different cultures in which they trade. Failure to adjust to different environments can lead to significant costs and poor sales.

4.1 Product risks

Companies may face government legislation or action in any jurisdiction that extend over its products. Important areas may include the following:

4.1.1 Legal risks

(a)   Determination of minimum **technical standards** that the goods must meet, eg noise levels, contents and so on.

(b)   **Standardisation measures** such as packaging sizes.

(c)   **Pricing regulations**, including credit (eg, some countries require importers to deposit payment in advance and may require the price to be no lower than those of domestic competitors).

(d)   **Restrictions on promotional messages**, methods and media.

(e)   **Product liability**. Different countries have different rules regarding product liability (ie the manufacturer's/retailer's responsibility for defects in the product sold and/or injury caused). US juries are notoriously generous in this respect.

(f)   **Acceptance of international trademark, copyright and patent conventions**. Not all countries recognise such international conventions.

Businesses that fail to comply with the law run the risk of **legal penalties** and accompanying **bad publicity**. Companies may also be forced into legal action to counter claims of allegedly bad practice that is not actually illegal; as the McDonalds case demonstrates, even a victory in such an action cannot prevent much bad publicity.

The issues of legal standards and costs have very significant implications for companies that trade internationally. Companies that meet a strict set of standards in one country may face accusations of **hypocrisy** if their practices are laxer elsewhere. Ultimately higher costs of compliance, as well as costs of labour may mean that companies **relocate** to countries where costs and regulatory burdens are lower.

Bear in mind that organisations may also face legal risks from lack of legislation (or lack of enforcement of legislation) designed to protect them.

CASE STUDY

The Welsh company Performance Practitioners devised a new product, the Sales Activator, for the global sales development market. This product needed to be protected from imitators, particularly as it gave access to new markets overseas.

Performance Practitioners found that it was essential to obtain expert advice. The company decided on a portfolio of measures. Copyright protection was free, but a weak form of protection in many environments. The company also registered the Sales Activator as a trademark and communicated its intellectual property rights at every opportunity.

However Performance Practitioners had to risk not being able to take effective action to protect its rights if it wanted to operate in some markets. In some countries it can take months for an intellectual property case to come to court. Performance Practitioners also had to consider the need to limit costs because of its desire to invest in the rest of its business. Therefore some options, like global patent protection, were too expensive. Nevertheless the company needed enough funds to police its rights. The ability to protect intellectual property is diminished if a company cannot afford to take offenders to court.

Exam alert

Legal risk will bear particularly hard on organisations in very regulated sectors, such as financial services.

4.1.2 Products and cultural differences

National culture may have a **significant impact** on the **demand for products**. For example consumers in some countries prefer front-loading washing machines and others prefer top-loading washing machines. In some countries the lack of electricity will restrict the demand for electronic items.

Products also have **symbolic and psychological aspects** as well as physical attributes. As a result, entry into a market with a different set of cultural, religious, economic, social and political assumptions may cause extreme consumer reactions.

Some products are extremely sensitive to the **environmental differences**, which bring about the need for adaptation; others are not at all sensitive to these differences, in which case standardisation is possible.

Environmentally sensitive	Environmentally insensitive
Adaptation necessary	Standardisation possible
• Fashion clothes • Convenience foods	• Industrial and agricultural products • World market products, eg jeans

4.2 Dealing with product risks

4.2.1 Legal risks

One aspect of minimising problems is social and commercial good citizenship, **complying with best practice** and being responsive to **ethical concerns**. Often what is considered good practice at present is likely to acquire some regulatory force in the future. In addition, compliance with voluntary codes, particularly those relating to best practice or relations with consumers, can be **marketed positively**.

Companies may also wish to take all possible steps to avoid the bad publicity resulting from a court action. This includes implementing systems to make sure that the company **keeps abreast** of **changes in the law**, and staff are kept fully informed. Internal procedures may be designed to minimise the risks from legal action.

4.2.2 Cultural differences

The most important thing a business can do is to make the right decision on whether to **standardise** or **adapt products**.

Businesses need to be aware of the arguments in favour of standardisation, most of which link in with economies of scale:

- Production concentrated on one country
- Avoidance of product modification costs
- Standardisation of promotion, distribution and other aspects of marketing mix
- Promotion of global brand

At the same time businesses need to be aware of the different ways in which products can be adapted:

- **Fulfilling the same function under different conditions**, such as an electrical device being adapted to conform to a different voltage

- **Marketing an unchanged product to fulfil a different need**, as when garden implements are promoted as agricultural equipment in less-developed countries

4.3 Cultural risks

Where a business trades with, or invests in, a foreign country the existence of different customs, laws and language can create wider problems than those related to product preferences. Communication between parties can be hindered, and potential deals put into jeopardy by ignorance of the expected manner in which such transactions should be conducted.

The following areas may be particularly important.

(a) The **cultures and practices of customers** and consumers in individual markets

(b) The **media and distribution systems** in overseas markets

(c) The **different ways of doing business** (eg it is reputed that Japanese companies are concerned to avoid excessive legalism) in overseas markets

(d) The degree to which a firm can use its own '**national culture**' as a selling point

CASE STUDY

Assumptions about particular cultures can also be dangerous. *Accountancy* magazine ran a series about the major cultural issues involved in dealing with particular countries. Its article on Greece suggested that 'unorthodox' methods might be required to be successful there:

'The concept of a bribe is one that is well understood in Greece.'

Unsurprisingly the magazine received a number of complaints about this article.

4.4 Dealing with cultural risks

4.4.1 Deciding which markets to enter

Making the right choices about which markets to enter is a key element in dealing with cultural risk. When deciding what types of country it should enter (in terms of environmental factors, economic development, language used, cultural similarities and so on), the major criteria for this decision should be as follows.

(a) **Market attractiveness**. This concerns such indicators as GNP/head and forecast demand.

(b) **Competitive advantage**. This is principally dependent on prior experience in similar markets, language and cultural understanding.

(c) **Risk**. This involves an analysis of political stability, the possibility of government intervention and similar external influences.

4.4.2 Use of control systems

Local conditions and the scale of operations will influence the organisation structure of companies trading internationally. Conglomerates with widely differing product groups may organise globally by product, with each operating division having its own geographic structure suited to its own needs.

Companies with more integrated operations may prefer their top-level structure to be broken down **geographically** with product management conducted locally.

Very large and complex companies may be organised as a **heterarchy,** an organic structure with significant local control.

4.4.3 Degree of centralisation

Central control may be appropriate if the volume of international business or the company's experience in international operations is low. Centralisation can **promote efficiency** and prevent duplication of effort between regions. Even when operations are on a limited scale, when conformity with demanding technical standards is required, some central control may be necessary. Thus, a largely autonomous foreign subsidiary may have to accept supervision of its quality assurance or financial reporting functions.

If business is done globally, a form of **regional organisation** may be appropriate if there is some measure of social and economic integration within regions. The need for rapid response to local opportunities and threats may be served by a significant measure of **decentralisation**. National political and cultural sensitivities may reinforce this, but a shortage of local talent may limit it.

4.4.4 Management of human resources

For an international company, which has to think globally as well as act locally, there are a number of problems.

- Do you employ mainly **expatriate staff** to control local operations?

- Do you employ **local managers**, with the possible loss of central control?

- Is there such a thing as the **global manager**, equally at home in different cultures?

Section summary

Businesses need to ensure they **manage the varying legal requirements** that affect products in different countries.

A key decision when dealing with product risk is whether to **adapt the products for local markets**.

Cultural risk also affects the way organisations are managed and staffed. Businesses should take cultural issues into account when deciding **where** to **sell abroad**, and how much to **centralise** activities.

5 Trading and credit risks

Introduction

In this section we briefly recap on the methods used by businesses to manage risks affecting trading and the collection of debts from overseas customers.

5.1 Trading risks

Both domestic and international traders will face trading risks, although those faced by the latter will generally be greater due to the increased distances and times involved. The types of trading risk include:

(a)   **Physical risk** – the risk of goods being lost or stolen in transit, or the documents accompanying the goods going astray

(b)   **Credit risk** – the possibility of payment default by the customer. This is discussed further below

(c)   **Trade risk** – the risk of the customer refusing to accept the goods on delivery (due to sub-standard/inappropriate goods), or the cancellation of the order in transit

(d)   **Liquidity risk** – the inability to finance the credit

Such risks may be reduced with the **help** of **banks, insurance companies, credit reference agencies** and government agencies, such as the UK's Export Credit Guarantee Department (ECGD).

Other ways to reduce these risks include risk **transfer.** A business shipping parcels overseas may agree a contract obligating the courier to pay for losses in excess of its statutory liability.

5.2 Credit risks

KEY TERM

CREDIT RISK is the possibility that a loss may occur from the failure of another party to perform according to the terms of a contract.

(CIMA Official Terminology)

You will have covered the elements of a basic credit risk or debtor management strategy in some detail in your earlier studies. Briefly these are:

- Assess the **creditworthiness** of new customers before extending credit, by obtaining trade, bank and credit agency references and making use of information from financial statements and salesmen's reports.

- Set **credit limits** and **credit periods** in line with those offered by competitors, but taking account of the status of individual customers.

- Set up a system of **credit control** that will ensure that credit checks and terms are being adhered to.

5.3 International credit risk management

Where a company trades overseas, the risk of bad debts is potentially increased by the lack of direct **contact** with, and **knowledge** of, the **overseas customers** and the business environment. Whilst the basic methods of minimising foreign credit risk will be as above, we shall here consider the additional options available to the exporter.

There are a number of methods of reducing the risks of bad debts in foreign trade.

Export factoring	Essentially the same as factoring domestic trade debts.
Forfaiting	Medium-term export finance by the **purchase of financial instruments** such as bills of exchange or letters of credit on a **non-recourse basis by a forfaiter**.
Documentary credits	**Risk-free method** of obtaining payment, also a method of obtaining short-term finance from a bank, for **working capital**. as a bank might agree to discount or negotiate a letter of discount.
International credit unions	Organisations or **associations of finance houses or banks** in different countries (in Europe). The finance houses or banks have reciprocal arrangements for providing **instalment credit finance**.
Export credit insurance	Insurance against the **risk of non-payment by foreign customers** for export debts.
Acceptance credits	**Short-term finance** by a bank agreeing to accept bills of exchange drawn on itself. The bills can be discounted to **provide immediate finance**.
Export merchants	Export merchants **buy goods from manufacturers** and then export them. The manufacturer **receives payment quickly** and the export merchant **bears the risk of bad debts**.
Government departments	Government departments supply **support for banks** who **provide finance** to exporters of **capital goods**.

Section summary

The risks faced by exporters include those arising from **general business and trading conditions**.

Management of **credit risk** is of particular importance to exporters and various instruments and other arrangements are available to assist in this, such as documentary credits, bills of exchange, export credit insurance, export factoring and forfaiting.

Chapter Roundup

✓ Many business risks have an **international dimension**.

✓ **Economic exposure** can be hedged by **matching assets and liabilities** and **diversification**.

✓ **Translation exposure,** the risk of apparent losses appearing when accounting results are translated, probably does not need to be hedged.

✓ Multinationals can take various measures to combat the risks of **political interference** or **turbulence** including agreements with governments, insurance, and location elsewhere of key parts of the production process.

✓ Businesses need to ensure they **manage the varying legal requirements** that affect products in different countries.

✓ A key decision when dealing with product risk is whether to **adapt the products for local markets**.

✓ **Cultural risk** also affects the way organisations are managed and staffed. Businesses should take cultural issues into account when deciding **where** to **sell abroad**, and how much to **centralise** activities.

✓ The risks faced by exporters include those arising from **general business and trading conditions**.

✓ Management of **credit risk** is of particular importance to exporters and various instruments and other arrangements are available to assist in this, such as documentary credits, bills of exchange, export credit insurance, export factoring and forfaiting.

Quick Quiz

1   What is physical trading risk?

2   Fill in the blank.

    .... is the possibility that a loss may occur from the failure of another party to accept the goods on delivery.

3   Which of the following is not a type of currency risk?

    A   Credit risk
    B   Economic risk
    C   Transaction risk
    D   Translation risk

4   Which of the following is more likely to be sensitive to the local cultural environment?

    Convenience foods ☐

    Jeans ☐

5   Give three examples of restrictions that may be defined as political risk.

6   By what methods do governments impose exchange controls?

7   Fill in the blank.

    .... risk is the risk that companies will fail to finance the credit they give to customers.

8   Give four examples of ways companies can overcome exchange controls.

9   Fill in the blank.

    .... are short-term finance by a bank agreeing to accept bills of exchange drawn on itself. The bills can be discounted to provide immediate finance.

Answers to Quick Quiz

1   The risk of goods being lost or stolen in transit, or the documents accompanying the goods going astray

2   **Trade risk** is the possibility that a loss may occur from the failure of another party to accept the goods on delivery

3   A   Credit risk

4   Convenience foods (Jeans are standard across many countries)

5   •   Quotas
     •   Exchange controls
     •   Tax regulations
     •   Restrictions on the use of local resources
     •   Legal standards
     •   Ownership rules

6   •   Rationing the supply of foreign exchange
     •   Restricting the types of transaction for which payments abroad are allowed

7   **Credit risk** is the risk that companies will fail to finance the credit they give to customers.

8   •   Selling goods or services to subsidiary
     •   Charging a royalty on goods sold by subsidiary
     •   Interest rate manipulation
     •   Management charges

9   **Acceptance credits** are short-term finance by a bank agreeing to accept bills of exchange drawn on itself. The bills can be discounted to provide immediate finance.

Answers to Questions

10.1 Political risk

To: Board of directors
From: Accountant
Date: 17 December 20X8
Subject: The evaluation of political risk in investment decisions

The measurement of political risk

Political risk in foreign investment could be defined as the threat that a foreign government will change the rules of the game after the investment has been made. There are various agencies that can provide risk scores for different countries, but the key problem for all such approaches is that the scores that they use will always be subjective.

Weaknesses of approach

Considering the data that is being used in this case in more detail, there are a number of weaknesses that should be recognised.

(a)   **Economic performance** is one of the most heavily weighted factors. However it can be argued that this is not really a component of political risk.

(b)   There is **no information** as to how the **weightings have been arrived** at.

(c)   A number of factors that could have been included have been ignored. These include:

- Cultural homogeneity
- Quality of infrastructure
- Legal system
- Record on nationalisation
- Currency stability

Other methods of evaluation

The directors should also consider some of the other approaches to the evaluation of political risk. These include:

(a)   Seeking the **views of individuals** with direct experience of the countries in question, such as academics, diplomats and journalists

(b)   **Social** as well as **economic analysis**

The decision about which country to invest in

The evaluation of political risk must obviously form some part of the decision about which country to invest in. However, the use of this type of data to evaluate political risk in this context can be misleading for the following reasons:

(a)   **Microrisks**

These scores are valid at the macro level, but they do not measure the risk that is faced at the micro level by the industry or firm. Certain industries, such as mining and agriculture are more prone to political risk than are others. Some activities will be welcomed by countries due to the perceived benefits that their presence can bring. Examples of this can be seen in the UK economy where the activities of the multinational biotechnology companies are being severely restricted, while investment by Japanese microchip companies is welcomed and assisted.

(b)   **Emphasis on political features**

It can lead to an over-emphasis on the political features of the host country while neglecting other vital considerations such as the strategic fit of the new investment with the company's other operations.

Conclusion

This type of data therefore has relevance to the investment decision, but should not form the sole basis on which the decision is made. Although Forland comes out best in the overall scores, it has the **worst level** of **economic performance**. If the subsidiary is being developed with a view to serving primarily the local market, then this factor should receive a higher weighting in the overall decision making process since it will have a significant impact on the expected cash flow that will be generated.

Now try this question from the Exam Question Bank

Number	Level	Marks	Time
Q14	Examination	25	45 mins

TRANSACTION RISK I

In this chapter and the next we see how business that undertake transactions may be liable to risks arising from short-term exchange rate movements.

Before we look at how these risks and what can be done to manage it, you need a good understanding of exchange rate theory and must be comfortable with basic exchange rate calculations. Section 1 therefore deals with these calculations. In Section 2 we examine the factors influencing movements in exchange rates.

In Section 3 we demonstrate how transaction risks can affect a business before moving on to discuss the simpler ways of managing the risk in the rest of the chapter.

The temptation with transaction risk is to go very quickly through the topics covered in this chapter and spend more time on the more difficult techniques covered in the next chapter, Chapter 12. However a number of the topics covered in this chapter will certainly be covered in exam questions.

Remember also that although risks will be tested numerically (by calculation or interpretation) there will also be a significant written element in every question. You therefore will need to be able to explain what the key risks are and describe the techniques for dealing with them.

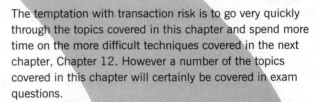

topic list	learning outcomes	syllabus references	ability required
1 Exchange rates	D2(c)	D2(v)	analysis
2 Factors influencing exchange rates	D2(c)	D2(v)	analysis
3 Transaction risk	D2(a),(b)	D1(ii)	evaluation
4 Managing transaction risk	D2(a),(b)	D2(viii)	evaluation
5 Forward exchange contracts	D2(a),(b)	D2(iii)	evaluation
6 Money market hedging	D2(a),(b)	D2(iii)	evaluation
7 Choosing a hedging method	D2(a),(b)	D2(iii)	evaluation

1 Exchange rates

Introduction

We start off with the basics of exchange rates – the definitions you need to know and the calculations you need to be able to do. This section gives you lots of practice in tackling the important calculations.

1.1 Spot rates

KEY TERM

The SPOT RATE is the current rate (typically of interest or currency exchange) available in the market today.

(CIMA Official Terminology)

The **spot rate** is the rate of exchange in currency for **immediate delivery.**

1.2 Paying foreign suppliers

If an importer has to pay a foreign supplier in a foreign currency, it might ask its bank to sell it the required amount of the currency. The bank will sell the currency at a selling rate known as the **bid price.**

Example: Paying foreign suppliers

A European trading company has imported goods for which it must now pay US$10,000. The bank agrees to sell US$10,000 to the company at a bid price of $1.7935 for €1.

The bank will charge the company:

$$\frac{\$10,000}{\$1.7935 \text{ per } €1} = €5,575.69$$

1.3 Receiving foreign currency from customers

If an exporter is paid in a foreign currency, it might ask its bank to buy the currency from it. The bank will buy the currency at a buying rate known as the **offer price.**

Example: Receiving foreign currency from customers

A European trading company has exported goods for which it has received US$20,000. The bank agrees to buy US$20,000 from the company at an offer price of $1.8075 for €1.

The bank will pay the exporter:

$$\frac{\$20,000}{\$1.8075 \text{ per } €1} = €11,065.01$$

1.4 Division and multiplication of exchange rates

Students often find it difficult to know when to divide and when multiply by the exchange rates quoted. The rules are:

- If the exchange rate is quoted as Home currency 1 unit to Foreign currency X units, you **divide** the foreign currency amount by the rate quoted

- If the exchange rate is quoted as Foreign currency 1 unit to Home currency X units, you **multiply** the foreign currency amount by the rate quoted

If a rate is quoted as A$/B$, then A$/B$ is the number of B$ to each A$.

If therefore a rate is quoted at 2 £/$ it means $2 per £1.

Example: Division and multiplication of exchange rates

A UK company is about to enter two transactions, receiving an amount of €4,000,000 from a Dutch company and paying an amount of $3,000,000 to an American company. Current exchange rates are: €1 = £0.8 and £1 = $2.0

Required

Calculate what the company will receive and pay in £.

Solution

(a) As the rate of exchange between £ and € is quoted as €1 = £0.8, you **multiply** by it, so:

4,000,000 × 0.8 = £3,200,000 receipt.

(b) As the rate of exchange between £ and $ is quoted as £1 = $2.0, you divide by it, so:

$$\frac{3,000,000}{2.0} = £1,500,000 \text{ payment.}$$

Question 11.1	Exchange rate arithmetic

Learning outcome D2(c)

A German company is about to enter two transactions paying an amount of £4,000,000 to a UK company and receiving an amount of $3,000,000 from an American company. Current exchange rates are: €1 = £0.8 and $1 = €0.6.

Required

Calculate what the company will receive and pay in €.

1.5 Currency quotes

If a currency is quoted at £1:$1.50, the $ is the TERM CURRENCY (the REFERENCE CURRENCY), the £ is the BASE CURRENCY.

A bank expects to make a profit from selling and buying currency, and it does so by quoting or offering a rate for selling a currency which is different from the rate for buying the currency.

1.6 Selling low and buying high

When considering the prices banks are using, remember that the bank will **sell** the **term/reference currency low**, and **buy** the **term/reference currency high**. For example if a UK bank is buying and selling dollars, the selling price may be $1.41, the buying price may be $1.43.

If the bank is selling the base currency, then it will **buy** the base currency **low**, and **sell** the base currency **high**. Thus a US bank may sell £ at $1.47 per £ and buy £ at $1.45 per £.

Question 11.2

Learning outcome D2(c)

The current exchange rate is £1 = $1.5150 – $1.5200

Required

Calculate the rate at which:

(a)   A US bank would sell a US customer £
(b)   A British bank would buy $ from a British customer

1.7 Bid-ask spread

KEY TERM

BID-ASK SPREAD (BID-OFFER SPREAD) is the difference between the buying and selling price of a traded commodity or financial instrument.

The size of the spread depends on **processing and storage costs**, **currency volatility** and the **volume of transactions in the market**. The higher the volatility and the lower the volume of transactions, the greater the spread will be.

Question 11.3

Learning outcome D2(c)

Calculate how much or their own currency exporters would receive or how much of their own currency importers would pay in each of the following situations, if they were to exchange their own currency with another currency at the spot rate.

(a)   A UK exporter receives a payment from a Danish customer of 150,000 kroners.
(b)   A German importer buys goods from a Japanese supplier and pays 1 million yen.

Spot rates are as follows.

	Bank sells		Bank buys
Denmark Kr per £1	9.4340	–	9.5380
Japan ¥ per €1	203.65	–	205.78

1.8 Direct and indirect currency quotes

KEY TERMS

A **DIRECT QUOTE** is the amount of domestic currency which is equal to one foreign currency unit. An **INDIRECT QUOTE** is the amount of foreign currency which is equal to one domestic currency unit.

Currencies may be quoted in either direction. In most countries, direct quotes are more common although in the UK indirect quotes are invariably used.

For example the US dollar and Swiss Franc may be quoted as $1 = SFr1.723 or SFr1 = $0.580. One rate is simply the reciprocal of the other.

Exam skills

Exchange rates given in the examination could be as quoted in any currencies. Because of these complications you should always double-check which rate you are using when choosing between the bid or offer rate. One sure method is to recognise that the bank makes money out of the transaction and will therefore offer you the worse of the two possible rates!

1.9 Forward rates

KEY TERM

FORWARD EXCHANGE RATE is an exchange rate set for the exchange of currencies at some future date.

(*CIMA Official Terminology*)

A forward exchange rate might be higher or lower than the spot rate. If it is higher, the quoted currency will be cheaper forward than spot.

Example: Forward rates

In the case of Swiss Francs and £ (i) the spot rate is £1 = 2.156 – 2.166 Swiss Francs and (ii) the three months forward rate is 2.207 – 2.222:

(a)   A bank would sell 2,000 Swiss Francs:

   (i)   At the spot rate, now, for (**selling** the **term** currency, the Swiss Franc, **low**)

$$\left(\frac{2,000}{2.156}\right) = £927.64$$

   (ii)   In three months time, under a forward contract, for $\left(\frac{2,000}{2.207}\right) = £906.21$

(b)   A bank would buy 2,000 Swiss Francs:

   (i)   At the spot rate, now, for (**buying** the **term** currency, the Swiss Franc, **high**) $\left(\frac{2,000}{2.166}\right) = £923.36$

   (ii)   In three months time, under a forward contract, for $\left(\frac{2,000}{2.222}\right) = £900.09$

In this situation, the Swiss Franc is expected to weaken and would be worth less against sterling in a forward contract than at the current spot rate. You would need Fr 2.207 to buy £1 from the bank whereas at spot you would only need Fr 2.156. We say that the Swiss Franc is quoted **forward cheaper**, or 'at a **discount**', against sterling.

Alternatively the Swiss Franc may be expected to strengthen against sterling so that it is worth more against sterling in a forward contract (say you need to pay Fr 2.000 to buy £1 in the forward contract). If the forward rate is **more expensive** than the spot rate, then it is 'at a **premium**' to the spot rate.

Question 11.4   Forward contracts

Learning outcome D2(c)

An American company is committed to making a payment to a UK supplier in three months' time of £8,000,000. The finance director is worried about the possibility of adverse exchange rate movements and wants to take out a forward contract. The three month forward rate at present is £1 = $1.9250 – 1.9300.

Required

Calculate how much the company will pay in dollars if it enters the forward rate agreement.

1.10 Premiums and discounts

Sometimes the forward rates are quoted at an **annual premium or discount** to the spot rate. How you calculate the premium or discount depends on whether the currency is quoted in **direct** or **indirect** terms.

(a)   If the exchange rate is calculated in indirect terms the formula will be:

$$\% \text{ Forward Premium/(Discount)} = \frac{360}{n} \times \frac{(\text{Spot rate} - \text{Forward rate})}{\text{Forward rate}} \times 100\%$$

(b)   If the exchange rate is calculated in direct terms the formula will be:

$$\% \text{ Forward Premium/(Discount)} = \frac{360}{n} \times \frac{(\text{Forward rate} - \text{Spot rate})}{\text{Spot rate}} \times 100\%$$

> ### Example: Spot and forward rates
>
> Using the spot rate of £1 = 2.156 – 2.166 Swiss Francs and three months forward rate of 2.207–2.222, the rates are quoted (from the UK perspective) using the indirect method.
>
> $$\text{Forward Premium/(Discount)} = \frac{360}{90} \times \frac{(2.156 - 2.207)}{2.207} \times 100\%$$
>
> $$= -9.25\%$$
>
> From the Swiss perspective, the rates are quoted using the direct method:
>
> $$\text{Forward Premium/(Discount)} = \frac{360}{90} \times \frac{(2.207 - 2.156)}{2.156} \times 100\%$$
>
> $$= 9.46\%$$
>
> The forward rate for the Swiss franc is at a 9.25% discount to spot, and the forward rate for sterling is at a 9.46% premium to spot.

Question 11.5   Spot and forward rates compared

Learning outcome D2(c)

The current spot exchange rate is $1 = €0.6000 and the 6 month forward rate is 0.6300.

Required

Calculate how the forward rate is quoted in relation to spot rate from:

(a)   The European perspective
(b)   The American perspective

If forward rates are quoted at a premium or discount to spot rate (rather than the absolute value of the forward rate being given) you should **deduct the premium** and **add the discount**.

Example: Premiums and discounts

The spot rate is quoted at £1 = €1.1500 – 1.1555 and at a 3 months forward premium of 0.0004 – 0.0003. Calculate the rate that a French company that is looking to buy £ under a 3 months forward contract would obtain.

Solution

As the £ is the base currency, the bank would sell the French company £ at the higher rate, 1.1555.

Deducting the premium from that rate gives a forward rate of 1.1555 – 0.0003 = 1.1552

| Question 11.6 | Premiums and discounts |

Learning outcome D2(c)

The spot rate is quoted at $1 = €0.7700 – 0.7735 and at a 3 months forward discount of 0.0003 – 0.0004. Calculate the rate that an American company that is looking to sell € under a 3 months forward contract would obtain.

Section summary

Currencies are quoted at Base currency 1 unit = Term currency X units

The **spot rate** is the rate at which currencies are currently quoted on the foreign exchange markets. The **forward rate** is the rate at which currencies will be exchanged on a set future date.

2 Factors influencing exchange rates

Introduction

In this section we deal with the factors that cause exchange rates to move, and hence the factors that influence the level of transaction risk the business faces.

2.1 Currency supply and demand

The exchange rate between two currencies – ie the buying and selling rates, both 'spot' and forward – is determined primarily by **supply and demand** in the foreign exchange markets. Demand comes from individuals, firms and governments who want to buy a currency and supply comes from those who want to sell it.

Supply and demand for currencies are in turn influenced by:

- The rate of inflation, compared with the rate of inflation in other countries
- Interest rates, compared with interest rates in other countries
- The balance of payments
- Sentiment of foreign exchange market participants regarding economic prospects
- Speculation
- Government policy on intervention to influence the exchange rate

Other factors influence the exchange rate through their relationship with the items identified above. For example:

(a) **Total income and expenditure** (demand) in the domestic economy determines the demand for goods, including:

(i) Imported goods

(ii) Goods produced in the country which would otherwise be exported if demand for them did not exist in the home markets

(b) **Output capacity** and the **level of employment** in the domestic economy might influence the balance of payments, because if the domestic economy has full employment already, it will be unable to increase its volume of production for exports.

(c) The **growth in the money supply** influences interest rates and domestic inflation.

2.2 Interest rate parity/ Expectations theory

KEY TERM

INTEREST RATE PARITY method is a method of predicting foreign exchange rates based on the hypothesis that the difference between the interest rates in the two countries should offset the difference between the spot rates and the forward foreign exchange rates over the same period. *(CIMA Official Terminology)*

Under interest rate parity the difference between spot and forward rates **reflects differences in interest rates.** If this were not so, then investors holding the currency with the lower interest rates would switch to the other currency, ensuring that they would not lose on returning to the original currency by fixing the exchange rate in advance at the forward rate. If enough investors acted in this way, forces of supply and demand would lead to a change in the forward rate to prevent such risk-free profit making.

The principle of **interest rate parity** links the foreign exchange markets and the international money markets. The principle can be stated as follows.

EXAM

$$\text{Future spot rate A\$/B\$} = \text{Spot A\$/B\$} \times \frac{1 + \text{nominal country B interest rate}}{1 + \text{nominal country A interest rate}}$$

Note that the term 'forward rate' is used here as meaning the expected future spot rate and will not necessarily coincide with the 'forward exchange rate' currently quoted.

2.3 Purchasing power parity

KEY TERM

PURCHASING POWER PARITY theory states that the exchange rate between two currencies is the same in equilibrium when the purchasing power of currency is the same in each country.

(CIMA Official Terminology)

Interest rate parity should not be confused with **purchasing power parity**. Purchasing power parity theory predicts that the exchange value of foreign currency depends on the relative purchasing power of each currency in its own country and that **spot exchange rates will vary over time according to relative price changes**.

Formally, purchasing power parity can be expressed in the following formula.

EXAM

$$\text{Future spot rate A\$/B\$} = \text{Spot A\$/B\$} \times \frac{1 + \text{country B inflation rate}}{1 + \text{country A inflation rate}}$$

CASE STUDY

An amusing example of purchasing power parity is the Economist's Big Mac index. Under PPP movements in countries' exchange rates should in the long-term mean that the prices of an identical basket of goods or services are equalised. The McDonalds Big Mac represents this basket.

The index compares local Big Mac prices with the price of Big Macs in America. This comparison is used to forecast what exchange rates should be, and this is then compared with the actual exchange rates to decide which currencies are over and under-valued.

2.4 The Fisher effect

The term **Fisher effect** is sometimes used in looking at the relationship between **interest** rates and expected rates of **inflation**.

According to the **international Fisher effect**, interest rate differentials between countries provide an unbiased predictor of future changes in spot exchange rates. The currency of countries with relatively high interest rates is expected to depreciate against currencies with lower interest rates, because the higher interest rates are considered necessary to compensate for the anticipated currency depreciation. Given free movement of capital internationally, this idea suggests that the real rate of return in different countries will equalise as a result of adjustments to spot exchange rates.

The Fisher effect can be expressed as:

$$\frac{1 + r_f}{1 + r_{uk}} = \frac{1 + i_f}{1 + i_{uk}}$$

where r_f is the nominal interest rate in the foreign country, with inflation rate i_f

r_{uk} is the nominal interest rate in the home country, with inflation rate i_{uk}

You may need to bring these concepts into answers in this paper; they will also often be very significant for major calculations in the *Financial Strategy* paper.

Section summary

Factors influencing the exchange rate include the comparative rates of inflation in different countries (**purchasing power parity**), comparative interest rates in different countries (**interest rate parity**), the underlying balance of payments, speculation and government policy on managing or fixing exchange rates.

3 Transaction risk

Introduction

In this section we show what impact transaction risk can have on a business.

KEY TERM

TRANSACTION RISK is the risk of adverse exchange rate movements occurring in the course of **normal international trading transactions**.

Transaction risk arises when the prices of imports or exports are fixed in foreign currency terms and there is movement in the exchange rate between the date when the price is agreed and the date when the cash is paid or received in settlement.

Much international trade involves credit. An importer will take credit often for several months and sometimes longer, and an exporter will grant credit. One consequence of taking and granting credit is that international traders will know in advance about the receipts and payments arising from their trade. They will know:

- Which foreign currency they will receive or pay
- When the receipt or payment will occur

- How much of the currency will be received or paid

The great danger to profit margins is in the **movement in exchange rates**. The risk faces:

- Exporters who invoice in a foreign currency
- Importers who pay in a foreign currency

Question 11.7

Exchange rate movements

Learning outcomes D2(c)

Bulldog, a UK company, buys goods from Redland which cost 100,000 Reds (the local currency). The goods are re-sold in the UK for £32,000. At the time of the import purchase the exchange rate for Reds against sterling is £1 = 3.5650 – 3.5800 Reds.

Required

(a)   What is the expected profit on the re-sale?

(b)   What would the actual profit be if the spot rate at the time when the currency is received has moved to:

    (i)   3.0800 – 3.0950

    (ii)   4.0650 – 4.0800?

Ignore bank commission charges.

Section summary

Transaction risk is the short-term exchange risk that arises out of undertaking specific transactions in different currencies.

4   Managing transaction risk

5/10

Introduction

We now start looking at some of the more straightforward ways in which businesses deal with transaction risk

4.1 Hedging transaction risk

KEY TERM

HEDGE is a transaction to reduce or eliminate an exposure to risk.   *(CIMA Official Terminology)*

We shall now look at the various means by which a business can hedge or manage the transaction risk that has a direct effect on immediate cash flows.

Exam skills

Don't forget also that deciding not to hedge exposure may be legitimate. The costs may be considered too great, or the chances of adverse exchange rate movements may be too low.

4.2 Direct risk reduction methods

The **forward exchange contract** is perhaps the most important method of obtaining cover against risks, where a firm decides that it does not wish to speculate on foreign exchange (covered in Section 5). Another frequently used method is employing market investments and loans to hedge against risk (discussed in Section 6). However, there are **other methods of reducing risk** which we shall consider below. Alternatively, a firm could simply **reduce its operations** in, or dealings with, overseas countries.

4.3 Currency of invoice

One way of avoiding exchange risk is for an exporter to **invoice his foreign customer in his own domestic currency**, or for an importer to arrange with his foreign supplier to be invoiced in his domestic currency.

(a)   If an exporter is able to quote and invoice an overseas buyer in sterling, then **the foreign exchange risk is in effect transferred to the overseas buyer.**

(b)   Similarly, an importer may be able to persuade the overseas supplier to **invoice in sterling** rather than in a foreign currency.

Although either the exporter or the importer avoids exchange risk in this way, only one of them can. The other must accept the exchange risk, since there will be a period of time elapsing between agreeing a contract and paying for the goods (unless payment is made with the order). Who bears the risk may depend on bargaining strength.

An alternative method of achieving the same result is to negotiate contracts expressed in the foreign currency but specifying **a fixed rate of exchange** as a condition of the contract.

Exam alert

You may be asked in the exam how invoicing policy might change if financing arrangements change.

4.4 Matching receipts and payments

A company can reduce or eliminate its foreign exchange transaction risk exposure by matching receipts and payments. Wherever possible, a company that expects to make payments and have receipts in the same foreign currency should plan to **offset its payments against its receipts in the currency**. The process of matching is made simpler by having **foreign currency accounts** with a bank.

Offsetting (matching payments against receipts) will be **cheaper** than arranging a forward contract to buy currency and another forward contract to sell the currency, provided that:

- Receipts occur before payments:
- The time difference between receipts and payments in the currency is not too long

Any **differences** between the amounts receivable and the amounts payable in a given currency may be covered by a **forward exchange contract** to buy/sell the amount of the difference.

Exam alert

The examiner has commented that weak students often neglect natural hedges such as sales and purchases in the same currency, and focus solely on derivatives as the way to manage currency risks.

4.5 Leads and lags

Companies might try to use:

- **Lead payments**: payments in advance, or
- **Lagged payments**: delaying payments beyond their due date

in order to take advantage of foreign exchange rate movements. With a lead payment, paying in advance of the due date, there is a finance cost to consider. This is the interest cost on the money used to make the payment, but early settlement discounts may become available.

4.6 Netting

Unlike matching, netting is not technically a method of managing exchange risk. However, it is conveniently dealt with at this stage. The objective is simply to save transactions costs by netting off inter-company balances before arranging payment. Many **multinational groups** of companies engage in **intra-group trading**. Where related companies located in different countries trade with one another, there is likely to be inter-company indebtedness denominated in different currencies.

NETTING is a process in which credit balances are netted off against debit balances so that only the reduced net amounts remain due to be paid by actual currency flows.

In the case of **bilateral netting,** only two companies are involved. The lower balance is netted off against the higher balance and the difference is the amount remaining to be paid.

Example: Bilateral netting

A and B are respectively UK and US based subsidiaries of a Swiss based holding company. At 31 March 20X5, A owed B SFr300,000 and B owed A SFr220,000. Bilateral netting can reduce the value of the intercompany debts: the two intercompany balances are set against each other, leaving a net debt owed by A to B of SFr 80,000 (SFr300,000 – 220,000).

4.7 Multilateral netting

As you will have guessed, **multilateral netting** is a more complex procedure in which the debts of more than two group companies are netted off against each other. There are different ways of arranging multilateral netting. The arrangement might be co-ordinated by the company's own central treasury or alternatively by the company's bankers.

Section summary

Basic methods of hedging risk include **matching receipts and payments**, **invoicing in own currency**, and **leading and lagging** the times that cash is received and paid.

5 Forward exchange contracts   5/10

Introduction

This section looks at forward exchange contracts, which are a simple and very common way of hedging transaction risk.

5.1 Forward exchange contracts

KEY TERM

A FORWARD EXCHANGE CONTRACT is:

(a)   An immediately firm and binding contract between a bank and its customer

(b)   For the purchase or sale of a specified quantity of a stated foreign currency

(c)   At a rate of exchange fixed at the time the contract is made

(d)   For performance (delivery of the currency and payment for it) at a future time which is agreed upon when making the contract. (This future time will be either a specified date, or any time between two specified dates.)

Forward exchange contracts hedge against transaction exposure by allowing a trader who knows that he will have to buy or sell foreign currency at a date in the future, to make the purchase or sale at a **predetermined rate of exchange**. The trader will therefore know in advance:

*   How much local currency he will receive (if he is selling foreign currency to the bank)
*   How much local currency he must pay (if he is buying foreign currency from the bank)

5.1.1 Advantages of forward exchange contracts

*   They are **transacted over the counter**, and are not subject to the requirements of a trading exchange.
*   They can in theory be for **any amount**.
*   The length of the contract can be **flexible**, but contracts are generally for less than two years.

5.1.2 Disadvantages of forward exchange contracts

*   The organisation doesn't have the **protection** that trading on an exchange brings.
*   The contracts are **difficult to cancel** as they are contractual obligations (discussed below).
*   There is a risk of **default** by the counterparty to the contract (discussed below).

5.2 Forward rates and future exchange rate movements

Interest rate parity predicts that the forward rate is the spot price ruling on the day a forward exchange contract is made plus or minus the interest differential for the period of the contract. **It is wrong to think of a forward rate as a forecast of what the spot rate will be on a given date in the future**. It will be a coincidence if the forward rate turns out to be the same as the spot rate on that future date.

However the spot rate is likely to move in the direction indicated by the forward rate. Currencies with high interest rates are likely to depreciate in value against currencies with lower interest rates: the attraction of higher interest persuades investors to hold amounts of a currency that is expected to depreciate.

5.3 Expectations theory of forward exchange rates

On the assumption that risk is absent, the **expectations theory of forward exchange rates** predicts that **the percentage difference between forward and spot rates now equals the expected change in spot rates over the period.**

Thus, given expectations of interest rates and inflation rates, the spot rate three months from now is expected to equal the three-months forward rate quoted now, for example. Because on average the forward rate equals the future spot rate, and overestimates it about as often as it underestimates it, the forward market is said to be an **unbiased predictor** of exchange rates.

5.4 Fixed and option contracts

A forward exchange contract may be either **fixed** or **option**.

(a)   **'Fixed'** means that performance of the contract will take place on a specified date in the future. For example, a two months forward **fixed** contract taken out on 1 September will require performance on 1 November.

(b)   **'Option'** means that performance of the contract may take place, at the option of the customer, either

(i)   At any date from the contract being made up to and including a specified final date for performance, or

(ii)   At any date between two specified dates

They can be used bit by bit.

Option forward exchange contracts are different from **currency options**, which are explained later. Option forward exchange contracts must be performed at some time.

Example: Forward exchange contracts

A UK importer knows on 1 April that he must pay a foreign seller 26,500 Swiss francs in one month's time, on 1 May. He can arrange a forward exchange contract with his bank on 1 April, whereby the bank undertakes to sell the importer 26,500 Swiss francs on 1 May, at a fixed rate of, say, 2.64 Swiss francs to the £.

The UK importer can be certain that whatever the spot rate is between Swiss francs and sterling on 1 May, he will have to pay on that date, at this forward rate.

$$\frac{26,500}{2.64} = £10,037.88$$

(a)   If the spot rate is lower than 2.64, the importer would have successfully protected himself against a weakening of sterling, and would have avoided paying more sterling to obtain the Swiss francs.

(b)   If the spot rate is higher than 2.64, sterling's value against the Swiss franc would mean that the importer would pay more under the forward exchange contract than he would have had to pay if he had obtained the francs at the spot rate on 1 May. He cannot avoid this extra cost, because a forward contract is binding.

Question 11.8   Forward exchange contracts

Learning outcomes D2(a), (b)

A German exporter will receive an amount of $1,500,000 from a US customer in three months' time. He can arrange a forward exchange contract to cover this transaction. The current spot rate is $1 = €0.7810 – 0.7840 and the 3 month forward rate is quoted at 0.0005 – 0.0003 premium.

Required

Calculate how much the exporter will receive under the terms of the forward contract.

5.5 What happens if a customer cannot satisfy a forward contract?

A customer might be unable to satisfy a forward contract for any one of a number of reasons.

(a)   An **importer** might find that:

   (i)   His supplier **fails to deliver the goods as specified**, so the importer will not accept the goods delivered and will not agree to pay for them

   (ii)   The **supplier sends fewer goods** than expected, perhaps because of supply shortages, and so the importer has less to pay for

   (iii) The **supplier is late with the delivery**, and so the importer does not have to pay for the goods until later than expected

(b)   An **exporter** might find the same types of situation, but in reverse, so that he does not receive any payment at all, or he receives more or less than originally expected, or he receives the expected amount, but only after some delay.

5.6 Close-out of forward contracts

If a customer cannot satisfy a forward exchange contract, the bank will make the customer fulfil the contract.

(a)   If the customer has arranged for the bank to **buy** currency but then cannot deliver the currency for the bank to buy, the bank will:

   (i)   **Sell currency** to the customer **at the spot rate** (when the contract falls due for performance)
   (ii)   Buy **the currency back**, under the terms of the forward exchange contract

(b)   If the customer has contracted for the bank to **sell** him currency, the bank will:

   (i)   **Sell the customer** the **specified amount of currency** at the forward exchange rate
   (ii)   **Buy back the unwanted currency** at the spot rate

Exam skills

It may seem a pedantic point, but don't confuse forward contracts (currency risk management) with forward rate agreements (interest risk management).

Section summary

A **forward contract** specifies in advance the rate at which a specified quantity of currency will be bought and sold.

6 Money market hedging

Introduction

Some businesses use the financial markets to create a hedge arrangement that is likely to have a similar impact to forward contracts.

6.1 Using the money market

Because of the close relationship between forward exchange rates and the interest rates in currencies, it is possible to 'manufacture' a forward rate by using the spot exchange rate and money market lending or borrowing. This technique is known as a **money market hedge** or **synthetic forward**.

6.2 Hedging payments

Suppose a British company needs to **pay** a Swiss creditor in Swiss francs in three months time. It does not have enough cash to pay now, but will have sufficient in three months time. Instead of negotiating a forward contract, the company could:

- Borrow the appropriate amount in pounds now

- Convert the pounds to francs immediately

- Put the francs on deposit in a Swiss franc bank account

- When the time comes to pay the creditor:
    - Pay the creditor out of the franc bank account
    - Repay the pound loan account

The effect is exactly the same as using a forward contract, and will usually cost almost exactly the same amount. If the results from a money market hedge were very different from a forward hedge, speculators could make money without taking a risk. Therefore market forces ensure that the two hedges produce very similar results.

Example: Money market hedge 1

A UK company owes a Danish creditor Kr3,500,000 in three months time. The spot exchange rate is £1 = Kr 7.5509 – 7.5548. The company can borrow in sterling for 3 months at 8.60% per annum and can deposit kroners for 3 months at 10% per annum.

Required

Calculate the cost in pounds with a money market hedge.

Solution

	UK	@ 7.5509	Denmark
Now	£452,215	←	Kr3,414,634
	↓ @ 1.0215**		↓ @ 1.025*
3 months	£461,938		Kr3,500,000

* $\dfrac{3}{12} \times 10\% = 2.5\%$

** $\dfrac{3}{12} \times 8.6\% = 2.15\%$

Cost of hedge = £461,938

| Question 11.9 | Money market hedge 1 |

Learning outcomes D2(a), (b)

A Thai company owes a New Zealand Company NZ$ 3,000,000, payable in 3 months time. The current exchange rate is NZ $1 = Thai Baht 19.0300 – 19.0500.

The Thai company elects to use a money market hedge to manage the exchange risk.

The current borrowing and investing rates in the two countries are:

	New Zealand %	Thailand %
Investing	2.5	4.5
Borrowing	3.0	5.2

Required

Calculate the cost to the Thai company of using a money market hedge.

6.3 Hedging receipts

A similar technique can be used to cover a foreign currency **receipt** from a debtor. To manufacture a forward exchange rate, follow the steps below.

- Borrow an appropriate amount in the foreign currency today

- Convert it immediately to home currency

- Place it on deposit in the home currency

- When the debtor's cash is received:

    - Repay the foreign currency loan
    - Take the cash from the home currency deposit account

Exam alert

Variations on these money market hedges are possible.

| Example: Money market hedge 2 |

A UK company is owed SFr 2,500,000 in three months time by a Swiss company. The spot exchange rate is £1 = SFr 2.2498 – 2.2510. The company can deposit in Sterling for 3 months at 8.00% per annum and can borrow Swiss Francs for 3 months at 7.00% per annum. What is the receipt in pounds with a money market hedge?

| Solution |

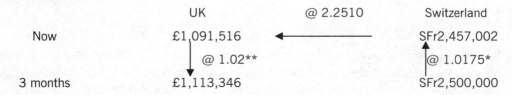

	UK	@ 2.2510	Switzerland
Now	£1,091,516	←	SFr2,457,002
	@ 1.02** ↓		↑ @ 1.0175*
3 months	£1,113,346		SFr2,500,000

$$* \frac{3}{12} \times 7\% = 1.75\%$$

$$** \frac{3}{12} \times 8\% = 2\%$$

Receipt = £1,113,346

Question 11.10   Money market hedge 2

Learning outcomes D2(a), (b)

An Australian company is due to receive ¥ 15,000,000 from a Japanese company, payable in four months' time. The current exchange rate is Aus $1 = ¥ 62.6000 – 62.8000.

The Australian company elects to use a money market hedge to manage the exchange risk.

The current borrowing and investing rates in the two countries are:

	Australia %	Japan %
Investing	4.5	2.7
Borrowing	6.0	3.3

Required

Calculate the amount the Australian company will receive if it uses a money market hedge.

6.4 Forward exchange contracts versus money market hedge

Is one of these methods of cover likely to be cheaper than the other? The answer is perhaps, but not by much. There will be very little difference between borrowing in foreign currency and repaying the loan with currency receivables and borrowing in sterling and selling forward the currency receivables. This is because the premium or discount on the forward exchange rate reflects the interest differential between the two countries.

6.5 Arbitrage profits

KEY TERM

ARBITRAGE is the simultaneous purchase and sale of a security in different markets with the aim of making a risk-free profit through the exploitation of any price differences between the two markets.

(CIMA Official Terminology)

Arbitrage means exploiting differences:

- Between two markets, selling in one market, buying in another

- Between two products, where similarities between those products suggest they should be traded at the **same price**

Arbitrage differences are **short-term**. As others see the differences and exploit them, prices will converge, and the opportunities for exploiting differences will disappear as equilibrium is reached.

6.5.1 Arbitrage and exchange rates

Interest rate parity suggests that the spot rate in a year forward will reflect differences in interest rates. If however the difference between the spot rate now and the forward rate being offered now does not reflect differences in the two countries' interest rates, investors can exploit differences. They can:

- Borrow in Currency A

- Deposit what they have borrowed in Currency B for a period of a time

- Take out a forward contract to sell Currency B at the end of the period

- At the end of the period, liquidate the investment and convert the Currency 2 proceeds to Currency 1 under the forward contract

- Repay the amount borrowed in Currency 1 and retain the surplus

Section summary

Money market hedging involves borrowing in one currency, converting the money borrowed into another currency and putting the money on deposit until the time the transaction is completed, hoping to take advantage of favourable interest rate movements.

7 Choosing a hedging method

Introduction

This section shows what you may be asked to do in the exam, comparing different methods of hedging and recommending which is most appropriate.

7.1 Choice of methods

When a company expects to receive or pay a sum of foreign currency in the next few months, it can choose between using the **forward exchange market** and the **money market** to hedge against the foreign exchange risk. The cheaper option available is the one that ought to be chosen. Other methods may also be possible, such as making **lead payments**.

Example: Choosing the cheapest method

Trumpton, a UK company, has bought goods from a US supplier, and must pay $4,000,000 for them in three months time. The company's finance director wishes to hedge against the foreign exchange risk, and the three methods which the company usually considers are:

- Using forward exchange contracts
- Using money market borrowing or lending
- Making lead payments

The following annual interest rates and exchange rates are currently available.

	US dollar		Sterling	
	Deposit rate	Borrowing rate	Deposit rate	Borrowing rate
	%	%	%	%
1 month	7	10.25	10.75	14.00
3 months	7	10.75	11.00	14.25

	£1 = $
Spot	1.8625 – 1.8635
1 month forward	1.8565 – 1.8577
3 months forward	1.8445 – 1.8460

Which is the cheapest method for Trumpton? Ignore commission costs. (The bank charges for arranging a forward contract or a loan.)

Solution

The three choices must be compared on a similar basis, which means working out the cost of each to Trumpton either **now** or **in three months time**. Here the cost to Trumpton in three months' time will be determined.

Choice 1: the forward exchange market

Trumpton must buy dollars in order to pay the US supplier. The exchange rate in a forward exchange contract to buy $4,000,000 in three months time (bank sells) is £1 = $1.8445

The cost of the $4,000,000 to Trumpton in three months time will be:

$$\frac{\$4,000,000}{1.8445} = £2,168,609.38$$

This is the cost **in three months**.

Choice 2: the money markets

Using the money markets involves lending (depositing) in the foreign currency, as Trumpton will eventually pay the currency.

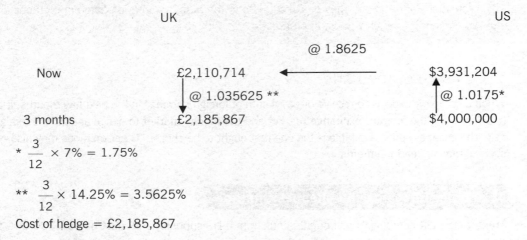

	UK		US
		@ 1.8625	
Now	£2,110,714	←	$3,931,204
	@ 1.035625 **		@ 1.0175*
3 months	£2,185,867		$4,000,000

$$* \ \frac{3}{12} \times 7\% = 1.75\%$$

$$** \ \frac{3}{12} \times 14.25\% = 3.5625\%$$

Cost of hedge = £2,185,867

Choice 3: lead payments

Lead payments should be considered when the currency of payment is expected to strengthen over time, and is quoted forward at a premium on the foreign exchange market.

Here, the cost of a lead payment (paying $4,000,000 now) would be:

$4,000,000 ÷ 1.8625 = £2,147,651.01

The cost in three months' time is the cost of lost interest:

£2,147,651 × (1 + 0.11/4) = £2,206,711

In this example, the present value of the costs are as follows.

	£
Forward exchange contract	2,168,609
Money markets	2,185,867
Lead payment	2,206,711

Question 11.11

Hedging

Learning outcomes D2(a), (b)

Weft is an importer/exporter of textiles and textile machinery. It is based in the UK but trades extensively with countries throughout Europe, particularly in the eurozone. It has a small subsidiary based in Germany. The company is about to invoice a customer in Germany for 750,000 euros, payable in three months' time. Weft's treasurer is considering two methods of hedging the exchange risk. These are:

Method 1

Borrow €750,000 for three months, convert the loan into sterling and repay the loan out of eventual receipts. The interest payable on the loan will be purchased in the forward exchange market.

Method 2

Enter into a 3-month forward exchange contract with the company's bank to sell €750,000.

The spot rate of exchange is £1 = €1.6006

The 3-month forward rate of exchange is £1 = €1.5935

Annual interest rates for 3 months' borrowing and lending are: euro 3%, sterling 5%.

Required

(a)   Which of the two methods is the most financially advantageous for Weft?

(b)   What are the other factors to consider before deciding whether to hedge the risk using the foreign currency markets?

Section summary

In the exam you may be asked to see what the results are of using a number of different hedging methods, and identify the cheapest.

Chapter Roundup

✓   Currencies are quoted at Base currency 1 unit = Term currency X units

✓   The **spot rate** is the rate at which currencies are currently quoted on the foreign exchange markets. The **forward rate** is the rate at which currencies will be exchanged on a set future date.

✓   Factors influencing the exchange rate include the comparative rates of inflation in different countries (**purchasing power parity**), comparative interest rates in different countries (**interest rate parity**), the underlying balance of payments, speculation and government policy on managing or fixing exchange rates.

✓   **Transaction risk** is the short-term exchange risk that arises out of undertaking specific transactions in different currencies.

✓   Basic methods of hedging risk include **matching receipts and payments**, **invoicing in own currency**, and **leading and lagging** the times that cash is received and paid.

✓   A **forward contract** specifies in advance the rate at which a specified quantity of currency will be bought and sold.

✓   **Money market hedging** involves borrowing in one currency, converting the money borrowed into another currency and putting the money on deposit until the time the transaction is completed, hoping to take advantage of favourable interest rate movements.

✓   In the exam you may be asked to see what the results are of using a number of different hedging methods, and identify the cheapest.

Quick Quiz

1   A Danish company intends to buy goods from its UK supplier worth £1,200,000.

The current exchange rate is £1 = DKr 8.5320 – 8.5380. How much in DKr will the goods cost the Danish company?

2   Which factors influence the supply and demand for currencies?

3   The principle of purchasing power parity must always hold.

True   ☐

False   ☐

4   A company might make payments earlier or later in order to take advantage of exchange rate movements. What is this called?

A   Smoothing
B   Hedging
C   Leading and lagging
D   Matching

5   Define a 'forward exchange rate'.

6   Fill in the boxes in the diagram with (A) to (E), to indicate which factors are linked by which theory.

(A)   Purchasing power parity theory

(B)   Expectations theory

(C)   Fisher effect

(D)   International Fisher effect

(E)   Interest rate parity

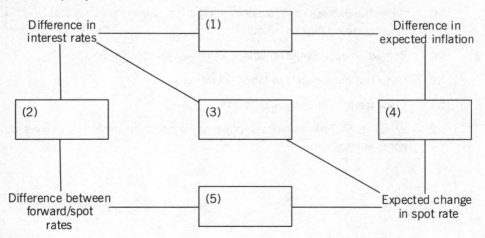

7   Fill in the blanks

(a)   Forward rate cheaper than spot rate quoted at a ....

(b)   Forward rate more expensive than spot rate quoted at a ....

8   What steps can be taken in money markets to cover a foreign currency receipt in the future from a debtor?

9   What steps can be taken in money markets to cover a foreign currency payment in the future to a creditor?

Answers to Quick Quiz

1 As the £ is the base currency, the bank will sell £ high. The amount in £ should be multiplied by the exchange rate:

   1,200,000 × 8.5380 = DKr10,245,600

2 (a) Relative rates of inflation
   (b) Relative interest rates
   (c) The balance of payments position
   (d) Market sentiment
   (e) Speculation
   (f) Government policy

3 False. In reality, for example prices of commodities do differ significantly in different countries.

4 C Leading and lagging

5 An exchange rate set for the exchange of currencies at some future date

6 (1) C Fisher effect
   (2) E Interest rate parity
   (3) D International Fisher effect
   (4) A Purchasing power parity
   (5) B Expectations theory

7 (a) Forward rate cheaper than spot rate quoted at a **discount**
   (b) Forward rate more expensive than spot rate quoted at a **premium**

8 (a) Borrow an appropriate amount in the foreign currency today

   (b) Convert it immediately to home currency

   (c) Place home currency on deposit

   (d) When the debtor's cash is received, repay the foreign currency loan and take the cash from the home currency deposit account

9 (a) Borrow an appropriate amount in the home currency now

   (b) Convert it immediately to foreign currency

   (c) Place foreign currency on deposit

   (d) When creditor has to be paid, pay creditor out of the foreign currency deposit account and repay home currency loan

Answers to Questions

11.1 Exchange rate arithmetic

(a) As the rate of exchange between £ and € is quoted as €1 = £0.8, you divide by it, so:

4,000,000/0.8 = €5,000,000 payment

(b) As the rate of exchange between € and $ is quoted as $1 = €0.6, you multiply by it, so:

3,000,000 × 0.6 = €1,800,000 receipt.

11.2 Bank selling and buying

(a) Here the £ that the bank is selling is the **base** currency, so that the bank would **sell** it **high** at 1.5200
(b) Here the $ the bank is buying is the **term** currency, so that the bank would **buy** it **high**, also at 1.5200

11.3 Exchange of currency

(a) The bank is being asked to buy the Danish kroners and will give the exporter:

$$\frac{150,000}{9.5380} = £15,726.57 \text{ in exchange}$$

(b) The bank is being asked to sell the yen to the importer and will charge for the currency:

$$\frac{1,000,000}{203.65} = €4,910.39$$

11.4 Forward contracts

- As the £ is the **base** currency, the bank will **sell** the company £ the company needs at the **higher rate**, so the rate used in the contract is 1.9300

- As the $ is the **home** currency, and is quoted at £1 = $X, you have to **multiply** by the rate used:

8,000,000 × 1.9300 = $15,440,000

11.5 Spot and forward rates compared

(a) From the European perspective the rates are quoted using the direct method

$$\text{Forward Premium/(Discount)} = {}^{360}/_{180} \times \frac{0.6300 - 0.6000}{0.6000} = 10\%$$

From the European perspective, the dollar is quoted at a 10% premium to spot.

(b) From the American perspective, the rates are quoted using the indirect method

$$\text{Forward Premium/(Discount)} = {}^{360}/_{180} \times \frac{0.6000 - 0.6300}{0.6300} = -9.52\%$$

From the American perspective, the euro is quoted at a 9.52% discount to spot.

11.6 Premiums and discounts

As the € is the term currency, the US bank would buy the € at the higher rate, 0.7735

Adding the discount to that rate gives a forward rate of 0.7735 + 0.0004 = 0.7739

11.7 Exchange rate movements

(a) Bulldog must buy Reds to pay the supplier, and so the bank is selling Reds. The expected profit is as follows.

	£
Revenue from re-sale of goods	32,000.00
Less cost of 100,000 Reds in sterling (÷ 3.5650)*	28,050.49
Expected profit	3,949.51

(b) (i) If the actual spot rate for Bulldog to buy and the bank to sell the Reds is 3.0800, the result is as follows.

	£
Revenue from re-sale	32,000.00
Less cost (100,000 ÷ 3.0800)*	32,467.53
Loss	(467.53)

   (ii) If the actual spot rate for Bulldog to buy and the bank to sell the Reds is 4.0650, the result is as follows.

	£
Revenue from re-sale	32,000.00
Less cost (100,000 ÷ 4.0650)*	24,600.25
Profit	7,399.75

* The bank **sells** Bulldog the **term** currency (Reds) at the **lower** rate.

This variation in the final sterling cost of the goods (and thus the profit) illustrates the concept of transaction risk.

11.8 Forward exchange contracts

As $ is the base currency, the German bank will buy $ at the lower rate 0.7810.

The premium should be deducted from this rate 0.7810 − 0.0005 = 0.7805.

As the $ is the base currency, multiply the amount in $ by the forward rate:

1,500,000 × 0.7805 = €1,170,750

11.9 Money market hedge 1

	Thailand		New Zealand
Now	Bt56,795,022	@ 19.0500 ←	$2,981,366
	↓ @ 1.013**		↑ @ 1.00625*
3 months	Bt57,533,357		$3,000,000

* $\dfrac{3}{12} \times 2.5\% = 0.625\%$

** $\dfrac{3}{12} \times 5.2\% = 1.3\%$

Cost of hedge = Bt57,533,357

11.10 Money market hedge 2

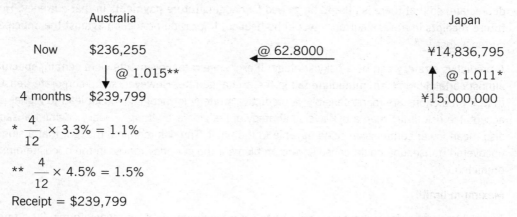

Australia   Japan

Now $236,255   @ 62.8000   ¥14,836,795

          ↓ @ 1.015**   ↑ @ 1.011*

4 months $239,799   ¥15,000,000

* $\dfrac{4}{12} \times 3.3\% = 1.1\%$

** $\dfrac{4}{12} \times 4.5\% = 1.5\%$

Receipt = $239,799

11.11 Hedging

(a)   **Method 1**

Weft borrows €750,000.

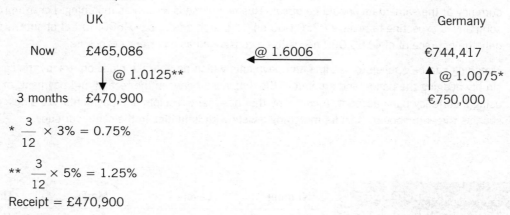

UK   Germany

Now   £465,086   @ 1.6006   €744,417

          ↓ @ 1.0125**   ↑ @ 1.0075*

3 months   £470,900   €750,000

* $\dfrac{3}{12} \times 3\% = 0.75\%$

** $\dfrac{3}{12} \times 5\% = 1.25\%$

Receipt = £470,900

Method 2

The exchange rate is fixed in advance at €1.5935 by the forward contract. Cash received in three months is converted to produce €750,000/1.5935 = £470,662.

Conclusion

On the basis of the above calculations, Method 1 gives a slightly higher receipt. However, the difference is quite small, and banker's commission has been excluded from the calculation.

(b)   **Factors to consider before deciding whether to hedge foreign exchange risk using the foreign currency markets**

Defensive strategy

The company should have a clear strategy concerning how much foreign exchange risk it is prepared to bear. A highly risk-averse or 'defensive' strategy of hedging all transactions can be **expensive** in terms of **commission costs**, but recognises that exchange rates are unpredictable, can be volatile and so can cause severe losses unless the risk is hedged.

Predictive strategy

An alternative **'predictive' strategy** recognises that if all transaction exposures are hedged, the chance of making gains from favourable exchange rate movements is lost. It might be possible to predict the future movement in an exchange rate with some confidence. The company could therefore **attempt to forecast foreign exchange movements** and only hedge those transactions where **losses from currency exposures**

are **predicted**. For example, if inflation is high in a particular country, its currency will probably depreciate, so that there is little to be gained by hedging **future payments** in that currency. However, **future receipts** in a weak currency would be hedged, to provide protection against the anticipated currency loss.

A predictive strategy can be a risky strategy. If exchange rate movements were certain, **speculators** would almost certainly force an **immediate fall** in the exchange rate. However, some corporate treasurers argue that, if predictions are made sensibly, a predictive strategy for hedging should lead to higher profits within acceptable risk limits than a risk-averse strategy of hedging everything. Fewer hedging transactions will also mean lower commission costs payable to the bank. The risk remains, though, that a single large uncovered transaction could cause severe problems if the currency moves in the opposite direction to that predicted.

Maximum limit

A sensible strategy for a company could be to set a **maximum limit**, in money terms, for a **foreign currency exposure**. Exposures above this amount should be hedged, but below this limit a predictive approach should be taken or, possibly, all amounts could be left unhedged.

Offsetting

Before using any technique to hedge foreign currency transactions, **receipts and payments** in the same currency at the same date should be **offset**. This technique is known as matching. For example, if the company is expecting to receive €750,000 on 31 March and to pay €600,000 at about the same time, only the net receipt of €150,000 needs to be considered as a currency exposure.

Matching can be applied to receipts and payments which do not take place on exactly the same day by simply hedging the period and amount of the difference between the receipt and payment, or even by using a currency bank account. A company that has many receipts and payments in a single currency such as the euro should consider **matching assets with liabilities** in the same currency.

Now try this question from the Exam Question Bank

Number	Level	Marks	Time
Q15	Examination	25	45 mins

TRANSACTION RISK II

In this chapter, we extend our discussion of **currency risk management** and consider some of the variety of **derivatives** which are now available for managing **financial risks** of various kinds.

Using the methods described in this chapter will ensure that you set out your workings clearly and should be able to gain marks for the straightforward areas easily. Don't worry too much if you don't feel you've mastered all the complexities in this chapter. Being able to describe these methods, discuss their advantages and disadvantages and knowing the steps for setting up contracts should guarantee you most of the marks.

topic list	learning outcomes	syllabus references	ability required
1 Currency futures	D2(a), (b)	D2(iii)	evaluation
2 Currency options	D2(a), (b)	D2(iii)	evaluation
3 Currency swaps	D2(a), (b)	D2(iii)	evaluation

1 Currency futures

Introduction

The first derivatives we'll discuss are currency futures, which have a similar impact to forward agreements.

KEY TERM

A CURRENCY FUTURE is a standardised contract to buy or sell a fixed amount of currency at a fixed rate at a fixed future date:

- Buying the futures contract means receiving the contract currency
- Selling the futures contract means supplying the contract currency

1.1 Development of currency futures

The currency futures markets have grown rapidly as more and more speculators have become involved and this has increased short-term volatility. The only risk to hedgers is that the futures market does not always provide a perfect hedge. This can result from two causes.

(a) Amounts must be **rounded to a whole number of contracts**, causing inaccuracies.

(b) **Basis risk** is the risk that the futures contract price may move by a different amount from the price of the underlying currency or commodity. The actions of speculators may increase basis risk.

When deciding to use futures to hedge currency risk, you need to consider the following when setting up the hedge:

- Which type of futures contract – are you looking for a **buy or sell** contract?
- Which contract out of a number of contracts with **different settlement dates**?

1.2 Which type of contract?

One of the limitations of currency futures is that currencies can only be bought or sold on exchanges for US dollars there are **no** US dollars traded currency futures. The basic rules are given below.

(a) If you are going to make a payment in a foreign currency (not American dollars) on a future date, you will need to buy that currency. To hedge: take the following action.

Buy the appropriate **foreign currency futures** contracts **now** (just as you would with a forward contract)

Sell the same number of **foreign currency futures** contracts on the date that you buy the actual currency (closing out)

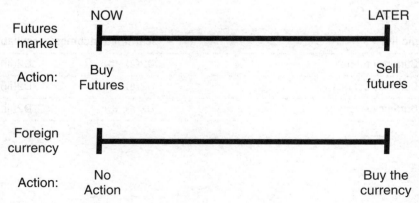

(b) If you are going to receive monies in a foreign currency on a future date, you will need to sell that currency. To hedge take the following steps:

 Sell the appropriate **foreign currency futures** contracts **now**

 Buy the same number of **foreign currency futures** contracts on the date that you sell the actual currency

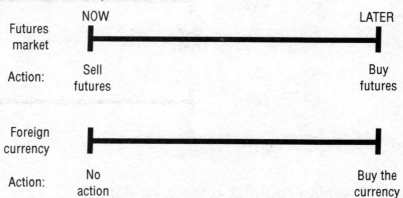

	NOW		LATER
Futures market			
Action:	Sell futures		Buy futures
Foreign currency			
Action:	No action		Buy the currency

(c) If you are from outside America and are going to make a payment in American dollars on a future date, you will need to buy American dollars. To hedge you cannot buy American dollar futures, so therefore you will have to sell your own currency's futures

 Sell your **home currency futures** contracts **now**

 Buy the same number of **home currency futures** contracts on the date that you buy the dollars

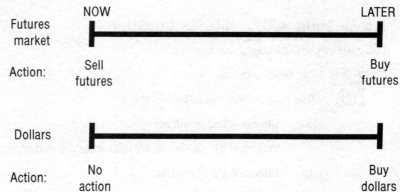

	NOW		LATER
Futures market			
Action:	Sell futures		Buy futures
Dollars			
Action:	No action		Buy dollars

(d) If you are from outside America and are going to receive an amount in American dollars on a future date, you will need to sell American dollars. To hedge you cannot sell American dollar futures so that you will have to buy your own currency's futures:

Buy the appropriate **home currency futures** contracts **now**

 Sell the same number of **home currency futures** contracts on the date that you receive dollars

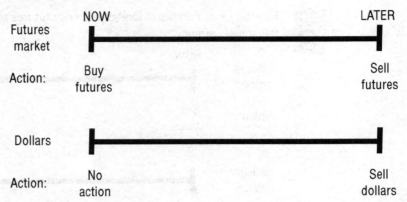

1.3 Which contract settlement date?

Currency futures are traded for a period of about nine months before the settlement date is reached. To hedge currency receipts and payments a futures contract must have a **settlement date after** the date that the actual **currency is needed**. Usually the best hedge is achieved by selecting the contract which matures **next after** the actual cash is needed.

1.4 Contract prices

All currency futures are priced in US$, for example $/€, $/£.

1.5 Dealing with a futures question

A number of possible stages are involved.

 The setup process

This may involve the following steps.

(a) **Choose which contract**

You must choose an expiry date after the underlying exposure.

(b) **Choose type of contract**

A €125,000 contract will be used to buy or sell €. If the company owes €, it will wish to buy € so will **buy € futures**.

However a UK company receiving $ will wish to sell $ or buy £. As the contract size is quoted in £, £62,500, the company will **buy £ futures**.

(c) **Choose number of contracts**

You need to divide the amount being hedged by the size of contract, rounding to the nearest whole contract.

You may also need to calculate how much of the currency of the future is needed. You do this by using today's price for the futures contract to convert the amount being hedged into the currency of the futures contract, and then divide by the size of the futures contract.

Estimate the closing futures price

You should be given this in the question.

Hedge outcome

(a) **Calculate futures market outcome**

This will be:

Movement in rate × Value of one contract × Number of contracts

(b) **Calculate net outcome**

Spot market payment or receipt translated at closing rate
+ Futures market profit/(loss)

The currency used for this calculation will be the opposite to the currency of the receipt/payment being hedged. Ultimately therefore, unless a dollar receipt or payment is being hedged, the value of the futures profit or loss will also have to be converted using the **closing spot rate**.

The gain or loss on the future will accrue during the contract. For exam purposes you will take this gain or loss when the contract is terminated.

Example: Futures contract

A US company buys goods worth €720,000 from a German company payable in 30 days. The US company wants to hedge against the € strengthening against the dollar.

Current spot is €1 = $0.9215 – 0.9221 and the futures rate is 0.9245.

The standard size of a 3 month € futures contract is €125,000.

In 30 days time the spot is 0.9345 – 0.9351.

Closing futures price will be 0.9367.

Evaluate the hedge.

Solution

Setup

(a) **Which contract?**

We assume that the three month contract is the best available.

(b) **Type of contract**

We need to buy € or sell $.
As the futures contract is in €, we need to buy futures.

(c) **Number of contracts**

$$\frac{720,000}{125,000} = 5.76, \text{ say 6 contracts}$$

Closing futures price

We're told it will be 0.9367

Hedge outcome

(a) **Outcome in futures market**

Opening futures price	0.9245	Buy at low price
Closing futures price	0.9367	Sell at high price
Movement	0.0122	Profit
Futures profit/loss	0.0122 × $125,000 × 6 contracts = $9,150	

(b) **Net outcome**

	$
Spot market payment (720,000 × 0.9351)	673,272
Futures market profit	(9,150)
	664,122

In this instance the risk feared was the risk that the payment would go up in $ terms, as you needed more $ to buy each € that you needed to pay the European supplier.

This risk has materialised as in the end you need to pay $0.9351 to buy each € rather than $0.9221.

Buying the € futures has mitigated this loss because at the end you can sell them for more than you paid because € have become more valuable.

KEY POINT

Remember the following table.

Transaction on future date		Now		On future date	
Receive	currency	Sell	currency futures	Buy	currency futures
Pay	currency	Buy	currency futures	Sell	currency futures
Receive	$	Buy	currency futures	Sell	currency futures
Pay	$	Sell	currency futures	Buy	currency futures

1.6 Choosing between forward contracts and futures contracts

A futures market hedge attempts to achieve the same result as a forward contract, that is to fix the exchange rate in advance for a future foreign currency payment or receipt. As we have seen, hedge inefficiencies mean that a futures contract can only fix the exchange rate subject to a margin of error.

Forward contracts are agreed **'over the counter'** between a bank and its customer. Futures contracts are standardised and traded on futures exchanges. This results in the following advantages and disadvantages.

1.6.1 Advantages of currency futures

(a) **Transaction** costs should be **lower** than for forward contracts.

(b) The **exact date** of **receipt** or **payment** of the currency does **not have to be known**, because the futures contract does not have to be closed out until the actual cash receipt or payment is made. In other words, the futures hedge gives the equivalent of an 'option forward' contract, limited only by the expiry date of the contract.

(c) Because future contracts are traded on exchange regulated markets, **counterparty risk** should be **reduced** and buying and selling contracts should be easy.

1.6.2 Disadvantages of currency futures

(a)   The **contracts cannot be tailored** to the user's exact requirements.

(b)   **Hedge inefficiencies** are **caused** by having to deal in a whole number of contracts and by **basis risk**.

(c)   **Only a limited number of currencies** are the subject of futures contracts (although the number of currencies is growing, especially with the rapid development of Asian economies).

(d)   The **procedure for converting** between two currencies neither of which is the US dollar is twice as complex for futures as for a forward contract.

(e)   Using the market will involve various **costs**, including brokers' fees.

In general, the disadvantages of futures mean that the market is much smaller than the currency forward market.

Question 12.1	Futures

Learning outcomes D2(a), (b)

Allbrit plc, a company based in the UK, imports and exports to the USA. On 1 May it signs three agreements, all of which are to be settled on 31 October:

(a)   A sale to a US customer of goods for $205,500
(b)   A sale to another US customer for £550,000
(c)   A purchase from a US supplier for $875,000

On 1 June the spot rate is £1 = 1.5500 – 1.5520 $ and the October forward rate is at a premium of 4.00 – 3.95 cents per pound. Sterling futures contracts are trading at the following prices:

Sterling futures (IMM) Contract size £62,500

Contract settlement date	Contract price $ per £1
Jun	1.5370
Sep	1.5180
Dec	1.4970

Tick size is $6.25.

Required

(a)   Calculate the net amount receivable or payable in pounds if the transactions are covered on the forward market.

(b)   Demonstrate how a futures hedge could be set up and calculate the result of the futures hedge if, by 31 October, the spot market price for dollars has moved to 1.5800 – 1.5820 and the sterling futures price has moved to 1.5650.

Section summary

Currency futures are contracts for the sale or purchase at a set future date of a set quantity of currency. A step-by-step approach can be used to deal with complications.

2 Currency options

Introduction

Like interest rate options, currency options allow businesses to take advantage of favourable movements in rates, whilst limiting the impact of adverse changes.

2.1 Currency options

KEY TERM

A **CURRENCY OPTION** is an agreement involving an option, but not an obligation, to buy or to sell a certain amount of currency at a stated rate of exchange (the exercise price) at some time in the future.

A forward exchange contract is an agreement to buy or sell a given quantity of foreign exchange, which **must be carried out** because it is a binding contract. However, some exporters might be uncertain about the amount of currency they will earn in several months' time.

An alternative method of obtaining foreign exchange cover, which overcomes much of this problem, is the **currency option**. A currency option **does not have to be exercised**. Instead, when the date for exercising the option arrives, the importer or exporter can either exercise the option or let the option lapse.

The exercise price for the option may be the same as the current spot rate, or it may be more favourable or less favourable to the option holder than the current spot rate.

As with other types of option, buying a currency option involves **paying a premium**, which is the most the buyer of the option can lose.

2.2 Types of option

Companies can choose whether to buy:

(a)   A tailor-made currency option from a bank, suited to the company's specific needs. These are **over-the-counter** (OTC) or **negotiated** options, or

(b)   A standard option, in certain currencies only, from an options exchange. Such options are **traded** or **exchange-traded** options.

2.3 The uses of currency options

The purpose of currency options is to reduce or eliminate exposure to currency risks, and they are particularly useful for companies in the following situations:

(a)   Where there is **uncertainty** about **foreign currency receipts or payments**, either in timing or amount. Should the foreign exchange transaction not materialise, the option can be sold on the market (if it has any value) or exercised if this would make a profit.

(b)   To **support the tender** for an **overseas contract**, priced in a foreign currency.

(c)   To allow **the publication of price lists** for its goods in a foreign currency.

(d)   To protect the import or export of **price-sensitive goods**.

In both situations (b) and (c), the company would not know whether it had won any export sales or would have any foreign currency income at the time that it announces its selling prices. It cannot make a forward exchange contract to sell foreign currency without becoming exposed in the currency.

2.4 Comparison of currency options with forward contracts and futures contracts

We have seen that a hedge using a currency future will produce approximately the same result as a currency forward contract, subject to hedge inefficiencies. When comparing currency options with forward or futures contracts we usually find the following.

(a)   If the currency movement is adverse, the option will be exercised, but the hedge will not normally be quite as good as that of the forward or futures contract; this is because of the **premium cost of the option**.

(b)   If the currency movement is favourable, the option will not be exercised, and the result will normally be better than that of the forward or futures contract; this is because the option allows the holder to **profit from the improved exchange rate**.

2.5 Put and call options

KEY TERMS

There are two types of currency option, both of which can be bought and sold.

(a)   CALL OPTIONS give the **buyer** of the option the **right** to **buy** the underlying **currency** at a **fixed rate of exchange** (and the **seller** of the option would be **required** to **sell** the underlying **currency** at that rate).

(b)   PUT OPTIONS give the **buyer** of the option the **right** to **sell** the underlying **currency** at a **fixed rate of exchange** (and the **seller** of the option would be **required** to **buy** the underlying **currency** at that rate).

2.5.1 Choosing the correct type of option

The vast majority of options examples which we consider are concerned with **hedgers** who **purchase** options in order to reduce risk. We are seldom concerned with option writers who sell options.

So, given that we are normally going to *purchase* options, should we **purchase puts or calls**?

(a)   A **US company receiving £** in the future and hence wishing to **sell £** in the future can hedge by **purchasing £ put options** (ie options to sell £).

(b)   A **US company paying £** in the future and hence wishing to **buy £** in the future can hedge by **purchasing £ call options** (ie options to buy £).

(c)   A **UK company receiving $** in the future and hence wishing to **sell $** in the future cannot hedge by purchasing $ put options as they don't exist. They therefore have to **purchase £ call options**.

(d)   A **UK company paying $** in the future and hence wishing to **buy $** in the future cannot hedge by purchasing $ call options as they don't exist. They therefore have to **purchase £ put options**.

KEY POINT

Transaction on future date		Now		Option on future date	
Receive	currency	Buy	currency put	Sell	currency
Pay	currency	Buy	currency call	Buy	currency
Receive	$	Buy	currency call	Buy	currency
Pay	$	Buy	currency put	Sell	currency

Exam alert

Note that this table only applies to **traded** options. It would be possible to purchase a dollar put or call option over-the-counter.

2.6 Choosing the price and the number of contracts to be used

A problem arises when a non-US company wishes to buy or sell US dollars using traded options. The amount of US dollars must first be converted into the home currency. For this purpose the best exchange rate to use is the **exercise price**, which means that the number of contracts may vary according to which exercise price is chosen.

2.7 Closing out when traded options still have time to run

In practice, most traded options are **closed out**, like futures contracts, because the date when the cash is required does not match the option expiry date.

Exam skills

The position with options is equivalent to the position with **futures**; the expiry date of options must be **on** or **after** the date of the key event. Thus if you were told a company was receiving a payment on 10 September, and you were given a choice of using June, September or December options:

- You could most likely choose September as that expires soonest after 10 September (on 30 September)

- You could choose December

- You would not choose June (as June options expire before 10 September, the date on which you will receive the payment)

2.8 Option calculation

Because of the complications, it is best to use a similar method to the method we used for futures to assess the impact of options.

Set up the hedge

(a)   Choose contract date
(b)   Decide whether put or call option required
(c)   Decide which exercise or strike price applies
(d)   How many contracts
(e)   Calculate premium (Price in table × 0.01) × Size of contract × Number of contracts

The premium may need to be converted using the spot rate

Ascertain closing price

You should be given this.

Calculate outcome of hedge

You may have to calculate the outcome under more than one closing spot rate.

(a)   Outcome in options market. This will include:

    (i)   Exercising the option
    (ii)   Cash flows on exercise
    (iii)   Converting amount uncovered/overcovered at spot rate

(b)   Net outcome

Example: Currency options

A UK company owes a US supplier $2,000,000 payable in July. The spot rate is £1 = $1.5350–1.5370 and the UK company is concerned that the $ might strengthen.

The details for $/£ £31,250 options (cents per £1) are as follows.

Premium cost per contract

		Calls			Puts	
Strike price	June	July	August	June	July	August
1.4750	6.34	6.37	6.54	0.07	0.19	0.50
1.5000	3.86	4.22	4.59	0.08	0.53	1.03
1.5250	1.58	2.50	2.97	0.18	1.25	1.89

Show how traded currency options can be used to hedge the risk at 1.525. Calculate the sterling cost of the transaction if the spot rate in July is:

(a)   1.46–1.4620

(b)   1.61–1.6120

Solution

Set up the hedge

(a)   Which date contract? July

(b)   Put or call? Put, we need to put (sell) pounds in order to generate the dollars we need

(c)   Which strike price? 1.5250

(d)   How many contracts

$$\frac{2,000,000 \div 1.525}{31,250} \approx 41.97, \text{ say 42 contracts}$$

(e)   Use July Put figure for 1.5250 of 1.25. Remember it has to be multiplied by 0.01.

Premium = (1.25 × 0.01) × Contract size × Number of contracts

Premium = 0.0125 × 31,250 × 42
         = $16,406 ÷ 1.5350 (to obtain premium in £)
         = £10,688

We need to pay the option premium in $ now. Therefore the bank sells low at 1.5350.

Closing spot and futures prices

Case (a) $1.46
Case (b) $1.61

Assume here the price to use for options calculation is the same as the closing spot rate.

Outcome

(a) **Options market outcome**

Strike price put	1.5250	1.5250
Closing price	1.46	1.61
Exercise?	Yes	No
Outcome of options position (31,250 × 42)	£1,312,500	–

Balance on spot market

	$
Exercise option (31,250 × 42 × 1.5250)	2,001,563
Value of transaction	2,000,000
Balance	1,563

Translated at spot rate $\dfrac{1,563}{1.46}$ = £1,071

(b) **Net outcome**

	£	£
Spot market outcome translated at closing spot rate $\dfrac{2,000,000}{1.61}$	–	(1,242,236)
Options position	(1,312,500)	–
Difference in hedge at closing rate	1,071	
The difference is a receipt as the amount owed was over-hedged.		
Premium (remember premium has to be added in separately as translated at the opening spot rate)	(10,688)	(10,688)
	(1,322,117)	(1,252,924)

Exam skill

You are most likely to be told in the question which strike or exercise price to use. If you aren't, and are told in the question what the closing rate was, choose a strike price which will mean that the option is exercised.

Question 12.2

Learning outcomes D2(a), (b)

Edted is a UK company that has purchased goods worth $2,000,000 from an American supplier. Edted is due to make payment in three months' time. Edted's treasury department is looking to hedge the risk using an over-the-counter option, A three month dollar call option has a price of 1.4800.

Required

Ignoring premium costs, calculate the cost to Edted if the exchange rate at the time of payment is:

(a) £1 = $1.4600
(b) £1 = $1.5000

Question 12.3

Learning outcomes D2(a), (b)

Vinnick, an American company purchases goods from Santos, a Spanish company, on 15 May on 3 months credit for €600,000.

Vinnick is unsure in which direction exchange rates will move so has decided to buy options to hedge the contract at a rate of $1 = €0.7700.

The details for €10,000 options at 0.7700 are as follows.

	Calls			Puts	
July	August	September	July	August	September
2.55	3.57	4.01	1.25	2.31	2.90

The current spot rate is 0.7800.

Required

Calculate the dollar cost of the transaction if the spot rate in August is:

(a)   0.7500
(b)   0.8000

2.9 Drawbacks of currency options

- The cost depends on the expected volatility of the exchange rate.
- Options must be paid for as soon as they are bought.
- Tailor-made options lack negotiability.
- Traded options are not available in every currency.

2.10 Graphical illustration of currency options

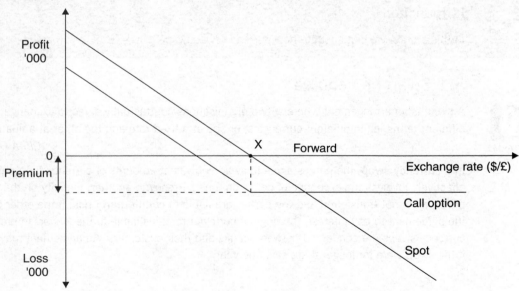

Currency call option, forward and spot markets: profit/loss profile

Suppose that a UK-based company expects to receive an amount of export income in dollars ($) in three months' time. This graph illustrates the profit/loss profile of different strategies.

(a) Selling dollars and buying sterling in the **forward market** eliminates all uncertainty. The outcome is represented by a horizontal line.

(b) Relying on the **spot market** results in a net gain or loss compared with the forward market if the spot exchange rate in three months' time turns out to be below or above $X per pound respectively.

(c) If a **call option** is used, it will not be exercised if the exchange rate is less than $X per pound. A currency call option reduces the potential gain compared with the spot market strategy (b) by the amount of the premium on the option, but has the advantage that potential losses are contained as they will not exceed the value of the premium.

2.11 Option premiums

The level of currency option premiums depends upon the following factors:

- The **exercise price**
- The **maturity of the option**
- The **volatility** of exchange and interest rates
- **Interest rate differentials**, affecting how much banks charge

Section summary

Currency options protect against **adverse exchange rate movements** while allowing the investor to take advantage of favourable exchange rate movements. They are particularly useful in situations where the cash flow is not certain to occur (eg when tendering for overseas contracts).

A currency **call** option is a right to **buy** the underlying instrument.

A currency **put** option is a right to **sell** the underlying instrument.

3 Currency swaps

Introduction

In this section we demonstrate how currency swaps work.

3.1 Swap procedures

KEY TERM

A SWAP is an arrangement whereby two organisations contractually agree to exchange payments on different terms, eg in different currencies, or one at a fixed rate and the other at a floating rate.

(CIMA Official Terminology)

In a **currency swap**, the parties agree to swap equivalent amounts of currency for a period. This effectively involves the exchange of debt from one currency to another. Liability on the main debt (the principal) is not transferred and the parties are liable to **counterparty risk**: if the other party defaults on the agreement to pay interest, the original borrower remains liable to the lender. In practice, most currency swaps are conducted between banks and their customers. An agreement may only be necessary if the swap were for longer than, say, one year.

Example: Currency swap

Consider a UK company X with a subsidiary Y in France which owns vineyards. Assume a spot rate of £1 = 1.6 Euros. Suppose the parent company X wishes to raise a loan of 1.6 million Euros for the purpose of buying another French wine company. At the same time, the French subsidiary Y wishes to raise £1 million to pay for new up-to-date capital equipment imported from the UK. The UK parent company X could borrow the £1 million sterling and the French subsidiary Y could borrow the 1.6 million euros, each effectively borrowing on the other's behalf. They would then swap currencies.

3.2 Benefits of swaps

(a) **Flexibility**

Swaps are **easy to arrange** and are **flexible** since they can be arranged in any size and are reversible.

(b) **Cost**

Transaction costs are low, only amounting to legal fees, since there is no commission or premium to be paid.

(c) **Market avoidance**

The parties can **obtain the currency they require** without subjecting themselves to the **uncertainties** of the foreign exchange markets.

(d) **Access to finance**

The company can gain **access to debt finance in another country** and currency where it is little known, and consequently has a poorer credit rating, than in its home country. It can therefore take advantage of lower interest rates than it could obtain if it arranged the currency loan itself.

(e) **Financial restructuring**

Currency swaps may be used to **restructure the currency base** of the company's liabilities. This may be important where the company is trading overseas and receiving revenues in foreign currencies, but its borrowings are denominated in the currency of its home country. Currency swaps therefore provide a means of reducing exchange rate exposure.

(f) **Conversion of debt type**

At the same time as exchanging currency, the company may also be able to **convert fixed rate debt** to **floating rate or vice versa**. Thus it may obtain some of the benefits of an interest rate swap in addition to achieving the other purposes of a currency swap.

(g) **Liquidity improvement**

A currency swap could be used to **absorb excess liquidity** in one currency which is not needed immediately, to create funds in another where there is a need.

3.3 Disadvantages of swaps

(a) **Risk of default by the other party to the swap (counter party risk)**

If one party became **unable to meet its swap payment obligations**, this could mean that the other party risked having to make them itself.

(b) **Position or market risk**

A company whose main business lies outside the field of finance should **not increase financial risk** in order to make **speculative gains**.

(c) **Sovereign risk**

There may be a risk of **political disturbances or exchange controls** in the country whose currency is being used for a swap.

(d) **Arrangement fees**

Swaps have arrangement fees payable to third parties. Although these may appear to be cheap, this is because the intermediary accepts **no liability** for the swap. (The third party does however suffer some spread risk, as they warehouse one side of the swap until it is matched with the other, and then undertake a temporary hedge on the futures market.)

Example: Currency swap

STEP 1

Edted, a UK company, wishes to invest in Germany. It borrows £20 million from its bank and pays interest at 5%. To invest in Germany, the £20 million will be converted into euros at a spot rate of £1 = €1.5. The earnings from the German investment will be in euros, but Edted will have to pay interest on the swap. The company arranges to swap the £20 million for €30 million with Gordonbear, a company in the Euro currency zone. Gordonbear is thus the counterparty in this transaction. Interest of 6% is payable on the €30 million. Edted can use the €30 million it receives to invest in Germany.

STEP 2

Each year when interest is due:

(a) Edted receives from its German investment cash remittances of €1.8 million (€30 million × 6%).

(b) Edted passes this €1.8 million to Gordonbear so that Gordonbear can settle its interest liability.

(c) Gordonbear passes to Edted £1 million (£20 million × 5%).

(d) Edted settles its interest liability of £1 million with its lender.

STEP 3

At the end of the useful life of the investment the original payments are reversed with Edted paying back the €30 million it originally received and receiving back from Gordonbear the £20 million. Edted uses this £20 million to repay the loan it originally received from its UK lender.

Section summary

Currency swaps effectively involve the exchange of debt from one currency to another.

Currency swaps can provide a **hedge** against exchange rate movements for longer periods than the forward market, and can be a means of obtaining finance from new countries.

Chapter Roundup

✓   **Currency futures** are contracts for the sale or purchase at a set future date of a set quantity of currency. A step-by-step approach can be used to deal with complications.

✓   **Currency options** protect against **adverse exchange rate movements** while allowing the investor to take advantage of favourable exchange rate movements. They are particularly useful in situations where the cash flow is not certain to occur (eg when tendering for overseas contracts).

✓   A currency **call** option is a right to **buy** the underlying instrument.

✓   A currency **put** option is a right to **sell** the underlying instrument.

✓   **Currency swaps** effectively involve the exchange of debt from one currency to another.

✓   Currency swaps can provide a **hedge** against exchange rate movements for longer periods than the forward market, and can be a means of obtaining finance from new countries.

Quick Quiz

1   What does *CIMA Official Terminology* define as 'a right of an option holder to buy or sell a specific asset on predetermined terms on, or before, a future date'.

2   In the context of currency options, a put option gives the option buyer the right to buy the underlying currency at a fixed rate of exchange.

   True   ☐

   False   ☐

3   Futures market outcome = ?

4   Complete the following table using Buy or Sell.

Transaction on future date		Now	On future date
Receive	currency	currency futures	currency futures
Pay	currency	currency futures	currency futures
Receive	$	currency futures	currency futures
Pay	$	currency futures	currency futures

5   Complete the following table using Buy or Sell.

Transaction on future date		Now	Option on future date
Receive	currency		
Pay	currency		
Receive	$		
Pay	$		

6   What are the key stages in setting up an option hedge?

7   What is the significance of a settlement date in futures?

8   What are the main factors affecting the level of option premiums?

9   Fill in the blank.

   .... risk is the risk of one party on a swap defaulting on the arrangement.

10   Swaps, like other derivatives, can be used as methods of speculation.

   True   ☐

   False   ☐

Answers to Quick Quiz

1   An option

2   False. This is true of a call option, not a put option.

3   Movement in rate × Value of one contract × Number of contracts

4

Transaction on future date		Now		On future date	
Receive	currency	Sell	currency futures	Buy	currency futures
Pay	currency	Buy	currency futures	Sell	currency futures
Receive	$	Buy	currency futures	Sell	currency futures
Pay	$	Sell	currency futures	Buy	currency futures

5

Transaction on future date		Now		Option on future date	
Receive	currency	Buy	currency put	Sell	currency
Pay	currency	Buy	currency call	Buy	currency
Receive	$	Buy	currency call	Buy	currency
Pay	$	Buy	currency put	Sell	currency

6   • Choose contract date   • No of contracts
     • Put or call options   • Premium
     • Strike price

7   A settlement date is the date when trading on a futures contract stops and all accounts are settled.

8   • Exercise price   • Volatility of exchange/interest rates
     • Maturity of option   • Interest rate differentials

9   **Counterparty** risk is the risk of one party on a swap defaulting on the arrangement.

10   True

Answers to Questions

12.1 Futures

(a) Before covering any transactions with forward or futures contracts, match receipts against payments. The sterling receipt does not need to be hedged. The dollar receipt can be matched against the payment giving a net payment of $669,500 on 31 October.

The appropriate spot rate for buying dollars on 1 May (bank sells low) is 1.5500. The forward rate for October is *spot – premium* = 1.5500 – 0.0400 = 1.5100.

Using a forward contract, the sterling cost of the dollar payment will be 669,500/1.5100 = £443,377. The net cash received on October 31 will therefore be £550,000 – 443,377 = £106,623.

(b) **Set up**

 STEP 1

   (a) **Which contract**

      December contracts

   (b) **Type of contract**

      Sell sterling futures in May, we sell the sterling in order to buy the $ that we need

   (c) **Number of contracts**

      Here we need to convert the dollar payment to £ as contracts are in £.

      Using December futures price

$$\frac{669,500}{1.4970} = = £447,228$$

      No of contracts $= \dfrac{£447,228}{62,500}$

      = 7.16 contracts, round to 7

 STEP 2 **Closing futures price**

1.5650 given in question

 STEP 3 **Result of futures market**

   (a) **Futures market outcome**

Opening futures price	1.4970	Sell
Closing futures price	1.5650	Buy
Movement	0.0680	Loss

      Futures market loss = 0.0680 × 62,500 × 7 = $29,750

   (b) **Net outcome**

	$
Spot market payment	(669,500)
Futures market loss	(29,750)
	(699,250)
Translated at closing spot rate	1.5800
The bank sells low hence we use the rate of 1.5800	£442,563

12.2 Currency options 1

As the option is an over-the-counter option, it is possible to have a dollar call option and to cover the exact amount.

(a) If the exchange rate is 1.4600, the option will be exercised and the cost will be:

$$\frac{2,000,000}{1.4800} = £1,351,351$$

(b) If the exchange rate is 1.5000, the option will not be exercised, and the cost will be:

$$\frac{2,000,000}{1.5000} = £1,333,333$$

12.3 Currency options 2

Set up the hedge

(a) Which date contract? August

(b) Put or call? Call, we need to buy euros

(c) Which strike price? 0.7700

(d) How many contracts

$$\frac{600,000}{10,000} = 60$$

(e) Use August call figure of 3.57. Remember it has to be multiplied by 0.01.

Premium $=$ (3.57 × 0.01) × Contract size × Number of contracts

Premium $=$ 0.0357 × 10,000 × 60
$=$ \$21,420

Closing spot and futures prices

Case (a) 0.75
Case (b) 0.80

Assume here the price to use for options calculation is the same as the closing spot rate.

Outcome

(a) **Options market outcome**

Strike price call	0.77	0.77
Closing price	0.75	0.80
Exercise?	Yes	No
Outcome of options position	€600,000	–

(b) **Net outcome**

	$	$
Spot market outcome translated at closing spot rate $\dfrac{600,000}{0.80}$	–	(750,000)
Options position $\dfrac{600,000}{0.77}$	(779,221)	–
Premium	(21,420)	(21,420)
	(800,641)	(771,420)

Now try these questions from the Exam Question Bank

Number	Level	Marks	Time
Q16	Examination	25	45 mins
Q17	Examination	25	45 mins
Q18	Examination	20	36 mins

RISK AND CONTROL IN INFORMATION SYSTEMS

Part D

INFORMATION STRATEGY AND SYSTEMS

 In this chapter we concentrate on information strategies and systems, beginning with the importance of information to organisations.

The remainder of this chapter focuses on the high-level controls over the provisions of information and over the technology that provides it.

We will firstly consider how organisations develop information strategies to support management and internal control requirements and then examine the various information systems that organisations operate.

We also need to look at the different ways of structuring the information function.

This chapter ends with outsourcing, examining the advantages and disadvantages and also considering the criteria for selecting outsourcing partners and for managing on-going relationships.

The examiner has stated that the areas covered by chapter 13 and 14 are likely to be examined in the context of a broader question covering other topics.

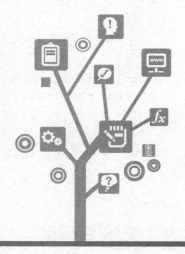

topic list	learning outcomes	syllabus references	ability required
1 Information requirements	E1(a), (b)	E1(i)	evaluation
2 The value of information	E1(a), (b)	E1(i)	evaluation
3 Information strategy	E1(a)	E1(ii)	evaluation
4 Developing an information strategy	E1(a)	E1(ii)	evaluation
5 Types of information system	E1(b)	E1(iii)	evaluation
6 Evaluating information systems	E1(b)	E1(i), (iii)	evaluation
7 Information systems provision and staffing	E1(c)	E1(iv)	evaluation
8 Organising and assessing the IT department	E1(c)	E1(iv)	evaluation
9 Outsourcing	E1(c)	E1(v), (x)	evaluation

1 Information requirements

Introduction

In this section, we consider what information is and why organisations need information. Information is needed for recording transactions, measuring performance, decision-making, planning and control. We also look at the types of information (strategic, tactical and operational) and the qualities of good information.

1.1 Needs for information

KEY TERMS

DATA is the raw material for data processing. Data consists of numbers, letters and symbols and relates to facts, events, and transactions. INFORMATION is data that has been processed in such a way as to be meaningful to the person who receives it.

An INFORMATION SYSTEM is 'an organisational and management solution, based on information technology, to any challenge posed by the environment'.

All organisations require information for a range of purposes, which are discussed below.

1.1.1 Planning

Planning requires a knowledge of the available resources, possible time-scales and the likely outcome under alternative scenarios. Information is required that helps **decision-making**, and how to implement decisions taken.

1.1.2 Controlling

Once a plan is implemented, its actual performance must be controlled. Information is required to assess **whether it is proceeding as planned** or whether there is some unexpected deviation from plan. It may consequently be necessary to take some form of corrective action.

1.1.3 Recording transactions

Information about **each transaction or event** is required. Reasons include:

(a)   Documentation of transactions can be used as **evidence** in a case of dispute.

(b)   There may be a **legal requirement** to record transactions, for example for accounting and audit purposes.

(c)   **Operational information** can be built up, allowing control action to be taken.

1.1.4 Performance measurement

Just as individual operations need to be controlled, so overall performance must be measured. **Comparisons against budget or plan** are able to be made. This may involve the collection of information on, for example, costs, revenues, volumes, time-scale and profitability.

1.1.5 Decision-making

Information is needed to optimise decision-making for **strategic planning, management control** and **operational control**.

1.2 Data capture

Data capture refers to the media or input device from which the data is obtained. Data can be in

- **Machine form**, which uses IT to capture the data correctly eg a bar code scanner; its advantages are speed, accuracy, large volume capabilities

- **Human sensible form**, which requires human intervention for data to be input to an IT medium; its advantages are flexibility and ease of understanding

The data capture mechanism needs to be appropriate for the type of organisation. In addition the quality of the output is **dependent** on the quality of input. In other words:

RUBBISH IN = RUBBISH OUT

1.3 Types of information

1.3.1 Strategic information

Strategic information is used to **plan** the **objectives** of the **organisation**, and to **assess** whether the objectives are being met in practice. Such information includes overall profitability, the profitability of different segments of the business, future market prospects, the availability and cost of raising new funds, total cash needs, total manning levels and capital equipment needs.

Strategic information is:

- Derived from both **internal and external** sources
- **Summarised** at a high level
- Relevant to the **long-term**
- Concerned with the **whole organisation**
- Often prepared on an **'ad hoc'** basis
- Both **quantitative and qualitative**
- **Uncertain**, as the future cannot be accurately predicted

1.3.2 Tactical information

Tactical information is used to decide **how the resources of the business should be employed**, and to **monitor** how they are being and have been employed. Such information includes productivity measurements (output per hour), budgetary control or variance analysis reports, and cash flow forecasts, staffing levels and profit results within a particular department of the organisation, labour turnover statistics within a department and short-term purchasing requirements.

Tactical information is:

- Primarily generated internally (but may have a limited external component)
- **Summarised at a lower level**
- Relevant to the **short and medium term**
- Concerned with **activities or departments**
- Prepared **routinely and regularly**
- Based on **quantitative** measures

1.3.3 Operational information

Operational information is used to ensure that **specific operational tasks** are planned and carried out as intended.

Operational information is:

- Derived from **internal** sources such as transaction recording methods
- **Detailed**, being the processing of raw data (for example transaction reports listing all transactions in a period)
- Relevant to the **immediate term**
- **Task-specific**
- Prepared very **frequently**
- Largely **quantitative**

1.4 The qualities of good information

'Good' information is information that adds to the understanding of a situation. The qualities of good information are outlined in the following table. You can use the mnemonic ACCURATE to help you remember the qualities of good information.

Quality	Example
Accurate	Figures should add up, the degree of rounding should be appropriate, there should be no typos, items should be allocated to the correct category, assumptions should be stated for uncertain information.
Complete	Information should include everything that it needs to include, for example external data if relevant, comparative information or qualitative information as well as quantitative. Sometimes managers or strategic planners will need to build on the available information to produce a forecast using assumptions or extrapolations.
Cost-beneficial	It should not cost more to obtain the information than the benefit derived from having it. Providers of information should be given efficient means of collecting and analysing it. Presentation should be such that users do not waste time working out what it means.
User-targeted	The needs of the user should be borne in mind, for instance senior managers need strategic summaries periodically, junior ones need detail.
Relevant	Information that is not needed for a decision should be omitted, no matter how 'interesting' it may be.
Authoritative	The source of the information should be a reliable one (not, for instance, 'Joe Bloggs Predictions Page' on the Internet unless Joe Bloggs is known to be a reliable source for that type of information). However, subjective information (eg expert opinions) may be required in addition to objective facts.
Timely	The information should be available when it is needed. It should also cover relevant time periods, the future as well as the past.
Easy to use	Information should be clearly presented, not excessively long, and sent using the right medium and communication channel (e-mail, telephone, hard-copy report etc).

Exam skills

You will not be asked simply to produce a list of the qualities of good information in the exam. Exam questions will expect you to be able to identify **the information problems** that a company is having, and to **suggest solutions**. These would include inadequate record – keeping that makes it difficult to calculate profitability. Better data collection systems, for example a shop introducing electronic point trade (EPOS) technology, may help.

1.5 Improvements to information

The table below contains suggestions as to how poor information can be **improved**.

Feature	Examples of possible improvements
Accurate	Use computerised systems with automatic input checks rather than manual systems.
	Allow sufficient time for collation and analysis of data if pinpoint accuracy is crucial.
	Incorporate elements of probability within projections so that the required response to different future scenarios can be assessed.
Complete	Include past data as a reference point for future projections.
	Include any planned developments, such as new products.
	Information about future demand would be more useful than information about past demand.
	Include external data.
Cost-beneficial	Always bear in mind whether the benefit of having the information is greater than the cost of obtaining it.
User-targeted	Information should be summarised and presented together with relevant ratios or percentages.
Relevant	The purpose of the report should be defined. It may be trying to fulfil too many purposes at once. Perhaps several shorter reports would be more effective.
	Information should include exception reporting, where only those items that are worthy of note – and the control actions taken by more junior managers to deal with them – are reported.
Authoritative	Use reliable sources and experienced personnel.
	If some figures are derived from other figures the method of derivation should be explained.
Timely	Information collection and analysis by production managers needs to be speeded up considerably, probably by the introduction of better information systems
Easy-to-use	Graphical presentation, allowing trends to be quickly assimilated and relevant action decided upon.
	Alternative methods of presentation should be considered, such as graphs or charts, to make it easier to review the information at a glance. Numerical information is sometimes best summarised in narrative form or vice versa.
	A 'house style' for reports should be devised and adhered to by all. This would cover such matters as number of decimal places to use, table headings and labels, paragraph numbering and so on.

Exam alert

Assessing the problems with the information provided for an investment appraisal could come up in part of a question, for which the above table could prove useful in generating ideas for your answer.

1.6 Information requirements in different sectors

The following table provides examples of the typical information requirements of organisations operating in different sectors.

Sector	Information type	Example(s)	General comment
Manufacturing	Strategic	Future demand estimates New product development plans Competitor analysis	The information requirements of commercial organisations are influenced by the need to make and monitor profit. Information that contributes to the following measures is important:
	Tactical	Variance analysis Departmental accounts Inventory turnover	• Changeover times • Number of common parts • Level of product diversity • Product and process quality
	Operational	Production reject rate Materials and labour used Inventory levels	
Service	Strategic	Forecast sales growth and market share Profitability, capital structure	Organisations have become more customer and results-oriented over the last decade. As a consequence, the difference between service and other organisations' information requirements has decreased. Businesses have realised that most of their activities can be measured, and many can be measured in similar ways regardless of the business sector.
	Tactical	Resource utilisation such as average staff time charged out, number of customers per hairdresser, number of staff per account Customer satisfaction rating	
	Operational	Staff timesheets Customer waiting time Individual customer feedback	
Public	Strategic	Population demographics Expected government policy	Public sector (and non-profit making) organisations often don't have one overriding objective. Their information requirements depend on the objectives chosen. The information provided often requires interpretation (eg student exam results are not affected by the quality of teaching alone).
	Tactical	Hospital occupancy rates Average class sizes Percent of reported crimes solved	

Sector	Information type	Example(s)	General comment
	Operational	Staff timesheets Vehicles available Student daily attendance records	Information may compare actual performance with: • Standards • Targets • Similar activities • Indices • Activities over time as trends
Non-profit/ charities	Strategic	Activities of other charities Government (and in some cases overseas government) policy Public attitudes	Many of the comments regarding public sector organisations can be applied to not-for-profit organisations. Information to judge performance usually aims to assess economy, efficiency and effectiveness.
	Tactical	Percent of revenue spent on admin Average donation 'Customer' satisfaction statistics	A key measure of efficiency for charities is the percentage of revenue that is spent on the publicised cause (eg rather than on advertising or administration).
	Operational	Households collected from/approached Banking documentation Donations	

1.7 Information systems, technology and management

KEY TERMS

INFORMATION SYSTEMS are systems at any level of an organisation that change goals, processes, products, services or environmental relationships with the aim of gaining competitive advantage.

STRATEGIC LEVEL INFORMATION SYSTEMS are systems used by senior managers for long-term decision making.

INFORMATION TECHNOLOGY describes the interaction of computer technology and data transmission technology in order to operate systems that satisfy the information needs of the organisation, including hardware, software and operating systems.

INFORMATION MANAGEMENT refers to the basic approach an organisation has to the management of its information systems, including:

- Planning IS/IT developments
- Organisational environment of IS
- Control
- Technology

- **Information systems** deal with **what information is needed and why**

- **Information management** deals with **who** needs the information, what their **needs** are and **what information** is therefore made **available to whom**, also **how information is protected**

- **Information is made available** in response to these needs; **information technology** deals with **how the information is transferred**

Section summary

Organisations **require information** for recording transactions, measuring performance, making decisions, planning and controlling.

There are three types of information: **strategic; tactical** and **operational**.

Strategic information is used to **plan** the **objectives** of the organisation and to **assess** whether the objectives are being met in practice.

Tactical information is used to decide **how the resources of the organisation should be employed**, and to **monitor** how they are being and have been employed.

Operational information is used to ensure that **specific operational tasks** are planned and carried out as intended.

'Good' information is information that adds to the **understanding** of a situation.

2 The value of information

Introduction

In this section we look at the factors that make information valuable. We also briefly examine the use of enterprise analysis to identify the key elements and attributes of organisational data and information.

2.1 Factors that make information a valuable commodity

Information is now recognised as a valuable resource, and a **key tool in the quest for a competitive advantage.**

Easy **access** to information, the **quality** of that information and **speedy methods of exchanging** the information have become essential elements of business success.

Organisations that make **good use of information** in decision making, and which use new technologies to access, process and exchange information are likely to be **best placed to survive** in increasingly competitive world markets.

2.2 The value of obtaining information

In spite of its value in a general sense, information which is **obtained but not used** has no actual value to the person that obtains it. A decision taken on the basis of information received also has no actual value. It is only the **action taken** as a result of a decision which realises actual value for a company. The cost of collecting information bears no relation to its value. An item of information which leads to an actual increase in profit of £90 is not worth having if it costs £100 to collect.

Question 13.1

Assessing the value of information

Learning outcome E1(a)

The value of information lies in the action taken as a result of receiving it. What questions might you ask in order to make an assessment of the value of information?

2.3 Enterprise analysis

KEY TERM

ENTERPRISE ANALYSIS involves examining the entire organisation in terms of structure, processes, functions and data elements to identify the key elements and attributes of organisational data and information.

Enterprise analysis is sometimes referred to as **business systems planning**. This approach involves the following steps.

STEP 1

Ask a large sample of managers about:

- How they use information
- Where they get information
- What their objectives are
- What their data requirements are
- How they make decisions
- The influence of the environment

STEP 2

Aggregate the findings from *Step 1* into subunits, functions, processes and data matrices. Compile a Process/data class matrix to show:

- What data classes are required to support particular organisational processes
- Which processes are the creators and users of data

STEP 3

Use the matrix to identify areas that information systems should focus on, eg on processes that create data.

Section summary

The **cost and value** of information are often not easy to quantify – but attempts should be made to do so.

---

3 Information strategy

Introduction

In this section we look at the importance of having an information strategy in place for information systems, technology and management.

3.1 Elements of information strategy

A business's information strategy consists of three elements:

- Information systems strategy
- Information technology strategy
- Information management strategy

KEY TERMS

The INFORMATION SYSTEMS (IS) STRATEGY refers to the long-term plan concerned with exploiting IS and IT either to support business strategies or create new strategic options. It needs to ensure that information is obtained, retained, distributed and made available for implementing strategy in all areas of an organisation's activities.

The IS strategy is supported by:

(a) The INFORMATION TECHNOLOGY (IT) STRATEGY which involves deciding how information needs will be met by balancing supply and demand of funds and facilities, and the development of programmes to supply IT.

BPP
LEARNING MEDIA

(b)   The INFORMATION MANAGEMENT (IM) STRATEGY which aims to ensure that **information** is **provided to users** and that **redundant information** is not being produced.

Exam alert

Question 1 of the specimen paper asked about how these three strategies should be developed in an organisation.

3.2 Why have an information strategy?

A strategy for IS and IT is **justified** on the grounds that IS/IT:

* Involves **high costs**
* Is **critical to the success** of many organisations
* Is now used as part of the commercial strategy in the battle for **competitive advantage**
* Impacts on **customer service**
* Affects **all levels of management**
* Affects the way **management information** is created and presented
* **Requires effective management** to obtain the maximum benefit
* Involves many **stakeholders** inside and outside the organisation

3.3 IS/IT/IM is a high cost activity

IT costs include **hardware and software costs**, **implementation costs** associated with a new systems development and **day-to-day costs** such as salaries and accommodation.

Many organisations invest large amounts of money in IS, but not always wisely. The unmanaged proliferation of IT is likely to lead to expensive mistakes. Two key benefits of IT, the ability to **share** information and the **avoidance of duplication**, are likely to be lost.

All IT expenditure should therefore require approval to ensure that it enhances rather than detracts from the overall information strategy.

3.4 IS/IT/IM is critical to the success of many organisations

When developing an IS/IT/IM strategy a firm should assess **how important IT is** in the provision of products and services. The role that IT fills in an organisation will vary depending on the type of organisation. IS/IT could be:

* A **support** activity
* A **key** operational activity
* **Potentially** very important
* A **strategic** activity (without IT the firm could not function at all)
* A source of **competitive advantage**

Ultimately a failure of computer systems to work can result in a failure of some organisations to function at all.

3.5 IT can impact significantly on the business context

IT is an **enabling** technology, and can produce dramatic changes in individual businesses and whole industries. For example, the deregulation of the airline industry encouraged the growth of computerised seat-reservation systems. IT can be both a **cause** of major changes in doing business and a **response** to them.

3.6 IT affects all levels of management

IT has become a routine feature of office life, **a facility for everyone to use**. IT is no longer used solely by specialist staff.

3.7 IT and its effect on management information

The use of IT has permitted the design of a range of information systems, which we shall look at later in this chapter.

IT permeates the different layers of management, as a routine feature of office life and a facility for everyone to use.

(a)   Senior managers can see **more precisely** what goes on at operational level.

(b)   Operational management can be **empowered by IT** (eg expert systems) to take decisions, which computers can support.

(c)   **Delayering**. IT renders redundant the information processing role of middle managers.

(d)   Use of IT requires so-called **intellective** skills, the ability to analyse and manipulate abstract data. These used to be management's concern.

(e)   Email systems and diary planning systems enable managers to **co-ordinate** their activities better.

IT has also had an effect on **production processes**. For example, Computer Integrated Manufacturing (CIM) changed the methods and cost profiles of many manufacturing processes. The techniques used to **measure and record costs** have also adapted to the use of IT.

3.8 Information systems and corporate/business strategy

It is widely accepted that an organisation's information system should **support** corporate and business strategy. In some circumstances an information system may have a greater influence and actually help **determine** corporate/business strategy. For example:

(a)   IS/IT/IM may provide a possible source of **competitive advantage**. This could involve new technology not yet available to others or simply using existing technology in a different way.

(b)   The information system may help in formulating business strategy by **providing information** from internal and external sources.

(c)   Developments in IT may provide **new channels** for distributing and collecting information, and /or for conducting transactions eg the Internet.

Some common ways in which IS/IT/IM have had a major impact on organisations are explained below.

(a)   **The type of products or services that are made and sold**

For example, consumer markets have seen the emergence of home computers, compact discs and satellite dishes for receiving satellite TV; industrial markets have seen the emergence of custom-built microchips, robots and local area networks for office information systems. Technological changes can be relatively minor, such as the introduction of tennis and squash rackets with graphite frames, fluoride toothpaste and turbo-powered car engines.

(b)   **The way in which products are made**

There is a continuing trend towards the use of automation and computer aided design and manufacture. The manufacturing environment is undergoing rapid changes with the growth of advanced manufacturing technology. These are changes in both apparatus and technique.

(c)   **The way in which services are provided**

High-street banks encourage customers to use 'hole-in-the-wall' cash dispensers, or telephone or Internet banking. Most larger shops now use computerised **Point of Sale terminals** at cash desks. Many organisations use **e-commerce**: selling products and services over the Internet.

(d)   **The way in which markets are identified**

Database systems make it much easier to analyse the market place.

(e)   **The way in which employees are mobilised**

Technology encourages workforce empowerment. Using technology frequently requires changes in working methods. This is a change in organisation.

(f)   **The way in which firms are managed**

An empowered workforce often leads to the 'delayering' of organisational hierarchies (in other words, the reduction of management layers).

(g)   The means and extent of **communications** with customers and suppliers.

Benefits of technological change might therefore be as follows.

- To **cut production costs** and so (probably) to **reduce sales prices** to the customer
- To develop **better quality** products and services
- To develop products and services that **did not exist before**
- To **provide** products or services to customers **more quickly or effectively**
- To **free staff** from repetitive work and to tap their creativity

Section summary

A **strategy for information management**, **systems and technology** is justified on the grounds that IS/IT is costly and vital for many organisations.

4 Developing an information strategy

Introduction

In this section we examine the variety of tools available for developing an information strategy, such as Critical Success Factors and Earl's three leg analysis.

4.1 Context of information strategy

An information strategy should be developed with the aim of ensuring IS/IT is utilised as efficiently and effectively as possible in the pursuit of organisational goals and objectives.

The inputs and outputs of the IS/IT strategic planning process are summarised on the following diagram.

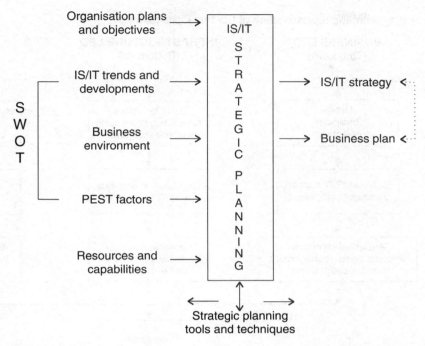

An IS strategy therefore deals with the integration of an organisation's information requirements and information systems planning with its **long-term overall goals** (customer service etc). It deals with what applications should be developed and where resources should be deployed.

4.1.1 Information technology strategy

The **IT strategy** leads on from the IS strategy above. It deals with the **technologies** of:

*   Computing
*   Communications
*   Data
*   Application systems

This provides a framework for the analysis and design of the **technological infrastructure** of an organisation. This strategy indicates how the information systems strategies that rely on technology will be **implemented**.

4.2 Establishing organisational information requirements

The identification of organisational information needs and the IS framework to satisfy them is at the heart of a strategy for IS and IT.

The IS and IT strategies should complement the overall strategy for the organisation. It follows therefore that the IS/IT strategy should be considered whenever the organisation prepares other long-term strategies such as marketing or production.

4.3 Earl's three leg analysis

The writer Earl devised a method for the development of IS strategies. His method identified three legs of IS strategy development.

*   Business led (top down emphasis, focuses on **business plans and goals**)
*   Infrastructure led (bottom up emphasis, focuses on **current systems**)
*   Mixed (inside out emphasis, focuses on **IT/IS opportunities**)

A diagrammatic representation of the three legs follows.

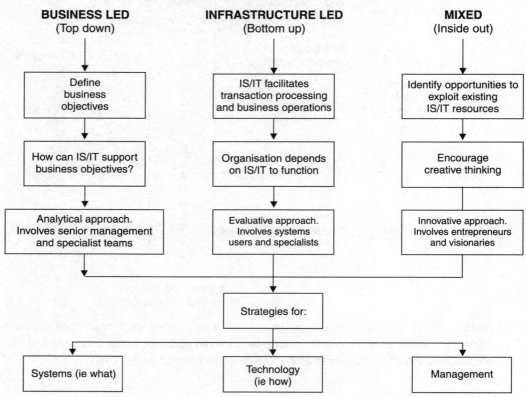

4.4 Critical success factors

The use of **critical success factors (CSFs)** can help to determine the information strategy of an organisation. CSFs are operational goals. If operational goals are achieved the organisation should be successful.

KEY TERM

A CRITICAL SUCCESS FACTOR is an element of organisational activity which is central to its future success. CSFs may change over time and may include items such as product quality, employee attitudes, manufacturing flexibility and brand awareness. *(CIMA Official Terminology)*

The CSF approach is sometimes referred to as the **strategic analysis** approach. The philosophy behind this approach is that managers should focus on a small number of objectives, and information systems should be focused on providing information to enable managers to monitor these objectives.

Example: CSFs

One of the **objectives** of an organisation might be to maintain a high level of service direct from inventory without holding uneconomic inventory levels. This is first quantified in the form of a **goal**, which might be to ensure that 95% of orders for goods can be satisfied directly from inventory, while minimising total holding costs and inventory levels.

CSFs might then be identified as the following.

- **Supplier performance** in terms of quality and lead times
- Reliability of inventory **records**
- **Forecasting** of demand variations

4.5 Parsons' six information systems strategies

The writer Parsons identified six possible generic Information IS strategies. These are outlined in the following table.

Generic strategy for IS	Comment
Centrally planned	The logic of this approach is that those planning IS developments should have an understanding of the overall strategic direction. Business and IS strategy are viewed as being closely linked.
Leading edge	There is a belief that innovative technology use can create competitive advantage, and therefore that risky investment in unproven technologies may generate large returns. The organisation must have the motivation and ability to commit large amounts of money and other resources. Users must be enthusiastic and willing to support new initiatives.
Free market	This strategy is based on the belief that the market makes the best decisions. The IS function is a competitive business unit, which must be prepared to achieve a return on its resources. The department may have to compete with outside providers.
Monopoly	The direct opposite to the free market strategy. This strategy is based upon the belief that information is an organisational asset that should be controlled by a single service provider.
Scarce resource	This strategy is based on the premise that information systems use limited resources, and therefore all IS development requires a clear justification. Budgetary controls are in place and should be adhered to. New projects should be subject to Cost Benefit Analysis (CBA).
Necessary evil	IS/IT is seen as a necessary evil of modern business. IS/IT is allocated enough resource only to meet basic needs. This strategy is usually adopted in organisations that believe that information is not important to the business.

4.6 Strategic grid and applications portfolio

McFarlan and McKenney provide a **strategic grid** to examine the strategic role of IT in an organisation. It classifies organisations into four types based on the current and future strategic importance of IT systems.

The strategic grid has been developed and adapted (by Peppard) into what is commonly known as the **applications portfolio**.

*Strategic importance of **current** information systems*

		Low	High
*Strategic importance of **planned** information systems*	High	Turnaround	Strategic
	Low	Support	Factory

(a)   Organisations in the **strategic** quadrant currently depend on IS/IT for competitive advantage, and expect to continue to do so.

(b)   Organisations in the **turnaround** quadrant do not currently view IS/IT as having strategic importance, but expect IS/IT will be strategically important in the future.

(c)   Organisations in the **support** quadrant see no strategic value in IS/IT.

(d)   Organisations in the **factory** quadrant see IS/IT as strategically significant at the moment, but predict this will not be the case in the future.

The **risk profile** connected to the use of IS/IT within the firm also changes as an organisation moves from the right hand quadrants to the left hand quadrants. Systems in support and key operational systems require maintenance either to fix when broken or to ensure systems do not break down.

When an organisation has systems or applications in development as they have potential to provide **strategic advantage,** the risk profile is greater. This then has implications for the management of risk and the need for an **IS/IT strategy,** including control over **systems development expenditure.**

Section summary

There are a range of methodologies and frameworks for establishing the information requirements of an organisation including **Critical Success Factors (CSFs)** and **Earl's three leg analysis**.

5 Types of information system

Introduction

In this section we consider the different types of information system available to organisations, including Executive Support Systems, Management Information Systems and Decision Support Systems.

5.1 Input, processes and output

In this section we shall examine different types of information systems. You need to remember that the three component parts of a system are:

(a)   **Input** – the systems are only as good as the data that is fed into them. Remember – Rubbish In, Rubbish Out. The **data capture process**, the means by which source data enters the system, needs to be appropriate.

(b)   **Processes** – we shall examine what different systems do in the rest of this section

(c)   **Output** – we shall discuss how system output, what systems produce, is assessed in the next section

5.2 Systems requirements

A modern organisation requires a **wide range of systems** to hold, process and analyse information. We will now examine the various information systems used to serve organisational information requirements.

System level	System purpose
Strategic	To help senior managers with long-term planning. Their main function is to ensure changes in the external environment are matched by the organisation's capabilities.
Management	To help middle managers monitor and control. These systems check if things are working well or not. Some management level systems support non-routine decision making such as 'what if?' analyses.
Knowledge	To help knowledge and data workers design products, distribute information and perform administrative tasks. These systems help the organisation integrate new and existing knowledge into the business and to reduce the reliance on paper documents.

System level	System purpose
Operational	To help operational managers track the organisation's day-to-day operational activities. These systems enable routine queries to be answered, and transactions to be processed and tracked.

The major **types of information system** are discussed below.

5.3 Executive Support Systems (ESS)

KEY TERMS

An EXECUTIVE SUPPORT SYSTEM (ESS) or EXECUTIVE INFORMATION SYSTEM (EIS) pools data from internal and external sources and makes information available to senior managers in an easy-to-use form. An ESS helps senior managers make strategic, unstructured decisions.

An ESS should provide senior managers with easy access to key **internal and external** information. The system summarises and tracks strategically critical information, possibly drawn from internal MIS and DSS, but also including data from external sources eg competitors, legislation, external databases such as Reuters.

An ESS is likely to have the following **features**.

- Flexibility
- Quick response time
- Sophisticated data analysis and modelling tools

5.4 Strategic Enterprise Management Systems (SEMS)

KEY TERM

STRATEGIC ENTERPRISE MANAGEMENT SYSTEMS (SEMS) OR STRATEGIC INFORMATION SYSTEMS help organisations make high-level strategic decisions.

SEMS assist organisations in **setting strategic goals**, **measuring performance** in the light of those goals, and **measuring** and **managing intellectual capital**. They can also be a great help in **activity-based management**, which you will have covered in your earlier studies.

5.5 Enterprise Resource Planning Systems (ERPS)

KEY TERM

The ENTERPRISE RESOURCE PLANNING SYSTEM (ERPS) is a software system designed to support and automate the business processes of medium and large enterprises. ERPS are accounting oriented information systems which aid in identifying and planning the enterprise wide resources needed to resource, make, account for and deliver customer orders. ERPS tend to incorporate a number of software developments such as the use of relational databases, object-oriented programming and open system portability.   (*CIMA Official Terminology*)

ERPS handle many aspects of operations including manufacturing, distribution, inventory, invoicing and accounting. They also cover **support functions** such as **human resource management** and **marketing**. **Supply chain management** software can provide links with **suppliers** and customer relationship management with **customers**.

ERPS thus operate **over the whole organisation** and **across functions**. All departments that are involved in operations or production are **integrated** into one system. Some ERPS software is custom-built, and often now ERPS software is written for organisations in particular industries. ERPS can be configured for organisations' needs and software adapted for circumstances. The data is made available in data warehouses, which can be used to produce customised reports containing data that is consistent across applications. They can **support performance measures** such as **balanced scorecard** and **strategic planning**.

ERPS should result in **lower costs** and lower **investment required** in assets. ERPS should increase **flexibility** and **efficiency of production**. Their disadvantages include cost, implementation time, and lack of scope for adaption to the demands of specific businesses. Also a **problem** with one function can affect all the other functions. ERPS linked in with supply chains can similarly be vulnerable to problems with any links in the chain, and switching costs may be high. The blurring of boundaries can also cause accountability problems.

5.6 Management Information Systems (MIS)

KEY TERM

MANAGEMENT INFORMATION SYSTEMS (MIS) convert data from mainly internal sources into information (eg summary reports, exception reports). This information enables managers to make timely and effective decisions for planning, directing and controlling the activities for which they are responsible.

An MIS provides regular reports and (usually) on-line access to the organisation's current and historical performance.

MIS usually transform data from underlying transaction processing systems into summarised files that are used as the basis for standard management reports.

MIS have the following characteristics:

- Support **structured** decisions at operational and management control levels
- Designed to report on **existing** operations
- Have **little analytical capability**
- Relatively **inflexible**
- Have an **internal** focus
- Not suitable for **strategic planning** and **decision-making**

Exam alert

You may see the term **Management Information System** used as an umbrella term for **all information systems** within an organisation.

5.7 Decision Support Systems (DSS)

KEY TERM

DECISION SUPPORT SYSTEMS (DSS) combine data and analytical models or data analysis tools to support decision making.

DSS are used by management to assist in making decisions on issues which are subject to high levels of uncertainty about the problem, the various **responses** which management could undertake or the likely **impact** of those actions.

DSS are intended to provide a wide range of alternative information gathering and analytical tools with a major emphasis upon **flexibility** and **user-friendliness**.

DSS have more analytical power than other systems enabling them to analyse and condense large volumes of data into a form that aids managers make decisions. The objective is to allow the manager to consider a number of **alternatives** and evaluate them under a variety of potential conditions.

5.8 Expert systems

KEY TERM

An **EXPERT SYSTEM** is a computer program that captures human expertise in a limited domain of knowledge.

Expert system software uses a knowledge base that consists of facts, concepts and the relationships between them on a particular domain of knowledge, and uses pattern-matching techniques to 'solve' problems.

A simple business example programmed into a credit check may be: 'Don't allow credit to a person who has no credit history and has changed address twice or more within the last three years'.

Many financial institutions now use expert systems to process straightforward **loan applications**. The user enters certain key facts into the system such as the loan applicant's name and most recent addresses, their income and monthly outgoings, and details of other loans. The system will then:

(a)   **Check the facts** given against its database to see whether the applicant has a good previous credit record.

(b)   **Perform calculations** to see whether the applicant can afford to repay the loan.

(c)   **Make a judgement** as to what extent the loan applicant fits the lender's profile of a good risk (based on the lender's previous experience).

(d)   **Suggest a decision** based on the results of this processing.

      This is why it is now often possible to get a loan or arrange insurance **over the telephone**, whereas in the past it would have been necessary to go and speak to a bank manager or send details to an actuary and then wait for him or her to come to a decision.

An organisation can use an expert system when a number of conditions are met.

- The problem is **well defined**.
- The expert can define **rules** by which the problem can be solved.
- The investment in an expert system is **cost-justified**.

The knowledge base of an expert system must be kept up-to-date.

Expert systems are not suited to high-level unstructured problems as these require information from a wide range of sources rather than simply deciding between a few known alternatives.

Exam skills

An exam question could ask you to explain how an expert system could be used as a control aid. Give some thought to this for different sorts of organisation, for example a local authority, a transport company, a manufacturer of fast-moving consumer goods, a firm of accountants and so on.

5.9 Knowledge Work Systems (KWS)

KEY TERMS

KNOWLEDGE WORK SYSTEMS (KWS) are information systems that facilitate the creation and integration of new knowledge into an organisation.

KNOWLEDGE WORKERS are people whose jobs consist of primarily creating new information and knowledge. They are often members of a profession such as doctors, engineers, lawyers and scientists.

KWS are information systems that facilitate the creation and integration of new knowledge into an organisation. They provide knowledge workers with tools such as:

- Analytical tools
- Powerful graphics facilities
- Communication tools
- Access to external databases
- A user-friendly interface

The workstations of knowledge workers are often designed for the specific tasks they perform. For example, a design engineer would require sufficient graphics power to manipulate 3-D Computer Aided Design (CAD) images; a financial analyst would require a powerful desktop computer to access and manipulate a large amount of financial data (an **investment workstation**).

Virtual reality systems are another example of KWS. These systems create computer generated simulations that emulate real-world activities. Interactive software and hardware (eg special headgear) provide simulations so realistic that users experience sensations that would normally only occur in the real world.

CASE STUDY

Virtual reality

Burger King have used virtual reality stores to test new store designs.
Volvo have used virtual reality test drives in vehicle development.

5.10 Office Automation Systems (OAS)

KEY TERM

OFFICE AUTOMATION SYSTEMS (OAS) are computer systems designed to increase the productivity of data and information workers.

OAS support the major activities performed in a typical office such as document management, facilitating communication and managing data. Examples include:

- Word processing, desktop publishing, and digital filing systems
- E-mail, voice mail, videoconferencing, groupware, intranets, schedulers
- Spreadsheets, desktop databases

5.11 Transaction Processing Systems (TPS)

KEY TERM

A TRANSACTION PROCESSING SYSTEM (TPS) performs and records routine transactions.

TPS are used for **routine tasks** in which data items or transactions must be processed so that operations can continue. TPS support most business functions in most types of organisations.

Exam alert

Information systems are likely to be regularly examined on this paper. Questions could include discussions of the features of particular systems, the systems most appropriate for a business type or the investment appraisal process.

Section summary

Organisations require different **types of information system** to provide **different levels** of information in a range of **functional areas**.

Major types of Information Systems include: Executive Support Systems (**ESS**), Strategic Enterprise Management Systems (**SEMS**), Enterprise Resource Planning Systems (**ERPS**), Management Information Systems (**MIS**), Decision Support Systems (**DSS**), Knowledge Work Systems (**KWS**), Office Automation Systems (**OAS**) and Transaction Processing Systems (**TPS**).

6 Evaluating information systems   5/10

Introduction

In this section, we look at the methods of evaluating information systems, such as cost-benefit analysis and balanced scorecard.

6.1 Cost-benefit analysis

Traditional cost-benefit investment appraisal methods such as net present value (NPV), internal rate of return and payback period can be used to evaluate computer systems.

However NPV analysis may have to be used with care. If, for example, systems development is being proposed because of threats to the current situation, investment in systems should be compared not with the current situation but the **projected situation** if the threats are realised. It is also important to **collect all the costs** involved including programming, training, **maintenance** and employee costs.

Cost-benefit analysis is most appropriate when **direct improvements** in productivity and performance are being sought. It should be possible to quantify benefits if efficiency and effectiveness are being pursued.

The main tangible costs will be **capital items, installation costs, development costs** and **changes in operational costs**.

6.2 Problems with cost-benefit analysis

The main problem with using traditional cost-benefit analysis to evaluate systems is that the costs and benefits tend to be derived from the accounting system. However a very important aspect of investment in systems is **improving the quality** of **operational and control information** and this cannot **easily be measured in accounting terms**. For example what cost can be placed on not having information? Other benefits such as improved **responsiveness** and **flexibility** may also be very difficult to measure.

The indirect benefits, **often strategic**, of better information are also very difficult to quantify. Organisations may find it very difficult to assess how much better information about customers has impacted upon customer service, or improved information about competitors yielded a competitive advantage. Internal benefits might include **improving the linkages** between **processes and activities, improved organisational performance** in areas other than those where the new systems are introduced, such as better customer service, and **intangible improvements** such as improved staff morale or better decision making.

Possible methods for dealing with unquantifiable benefits include:

- Carry out the NPV analysis using alternative values for intangibles

- Treat intangibles as options

- Calculate the NPV for the quantifiable cash flows. If it is positive, accept the investment. If it is negative, calculate the value of intangibles to make the net present value zero and assess whether these values appear to be realistic.

There are also less tangible costs such as:

- **Switching costs** – reduced efficiency, staff discontent with change

- **Locking in costs** – being locked into a single supplier and not being able to take advantage of subsequent better offers from other suppliers

- **Opportunity costs** – the investment in IT meaning that other investments cannot be undertaken

These considerations may also be important in F3 *Financial Strategy* if you are asked to undertake the investment appraisal of a major computer system.

6.3 Other methods

Along with financial analysis methods, other methods can be appropriate in different circumstances. These are discussed below.

6.3.1 Balanced scorecard

A balanced scorecard approach covering multiple goals is likely to be most appropriate if systems are meant to change fundamentally the way the organisation is **managed**, by for example removing constraints or increasing flexibility. If improvements are to result in better forecasting or planning, changes in the organisational structure may also be required. You covered this approach in detail in Chapter 7 so refer back to it if necessary.

6.3.2 Strategic analysis

Use of Porter's model to assess the impact of systems on competitive forces should be used if information systems are designed to help the organisation achieve **competitive advantage.**

6.3.3 Business case analysis

Business case analysis is helpful if systems are being used to **generate new business**. It needs to cover financial consequences, marketing and operational issues.

6.3.4 User requirements

Users' views are investigated in terms of their requirements, how much they will use the system and how much they are prepared to pay.

6.4 Technical and operational viability

As well as assessing viability in terms of financial value or benefits to the business, technical and operational issues must also be considered carefully.

Technical issues	Operational issues
Availability of technology	Availability, reliability and clarity of data
Skills necessary to use technology	Strong operational procedures
Changes in risk profile	Level of support and commitment
Compatibility with existing systems	Human resource implications
The systems' number of users and transaction/data volumes	Impacts on external stakeholders

6.5 Earl's grid

Earl devised a grid to identify suitability of systems in terms of:

Business value: based on system user requirements
Technical quality: cost, reliability and required maintenance

The grid provides a means of helping management to determine **priorities** and **resource allocations** and serve the needs of information users by providing good quality information on reliable and user-friendly systems.

Technical quality

		Low	High
		Low	*High*
Business value	*Low*	**DIVEST** This is a costly and unused system	**REASSESS** Why do users not value the system
	High	**RENEW** This will enhance its technical quality	**MAINTAIN AND ENHANCE** Upgrade system to maintain the position

Question 13.2   New information system

Learning outcome E1(b)

NEST is a national furniture retailer operating from 12 large showrooms on retail parks close to the principal motorways. The present management information system was set up in 20X0 and since that time the business has expanded rapidly. A new project for the design and implementation of a new system to meet current and future needs will commence soon. There is some urgency as the present system frequently 'crashes' leaving staff with the problem of explaining delays to dissatisfied customers. Staff turnover among systems personnel is high.

Required

Write a memorandum to the Head of Systems to explain the need for a cost-benefit assessment of the proposed new system.

Exam alert

Question 1 (b) in May 2010 asked students to discuss the strengths and weaknesses of a company's management information system.

Section summary

Although **cost-benefit analysis** should be used to evaluate information systems, the **wider operational and control issues** mean that other methods such as the **balanced scorecard** should also be used.

As well as fulfilling financial criteria, systems must also be **technically and operationally viable.**

7 Information systems provision and staffing

Introduction

In this section, we look at the staffing aspect of the information system, examining the roles of key personnel and other functions such as the steering committee and information centre.

7.1 Information Technology Infrastructure Library (ITIL)

The ITIL is a model for the provision of IT services that ensures the services provided are consistent with business strategy.

Key elements of **support** are:

- **Configuration** – **recording** and **reporting** on the system

- **Incident** – **resuming normal services** and **minimising the impact** of **major adverse events**

- **Change** – following a **standardised framework of actions** when changes are introduced to minimise the potential problems caused by changes

- **Release** – ensuring that **all aspects of change**, technical and non-technical, are considered

- **Problem** – **minimising the impact of incidents** and problems caused by shortcomings in the infrastructure and solving those problems

Key elements of **delivery** are:

- **Service level** – constantly seeking to **improve quality** and **meet business objectives**
- **Availability** – developing an IT structure that delivers **cost-effective and continuous availability**
- **Capacity** – providing **capacity** and **performance requirements** cost-effectively
- **Continuity** – **recovering IT** and **technical service facilities** within **agreed timescales**
- **Financial management** – **providing IT services** cost-effectively

7.2 Directing information systems

Most organisations choose to have an information systems department, or team responsible for the tasks and responsibilities associated with information systems.

The IS/IT director or manager would have responsibility for the following areas.

IS/IT director responsibility	Comment
IS/IT strategy development	The IS/IT strategy must complement the overall strategy of the organisation. The strategy must also be achievable given budgetary constraints. Returns on investments in IS/IT should be monitored.
IS/IT risk management	This is a wide ranging area including legal risks, such as ensuring compliance with relevant data protection legislation, ensuring adequate IS/IT security measures and disaster recovery arrangements.
Steering committee	The IS/IT director should play a key role in a steering committee set up to oversee the role of IS/IT within the organisation. There is more on steering committees later in this chapter.
IS/IT infrastructure	Standards should be set for the purchase and use of hardware and software within the organisation.
Ensuring employees have the IS/IT support and tools they require	Efficient links are required between IS/IT staff and the rest of the organisation. Technical assistance should be easily obtainable.

7.3 IS/IT steering committee

Organisations may set up a **steering committee** to oversee all information systems development. A steering committee might also be set up for a 'one-off' computer-related project.

7.4 Database administrator

A key information systems role is that of database administrator. A database administrator is responsible for all data and information held within an organisation.

7.5 Operations control

Operations control is concerned with ensuring IS/IT systems are working and available to users. Key tasks include:

- Maintaining the IS/IT infrastructure
- Maintaining and testing systems
- User documentation
- Monitoring network usage and managing network resources
- Keeping employees informed, eg advance warning of service interruptions
- Employee training
- Security measures eg ensuring anti-virus software updates are loaded
- Fault fixing

7.6 Information centre staff

KEY TERM

An INFORMATION CENTRE (IC) is a small unit of staff with a good technical awareness of computer systems, whose task is to provide a support function to computer users within the organisation.

Information centres, sometimes referred to as **support centres**, are particularly useful in organisations which use distributed systems and so are likely to have hardware, data and software scattered throughout the organisation.

7.6.1 Help

An IC usually offers a **Help Desk** to solve IT problems. Help may be via the telephone, e-mail, through a searchable knowledge base or in person.

7.6.2 Problem solving

The IC will **maintain a record of problems** and identify those that occur most often. If the problem is that users do not know how to use the system, training is provided.

If the problem is with the system itself, a solution is found, either by modifying the system or by **investment in new hardware or software**.

7.6.3 Improvements

The IC may also be required to consider the **viability of suggestions** for improving the system, and to bring these improvements into effect. It may have to find advice on **hardware** and **software purchase**, and **application development**.

7.6.4 Standards

The IC is also likely to be responsible for setting, and encouraging users to conform to, common **standards**.

(a) **Hardware standards** ensure that all of the equipment used in the organisation is compatible and can be put into use in different departments as needed.

(b) **Software standards** ensure that information generated by one department can easily be shared with and worked upon by other departments.

(c) **Programming standards** ensure that applications developed by individual end-users (for example complex spreadsheet macros) follow best practice and are easy to modify.

(d) **Data processing standards** ensure that certain conventions such as the format of file names are followed throughout the organisation. This facilitates sharing, storage and retrieval of information.

7.6.5 Security

The IC may help to preserve the security of data in various ways.

(a)   It may develop **utility programs** and **procedures** to ensure that back-ups are made at regular intervals.

(b)   The IC may **help to preserve the company's systems** from attack by computer viruses, for instance by ensuring that the latest versions of anti-virus software are available to all users, by reminding users regularly about the dangers of viruses, and by setting up and maintaining 'firewalls', which deny access to sensitive parts of the company's systems. We look at these issues in more detail in Chapter 14.

7.7 Shared service centre

A **shared service centre** is similar to an information centre in that it provides services needed by different business units. Services provided include **systems design**, **data processing**, **IT security**.

The difference between shared service centres and other information centres is that shared service centres are driven by **customer demand** rather than requirements to **centralise and control**. The customers specify the level of service that is formalised in a **service agreement**, just as it would be if the service was outsourced. The shared service centre aims to provide the quality services the customer units require rather than specifying the service these units must have.

Section summary

The **IS/IT manager** and the **IS/IT director** are responsible for strategy development, risk management and infrastructure.

The IS/IT **steering committee** makes decisions relating to the future use and development of IS/IT.

The **database administrator** is responsible for all data and information held within an organisation.

An **Information Centre (IC)** provides support for computer users within the organisation.

8   Organising and assessing the IT department

Introduction

In this short section, we consider how the IT department in an organisation could be organised – either centralised or decentralised. Organisations must consider what will work best in their specific circumstances.

KEY TERMS

A CENTRALISED IS/IT department involves all IS/IT staff and functions being based at a single central location, such as head office.

A DECENTRALISED IS/IT department involves IS/IT staff and functions being spread out throughout the organisation.

There is no single 'best' structure for an IS/IT department – an organisation should consider its IS/IT requirements and the merits of each structure.

8.1 Centralisation of IS/IT department

8.1.1 Advantages of a centralised IS/IT department

(a)   Assuming centralised processing is used, there is only one set of files. Everyone uses the **same data and information**.

(b)   It gives **better security/control** over data and files. It is easier to enforce standards.

(c)   Head office is in a **better position** to know what is going on.

(d)   There may be **economies of scale** available in purchasing computer equipment and supplies.

(e)   Computer staff are in a **single location**, and **more expert staff** are likely to be employed. Career paths may be more clearly defined.

8.1.2 Disadvantages of a centralised IS/IT department

(a)   Local offices might have to **wait** for IS/IT services and assistance.

(b)   **Reliance on head office**. Local offices are less self-sufficient.

(c)   A **system fault** at head office will impact across the organisation.

8.2 Decentralisation of IS/IT department

8.2.1 Advantages of a decentralised IS/IT department

(a)   IS/IT staff will be more **aware** of local business requirements.
(b)   Each office is more **self-sufficient**.
(c)   Offices are likely to have **quicker access** to IS/IT support/advice.
(d)   A decentralised structure is more likely to **facilitate accurate IS/IT cost/overhead allocations**.

8.2.2 Disadvantages of a decentralised IS/IT department

(a)   **Control** may be more **difficult** – different and uncoordinated information systems may be introduced.

(b)   Self-sufficiency may encourage a **lack of co-ordination** between departments.

(c)   **Increased risk of data duplication**, with different offices holding the same data on their own separate files.

8.3 Evaluation of the IT function

Methods of evaluation could include the following:

- User assessment of business focus from IT applications
- Degree of utilisation of support services by users
- Post evaluation review of implementation (degree of success)
- Success of the user groups – level of participation
- Improvement in level of user computer literacy
- Improvement in awareness of business issues of IT staff

Section summary

A **centralised IS/IT department** has the advantages of the **same information** being used, **better security and control**, and possibly **greater expertise**.

A **decentralised IS/IT department** has the advantages of **greater knowledge** of **local requirements** and **quicker responsiveness**.

9 Outsourcing

Introduction

In the final section of this chapter we look at the process of outsourcing an organisation's functions and the potential benefits and drawbacks of taking this course of action.

KEY TERM

OUTSOURCING is the use of external suppliers as a source of finished products, components or services. This is also known as contract manufacturing or subcontracting.   (*CIMA Official Terminology*)

9.1 Types of outsourcing

There are four **broad classifications** of outsourcing, as described in the following table.

Classification	Comment
Ad-hoc	The organisation has a short-term requirement for increased IS/IT skills. An example would be employing programmers on a short-term contract to help with the programming of bespoke software.
Project management	The development and installation of a particular IS/IT project is outsourced. For example, a new accounting system. (This approach is sometimes referred to as **systems integration.**)
Partial	Some IT/IS services are outsourced. Examples include hardware maintenance, network management or ongoing website management.
Total	An external supplier provides the vast majority of an organisation's IT/IS services; eg a third party owns or is responsible for IT equipment, software and staff.

9.2 Levels of service provision

The degree to which the provision and management of IS/IT services are transferred to the third party varies according to the situation and the skills of both organisations.

(a) **Time-share**

The vendor charges for access to an external processing system on a time-used basis. Software ownership may be with either the vendor or the client organisation.

(b) **Service bureaux**

Service bureaux usually focus on a specific function. Traditionally bureaux would provide the same type of service to many organisations eg payroll processing. As organisations have developed their own IT infrastructure, the use of bureaux has decreased.

(c) **Facilities management (FM)**

In the context of IS/IT, facilities management involves an outside agency managing the organisation's IS/IT facilities. All equipment usually remains with the client, but the responsibility for providing and managing the specified services rests with the FM company. FM companies operating in the UK include Accenture and Cap Gemini.

The following table shows the main features of each of the outsourcing arrangements described above.

	Outsourcing arrangement		
Feature	Timeshare	Service bureaux	Facilities Management (FM)
Management responsibility	Mostly retained	Some retained	Very little retained
Focus	Operational	A function	Strategic
Timescale	Short-term	Medium-term	Long-term
Justification	Cost savings	More efficient	Access to expertise; higher quality service provision. Enables management to concentrate on the areas where they do possess expertise.

9.3 Managing outsourcing arrangements

Managing outsourcing arrangements involves deciding what will be outsourced, choosing and negotiating with suppliers and managing the supplier relationship.

When considering whether to outsource a particular service the following questions are relevant.

(a)   Is the system of **strategic importance**? Strategic IS are generally not suited to outsourcing as they require a high degree of specific business knowledge that a third party IT specialist cannot be expected to possess.

(b)   Can the system be **relatively isolated**? Functions that have only limited interfaces are most easily outsourced eg payroll.

(c)   Do we know **enough about the system** to manage the outsourced service agreement? If an organisation knows very little about a technology it may be difficult to know what constitutes good service and value for money. It may be necessary to recruit additional expertise to manage the relationship with the other party.

(d)   Are our **requirements likely to change**? Organisations should avoid tying themselves into a long-term outsourcing agreement if requirements are likely to change.

(e)   What will be the **full costs of outsourcing**? The organisation needs to consider not just the fees the provider will charge, but also the costs of dealing with the provider, monitoring its activities, insuring against loss.

9.4 The tendering process

The organisation needs to make certain specifications about what it requires when inviting tenders for outsourcing. The most important decision is the **nature of the relationship** between the **organisation** and the **service provider**. This will depend on the **service** that has been **outsourced**.

(a)   If full facilities management is involved, and almost all management responsibility for IT/IS lies with the entity providing the service, then a close relationship between the parties is necessary (a '**partnership**'). The relationship is likely to be founded on broadly drawn, incentive-based contracts with the expectation that the customer and supplier will do business over many years.

(b)   On the other hand, if a **relatively simple function** such as payroll were outsourced, such a close relationship with the supplier would not be necessary. A 'typical' supplier-customer relationship is all that is required (although issues such as confidentiality need to be considered with payroll data). Contracts here are likely to be very detailed.

Requests for tender need to make clear the **required product delivery**, the **present** and **planned hardware** and **software configuration** and the **history and future expectations** of the organisation. The potential suppliers must understand how the bids will be **evaluated**.

9.4.1 Service level agreement

A key factor when choosing and negotiating with external vendors is the contract offered and subsequently negotiated with the supplier. The contract is sometimes referred to as the **Service Level Contract** (SLC) or **Service Level Agreement** (SLA).

The key elements of the contract are described in the following table.

Contract element	Comment
Timescale	When does the contract expire? Is the timescale suitable for the organisation's needs or should it be renegotiated?
Service level	The contract should clearly specify **minimum levels of service** to be provided. Penalties should be specified for failure to meet these standards. Relevant factors will vary depending on the nature of the services outsourced but could include: • Response time to requests for assistance/information • System 'uptime' percentage • Deadlines for performing relevant tasks
Exit route	Arrangements for an exit route, addressing how transfer to another supplier, or the move back in-house, would be conducted.
Software ownership	Relevant factors include: Software licensing and security If the arrangement includes the development of new software who owns the copyright?
Dependencies	If related services are outsourced the level of service quality agreed should group these services together.
Employment issues	If the arrangement includes provision for the organisation's IT staff to move to the third party, employer responsibilities must be specified clearly.

9.4.2 Dealing with the supplier

The organisation also needs to decide the roles of the staff who will deal with the outsourcing supplier. **The managers** and **staff involved** will be **responsible** for **managing service level** and **delivery** and business development. They will need to have the **technical capability** to assess the performance of the provider, but will also need to have the necessary **contract management skills**.

The **degree of monitoring** required will also need to be considered carefully. Heavy monitoring could mean internal costs are **high**, but on the other hand risk will be low as problems should be identified early. Loose monitoring focused on end results will have lower costs, but problems will not be picked up until the end of the process or, worst of all, picked up by customers.

9.4.3 Changeover arrangements

Over time the services outsourced may be re-tendered and the supplier changed. The changeover may present certain problems that need to be anticipated, with the initial contract including the necessary provisions. Possible problems include:

(a)   **Loss of copyright** on **own software** run by vendor. Explicit contract clauses should cover the **ownership of the software**, its **security** and its **confidentiality**.

(b)   **Loss of copyright** on **software** vendor develops as part of outsourcing. Again the contract needs to be clear, although here considerations of cost, product value and exclusivity will influence who holds the copyright.

(c)   **Dependence on supplier** for IT for which supplier has **exclusive rights**. To avoid this the organisation should only use what they own, have right to, is publicly available or easily replaced.

(d)   **Partial transfer** to another supplier. **Separate contracts** for separate services should be drawn up to minimise problems when the original supplier is still supplying some services, but others have been transferred to a new supplier.

| Question 13.3 | Outsourcing |

Learning outcome E1(c)

Do any organisations with which you are familiar use outsourcing? What is the view of outsourcing in the organisation?

9.5 Advantages of outsourcing arrangements

The **advantages** of outsourcing are as follows.

(a)   Outsourcing can remove uncertainty about **cost**, as there is often a long-term contract where services are specified in advance for a **fixed price**. If computing services are inefficient, the costs will be borne by the FM company. This is also an incentive to the third party to provide a high quality service.

(b)   Long-term contracts (maybe up to ten years) encourage **planning** for the future.

(c)   Outsourcing can bring the benefits of **economies of scale**. For example, an FM company may conduct research into new technologies that benefits a number of their clients.

(d)   A specialist organisation is able to retain **skills and knowledge**. Many organisations would not have a sufficiently well-developed IT department to offer IT staff opportunities for career development. Talented staff would leave to pursue their careers elsewhere.

(e)   New skills and knowledge become available. A specialist company can **share** staff with **specific expertise** between several clients. This allows the outsourcing company to take advantage of new developments without the need to recruit new people or re-train existing staff, and without the cost.

(f)   **Flexibility** (contract permitting). Resources may be able to be scaled up or down depending upon demand. For instance, during a major changeover from one system to another the number of IT staff needed may be twice as large as it will be once the new system is working satisfactorily.

(g)   An outsourcing organisation is more able to arrange its work on a **project** basis, whereby some staff will expect to be moved periodically from one project to the next.

9.6 Disadvantages of outsourcing arrangements

Some possible **drawbacks** are outlined below.

(a)   It is arguable that information and its provision is an **inherent part of the business** and of management. Unlike office cleaning, or catering, an organisation's IT services may be too important to be contracted out because of the potential financial implications and risks to reputation of loss of service. Information is at the heart of management.

(b)   A company may have highly **confidential information** and to let outsiders handle it could be seen as **risky** in commercial and/or legal terms.

(c)   If a third party is handling IS/IT services there is no onus upon internal management to keep up with new developments or to suggest new ideas. Consequently, opportunities to gain **competitive advantage** may be missed. Any new technology or application devised by the third party is likely to be available to competitors.

(d)   An organisation may find itself **locked in** to an unsatisfactory contract. The decision may be very difficult to reverse. If the service provider supplies unsatisfactory levels of service, or cannot respond quickly enough to changing circumstances, the effort and expense the organisation would incur to rebuild its own computing function or to move to another provider could be substantial.

(e)   The use of an outside organisation does **not encourage awareness** of the potential **costs** and benefits of IS/IT within the organisation. If managers cannot manage in-house IS/IT resources effectively, then it could be argued that they will not be able to manage an arrangement to outsource effectively either.

9.7 Insourcing

Outsourcing involves purchasing information technology expertise from outside the organisation. Several factors have led some to believe this is not the best solution in today's environment.

Insourcing involves recruiting IS/IT staff internally, from other areas of the business, and teaching these business-savvy employees about technology. The logic behind the idea is that it is easier (and cheaper) to **teach technical skills to business people** than to teach business skills to technical people.

Supporters of insourcing believe it has the potential to:

- Create a better quality workforce that combines both technical and business skills
- Reduce costs
- Improve relationships and communication between IT staff and other departments
- Increase staff retention – through providing an additional career path

Possible disadvantages include:

- Risk that non-technical employees will not pick up the IS/IT skills required
- Finding staff willing to make the change
- Replacing staff who do make the switch

Section summary

Outsourcing is the contracting out of operations or services. There are various outsourcing options available, with different levels of control maintained 'in-house'. Outsourcing has **advantages** (eg use of highly skilled people) and **disadvantages** (eg lack of control).

Chapter Roundup

✓ Organisations **require information** for recording transactions, measuring performance, making decisions, planning and controlling.

✓ There area three types of information: **strategic; tactical** and **operational**.

✓ **Strategic information** is used to **plan** the **objectives** of the organisation and to **assess** whether the objectives are being met in practice.

✓ **Tactical information** is used to decide **how the resources of the organisation should be employed**, and to **monitor** how they are being and have been employed.

✓ **Operational information** is used to ensure that **specific operational tasks** are planned and carried out as intended.

✓ 'Good' information is information that adds to the **understanding** of a situation.

✓ The **cost and value** of information are often not easy to quantify – but attempts should be made to do so.

✓ A **strategy for information management, systems and technology** is justified on the grounds that IS/IT is costly and vital for many organisations.

✓ There are a range of methodologies and frameworks for establishing the information requirements of an organisation including **Critical Success Factors (CSFs)** and **Earl's three leg analysis**.

✓ Organisations require different **types of information system** to provide **different levels** of information in a range of **functional areas**.

✓ Major types of Information Systems include: Executive Support Systems (**ESS**), Strategic Enterprise Management Systems (**SEMS**), Enterprise Resource Planning Systems (**ERPS**), Management Information Systems (**MIS**), Decision Support Systems (**DSS**), Knowledge Work Systems (**KWS**), Office Automation Systems (**OAS**) and Transaction Processing Systems (**TPS**).

✓ Although **cost-benefit analysis** should be used to evaluate information systems, the **wider operational** and **control issues** mean that other methods such as the **balanced scorecard** should also be used.

✓ As well as fulfilling financial criteria, systems must also be **technically and operationally viable**.

✓ The **IS/IT manager** and the **IS/IT director** are responsible for strategy development, risk management and infrastructure.

✓ The **IS/IT steering committee** makes decisions relating to the future use and development of IS/IT.

✓ The **database administrator** is responsible for all data and information held within an organisation.

✓ An **Information Centre (IC)** provides support for computer users within the organisation.

✓ A **centralised IS/IT department** has the advantages of the **same information** being used, **better security and control**, and possibly **greater expertise**.

✓ A **decentralised IS/IT department** has the advantages of **greater knowledge** of **local requirements** and **quicker responsiveness**.

✓ **Outsourcing** is the contracting out of operations or services. There are various outsourcing options available, with different levels of control maintained 'in-house'. Outsourcing has **advantages** (eg use of highly skilled people) and **disadvantages** (eg lack of control).

Quick Quiz

1   List five characteristics each of strategic information, tactical information and operational information.

2   Fill in the blank.

.... is data that has been processed in such a way as to be meaningful to the person who receives it.

3   Fill in the blank.

An .... is an organisational and management solution, based on information technology, to any challenge posed by the environment.

4   Complete the mnemonic A C C U R A T E in respect of the qualities of good information.

5   Give three factors that make information valuable.

6   A system that pools data from internal and external sources and makes information available to senior managers in an easy to use form is called an executive support system.

True   ☐

False   ☐

7   Fill in the blank.

.... are systems that combine data and analytical models or data analysis tools to support semi-structured and unstructured decision-making.

8   Match the following examples of systems to the types of system that they are.

A	Inventory control	1	ESS
B	Electronic calendars	2	MIS
C	Engineering work stations	3	DSS
D	Order tracking	4	KWS
E	Sales region analysis	5	OAS
F	Human resource planning	6	TPS

9   Fill in the blank.

An .... is a small unit of staff with a good technical awareness of computer systems, whose task is to provide a support function to computer users within the organisation.

10   List three advantages of a decentralised IS/IT department.

11   'Information systems that are strategically important should be outsourced to ensure those working with these systems have excellent technical knowledge'.

True   ☐

False   ☐

Answers to Quick Quiz

1

Strategic information	Tactical information	Operational information
Derived from both internal and external sources	Primarily generated internally (but may have a limited external component)	Derived from internal sources
Summarised at a high level	Summarised at a lower level	Detailed, being the processing of raw data
Relevant to the long term	Relevant to the short and medium term	Relevant to the immediate term
Concerned with the whole organisation	Concerned with activities or departments	Task-specific
Often prepared on an 'ad hoc' basis	Prepared routinely and regularly	Prepared very frequently
Both quantitative and qualitative	Based on quantitative measures	Largely quantitative
Uncertain, as the future cannot be predicted accurately		

2   **Information** is data that has been processed in such a way as to be meaningful to the person who receives it.

3   An **information system** is an organisational and management solution, based on information technology, to any challenge posed by the environment.

4   **A**ccurate

Complete

Cost-beneficial

User-targeted

Relevant

Authoritative

Timely

Easy to use

5   • The source of the information
   • The ease of assimilation
   • Accessibility

6   True

7   **Decision Support Systems** are systems that combine data and analytical models or data analysis tools to support semi-structured and unstructured decision-making.

8   A2; B5; C4; D6; E3; F1

9   An **information centre** is a small unit of staff with a good technical awareness of computer systems, whose task is to provide a support function to computer users within the organisation.

10   • Each office can introduce an information system specially tailored for its individual needs.
   • Local offices are more self-sufficient.
   • Offices are likely to have quicker access to IS/IT support/advice.
   • A decentralised structure is more likely to facilitate accurate IS/IT cost/overhead allocations.

11   False. Strategic IS are generally not suited to outsourcing as they require a high degree of specific business knowledge that a third party IT/IS specialist cannot be expected to possess.

Answers to Questions

13.1 Assessing the value of information

(a) What information is provided?

(b) What is it used for?

(c) Who uses it?

(d) How often is it used?

(e) Does the frequency with which it is used coincide with the frequency of provision?

(f) What is achieved by using it?

(g) What other relevant information is available which could be used instead?

An assessment of the value of information can be derived in this way, and the cost of obtaining it should then be compared against this value. On the basis of this comparison, it can be decided whether certain items of information are worth having. It should be remembered that there may also be intangible benefits which may be harder to quantify.

13.2 New information system

MEMORANDUM

To: Head of systems

From: Accountant

Date: 24 July 20X4

Re: Cost-benefit assessment of the proposed new system

The primary purpose of the cost-benefit assessment is to ensure that the **benefits are greater** than the **costs**.

It is important to include both **capital and revenue costs** and to cover all of the setting up, running and maintenance expenses. Costs should include the following.

(a) Hardware, software, computer room modifications, cabling and ancillary equipment (for example modems).

(b) Set-up costs for analysis, design, specification, programming etc, file conversion; to training implementation and testing, staff recruitment.

(c) Ongoing costs: wages of systems staff, telecoms costs, power, consumables, further training, fallback facilities.

(d) Investment in training will be particularly important as part of a strategy to reduce staff turnover.

Benefits are much harder to express quantitatively but there are some that will be of particular value to NEST.

(a) **Improved customer satisfaction**: a higher level of reliability of the system will increase customer confidence and goodwill and reduce customer complaints.

(b) **Higher staff morale** resulting from improved self-esteem and teamworking with the new reliable system.

(c) The **saving of valuable time** spent resolving the consequences of current 'crashes'. This in turn may bring the further benefits of higher sales and improved inventory control.

(d) **Improved decision making** based on high quality information.

Capital investment appraisal techniques can help to evaluate the project, using payback period, accounting rate of return or discounted cash flow methods.

Whilst it is impossible to eliminate the risks associated with the project entirely, careful assessment of the costs and benefits will give the company confidence to proceed with the required new system.

13.3 Outsourcing

One view of outsourcing is given below.

The PA Consulting Group's annual survey of outsourcing found that 'on average the top five strategic outsourcers out-performed the FTSE by more than 100 per cent over three years; the bottom five under-performed by more than 66%'.

However the survey revealed that of those organisations who have opted to outsource IT functions, only five per cent are truly happy with the results. A spokesman for the consultants said that this is because most people fail to adopt a proper strategic approach, taking a view that is neither long-term nor broad enough, and taking outsourcing decisions that are piecemeal and unsatisfactory.

This lack of prescience is compounded by a failure to take a sufficiently rigorous approach to selection, specification, contract drafting and contract management.

The survey found that a constant complaint among many of those interviewed is the lack of ability of outsourcing organisations to work together.

25 per cent of those asked would bring the functions they had outsourced back in-house if it were possible.

Now try these questions from the Exam Question Bank

Number	Level	Marks	Time
Q19	Examination	25	45 mins
Q20	Examination	25	45 mins
Q21	Examination	25	45 mins

INFORMATION OPERATIONS

In this chapter, we shall be looking at the risks that organisations face and the main controls that can be used to deal with these risks. Key risks relate to design, implementation, operation and maintenance of systems.

The first section of this chapter examines the risks to information operations. The sections following on examine in detail the controls that can be implemented to mitigate these risks. We firstly cover the general framework within which operational controls apply and then consider the personnel who implement those controls. In sections 4 to 8 we look at controls that are designed to counter various threats to operations.

The last section of the chapter deals with systems development. We concentrate on the controls that should prevent the system being poorly designed and inadequately tested, and the staff who operate it being inadequately briefed. Many stages of the systematic approach to development that we discuss in this chapter can also be applied to any system, not just IT.

Although this chapter covers the main general threats that the use of information technology systems can create, new specific threats are being publicised all the time so it is certainly worth reading IT supplements in newspapers or specialist magazines to gain further understanding of how best to tackle threats to systems.

topic list	learning outcomes	syllabus references	ability required
1 Operational risks of information systems	E1(e)	E1(viii)	evaluation
2 Control framework	E1(d), (e)	E1(vii), (xi)	evaluation
3 Personnel controls	E1(d), (e)	E1(vii), (xi)	evaluation
4 Contingency controls and disaster planning	E1(d), (e)	E1(vi), (xi)	evaluation
5 Access controls	E1(d), (e)	E1(vii), (xi)	evaluation
6 Integrity and backup controls	E1(d), (e)	E1(vi), (vii), (xi)	evaluation
7 Theft and fraud prevention	E1(d), (e)	E1(vii), (xi)	evaluation
8 Internet and e-mail	E1(d), (e)	E1(ix), (xi)	evaluation
9 Systems development controls	E1(e)	E1(xii)	evaluation

1   Operational risks of information systems

Introduction

In this section, we consider the various risks to information operations. These range from physical factors, data integrity, fraud, Internet usage and systems development.

1.1 Risks of physical damage

1.1.1 Natural threats

Fire is the **most serious hazard** to computer systems. Destruction of data can be even more costly than the destruction of hardware.

Water is a serious hazard. In some areas flooding is a natural risk, for example in parts of central London and many other towns and cities near rivers or coasts. Basements are therefore generally not regarded as appropriate sites for large computer installations.

Wind, rain and storms can all cause substantial **damage to buildings**. In certain areas the risks are greater, for example the risk of typhoons in parts of the Far East. Many organisations make heavy use of prefabricated and portable offices, which are particularly vulnerable. Cutbacks in maintenance expenditure may lead to leaking roofs or dripping pipes.

Lightning and electrical storms can play havoc with power supplies, causing power failures coupled with power surges as services are restored. Minute adjustments in power supplies may be enough to affect computer processing operations (characterised by lights which dim as the country's population turns on electric kettles following a popular television programme).

1.1.2 Human threats

Organisations may also be exposed to physical threats through the actions of humans. **Political terrorism** is the main risk, but there are also threats from individuals with **grudges.** Staff are a physical threat to computer installations, whether by spilling a cup of coffee over a desk covered with papers, or tripping and falling doing some damage to themselves and to an item of office equipment.

1.2 Risks to data and systems integrity

The **risks** include:

- Human error

    - Entering incorrect transactions
    - Failing to correct errors
    - Processing the wrong files
    - Failing to follow prescribed security procedures

- Technical error such as malfunctioning hardware or software and supporting equipment such as communication equipment, normal and emergency power supplies and air conditioning units

- Commercial espionage

- Malicious damage

- Industrial action

These risks may be particularly significant because of the nature of computer operations. The **processing** capabilities of a computer are **extensive**, and enormous quantities of data are processed without human intervention, and so without humans knowing what is going on. Information on a computer file **can be**

changed without leaving any physical trace of the change. In comparison, a change to a manual file would often involve leaving a trace – eg crossing out data on a card file to insert new data etc.

CASE STUDY

The IT Governance Institute in the USA has published guidance on IT controls (*IT Control Objectives for Sarbanes-Oxley*) that aims to help businesses comply with the Sarbanes-Oxley legislation. The guidance therefore emphasises the role of information technology in the internal control system operating over disclosure and financial reporting. IT controls need to be changed as financial reporting processes change, and ensure **consistency** between different units.

1.3 Risks of fraud

Computer fraud usually involves the theft of funds by **dishonest use** of a computer system. The type of computer fraud depends on the point in the system at which the fraud is perpetrated.

(a)   **Input fraud**

Data input is falsified; good examples are putting a **non-existent employee** on the salary file or a non-existent supplier to the purchases file.

(b)   **Processing fraud**

A programmer or someone who has broken into this part of the system may **alter a program**. For example, in a large organisation, a 'patch' might be used to change a program so that 10 pence was deducted from every employee's pay cheque and sent to a fictitious account to which the perpetrator had access. A 'patch' is a change to a program which is characterised by its speed and ease of implementation.

(c)   **Output fraud**

Output documents may be **stolen or tampered with** and control totals may be altered. Cheques are the most likely document to be stolen, but other documents may be stolen to hide a fraud.

(d)   **Fraudulent use of the computer system**

Employees may feel that they can use the computer system for their **own purposes** and this may take up valuable processing time. This is probably quite rare, but there was a case of a newspaper publisher's computer system being used by an employee to produce another publication!

1.3.1 Recent developments increasing the risk of fraud

Over the last few years there have been rapid developments in all aspects of computer technology and these have increased the opportunities that are available to commit a fraud. The most important of the recent developments are as follows.

(a)   **Computer literacy**

The proportion of the population which is computer literate is growing all the time. Once people know how to use a computer, the dishonest ones among them may attempt computer fraud.

(b)   **Communications**

The use of telephone links and other public communication systems has increased the ability of people outside the organisation to break into the computer system. These 'hackers' could not have operated when access was only possible on site.

(c)   **Reduction in internal checks and documentation**

The more computers are used, the fewer the tasks left to personnel to carry out. A consequence of this is often a **reduction** in the number of **internal checks** carried out for any transaction. As many data entries occur automatically, documentation is also reduced.

(d) **Real-time processing**

Immediate processing of transactions means **access** and **input** must be well-controlled.

(e) **Technical change**

Improvements in the **quality of software** and the increase in **implementation of good software** has not kept pace with the improvements in hardware. Distributed systems and networked PCs have become very common but this has caused the control over central databases and programs to be relaxed.

1.3.2 Other deliberate actions

Data and/or systems may be threatened by deliberate actions other than fraud, for example **commercial espionage**, **malicious damage** or **industrial action**.

1.4 Internet risks

Establishing organisational links to the Internet brings numerous security dangers.

(a) Corruptions such as **viruses** on a single computer can spread through the network to all of the organisation's computers.

(b) **Disaffected employees** have much greater potential to do **deliberate damage** to valuable corporate data or systems because the network could give them access to parts of the system that they are not really authorised to use.

(c) If the organisation is linked to an external network, persons outside the company (**hackers**) may be able to get into the organisation's internal network, either to steal data or to damage the system.

(d) Employees may **download inaccurate information** or imperfect or **virus-ridden software** from an external network. For example 'beta' (free trial) versions of forthcoming new editions of many major packages are often available on the Internet, but the whole point about a beta version is that it is not fully tested and may contain bugs that could disrupt an entire system.

(e) Information transmitted from one part of an organisation to another may be **intercepted**. Data can be 'encrypted' (scrambled) in an attempt to make it unintelligible to eavesdroppers.

(f) The **communications link itself may break down or distort data**. The worldwide telecommunications infrastructure is improving thanks to the use of new technologies, and there are communications 'protocols' governing the format of data and signals transferred.

1.4.1 Hacking

Hacking involves attempting to gain unauthorised access to a computer system, usually through telecommunications links.

Hackers require only limited programming knowledge to cause large amounts of damage. The fact that billions of bits of information can be transmitted in bulk over the public telephone network has made it **hard to trace** individual hackers, who can therefore make repeated attempts to invade systems. Hackers, in the past, have mainly been concerned to **copy** information, but a recent trend has been their desire to **corrupt it**.

Phone numbers and passwords can be guessed by hackers using **electronic phone directories** or number generators and by software which enables **rapid guessing** using hundreds of permutations per minute.

Default passwords are also available on some electronic bulletin boards and sophisticated hackers could even try to 'tap' messages being transmitted along phone wires (the number actually dialled will not be scrambled).

1.4.2 Viruses

KEY TERM

A VIRUS is a piece of software which infects programs and data and possibly damages them, and which replicates itself.

Viruses need an **opportunity to spread**. The programmers of viruses therefore place viruses in the kind of software which is most likely to be copied. This includes:

- Free software (for example from the Internet)

- Pirated software (cheaper than original versions)

- Games software (wide appeal)

- **E-mail attachments**. E-mail has become the most common means of spreading the most destructive viruses. The virus is often held in an attachment to the e-mail message. Recent viruses have been programmed to send themselves to all addresses in the user's electronic address book.

1.4.3 Denial of service attack

A fairly new threat, relating to Internet websites and related systems is the '**Denial of Service (DoS)**' attack. A denial of service attack is characterised by an attempt by attackers to prevent legitimate users of a service from using that service. Examples include attempts to:

- 'Flood' or bombard a site or network, thereby preventing legitimate network traffic (major sites, such as Amazon.com and Yahoo! have been targeted in this way)

- Disrupt connections between two machines, thereby preventing access to a service

- Prevent a particular individual from accessing a service

1.5 Data protection risks

1.5.1 Data protection legislation

In recent years, there has been a growing fear that the ever-increasing amount of **information** about individuals held by organisations could be misused. In particular, it was felt that an individual could easily be harmed by the existence of computerised data about him or her which was inaccurate or misleading and which could be **transferred to unauthorised third parties** at high speed and little cost. During the 1980s and 1990s individuals were therefore **given more protection** from organisations holding data about them.

1.5.2 Consequences of failure to comply with legislation

Organisations may be subject to sanctions if they breach individuals' rights.

(a) A data subject may seek **compensation** through the courts for damage and any associated distress caused by the **loss**, **destruction** or **unauthorised disclosure** of data about himself or herself or by **inaccurate data** about himself or herself.

(b) A data subject may apply to the courts for **inaccurate data** to be **put right** or even **wiped off** the data user's files altogether.

(c) A data subject may obtain **access** to personal data of which he or she is the subject. (This is known as the 'subject access' provision.) In other words, a data subject can ask to see his or her personal data that the data user is holding.

(d) A data subject can **sue** a data user for any **damage or distress** caused to him by personal data about him that is **incorrect** or **misleading** as to matter of **fact** (rather than opinion).

1.5.3 Compliance with data protection legislation

Measures could include the following.

- **Obtain consent from individuals** to hold any sensitive personal data you need.
- **Supply individuals** with a **copy of any personal data** you hold about them if so requested.
- Consider if you may need to **obtain consent** to **process personal data**.
- Ensure you **do not pass on personal data** to unauthorised parties.

1.6 Systems development risks

If systems development is not controlled properly, the following problems could develop:

- Unauthorised changes to systems
- Development of systems that do not provide required information for management decision-making
- Programs being changed without adequate planning and testing
- Poor systems being allowed to become active
- Development of systems that are not flexible enough to cope with changes in circumstances
- Loss of confidence among managers, staff and customers
- Increased risk of fraud or problems with data protection legislation
- Excessive costs
- Lack of audit trail

We look at systems development in detail in Section 9 of this chapter.

1.7 Risk assessment

As with other risks, a key part of IT risk assessment will be determining the **likelihood and consequences** of risks materialising. The USA's Information Systems Audit and Control Association has published guidance suggesting that a number of factors will indicate that risks are significant:

Technology	Complex, unique, customised, developed in-house
People	Inexperienced, lack of training, limited number of people, high staff turnover
Processes	Decentralised, multi-location ad hoc
Past experience	History of problems including processing errors, system outages, data corruption
Financial reports	Direct significance, used for initiating and recording amounts in the financial reports

1.8 Combating risks and security

KEY TERM

SECURITY, in information management terms, means the protection of data from accidental or deliberate threats which might cause unauthorised modification, disclosure or destruction of data, and the protection of the information system from the degradation or non-availability of services.

Security refers to **technical** issues related to the computer system, psychological and **behavioural** factors in the organisation and its employees, and protection against the unpredictable occurrences of the **natural world**.

Security can be subdivided into a number of aspects.

Prevention	It is in practice impossible to prevent all threats cost-effectively.
Detection	Detection techniques are often combined with prevention techniques: a log can be maintained of unauthorised attempts to gain access to a computer system.
Deterrence	As an example, computer misuse by personnel can be made grounds for disciplinary action.

Recovery	If the threat occurs, its consequences can be contained (for example checkpoint programs).
Correction	These ensure the vulnerability is dealt with (for example, by instituting stricter controls).
Avoidance	This might mean changing the design of the system.

We examine the controls to mitigate the risks to information operations in the remainder of this chapter.

The international security standard, ISO 7799 groups its recommendations under the following headings.

CASE STUDY

(a)   **Business continuity planning**. This means that there should be measures to ensure that if major failures or disasters occur, the business will not be completely unable to function.

(b)   **Systems access control.** This includes protection of information, information systems, networked services, detection of unauthorised activities and security when using the systems.

(c)   **Systems development and maintenance**. This includes security measures and steps to protect data in operational and application systems and also ensuring that IT projects and support are conducted securely.

(d)   **Physical and environmental security.** Measures should be taken to prevent unauthorised access, damage and interference to business premises, assets, information and information facilities and prevention of theft.

(e)   **Compliance** with any relevant legal requirements and also with organisational policies in standards. There is no point in having them if they are not enforced.

(f)   **Personnel security**. This covers issues such as recruitment of trustworthy employees, and also reporting of security-related incidents. Training is particularly important, with the aim that users are aware of information security threats and concerns and are equipped to comply with the organisation's security policy.

(g)   **Security organisation**. It should be clear who has responsibility for the various aspects of information security. Additional considerations will apply if facilities and assets are accessed by third parties or responsibility for information processing has been outsourced.

(h)   **Computer and network management**. This includes ensuring continuity of operations and minimising the risk of systems failures, also protecting the integrity of systems and safeguarding information, particularly when exchanged between organisations. Particularly important is protection from viruses.

(i)   **Asset classification and control**. Information is an asset, just like a machine, building or a vehicle, and security will be improved if information assets have an 'owner', and are classified according to how much protection they need.

(j)   **Security policy**. A written document setting out the organisation's approach to information security should be available to all staff.

Section summary

Risks to data and systems include **physical risks** such as fire and water and **risks** through **human error or fraud**.

Internet links have resulted in additional risks including **hacking** and **viruses**.

Risks arising from **systems development** include the risks that the system will have **inadequate security**, and will **not meet the users' requirements**.

2 Control framework

Introduction

In this section we cover the control framework, looking at two popular frameworks – CobiT and SAC/e-SAC. We also consider an example information security policy statement.

2.1 Developing an approach to control

There are a number of possible frameworks the organisation can follow in developing its information technology. CobiT and SAC/e-SAC are popular frameworks, which are discussed in detail below.

2.2 CobiT framework

CobiT stands for Control Objectives for Information and Related Technologies. The overall aim of CobiT is to ensure that the **objectives of an organisation** are met by providing **appropriate IT systems**. This means ensuring that IT systems provide appropriate returns to the business without too high a risk of systems providing poor or inaccurate data.

The main objective of CobiT is to try to assist management **balance risk and control** investments in an unpredictable IT environment. The aim is to ensure that **sufficient investment** is made in IT; too little would introduce too much risk in terms of lack of information or inaccuracies in processing; too much investment would not be cost-effective.

CobiT follows the idea of top down planning for systems in that:

- CobiT defines **high level control objectives** (similar to Critical Success Factors) for each IT process
- IT processes are linked to **specific detailed control objectives** (similar to Performance Indicators)
- Control objectives are **supported by auditing guidelines** that show how they can be checked

Overall, CobiT attempts to provide appropriate emphasis on IT by providing an IT governance system within the organisation.

CobiT uses the principles of balanced scorecard in four key areas:

(a) **Providing benchmarks for IT control practices** (also called **maturity models**). With a maturity model, an organisation can **compare itself** against other similar companies, and hopefully with companies with better IT systems, as well as making comparison against international standards. Scoring is provided against a range of IT processes. The result of the scoring will indicate areas for improvement of IT systems within an organisation.

(b) **Critical success factors** to get IT processes under control will be stated. The CSFs define the most important things that management must do in the areas of strategy, technology, the organisation and procedures.

(c) **Key performance indicators** will show whether IT processes have achieved their objectives in terms of **supplying reliable information** at the **correct time**, providing appropriate **confidentiality and integrity** of data transfer, **complying** with **legal and internal requirements** and doing all of these **cost-effectively**.

(d) **Provision of detailed performance indicators** will determine how well IT processes are performing and allowing goals to be reached by those systems.

You can find out more about CobiT on the Information Systems Audit and Control Association's (ISACA) website: www.isaca.org/.

2.3 SAC and e-SAC

Systems Auditability and Control (SAC) and its development, **Electronic Systems Assurance and Control (e-SAC)** are alternative frameworks for dealing with information technology risks. These are described as:

- Fraud
- Error
- Business interruption
- Lack of efficiency and effectiveness

The internal control system consists of:

- Control environment
- Manual and automated systems
- Control procedures

and control procedures consist of prevent/detect/correct, discretionary/non-discretionary, voluntary/mandatory, manual/automated, and application/general controls.

SAC/e-SAC provides a framework for **analysing the application and operation of controls**, and whether the controls can be overridden.

2.4 Developing a security policy

Information security is an important responsibility for all levels of management. A security policy is needed, not simply a collection of measures adopted *ad hoc*. Developing a security policy would involve normal risk management procedures including **identification**, **quantification** and **prioritisation** of risks, **costing, selection** and **implementation** of **counter measures** and drawing up of **contingency plans**.

CASE STUDY

The International Federation of Accountants in its Information Technology Guideline 1 *Managing security of information* included an example Information Security Policy statement.

INFORMATION SECURITY POLICY STATEMENT EXAMPLE

- The purpose of the Information Security Policy is to protect the organisation's information assets from all types of threats, whether internal or external, deliberate, or accidental. Information systems security is critical to the organisation's survival.

- The Chief Executive Officer supports and has approved the Information Security Policy.

- It is the Policy of the organisation to ensure that:

    - Assets will be classified as to the level of protection required

    - Information will be protected against unauthorised access

    - Confidentiality of information will be assured

    - Integrity of information will be maintained

    - Personnel security requirements will be met

    - Physical, logical, and environmental security (including communications security) will be maintained

    - Legal, regulatory, and contractual requirements will be met

    - Systems development and maintenance will be performed using a life cycle methodology

    - Business continuity plans will be produced, maintained, and tested

    - Information security awareness training will be provided to all staff

    - All breaches of information systems security, actual or suspected, will be reported to, and promptly investigated by Information Systems Security

    - Violations of Information Security Policy will result in penalties or sanctions

- Standards, practices, and procedures will be produced, and measures implemented to support the Information Security Policy. These may include, but are not limited to, virus protection, passwords, and encryption.

- Business requirements for the availability of information and information systems will be met.

- The roles and responsibilities regarding information security are defined for:

  - Executive management
  - Information systems security professionals
  - Data owners
  - Process owners
  - Technology providers
  - Users
  - Information systems auditors

- The Information Systems Security function has direct responsibility for maintaining the Information Security Policy and providing guidance and advice on its implementation.

- All managers are directly responsible for implementing the Information Security Policy within their areas of responsibility, and for adherence by their staff.

- It is the responsibility of each employee to adhere to the Information Security Policy.

Section summary

Organisations need to adopt a **control framework** and develop a **security policy**. CobiT and SAC/e-SAC are popular frameworks.

---

3 Personnel controls

Introduction

In this section we look at personnel controls which help mitigate the risks over information operations.

3.1 Management responsibilities

Responsibility for information technology should be clearly set down within the remit of every layer of management.

Organisation level	Examples of responsibilities
Top management	Establish **ownership of security and continuity**.
	Specify work of **audit committee** and **internal and external auditors**.
	Initiate and approve **contingency plan**.
	Act on all incidents of known **violation** of management **security policy** (such as illegal and unethical transactions).

Organisation level	Examples of responsibilities
User management	Establish **security function and strategy**.
	Establish **procedures** (for example, **segregation of duties** or **authorisation procedures**).
	Strive to employ, train and develop **competent** and **trustworthy personnel** with clear lines of authority and responsibility.
	Establish **risk assessment procedures**, **monitor system weaknesses** and **assess contingency plans**.
	Ensure **information security audits** are carried out and recommendations actioned.
	Establish **physical and access controls** to assets and data.
	Establish and maintain **checkpoints** and balances.
	Monitor compliance with controls through **scheduled and unscheduled audits**.
Data processing manager	Ensure that hardware, software and computer operations **meet security requirements.**
Personnel departments	Establish **terms of employment** and **screening procedures** consistent with company and department security aims.
	Include security in **job performance appraisals** and apply appropriate rewards and disciplinary measures.

3.2 Personnel security planning

Certain employees will always be placed in a position of trust, for example senior systems analysts, the database administrator and the computer security officer. With the growth of networks, almost all employees may be in a position to do damage to a computer system.

Although most employees are honest and well-intentioned, if they wish to do so, it may be relatively easy for individuals to compromise the security of an organisation.

The types of measure that can be used to control the personnel risk are as follows.

- Careful recruitment including taking up of references
- Job rotation
- Supervision and observation by a superior
- Review of computer usage (for example via systems logs)
- Enforced vacations

Termination procedures, restricting their access to sensitive data, are required for employees about to leave an organisation. Management should also consider the possible effects of industrial action directed at computer processing.

3.3 Division of responsibilities in the data processing department

If the organisation has a separate data processing department, the principle of division of responsibilities states that work is divided between systems analysts, programmers and operating staff, and that operations jobs are divided between data control, data preparation and computer room operations etc. The functions of an organisation structure, as far as control is concerned, are twofold.

(a) To **assign** the **responsibility** for certain tasks to specific jobs and individuals. A person in a given job has the responsibility for ensuring that certain controls are applied.

(b) To **prevent deliberate error**. It is easier for a person to commit fraud if he can input data, write programs and operate the computer all by himself.

3.4 Computer support department

In environments where there is a lot of end-user computing, the computer will be more of a support service than having responsibility for processing data itself. The services provided might include **user** and **software support**, **change and configuration management**, **backups**, **documentation** and **maintenance.** The controls over this department should ensure that its activities **enhance security.**

3.5 End-user computing

In the case of typical end user-based operations it is difficult to apply **segregation of duties**. The same person who operates the computer also **inputs data**, and may even **write his or her own programs** for it.

In these cases, however, it is still essential that the data being processed is not such as to have a bearing on the assets of the business. For example, if a PC were to be used for a sales ledger system or payroll system, the person responsible for data input and operating the PC must not be allowed to **design the system** nor **write its programs**, and there must also be suitable internal (and external) **audit checks** of the system.

Section summary

Personnel controls should include making **responsibility** for information systems an integral part of the manager's role, and appropriate **segregation of duties**.

4 Contingency controls and disaster planning

Introduction

In this section, we look at physical security and examine in detail the important controls of contingency planning and business continuity planning.

4.1 Minimising physical threats

Physical security comprises two sorts of controls.

- Protection against **natural** and man-made **disasters**, such as fire, flood or sabotage
- Protection against **intruders** gaining physical access to the system

A proper **fire safety plan** is an essential feature of security procedures, in order to prevent fire, detect fire and put out the fire. Fire safety includes:

- **Site preparation** (for example, appropriate building materials, fire doors)
- **Detection** (for example, **smoke detectors**)
- **Extinguishing** (for example, **sprinklers**)
- **Training** for staff in observing **fire safety procedures**

Flooding and water damage can be countered by the use of **waterproof ceilings and floors** together with the provision of **adequate drainage**.

Keeping up maintenance programmes can counter the leaking roofs or dripping pipes that result from **adverse weather conditions**. The problems caused by power surges resulting from lightning can be countered by the use of **uninterrupted (protected) power supplies**. This will protect equipment from fluctuations in the supply. Power failure can be protected against by the use of a **separate generator**.

Threats from terrorism can be countered by **physical access controls** and consultation with police and fire authorities.

Accidental damage can be avoided by **sensible attitudes to office behaviour** and **good office layout**.

4.2 Contingency planning

KEY TERMS

A CONTINGENCY is an unscheduled interruption of computing services that requires measures outside the day-to-day routine operating procedures.

A CONTINGENCY PLAN is a plan, formulated in advance, to be implemented upon the occurrence of certain specific future events.   *(CIMA Official Terminology)*

The preparation of a **contingency plan** (also known as a **disaster recovery plan**) is one of the stages in the development of an organisation-wide security policy. A contingency plan is necessary in case of a major **disaster,** or if some of the **security measures** discussed elsewhere **fail**.

A **disaster** occurs where the system for some reason breaks down, leading to potential **losses** of equipment, data or funds. The system **must recover as soon as possible** so that further losses are not incurred, and current losses can be rectified.

Question 14.1	Systems breakdown

Learning outcome E1(e)

What actions or events might lead to a computer system breakdown?

Any disaster recovery plan must therefore provide for:

(a)   **Standby procedures** so that some operations can be performed while normal services are disrupted
(b)   **Recovery procedures** once the cause of the breakdown has been discovered or corrected
(c)   **Personnel management** policies to ensure that (a) and (b) above are implemented properly

4.3 Contents of a contingency plan

The contents of a contingency (or disaster recovery) plan will include the following.

Section	Comment
Definition of responsibilities	It is important that somebody (a manager or co-ordinator) is designated to take control in a crisis. This individual can then delegate specific tasks or responsibilities to other designated personnel.
Priorities	Limited resources may be available for processing. Some tasks are more important than others. These must be established in advance. Similarly, the recovery programme may indicate that certain areas must be tackled first.
Backup and standby arrangements	These may be with other installations, with a company that provides such services (eg maybe the hardware vendor), or reverting to manual procedures.
Communication with staff	The problems of a disaster can be compounded by poor communication between members of staff.
Public relations	If the disaster has a public impact, the recovery team may come under pressure from the public or from the media.
Risk assessment	Some way must be found of assessing the requirements of the problem, if it is contained, with the continued operation of the organisation as a whole.

The contingency plan is dependent on effective **back-up procedures** for data and software, and arrangements for replacement – and even alternative premises.

The plan must cover all activities from the initial response to a 'disaster', through to damage limitation and full recovery. Responsibilities must be clearly spelt out for all tasks.

4.4 Business continuity planning

KEY TERM

BUSINESS CONTINUITY PLANNING is the creation and validation of a practised logistical plan for an organisation to recover and restore partially or completely interrupted critical functions within a predetermined time after a disaster or extended disruption.

A completed business continuity planning cycle results in a formal printed manual. For a small organisation, this manual could consist of a printed manual stored safely away from the organisation's main location, containing the contact details for crisis management staff, general staff, customers, suppliers, the location of offsite data backup storage media and other vital materials.

Organisations need to ensure that their manual is realistic and easy to use in a crisis. Therefore business continuity planning sits alongside contingency planning and is part of the risk management process.

CASE STUDY

In 2004, the UK enacted the Civil Contingencies Act 2004, which requires all emergency services and local authorities to actively prepare and plan for emergencies. Local authorities also have a legal obligation to actively lead promotion of business continuity practices amongst their geographical areas.

4.5 Hardware duplication

Hardware duplication may be required to permit a system to function in case of breakdown.

The provision of **back-up computers** tends to be quite costly, particularly where these systems have no other function. Many organisations will use **several smaller computer systems** and find that a significant level of protection against system faults can be provided by **shifting operations** to one of the systems still functioning.

Where an organisation has only a single system to rely on, recourse to a back-up facility is unavailable. In these instances one response would be to negotiate a **maintenance contract** which provides for back-up facilities.

Section summary

Organisations should have systems in place for dealing with the **most common natural threats** of fire, water and weather interruptions.

Contingency plans for major disruptions should include **standby and recovery** procedures.

5 Access controls

Introduction

In this section we examine access controls. These can range from looks on doors to passwords to restrict access to systems to authorised personnel only.

5.1 Examples of access controls

Access controls are designed to prevent intruders getting near to computer equipment and/or storage media.

(a)   **Personnel**, including receptionists and, outside working hours, security guards, can help control human access.

(b)   **Door locks** can be used where frequency of use is low. (This is not practicable if the door is in frequent use.)

(c)   Locks can be combined with:

    (i)   A **keypad system**, requiring a code to be entered.

    (ii)   A **card entry system**, requiring a card to be 'swiped'.

(d)   **Intruder alarms are vital**.

(e)   Even if intruders get past the physical controls a system of **effective passwords** should prevent them being able to access the systems.

The best form of access control would be one which **recognised** individuals immediately, without the need for personnel or cards. However, machines which can identify a person's fingerprints or scan the pattern of a retina are **expensive**, so are used only in highly sensitive industries, eg defence.

It may not be cost-effective or practical to use the same access controls in all areas. The **security requirements of different departments** should be estimated, and appropriate measures taken. Some areas will be very restricted, whereas others will be relatively open.

CASE STUDY

Care is needed to ensure access controls can cope with variations from the normal routine.

Wake County in the USA used a central computer to lock and unlock 50 of its buildings in and around Raleigh. The Wake Country Animal Shelter was closed on Easter weekend, but the computer didn't know that. The doors were unlocked at the normal opening time and several animals went missing from the shelter.

5.2 Passwords

KEY TERM

PASSWORDS are a set of characters which may be allocated to a person, a terminal or a facility which are required to be keyed into the system before further access is permitted.

Unauthorised persons may **circumvent physical access controls**. A **logical access system** can prevent access to data and program files, by measures such as the following.

(a)   Identification of the user

(b)   Authentication of user identity

(c)   Checks on user authority

Passwords can be applied to data files, program files and to parts of a program.

(a)   One password may be **required to read** a **file**, but another to **write new data** to it.

(b)   The terminal user can be **restricted** to the **use of certain files** and programs (eg in a banking system, junior grades of staff are only allowed to access certain routine programs).

If what is entered matches a password issued to an authorised user or is valid for that particular terminal the system permits access. Otherwise the system does **not allow access,** the terminal may **lock** and the **attempted unauthorised access** should be **recorded**.

Keeping track of **failed attempts** can alert managers to repeated efforts to break into the system; in these cases the culprits might be caught, particularly if there is an apparent pattern to their efforts.

The following is a good example of the sort of code that organisations might issue on use of passwords.

Best Password Practice

CASE STUDY

> Here is a checklist of points to be observed by computer users to whom passwords have been allocated.
>
> •   Keep your password secret. Do not reveal it to anyone else.
>
> •   Do not write it down. The second easiest way of revealing a password is to write it on an adhesive label and stick this to the VDU, the desk beneath the keyboard, the inside of a desk drawer or the underside of an overhead filing cabinet.
>
> •   Change your password regularly.

- Change and use your password discreetly. Even though a password does not show up on screen, it is easy for onlookers to see which keys are being used. (FRED is a popular password for this reason; the relevant keys are close together on a QWERTY keyboard.)

- Do not use an obvious password. (FRED is an obvious password. Your name or nickname is another.)

- Change your password if you suspect that anyone else knows it.

Section summary

Physical access control attempts to stop **intruders** or other unauthorised persons getting near to computer equipment or storage media. Important aspects are **door locks** and **card entry systems**. **Passwords** are an important access control, although they can be ineffective if the system is simple or if users are careless.

6 Integrity and backup controls

Introduction

In this section, we consider controls over the integrity and back-up of information. Controls over integrity encompass input controls, processing controls and output controls.

6.1 Integrity controls

KEY TERMS

DATA INTEGRITY in the context of security is preserved when data is the same as in source documents and has not been accidentally or intentionally altered, destroyed or disclosed.

SYSTEMS INTEGRITY refers to system operation conforming to the design specification despite attempts (deliberate or accidental) to make it behave incorrectly.

Data will maintain its **integrity** if it is **complete** and **not corrupted**. This means that:

(a) The original **input** of the data must be controlled in such a way as to ensure that the results are complete and correct.

(b) Any **processing and storage** of data must maintain the **completeness** and **correctness** of the data captured.

(c) Reports or other **output** should be set up so that they, too, are complete and correct.

6.1.1 Input controls

Input controls should ensure the **accuracy, completeness and validity** of input.

(a) **Data verification** involves ensuring data entered matches source documents.

(b) **Data validation** involves ensuring that data entered is not incomplete or unreasonable. Various checks can be used, depending on the data type.

    (i) **Check digits**. A digit calculated by the program and added to the code being checked to validate it eg modulus 11 method.

    (ii) **Control totals**. For example, a batch total totalling the entries in the batch.

    (iii) **Hash totals**. A system generated total used to check the reasonableness of numeric codes entered.

(iv)   **Range checks**. Used to check the value entered against a sensible range, eg account number for statement of financial position items must be between 5,000 and 9,999.

(v)   **Limit checks**. Similar to a range check, but usually based on an upper limit eg must be less than 999,999.99.

Data may be **valid** (for example in the **correct format**) but still **not match source documents**.

6.1.2 Processing controls

Processing controls should ensure the **accuracy and completeness of processing**. Programs should be subject to development controls and to rigorous testing. **Periodic running of test data** is also recommended.

Processing controls should also include:

- **Standardisation procedures**, for example a chart of accounts

- **Agreements within the system**, for example agreeing the total of balances on subsidiary ledgers to the control totals

6.1.3 Output controls

Output controls should ensure the **accuracy**, **completeness** and **security of output**. The following measures are possible.

- A list of all transactions processed
- Pre-printed stationery
- Suspense accounts which are investigated and cleared regularly
- Investigation and follow-up of **error reports** and **exception reports**
- Batch controls to ensure all items processed and returned
- Controls over distribution/copying of output
- Labelling of disks/tapes

6.2 Back-up controls

KEY TERM

BACK-UP means to make a copy in anticipation of future failure or corruption. A back-up copy of a file is a duplicate copy kept separately from the main system and only used if the original fails.

The **purpose of backing up data** is to ensure that the most recent usable copy of the data can be recovered and restored in the event of loss or corruption on the primary storage media.

Back-up controls aim to maintain system and data integrity. We have classified back-up controls as an integrity control rather than a contingency control because back-ups should be part of the **day-to-day procedures** of all computerised systems.

6.3 Audit trail

The original concept of an audit trail is to enable a manager or auditor to follow transactions stage-by-stage through a system to ensure that they have been processed correctly. The intention is to **identify errors** and **detect fraud**.

Modern integrated computer systems have cut out much of the time-consuming stage-by-stage working of older systems, but there should still be some **means of identifying individual records** and the **input and output documents** associated with the processing of any individual transaction.

KEY TERM

An AUDIT TRAIL is a record showing who has accessed a computer system and what operations that individual has performed. Audit trails are useful both for maintaining security and for recovering lost transactions. Accounting systems include an audit trail component that is able to be output as a report.

In addition, there are separate audit trail software products that enable network administrators to monitor use of network resources.

An audit trail should be provided so that every transaction on a file contains a **unique reference** (eg a sales system transaction record should hold a reference to the customer order, delivery note and invoice).

Section summary

Integrity controls include **input controls** (over accuracy, completeness and validity), **processing controls** (over accuracy and completeness) and **output controls** (over accuracy, security and completeness).

Critical data should be regularly backed up and stored separately. An **archiving policy** should ensure that data is preserved in the long-term.

7   Theft and fraud prevention   5/10

Introduction

In this section we look at the controls used to prevent theft and fraud, which are key risks in information operations.

7.1 Computer theft

As computer equipment becomes **smaller** and **more portable**, it can be 'smuggled' out of buildings with greater ease. Indeed much equipment is specifically **designed for use off-site**.

A **log of all equipment** should be maintained. The log should include the **make, model** and **serial number** of each item, together with some other organisation-generated code which identifies the **department** which owns the item, the **individual** responsible for the item and its **location**. Anyone taking any equipment off-site should book it out and book it back in. **Smaller items** of equipment, such as laptop computers and CDs, should always be **locked securely away**.

Question 14.2	Theft prevention

Learning outcome E1(e)

You are the chief accountant at your company. Your department, located in an open-plan office, has five networked desktop PCs and two laser printers.

You have just read an article suggesting that the best form of security is to lock hardware away in fireproof cabinets, but you feel that this is impracticable. Identify any alternative security measures which you could adopt to protect the hardware.

7.1.1 Software piracy

An organisation can face problems through **unlicensed use** of software by staff on its own machines, or its staff or others illegally making copies for their own use of the software it owns itself. Unlicensed software will lack **warranties**, is more likely to contain **viruses**, and could result in **legal action** for breach of copyright.

Record keeping is the most important control **preventing** the **unlicensed use** of software:

- Buying from **reputable dealers**

- **Maintaining records** of **software purchase and licensing**, identifying the software being used on each machine

- Maintaining a **central secure store** of **disks**

- **Spot inventory checks** to confirm that all software being used is licensed. This should cover **product name**, **version number**, and **serial number**.

7.2 Computer fraud

We have seen that **computer fraud usually involves the theft of funds by dishonest use of a computer system**.

The management of every company must be conscious of the possibility and costs of computer fraud and everything must be done to prevent it. Employees (including directors) are the most likely perpetrators of fraud. A dishonest employee will be rare, but temptation should be avoided by giving **no opportunity or motive** to staff.

7.2.1 Fraud prevention

The UK's Audit Commission suggested six measures as being particularly important in the prevention and detection of computer fraud:

- **Involvement of internal audit**
- **Computer audit skills** in the internal audit function
- Rigorously implemented **computer security policy**
- All staff being given **computer awareness training**
- **Risk analysis** focusing on activities and functions most prone to abuse
- **Staff being employed** to **ensure compliance** with the organisation's computer security policy

In addition, organisations can take additional steps.

(a)   **Instigate stringent controls** at the **periphery of the financial system**, at all points where money leaves the company.

(b)   Program the computers to **change the controls** operated over **specific transactions.**

It is possible to **use expert systems** to monitor fraud. Barclaycard has installed an expert system to monitor credit card transactions. It has been fed with information relating to credit card frauds perpetrated over a twenty year period. The expert system can therefore 'recognise' suspicious buying patterns.

Section summary

Organisations should ensure **detailed records** are kept of all computer equipment and software and **theft prevention measures** such as locking items away are in place.

Important **fraud prevention methods** include **security policy, training** and **internal audit.**

8   Internet and e-mail

Introduction

In this section we look at the controls over the use of the Internet and e-mail by organisations. We will also look at the use of intranets and extranets and the benefits of these to organisations, provided relevant controls are also put in place over their use.

8.1 Risks of Internet

We discussed in Section 1 of this chapter the possible dangers of establishing links to the Internet, which are amongst the most serious risks that organisations face. The main risks are from **viruses** and **hackers**. We discuss now the controls that can be implemented to mitigate against these and other risks associated with the use of the Internet by organisations.

Exam alert

Questions on the risks faced by companies that trade over the Internet are likely to come up very regularly in the exam.

8.2 Protecting against viruses

The main protection against viruses is **anti-virus software**. Anti-virus software, such as McAfee or Norton searches systems for viruses and removes any that are found. **On-access virus scanning** prevents infection by disallowing access to infected items.

Anti-virus programs include an **auto-update feature** that enables the program to **download profiles** of new viruses, enabling the software to check for all **known** or existing viruses. Very new viruses may go undetected by anti-virus software (until the anti-virus software vendor updates their package – and the organisation installs the update).

Personnel policies are also important in dealing with viruses.

(a)   Staff's **information technology training** should include dealing with viruses.

(b)   **Disciplinary procedures** should be used against staff who use unauthorised software on the network.

External e-mail links can be protected by virus checking all messages, and preventing files of a certain type being sent via e-mail (eg .exe files, as these are the most common means of transporting a virus).

Controls we have discussed in other contexts can also be used to **combat viruses**, also other attempts to **hack** into the system.

(a)   **Monitoring and trading**. Reviewing the network regularly, emphasising to staff the importance of **vigilance** and fully investigating **deliberate attempts** to breach security.

(b)   **Backups.** All software including operating system software should be write-protected and stored in a safe place.

(c)   **Contingency plans.** Plans should specify how the virus should be **contained**. The infected terminals may have to be disconnected from the network and disk interchange between PCs suspended. **Recovery procedures** may include restoration of hard disks, checking data to see whether it has been corrupted and thoroughly checking all infected objects.

8.3 Encryption and other safety measures

ENCRYPTION involves scrambling the data at one end of the line, transmitting the scrambled data, and unscrambling it at the receiver's end of the line.

8.3.1 Encryption

Encryption aims to ensure the security of data during transmission. It involves the translation of data into secret code. To read an encrypted file, you must have access to a secret key or password that enables you to decrypt it. Unencrypted data is called **plain text**; encrypted data is referred to as **cipher text**.

Encryption is the only secure way to **prevent eavesdropping** (since eavesdroppers can get round password controls, by tapping the line or by experimenting with various likely passwords).

8.3.2 Firewalls

Firewalls disable part of the communications technology to **prevent unwelcome access** into the computer system. Firewalls allow public access to some parts of the computer system, whilst denying access to other parts inside the firewall. The organisation locates software and files for public use on a dedicated web server. All users are required to enter the site through a single gateway, where scans occur for the presence of viruses and spam email. Access to the rest of the system is controlled by **passwords**.

However a determined hacker may be able to bypass these precautions.

8.3.3 Other safety measures

More sophisticated encryption techniques include:

(a)   **Digital signature.** This is **encryption** by means of private keys, ensuring the senders are who they claim to be and providing evidence should the sender later claim the order was never made.

(b)   **Digital envelope.** This involves sending the key used to encrypt the message separately from the encrypted message.

Authentication is a technique for making sure that a message has come from an authorised sender. Authentication involves adding an extra field to a record, with the contents of this field derived from the remainder of the record by applying an algorithm that has previously been agreed between the senders and recipients of data.

Dial-back security operates by requiring the person wanting access to the network to dial into it and identify themselves first. The system then dials the person back on their authorised number before allowing them access.

Exam skills

If you are asked to recommend controls you must ensure that your recommendations are well-explained and are pertinent to the organisation described in the question scenario.

8.4 E-mail

E-mail can impose **legal** and **security** problems, and is often the gateway through which viruses can enter systems. To combat these risks, organisations should enforce strict policies.

(a)   **Limits** should be imposed on the personal use of e-mail. A blanket prohibition may not work, as employees will use web services instead. A possible solution would be to provide a secondary personal e-mail address with limitations such as a prohibition on attachments.

(b)   The policy should prohibit the sending of **defamatory**, **abusive**, **sexist** or **racist messages**, or downloading **offensive material**.

(c)   E-mails to external customers should give the **company's name, address, telephone number** and **fax number** and **full name** of the person sending the e-mail. They should include a **disclaimer**.

(d)   The sending of **confidential information** to external sources should be **prohibited** if possible. If it has to be sent, it should be encrypted or password-protected.

(e)   Ideally **external e-mails** should contain **matters of fact** only.

(f)   Employees should be advised that e-mails may have to be **disclosed** in court, and hence they should not delete sensitive e-mails from the system, and should keep hard copies of sensitive e-mails. If there is a legal dispute, employees should not discuss it over e-mail.

(g)   All **attachments** to e-mails received should be **copied**, and **checked** for viruses.

(h)   Security software should be used to **analyse attachments** for viruses and e-mails themselves for sensitive words or abusive language. **Electronic limits** can also be placed on the types of attachment specific users can send out.

(i)   All **e-mails received** should be **scanned** for viruses.

8.5 Benefits of Internet

Provided they have proper procedures in place for dealing with risk, the benefits to organisations of the Internet can of course be great.

(a)   **The Internet reduces transaction costs and thus stimulates economic activity**. According to one US calculation, a banking transaction via the Internet costs 1 cent, 27 cents at an ATM (automated teller machine) and 52 cents over the telephone. Significant savings can be enjoyed by small-scale or even single customers.

(b)   The Internet **reduces costs for vendors**. Savings can be achieved through **economies of scale** (becoming a high volume global supplier with low costs) and **economies of scope** (through product specialisation). Links between vendors, intermediaries and manufacturer minimise the need for inventory and ensure that delivery, installation and after-sales service can all be arranged automatically. Certain goods, for example computer software or music, can be **delivered electronically,** reducing delivery and insurance costs and increasing the timeliness of delivery.

(c)   **Marketing can be targeted** at selected customers based on customer registration information or past purchase history. The internet also offers **innovative marketing alternatives** such as product demonstrations, detailed user manuals and cross-selling of services.

(d)   **The speed, range and accessibility of information on the Internet, and the low cost of capturing and distributing it, create new commercial possibilities**. Businesses can focus on **niche product/service supply issues** thus attracting specialised buyers and sellers. In turn they acquire more expertise that generates continued customer loyalty and participation.

8.6 Benefits of Intranets and Extranets

KEY TERM

An INTRANET is an internal network used to share information. Intranets utilise Internet technology and protocols. The firewall surrounding an intranet fends off unauthorised access.

The idea behind an 'intranet' is that organisations set up their own **mini version of the Internet.** Intranets use a combination of the organisation's own networked computers and Internet technology. Each employee has a browser, used to access a server computer that holds corporate information on a wide variety of topics, and in some cases also offers access to the Internet.

Potential applications include company newspapers, induction material, online procedure and policy manuals, employee web pages where individuals post details of their activities and progress, and **internal databases** of the corporate information store.

Most of the **cost** of an intranet is the **staff time** required to set up the system.

The **benefits** of intranets are diverse.

(a)   Savings accrue from the **elimination of storage**, **printing** and **distribution** of documents that can be made available to employees on-line.

(b)   Documents on-line are often **more widely used** than those that are kept filed away. This means that there are **improvements in productivity** and **efficiency**.

(c)   It is much **easier to update** information in electronic form.

(d)   Wider access to corporate information should open the way to **more flexible working patterns**, eg material available on-line may be accessed from remote locations.

KEY TERM

An EXTRANET links the intranets of related organisations – for example within a supply chain – for their mutual benefit. Extranets can be used to share inventory and price information.

Section summary

To combat risks from using the Internet, organisations should have **virus protection software** and **encryption procedures**, and also take measures against the security and legal risks of using **e-mail**.

9   Systems development controls

Introduction

In this section we look at the controls over systems development. Controls over each stage of systems development are vital to ensure that new systems are put in place effectively.

In your previous studies you will have looked at systems development in detail. We summarise below the main points before going on to talk about control and audit of development and implementation.

9.1 Systems development life cycle (SDLC)

The SDLC is a disciplined approach to systems upgrades intended to reduce the possibility of ending up with a system that fails to meet the needs of the organisation and wastes time and money.

SYSTEMS DEVELOPMENT LIFE CYCLE	
Feasibility study	Briefly review the existing system
	Identify possible alternative solutions
Systems investigation	Obtain details of current requirements and user needs such as data volumes, processing cycles and timescales
	Identify current problems and restrictions
Systems analysis	Consider why current methods are used and identify better alternatives
Systems design	Determine what inputs, processing and storage facilities are necessary to produce the outputs required
	Consider matters such as program design, file design and security
	Prepare a detailed specification of the new system
	Test system fully
Systems implementation	Write or acquire software, test it, convert files, install hardware and start running the new system

The cycle begins again when a review suggests that it is becoming difficult for an installed system to continue to meet current objectives through routine maintenance.

Exam alert

A question on systems development could require discussion of project management issues as well as controls over, and the audit of, the development process itself.

9.2 Control framework

Major systems development must take place within a clearly defined control framework, containing the following elements.

9.2.1 Steering committee

A steering committee is responsible for overseeing the project development, reporting to the board. It should include:

Personnel	Responsibilities
Project sponsor	Senior manager, possibly head of IT, responsible for leading the project and the committee. Responsible for investment of resources into the project and the achievement of the project's business objectives.
Project manager	Responsible for planning, recruiting project team, overseeing daily progress of project, co-ordinating project activities and communicating progress. Project manager should ensure resources are used efficiently.
IT specialists	Internal staff or IT consultants, responsible for developing and implementing the system.
User representatives	Staff from relevant operational areas, advising on needs and usability and implementation of system. They should be involved in systems testing and should sign system off.
Internal audit	The head of internal audit and/or auditors with IT knowledge, assessing adequacy of systems testing and internal controls.

9.2.2 The project team

The project team will include internal and external IT specialists as well as user representatives. It will be responsible for the detailed planning, design, development and implementation work on the new system. Key tasks include:

- Defining deliverables
- Planning, timetabling and resourcing
- System testing
- User group education
- Approval of final systems design
- Systems implementation

9.2.3 Design criteria

As well as fulfilling the specific objectives, all systems must fulfil certain **criteria** that need to be considered at the design stage, such as **data security, authorisation and acceptance of design by all involved**.

9.2.4 Board involvement

As well as review by the steering committee, the **board or audit committee** must also **supervise the project**. This should include approval of the project's **objectives** and major **expenditure decisions** and **regular review** of progress, using evidence provided by **internal audit**.

This control framework may be used for other investment decisions.

9.2.5 Resource planning and allocation

Sufficient funds and **personnel** will be required to carry the project through.

9.2.6 Risk management

The specific risks relating to the project clearly need to be **identified and assessed**, and risks and consequences monitored throughout the period.

9.3 Developing a testing strategy

To ensure a coherent, effective approach to testing, a testing plan should be developed. This plan would normally form part of the overall software development quality plan.

A testing strategy should cover the following areas.

Testing strategy area	Comment
Strategy approach	A testing strategy should be formulated that details the approach that will be taken to testing, including the tests to be conducted and the testing tools/techniques that will be used.
Test plan	A test plan should be developed that states: • What will be tested • When it will be tested (sequence) • The test environment
Test design	The logic and reasoning behind the design of the tests should be explained.
Performing tests	Detailed procedures should be provided for all tests. This explanation should ensure tests are carried out consistently, even if different people carry out the tests.
Documentation	It must be clear how the results of tests are to be documented. This provides a record of errors, and a starting point for error correction procedures.
Re-testing	The re-test procedure should be explained. In many cases, after correction, all aspects of the software should be re-tested to ensure the corrections have not affected other aspects of the software.

The presence of 'bugs' or errors in the vast majority of software/systems demonstrates that even the most rigorous testing plan is unlikely to identify all errors. The limitations of software testing are outlined below.

Limitation	Comment
Poor testing process	The test plan may not cover all areas of system functionality. Testers may not be adequately trained. The testing process may not be adequately documented.
Inadequate time	Software and systems are inevitably produced under significant time pressures. Testing time is often 'squeezed' to compensate for project over-runs in other areas.
Future requirements not anticipated	The test data used may have been fine at the time of testing, but future demands may be outside the range of values tested. Testing should allow for future expansion of the system.
Inadequate test data	Test data should test 'positively' – checking that the software does what it should do, and test 'negatively' – that it doesn't do what it shouldn't. It is difficult to include the complete range of possible input errors in test data.
Software changes inadequately tested	System/software changes made as a result of testing findings or for other reasons may not be adequately tested as they were not in the original test plan.

9.4 Stages of testing

A system must be **thoroughly tested before implementation** – a system that is not thoroughly tested may 'go live' with faults that cause disruption and prove costly. The scope of tests and trials will vary depending on the size and purpose of the system.

Four basic stages of testing can be identified:

- System logic
- Program testing
- System testing
- User acceptance testing

9.4.1 Testing system logic

Before any programs are written, the **logic devised** by the **systems analyst** should be checked. This process would involve the use of flow charts or structure diagrams such as data flow diagrams to plot the path of **different types of data** and **transactions**.

9.4.2 Program testing

Program testing involves **processing test data** through all programs. Test data should be of the type that the program will be required to process and should include invalid/exceptional items to test whether the program reacts as it should.

9.4.3 System testing

When it has been established that individual programs and interfaces are operating as intended, overall system testing should begin. System testing has a wider focus than program testing. System testing should extend beyond areas already tested, to cover:

- **Input documentation** and the practicalities of input eg time taken
- **Flexibility of system** to allow amendments to the 'normal' processing cycle
- **Ability to produce information** on time
- Ability to cope with **peak system resource requirements** eg transaction volumes, staffing levels
- **Viability of operating procedures**

System testing will involve testing both **before installation** (known as off-line testing) and **after implementation** (on-line testing). As many problems as possible should be identified before implementation, but it is likely that some problems will only become apparent when the system goes live.

9.4.4 User acceptance testing

KEY TERM

USER ACCEPTANCE TESTING is carried out by those who will use the system to determine whether the system meets their needs. These needs should have previously been stated as acceptance criteria. The aim is for the customer to determine whether or not to accept the system.

It is vital that users are involved in system testing to ensure the system operates as intended when used in its operating environment. Any problems identified should be corrected. This will improve system efficiency and should also encourage users to accept the new system as an important tool to help them in their work.

9.5 Training

Staff training in the use of information systems and information technology is essential if the return on investment in IS/IT is to be maximised.

Training will be needed when:

- A new system is implemented
- An existing system is significantly changed
- Job specifications change
- New staff are recruited
- Skills have been forgotten

9.6 Documentation

9.6.1 Technical manual

The technical manual is produced as a **reference tool** for those involved in producing and installing the system. The technical manual should be referred to when future modifications are made to the system. It should be updated whenever system changes are made.

9.6.2 User manual

The system should be documented from the point-of-view of **users**. User documentation is used to **explain** the system to users and in training. It provides a **point of reference** should the user have problems with the system. Much of this information may be available **on-line** using context-sensitive help eg 'Push F1 for help'.

9.7 File conversion and changeover

9.7.1 File conversion procedures

KEY TERM

FILE CONVERSION means converting existing files into a format suitable for the new system. When a new system is introduced, files must be created that conform to the requirements of that system.

It is essential that the 'new' converted files are accurate. Various checks can be utilised during the conversion process, including **one-to-one checking** or **sample checking**.

Once the new system has been fully and satisfactorily tested the changeover can be made. This may be according to one of four approaches.

9.7.2 Direct changeover

The old system is **completely replaced** by the new system **in one move**.

This may be unavoidable where the two systems are substantially different, or where the costs of parallel running are too great.

While this method is comparatively **cheap** it is **risky** (system or program corrections are difficult while the system has to remain operational).

9.7.3 Parallel running

The **old and new** systems are **run in parallel** for a period of time, both processing current data and enabling cross checking to be made.

This method provides a **degree of safety** should there be problems with the new system. However, if there are differences between the two systems cross-checking may be difficult or impossible.

There is a **delay** in the actual implementation of the new system, a possible indication of **lack of confidence,** and a need for **more staff** to cope with both systems running in parallel.

9.7.4 Pilot operation

Pilot operation involves selecting part or parts of an organisation (eg a department or branch) to operate running the new system in parallel with the existing system. When the branch or department piloting the system is satisfied with the new system, they cease to use the old system. The new system is then piloted in another area of the organisation.

Pilot operation is **cheaper** and **easier to control** than running the whole system in parallel, and provides a **greater degree of safety** than a direct changeover.

9.7.5 Phased changeover

Phased changeover involves **selecting a complete section** of the system for a **direct changeover**, for example the purchase ledger in an accounting system. When this part is running satisfactorily, another part is switched – until eventually the whole system has been changed.

A phased series of direct changeovers is less risky than a single direct changeover, as any problems and disruption experienced should be isolated in an area of operations.

9.8 Post-implementation review

A **post-implementation review** should establish whether the **objectives** and **targeted performance criteria** have been met, and if not, why not, and what should be done about it.

In appraising the operation of the new system immediately after the changeover, comparison should be made between **actual and predicted performance**. This will include:

- Consideration of **throughput speed** (time between input and output)
- Use of computer **storage** (both internal and external)
- The number and type of **errors/queries**
- The **cost** of processing (data capture, preparation, storage and output media, etc)

The review also needs to cover more qualitative aspects of whether **users' needs** have been fulfilled.

The post-implementation measurements should **not be made too soon** after the system goes live, or else results will be abnormally affected by 'teething' problems, lack of user familiarity and resistance to change.

Recommendations should be made as to any **further action** or steps which should be taken to improve performance.

The report should also make **recommendations** on **wider issues**, including improvements in **systems development** and overall **project management procedures**.

9.9 Audit of systems development

In this section, we discuss briefly the audit of systems development. The audit of systems by internal audit is covered in detail in Chapter 16, to which you should refer if necessary.

Auditors have a very important role in the development of major systems, and significant audit involvement can help ensure control procedures operate and avoid the problems discussed above. Auditors are likely to be involved in three main areas in the audit of systems development.

9.9.1 Assessing adequacy of control framework

Auditors will wish to see in advance that development will take place within a control framework, including **appropriate staffing** and **regular review** by senior management.

9.9.2 Development process

Auditors will be particularly concerned with the following areas.

(a) **Feasibility study**

Auditors should confirm that the project is **justified on financial** and other **relevant grounds**, and that there is evidence that a **number of options** have been **considered**. They will also check that the **timescale** for **project completion** is **realistic**. Auditors should also follow the results of the **feasibility study through**, to confirm that the contract specification is based on the feasibility study.

(b) **Suppliers**

Auditors will wish to check that **suppliers** are **reputable**, and that the contract is **tight**. They will ascertain that **delivery schedules and timetables** have been agreed.

(c) **System design**

Auditors must be one of the parties consulted at the **design stage** for **approval** before the development is allowed to proceed. They will be most concerned that **appropriate data security** and **authorisation procedures** are built into the design, also that the system will produce **adequate and accurate information**. In addition they will review the design to confirm that there are no obvious problems with data collection, input, processing and output.

Auditors will be concerned with controls over the **data used in development** and that changes to data are authorised. They should check that the programmers are **following formal program specifications**. They will also be concerned that there is a **full information trail** for the design process and that the project has been **endorsed** by the development team **and** users of the system.

(d) **System testing**

With testing, auditors will require that all aspects, not just software, are tested and **testing** is carried out by the systems development team, programmers and users.

At the testing stage auditors will also wish to carry out their own testing on controls, or at any rate obtain assurance that controls have been tested. They will be primarily concerned to test the operation of controls that ensure the system is **reliable, produces accurate data and is secure**. They will also be concerned with how easy the system will be to audit.

(e) **Implementation**

Auditors will check that staff have been **fully trained** and **support documentation** is complete.

Auditors will confirm in advance that **file conversion** has been properly planned, and the implementation plan allows sufficient time for implementation of each aspect of the system.

9.9.3 After installation

As well as checking that the **post-completion review** has been **carried out**, auditors should themselves review the system development as part of an ongoing review of the organisation's project management procedures.

Exam alert

Systems development is likely to be a topic that will come up frequently and will probably include an audit element.

CASE STUDY

Some of the UK government's biggest computer projects have spiralled out of control. Some projects are years behind schedule and costs have escalated, while others have been scaled back or scrapped altogether. One of the projects, a £13 billion plan to computerise all patient medical records and link general practitioners to hospitals, is years late, having been originally estimated to cost £2.3 billion. A top NHS executive admitted in April 2010 that the full systems originally promised will not be delivered. Only around half of London's acute hospitals will receive the central patient administration software.

Section summary

The key stages of the **systems development lifecycle** are **feasibility study**, **systems investigation**, **systems analysis**, **systems design**, **systems implementation**, **systems control**.

A system must be thoroughly **tested** to ensure it operates as intended. The nature and scope of testing will vary depending on the size and type of the system and user acceptance testing.

Four basic **stages of testing** can be identified: system logic, program testing, system testing and user acceptance testing.

There are four approaches to **changeover**: direct changeover, parallel running, pilot operations and phased changeover. These vary in terms of time required, cost and risk.

A **post-implementation review** should be carried out to see whether the targeted performance criteria have been met, and to review costs and benefits. The review should culminate in the production of a **report**.

Auditors should monitor systems development carefully. They should confirm the **appropriate control framework** is in place over developments, that **system development standards** are being followed, and that the system contains **controls** over **completeness**, **security** and **accuracy** of data.

Chapter Roundup

✓ Risks to data and systems include **physical risks** such as fire and water and **risks** through **human error or fraud**.

✓ **Internet links** have resulted in additional risks including **hacking** and **viruses**.

✓ Risks arising from **systems development** include the risks that the system will have **inadequate security**, and will **not meet the users' requirements**.

✓ Organisations need to adopt a **control framework** and develop a **security policy**. CobiT and SAC/e-SAC are popular frameworks.

✓ **Personnel controls** should include making **responsibility** for information systems an integral part of the manager's role, and appropriate **segregation of duties**.

✓ Organisations should have systems in place for dealing with the **most common natural threats** of fire, water and weather interruptions.

✓ **Contingency plans for major disruptions** should include **standby and recovery** procedures.

✓ **Physical access control** attempts to stop **intruders** or other unauthorised persons getting near to computer equipment or storage media. Important aspects are **door locks** and **card entry systems**. **Passwords** are an important access control, although they can be ineffective if the system is simple or if users are careless.

✓ **Integrity controls** include **input controls** (over accuracy, completeness and validity), **processing controls** (over accuracy and completeness) and **output controls** (over accuracy, security and completeness).

✓ **Critical data** should be regularly backed up and stored separately. An **archiving policy** should ensure that data is preserved in the long-term.

✓ Organisations should ensure **detailed records** are kept of all computer equipment and software and **theft prevention measures** such as locking items away are in place.

✓ Important **fraud prevention methods** include **security policy, training** and **internal audit.**

✓ To combat risks from using the Internet, organisations should have **virus protection software** and **encryption procedures**, and also take measures against the security and legal risks of using **e-mail**.

✓ The key stages of the **systems development lifecycle** are **feasibility study, systems investigation, systems analysis, systems design, systems implementation, systems control**.

✓ A system must be thoroughly **tested** to ensure it operates as intended. The nature and scope of testing will vary depending on the size and type of the system and user acceptance testing.

✓ Four basic **stages of testing** can be identified: system logic, program testing, system testing and user acceptance testing.

✓ There are four approaches to **changeover**: direct changeover, parallel running, pilot operations and phased changeover. These vary in terms of time required, cost and risk.

✓ A **post-implementation review** should be carried out to see whether the targeted performance criteria have been met, and to review costs and benefits. The review should culminate in the production of a **report**.

✓ Auditors should monitor systems development carefully. They should confirm the **appropriate control framework** is in place over developments, that **system development standards** are being followed, and that the system contains **controls** over **completeness, security** and **accuracy** of data.

Quick Quiz

1   Give five examples of recent developments that have increased the risk of computer fraud.

2   List three physical access control methods.

3   Fill in the blank.

     .... enables valid files to be restored in the case of future corruption or failure.

4   Why should certain duties be segregated between staff members?

5   Fill in the blank.

     .... involves scrambling data at one end of the communications link, transmitting the scrambled data, then receiving and unscrambling the data at the other end of the link.

6   What is the most common method of spreading a virus?

7   Fill in the blanks.

     Input controls in a computerised information system ensure the ....,
     .... and .... of input.

8   List four different stages of testing applications through a systems development project.

9   Fill in the blank.

     A .... establishes whether the systems objectives and targeted performance criteria have been met.

10   End-user computing strengthens segregation of duties.

     True   ☐

     False ☐

Answers to Quick Quiz

1   • Increased computer literacy
    • Use of telephone and other public communication systems
    • Reduction in internal checks and documentation
    • Increased real-time processing
    • Differing speed of developments in hardware and software

2   • Personnel (security guards)
    • Mechanical devices (eg keys)
    • Electronic devices (eg card-swipe systems, PIN keypads)

3   A **back-up** enables valid files to be restored in case of a future corruption or failure.

4   To reduce the opportunity for fraud and/or malicious damage.

5   **Encryption** involves scrambling data at one end of the communications link, transmitting the scrambled data, then receiving and unscrambling the data at the other end of the link.

6   E-mail

7   Input controls in a computerised information system ensure the **accuracy**, **completeness** and **validity** of input.

8   • System logic
    • Program testing
    • System testing
    • User acceptance testing

9   A **post-implementation** audit establishes whether the system objectives and targeted performance criteria have been met.

10   False. End-user computing makes segregation of duties more difficult.

Answers to Questions

14.1 Systems breakdown

System breakdowns can occur in a variety of circumstances, for example:

(a) Fire destroying data files and equipment

(b) Flooding

(c) A computer virus completely destroying a data or program file or damaging hardware

(d) A technical fault in the equipment

(e) Accidental destruction of telecommunications links (eg builders severing a cable)

(f) Terrorist attack

(g) System failure caused by software bugs which were not discovered at the design stage

(h) Internal sabotage (eg logic bombs built into the software)

14.2 Theft prevention

(a) **'Postcode'** all pieces of hardware. Invisible ink postcoding is popular, but visible marking is a better deterrent. Soldering irons are ideal for writing on plastic casing.

(b) **Mark the equipment** in other ways. Some organisations spray their hardware with permanent paint, perhaps in a particular colour (bright red is popular) or using stencilled shapes.

(c) Hardware can be **bolted to desks**. If bolts are passed through the desk and through the bottom of the hardware casing, the equipment can be rendered immobile.

(d) Ensure that the organisation's **standard security procedures** (magnetic passes, keypad access to offices, signing in of visitors etc) are followed.

<table>
<tr><td>**Now try these questions from the Exam Question Bank**</td><td>**Number**</td><td>**Level**</td><td>**Marks**</td><td>**Time**</td></tr>
<tr><td></td><td>Q22</td><td>Introductory</td><td>N/A</td><td>25 mins</td></tr>
<tr><td></td><td>Q23</td><td>Examination</td><td>25</td><td>45 mins</td></tr>
</table>

AUDIT AND REVIEW

Part E

INTERNAL AUDIT

In the last part of this Text we focus on the role of internal audit. Internal audit's role is to provide **feedback** potentially on all the other controls and systems we have discussed in this Text. This feedback helps the audit committee and board monitor the organisation's activities effectively and insist on corrective action.

In this chapter, we introduce the work of internal audit, describing its role and the various types of audit it undertakes and how the work of internal audit should be assessed.

We then take a look at the relationship between internal and external audit work, and the implications of internal audit work for the external audit process.

We end this chapter with a consideration of the ethical issues which could affect internal auditors.

topic list	learning outcomes	syllabus references	ability required
1 The role of internal audit	C2(a)	C2(i)	evaluation
2 Types of internal audit assignments	C2(a)	C2(ii)	evaluation
3 Internal and external audit	C2(e)	C2(i), (vi)	evaluation
4 Standards for internal audit and ethical considerations	C2(a), C3(b)	C2(iv), C3(ii)	evaluation

1 The role of internal audit

Introduction

In this section, we examine the role of the internal audit department as a monitoring activity established by the management of an organisation.

KEY TERM

INTERNAL AUDIT is an independent appraisal function established within an organisation to examine and evaluate its activities as a service to the organisation. The objective of internal auditing is to assist members of the organisation in the effective discharge of their responsibilities. To this end, internal auditing furnishes them with analyses, appraisals, recommendations, counsel and information concerning the activities reviewed.   *(Institute of Internal Auditors)*

INTERNAL AUDIT is an appraisal or monitoring activity established by management and directors for the review of the accounting and internal control systems as a service to the entity. It functions by, amongst other things, examining, evaluating and reporting to management and the directors on the adequacy and effectiveness of components of the accounting and internal control systems. *(Auditing Practices Board)*

1.1 The need for internal audit

The 1999 UK Turnbull report on internal control stated that listed companies without an internal audit function should **annually review** the need to have one, and listed companies with an internal audit function should **annually review** its **scope, authority** and **resources**.

Turnbull states that the need for internal audit will depend on:

*   The **scale, diversity** and **complexity** of the company's activities
*   The **number of employees**
*   **Cost-benefit considerations**
*   **Changes** in the organisational structures, reporting processes or underlying information systems
*   **Changes** in **key risks**
*   **Problems** with **internal control systems**
*   An **increased number** of **unexplained** or **unacceptable** events

Although there may be alternative means of carrying out the routine work of internal audit, those undertaking the work may be involved in operations and hence lack **objectivity**.

CASE STUDY

WorldCom in the United States was the company involved in one of the most high profile accounting scandals of the last few years. The company's Chief Financial Officer, Controller and Director of General Accounting used fraudulent accounting methods to cover up its declining earnings to increase the share price.

The fraud was discovered by the company's internal auditors who uncovered a massive $3.8 billion in fraud. By the end of 2003, it was estimated that the company's total assets had been inflated by some $11 billion. The company subsequently filed for bankruptcy.

1.2 Objectives of internal audit

The role of the internal auditor has expanded in recent years as internal auditors seek to monitor all aspects (not just accounting) of the business, and add value to their organisation. The work of the internal auditor is still prescribed by management, but it may cover the following broad areas.

(a)   **Review of the accounting and internal control systems**. The establishment of adequate accounting and internal control systems is a responsibility of management and the directors. Internal audit is often assigned specific responsibility for the following tasks.

(i)   **Reviewing** the design of the systems

(ii)   **Monitoring** the operation of the systems by risk assessment and detailed testing

(iii)   **Recommending** cost effective improvements

Review will cover both financial and non-financial controls.

(b)   **Examination of financial and operating information**. This may include review of the means used to identify, measure, classify and report such information and specific enquiry into individual items including detailed testing of transactions, balances and procedures.

(c)   **Review** of the **economy**, **efficiency** and **effectiveness** of operations.

(d)   **Review of compliance** with laws, regulations and other external requirements and with internal policies and directives and other requirements including appropriate authorisation of transactions.

(e)   **Review of the safeguarding of assets**.

(f)   **Review of the implementation of corporate objectives**. This includes review of the effectiveness of planning, the relevance of standards and policies, the company's corporate governance procedures and the operation of specific procedures such as communication of information.

(g)   **Identification of significant business** and financial **risks, monitoring** the **organisation's overall risk management policy** to ensure it operates effectively, and **monitoring** the **risk management strategies** to ensure they continue to operate effectively.

(h)   **Special investigations** into particular areas, for example suspected fraud.

Exam skills

In the exam you could be asked for a general description of the role of internal audit. Internal audit's role in the risk management process needs to be stressed when answering such a question. However don't forget that risk needs to be seen widely. Internal audit can also review efficiency and waste levels as well as examining how the organisation deals with financial and asset security risks.

1.3 Internal audit and risk management

Internal audit will play a significant part in the organisation's risk management processes, being required to assess and advise on how risks are countered. Internal audit's work will be influenced by the organisation's **appetite** for bearing risks, but internal audit will assess:

- The **adequacy of the risk management and response processes** for identifying, assessing, managing and reporting on risk

- The risk management and control **culture**

- The appropriateness of **internal controls** in operation to **limit risks**

- The **operation and effectiveness** of the **risk management processes**, including the internal controls

The areas auditors will concentrate on will depend on the **scope** and **priority** of the assignment and the **risks identified**. Where the risk management framework is insufficient, auditors will have to rely on their own **risk assessment** and will focus on **recommending an appropriate framework**. Where a framework for risk management and control is embedded in operations, auditors will aim to use **management assessment of risks** and concentrate on **auditing the risk management processes**.

A key part of internal audit's role in control systems is to provide feedback that influences the **design and operation** of **internal control systems**. Internal audit recommendations need to be seen in the context of the organisation's **strategic objectives** and **risk appetite.**

However you should remember that internal audit has a primarily monitoring and review role.

Internal auditors should be **checking that day-to-day control procedures such as monitoring** of **transactions are being carried out**, rather than carrying out these control procedures themselves. If they had day-to-day responsibilities, they would be **part of the control system** rather than reviewers of it, and therefore be unable to give an independent opinion on its operation.

The risk management function will be responsible for **building a risk aware culture** throughout the organisation by **information provision and training**. Risk management will provide **guidelines on overall risk policy and coordinate the various functional activities that deal with risks**.

Risk management will also be responsible for **designing risk analysis procedures and risk response processes**. They should ensure not only their **recommendations** for improvements, but the recommendations of the board, board committees and internal audit functions are **implemented**.

Exam alert

You may be asked in the exam about the inter-relationship between these two functions and their relationships to other parts of control systems (internal controls, corporate governance).

1.4 CIMA guide on internal audit

CIMA has published a guide on internal audit, *Internal audit – a guide to good practice for internal auditors and their customers*. The guide stresses the importance of the internal audit function being properly resourced and supported by the highest levels of the organisation's management.

The guide states that the following conditions are needed for internal audit to function well:

- The **aims** of internal audit are **agreed** by the board.

- Internal audit **covers all areas** of controls, and not just accounting controls.

- Internal audit has whatever **access is necessary** to people and documents.

- The head of internal audit has **clear access to the chairman and chief executive** of the organisation, as well as to the chairman of the audit committee.

- The head of internal audit **reports** to a **senior director**.

- The internal audit department is **independent** of executive management.

- Internal audit fulfils the requirements of **auditing standards** and **best practice**.

- Internal audit is **consulted** if there are likely to be **significant changes** in the business or control systems.

- Internal auditors do **not** have **operational involvement** in areas outside internal audit.

- The results of internal audit's work are **clearly communicated**, and its recommendations acted upon by senior management.

- Internal audit's performance is **regularly assessed**.

1.5 Role of head of internal audit

As well as organising the internal audit function, and supervising staff, the head of internal audit will be responsible for determining **internal audit strategy** and preparing the **overall audit plan**, working with the audit committee. The head of internal audit will also be responsible for reporting the results of internal audit work to the audit committee.

Reporting to, and working with the audit committee, should help to ensure the independence of the head of internal audit and internal audit department from the finance director and the chief executive.

Section summary

The role of internal audit will **vary** according to the **organisation's objectives** but is likely to include review of **internal control systems, risk management, legal compliance** and **value for money**.

2 Types of internal audit assignments

Introduction

In this section we look at the various types of audit that can be performed by internal auditors which range from systems audits to value for money work. At the end of this section we also briefly look at how the performance of internal audit work can be assessed.

2.1 Transactions audits

Transactions audits are (sometimes extensive) audits of the individual transactions of a business. They generally take excessive time and fail to give enough assurance on the overall processes and systems that organisations employ. However transactions audits may still be used to give assurance on occasions if for example the **accounting systems** have **broken down** or **major fraud** is **suspected**.

2.2 Systems audits

KEY TERM

SYSTEMS AUDIT is the audit of the internal controls within a system.

This is the type of audit most commonly associated with the job of auditing. As its name implies, it is the **audit of any system**, although the term is commonly associated with the audit of accounting systems, such as cash and cheques, sales and receivables, non-current asset records and so on.

The focus of systems-based auditing is on the functioning of all the companies' systems, covering financial and other areas. The priority given to each system will depend on the **risks** that the systems address and the **resources** needed to audit them.

Systems audits cover two areas of assurance.

2.2.1 Assurance on the design of the internal control system

Internal auditors will need to establish:

- The **desired balance** between **prevention** and **detection controls**
- The balance between **costs and benefits**
- The importance of **specific control objectives**

2.2.2 Assurance on the operation of the internal control system

A systems audit tests and evaluates the internal controls within the system, to determine the following.

- How **good** are the **internal controls**?
- What **weaknesses** might there be in the system of internal controls?
- What **reliance** can management place on the internal controls

The auditors must therefore investigate the nature of the control procedures within a system, and how well these procedures operate in practice. The objectives the audits will focus on include:

- Suitable and accurate management information
- Compliance with procedures, laws and regulations

- Safeguarding assets
- Securing economies and efficiencies
- Accomplishing objectives

The systems audit would include consideration of all the stages of the internal controls process identified below.

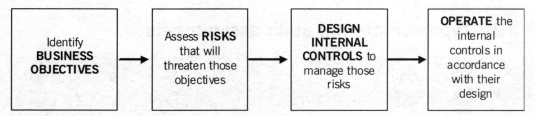

2.2.3 Weaknesses of systems audits

One criticism of systems-based audits is that they concentrate on whether existing systems are operating as intended. Auditors do not question the **underlying assessment** of risks that led to the systems being established, or whether the systems that were designed adequately address those risks. Risk-based audits (see below) are needed to ascertain whether the risk management processes are sufficient to **assess and manage risks**.

2.2.4 Compliance audits

KEY TERM

A COMPLIANCE AUDIT is the audit of specific activities in order to determine whether performance is in conformity with a predetermined contractual, regulatory or statutory requirement.

(CIMA Official Terminology)

The terms systems and compliance audits are used interchangeably, but in a stricter sense, compliance audits check whether activities fulfil **internal procedures,** contract terms, regulations or laws.

2.3 Risk-based audits

Risk-based audits are a development of systems audits, with the main focus being on the assessment of risks. Auditors will again be concerned to see that managers have made **adequate responses to risks**, have **designed robust risk management processes and internal control systems**, and that these risk management processes and controls operate to mitigate the risks.

The starting point for a risk audit is to identify **business objectives** and the **risks** that may prevent the organisation achieving those objectives. Then the auditors consider the organisation's **risk tolerance** and consider whether the risk management process appears to be **adequate** and **effective** for dealing with risks. If the **risk management processes** appear **sound**, the auditors will look to use management assessment of risks to determine their work; however if they are not sound the auditors will have to rely on their own assessments of risk whilst suggesting improvements.

Having taken an overall view earlier in the audit, auditors will concentrate on the **adequacy of risk management processes** and **controls** for each area to be covered, determine whether these processes are operating as intended, and seek to promote improvements where processes are inadequate or not operating as required.

2.4 Audit of accounting systems

The considerations relating to systems audits are particularly relevant to internal audit work on the major accounting areas. The auditors will be looking for evidence that **controls such as authorisations and reconciliations have been performed**, either by **observing** those controls being performed or **inspecting** documentary evidence. Other important work will include:

- Checking correctness of calculations and entry on documents
- Comparing documents from different sources for consistency
- Seeing whether the required documents have been completely maintained
- Inspecting security of assets

The appendix to Chapter 6 gives details about how individual accounting areas are audited and you may wish to revisit it now.

2.5 Operational audit assignments

Operational audits are a vital part of the **operational control process**, designed to confirm **adequacy and implementation** of control and risk management policies.

There are two aspects of an operational assignment:

- Ensure policies are **adequate**
- Ensure policies **work effectively**

2.5.1 Adequacy

The internal auditor will have to review the policies of a particular department by:

- **Reading** them
- **Discussion** with members of the department

Then the auditor will have to assess whether the policies are adequate, and possibly advise the board of improvements which could be made.

2.5.2 Effectiveness

The auditor will then have to examine the effectiveness of the controls by:

- **Observing them** in operation
- **Testing them**

2.6 Value for money and best value audits

Value for money audits focus on whether organisations have achieved economy, efficiency and effectiveness in their operations. Best value audits focus on challenge, consultation, comparison and competition.

2.6.1 Value for money audits

KEY TERM

A **VALUE FOR MONEY AUDIT** is an investigation into whether proper arrangements have been made for securing economy, efficiency and effectiveness in the use of resources.   (*CIMA Official Terminology*)

The three Es can be defined as follows.

(a) **Economy**

Attaining the **appropriate quantity and quality** of physical, human and financial resources (**inputs**) at **lowest cost**. An activity would not be economic if, for example, there was over-staffing or failure to purchase materials of requisite quality at the lowest available price.

(b) **Efficiency**

This is the relationship between **goods or services produced** (**outputs**) and the **resources** used to produce them. An efficient operation produces the maximum output for any given set of resource inputs; or it has minimum inputs for any given quantity and quality of product or service provided.

(c) **Effectiveness**

This is concerned with how well an **activity** is **achieving its policy objectives** or other intended effects.

The internal auditors will **evaluate these three factors** for any given business system or operation in the company. Value for money can often only be judged by **comparison**. In searching for value for money, present methods of operation and uses of resources must be **compared with alternatives**.

CASE STUDY

In the UK, the National Audit Office has two roles. It audits the accounts of all government departments and also reports to Parliament on the economy, efficiency and effectiveness with which these bodies have used public money. A recent VFM report published in February 2009 was about the efficiency of radio production at the BBC.

2.6.2 Best value audits

'Best value' is a new performance framework introduced into local authorities by the UK government. They are required to publish annual best value performance plans and review all of their functions over a five year period.

As part of 'Best value' authorities are required to strive for continuous improvement by implementing the '4 Cs':

- **Challenge**. How and why is a service provided?

- **Compare**. Make comparisons with other local authorities and the private sector.

- **Consult**. Talk to local taxpayers and service users and the wider business community in setting performance targets.

- **Compete**. Embrace fair competition as a means of securing efficient and effective services.

One of internal audit's **standard roles** in an organisation is to **provide assurance that internal control systems are adequate to promote the effective use of resources and that risks are being managed properly**.

In relation to best value, **this role can be extended** to ensure that the local authority has arrangements in place to achieve best value, that the risks and impacts of best value are incorporated into normal audit testing and that the authority keeps abreast of best value developments.

2.7 Management audits

KEY TERM

MANAGEMENT AUDIT is an objective and independent appraisal of the effectiveness of managers and the corporate structure in the achievement of entity objectives and policies. Its aim is to identify existing and potential management weaknesses and to recommend ways to rectify them. (*CIMA Official Terminology*)

2.7.1 Purpose of management audit

A management audit might be thought of as a **non-routine investigation** into the performance of a manager or group of managers which, unlike financial audits by internal or external auditors, attempts to look at all aspects of the management performance, and does not concentrate solely on financial matters.

2.7.2 Carrying out a management audit

Like any other audit, a management audit involves deciding the **audit objectives** (which managers to audit, what aspects of their work and so on), **carrying out an investigation, gathering evidence and reporting the results.**

Management audits can cover a wide variety of situations, for example to consider whether management policies are being applied to purchase of company cars, promotions and the sale of non-current assets no longer in use.

2.7.3 Management audit and the three Es

Auditing of a manager's efficiency and economy calls for obtaining evidence on whether the manager has used his or her **resources** (labour, materials, non-current assets, other assets, and management information) in the **best way** and without overspending and waste.

Similarly, auditing of a manager's **effectiveness** in his or her job calls for obtaining evidence on whether a manager has had a **clear objective** (or objectives) and **sufficient authority** and **resources** to achieve that **objective**, and whether the objective (or objectives) have in fact been **achieved**.

Audits of **economy** can also be much more detailed. The auditors can look into the items of expenditure incurred by a manager, to assess whether they have been excessive, or perhaps inadequate.

Exam alert

Management audit may be part of a wider question on management control systems and methods.

2.8 Social and environmental audits

Social and environmental audits are designed to ascertain whether the organisation is complying with **codes of best practice** or **internal guidelines** or is fulfilling the wider requirements of being a **good corporate citizen**.

2.8.1 Social audits

The process of checking whether an organisation has achieved set targets may fall within a social audit that a company carries out. Social audits may cover sustainable use of resources, health and safety compliance, labour conditions and equal opportunities.

Social audits will involve:

- Establishing whether the organisation has a **rationale** for engaging in socially responsible activity

- Identifying that all current environment programmes are **congruent** with the mission of the company

- **Assessing objectives and priorities** related to these programmes

- **Evaluating company involvement** in such programmes past, present and future

Whether or not a social audit is used depends on the degree to which social responsibility is part of the **corporate philosophy**. A cultural awareness must be achieved within an organisation in order to implement environmental policy, which requires Board and staff support.

2.8.2 Environmental audits

KEY TERM

An ENVIRONMENTAL AUDIT is a systematic, documented, periodic and objective evaluation of how well an entity, its management and equipment are performing with the aim of helping to safeguard the environment by facilitating management control of environmental practices and assessing compliance with entity policies and external compliance with entity policies and external regulations.

(CIMA Official Terminology)

An environmental audit might be undertaken as part of obtaining or maintaining the BSI's ISO 14001 standard.

Auditors will mainly be concerned with the following:

- Board and management having **good understanding** of the environmental impact and related legislation of the organisation's activities in areas such as buildings, transport, products, packaging and waste

- Adoption and communication of adequate policies and procedures to ensure **compliance with relevant standards and laws**

- Adoption and **review of progress** against quantifiable targets

- Assessment of whether **progress** is being made **economically and efficiently**

- **True, fair and complete reporting** of environmental activities

Exam alert

Environmental auditing's increased importance as an area for internal audit work was reflected by its inclusion in Question 1 of the specimen paper.

2.9 Assessing the performance of internal audit

The performance of internal audit can be judged by various criteria. The Institute of Internal Auditors has issued standards for internal auditors which can be used in this assessment and which we discuss in more detail in Section 4 below.

As mentioned in Section 1, the board or audit committee of the organisation should conduct an annual review of the internal auditors' work in line with the Turnbull guidance. The reviews should include the following areas:

2.9.1 Scope of work

The review will be particularly concerned with the work done to test:

- The **adequacy, effectiveness** and value for money of internal control
- Risk assessment and management processes
- **Compliance with laws, regulations** and **policies**
- **Safeguarding** of assets
- **Reliability** of information
- **Value for money**
- **Attainment** of organisation's **objectives** and **goals**

It should be possible to see from the plans that internal audit submits to the audit committee that internal audit's work does forward the organisation's aims and that internal audit is **responsive** to organisational change.

2.9.2 Authority

The review should cover the formal **terms of reference** and assess whether they are adequate.

It should consider whether there are senior personnel in the organisation who can ensure that the scope of internal audit's work is **sufficiently broad**, that there is **adequate consideration** of **audit reports** and **appropriate action** on audit findings and recommendations.

2.9.3 Independence

The review should consider carefully whether there are **adequate safeguards** in place to ensure the independence of internal audit. These include reporting by the head of internal audit to the audit committee, dismissal of the head of internal audit being the responsibility of the board or audit committee, internal auditors not assuming operational responsibilities and internal auditors being excluded from systems, design, installation and operation work.

2.9.4 Resources

Again the review should consider the documentation provided by internal audit and confirm that resourcing plans indicate that there will be **sufficient resources** to review all areas. This should be assessed not just in terms of the hours set aside but also physical resources such as computers, and also of course the necessary **knowledge, skills and disciplines**.

Exam alert

You could be asked how the effectiveness of internal audit should be assessed. Remember the assessment should reflect the objectives of internal audit; hence a range of measures is likely to be used.

2.9.5 Value for money

The UK's Chartered Institute of Public Finance and Accountancy (CIPFA) has highlighted the need to look at internal audit from the point of view of value for money. The review should consider the **economy, efficiency and effectiveness** (the 3Es) of internal audit.

Section summary

Internal audit work can cover a range of different types of audit, the most common of which are **transactions** audits and **systems audits**.

Other assignments include **value for money audits** (focusing on **economy**, **efficiency** and **effectiveness**), **best value audits** (which are specific to UK local authorities), **management audits**. **Social** and **environmental audits** have also been given a higher profile in recent years.

Formal **quality control procedures** should be used to assess the work of internal audit, which should also consider the **value for money** provided by the internal audit function.

3 Internal and external audit

Introduction

In this section we look at the role of external auditors and their relationship with internal auditors. It is important to understand the differences between internal and external auditors in terms of their objectives, reporting responsibilities, scope of work and relationship to the organisation.

KEY TERM

EXTERNAL AUDIT is a periodic examination of the books of account and records of an entity carried out by an independent third party (the auditor), to ensure that they have been properly maintained, are accurate and comply with established concepts, principles, accounting standards, legal requirements and give a true and fair view of the financial state of the entity.   (*CIMA Official Terminology*)

3.1 Differences between internal and external audit

The following table highlights the differences between internal and external audit.

	Internal audit	External audit
Objective	Internal audit is an activity designed to **add value** and improve an **organisation's operations**.	External audit is an exercise to enable auditors to **express an opinion on the financial statements**.
Reporting	Internal audit reports to the **board of directors**, or others charged with governance, such as the audit committee.	The external auditors report to the **shareholders**, or members, of a company on the stewardship of the directors.
Scope	Internal audit's work relates to the **operations of the organisation**.	External audit's work relates to the **financial statements**.
Relationship with the organisation	Internal auditors are very often **employees of the organisation**, although sometimes the internal audit function is **outsourced**.	External auditors are **independent of the company and its management**. They are appointed by the shareholders.

The table shows that although some of the procedures that internal audit undertake are very similar to those undertaken by the external auditors, the whole **basis** and **reasoning** of their work is fundamentally **different**.

The **difference** in **objectives** is particularly important. Every definition of internal audit suggests that it has a **much wider scope** than external audit, which has the objective of considering whether the accounts give a true and fair view of the organisation's financial position.

3.2 External audit process

As stated in the definition above, the external audit process is undertaken to conclude whether an entity's financial statements are **true and fair**. The external audit provides assurance to shareholders because it is **independent** and **impartial**. In many countries, external audits are required by legislation for most companies. For example, in the UK, this legislation is provided by the Companies Act 2006.

External audits have to be carried out in accordance with strict standards and legislation. **International Standards on Auditing (ISAs)** are prepared by the International Auditing and Assurance Standards Board, a part of the International Federation of Accountants, and provide guidance to external auditors on different aspects of the audit process. Examples of ISAs include ISA 300 *Planning an audit of financial statements* and ISA 570 *Going concern*.

3.2.1 Planning

The external audit process begins with **planning**. The purpose of this stage is to gain an understanding of the entity being audited and to identify any potential **risks** which could result in material misstatements in the financial statements. This stage is characterised by the use of analytical procedures and documentation and testing of systems such as sales and purchases.

3.2.2 Fieldwork

Once planning and risk assessment are completed, the auditor undertakes **audit fieldwork** to gain **audit evidence** to support the figures disclosed in the accounts. Depending on whether reliance can be placed on controls, this will involve either tests of controls and minimum substantive work or a wholly substantive-based audit.

3.2.3 Completion

The audit **completion** stage is a key stage of the audit involving the use of analytical review, work on going concern and a review of events occurring after the end of the reporting period. After this stage, the auditors will issue their audit report which contains their opinion on the financial statements. A by-product of the external audit is the **report to management** (also commonly referred to as the **letter of weakness** or **management letter**) which sets out control weaknesses found during the audit and recommendations to mitigate them.

The following diagram summarises the external audit process.

Chronology of an audit

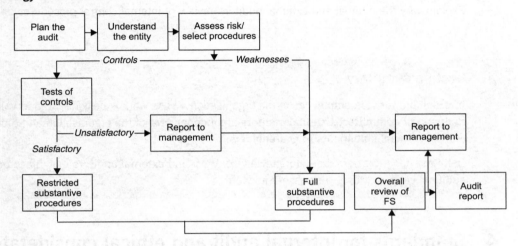

CASE STUDY

A survey by the Institute of Chartered Accountants in England and Wales that was published in April 2010 suggested that the audit report did not provide helpful information. External auditors should express a more subjective view to help investors and regulators make decisions.

Audit report users considered that the external audit report was a compliance document and that standardisation meant that they were unable to judge the quality of external audit firms. Instead there should be more detail in the audit report about the risks companies faced.

However bankers and auditors were unhappy about giving subjective opinions, fearing that it could increase the likelihood that they would be sued.

3.3 Relationship between external and internal audit

Co-ordination between the external and internal auditors of an organisation will minimise duplication of work and encourage a wide coverage of audit issues and areas. Examples include attendance at inventory or cash counts, systems audits, operational audits.

However, before the external auditors can place reliance on the work of the internal auditors, they must assess the internal audit function, as with any part of the system of internal control. Guidance on this is provided by ISA 610 *Considering the work of internal auditing*. The following important criteria will be considered by the external auditors.

- Organisational status
- Scope of function

- Technical competence
- Due professional care

Question 15.1

Learning outcome C2(a)

The growing recognition by management of the benefits of good internal control, and the complexities of an adequate system of internal control have led to the development of internal auditing as a form of control over all other internal controls. The emergence of internal auditors as specialists in internal control is the result of an evolutionary process similar in many ways to the evolution of independent auditing.

Required

Explain why the internal and external auditors' review of internal control procedures differ in purpose.

Section summary

Internal auditors are **employees** of the organisation whose work is designed to **add value** and who report to the **audit committee. External auditors** are **independent** of the organisation and their role is to **report on the financial statements to shareholders**.

Both internal and external auditors review controls, and **external auditors** may **place reliance on internal auditors' work** providing they assess its worth.

---

4 Standards for internal audit and ethical considerations

Introduction

In this final section, we look at standards in place for internal audit and also examine ethical considerations for internal auditors.

4.1 IIA Standards

Whatever the scope of internal audit all staff should be aware of the standards to which they are working.

The Institute of Internal Auditors has produced a series of standards covering all areas of internal auditing. The standards comprise five general standards supported by more specific standards with accompanying guidance.

4.2 Professional proficiency

Internal audits should be performed with **proficiency** and **due professional care**. There are specific standards on the following areas.

- Appropriate staffing
- Knowledge, skills and disciplines
- Supervision
- Compliance with professional standards
- Human relations and communications
- Continuing education
- Due professional care

4.3 Scope of work

The scope of internal audit's work should include **assessment** of the **adequacy** and **effectiveness** of the internal control system and quality of performance. The assessment should include consideration of whether the organisation has met the following objectives.

- Reliability and integrity of information
- Compliance with policies, plans, procedures, laws and regulations
- Safeguarding of assets
- Economical and efficient use of resources
- Accomplishment of established objectives and goals for operations and programmes

4.4 Performance of audit work

Performance should include the following stages.

- Planning the audit
- Examining and evaluating information
- Communicating results
- Follow up of work

4.5 Management of internal audit

The chief internal auditor should manage the internal audit department properly. If the department is running well, it should have the following features.

- A statement of purpose, authority and responsibility
- Thorough planning
- Written policies and procedures
- A programme for personnel management and development
- Co-ordination with external auditors
- A quality assurance system

4.6 Ethical issues – independence and objectivity

We looked at ethics in detail in Chapter 4.

Internal auditors should be independent of the activities audited. This involves having **sufficient status** within the organisation and **objectivity**.

Although an internal audit department is part of an organisation, it should be **independent** of the **line management** whose sphere of authority it may audit. The department should therefore report to the board or to a special internal audit committee and not to the finance director.

The reason for this is best seen by thinking about what could happen if the internal audit department reported some kind of irregularity to a finance director without realising that the finance director was actually involved. The director would take the report and decide that it was all very interesting, but not worth pursuing. A very different line might be taken by another, independent director!

Internal auditors should also have **appropriate scope** in carrying out their responsibilities, and unrestricted access to records, assets and personnel.

CASE STUDY

Spencer Pickett in the *Internal Auditing Handbook* suggests that the concept of independence involves a number of key qualities:

Objectivity	Judgements are made in a state of detachment from the situation or decision
Impartiality	Not taking sides, in particular not being influenced by office politics in determining the work carried out and the reports given
Unbiased views	Avoiding the perception that internal audit is out to 'hit' certain individuals or departments
Valid opinion	The audit opinion should be based on all relevant factors, rather than being one that pleases everyone
No spying for management	Again internal audit should serve the whole organisation; also managers who want their staff targeted might be trying to cover up their own inadequacies
No no-go areas	Being kept away from certain areas will fatally undermine the usefulness of internal audit and mean that aggressive (incompetent?) managers are not checked
Sensitive areas audited	Internal audit must have the abilities and skills to audit complex areas effectively
Senior management audited	Internal audit must cover the management process and not just audit the detailed operational areas
No backing-off	Audit objectives must be pursued fully in a professional manner and auditors must not allow aggressive managers to deflect them from doing necessary work and issuing valid opinions

Question 15.2

Reporting to board

Learning outcome C3(b)

Explain the reasons why internal auditors should or should not report their findings on internal control to the board of directors.

Question 15.3

Independence

Learning outcomes C2(a), C3(b)

KEY TERM

KEY TERM key terms are styled with Key term text character style. Key terms may appear anywhere within the text and are highlighted with an icon. THE KEY TERM IS IN SMALL CAPITALS, SO PLEASE TYPE ONLY THE FIRST LETTER WITH A CAPITAL!

Suppose the same audit firm offered both internal and external audit services to the same client by virtue of the client outsourcing its internal audit function.

(a)   What do you think are the independence issues?
(b)   Why should the issues affect the external audit team rather than the internal audit team?

Section summary

Internal audit standards cover **professional proficiency, scope of work, performance, management**, and most importantly **independence**.

Chapter Roundup

✓ The role of internal audit will **vary** according to the **organisation's objectives** but is likely to include review **of internal control systems, risk management, legal compliance** and **value for money.**

✓ Internal audit work can cover a range of different types of audit, the most common of which are **transactions audits** and **systems audits.**

✓ Other assignments include **value for money audits** (focusing on **economy, efficiency** and **effectiveness**), **best value audits** (which are specific to UK local authorities), **management audits. Social** and **environmental audits** have also been given a higher profile in recent years.

✓ Formal **quality control procedures** should be used to assess the work of internal audit, which should also consider the **value for money** provided by the internal audit function.

✓ **Internal auditors** are **employees** of the organisation whose work is designed to **add value** and who report to the **audit committee. External auditors** are **independent** of the organisation and their role is to **report on the financial statements to shareholders.**

✓ Both internal and external auditors review controls, and **external auditors** may **place reliance on internal auditors' work** providing they assess its worth.

✓ Internal audit standards cover **professional proficiency, scope of work, performance, management,** and most importantly **independence.**

Quick Quiz

1 Fill in the blank.

A .... is the audit of specific activities in order to determine whether performance conforms with a predetermined contractual, regulatory, or statutory requirement.

2 What are the main elements of internal audit's review of the accounting and control systems?

3 Link the value for money 'E' with its definition.

   (a) Economy

   (b) Efficiency

   (c) Effectiveness

   (i) The relationships between the goods and services produced (outputs) and the resources used to produce them.

   (ii) The concern with how well an activity is achieving its policy objectives or other intended effects.

   (iii) Attaining the appropriate quantity and quality of physical, human and financial resources (inputs) at lowest cost.

4 In the context of best value audits which of the following is not one of the four C's?

   A Challenge
   B Compare
   C Consult
   D Compute

5 What sort of areas might be covered by a social audit?

6 Name three key differences between internal and external audit.

7   What matters would the external auditors consider when assessing the internal audit function?

8   It is possible to buy in an internal audit service from an external organisation.

True   ☐

False   ☐

Answers to Quick Quiz

1   A **compliance audit** is the audit of specific activities in order to determine whether performance conforms with a predetermined contractual, regulatory or statutory requirement.

2   • Reviewing the design of systems
     • Monitoring the operation of systems by risk assessment and detailed testing
     • Recommending cost effective improvements

3   (a)(iii), (b)(i), (c)(ii)

4   D   Compute. Compete is the C missing from the list in the question.

5   • Sustainable use of resources
     • Compliance with health and safety
     • Labour conditions
     • Equal opportunities

6   External report to members, internal to directors
     External report on financial statements, internal on systems, controls and risks
     External are independent of the company, internal often employed by it

7   • Organisational status
     • Scope of function
     • Technical competence
     • Due professional care

8   True

Answers to Questions

15.1 Internal and external audit

The internal auditors **review and test the system of internal control** and report to management in order to **improve the information** received by managers and to help in their task of running the company. The internal auditors will recommend changes to the system to make sure that management receive objective information that is efficiently produced. The internal auditors will also have a duty to search for and discover fraud.

The external auditors **review the system of internal control** in order to **determine the extent of the substantive work** required on the year-end accounts. The external **auditors report** to the **shareholders** rather than the managers or directors. It is usual, however, for the external auditors to issue a letter of weakness to the managers, laying out any areas of weakness and recommendations for improvement in the system of internal control. The external auditors report on the **truth and fairness** of the financial statements, not directly on the system of internal control. The auditors do not have a specific duty to detect fraud, although they should plan the audit procedures so as to have reasonable assurance that they will detect any material misstatement in the accounts on which they give an opinion.

15.2 Reporting to board

A high level of independence is achieved by the internal auditors if they report directly to the Board. However, there may be problems with this approach.

(1)   The members of the Board may **not understand all the implications** of the internal audit reports when accounting or technical information is required.

(2)   The Board may **not have enough time** to spend considering the reports in sufficient depth. Important recommendations might therefore remain unimplemented.

A way around these problems might be to delegate the review of internal audit reports to an **audit committee**, which would act as a kind of sub-committee to the main board. The audit committee should be made up largely of non-executive directors who have more time and more independence from the day-to-day running of the company, and who possess the necessary financial knowledge.

15.3 Independence

(a)   External auditors are employed to give an assurance to the members of a company about the stewardship of the directors and the management of that entity. They are **independent verifiers**. If the firm provides internal audit services to the entity, two issues arise:

(i)   Internal auditors report to the directors so there is a **link between the firm and the directors** which is a block to independence.

(ii)   The firm provides 'other services' to an external audit client, and the partners must consider whether this affects their objectivity in relation to the audit, and renders them no longer impartial.

(b)   The issues arise for the external audit team as independence is a key ethical issue for external auditors. As internal auditors provide a service to the directors, by whom they are employed, the issue of independence is a more tricky issue. It relates more to 'independence in the mind'. Internal auditors are not required to be 'seen to be independent' in the same way that external auditors are.

Now try these questions from the Exam Question Bank

Number	Level	Marks	Time
Q24	Introductory	N/A	30 mins
Q25	Examination	20	36 mins
Q26	Examination	25	45 mins

INTERNAL AUDIT REVIEW AND REPORTING

 We looked at the role of internal audit in the previous chapter and considered its relationship with external audit. In this chapter, our focus is on the work performed by internal auditors when carrying out an assignment and the reporting of their findings to the audit committee.

Fist we consider the necessity of planning and risk assessment. Each level of planning is vital to a well-directed internal audit function – it is important to focus on long-term strategic aims, and select the right areas to work on, as well as carrying out the most appropriate tests within those areas.

We also consider how internal auditors document the systems they are going to examine, through the use of flow charts and internal control questionnaires for example.

A key test used by internal auditors is sampling, which we will examine in some detail. They also use analytical review which help identify risky areas.

Computer-assisted audit techniques are used by internal auditors when auditing in a computerised environment, the main ones being audit software and test data.

The recording and control of internal audit is just as important as good planning so we will also consider this in this chapter.

We then examine the reporting of internal audit to the audit committee. We finish the text by looking at the high level of systems and controls that the management of all organisations should undertake.

16

topic list	learning outcomes	syllabus references	ability required
1 Audit planning	C1(a), C2(b)	C1(ii)	evaluation
2 Risk analysis	C2(c), (d)	C2(iii)	evaluation
3 Documenting systems	C1(a)	C1(ii)	evaluation
4 Audit evidence	C2(b)	C2(ii)	evaluation
5 Audit sampling and CAATs	C1(a), E1(e)	C1(ii), E1(xiii)	evaluation
6 Analytical review	C2(b)	C2(iii)	evaluation
7 Internal audit control and reporting	C2(c), (d)	C2(iii)	evaluation
8 The audit committee	C1(a), C3(a)	C1(i), C3(i)	evaluation
9 Management review of internal controls	C1(a), C3(a)	C1(i), C3(i)	evaluation

1 Audit planning

Introduction

In this section, we consider the need for internal auditors to plan their work through the preparation of strategic, tactical and operational plans.

1.1 Aims of audit planning

As with any other activity or enterprise, an internal audit department must plan its work carefully if it is to achieve the audit objectives efficiently and effectively. The aim of audit planning is:

(a) **Decide priorities** for audit work
(b) **Establish objectives** (and apply control measures to ensure that objectives are achieved)
(c) Ensure that audit resources are used **efficiently**, **effectively** and **cost-effectively**

1.2 Strategic audit planning

The strategic plan sets out audit objectives in broad terms, including areas to be covered, frequency of coverage and rough estimates of resource requirements.

Usually, the strategic plan covers a period of two to five years. It must be **regularly reviewed** and adjusted in the light of any changes of audit requirements or any information arising out of audit work.

1.2.1 Selecting areas for investigation

The internal auditors then have to consider what areas need to be investigated. Sometimes management will instruct them to look into a certain topic, but for the most part, the internal auditors need some yardstick which they can use to determine whether some segment of the company is important enough to merit investigation. By segment of the company we mean, for example, a specific function or business process, or a transactions flow, or even the work of a physical department located somewhere in the building.

Suppose the internal auditors are considering whether the work of a section which authorises invoices for payment is worth investigation. The criteria which they should bear in mind while making this judgement are as follows.

(a) **Financial**

The volume and size of income and expenditure transactions, or the value of assets

(b) **Internal control**

The existence or otherwise of controls

(c) **Probity**

Whether there is any evidence of past inaccuracies or fraud

(d) **Business goals**

Whether the organisation has laid down explicit objectives and policies against which its achievements can be measured

(e) **Business effects**

Whether the business generates any consequences, internal or external, which need to be investigated

(f)   **Value for money**

Whether there is likely to be any waste which can be eliminated

(g)   **Special investigations**

Whether management has requested the internal audit department to undertake any specific tasks

1.3 Tactical audit planning

Once the internal auditors have set out their strategic plan, and agreed it with management, it is necessary to prepare a **tactical plan**.

In many ways a tactical audit plan is the easiest type of audit plan to draw up. Basically, it takes the **areas of work** laid down in the strategic plan and matches them to audit resources and timetables. It covers a period of about six months to a year, and will include the following features.

*   **Programme** of internal audits to be carried out
*   Detailed definition of the **objectives** of each audit
*   Detailed **allocation** of audit **resources**

1.4 Operational audit planning

An operational internal audit plan will be drawn up for each **individual audit**. It is based on the **objectives** as broadly indicated in the strategic plan, on resource and timetabling considerations within the tactical plan, on results of previous audits, and any other relevant data. When completed, it should show:

*   **Detailed audit objectives**
*   The **extent of coverage** and areas to be given emphasis
*   **Target dates** for individual stages of the audit
*   **Names of auditors** responsible for or involved in the completion of the audit

Section summary

An internal audit department should plan its work carefully through the preparation of **strategic**, **tactical** and **operational plans**.

2 Risk analysis   5/10

Introduction

In this section, we look at risk assessment and why internal auditors must undertake this important task.

2.1 Business risk

In Part A of this Study Text we looked at the different risks organisations face. Internal audit will often start their assessment by considering **business risk**.

KEY TERM

BUSINESS RISK is the risk relating to activities carried out within an entity arising from structure, systems, people, products or processes.   (*CIMA Official Terminology*)

The internal auditors, when planning their audit work, will try to concentrate on those areas and activities of the business which represent the highest **business risk**. There are many different ways of assessing business risk, but the CIMA document *A Framework for Internal Control* offers one approach. This approach would be used by internal audit or by executive management.

2.2 Assessment of business risks

An appendix to the CIMA document splits the assessment of business risks into three parts.

- Inherent risk
- Quality of control
- Risk formula

2.2.1 Inherent risk

KEY TERM

INHERENT RISK is the level of risk relating to an activity irrespective of the quality of the associated control system or the effectiveness of management.

The document then lists factors which might be taken into account when assessing inherent risk.

- **Relative size of the unit**, with reference to operational budget, capital employed and volume of transactions

- The **nature of the transactions**, taking account of unit values and convertibility

- **Complexity** of operations

- **Convertibility of assets**, with reference to liquidity, desirability, portability etc

- The extent of reliance on **computerised systems**

- **Sensitivity** to political exposure and adverse publicity

2.2.2 Quality of control

KEY TERM

QUALITY OF CONTROL is the assessment of the adequacy of control that an error or misstatement would not be prevented, or detected and corrected on a timely basis by the internal control system. This concept is similar to **control risk**.

Quality of control takes into account the following factors.

- **Managerial effectiveness**, including the competence and integrity of managerial and supervisory personnel

- The **extent of change** since the last review, such as the following.

    - Changes to the accounting system or procedures
    - Changes in key personnel
    - High staff turnover
    - Rapid growth
    - Pressure on management to meet objectives

- **Time elapsed** since the last review.

2.2.3 Risk formula

Risks can be formally assessed by using an **index** which is applied to the areas under consideration and provides a kind of ranking as to which business activities are most at risk and therefore most in need of examination.

The CIMA document gives an example of such a risk assessment system. Each value is multiplied by its weighting and the results added together to give a total inherent risk (A to F) and total quality of control (G to J). These two figures are then multiplied together to produce the overall business risk of each activity. The higher the rating, the higher the business risk. In the CIMA example, factors are weighted to give a maximum of 10 for each inherent and control risk, giving a maximum overall business risk of 100 (10×10), which gives a form of indexation.

Risk assessment: factors, values and weightings

Factor		Values	Weighting
Inherent risk			
A	Size of unit: in terms of operational budget, capital employed, volume and value of output	1 – Insignificant 2 – Small 3 – Medium 4 – Large	0.5
B	Nature of output: in terms of unit value and convertibility eg transactions	1 – Minimal 2 – Low risk 3 – Medium risk 4 – High risk	0.5
C	Complexity of operation	1 – Simple to 4 – Extremely complex	0.5
D	Convertibility of assets: in terms of liquidity, desirability, portability etc	1 – Minimal 2 – Low risk 3 – Medium risk 4 – High risk	0.5
E	Extent of computerisation	1 – Minimal use 2 – Moderate use 3 – Larger or complex systems 4 – Total reliance on systems	0.25
F	Sensitivity to public and political exposure	1 – Not sensitive 2 – Some sensitivity 3 – Significant 4 – High profile	0.25
Quality of control			
G	Adequacy of control (as at last review)	1 – Adequate 2 – Minor reservations 3 – Major reservations 4 – No controls (or not previously reviewed)	1.0
H	Managerial effectiveness	1 – Totally effective 2 – Minor reservations 3 – Major reservations 4 – Ineffective (or not previously reviewed)	0.5
I	Change factor (since last review)	1 – No change 2 – Minor change 3 – Moderate change 4 – Significant change	0.5
J	Elapsed time since last review	1 – Less than 1 year 2 – 1-2 years 3 – 2-3 years 4 – More than 3 years	0.5

Question 16.1   Risk assessment

Learning outcome C1(a)

Using the risk assessment table above, work out an overall risk factor for the following two departments, showing the inherent and control risk factors.

Factor	Dept X	Dept Y
A	2	4
B	3	3
C	1	4
D	4	3
E	4	3
F	1	3
G	3	1
H	2	2
I	1	4
J	4	2

Clearly this technique is far from perfect. The factors, point ranges and weighting factors all have to be **determined judgementally** by the internal auditors and so does the marking index awarded. Nevertheless, many internal audit departments do use risk indexation, on the grounds that any attempt at evaluating risk is better than no attempt, and at least it provides a basis for directing audit resources towards what appear to be the areas of highest risk.

2.3 Business risk – an alternative view

As we mentioned in Chapter 1, there are various ways of defining business risk. Another definition is discussed below.

KEY TERM

BUSINESS RISK is the threat that an event or action will adversely affect an organisation's ability to achieve its business objectives and execute its strategies effectively. It is the potential for events, actions or inactions to result in the failure of a business to meet its key business objectives, or its failure to define objectives that are responsive to key stakeholders.

Different types of business risks will be considered. An important distinction in an analysis of business risk is likely to be between **environment risks** (those that affect the external environment), and **process risks** (which affect a company's internal activities).

An audit of financial information based on business risks would then consider how the business risks might affect the **processing of data**, how it might cause **inaccuracy and incompleteness** of **processing** or affect its timeliness. In turn **how data** is processed will **affect** the **preparation** of, and **disclosures** in, the financial statements.

Having considered the possible consequences of business risks, the introduction of business processes to manage those risks and a sound control environment can then be considered.

2.4 Other elements in risk assessment

As well as these considerations, other factors that may determine the extent of audit work include:

- The **volume of transactions**
- The **impact on business continuity**
- The **likelihood and consequences of risks materialising**

Exam alert

May 2010 Question 4 asked about the auditor risk assessment of IT systems.

Section summary

Business risk can be assessed as two components, **inherent risk** and **quality of control** (or **control risk**).

The internal auditors may use the technique of **risk analysis** to assist them in drawing up a strategic plan.

3 Documenting systems

Introduction

In this section we consider how internal auditors can document the systems they are going to test. They can do this using a variety of tools, from simple narrative notes to complex flowcharts to internal control questionnaires.

There are several techniques for recording systems. One or more of the following may be used depending on the complexity of the system.

- Narrative notes
- Flowcharts
- Questionnaires
- Checklists

We will look at the use of questionnaires here in more detail. There are two types, each with a different purpose.

- **Internal Control Questionnaires (ICQs)** are used to ask whether controls exist which meet specific control objectives.

- **Internal Control Evaluation Questionnaires (ICEQs)** are used to determine whether there are controls which prevent or detect specified errors or omissions.

3.1 Internal Control Questionnaires (ICQs)

The major question which internal control questionnaires are designed to answer is 'How good is the system of controls?'

Although there are many different forms of ICQ in practice, they all conform to the following basic principles:

(a)   A list of questions designed to determine whether desirable controls are present
(b)   Each of the major transaction cycles is covered

Since it is the primary purpose of an ICQ to evaluate the system rather than describe it, one of the most effective ways of designing the questionnaire is to phrase the questions so that all the answers can be given as 'YES' or 'NO' and a 'NO' answer indicates a weakness in the system. An example would be:

Are purchase invoices checked to goods received notes before being passed for payment?   YES/NO/Comments

A 'NO' answer to that question clearly indicates a weakness in the company's payment procedures.

3.2 Internal Control Evaluation Questionnaires (ICEQs)

ICEQs are designed to assess whether specific errors (or frauds) are possible rather than to establish whether certain desirable controls are present.

This is achieved by reducing the control criteria for each transaction stream down to a handful of key questions (or control questions). These questions concentrate on the significant errors or omissions that could occur at each phase of the appropriate cycle if controls are weak. An example question for the purchases cycle would be:

> Is there reasonable assurance that:
>
> • Receipt of goods or services is required in order to establish a liability?

Each key control question is supported by detailed control points to be considered. For example, for the key control question above, the detailed control points to be considered could include:

> • Is segregation of duties satisfactory?
>
> • Are controls over relevant master files satisfactory?
>
> • Is there a record that all goods received have been checked for weight or number and quality and damage?

Alternatively, ICEQ questions can be phrased so that the weakness which should be prevented by a key control is highlighted, such as the following:

		Comments or explanation of 'yes' answer
Question	*Answer*	
Can goods be sent to unauthorised suppliers?		

In these cases a 'YES' answer would require an explanation, rather than a 'NO' answer.

Section summary

Internal auditors can record the entity's systems through the use of **narrative notes**, **flowcharts**, **questionnaires** or **checklists**.

4 Audit evidence

Introduction

In this section we shall look at the audit evidence auditors have gathered that **enables** them to express an opinion.

4.1 Audit evidence and audit tests

Audit evidence includes all the information contained within the accounting records underlying the financial statements, and other information gathered by the auditors, such as confirmations from third parties. Auditors **do not look at all the information** that might exist. They will often select samples, as we shall see in Section 5.

In order to reach a position in which they can express an opinion, the auditors need to gather evidence from various sources. There are two types of test which they will carry out.

KEY TERM

TESTS OF CONTROLS are performed to obtain audit evidence about the effectiveness of the:

- **Design** of the accounting and internal control systems, ie whether they are suitably designed to prevent or detect and correct material misstatements

- **Operation** of the internal controls throughout the period

SUBSTANTIVE PROCEDURES are tests to obtain audit evidence to detect material misstatements in the accounts. They are generally of two types:

- Analytical procedures

- Other substantive procedures such as tests of detail of transactions and balances, review of minutes of directors' meetings and enquiry

The International Audit and Assurance Standards Board's ISA 500 *Audit evidence* requires auditors to 'design and perform audit procedures that are appropriate in the circumstances for the purpose of obtaining sufficient appropriate audit evidence'.

4.2 Sufficient appropriate audit evidence

'Sufficiency' and 'appropriateness' are interrelated and apply to both tests of controls and substantive procedures.

- **Sufficiency** is the measure of the **quantity** of audit evidence.

- **Appropriateness** is the measure of the **quality** or **reliability** of the audit evidence.

The **quantity** of audit evidence required is affected by the **level of risk** in the area being audited. It is also affected by the **quality** of evidence obtained. If the evidence is high quality, the auditor may need less than if it were poor quality. However, obtaining a high quantity of poor quality evidence will not cancel out its poor quality. The following generalisations may help in assessing the **reliability** of audit evidence.

QUALITY OF EVIDENCE	
External	Audit evidence from **external sources** is more reliable than that obtained from the entity's records.
Auditor	Evidence obtained **directly by auditors** is more reliable than that obtained indirectly or by inference
Entity	Evidence obtained from the entity's records is more reliable when related **control systems operate effectively**
Written	Evidence in the form of **documents (paper or electronic)** or **written representations** are more reliable than oral representations
Originals	Original documents are more reliable than photocopies, or facsimiles

Auditors will often use information produced by the entity when obtaining audit evidence, although this will not always be a strong form of audit evidence. When doing so, the ISA requires that the auditor 'obtain audit evidence about the **accuracy and completeness** of the information'. This may be achieved by testing controls in the related area, or by other methods, for example, computer assisted audit techniques (see below).

Exam alert

You may be asked to consider how strong certain evidence is from the auditor's viewpoint.

4.3 Financial statement assertions

Audit tests are designed to obtain evidence about the financial statement assertions. Although they are most relevant to the work of the external auditors, they have relevance to some of the work carried on by internal audit.

ISA 315 states that 'the auditor should use assertions for **classes of transactions**, **account balances**, and **presentation and disclosures** in sufficient detail to form the basis for the assessment of risks of material misstatement and the design and performance of further audit procedures'. It gives examples of assertions in these areas.

Assertions used by the auditor	
Assertions about **classes of transactions** and events for the period under audit	**Occurrence**: transactions and events that have been recorded have occurred and pertain to the entity.
	Completeness: all transactions and events that should have been recorded have been recorded.
	Accuracy: amounts and other data relating to recorded transactions and events have been recorded appropriately.
	Cutoff: transactions and events have been recorded in the correct accounting period.
	Classification: transactions and events have been recorded in the proper accounts.
Assertions about **account balances** at the period end	**Existence**: assets, liabilities and equity interests exist.
	Rights and obligations: the entity holds or controls the rights to assets, and liabilities are the obligations of the entity.
	Completeness: all assets, liabilities and equity interests that should have been recorded have been recorded.
	Valuation and allocation: assets, liabilities, and equity interests are included in the financial statements at appropriate amounts and any resulting valuation or allocation adjustments are appropriately recorded.
Assertions about **presentation and disclosure**	**Occurrence and rights and obligations**: disclosed events, transactions and other matters have occurred and pertain to the entity.
	Completeness: all disclosures that should have been included in the financial statements have been included.
	Classification and understandability: financial information is appropriately presented and described, and disclosures are clearly expressed.
	Accuracy and valuation: financial and other information are disclosed fairly and at appropriate amounts.

4.4 Audit procedures

Auditors obtain evidence by one or more of the following procedures, sometimes referred to as **analytical review**.

PROCEDURES	
Inspection of assets	Inspection of assets that are recorded in the accounting records confirms existence, gives evidence of valuation, but does not confirm rights and obligations
	Confirmation that assets seen are recorded in accounting records gives evidence of completeness

PROCEDURES	
Inspection of documentation	Confirmation to documentation of items recorded in accounting records confirms that an asset exists or a transaction occurred. Confirmation that items recorded in supporting documentation are recorded in accounting records tests completeness
	Cut-off can be verified by inspecting reverse population ie checking transactions recorded after the date of the statement of financial position to supporting documentation to confirm that they occurred after the balance sheet date
	Inspection also provides evidence of valuation/measurement, rights and obligations and the nature of items (presentation and disclosure). It can also be used to compare documents (and hence test consistency of audit evidence) and confirm authorisation
Observation	Involves watching a procedure being performed (for example, post opening)
	Of limited use, as only confirms procedure took place when the auditor was watching
Inquiry	Seeking information from client staff or external sources
	Strength of evidence depends on knowledge and integrity of source of information
Recalculation	Checking arithmetic of client's records, for example adding up ledger account
Reperformance	Independently executing procedures or controls, either manually or through the use of CAATs (see below)
Analytic review/ Analytical procedures	Evaluating and comparing financial and/or non-financial data for plausible relationships (see Section 6)
Confirmation	Confirmation means having the facts of one area confirmed by reference to another party or another source of evidence. The more independent the additional evidence is, the more reliable the confirmation
Reconciliation	Carrying out reconciliations can confirm the accounting records balance, or that the organisation has procedures in place to confirm the consistency of accounting records
Expert opinion	Expert opinion can be used as a source of confirmation in technical areas where the auditors lack expertise to be able to confirm the explanations given to them
Research into published material and reports	Auditors can use various types of reports, for example internal reports on efficiency, reports on the feasibility of computer systems, or research into industry figures for the operation being reviewed
Receiving the service	Internal audit may be able to gain direct experience of using the services provided by other departments. This may be directly, for example use of the computer support function, or internal audit may themselves act as customers to gain evidence on functions that deal with external customers
Mathematical models	Mathematical models can be used to check the reasonableness of certain business functions, for example use of inventory control models to check the reasonableness of stock ordering policies

PROCEDURES	
Questionnaires	Questionnaires can be a means of gaining evidence for comparisons, asking other functions within the organisations or external organisation detailed questions in order to be able to compare what they do with the operation under review
User satisfaction surveys	Obtaining feedback from customers who use the service/product can provide evidence into the success or otherwise of the service/product
Benchmarking	Comparing business units with other business units, competitors or best practice.

Section summary

Auditors must evaluate all types of audit evidence in terms of its **sufficiency** and **appropriateness**.

Tests of control concentrate on the **design** and **operation** of controls. **Substantive testing** aims to test all the **financial statement assertions**.

The **reliability** of audit evidence is influenced by its **source** and by its **nature**.

Audit evidence can be obtained by inspection, observation, enquiry and confirmation, computation and analytical review.

5 Audit sampling and CAATs

Introduction

Sampling is used by internal auditors because they cannot test every single item in a population. In this section we consider the various aspects of sample selection.

5.1 The need for sampling

Auditors cannot usually examine all the information available to them; it would be impractical to do so and using audit sampling will produce valid conclusions.

KEY TERMS

AUDIT SAMPLING involves the application of audit procedures to less than 100% of the items within an account balance or class of transactions such that all sampling units have a chance of selection. This will enable the auditor to obtain and evaluate audit evidence about some characteristic of the items selected in order to form or assist in forming a conclusion concerning the population.

The POPULATION is the entire set of data from which a sample is selected and about which an auditor wishes to draw conclusions.

Some testing procedures do **not** involve sampling, such as:

- **Testing 100%** of items in a population (this should be obvious)
- Testing all items with a **certain characteristic** as selection is not representative

5.2 Sample selection

One method of sample selection is random selection. The auditor may alternatively select certain items from a population because of specific characteristics they possess. The results of items selected in this way cannot be projected onto the whole population but may be used in conjunction with other audit evidence concerning the rest of the population.

- **High value or key items.** The auditor may select high value items or items that are suspicious, unusual or prone to error.

- **All items over a certain amount.** Selecting items this way may mean a large proportion of the population can be verified by testing a few items.

- **Items to obtain information** about the business, the nature of transactions, or the accounting and control systems.

- **Items to test procedures,** to see whether particular procedures are being performed.

5.3 Use of computer-assisted audit techniques

The overall objectives and scope of an audit do not change when an audit is conducted in a computerised environment. The auditors will still check the main controls over the system such as security, authorisation, data validity and contingency plans (covered earlier in this chapter). However, the application of auditing procedures may require auditors to consider techniques that use the computer as an audit tool. These uses of the computer for audit work are known as **computer-assisted audit techniques (CAATs).**

(a)   The absence of input documents or the lack of a visible audit trail may require the use of CAATs in the application of tests of control and substantive procedures.

(b)   The effectiveness and efficiency of auditing procedures may be improved through the use of CAATs.

CAATs may be used in performing various auditing procedures, including the following.

(a)   **Tests of details of transactions and balances**, for example the use of audit software to test all (or a sample) of the transactions in a computer file

(b)   **Analytical review procedures**, for example the use of audit software to identify unusual fluctuations or items

(c)   **Tests of computer information system controls**, for example the use of test data to test access procedures to the program libraries, or the functioning of a programmed procedure

There are two particularly common types of CAAT: **audit software** and **test data**, which we look at in more detail below.

Exam alert

Use of computers on audits is now common practice. You will be expected to consider the company aspects of auditing as a matter of course. Therefore in answering questions on obtaining evidence, remember to include reference to CAATs if they seem relevant.

5.3.1 Audit software

Audit software consists of **computer programs** used by the auditors, as part of their auditing procedures, to **process data of audit significance** from the entity's accounting system. Regardless of the source of the programs, the auditor should substantiate their validity for audit purposes prior to use.

Examples of uses of audit software are:

- Interrogation software, which accesses data files and performs complex calculations
- Comparison programs which compare versions of a program
- Interactive software for interrogation of on-line systems
- Resident software to select transactions for review as they are processed
- Simulation to simulate the operation of the organisation's systems

5.3.2 Test data

Test data techniques are used in conducting audit procedures by entering data (eg a sample of transactions) into an entity's computer system, and comparing the results obtained with predetermined results. Examples include:

(a) Test data used to test **specific controls** in computer programs. Examples include on-line password and data access controls.

(b) Test transactions selected from previously processed transactions or created by the auditors to test **specific processing characteristics** of an entity's computer system. Such transactions are generally processed separately from the entity's normal processing. Test data can for example be used to check the controls that prevent the processing of **invalid data** by entering data with say a non-existent customer code or worth an unreasonable amount, or a transaction which may if processed break customer credit limits.

(c) Test transactions used in an **integrated test facility**. This is where a 'dummy' unit (eg a department or employee) is established, and to which test transactions are posted during the normal processing cycle.

A significant problem with test data is that any resulting corruption of data files has to be corrected. This is difficult with modern real-time systems, which often have built-in (and highly desirable) controls to ensure that data entered **cannot** be easily removed without leaving a mark.

Other problems with **test data** are that it only tests the operation of the system at a **single point of time**, and auditors are only testing controls in the programs being run and controls which they know about. The problems involved mean that test data is being used less as a CAAT.

Question 16.2	Invisible evidence

Learning outcome E1(e)

Try to think of examples of where visible evidence may be lacking in the accounting process.

5.3.3 Embedded audit facilities

To allow a continuous review of the data recorded and the manner in which it is treated by the system, it may be possible to use CAATs referred to as **'embedded audit facilities'**.

An embedded facility consists of audit modules that are incorporated into the computer element of the enterprise's accounting system. Two frequently encountered examples are **Integrated Test Facility** (ITF) and **Systems Control and Review File** (SCARF).

EXAMPLES OF EMBEDDED AUDIT FACILITIES	
Integrated test facility (ITF)	Creates a **fictitious entity** within the company application, where transactions are posted to it alongside regular transactions, and actual results of the fictitious entity compared with what it should have produced
Systems control and review file (SCARF)	Allows auditors to have transactions with particular characteristics (for example, above a **certain amount**) from **specific ledger accounts** posted to a file for later auditor review

| Question 16.3 | CAATs |

Learning outcome E1(e)

(a) Outline the major types of CAATs and describe the potential benefits that might be derived from using them.

(b) Explain what is meant by a 'test pack' of data.

(c) Briefly explain the use that the auditors could make of such a test pack when examining a sales ledger system maintained on a computer system.

(d) Briefly outline the main practical problems encountered when using a test pack.

Section summary

The main stages of **audit sampling** are determining **objectives** and **population**, determining **sample size**, choosing the method of **sample selection**, **analysing the results** and **projecting errors**.

CAATs can be used to assist in sample selection. The main types of CAATs are **audit software** and **test data**.

6 Analytical review

Introduction

In this section we consider the use of analytical review by internal auditors as a test to aid their understanding of the organisation and to identify areas of risk.

6.1 Analytical review and analytical procedures

KEY TERM

ANALYTIC REVIEW or ANALYTICAL REVIEW is an audit technique used to help analyse data to identify trends, errors, fraud, inefficiency and inconsistency. Its purpose is to understand what has happened in a system, to compare this with a standard and to identify weaknesses in practice or unusual situations that may require further investigation. The main methods of analytical review are ratio analysis, non-financial performance analysis, internal and external benchmarking and trend analysis. While the purpose of analytical review in external audit is to understand financial performance and position and to identify areas for more in-depth audit treatment, analytical review in internal audit aims to better understand the control environment and identify potential control weaknesses. (*CIMA Official Terminology*)

Analytical review is an exercise that can be carried out either during or at the end of substantive procedures in a systems audit. It is regarded as being a form of substantive testing as well as a final review procedure.

The term 'analytical review' refers to a review of the financial accounts that have been prepared, to decide whether they appear to make sense and are **coherent** and **consistent**.

6.2 Nature and purpose of analytical procedures

Analytical procedures include:

(a) The consideration of comparisons with:

(i) **Similar information** for prior periods

(ii)   **Anticipated results** of the entity, from budgets or forecasts

(iii) **Predictions** prepared by the auditors

(iv)   **Industry information**, such as a comparison of the client's ratio of sales to trade accounts receivable with industry averages, or with the ratios relating to other entities of comparable size in the same industry.

(b)   Those between **elements of financial information** that are expected to **conform to a predicted pattern** based on the **entity's experience**, such as the relationship of gross profit to sales.

(c)   Those between **financial information** and **relevant non-financial information**, such as the relationship of payroll costs to number of employees.

A variety of methods can be used to perform the procedures discussed above, ranging from **simple comparisons** to **complex analysis** using statistics, on an organisation level, branch level or individual account level. The choice of procedures is a matter for the auditors' professional judgement and is dependent on the **quality of the data**.

As well as helping to determine the **nature, timing and extent** of **other audit procedures,** such analytical procedures may also indicate **aspects of the business** and **risks** of which the auditors were previously unaware. Auditors are looking to see if developments in the business have had the expected effects. They will be particularly interested in changes in areas where problems have occurred in the past.

6.3 Using analytical procedures

Auditors will consider the **plausibility** and **predictability** of the relationships being tested. Some relationships are strong, for example between selling expenses and sales in business where the sales force is mainly paid by commission. Relationships may be more **problematic** during **times of business change**.

6.4 Ratio analysis

Ratio analysis is the **analysis** of the **relationships** between **items of financial data**, or between financial and non-financial data such as labour cost per employee.

The following factors should be considered when deciding how much use to make of ratio analysis.

(a)   Ratios mean very little when **used in isolation**. Ratios should be calculated for previous periods and for comparable companies. This may involve a certain amount of initial research, but subsequently it is just a matter of adding new statistics to the existing information on file each year.

(b)   Ratios should be calculated on a **consistent basis**. Changing the calculation (for example by using average receivables to calculate receivables turnover when in previous years closing receivables were used) may mean comparisons cannot be made over time.

(c)   There should be a **correlation** between the items involved. For example, sales commission will obviously vary directly with sales, whereas most administration costs will not.

(d)   In general the more **detailed** the ratio analysis is, the better. For example, ratio analysis should be applied to individual outlets in a retail chain, because in the aggregated figures the trends and fluctuations of some outlets may be masked by those of others.

(e)   Some ratios may be distorted by **single or unusual items**. For example, if a business has one very large customer, the receivables turnover ratio may be significantly affected by which side of the year-end the customer pays.

Exam skills

Remember that a key skill in ratio analysis is selecting the right ratios to calculate. In this paper you need to calculate ratios that indicate risk levels or that show how well controls are working. You will not get credit for calculations that don't add any value.

6.5 Trend and relationship analysis

Trend analysis is the analysis of changes in a given item over time. It can take various forms.

- Period by period comparisons
- Weighted/moving averages
- Regression analysis

Consideration of the **inter-relationship of elements of the accounts** which might be expected to conform to a predictable pattern is an important example of trend analysis.

For example, payables and purchases: if a company's purchases increase by 50% from one year to the next, then it is reasonable to expect that its payables figure will also increase by something in the region of 50%.

6.6 Reasonableness tests

The aim of reasonableness tests is to develop a prediction for an item based on relationships with other financial and non-financial data. Examples of reasonableness tests include the following.

6.6.1 Comparison with similar firms

These involve comparing the company's financial information with similar information produced by other companies within the same industry.

6.6.2 Comparison with budgets

Explanations should be obtained for all major variances analysed using a standard costing system. Variances that relate to over or under absorption of overheads are particularly important, since these may affect inventory valuations.

6.6.3 Comparison with other financial information

The following are examples of tests on types of expenditure.

- Rent with annual rent per rental agreement
- Interest payable on loans with outstanding balance and interest rate
- Hire or leasing charges with agreed annual rate.

6.6.4 Comparison with non-financial information

Examples include the following.

- Rent with space occupied
- Wages and salaries with employee numbers
- Cost of sales with production volumes
- Motor expenses with delivery miles

6.6.5 Credibility checks

In a small organisation for example it may be quite easy to relate the annual salaries bill to the total of individual pay cheques.

6.6.6 General business review

Auditors should seek to enhance their knowledge of the organisation by **review** of **board minutes, talking** with employees at all levels, and keep an eye on **industry or local trends**, including known disturbances of the trading pattern (for example strikes, depot closures, failure of suppliers).

Section summary

Analytical review assists internal auditors in identifying control weaknesses and areas of risk.

7   Internal audit control and reporting

Introduction

The end-product of an internal audit is the internal audit report presented to senior management. Reports should therefore be appropriately set out, as discussed in this section.

7.1 Control of internal audits

The main features of control will be the **management** and **supervision** of the **internal audit staff** and the **review** of their work.

7.2 Management of internal audits

Any work delegated to assistants should be directed, supervised and reviewed in a manner which provides reasonable assurance that such work is performed competently.

7.3 Objectives of reporting

7.3.1 Recommendations for change

The most important element of internal audit reporting is to **promote change** in the form of either **new or improved controls**. Descriptions of failings should promote change by emphasising the problems that need to be overcome and advising management on the steps needed to improve risk management strategies.

7.3.2 Assisting management identification of risk and control issues

The auditors' report can emphasise the **importance of control issues** at times when other issues are being driven forward, for example new initiatives. Auditors can also help managers assess the effect of unmitigated risk. If auditors find that the internal control system is sound, then resources can be directed towards other areas.

7.3.3 Ensuring action takes place

Auditors should aim to have their **recommendations agreed by operational managers** and staff, as this should enhance the chances of their being actioned.

7.4 Forms of report

There are **no formal requirements** for internal audit reports as there are for the external audit. One clear way of presenting observations and findings in individual areas is as follows:

- **Business objective** that the manager is aiming to achieve
- **Operational standard**
- The **risks** of current practice
- **Control weaknesses** or lack of application of controls
- The **causes** of the weaknesses
- The **effect** of the weaknesses
- **Recommendations** to solve the weaknesses

Section summary

Reports on the results of internal audits should highlight the **risks** identified, the **weaknesses** found in controls, the **consequences** of the problems found and **recommendations** for improvements.

8 The audit committee

Introduction

The audit committee was mentioned in Chapter 3. In this section we look at its role in more detail.

KEY TERM

The AUDIT COMMITTEE is a formally constituted committee of an entity's main board of directors whose responsibilities include: monitoring the integrity of any formal announcements on financial performance including financial statements; reviewing internal financial controls, internal control and risk management systems; monitoring the effectiveness of the internal audit function; making recommendations in respect of the appointment or removal of the external auditor; reviewing and monitoring auditor independence and the effectiveness of the audit process. *(CIMA Official Terminology)*

The UK's Cadbury committee summed up the benefits that an audit committee can bring.

'If they operate effectively, audit committees can bring significant benefits. In particular, they have the potential to:

(a)   improve the quality of financial reporting, by reviewing the financial statements on behalf of the Board;

(b)   create a climate of discipline and control which will reduce the opportunity for fraud;

(c)   enable the non-executive directors to contribute an independent judgement and play a positive role;

(d)   help the finance director, by providing a forum in which he can raise issues of concern, and which he can use to get things done which might otherwise be difficult;

(e)   strengthen the position of the external auditor, by providing a channel of communication and forum for issues of concern;

(f)   provide a framework within which the external auditor can assert his independence in the event of a dispute with management;

(g)   strengthen the position of the internal audit function, by providing a greater degree of independence from management;

(h)   increase public confidence in the credibility and objectivity of financial statements.'

Audit committees are now compulsory for companies trading on the New York Stock Exchange.

In order to be effective, the audit committee has to be well-staffed. The UK's Smith committee recommended that the **audit committee** should consist entirely of **independent non-executive directors** (excluding the chairman), and should include at least one member with **significant and recent financial experience**.

8.1 Review of internal audit

The review should cover the following aspects of internal audit.

- **Standards** including **objectivity**, **technical knowledge** and **professional standards**
- **Scope** including how much emphasis is given to different types of review
- **Resources**
- **Reporting arrangements**
- **Work plan**, especially review of controls and coverage of high risk areas
- **Liaison** with external auditors
- **Results**

The head of internal audit should have direct access to the audit committee.

8.2 Review of internal control

The audit committee should play a significant role in reviewing internal control.

(a)   Committee members can use their own experience to **monitor** continually the **adequacy** of **internal control systems**, focusing particularly on the control environment, management's attitude towards controls and overall management controls.

(b)   The audit committee's review should cover **legal compliance** and **ethics**, for example listing rules or environmental legislation. Committee members should check that there are systems in place to promote compliance. They should review reports on the operation of **codes of conduct** and review violations.

(c)   The committee should also address the risk of **fraud**, ensuring employees are aware of risks and that there are mechanisms in place for staff to report fraud, and fraud to be investigated.

(d)   Each year the committee should be responsible for **reviewing the company's statement on internal controls** prior to its approval by the board.

(e)   The committee should consider the **recommendations of the external auditors** in the management letter and management's response. Because the committee's role is ongoing, it can also ensure that recommendations are publicised and see that actions are taken as appropriate.

(f)   The committee may play a **more active supervisory role**, for example reviewing major transactions for reasonableness.

8.3 Review of financial statements and systems

The committee should review both the **quarterly** (if published) and **annual accounts**. This should involve assessment of the judgements made about the overall appearance and presentation of the accounts, key accounting policies and major areas of judgement.

As well as reviewing the accounts, the committee's review should cover the financial reporting and budgetary systems. This involves considering **performance indicators** and **information systems** that allow **monitoring** of the **most significant business and financial risks**, and the progress towards financial objectives. The systems should also highlight developments that may require action (for example large variances), and communicate these to the right people. If the board does not have a separate risk committee, the audit committee's review may be extended to cover non-financial internal controls and risk management.

8.4 Liaison with external auditors

The audit committee's tasks here will include:

(a)   Being responsible for making recommendations about the **appointment or removal of the external auditors** as well as fixing their remuneration.

(b)   Considering whether there are **any other threats to external auditor independence.** In particular the committee should consider **non-audit services** provided by the external auditors, paying particular attention to whether there may be a **conflict of interest.**

(c)   **Discussing the scope of the external audit** prior to the start of the audit. This should include consideration of whether external audit's coverage of all areas and locations of the business is fair, and how much external audit will rely on the work of internal audit.

(d)   Acting as a **forum for liaison** between the external auditors, the internal auditors and the finance director.

(e)   **Helping the external auditors to obtain the information** they require and in resolving any problems they may encounter.

(f)   **Making themselves available** to the external auditors for consultation, with or without the presence of the company's management.

(g)   Dealing with any **serious reservations** which the external auditors may express either about the accounts, the records or the quality of the company's management.

8.5 Review of risk management

The audit committee can play an important part in the review of risk recommended by the Turnbull report. This includes confirming that there is a **formal policy** in place for **risk management** and that the policy is backed and regularly monitored by the board. They should also **review** the **arrangements**, including training, for ensuring that managers and staff are aware of their responsibilities. They should use their own knowledge of the business to confirm that risk management is updated to **reflect current positions and strategy.**

8.6 Investigations

The committee will also be involved in implementing and reviewing the results of **one-off investigations**. The Cadbury report recommends that audit committees should be given specific authority to investigate matters of concern, and in doing so have access to sufficient resources, appropriate information and outside professional help.

Section summary

Audit committees of **independent, non-executive directors** should liaise with **external audit, supervise internal audit**, and **review** the **annual accounts** and **internal controls**.

9 Management review of internal controls

Introduction

We have already mentioned in the previous section the importance of management's review of internal controls. In this section we shall look in more detail at management's review of internal controls since it is effectively the last stage of the audit process.

9.1 Review of internal controls

The UK's **Turnbull committee**. suggested that review of internal controls should be an **integral part** of the **company's operations**; the board, or board committees, should actively consider reports on control issues from others operating internal controls.

In particular the board should consider:

(a) The identification, evaluation and management of all **key risks** affecting the organisation

(b) The **effectiveness of internal control**; again that does not just mean financial controls but also operational, compliance and risk management controls

(c) **Communication** to employees of risk objectives with targets and indicators

(d) The **action taken** if any **weaknesses** are found

The report recommends that when assessing the **effectiveness of internal control**, boards should consider the following:

(a) The **nature** and **extent** of the **risks** which face the company and which it regards as **acceptable** for the company to bear within its particular business

(b) The **threat** of such **risks becoming** a **reality**

(c) If that happened, the company's ability to **reduce** the **incidence** and **impact** on the business and to adapt to changing risks or operational deficiencies

(d) The **costs and benefits** related to operating relevant controls

Question 16.4	Internal control review

Learning outcome C1(a)

What sort of information would help the board carry out an effective review of internal control?

9.2 Annual review of controls

In addition, when directors are considering annually the disclosures they are required to make about internal controls, they should conduct an **annual review** of internal control. This should be wider-ranging than the regular review; in particular it should cover:

(a) The **changes** since the last **assessment** in **risks** faced, and the company's **ability** to **respond** to **changes** in its business environment

(b) The **scope** and **quality** of management's monitoring of risk and internal control, and of the work of internal audit, or consideration of the need for an internal audit function if the company does not have one

(c) The **extent** and **frequency** of reports to the board

(d)   **Significant controls**, **failings** and **weaknesses** which have or might have material impacts upon the accounts

(e)   The **effectiveness** of the **public reporting** processes

In an appendix Turnbull provides more detailed guidance on what should be assessed as part of the regular review of internal controls:

Risk assessment	• Does the organisation have clear objectives and have they been communicated to provide direction to employees (examples include performance targets)?
	• Are significant risks identified and assessed on an ongoing basis?
	• Do managers and employees have a clear understanding of what risks are acceptable?
Control environment and control activities	• Does the board have a risk management policy and strategies for dealing with significant risks?
	• Do the company's culture, code of conduct, human resource policies and performance reward systems support the business objectives and risk management and control systems?
	• Does senior management demonstrate commitment to competence, integrity and fostering a climate of trust?
	• Are authority, responsibility and accountability defined clearly?
	• Are decisions and actions of different parts of the company appropriately coordinated?
	• Does the company communicate to its employees what is expected of them and the scope of their freedom to act?
	• Do company employees have the knowledge, skills and tools necessary to support the company's objectives and manage risks effectively?
	• How are processes and controls adjusted to reflect new or changing risks or operational deficiencies?
Information and communication	• Do managers receive timely, relevant and reliable reports on progress against business objectives and risks to provide the information needed for decision-making and review processes?
	• Are information needs and systems reassessed as objectives and related risks change or reporting deficiencies are identified?
	• Do reporting procedures communicate a balanced and understandable account of the company's position and prospects?
	• Are there communication channels for individuals to report suspected breaches of law or regulations or other improprieties?

Monitoring	• Are there ongoing embedded processes for monitoring the effective application of the policies, processes and activities relating to internal control and risk management?
	• Do these processes monitor the company's ability to re-evaluate risks and adjust controls effectively in response to changes in objectives, business and environment?
	• Are there effective follow-up procedures to ensure action is taken in response to changes in risk and control assessments?
	• Are there specific arrangements for management monitoring and reporting to the board matters of particular importance (including fraud or illegal acts)?

9.3 Reporting on risk management

Per the Turnbull report the board should disclose as a minimum in the accounts, the existence of a **process** for **managing risks**, how the board has **reviewed** the **effectiveness** of the process and that the **process accords** with the **Turnbull guidance**. The board should also include:

(a) An **acknowledgement** that they are responsible for the company's system of internal financial control and reviewing its effectiveness

(b) An **explanation** that such a system is designed to **manage** rather than eliminate the risk of **failure to achieve business objectives**, and can only provide **reasonable** and not absolute **assurance** against material misstatement or **loss**

(c) A **summary** of the process that the **directors** (or a board committee) have **used to review the effectiveness** of the system of internal financial control and consider the need for an internal audit function if the company does not have one. There should also be disclosure of the process the board has used to deal with **material internal control aspects** of **any significant problems** disclosed in the annual accounts

(d) **Information** about those **weaknesses** in internal financial control that have resulted in material losses, contingencies or uncertainties which require disclosure in the financial statements or the external auditor's report on the financial statements

9.4 Significance of Turnbull recommendations

The system recommended by the Turnbull report is notable because of the following.

(a) It is **forward looking**.

(b) It is **open**, requiring appropriate disclosures to all stakeholders in the company about the risks being taken.

(c) It does **not seek** to **eliminate risk**. It is constructive in its approach to opportunity management, as well as concerned with 'disaster prevention'. To succeed companies are not required to take fewer risks than others but they do need a good understanding of what risks they can handle.

(d) It **unifies all business units** of a company into an integrated risk review, so that the same 'language' of risk (risk terminology) is applied throughout the company.

(e) It is **strategic**, and driven by business objectives and sound business practice, particularly the need for the company to adapt to its changing business environment.

(f) It should be **re-evaluated on a regular basis**.

(g) It should be **durable**, evolving as the business and its environment changes.

(h)   In order to create shareholder value, a company needs to **manage the risks** it faces and
       communicate to the capital markets how it is carrying out this task. Communication of risks helps
       shareholders make informed decisions.

All the main points in the Turnbull report are brought together in the Appendix to this chapter.

Section summary

The board should **review internal controls and risk management regularly** and carry out a wider-ranging
annual review.

Chapter Roundup

- ✓ An internal audit department should plan its work carefully through the preparation of **strategic**, **tactical** and **operational plans**.

- ✓ Business risk can be assessed as two components, **inherent risk** and **quality of control** (or **control risk**).

- ✓ The internal auditors may use the technique of **risk analysis** to assist them in drawing up a strategic plan.

- ✓ Internal auditors can record the entity's systems through the use of **narrative notes**, **flowcharts**, **questionnaires** or **checklists**.

- ✓ Auditors must evaluate all types of audit evidence in terms of its **sufficiency** and **appropriateness**.

- ✓ **Tests of control** concentrate on the **design** and **operation** of controls. **Substantive testing** aims to test all the **financial statement assertions**.

- ✓ The **reliability** of audit evidence is influenced by its **source** and by its **nature**.

- ✓ **Audit evidence** can be obtained by **inspection, observation, enquiry and confirmation, computation** and **analytical review**.

- ✓ The main stages of **audit sampling** are determining **objectives** and **population**, determining **sample size**, choosing the method of **sample selection, analysing the results** and **projection errorss**.

- ✓ **CAAT's** can be used to assist in sample selection. The main types of CAAT's are **audit software** and **test data**.

- ✓ **Analytical review** assists internal auditors in identiyfing weaknesses and areas of risk.

- ✓ Reports on the results of internal audits should highlight the **risks** identified, the **weaknesses** found in controls, the **consequences** of the problems found and **recommendations** for improvements.

- ✓ Audit committees of **independent, non-executive directors** should liaise with **external audit, supervise internal audit**, and **review** the **annual accounts** and **internal controls**.

- ✓ The board should **review internal controls and risk management regularly** and carry out a wider-ranging **annual review**.

Quick Quiz

1   What criteria should the internal auditors bear in mind when deciding which areas should be covered in a strategic audit plan?

2   What are the two main types of CAATs used by auditors?

3   Identify the significant relationships between pairs of items in the list of items below.

(a)	payables	(b)	interest	(c)	purchases	(d)	sales
(e)	amortisation	(f)	loans	(g)	receivables	(h)	intangibles

4   What considerations should be taken into account when using ratio analysis?

5   The audit committee should consist wholly of executive directors.

True   ☐

False   ☐

6   Fill in the blank.

.... risk is the level of risk relating to an activity irrespective of the quality of the associated control system or the effectiveness of management.

Answers to Quick Quiz

1   • Financial   • Business effects
        • Internal control   • Value for money
        • Probity   • Special investigations
        • Business goals

2   Audit software
        Test data

3   (a)   (c)
        (b)   (f)
        (d)   (g)
        (e)   (h)

4   • Ratios should be used for comparison
        • Ratios should be calculated on a consistent basis
        • There should be a correlation between the items involved
        • The more detailed the ratio analysis is, the better
        • Some ratios may be distorted by large or unusual items

5   False. The audit committee should consist of non-executive directors.

6   **Inherent risk** is the level of risk relating to an activity irrespective of the quality of the associated control system or the effectiveness of management.

Answers to Questions

16.1 Risk assessment

		Department X		Department Y	
			Index ×		Index ×
Factor	Index		weighting	Index	Weighting
A	2		1.00	4	2.00
B	3		1.50	3	1.50
C	1		0.50	4	2.00
D	4		2.00	3	1.50
E	4		1.00	3	0.75
F	1		0.25	3	0.75
Total inherent risk			6.25		8.50
G	3		3.00	1	1.00
H	2		1.00	2	1.00
I	1		0.50	4	2.00
J	4		2.00	2	1.00
Total control risk			6.50		5.00

Overall business risk

Dept X = 6.25 × 6.50 = 40.625
Dept Y = 8.50 × 5.00 = 42.500

Department Y is higher risk due to its size and complexity, but Department X is not far behind due to the convertibility of its assets and concerns about its controls as previously reviewed. Both departments are probably due for examination by internal audit in the near future.

16.2 Invisible evidence

(a)   **Input documents** may be non-existent where sales orders are entered on-line. In addition, accounting transactions, such as discounts and interest calculations, may be generated by computer programs with no visible authorisation of individual transactions.

(b)   The system may not produce a visible audit trail of **transactions processed** through the computer. Delivery notes and suppliers' invoices may be matched by a computer program. In addition, programmed control procedures, such as checking customer credit limits, may provide visible evidence only on an exception basis. In such cases, there may be no visible evidence that all transactions have been processed.

(c)   **Output reports** may not be produced by the system. In addition, a printed report may only contain summary totals while supporting details are kept in computer files.

16.3 CAATs

(a)   Audit techniques that involve, directly or indirectly, the use of a client's computer are referred to as Computer Assisted Audit Techniques (CAATs), of which the following are two principal categories.

   (i)   **Audit software**: computer programs used for audit purposes to examine the contents of the client's computer files

   (ii)   **Test data**: data used by the auditors for computer processing to test the operation of the enterprise's computer programs

The benefits of using CAATs are as follows.

(i)   By using **computer audit programs**, the auditors can **scrutinise large volumes of data** and concentrate skilled manual resources on the investigation of results, rather than on the extraction of information.

(ii)   Once the programs have been written and tested, the **costs of operation** are **relatively low**, indeed the auditors do not necessarily have to be present during its use (though there are frequently practical advantages in the auditors attending).

(b)   A **'test pack'** consists of **input data submitted by the auditors** for **processing** by the enterprise's computer based accounting system. It may be processed during a normal production run ('live') or during a special run at a point in time outside the normal cycle ('dead').

The primary use of the test pack is in **testing of application controls**. The data used in the test pack will often contain items which should appear in exception reports produced by the system. The results of the processed test pack will be compared with the expected results.

(c)   The auditors could use a test pack to test the sales ledger system by including data in the pack which would normally be processed through the system, such as:

(i)   Sales
(ii)   Credits allowed
(iii)   Cash receipts
(iv)   Discounts allowed

The processing of the input would involve:

(i)   **Production of sales invoices** (with correct discounts)

(ii)   **Production of credit notes**

(iii)   **Posting of cash received**, invoices and credit notes to individual customer accounts to appear on statements

(iv)   **Posting all transactions** to the sales ledger control account and producing balances

The result produced would be compared with those predicted in the test pack. Errors should appear on exception reports produced by the computer, for example, a customer credit limit being breached.

(d)   The practical problems involved in using a test pack are as follows.

(i)   In using 'live' processing there will be problems **removing or reversing the test data**, which might corrupt master file information.

(ii)   In using **'dead' processing** the auditors do not **test the system** actually used by the client.

(iii)   Any auditors who wish to design a test pack must have **sufficient skill in computing**, and also a thorough knowledge of the client's system.

(iv)   Any changes in the client's system will mean that the test pack will have to be **rewritten** which will be **costly** and **time-consuming**.

16.4 Internal control review

The UK's Institute of Internal Auditors suggests that the board needs to consider the following information in order to carry out an effective review.

•   The organisation's **Code of Business Conduct**

•   Confirmation that line managers are **clear as to their objectives**

•   The overall results of a **control self assessment** process by line management or staff

- **Letters of representation** ('comfort letters') on internal control from line management

- A **report** from the board on the **key procedures** which are designed to provide effective internal control

- **Reports from internal audit** on audits performed

- The audit committee's **assessment** of the **effectiveness of internal audit**

- Reports on **special reviews** commissioned by the audit committee from internal audit or others

- Internal audit's **overall summary opinion on internal control**

- The **external auditors' report on weaknesses** in the accounting and internal control systems and other matters, including errors, identified during the audit

- **Intelligence** gathered by board members during the year

- A **report on avoidable losses** by the finance director

- A **report on any material developments** since the date of the statement of financial position up to the present

- The board's proposed wording of **the internal control report** for publication

---

Now try these questions from the Exam Question Bank

Number	Level	Marks	Time
Q27	Examination	25	45 mins
Q28	Examination	50	90 mins

APPENDIX
MATHEMATICAL TABLES AND
EXAM FORMULAE

PRESENT VALUE TABLE

Present value of \$1 ie $(1+r)^{-n}$ where r = interest rate, n = number of periods until payment or receipt.

Periods (n)	Interest rates (r)									
	1%	**2%**	**3%**	**4%**	**5%**	**6%**	**7%**	**8%**	**9%**	**10%**
1	0.990	0.980	0.971	0.962	0.952	0.943	0.935	0.926	0.917	0.909
2	0.980	0.961	0.943	0.925	0.907	0.890	0.873	0.857	0.842	0.826
3	0.971	0.942	0.915	0.889	0.864	0.840	0.816	0.794	0.772	0.751
4	0.961	0.924	0.888	0.855	0.823	0.792	0.763	0.735	0.708	0.683
5	0.951	0.906	0.863	0.822	0.784	0.747	0.713	0.681	0.650	0.621
6	0.942	0.888	0.837	0.790	0.746	0.705	0.666	0.630	0.596	0.564
7	0.933	0.871	0.813	0.760	0.711	0.665	0.623	0.583	0.547	0.513
8	0.923	0.853	0.789	0.731	0.677	0.627	0.582	0.540	0.502	0.467
9	0.914	0.837	0.766	0.703	0.645	0.592	0.544	0.500	0.460	0.424
10	0.905	0.820	0.744	0.676	0.614	0.558	0.508	0.463	0.422	0.386
11	0.896	0.804	0.722	0.650	0.585	0.527	0.475	0.429	0.388	0.350
12	0.887	0.788	0.701	0.625	0.557	0.497	0.444	0.397	0.356	0.319
13	0.879	0.773	0.681	0.601	0.530	0.469	0.415	0.368	0.326	0.290
14	0.870	0.758	0.661	0.577	0.505	0.442	0.388	0.340	0.299	0.263
15	0.861	0.743	0.642	0.555	0.481	0.417	0.362	0.315	0.275	0.239
16	0.853	0.728	0.623	0.534	0.458	0.394	0.339	0.292	0.252	0.218
17	0.844	0.714	0.605	0.513	0.436	0.371	0.317	0.270	0.231	0.198
18	0.836	0.700	0.587	0.494	0.416	0.350	0.296	0.250	0.212	0.180
19	0.828	0.686	0.570	0.475	0.396	0.331	0.277	0.232	0.194	0.164
20	0.820	0.673	0.554	0.456	0.377	0.312	0.258	0.215	0.178	0.149

Periods (n)	Interest rates (r)									
	11%	**12%**	**13%**	**14%**	**15%**	**16%**	**17%**	**18%**	**19%**	**20%**
1	0.901	0.893	0.885	0.877	0.870	0.862	0.855	0.847	0.840	0.833
2	0.812	0.797	0.783	0.769	0.756	0.743	0.731	0.718	0.706	0.694
3	0.731	0.712	0.693	0.675	0.658	0.641	0.624	0.609	0.593	0.579
4	0.659	0.636	0.613	0.592	0.572	0.552	0.534	0.516	0.499	0.482
5	0.593	0.567	0.543	0.519	0.497	0.476	0.456	0.437	0.419	0.402
6	0.535	0.507	0.480	0.456	0.432	0.410	0.390	0.370	0.352	0.335
7	0.482	0.452	0.425	0.400	0.376	0.354	0.333	0.314	0.296	0.279
8	0.434	0.404	0.376	0.351	0.327	0.305	0.285	0.266	0.249	0.233
9	0.391	0.361	0.333	0.308	0.284	0.263	0.243	0.225	0.209	0.194
10	0.352	0.322	0.295	0.270	0.247	0.227	0.208	0.191	0.176	0.162
11	0.317	0.287	0.261	0.237	0.215	0.195	0.178	0.162	0.148	0.135
12	0.286	0.257	0.231	0.208	0.187	0.168	0.152	0.137	0.124	0.112
13	0.258	0.229	0.204	0.182	0.163	0.145	0.130	0.116	0.104	0.093
14	0.232	0.205	0.181	0.160	0.141	0.125	0.111	0.099	0.088	0.078
15	0.209	0.183	0.160	0.140	0.123	0.108	0.095	0.084	0.074	0.065
16	0.188	0.163	0.141	0.123	0.107	0.093	0.081	0.071	0.062	0.054
17	0.170	0.146	0.125	0.108	0.093	0.080	0.069	0.060	0.052	0.045
18	0.153	0.130	0.111	0.095	0.081	0.069	0.059	0.051	0.044	0.038
19	0.138	0.116	0.098	0.083	0.070	0.060	0.051	0.043	0.037	0.031
20	0.124	0.104	0.087	0.073	0.061	0.051	0.043	0.037	0.031	0.026

CUMULATIVE PRESENT VALUE TABLE

This table shows the present value of $1 per annum, receivable or payable at the end of each year for n years $\dfrac{1-(1+r)^{-n}}{r}$.

Periods (n)	Interest rates (r)									
	1%	**2%**	**3%**	**4%**	**5%**	**6%**	**7%**	**8%**	**9%**	**10%**
1	0.990	0.980	0.971	0.962	0.952	0.943	0.935	0.926	0.917	0.909
2	1.970	1.942	1.913	1.886	1.859	1.833	1.808	1.783	1.759	1.736
3	2.941	2.884	2.829	2.775	2.723	2.673	2.624	2.577	2.531	2.487
4	3.902	3.808	3.717	3.630	3.546	3.465	3.387	3.312	3.240	3.170
5	4.853	4.713	4.580	4.452	4.329	4.212	4.100	3.993	3.890	3.791
6	5.795	5.601	5.417	5.242	5.076	4.917	4.767	4.623	4.486	4.355
7	6.728	6.472	6.230	6.002	5.786	5.582	5.389	5.206	5.033	4.868
8	7.652	7.325	7.020	6.733	6.463	6.210	5.971	5.747	5.535	5.335
9	8.566	8.162	7.786	7.435	7.108	6.802	6.515	6.247	5.995	5.759
10	9.471	8.983	8.530	8.111	7.722	7.360	7.024	6.710	6.418	6.145
11	10.368	9.787	9.253	8.760	8.306	7.887	7.499	7.139	6.805	6.495
12	11.255	10.575	9.954	9.385	8.863	8.384	7.943	7.536	7.161	6.814
13	12.134	11.348	10.635	9.986	9.394	8.853	8.358	7.904	7.487	7.103
14	13.004	12.106	11.296	10.563	9.899	9.295	8.745	8.244	7.786	7.367
15	13.865	12.849	11.938	11.118	10.380	9.712	9.108	8.559	8.061	7.606
16	14.718	13.578	12.561	11.652	10.838	10.106	9.447	8.851	8.313	7.824
17	15.562	14.292	13.166	12.166	11.274	10.477	9.763	9.122	8.544	8.022
18	16.398	14.992	13.754	12.659	11.690	10.828	10.059	9.372	8.756	8.201
19	17.226	15.679	14.324	13.134	12.085	11.158	10.336	9.604	8.950	8.365
20	18.046	16.351	14.878	13.590	12.462	11.470	10.594	9.818	9.129	8.514

Periods (n)	Interest rates (r)									
	11%	**12%**	**13%**	**14%**	**15%**	**16%**	**17%**	**18%**	**19%**	**20%**
1	0.901	0.893	0.885	0.877	0.870	0.862	0.855	0.847	0.840	0.833
2	1.713	1.690	1.668	1.647	1.626	1.605	1.585	1.566	1.547	1.528
3	2.444	2.402	2.361	2.322	2.283	2.246	2.210	2.174	2.140	2.106
4	3.102	3.037	2.974	2.914	2.855	2.798	2.743	2.690	2.639	2.589
5	3.696	3.605	3.517	3.433	3.352	3.274	3.199	3.127	3.058	2.991
6	4.231	4.111	3.998	3.889	3.784	3.685	3.589	3.498	3.410	3.326
7	4.712	4.564	4.423	4.288	4.160	4.039	3.922	3.812	3.706	3.605
8	5.146	4.968	4.799	4.639	4.487	4.344	4.207	4.078	3.954	3.837
9	5.537	5.328	5.132	4.946	4.772	4.607	4.451	4.303	4.163	4.031
10	5.889	5.650	5.426	5.216	5.019	4.833	4.659	4.494	4.339	4.192
11	6.207	5.938	5.687	5.453	5.234	5.029	4.836	4.656	4.486	4.327
12	6.492	6.194	5.918	5.660	5.421	5.197	4.988	4.793	4.611	4.439
13	6.750	6.424	6.122	5.842	5.583	5.342	5.118	4.910	4.715	4.533
14	6.982	6.628	6.302	6.002	5.724	5.468	5.229	5.008	4.802	4.611
15	7.191	6.811	6.462	6.142	5.847	5.575	5.324	5.092	4.876	4.675
16	7.379	6.974	6.604	6.265	5.954	5.668	5.405	5.162	4.938	4.730
17	7.549	7.120	6.729	6.373	6.047	5.749	5.475	5.222	4.990	4.775
18	7.702	7.250	6.840	6.467	6.128	5.818	5.534	5.273	5.033	4.812
19	7.839	7.366	6.938	6.550	6.198	5.877	5.584	5.316	5.070	4.843
20	7.963	7.469	7.025	6.623	6.259	5.929	5.628	5.353	5.101	4.870

AREA UNDER THE NORMAL CURVE

This table gives the area under the normal curve between the mean and the point Z standard deviations above the mean. The corresponding area for deviations below the mean can be found by symmetry.

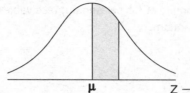

$Z = \frac{(x-\mu)}{\sigma}$	0.00	0.01	0.02	0.03	0.04	0.05	0.06	0.07	0.08	0.09
0.0	.0000	.0040	.0080	.0120	.0160	.0199	.0239	.0279	.0319	.0359
0.1	.0398	.0438	.0478	.0517	.0557	.0596	.0636	.0675	.0714	.0753
0.2	.0793	.0832	.0871	.0910	.0948	.0987	.1026	.1064	.1103	.1141
0.3	.1179	.1217	.1255	.1293	.1331	.1368	.1406	.1443	.1480	.1517
0.4	.1554	.1591	.1628	.1664	.1700	.1736	.1772	.1808	.1844	.1879
0.5	.1915	.1950	.1985	.2019	.2054	.2088	.2123	.2157	.2190	.2224
0.6	.2257	.2291	.2324	.2357	.2389	.2422	.2454	.2486	.2517	.2549
0.7	.2580	.2611	.2642	.2673	.2704	.2734	.2764	.2794	.2823	.2852
0.8	.2881	.2910	.2939	.2967	.2995	.3023	.3051	.3078	.3106	.3133
0.9	.3159	.3186	.3212	.3238	.3264	.3289	.3315	.3340	.3365	.3389
1.0	.3413	.3438	.3461	.3485	.3508	.3531	.3554	.3577	.3599	.3621
1.1	.3643	.3665	.3686	.3708	.3729	.3749	.3770	.3790	.3810	.3830
1.2	.3849	.3869	.3888	.3907	.3925	.3944	.3962	.3980	.3997	.4015
1.3	.4032	.4049	.4066	.4082	.4099	.4115	.4131	.4147	.4162	.4177
1.4	.4192	.4207	.4222	.4236	.4251	.4265	.4279	.4292	.4306	.4319
1.5	.4332	.4345	.4357	.4370	.4382	.4394	.4406	.4418	.4429	.4441
1.6	.4452	.4463	.4474	.4484	.4495	.4505	.4515	.4525	.4535	.4545
1.7	.4554	.4564	.4573	.4582	.4591	.4599	.4608	.4616	.4625	.4633
1.8	.4641	.4649	.4656	.4664	.4671	.4678	.4686	.4693	.4699	.4706
1.9	.4713	.4719	.4726	.4732	.4738	.4744	.4750	.4756	.4761	.4767
2.0	.4772	.4778	.4783	.4788	.4793	.4798	.4803	.4808	.4812	.4817
2.1	.4821	.4826	.4830	.4834	.4838	.4842	.4846	.4850	.4854	.4857
2.2	.4861	.4864	.4868	.4871	.4875	.4878	.4881	.4884	.4887	.4890
2.3	.4893	.4896	.4898	.4901	.4904	.4906	.4909	.4911	.4913	.4916
2.4	.4918	.4920	.4922	.4925	.4927	.4929	.4931	.4932	.4934	.4936
2.5	.4938	.4940	.4941	.4943	.4945	.4946	.4948	.4949	.4951	.4952
2.6	.4953	.4955	.4956	.4957	.4959	.4960	.4961	.4962	.4963	.4964
2.7	.4965	.4966	.4967	.4968	.4969	.4970	.4971	.4972	.4973	.4974
2.8	.4974	.4975	.4976	.4977	.4977	.4978	.4979	.4979	.4980	.4981
2.9	.4981	.4982	.4982	.4983	.4984	.4984	.4985	.4985	.4986	.4986
3.0	.4987	.4987	.4987	.4988	.4988	.4989	.4989	.4989	.4990	.4990
3.1	.4990	.4991	.4991	.4991	.4992	.4992	.4992	.4992	.4993	.4993
3.2	.4993	.4993	.4994	.4994	.4994	.4994	.4994	.4995	.4995	.4995
3.3	.4995	.4995	.4995	.4996	.4996	.4996	.4996	.4996	.4996	.4997
3.4	.4997	.4997	.4997	.4997	.4997	.4997	.4997	.4997	.4997	.4998
3.5	.4998									

This table can be used to calculate $N(d_1)$, the cumulative normal distribution functions needed for the Black-Scholes model of option pricing. If $d_1 > 0$, add 0.5 to the relevant number above. If $d_1 < 0$, subtract the relevant number above from 0.5.

EXAM FORMULAE

Annuity

Present value of an annuity of £1 per annum, receivable or payable for n years, commencing in one year, discounted at r% per annum:

$$PV = \frac{1}{r}\left[1 - \frac{1}{[1 + r]^n}\right]$$

Perpetuity

Present value of £1 per annum, payable or receivable in perpetuity, commencing in one year, discounted at r% per annum:

$$PV = \frac{1}{r}$$

Growing perpetuity

Present value of £1 per annum, receivable or payable, commencing in one year, growing in perpetuity at a constant rate of g% per annum, discounted at r% per annum:

$$PV = \frac{1}{r - g}$$

EXAM QUESTION AND ANSWER BANK

What the examiner means

The very important table below has been prepared by CIMA to help you interpret exam questions.

Learning objectives	Verbs used	Definition
1 Knowledge		
What are you expected to know	• List	• Make a list of
	• State	• Express, fully or clearly, the details of/facts of
	• Define	• Give the exact meaning of
2 Comprehension		
What you are expected to understand	• Describe	• Communicate the key features of
	• Distinguish	• Highlight the differences between
	• Explain	• Make clear or intelligible/state the meaning of
	• Identify	• Recognise, establish or select after consideration
	• Illustrate	• Use an example to describe or explain something
3 Application		
How you are expected to apply your knowledge	• Apply	• Put to practical use
	• Calculate/ compute	• Ascertain or reckon mathematically
	• Demonstrate	• Prove with certainty or to exhibit by practical means
	• Prepare	• Make or get ready for use
	• Reconcile	• Make or prove consistent/compatible
	• Solve	• Find an answer to
	• Tabulate	• Arrange in a table
4 Analysis		
How you are expected to analyse the detail of what you have learned	• Analyse	• Examine in detail the structure of
	• Categorise	• Place into a defined class or division
	• Compare and contrast	• Show the similarities and/or differences between
	• Construct	• Build up or compile
	• Discuss	• Examine in detail by argument
	• Interpret	• Translate into intelligible or familiar terms
	• Prioritise	• Place in order of priority or sequence for action
	• Produce	• Create or bring into existence
5 Evaluation		
How you are expected to use your learning to evaluate, make decisions or recommendations	• Advise	• Counsel, inform or notify
	• Evaluate	• Appraise or assess the value of
	• Recommend	• Propose a course of action

Guidance in our Practice and Revision Kit focuses on how the verbs are used in questions.

1 Types of risk

30 mins

Learning outcome B1(a)

Define the main types of risks that a company faces.

2 Azure Airline

45 mins

Learning outcomes B2(a), (b)

Azure, a limited liability company, was incorporated in Sepiana on 1 April 20X6. In May, the company exercised an exclusive right granted by the government of Pewta to provide twice weekly direct flights between Lyme, the capital of Pewta, and Darke, the capital of Sepiana.

The introduction of this service has been well advertised as 'efficient and timely' in national newspapers. The journey time between Sepiana and Pewta is expected to be significantly reduced, so encouraging tourism and business development opportunities in Sepiana.

Azure operates a refurbished 35 year old aircraft which is leased from an international airline and registered with the Pewtan Aviation Administration (the PAA). The PAA requires that engines be overhauled every two years. Engine overhauls are expected to put the aircraft out of commission for several weeks.

The aircraft is configured to carry 15 First Class, 50 Business Class and 76 Economy Class passengers. The aircraft has a generous hold capacity for Sepiana's numerous horticultural products (eg of cocoa, tea and fruit) and general cargo.

The six hour journey offers an in-flight movie, a meal, hot and cold drinks and tax-free shopping. All meals are prepared in Lyme under a contract with an airport catering company. Passengers are invited to complete a 'satisfaction' questionnaire which is included with the in-flight entertainment and shopping guide. Responses received show that passengers are generally least satisfied with the quality of the food – especially on the Darke to Lyme flight.

Azure employs 10 full-time cabin crew attendants who are trained in air-stewardship including passenger safety in the event of accident and illness. Flight personnel (the captain and co-pilots) are provided under a contract with the international airline from which the aircraft is leased. At the end of each flight the captain completes a timesheet detailing the crew and actual flight time.

Ticket sales are made by Azure and travel agents in Sepiana and Pewta. On a number of occasions Economy seating has been over-booked. Customers who have been affected by this have been accommodated in Business Class as there is much less demand for this, and even less for First Class. Ticket prices for each class depend on many factors, for example, whether the tickets are refundable/non-refundable, exchangeable/non-exchangeable, single or return, mid-week or weekend, and the time of booking.

Azure's insurance cover includes passenger liability, freight/baggage and compensation insurance. Premiums for passenger liability insurance are determined on the basis of passenger miles flown.

Required

(a)   Identify and explain the business risks facing Azure.   **(9 marks)**

(b)   Recommend how the risks identified in (a) could be managed and maintained at an acceptable
         level by Azure.   **(9 marks)**

(c)   Recommend FOUR measure of operational performance and the evidence that should be available
         to provide assurance on their accuracy.   **(7 marks)**

Note: You should assume it is 5 December 20X6.   **(Total = 25 marks)**

3 Bonus schemes

45 mins

Learning outcome B3(a)

It has been suggested that optimal bonus schemes for profit centre managers promise significant rewards for the achievement of challenging targets in areas they can influence. These schemes balance short-term pressure with incentives to maintain a long-term focus and protect managers from the distorting effects of uncontrollable factors.

It has also been suggested that many bonus schemes have additional features with different motivational effects.

The following are possible features of bonus schemes.

- Limiting the range of performance within which rewards are linked to results, in particular ignoring losses and limiting maximum payments

- Linking incentive payments wholly or partly to the profit of the organisation as a whole

Required

(a) (i) Explain why bonus schemes might include these features.
    (ii) Explain the effects of incorporating these features in bonus schemes. **(16 marks)**

Bonus schemes are normally designed to motivate full-time employees who have no other employment and are wholly dependent upon the organisation for their income. Part-time employees and short-term employees might not be included.

Required

(b) Describe and advise on the possible features of bonus schemes which are designed to motivate non-executive directors who are part-time, remunerated by fees under contracts for a fixed number of years and required by corporate governance codes to maintain independence. **(9 marks)**

(Total = 25 marks)

4 Integrated Broadcasting Organisation

45 mins

Learning outcomes B2(a), (b), 3(a)

Ben Jackson has recently been appointed as Managing Director of the Integrated Broadcasting Organisation (IBO), the biggest broadcaster in a large European country, Tara. Ben Jackson has previously worked for this company in a senior management role, was then headhunted to be Chief Executive of one of IBO's main rivals. He has recently been recruited back to IBO.

Background

IBO runs national television and radio channels, and also broadcasts worldwide through satellite. Its drama and comedy productions enjoy a high international reputation and IBO gains significant income from sales of these productions on DVD and to foreign broadcasters. Its other major sources of income include a levy on sales of radios and televisions, programme sponsorship, donations to benefit specific programming strands such as education and subscription channels dedicated to its old shows and national sporting events. IBO has competitors in Tara in both radio and television broadcasting, that are funded by advertising, digital subscription and other commercial activities. These include the Network Group, which owns a commercial television group as well as Tara's biggest selling newspaper, the Daily Network. All the major broadcasters are currently investing heavily in new media technologies to command higher subscription uptake. Technology is also developing so that laptops and mobile phones are increasingly being used as TV devices.

Corporate governance

IBO is governed by a Management Board consisting of the Managing Director, seven other executive directors and eight trustees. Details of the trustees are as follows:

- Liz Shaw, a member of the Council of the Advertising Authority which enforces advertising standards in Tara

- Peri Brown, managing director of a large independent production company in IBO's home country that supplies programmes to IBO

- Jamie McCrimmon, a member of the Upper House of Tara's legislature who represents the governing party

- Ian Chesterton, chair of Tara's Arts Council

- Harry Sullivan, a non-executive director of the Network Group

- Steven Taylor, who is on the board of Tara's Integrated Transport Authority

- Victoria Waterfield, who is on the executive committee of the Civic Values Trust, which sponsors a number of IBO's education programmes

- Zoe Herriot, who is a well-known economist and Vice-Chancellor of Tara's Arts authority

The major board committees are:

- Remuneration which is staffed solely by trustees

- Appointments, Audit, Finance, Strategy and Editorial Standards which are staffed 50:50 by trustees and Executive Directors

Ben Jackson has reservations about these arrangements and wishes to introduce a model of corporate governance that is based on internationally accepted guidance such as the Combined Code.

Required

(a) Analyse the strategic risks faced by IBO and explain the role that the Management Board should take in managing those risks. **(15 marks)**

(b) Prepare a memo advising Ben Jackson of shortcomings in the current governance arrangements and recommending improvements. **(10 marks)**

(Total = 25 marks)

5 Governance and controls   45 mins

Learning outcome B3(a)

Corporate governance issues first came to prominence in the late 1980s and early 1990s, and triggered the requirement for companies with shares traded on the main stock market to have a system of corporate governance in place.

Required

(a) Discuss the main issues that triggered the requirement for systematised corporate governance in large public companies. **(10 marks)**

A UK public company has an official listing for its shares, which are traded on the London Stock Exchange. The company has a small head office, including a non-executive chairman, a chief executive and a finance director. There are three major business divisions, each headed by a main board member, and each business division consists of a number of operating units (subsidiaries). The management structure is largely decentralised, and many operating and spending decisions are taken at operating unit level. Operations are carried on throughout Europe. The board consists of five executive directors, a non-executive chairman, and five non-executive directors. There is no internal audit department.

The board is required to make an annual statement in its report and accounts about the effectiveness of its internal controls.

Required

(b)   Explain what the board should do before it is in a position to make a statement about the effectiveness of its internal controls. Give particular attention to the responsibilities of different people for control, the need for a control environment, the evaluation of risks, risk management, the information and communication systems, control procedures and monitoring and corrective action.   **(15 marks)**

(Total = 25 marks)

6 Divisionalised structures

45 mins

Learning outcome A1(a)

Divisionalised structures are normal in large firms, and occur even when centralised structures would be feasible.

Required

(a)   Explain and discuss the arguments for divisionalised structures in large firms.   **(7 marks)**

(b)   Explain the costs and potential inefficiencies of a divisionalised structure.   **(8 marks)**

(c)   Explain how adoption of a divisionalised structure changes the role of top management and their control of subordinates.   **(10 marks)**

(Total = 25 marks)

7 Fraud and codes of conduct

45 mins

Learning outcomes A1(c), B3(b)

(a)   Explain how management control systems can help to minimise the risk of fraud in purchasing.

(10 marks)

Some codes of conduct appear to have a double standard. One such is quoted below.

Customer and supplier relations

The company does not seek to gain any advantage through the improper use of business courtesies or other inducements. Good judgement and moderation must be exercised to avoid misinterpretation and adverse effect on the reputation of the company and its employees. Offering, giving, soliciting or receiving any form of bribe is prohibited.

Business courtesies

Gifts, favours and entertainment may be given in the following circumstances.

(i)   If they are consistent with customary business practices.
(ii)   If they are not excessive in value and cannot be construed as a bribe or payoff.
(iii)   If they are not in contravention of applicable law or ethical standards.
(iv)   If they will not embarrass the company or the employee if publicly disclosed.

Gifts, favours, entertainment or other inducements may not be accepted by employees from any person or organisation that does or seeks business with, or is a competitor of, the company, except as common courtesies usually associated with customary business practices. An especially strict standard applies when suppliers are involved. Favours or entertainment, appropriate in our sales programmes may not be appropriate or acceptable from suppliers. It is never acceptable to accept a gift in cash or cash equivalent.

Required

(b)   Discuss the acceptability of the above code of conduct. If you consider it appropriate, recommend with reasons any amendments you would wish to see in the code of conduct.   **(15 marks)**

(Total = 25 marks)

8 Controls over cash and cheques   45 mins

Learning outcome B2(d)

List the types of control which may exist over the system for handling cash and cheques.

9 Pacific Group   45 mins

Learning outcomes B1(b), 2(d)

Pacific Group (PG), a limited liability company, is a publisher of a monthly magazine 'Sea Discovery'. Approximately 70% of the magazine's revenue is derived from advertising, the remainder being subscription income.

Individual advertisements, which may be quarter, half or whole page, are priced at $750, $1,250 and $2,000, respectively. Discounts of 10% to 25% are given for repeat advertisements and to major advertising customers.

PG's management has identified the following risks relating to its advertising revenues:

(i)   Loss of revenue through failure to invest in developments which keep the presentation of advertisements up to date with competitor publications (such as 'The Deep')

(ii)   Business being accepted from customers who default on the amounts they own but who fulfill the criteria for allowing credit established by PG's credit control department

(iii)   Published advertisements may not be invoiced due to incomplete data transfer between the editorial and invoicing departments

(iv)   Individual advertisements are not charged for at approved rates – either in error or due to arrangements with the advertisers. In particular, the editorial department does not notify the invoicing department of reciprocal advertisement arrangements, whereby advertising customers provide PG with other forms of advertising (such as website banners)

(v)   Individual advertisers refuse to pay for the inaccurate production of their advertisement

(vi)   Cash received at a front desk, which is significant, may not be passed to cashiers, or be misappropriated

(vii)   The risk of error arising from unauthorised access to the editorial and invoicing systems

(viii) The risk that the editorial and invoicing systems are not available

(ix)   The computerised transfer of accounting information from the invoicing system to the general ledger may be incomplete or inaccurate

(x)   The risk that PG may be sued for advertisements which do not meet the National Standards Authority's 'Code of Advertising'

Risks are to be screened out, as 'non-applicable', if they meet any of the following criteria:

(1)   The effect of the risk can be quantified and is less than $5,000
(2)   The risk is mitigated by an effective risk strategy eg insurance
(3)   The risk is likely to be low or its effect insignificant

Those risks not screened out, called 'applicable risks', will require further consideration and are to be actively managed.

Required

(a)   For each of the above risks identified by management, explain, with a reason, whether it should be considered as an 'applicable risk'.   **(15 marks)**

(b)   Recommend suitable internal controls to manage the applicable risks identified in (a).   **(10 marks)**

(Total = 25 marks)

10 Print room   45 mins

Learning outcomes A1(b), (d)

A local authority has recently extended its budgetary control and responsibility accounting system. A series of quarterly cost control reports has been installed in which each department manager receives a report for his/her department; a copy is also passed to a senior executive who controls a number of departments.

The printing department has just come 'on-line' with this system. This department deals with printing notices and letters to the local community, documents for in-company training, a new monthly magazine and all printing for other mailshots.

The print room labour consists of a manager and one other member of staff who has recently been appointed to cope with the increased demand arising from the introduction of the monthly magazine. In preparing the budget it was assumed that the new member of staff would be appointed on 1 March but the magazine was launched earlier than expected, resulting in production commencing on 2 January. However, the new member of staff was not appointed until 1 February. In addition to the manager and permanent member of staff, casual labour is appointed on a week to week basis to cope with excess demand. However, the casual labour is not used to produce the new magazine.

Shown below is the print-out of the first cost control report for the printing department. The manager had not been consulted over the budget and did not know the cost control report was being prepared.

The senior executive with responsibility for this department sent a strongly worded memo to the manager pointing out that any spending more than 5% above budget would not be tolerated. He requested an immediate explanation for the serious overspend.

COST CONTROL REPORT – PRINTING DEPARTMENT
QUARTER ENDING 31 MARCH 20X5

	Budget	Actual	Difference (over)/under
Print orders/copies	10,000	15,000	(5,000)
	£	£	£
Department expenses			
Supervisory salary	2,500	2,625	(125)
Wages (permanent staff)	700	1,400	(700)
Wages (casual)	1,500	2,500	(1,000)
Equipment deprecation	1,000	1,000	–
Repairs to equipment	100	20	80
Heating and power	500	600	(100)
Materials (paper)	10,000	17,000	(7,000)
Materials other	1,000	1,200	(200)
Allocated administrative costs	2,000	2,500	(500)
	19,300	28,845	(9,545)

Required

(a)   Identify any details or practices used in the preparation of the cost control report which may be inappropriate and recommend any corrections or extensions to them which may make the cost control report and procedure more effective. You may include numerical illustrations and comment on specific costs but you are not required to reproduce the report or calculate any values.

(17 marks)

(b)   Describe how the department manager's behaviour is likely to be affected by the report and the memo from the senior executive, if he/she is unaware of your points in (a) above.   **(8 marks)**

(Total = 25 marks)

11 JIT   45 mins

Learning outcomes A1(b), (d)

'Japanese companies that have used just-in-time (JIT) for five or more years are reporting close to a 30% increase in labour productivity, a 60% reduction in inventories, a 90% reduction in quality rejection rates, and a 15% reduction in necessary plant space. However, implementing a just-in-time system does not occur overnight. It took Toyota over twenty years to develop its system and realise significant benefits from it.'

Source: Sumer C Aggrawal, *Harvard Business Review*

Required

(a)   Describe JIT, and explain how the benefits claimed for JIT in the above quotation are achieved and why it takes so long to achieve those benefits.   **(15 marks)**

(b)   Explain how management information systems in general (and management accounting systems in particular) should be developed in order to facilitate and make best use of JIT.   **(10 marks)**

(Total = 25 marks)

12 Measuring risk   36 mins

Learning outcome D1(a)

(a)   Explain the difference between financial and non-financial (operating) risk.   **(3 marks)**

(b)   Describe the different ways that could be used for measuring risk in a project investment.

(6 marks)

Sternum is considering a two-year project to make and sell a single product. It has been estimated that the product will sell for £10 per unit, and will have a variable cost of £4 per unit. Directly attributable annual fixed costs would be £150,000 for any volume of annual production.

The marketing department has produced the following estimates of sales each year.

Year 1		Units sold	Probability
		50,000	0.8
		70,000	0.2

Year 2	Units sold in year 1	Units sold in year 2	Probability
	50,000	20,000	0.4
	50,000	40,000	0.6
	70,000	50,000	0.3
	70,000	60,000	0.7

The initial cost of the investment would be £200,000 at the start of the project.

Ignore taxation and inflation, and ignore any working capital investment.

The company has a cost of capital of 10%.

Required

(c) (i) Calculate the expected net present value of the project.

(ii) Calculate by how much would the initial capital expenditure need to exceed the estimate before the expected value of the project became negative.

(iii) Calculate by how much would the expected sales volume need to fall short of the estimate before the expected value of the project became negative.

(iv) Describe an alternative approach to risk assessment in this example, other than sensitivity analysis. **(11 marks)**

(Total = 20 marks)

13 Burnett

31 mins

Learning outcomes D2(a), (b), (d)

Burnett currently has a small overdraft and it expects that for the next two years the normal operating cash costs will equal its operating cash revenues. It cannot increase its overdraft.

In addition to normal operating revenues it is expecting to receive the sum of $10 million in March (exactly three months from now) from the sale of one of its subsidiaries. The contract for the sale of the subsidiary has already been finalised with a highly reputable, and financially strong, blue chip company.

The money is to be used to fund the purchase of a property as part of Burnett's strategy of relocating its activities. This contract has also been finalised with a contractual purchase price of $10.3 million and with completion to take place in September (exactly nine months from now).

Burnett is contractually committed to both the sale and the purchase and regards both the March cash inflow and the September cash outflow as being certain.

Burnett intends to invest, for the six month (183 day) period, all the funds when received in March. Because of the tight cash flow position Burnett must rely on receiving a good return on the $10 million. However interest rates in March might be considerably lower than their current level. It is suggested that a forward rate agreement (FRA) will minimise interest rate risks. FRAs currently available for a sum of $10 million are:

	LIBOR %
6V9	7.00 – 7.30
3V9	7.10 – 7.40
3V6	7.50 – 7.80

Over the next two years Burnett is hoping to expand and hence its hedging arrangements may become more complex. Burnett's finance director is considering whether Burnett ought to be using options.

Required

(a) Explain what a FRA is and demonstrate (without calculations) how Burnett should attempt to minimise its interest rate risks by using a FRA. Recommend which FRA is appropriate for Burnett's circumstances and identify the appropriate interest rate. **(6 marks)**

(b) Discuss the relative advantages of using exchange-traded interest rate options and over-the-counter (OTC) interest rate options. **(4 marks)**

(c) Identify the main determinants of interest rate option prices, and discuss whether or not the OTC options are likely to be expensive. **(7 marks)**

(Total = 17 marks)

14 Ferry
45 mins

Learning outcomes B1(a),(b)

In July 20X0, Ferry purchased exclusive rights to operate a car and passenger ferry route until December 20X9. This offers an alternative to driving an additional 150 kilometres via the nearest bridge crossing. There have been several ambitious plans to build another crossing but they have failed through lack of public support and government funds.

Ferry refurbished two 20-year old roll on, roll off ('Ro-Ro') boats to service the route. The boats do not yet meet the emission standards of Environmental Protection Regulations which come into force in two years' time, in 20X6. Each boat makes three return crossings every day of the year, subject to weather conditions, and has the capacity to carry approximately 250 passengers and 40 vehicles. The ferry service carried 70,000 vehicles in the year to 31 December 20X3 (20X2: 58,000; 20X1: 47,000).

Hot and cold refreshments and travel booking facilities are offered on the one hour crossing. These services are provided by independent businesses on a franchise basis.

Ferry currently receives a subsidy from the local transport authority as an incentive to increase market awareness of the ferry service and its efficient and timely operation. The subsidy increases as the number of vehicles carried increases and is based on quarterly returns submitted to the authority. Ferry employs 20 full-time crew members who are trained in daily operations and customer-service, as well as passenger safety in the event of personal accident, collision or breakdown.

The management of Ferry is planning to apply for a recognized Safety Management Certificate (SMC) in 20X5. This will require a ship audit including the review of safety documents and evidence that activities are performed in accordance with documented procedures. A SMC valid for five years will be issued if no major nonconformities have been found.

Required

(a) Identify and explain the business risks facing Ferry which should be assessed. **(12 marks)**

(b) Describe the processes by which the risks identified in (a) could be managed and maintained at an acceptable level by Ferry. **(13 marks)**

(Total = 25 marks)

15 OX
45 mins

Learning outcomes D2(a), (b), (d)

OX plc has export orders from a company in Singapore for 250,000 china cups, and from a company in Indonesia for 100,000 china cups. The unit variable cost to OX of producing china cups is 55. The unit sales price to Singapore is Singapore $2.862 and to Indonesia, 2,246 rupiahs. Both orders are subject to credit terms of 60 days, and are payable in the currency of the importers. Past experience suggests that there is 50% chance of the customer in Singapore paying 30 days late. The Indonesian customer has offered to OX the alternative of being paid US $125,000 in 3 months time instead of payment in the Indonesian currency. The Indonesian currency is forecast by OX's bank to depreciate in value during the next year by 30% (from an Indonesian viewpoint) relative to the US dollar.

Whenever appropriate, OX uses option forward foreign exchange contracts.

Foreign exchange rates (mid rates)

	$Singapore = $US1	$US = £1	Rupiahs = £1
Spot	2.1378	1.4875	2,481
1 month forward	2.1132	1.4963	No forward
2 months forward	2.0964	1.5047	market exists
3 months forward	2.0915	1.5105	

Assume that any foreign currency holding in the UK will be immediately converted into sterling.

	Money market rates (% per year)	
	Deposit	Borrowing
UK clearing bank	6	11
Singapore bank	4	7
Euro-dollars	7½	12
Indonesian bank	15	Not available
Euro-sterling	6½	10½
US domestic bank	8	12½

These interest rates are fixed rates for either immediate deposits or borrowing over a period of two or three months, but the rates are subject to future movement according to economic pressures.

Required

(a)   Using what you consider to be the most suitable way of protecting against foreign exchange risk, calculate the sterling receipts that OX can expect from its sales to Singapore and to Indonesia, without taking any risks.

All contracts, including foreign exchange and money market contracts, may be assumed to be free from the risk of default. Transactions costs may be ignored. **(13 marks)**

(b)   If the Indonesian customer offered another form of payment to OX, immediate payment in US dollars of the full amount owed in return for a 5% discount on the rupiah unit sales price, calculate whether OX is likely to benefit from this form of payment. **(7 marks)**

(c)   Discuss the advantages and disadvantages to a company of invoicing an export sale in a foreign currency. **(5 marks)**

(Total = 25 marks)

16 BS   45 mins

Learning outcomes D2(a), (b), (d)

BS is an importer/exporter of heavy machinery for a variety of industries. It is based in the UK but trades extensively with the USA. Assume that you are a newly appointed management accountant with BS. The company does not have a separate treasury function and it is part of your duties to assess and manage currency risks. You are concerned about the recent fluctuations in the exchange rate between US$ and sterling and are considering various methods of hedging the exchange risk involved. Assume it is now the end of March. The following transactions are expected on 30 June.

	£
Sales receipts	450,000
Purchases payable	250,000

Economic data

- The spot rate of exchange is £1 = US$1.6540-1.6590.
- The premium on the three-month forward rate of exchange is 0.82-0.77 cents.
- Annual interest rates for three months' borrowing are: USA 6 per cent; UK 9 per cent.
- Annual interest rates for three months' lending are: USA 4 per cent; UK 6.5 per cent.
- Option prices (cents per £, contract size £12,500):

	Calls		Puts	
Exercise price $	June	September	June	September
1.60	–	15.20	–	–
1.65	2.65	7.75	–	3.45
1.70	1.70	3.60	–	9.32

Assume that there are three months from now to expiry of the June contracts.

Required

(a) Calculate the net sterling receipts that BS can expect from its transactions if the company hedges the exchange risk using each of the following alternatives:

(i) The forward foreign exchange market

(ii) The money market

Accompany your calculations with brief explanations of your approach and recommend the most financially advantageous alternative for BS plc. Assume transaction costs would be 0.2 per cent of the US$ transaction value under either method, paid at the beginning of the transaction (ie now). **(8 marks)**

(b) Explain the factors the company should consider before deciding to hedge the risk using the foreign currency markets, and identify any alternative actions available to minimise risk. **(5 marks)**

(c) Discuss the relative advantages and disadvantages of using foreign currency options compared with fixed forward contracts. To illustrate your arguments assume that the actual spot rate in three months' time is

(i) 1.6458 – 1.6513
(ii) 1.7045 – 1.7100

And assess whether BS would have been better advised to hedge using options, rather than a fixed forward contract. **(12 marks)**

(Total = 25 marks)

17 Jennie   45 mins

Learning outcomes D2(a), (b), (d)

15 September data

Jennie, a German company, has made a large sale worth $5,000,000 to a US company, Ben Inc. Ben Inc is due to settle the amount it owes to Jennie in three months' time, on 15 December.

Currency Market Rates

Spot Rate $ per £1	1.5904 – 1.5912
Forward premium	0.0030 – 0.0023

Money Market Rates p.a.

Euro	2.6%
US	1.6%

Futures Prices (contract size = €125,000)

September	1.5897
December	1.5871

Currency options (contract size = €62,500; premia stated in cents per Euro)

	CALLS		PUTS	
Strike	September	December	September	December
1.5850	2.77	3.86	2.50	3.78
1.5900	2.54	3.61	2.75	4.07
1.5950	2.31	3.39	3.04	4.37
1.6000	2.08	3.02	3.34	4.86

Jennie receives the payment on 15 December when the spot rate is 1.6000.

The futures price when Jennie receives the payment is 1.5979.

Required

Recommend the most appropriate methods that Jennie can use to hedge its foreign exchange risk for the next three months. Your answer should include appropriate calculations to support your recommendation.

(Total = 25 marks)

18 Right   36 mins

Learning outcomes D2(a), (b), (d)

(a)   Identify and briefly explain the benefits of swaps to the corporate treasurer.   **(6 marks)**

(b)   Explain the types of risk associated with participating in swaps.   **(4 marks)**

Right wishes to borrow £3 million on a fixed interest rate basis for a period of three years. The treasurer has reported that the company can borrow at LIBOR plus 1% or issue three-year bonds at 6.5%. Herbert also wishes to borrow £3 million for three years, but at a floating rate. Its treasury department advises that it could issue fixed rate bonds at 6.0% or borrow at LIBOR plus 0.75%.

Required

(c)   Demonstrate how an interest rate swap would work to reduce borrowing costs for Right and Herbert. Assume that any arbitrage benefits are equally distributed to the two companies.   **(10 marks)**

(Total = 20 marks)

19 Facilities management   45 mins

Learning outcome E1(c)

The directors of DS are not satisfied with the GDC Ltd facilities management company which was contracted two years ago to run the IT system of the company. At that time, the existing in-house IT development and support department was disbanded and all control of IT systems handed over to GDC Ltd. The appointment of GDC Ltd was relatively rushed and although an outline contract was agreed, no detailed Service Level Agreement was produced.

Over the last few weeks the number of complaints received from staff regarding the service has been increasing and the provision of essential management reports has not been particularly timely.

A recent exchange of correspondence with GDC Ltd failed to resolve the matter. Staff at GDC Ltd recognised the fall in standards of service, but insisted that it has met its contractual obligations. DS's lawyers have confirmed that GDC Ltd is correct.

Key features of DS's contract with the GDC Ltd facilities management company:

The contract can be terminated by either party with three months' notice

GDC Ltd will provide IT services for DS, the services to include:

- Purchase of all hardware and software
- Repair and maintenance of all IT equipment
- Help desk and other support services for users
- Writing and maintenance of in-house software
- Provision of management information

Price charged to be renegotiated each year but any increase must not exceed inflation, plus 10%.

Required

(a)   Explain, from the point of view of DS, why it might have received poor service from GDC Ltd, even though GDC Ltd has met the requirements of the contract.   **(12 marks)**

(b)   Explain the courses of action now available to DS relating to the provision of IT services. Comment on the problems involved in each course of action.   **(13 marks)**

(Total = 25 marks)

20 Super Retail   **45 mins**

Learning outcomes E1(a),(c)

You have recently been appointed as a senior internal auditor at Super Retail, which operates a number of departmental stores across the UK. It currently retails only to customers who physically visit the stores. However, it operates a delivery system for purchases that are too large for customers to take home themselves, for example, for the furniture department and many of the electrical goods.

Super Retail is seeking to extend sales beyond customers who visit the stores and the directors are giving consideration to starting to trade via a website, within the country Super Retail operates in. They are considering options to achieve the aim of offering e-commerce from 1 April 20X7. (Assume it is now December 20X6). These options are:

(1)   Engaging specialists to build a website and employing additional staff to operate the ordering system. They would also expand their current delivery system to deal with the additional demand.

(2)   Option two is the same as option one, except that the company would use surface mail to deliver small goods, and would outsource the additional delivery requirement.

(3)   Outsourcing the entire 'e-commerce' business (website, order processing, delivery)

(4)   Purchasing an identified family Internet retailer which has a website and an existing contract with a delivery firm.

The strategy to consider outsourcing has been suggested by a director who is fairly new to the board. The other directors have no previous experience of outsourcing, and wonder what the advantages and disadvantages of such a strategy might be in practice.

The finance director has asked you to issue him with a report discussing any points which might be specifically relevant to Super Retail in this situation, including a discussion of the advantages and disadvantages of outsourcing, a risk analysis of the proposed strategy and the risks and costs associated with each of the options.

Required

(a)   As a senior internal auditor, draft the report for the finance director, discussing all the items that he has requested.   **(21 marks)**

(b)   Assume that Super Retail chooses Option 3. Discuss the implications that this option would have for the internal audit of Super Retail.   **(4 marks)**

(Total = 25 marks)

21 JS   **45 mins**

Learning outcomes E1(c), (d)

JS is a large manufacturing company. It operates from 10 different sites and produces a wide range of consumer goods. Within each site, each department (e.g. sales, production, inventory control) maintains its own independent computer-based Transaction Processing and Management Information Systems. The computer systems within a site, or on different sites, cannot communicate with each other. The lack of communication is a result of different system implementation dates, operating systems, hardware platforms and subsequent amendment by users of the software being used in each individual department.

JS is now experiencing significant increased demand for its products, and all systems, computerised and manual, are working excessively. A number of very large orders have recently been lost because managers made incorrect pricing and production decisions. This was surprising because managers obtained what they thought was up-to-date and accurate information from the company's computer systems when they were making the decisions. Subsequent investigation showed that the manager's decision-making process was not at fault: it was the information in the computer system itself that was incorrect.

Required

(a)   Explain why the information being provided by the computer systems could be incorrect. Make reference in your answer to the problems in JS's computer systems and the information being provided by the systems.

(12 marks)

(b)   Discuss how an information centre could help the company provide an acceptable standard of information to its managers.

(13 marks)

(Total = 25 marks)

22 Computer security
25 mins

Learning outcome E1(e)

Computer security is of vital importance to all organisations. Security is the means by which losses are controlled and therefore involves the identification of risks and the institution of measures to either prevent such risks entirely or to reduce their impact.

Required

Identify the main areas of risk which may arise in relation to a computer system.

23 Physical threats – contingency plan
45 mins

Learning outcome E1(e)

SCP Ltd is an engineering company which is about to implement a new production planning and control system. Following a strategic level review of the business, the board have decided that one of the company's critical success factors is the production of up-to-date and accurate information on internal (eg customer orders) and external (eg raw materials availability) factors, so that the company can respond quickly to changes in demand and other external circumstances. The new system will enable a rapid response to such information and will provide output for a range of production operations including machine loading, control of raw materials, production set-up, batch control, planned downtime and machine utilisation.

The system is seen as a 'mission-critical' one and the company is setting up a new computer centre, which will take responsibility for this system and also take over existing systems currently under the auspices of the finance, sales and personnel departments.

You have been asked to advise the company on the security aspects of the new computer centre.

Required

(a)   Describe the potential physical threats to make your client aware of and explain both the precautionary measures you would suggest and the techniques you would propose be implemented to control access to the computer centre.

(15 marks)

(b)   You also feel that a contingency plan is an essential aspect of the new computing facility.

Explain to the client the purpose of such a plan, how it might be developed, and the standby options which are available.

(10 marks)

(Total = 25 marks)

24 Outsourcing internal audit   30 mins

Learning outcome C2(c)

Internal audit has had an evolving role over recent years. It was highlighted as an important tool in corporate governance by the corporate governance reports of the 1990s. The Combined Code requires directors to review regularly the need for an internal audit function.

Another recent phenomenon in internal audit is the tendency of companies to outsource their internal audit function to the major accounting firms. One of the major reasons for this appears to be a perceived cost benefit.

Required

Discuss the advantages and disadvantages of outsourcing the internal audit function.

25 Audit and governance   36 mins

Learning outcomes B2(a), C2(a), (e), 3(a)

Required

(a) Explain the role of the external auditors in contributing towards a proper system of corporate governance, and describe what the relationship should be between the auditors and the audit committee.   **(7 marks)**

(b) Define what internal controls are and explain their purpose in a system of risk management.
                                                                      (6 marks)

(c) Explain what an internal audit department should contribute towards risk management, and describe the Turnbull Committee's recommendations on internal audit in listed companies?
                                                                      (4 marks)

(d) A recommendation of the Combined Code is that the positions of chief executive and chairman should not be held by the same person. Explain the reason for this recommendation.   **(3 marks)**

                                                                (Total = 20 marks)

26 Internal audit effectiveness   45 mins

Learning outcome C2(a)

As the newly-appointed finance director of a quoted company, you have just been asked by the chairman to advise him on the effectiveness of the existing internal audit department.

The chairman explained that internal audit has been established in the company for many years. The chief internal auditor, who has held this post for many years, has reported direct to the chairman. He has always had a right of access to the Board, and, since the establishment of an Audit Committee, has worked closely with that committee. However, there had been increasing friction in recent years between the chief internal auditor and your predecessor as finance director. Internal audit had been regarded by your predecessor as expensive, slow and ineffective.

Required

Write a report to the chairman explaining how the effectiveness of the internal audit department should be assessed. Your report should deal specifically with the following issues.

(a) What the objectives of internal audit should be.   **(6 marks)**
(b) Whether you should carry out the assessment yourself, or, if not, who should do so.   **(6 marks)**
(c) How the detailed work of gathering the appropriate information should be conducted.   **(4 marks)**
(d) The information required, and any specific financial or non-financial measures required. **(9 marks)**

                                                                (Total = 25 marks)

27 Analytical review

45 mins

Learning outcome C2(b)

You are a senior internal auditor at Patchit, a machine tool manufacturer. A draft set of financial statements for the year have been prepared by management, and it has fallen to you to examine the figures for reasonableness and at the same time identify significant audit areas which may require further work even though your systems audit during the year has proved satisfactory. You are aware of the fact that the company is at present contemplating an issue of £2,000,000 15% loan stock (redeemable in the year 20X0) in order to assist the remodelling of its present production facilities. The majority of the directors are in favour of making the issue but a few are reluctant to do so in view of the fact that the machine tools industry is subject to wide-ranging fluctuations in sales and profits.

Abbreviated financial statements for Patchit together with typical ratios for firms in the machine tool industry are as follows.

INCOME STATEMENTS FOR THE YEARS ENDED 31 DECEMBER

	20X2		20X1	
	£'000	£'000	£'000	£'000
Sales		23,500		20,500
Cost of goods sold		16,000		14,000
Gross profit		7,500		6,500
Selling expenses	2,700		1,900	
Administration expenses	2,300		2,600	
		5,000		4,500
Profit from operations		2,500		2,000
Interest paid		500		300
Net profit before taxation		2,000		1,700
Taxation		1,200		1,020
Net profit after taxation		800		680
Dividends paid		525		280
Profit for the year retained		275		400
Retained profit brought forward		6,090		5,690
Retained profit carried forward		6,365		6,090

STATEMENTS OF FINANCIAL POSITION AS AT 31 DECEMBER

	20X2		20X1	
	£'000	£'000	£'000	£'000
Total assets				
Tangible non-current assets (net)		6,315		5,600
Other non-current assets		800		750
		7,115		6,350
Current assets				
Inventory	5,100		3,200	*
Receivables	2,900		1,900	**
Prepayments	100		100	
Cash and bank	600		590	
		8,700		5,790
		15,815		12,140
Equity and liabilities				
Called up share capital				
Ordinary 50p shares authorised, issued and fully paid		350		350
Retained profits		6,365		6,090
		6,715		6,440
8% loan stock (20Y0 – 20Y3)		5,500		3,300
Current liabilities		3,600		2,400
		15,815		12,140

* (Inventory valuation at 31 December 20X0 was £2,500,000)

** (Receivables' balance at 31 December 20X0 totalled £1,700,000)

Typical industrial averages for 20X2 and 20X1 are as follows.

Gross profit on sales	34%	Acid test ratio	1.2:1
Net profit before tax on sales	11%	Average age of receivables	30 days
Net profit before tax on net assets employed	19.5%	Average age of inventory	73 days
Working capital ratio	2.5:1	Interest cover	8 times

Required

(a)   Review the above financial statements and industry averages and explain which main features therein require most attention during your forthcoming final audit.   **(12 marks)**

(b)   With regard to those areas which may cause you some concern, describe the main matters which you would need to investigate (a detailed audit programme is not required).   **(13 marks)**

(Total = 25 marks)

28 Stoy Toys   90 mins

Learning outcomes A2(b), B2(a), 3(a), C2(a)

Business background

Stoy Toys, a limited company, is a long-established manufacturer and distributor of children's toys. The company has expanded significantly over the last few years. The board is now contemplating seeking a stock market listing, probably in about 18 months' time. The majority (about 85%) of shares are held by members of the Stoy family who founded the company, although none of the Stoy family now take an active role in its management. The dividends paid to shareholders over the last few years have represented a fairly constant proportion of profits after tax.

The company's recent expansion has been largely due to having the rights to manufacture and distribute toys associated with the Puppy Pups television programme. This show, which features a family of mischievous but lovable puppies, has been a big success on children's television around the world. As a result Stoy has been able to expand significantly over the last few years.

As well as a marketing function, Stoy also has a product development function that researches the children's market and develops new toys. As a result the company has launched several new cuddly toys into the market over the last few years, aimed at younger children. However none of the other products launched has matched the initial success of the Puppy Pups, nor seem likely to have similar long-term appeal.

The most recent product concept to be developed by the product development function has been Attitude Girl. This represents the biggest product launch since the Puppy Pups. Attitude Girl represents diversification for Stoy in terms of:

•   Products – the company has not previously manufactured and sold dolls before

•   Market sector – the dolls are aimed at an older age range than the Puppy Pups and other recent products

In addition Attitude Girls will be sold in a package, complete with a number of accessories; the dolls will not be sold separately. The product launch will be tied in with the start of a cartoon series on European and American television about Attitude Girls and will coincide with the normal start of the increase in demand for toys leading up to Christmas. As with previous launches, the toys will be marketed extensively on major television channels; Stoy has not normally bought much advertising on smaller digital channels. Attitude Girls are the first toys that will not be manufactured in-house (see below).

One or two of the directors have doubts about this product. The view was expressed at the last board meeting that Attitude Girls would not be a major revenue earner and, 'We'd be better off buying the rights to manufacture Bagpuss.'

Board of Stoy Toys

The board of Stoy Toys currently consists of six executive directors, each with functional responsibilities. The board is chaired by the chief executive; there is no separate chairman. Stoy Toys' auditors have advised the board that if the company gains a listing, the local stock market's governance code will require that at least half of the board are independent non-executive directors. The chief executive has strongly expressed his unhappiness at this, saying that 'All non-executive directors will do is poke their noses in and interfere; they won't serve any purpose and will destroy board unity'.

However some of the shareholders of the founding family would like to see non-executive directors appointed whether or not Stoy Toys gains a listing. They have been increasingly unhappy about the way the board has been run over the last couple of years, believing that the other directors defer far too much to the chief executive's views. The shareholders suspect that a strong presence of non-executive directors could be a useful control on the activities of the board.

Directors' remuneration

Another aspect of the company that some shareholders are unhappy with is the directors' remuneration packages. Directors' basic salaries have increased significantly over the last few years, since the expansion resulting from the sales of the Puppy Pups. The directors are also paid a bonus of a maximum of 20% of salary, based largely on the sales and profits from products launched in the previous couple of years. The chief executive has argued that new products have the greatest strategic significance for Stoy Toys, since their success will justify the company seeking a stock market listing. The directors also receive very generous benefits in kind including expensive cars, health insurance and life assurance. The chief executive has expressed the view privately to other directors that they deserve generous rewards, as the expansion the company has enjoyed is due to their work, the founding family having failed to expand activities significantly when they managed the company.

Currently also all the directors have three year service contracts. The chief executive has argued strongly for these, stating that the company's strategy and operations would be significantly disrupted if any of the current board left suddenly. The shareholders have previously accepted this, but some of them are now wondering if long contracts are a good idea.

Management accounting systems

Whilst Stoy Toys has put considerable resources into developing and launching new products, the focus in its production activities has been heavily on cost control, with operational managers rewarded for meeting strict budget targets. However the chief management accountant has recently resigned saying he was fed up with being the 'budget bad cop, querying every last item with managers'. He also stated that the board had failed to invest in the up-to-date accounting systems necessary to support the implementation of strategy. A couple of directors have also queried the information provided at board meetings, saying that there is a lot of detail to go through, but it is difficult to see a clear overall picture of how the business is performing.

Product problems

The most recent product launch, of Stoy Toys' 'Techno Teddies' range, was not as successful as the board hoped, because of delays in production. These were caused by a failure to enforce internal quality standards, resulting in a major breakdown of a new machine and a delay in production of about two weeks. The operations director believes that the delay was entirely avoidable and the finance director has highlighted the extra costs and loss in expected revenues that resulted from this delay.

Internal audit

The external auditors have suggested that an internal audit function could help improve the efficiency of operations and contribute to preventing problems like those that delayed the launch of the Techno Teddies. However this suggestion has been dismissed by the chief executive who says that 'internal auditors are just tick and bash merchants who do work we pay the external auditors for'.

Outsourcing manufacture of Attitude Girls

Partly as a result of the delays in the last product launch, but mainly for reasons of cost, the board has decided to outsource the manufacture of Attitude Girls to a manufacturer based in the East Asian People's Republic. Although Stoy Toys has not outsourced to this country before, other toy manufacturers have, although a couple of large manufacturers have recently ceased outsourcing to this country and started producing in Europe again. The manufacture was put out to competitive tender, and the Operations Director has drawn up a service level agreement with the successful applicant, that he believes to be 'watertight'. This manufacturer offered to make the toys for a much lower cost than any of the other applicants; the board of Stoy Toys is currently waiting for details of production arrangements and practices, which the manufacturer was asked to provide by a week ago.

Required

(a)   Discuss the extent to which each of the following creates risks for the shareholders of Stoy Ltd:

(i)   Development of the Attitude Girls product
(ii)   Outsourcing of manufacture to the East Asian People's Republic
(iii)   Remuneration and service contracts of directors.   **(18 marks)**

(b)   Identify the problems with the current management accounting systems and information and recommend how the systems and the information provided can be improved.   **(12 marks)**

(c)   Discuss the ways in which the activities of non-executive directors can provide effective scrutiny over the board and the company's operations.   **(8 marks)**

(d)   As a consultant employed by Stoy Toys, prepare a memorandum to Stoy's board advising the directors of the benefits that a well-managed internal audit function could bring to Stoy. **(12 marks)**

(Total = 50 marks)

1 Types of risk

> **Top tips.** A simple revision question.

There are many different types of risk faced by commercial organisations, particularly those with international activities. They may be categorised under the following headings:

- General business risk
- Trading risk
- Cultural, country and political risk
- Currency (foreign exchange) risk
- Interest-rate risk
- Technological risk
- Fraud risk

General business risk

Business risk may be defined as **the potential volatility of profits caused by the nature and type of the business operations involved**.

Factors contributing to business risk will include:

- The type of industries/markets within which the business operates – the extent to which sales are vulnerable to changes in fashion, technology etc

- The state of the economy

- The actions of competitors

- The actions of unions or impact of government legislation

- The stage in a product's life cycle, with high risks in the introductory and declining stages

- The dependence upon inputs with fluctuating prices, eg wheat, oil etc

- The level of operating gearing – the proportion of fixed costs in total costs – the higher the level, the greater sales need to be made to break even

- The flexibility of production processes to adapt to different specifications or products

Trading risks

Both domestic and international traders will face trading risks, although those faced by the latter will generally be greater due to the increased distances and times involved. The types of trading risk include:

- **Physical risk** – the risk of goods being lost or stolen in transit, or the documents accompanying the goods going astray

- **Credit risk** – the possibility of payment default by the customer.

- **Trade risk** – the risk of the customer refusing to accept the goods on delivery (due to sub-standard/ inappropriate goods or other reasons), or the cancellation of the order in transit

- **Liquidity risk** – the inability to finance the credit

Cultural and political risk

Where a business trades with, or invests in, a foreign country **cultural risk** is introduced by the existence of **different customs, laws and language**. Communication between parties can be hindered, and potential deals put into jeopardy by ignorance of the expected manner in which such transactions should be conducted. **Political risk** is the risk that **political action** (exchange controls, tax changes, pricing regulations etc) will affect the position and value of a company.

Currency risk

Currency risk is the possibility of loss or gain due to **future changes in exchange rates**.

When a firm trades with an **overseas supplier** or customer, and the invoice is in the overseas currency, it will expose itself to exchange rate or currency risk. Movements in the foreign exchange rates will create risk in the settlement of the debt – ie the final amount payable/receivable in the home currency will be uncertain at the time of entering into the transaction.

Investment in a foreign country or borrowing in a foreign currency will also carry this risk.

Interest rate risk

As with foreign exchange rates, **future interest rates** cannot be easily predicted. If a firm has a significant amount of variable (floating)-rate debt, interest rate movements will give rise to uncertainty about the cost of servicing this debt.

Conversely, if a company uses a lot of fixed-rate debt, it will lose out if interest rates begin to fall.

Technological risk

All businesses depend to some extent on technology, either in the support of its business activities (eg the computers used by the accounts, stores and treasury departments), or more directly in its production or marketing activities.

As technology evolves and develops, firms can find themselves using out of date equipment and marketing methods, which may leave them at a **competitive disadvantage**. Products in a high-tech industry have very short life-cycles, and a firm must recognise and plan for continual replacement and upgrading of products if it is not to lose market share.

Fraud risk

All businesses run the risk of loss through the **fraudulent activities of its employees**, including management.

2 Azure Airline

Top tips. In (a) you would probably need to identify and explain half a dozen risks to gain full marks. The answer below contains more than this for illustration. Most of the risks identified below are signalled in the question. However, it is acceptable to use your general knowledge to identify a risk not signposted in the question, such as the fact that the price of fuel can escalate, and Azure needs fuel to operate.

In (b) you are asked for controls for the risks, and you must think widely about how the risks could be managed. For example, think about the lease contract. It must have contingencies and protections for Azure's operation in it.

It is important that you do not spend so much time on (a) and (b) that you do not attempt (c), even if you feel that it is hard. Again, use your common sense to think about practical measures in the airline industry. What performance factors are important to the company? The question indicates that efficiency and timeliness are important – think about how these could be measured.

Examiner's comments. When asked to 'identify' candidates must be brief and not copy out chunks of text from the question. Most candidates correctly identified the major business risks though fewer went on to explain them well. Far too many answers focused irrelevantly on competition. Candidates attempting (a) first, in isolation, tended to overrun. Marks awarded to (a) were restricted to the maximum available with not enough time being given to (b) and (c) or later questions.

Weaker candidates did not appreciate the business reality of the situation and the need to answer within the constraints imposed. For example, suggestions to 'buy a newer plane', 'buy another plane', 'employ own captain and co-pilot', were inappropriate to an entity operating just two days a week. Candidates should take note that they are provided with information relevant to the whole question. So for example, every item of information did not need to be translated into a risk in the answer to (a) and (b).

The reference to timesheets was a pointer to evidence requirements for (c). Even where this part was attempted many candidates did not read, or ignored, the underlined words and failed to answer the question set.

(a)   **Business risks**

(i)   **Leasing of equipment and specialist staff**

As Azure leases its equipment and the most specialised of its staff from another airline, there is a risk that its **equipment and/or pilots** could be **withdrawn** leaving it unable to operate.

(ii)   **Conditions of exclusive right**

The PAA requires Azure's aircraft engines be overhauled biannually. There is a risk that Azure will be **unable to meet this condition**, if the **lessor company does not agree** to regular overhaul, or that it will be **too expensive** for Azure to meet this requirement. It could then lose the right to operate, or its exclusivity, opening it up to competition. There may be other conditions which Azure has to meet, such as the two weekly flights being a minimum.

(iii)   **Necessary service suspension**

As Azure is required to overhaul its engines every two years, there will be a significant period every two years where Azure will either have to **incur the cost of leasing** other planes (assuming this is possible) or will have to **suspend services**. The cost of leasing other planes might be prohibitively expensive or the disruption to service might mean that conditions relating to the right to operate might not be met. As Azure only has one plane, service would also be interrupted if there was an emergency relating to the plane, such as fire or a crash.

(iv)   **Age of aircraft**

The aircraft being leased is old. This raises **operational risks** (it may not always be able to fly due to necessary maintenance), **finance risks** (it may require regular repair) and **compliance risks** (it may not meet environmental or safety standards, now or in the future).

(v)   **High proportion of expensive seats**

The plane leased by Azure has a **high proportion of empty expensive seats** and therefore **insufficient (overbooked) cheaper seats**. Although Azure can appease customers by upgrading them, this means the airline is operating well below capacity.

(vi)   **Cargo**

The flight route results in the airline carrying a large amount of horticultural produce. This raises various risks – that Azure might be liable to passengers if their **cargo deteriorates in transit**, that the airline might be **liable for any breaches of law** by its passengers (for example, if prohibited items are transferred into Pewta or Sepiana; (many countries prohibit the importation of animals or meat products or plants).

(vii)   **On-board services**

Customers are currently **dissatisfied with the food provision** on the flight and there is a risk that food prepared in Lyme may become **less appealing** and even dangerous when served on a Darke to Lyme flight (when it has been prepared a substantial time earlier, given a six hour flight, at least an hour's turn around time, and time for getting to the airline in the first place). If the food makes customers ill, Azure might be faced with compensation claims.

(viii) **Pricing**

There is a **complex system of pricing** and a large number of sales agents, and Azure is at risk of **operating at a sales value less than required** to cover costs (for example, if too many of the cheapest tickets are sold).

(ix) **Safety**

The airline industry has **stringent safety conditions** and Azure may face **customer boycotts** or difficulty in recruiting staff if safety requirements are not met, as well as the threat of not being allowed to fly.

(x) **Fuel**

The aircraft **cannot fly without fuel**, which can be a scarce or high-cost resource. If fuel prices escalate due to world conditions, the company might not be able to meet the costs of operating.

(b) **Managing risks**

(i) **Leasing of equipment and specialist staff**

Azure must ensure that the **terms of the contract** with the international airline ensure that aircraft and staff **cannot be withdrawn** without reasonable notice, and, that in the event of withdrawal, substitutes will be provided.

(ii) **Conditions of exclusive rights**

Azure must ensure that all staff are **aware of any conditions** and the **importance of meeting them**. However, this risk must simply be accepted as there is little Azure can do about conditions imposed on them by the governing body of their industry.

(iii) **Necessary service suspension**

Azure must have **contingency plans for service suspension**, such as ensuring their contract with the international airline ensures alternative aircraft will be made available to them in the event of maintenance or damage to the aircraft, or by making arrangements to lease from a different airline in the event of emergency. As a minimum, Azure must ensure that the airline they lease from would give them **financial compensation** in the event of aircraft or staff not being available, so that Azure's customers could be compensated.

(iv) **Age of aircraft**

Azure should have plans in place to be able to **lease/afford newer planes** if required to by law. Again, this could be written into their contract with the airline. Azure should **manage cash flow and borrowing facilities** so as to be able to afford ongoing maintenance when required.

(v) **High proportion of expensive seats**

Azure should negotiate a **reconfiguration of the plane** with the **lessor** so that business and first class seating could be reduced and more economy seats made available. If this is not possible with the current lessor, Azure should **investigate leasing differently configured planes** from a different company. If it is not feasible to adjust the plane seating, Azure should consider **its pricing and on-board facilities policies** to make business and first class seats more attractive to customers. As the seats are not being sold anyway, it is probable that a reduction in prices would increase overall revenue.

(vi) **Cargo**

Azure should **publish a cargo policy** to ensure that customers are aware of their legal obligations. They should ensure that staff are **sufficiently trained** to discuss the contents of baggage with customers and are aware what items Azure should not carry. They should insure against lost and damaged cargo.

(vii) **On-board services**

Azure should consider **entering into a contract with a company in Darke** to **provide food** for the Darke to Lyme journey. Obviously they must not breach any existing contract with the Lyme company and so in the meantime should review the type of food provided. For example, it might be safer to only offer cold food, for example sandwiches and cakes until a Darke contract can be set up. Even if a new contract is set up, it might still be best to offer cold food as there is less chance of health problems arising as a result of serving cold food rather than hot food.

(viii) **Pricing**

As discussed above, Azure should **review the pricing policy**. They should also **establish limits on how many of certain types of tickets** (non-refundable/single etc) can be issued for one flight and they should institute a **centralised system** to ensure that each agent is aware when limits have been reached. As the agents must be linked to a similar system already (to be aware of whether tickets are available for sale) this should not be too difficult to achieve.

(ix) **Safety**

The company should appoint a member of staff to be **specifically responsible for safety operations** (such as training, updating for legal requirements, educating passengers) and should ensure that staff are regularly appraised about safety issues.

(x) **Fuel**

The company could take out **hedging contracts** against the cost of fuel. Other than this, there is little they can do about this matter, and it is another risk that has to be accepted.

(c) **Measures of operational performance**

(i) **Passengers/flight**

The airline could have a **target number of passengers per flight** and must review actual numbers against target. Evidence of the number of passengers per flight will be easy to obtain as it will be a safety requirement that Azure maintains records concerning its passengers. **Evidence** will include ticketing information, check in records.

(ii) **Time of flight/check in**

The airline must have **target times for flight time** and check in time and review the percentage difference which occurs on a regular basis. The flight times can be obtained from the pilot's timesheet and the check in times could be monitored by asking passengers how long they have been waiting as they check in. **Evidence** will include timesheets, airport records.

(iii) **Customer satisfaction**

The airline should **record customer satisfaction** and have a target level of customer satisfaction which it hopes to achieve and maintain. This could be measured by customers completing questionnaires which ask them to rate the service, according to pre-designed ratings (for example, poor, adequate, good, excellent). **Evidence** will include the completed questionnaires.

(iv) **Safety**

The airline should have **targets for safety**, for example, no accidents/number of days or staff achieving safety qualifications. **Evidence** will include accident log books and staff certificates and training records.

3 Bonus schemes

Top tips. The biggest danger in (a) is the temptation to overrun on the time allowed for the solution, given the marks available. Bonus schemes are a recurring feature of this exam and most candidates should be able to write about them both from theoretical and personal knowledge without too much difficulty.

(b) requires much more thought – think about the key issue of independence for NEDs. As long as the features you suggest do not compromise independence or suggest awarding too generous bonuses you will be earning marks.

Examiner's comment. Common errors in part (a) were variants on failing to read the question carefully and plan an appropriate answer. Candidates were sensible to prepare for possible questions on bonus schemes but they must be prepared to answer the question actually asked, not the question on the topic they might have preferred.

(a) **Limiting the range of performance within which rewards are linked to results**

Many schemes do indeed limit the range of performance within which rewards are linked to results, in particular ignoring losses and limiting maximum payments.

Ignoring losses

Unless the organisation in question was operating in an extremely stable and predictable environment, it would be unacceptable to the vast majority of managers to be asked to participate in a remuneration system that might require them to reimburse their employer in the event of losses being incurred. In general, managers want to receive their standard salary, they do not want the threat of some of it being taken away if their organisation reports losses. If the organisation were to **impose penalties for poor performance**, managers may well **manipulate their targets to ensure that they did not suffer financially**.

Benefits and drawbacks of ignoring losses

If **losses are excluded** from the range of performance, **full participation** in the scheme is likely as no financial penalty (or negative bonus) can be imposed on a manager if levels of performance are particularly poor. Salaries will be viewed as fair payment for duties performed, with any bonus being regarded as a genuine reward for effort. Managers may **take unnecessary risks**, however, as they are under no financial risk themselves, and **poor levels of performance may be deliberately further depressed** to ensure easier future targets.

Capping maximum payments

Reasons for capping maximum payments include a desire by risk averse managers to **limit the organisation's maximum liability** and the **prevention of payments which shareholders might regard as excessive**.

Benefits and drawbacks of capping maximum payments

Capping maximum payments should ensure that managers **concentrate on improvements which will be sustainable year-on-year**. The financial incentive provided should be large enough to motivate without being excessive. Managers might feel **no incentive to improve performance beyond the cut-off level**, however, and they could be forced into **holding back for future periods profit-generating or cost-cutting strategies and ideas** once the maximum limit has been reached. A limit on maximum payments could also cause managers to feel **disempowered**, the message being sent out by the bonus system indicating that no matter how good their performance, the most they would receive is £X.

Linking incentive payments to the profits of the organisation as a whole

This is a **popular feature** in many bonus schemes for a number of **reasons**.

(i) Profit is a **widely-understood measure**, and the maximisation of organisational profit is generally accepted to be congruent with the goals of shareholders.

(ii) As **profit reporting forms** part of most organisation's **standard reporting procedures**, little additional work is required for profit to be used as the standard measure of performance (compared with more elaborate performance reward mechanisms which can generate substantial data collection costs).

(iii) It also provides a **basis for participation** in bonus schemes by service centre staff such as those of internal audit and IT departments, for whom the use of other measures can be much more problematic.

(iv) The profit reported by many profit centres will be **significantly affected** by **head office policies** on, for example, salary levels or stock valuation, and so overall organisational profit may be more objective.

(v) Rather than arguing over scarce resources, the use of organisational profit may persuade **profit centre managers** to **work together** to further the aims of the organisation as a whole.

(vi) As agents of the organisation's shareholders, **managers' rewards should be closely linked to the rewards of shareholders.**

Benefits of linking payments to organisational profits

(i) Inter-profit centre/-divisional **conflicts should be minimised**, with all parts of the organisation concentrating on group results.

(ii) Management attention should be focused on the need to **cut unnecessary expenditure.**

(iii) Management will **not be diverted from performing their regular duties** to agree on more elaborate performance-reward systems.

Drawbacks of linking payments to organisational profits

(i) If the proportion of the bonus that is linked to overall organisational performance is significant and other profit centres do not perform well, managers will get a **reduced bonus** payment or even no payment at all. Managers who consistently perform well and achieve their individual targets are likely to become demotivated if they receive no bonus because of poor levels of performance in other parts of the organisation.

(ii) Managers could feel that their **area of responsibility** is **too small** to have a substantial impact on group profits and may become demotivated.

(iii) Managers may **cut short-term, discretionary costs** in order to achieve current profit targets at the **expense of future profits**.

(b) **Bonus schemes for non-executive directors (NEDs)**

The design of bonus schemes for NEDs is **problematic**. If the bonus is **too small** the NEDs may **not be motivated** to do anything more than the minimum required to collect their fees. If the bonus is **too generous** they may **stop acting in the best interests of shareholders for fear of incurring the displeasure of the executive directors** and thereby jeopardizing their bonus payments.

A bonus scheme for NEDs will therefore need to include the following **features**.

(i)   It should ensure that **high quality and motivated NEDs** are recruited, thereby ensuring that shareholders will benefit from the appointment of the NEDs.

(ii)   The bonus should be paid either **in cash or in the companies' shares**. Such methods will motivate the NED without contravening the recommendation from the Hampel report that NEDs are not granted share options.

(iii)   The bonus scheme could be **linked to the long-term performance of the company**, rather than simply to the financial performance of the current period. A **balanced range of performance measures** such as increase in market share or stock market valuation in relation to competitors over a certain period of time (depending on the NEDs' length of contract) and so on should **encourage NEDs to take a broader view of corporate governance.**

(iv)   It is important that **good corporate governance is seen to be maintained**. Shareholders' prior approval of any bonus scheme should be obtained to avoid any impression that NEDs' bonuses are being offered as a *quid pro quo* for the executive directors' remuneration.

(v)   Any bonus scheme should be designed to provide an **incentive for the NED** to achieve **specific objectives** or complete specific tasks outside his normal duties as a NED.

Bonuses are justified for tasks such as carrying out competitor reviews or designing staff remuneration schemes, which will enhance the NED's understanding of the business without compromising his independence.

(vi)   Any **goal-oriented bonuses** should **be paid immediately following the work to which they relate**. Rolling up of bonus payments may silence any criticism from the NED as the payment date approaches.

4 Integrated Broadcasting Organisation

Top tips. The analysis in (a) is very similar to the threats part of a SWOT analysis which you may have encountered in other exams. The answer systematically looks at the threats to each source of income. Also important is whether IBO can generate a clear strategy; its variety of involvements and sources of income suggest it might not be.

Knowledge of the Combined Code can gain you some easy marks in (b) but there are other issues which require you to think beyond the guidance. What constitutes an unacceptable conflict of interest? How can trustees discharge their monitoring role effectively (arguably the monitoring role is even more important than it would be in a listed company given the nature of IBO)?

(a)   **Strategic risks**

Strategic risk relates to the **potential volatility of profits** caused by the nature and types of the business operations. It therefore concerns the fundamental and key decisions that the board takes about the organisation.

Threats to income

Levy

IBO's income from the **levy on television and radio sales** may be **threatened** if the government decides that the levy is politically unpopular and **abolishes it** or **reduces it in real terms**. IBO also faces the threat from a decline in radio and television sales, as viewers and listeners use other technology to obtain IBO's programmes.

Sponsorship

Sponsors may **withdraw sponsorship** from programmes or IBO as a whole if they feel their investment appears tainted because of ethical problems surrounding IBO. In the UK for example, Carphone Warehouse ceased sponsoring the programme Big Brother after a scandal. Sponsorship income may also be at risk if competitor action results in **audiences for IBO's programmes falling**.

Donations

Donation income may be threatened if donors believe that IBO is **not giving sufficiently high priority** to the programmes they wish to see on air, for example broadcasting them at times when the audience will be low. Like sponsors, donors may also be put off by the recent scandals surrounding IBO.

Subscriptions

Subscription income will depend on IBO's ability to **supply programmes** that audiences wish to pay for directly. The income from sports channel subscriptions may be most vulnerable if competitors acquire the rights to major sports.

Increased expenditure

New technologies

Because of the threats to income, IBO may have no choice but to **develop its services and technologies**. The expenditure and benefits of these may be uncertain; the technology investments may prove to be greater than expected as technology develops quicker than expected. Expenditure on new channels to attract a fresh, for example younger, audience may not be justified by the income received if the channels do not prove popular.

Rights

IBO may face a bidding war with an uncertain cost outcome if it wishes to **retain the rights to major sports**.

Confusion of strategic decision-making

The strategic decision-making process may also be a factor increasing the level of strategic risk. Because IBO has a number of **different key stakeholders** who provide **financial support** for its programmes and who are represented on its management board, its strategy has to satisfy all of them. This may lead to sub-optimal decisions being taken.

Role of Management Board

Risk appetite definition

The acceptability of the risks involved must be integral to the board, in particular the **strategy committee's**, decision-making. The **pay-off between risk and return** must be considered carefully, particularly where the benefits may be rather **less tangible** than the costs.

Risk and control management systems and environment

The board is responsible for establishing **appropriate risk management systems** that combat the main risks IBO faces. It is also responsible for overseeing the **environment** within which risk management takes place; is the focus on **innovation** and making programmes that may not be popular or is the focus on **achieving large audiences**. This needs to be communicated clearly to staff through **training and publicity**. The board is also responsible for ensuring that the IBO's **core values** are clearly stressed to staff and that they demonstrate their own **adherence** to these values. Clearly the IBO does have a management hierarchy, but the board also needs to ensure that the accountabilities and authorities within the hierarchy are understood.

Risk review

Review of major risk issues should be a **regular part of the board's agenda**. The board should review the risks, the strategies for identifying the risks and the controls and the other actions being taken to **reduce risks**. The board should obtain information by regular reports on different areas by senior managers and reports on key risk areas, also from staff expressing concerns. A better system of information gathering might have lead to the current problems being identified earlier. The board should also conduct an annual review covering longer-term issues such as **changes in risk** and the **scope of management monitoring**.

(b)   **To:** Ben Jackson
From: Consultant
Date: 26 November 20X7
Subject: Corporate governance arrangements

Introduction

You asked me to advise on current governance arrangements and to recommend appropriate improvements.

Lack of independent non-executive directors

Half of the Management Board are trustees, equivalent to non-executive directors (NEDs) in companies. However governance reports specify that half of the board should be not just NEDs but independent NEDs. A number of the trustees cannot be classified as independent because of their connections with key stakeholders in the IBO:

- Peri Brown, as managing director of a programme **supplier** to IBO

- Harry Sullivan, as a director of a **competitor** of IBO

- Jamie McCrimmon, as a **representative of the governing party of Tara**, which makes decisions on how the IBO is meant to be financed

- Victoria Waterfield, as Director of one of IBO's **main sources of finance**

Further non-executive directors therefore need to be appointed to ensure that the IBO has **sufficient independent trustees.**

Conflicts of interest

The analysis about non-executive directors must be taken further and questions asked whether it is appropriate that certain non-executive directors are on the Board at all. Directors have a **fiduciary duty** to act in accordance with the best interests of the organisation for which they are directors. It would appear to be impossible for Harry Sullivan to serve effectively both the IBO and its rival the Network Group; also Peri Brown has a duty as MD of the supplier which may conflict with the best interests of the IBO, if for example the supplier is tendering in competition with rivals. Since one of the three Is fundamental values of the IBO is **independence**, Jamie McCrimmon's position seems doubtful as it lays the IBO open to suspicions of party political influence, as there does not appear to be a representative from the opposition parties on the board.

It seems vital for the IBO to avoid accusations of political bias so Jamie McCrimmon should **resign from the board**. Harry Sullivan's conflict of interest is so fundamental that he too should **leave the board**. Peri Brown's conflict of interest is confined to the area of programmes that her production company makes. She can therefore remain on the board provided her position is **clearly disclosed** and she is **not involved in any decisions that affect her production company**.

Role of non-executive directors

The major corporate governance reports believe that NEDs should be involved in discussions about **strategy**; as directors they are responsible for supervising the company and the experience they bring from other companies is helpful. However governance reports also stress the monitoring role of NEDs, implying that their main role is to scrutinise rigorously the proposals made by NEDs. The involvement of trustees in the strategy committee may be a weakness, since if trustees are actively involved in setting strategy, they will then find it difficult to **criticise their own decisions**.

A trustee presence on the strategy committee may be valuable, but there should also be a strong trustee presence on the main board that is not involved in the strategy committee, and can therefore **monitor its activities effectively.** Possibly also the specification of the duties of trustees requires amendment to clarify their role in determining strategy.

Board committees

Although the IBO has established the main board committees, the membership of the appointments and audit committees are not in accordance with governance best practice. Best practice recommends that a majority of the members of the appointments committee should be **independent NEDs,** and all the members of the audit committee should be **independent NEDs,** as these committees play a vital role in scrutinising management.

The membership of these committees should therefore be **changed** to be in accordance with **governance best practice.**

Risk committee

Although other board committees deal with aspects of risk, IBO lacks a **risk committee.** Having a committee of directors and trustees specifically responsible for overseeing the risk arrangement framework should mean risk management is supervised more effectively, and that problems like those that have happened recently are avoided.

A separate risk committee should be established, staffed mainly by the trustees. Its remit should include approving **risk management strategy and risk management policy**, **reviewing reports on key risks, monitoring overall exposure to risk** and **assessing the effectiveness of risk management systems.**

5 Governance and controls

Top tips. The points in (a) are useful general background for any question on corporate governance. They provide a useful set of values and problems to benchmark an organisation's corporate governance arrangements.

(b) covers the responsibilities of different levels. Fundamentally the board's statement on internal controls will not be worth much unless the directors are sure that they are in proper control; the answer shows how onerous the responsibilities are. The question directs you quite closely on the points to consider, but it's worth noting that the points required are very similar to the main stages of the COSO 'cube', which you looked at in Chapter 2. The easiest points to forget are the overall environment, information and communication and monitoring and feedback.

(a)   Several different issues triggered moves towards systematised corporate governance.

   (i)   **Global investment**

   The trend towards global investment has meant that large investment institutions in the US in particular have been seeking to invest large amounts of capital in companies in other countries. US investors, expecting similar treatment from foreign companies that they received from US companies, have expressed concern about the **inadequacy of corporate governance in many countries.** Many of their concerns focused on the **lack of shareholder rights**, or the disregard for minority shareholder rights shown by major shareholders or the boards of foreign companies. The OECD has recognised that the demands and expectations of global investors would have to be met if the trend towards global investment (and efficient capital allocation) is to continue.

   (ii)   **Standards of financial reporting and auditing**

   In the late 1980s, there were a number of well-publicised corporate failures, which were unexpected because the financial statements of those companies had not given any indication of their financial problems. This raised questions about the **quality of external auditing** and the **effectiveness of professional auditing standards.**

(iii) **Agency problems**

There were also concerns that many large companies were being run for the **benefit of their executive directors and senior managers,** and not in the interests of shareholders. For example, there were concerns that acquisitions were sometimes made to increase the size of a company and the power of its chief executive, rather than as a means of adding shareholder value. These concerns raised the question of the **conflict of interest** between the board of directors and the shareholders. A particular concern was the powerful position of individuals holding the positions of both chairman and chief executive officer in their company, and the lack of 'balance' in boards of directors.

(iv) **Directors' remuneration**

There is a widely-held view that **executive directors** are **paid excessive amounts,** in terms of basic salary, 'perks' and incentives. Some directors appeared to receive high rewards even when the company performed badly or no differently from the 'average' of other companies. Although investment institutions did not object to high pay for talented executives, they believed that **incentive schemes** were **often badly conceived,** and that executives were being rewarded for performance that was not necessarily linked to the benefits provided to shareholders, for example in terms of a higher share price.

(v) **Insider dealing**

Although convictions for insider dealing have been rare, there was a suspicion that some directors might be using their **inside knowledge** about their company to make a personal gain by dealing in shares in the company. For example, directors might sell a large number of shares just ahead of a profits warning by their company, or buy shares just ahead of a public announcement that might be expected to boost the share price.

(b) **Control responsibilities**

(i) **Board**

The board of the parent company should meet regularly, and adopt a **schedule of matters** to be considered for decision, so ensuring that it **maintains control over strategic, financial, operational and compliance issues. The** investigation of these matters will probably be delegated to the audit committee, but the main board retains responsibility. The board will also exercise control through its approval of the annual budget and performance targets, and a system of **regular performance monitoring and reporting**.

(ii) **Audit committee**

The audit committee should meet regularly, and its remit should include a **review of the group's system of internal controls**, based on information obtained from both external sources (the external auditors) and internal sources.

(iii) **Operational management**

In order to issue its statement about the effectiveness of controls, the board of directors must obtain evidence of the **existence and effective operation of controls and procedures** throughout the group. Due to the decentralised nature of this company and the absence of an internal audit department, the confirmation of this evidence will probably have to come from the **senior managers of each operating unit**. The senior managers or directors of each operating unit would need to summarise the key internal control procedures, and provide written confirmation on a regular basis that these controls are in place and working well.

(iv)   **Financial**

As there is no internal audit department, head office staff (probably accounts staff) should visit operating units regularly, to carry out a **financial review**. The results of these reviews should be reported back to the **finance director** and the **audit committee.** The heads of operational units should also be required to report to the audit committee on the adequacy of their system of internal controls.

The need for a control environment

A suitable control environment should be provided by a combination of **culture and management style**, together with management control mechanisms. The necessary culture should be stimulated by the directors' **commitment to quality and competence,** and the adoption of ethical and behavioural standards throughout the group. Management control mechanisms should ensure that there are **clear lines of responsibility** running throughout the group, that **budgeting systems** are in place, and that **management information systems** exist for the provision of performance reports in a timely manner. Operating units should be given **clear and achievable targets** aligned with the group's overall objectives. There will be **some delegation of authority to spend**, but within clearly stated limits. All **divisions** should have at least one main board director actively involved, so that there is direct knowledge of operating units at main board level

Evaluation of risks

In considering the soundness of the system of internal controls, the board should consider the nature and extent of the risks facing the company, the extent and types of risk that it is reasonable for the company to bear, the likelihood of the risks materialising, the ability of the company to minimise the incidence and impact of risks when they do materialise and the costs and benefits of operating particular controls.

Risk management

The board should have a focus on the **control and containment of risks**, based on a cost/benefit approach. Controls are likely to include a board policy **not to invest in any operation outside specific areas of 'competence'**, so that acquisitions are not made that **alter the risk profile** of the company's businesses significantly. The main board should discuss all major proposed new ventures, and when a new venture is given the go-ahead, it should operate with **clear financial constraints**. The board should also consider **other risks on a regular basis**, such as the risk from **new technology**. The risk of **non-compliance with legal and regulatory requirements** might be controlled at head office level by the finance director. Insurance arrangements might also be controlled centrally.

Information and communication systems

The group should prepare budgets for each operating unit. The **budget** should be approved by the main board. There should be **regular budget reports comparing actual results** against the budget. The information system should report on performance in a way that **non-performing or under-performing units** can be identified as soon as possible. New operations and under-performing units should be monitored closely by the board, and the board should have a policy of closing down under-performing units that do not improve.

Control procedures

The group should have a range of control procedures in place. The external auditors should check that the **financial controls** are **operating effectively**. Controls include, a suitable **segregation of duties** in the accounts department, the **use of accounting controls** (such as bank reconciliations), and **suitable controls for computer systems** (password controls, physical security for cheque books and computer equipment, etc.).

Monitoring and corrective action

There should be **regular reports to the main board on internal controls**, and the audit committee should be **given responsibility for monitoring the control system**. The board should also **discuss the risk and control implications of major changes**, such as new acquisitions. Whenever a weakness or failure in the control system is discovered, **corrective action** should be taken. The finance director should have specific responsibility for explaining to the board any **weaknesses or deficiencies uncovered in the system of financial controls**.

6 Divisionalised structures

Top tips. Parts (a) and (b) can be answered from book knowledge, and this would have been perfectly acceptable. Part (c), however, looks at the question from a slightly different angle, which requires some thought. You will almost always find that questions in the Performance Strategy exam do this. Many candidates will leave out these parts of questions, so any sensible comments you can find to make will impress the examiner and make your paper stand out from the others. In part (c) it is very helpful to think of control as 'making sure that the right things get done by subordinates'.

Other points. Instead of repeating book knowledge, an alternative approach to part (a) might adopt Williamson's ideas about transaction cost economics. We have included both approaches. Matters that you may legitimately have mentioned in part (c) but which are not included in our answer are organisational culture and leadership style.

Examiner's comment. Common errors were: misreading part (a) and setting out the arguments for *and against* divisionalisation; writing about the *measurement* of divisional performance (marks were not available for expositions of ROI and RI); writing far too much in answer to parts (a) and (b). Marks were allowed if candidates answered part (c) from the perspective of top *divisional* management, although the question was intended to be about top *group* management.

(a) **Arguments for divisionalised structures in large firms**

(i) **Decision makers at divisional level** have **more awareness** of their markets and products and of local problems. They are closer to, and so have a better understanding of, day-to-day operational problems.

(ii) There is **greater speed of decision making** and response to changing events since there is no need to refer decisions upwards. This is valued by customers and is particularly important in a modern, rapidly changing environment.

(iii) Divisionalisation allows more **senior management** to **concentrate on strategic problems** affecting the organisation as a whole. They need not be burdened by large amounts of information that is not relevant to their role.

(iv) Divisionalisation helps more **junior managers** to **develop** in roles of responsibility. Divisional managers can be more adventurous and are better motivated.

Development of hierarchy

An alternative is to argue that the **complexity of the transactions** required for a business to operate **increases, transaction costs can be reduced by adopting some kind of hierarchy**. For example, a firm that only needs legal advice on very rare occasions will engage a firm of solicitors from outside (from the market). If, as that firm grows, it needs legal advice more and more it will eventually be cheaper to set up a full time legal department within the organisation (in an hierarchical structure).

As the **level of complexity increases** still further and we get into the realm of the 'large firms' envisaged in the question, the **cost savings are counterbalanced by the increasing costs of keeping control**. These costs arise because managers are prevented by the hierarchical division of responsibilities from taking the best decisions in their limited area of control, and because information tends to be lost or distorted as it passes through the hierarchy.

Development of M-form

This **leads to** the development of the **multi-divisional** or **organisation** which, by mixing the features of both divisions and hierarchies, has the following **advantages**.

(i) Each division has **quasi-autonomous** status: it is a separate business unit.

(ii) **Strategic decisions** are taken by **senior managers** (the hierarchy), while **operational decisions** are made by **divisional managers** (the market).

(iii) An **incentive mechanism** exists and is used to encourage divisional managers to share the interests of senior managers.

(iv) An **internal audit system** is in place, with performance measures to evaluate the success or otherwise of both managers and of divisions.

(v) There is a system of **allocating resources** whereby senior managers distinguish the most profitable alternatives from amongst all divisions.

(b) **The costs and potential inefficiencies of a divisionalised structure**

(i) **Duplication of functions and facilities**. It is perhaps wasteful for each division to have, say, its own management accounting department or production equipment.

(ii) In spite of Williamson's ideals, there will inevitably be some **loss of information** *needed* by the senior managers to take strategic decisions. At the extreme, for example, a divisional manager may be able to hide the truth about a division's poor performance from the top management, who would close down the division or change its manager if they were aware of the full story.

(iii) Competition between divisions may be healthy and encourage all divisions to do better. If divisions are dependent upon each other for input, processing or output, however, competition may cause them to take **decisions that are not in the interests of the organisation as a whole.**

(iv) **Senior management** may find that it is spending much of its **time resolving disputes between divisions** about, say, unfair transfer prices or biased allocation of capital investment, rather than concentrating on strategic issues.

As business conditions alter, the balance of power must be able to shift between the central authority and the divisions if the organisation as a whole is to be capable consistently of striking the optimum balance between integration and autonomy.

(c) **The role of top management and their control of subordinates**

In a centralised structure **senior managers** are responsible for both the strategic management of the organisation as a whole and for the day-to-day operations of the functions they represent. With a **divisionalised structure** these managers hand over the management of functions to their subordinates. Their role **becomes one more like that of an investor looking for a return on an investment.**

(i) They need to learn to **manage with 'hands off'**, on the basis of summary data, without getting involved in the day –to-day detail. The control system needs to develop appropriate **performance measures** that facilitate this approach. An **internal audit department** reporting directly to top management may be needed for reassurance that day to day operations are being properly managed.

(ii) Rather than fighting their own function's corner in matters such as transfer pricing and capital investment they need to be able to look at these issues from the **point of view of group interests** and **proper co-ordination** of the activities of the organisation as a whole.

(iii) They may need to develop **reward systems** for subordinates **that ensure goal congruence.**

(iv)   They will manage from the point of view of the changing environment in which the business as a whole operates, but their perspective of the environment and their subordinates' perspective may be different. **Mutual sharing of environmental data** will become essential.

A useful exposition of the problems of control in large diversified companies is provided by **Goold and Campbell** who identify three different styles of central management.

(i)   **Strategic planning**, which entails the centre participating in and influencing the strategies of the core businesses.

(ii)   **Financial control**, which focuses on annual profit targets rather than getting involved in the detail of how these are achieved.

(iii)   **Strategic control**, where the top management is concerned with the plans of its business units but believes in autonomy for business unit managers. Control is maintained through **financial targets** and **strategic objectives**, but top management do not advocate strategies or interfere in major decisions.

7 Fraud and codes of conduct

Top tips. The key point in (a) was a recognition of the risk of collusion between purchasing staff and suppliers. The answer should have concentrated on controls which minimised this risk, particularly authorisation and monitoring.

In (b) we have looked at the ways in which the code can be seen as acceptable and the ways in which it can be seen as unacceptable and have then suggested ways in which it could be improved.

You may have simply concentrated on the factors within the code that required amendment and have redrafted it, or alternatively you may have defined and justified the code as it stands. Any reasonable approach will be rewarded.

Examiner's comment. Common errors included repeating the code in the question without adding any substantial commentary and commenting that it was a contentious subject, without either agreeing with the existing approach or proposing an alternative.

(a)   The following features of the system should help minimise the risk of fraud.

(i)   **Risk assessment**

Examples of purchase fraud include **rigged tendering**, **goods being supplied** for **private purposes** and **fraudulent transactions** with **connected companies**. In setting up a control system therefore, management should be aware of what kinds of fraud the business may be at risk of experiencing.

One possible danger is **collusion** between the person authorising purchases and suppliers. Once purchases have been authorised, there may be nothing further that can be done to prevent fraud. The important controls therefore are normally those which are aimed at identifying unusual suppliers or circumstances.

(ii)   **Monitoring of suppliers**

The risk of collusion between suppliers and employees can be minimised in a number of ways.

(1)   The person using the goods should only be able to choose suppliers from an **approved list**.

(2)   The use of new suppliers should be **authorised** by **someone other** than the person using the goods. The person authorising new suppliers should be particularly wary of any of the following:

- Abnormal terms

- Suppliers providing goods which they would not normally supply

- Suppliers which appear small compared with the proposed volume of purchases

(3) In addition these should be **regular monitoring** by management of arrangements with suppliers. Warning signs should be investigated, such as suppliers handled directly by senior staff, or suppliers handled outside the normal control systems.

(iii) **Controls in the payment cycle**

(1) **Segregation of duties**

Segregation of duties can reduce certain risks. **Segregating** the **cheque-signing role** from the **payment authorisation** role can reduce the risk that payments are made out to certain types of bogus supplier, for example those with abbreviated names. Part of the process of reviewing suppliers can be carried out at the payment stage, by checking that **individual** or **total payments** do **not appear excessive**.

(2) **Documentation**

Requirements for **full documentation** should be linked to segregation of duties. Full documentation would include **purchase requisitions**, **purchase orders** and **purchase invoices**. These can help prevent purchases for private use.

Documentation of returns is also important; **credit notes** should always be obtained from suppliers when goods are returned in order to prevent stock losses through bogus returns.

(iv) **Contract management**

There are a number of different types of contract fraud including fixing the contract tendering process and undue payments in advance. Ways of preventing contract fraud include the following.

(1) An open **competitive tendering** process.

(2) Interim payments being made on **certification** from **independent valuers**.

(3) Any **changes to terms** being **authorised independently** of the person who deals with the contractors on a day to day basis.

(v) **Organisation and staff controls**

(1) **Personnel**

References should be obtained for all new staff, and details retained of previous employers so that possible collusion can be checked.

(2) **Ethics**

A **business code of ethics** can remind staff of what constitutes unreasonable inducements.

(vi) **Internal audit**

Internal audit can play a role in a number of the above checks, particularly the following.

(1) **Detailed checks** of documentation.
(2) **Scrutiny** of suppliers and payments for suspicious circumstances.

(b)   As with many codes of conduct adopted in practice, there are both acceptable and unacceptable aspects to the code in question.

Aspects of the code which are acceptable

(i)   The organisation has adopted a code of conduct which attempts to **conform** with **customary business practices**. It wishes to behave in a manner consistent with that of others in the market.

(ii)   The code appears to imply that employees can take **slight risks** and go beyond behaviour that might be construed as strictly correct in order to secure sales. It would be logical and reasonable to do this in order to gain a sales advantage.

(iii)   The conduct of the members of the staff working in the **purchasing function** is **controllable** by the organisation and so the organisation can determine the code of conduct which should apply. The code of conduct covering the **selling operation** has to meet the **expectations** of the **market** and **customers**, however. The organisation has **no control** over its **potential customers**, who can decide whether or not they should accept any gifts, favours or entertainment offered. That part of the code of conduct relating to the purchasing activity is therefore necessarily stricter and more stringent than the part relating to the sales activity.

(iv)   Any **gifts**, favours and entertainment **provided** by a **supplier benefits** an **employee** whereas those provided for **customers benefit** the **customer** rather than the employee (unless the entertainment is lavish). There are therefore stricter controls over purchasing staff than sales staff.

Aspects of the code which are unacceptable

(i)   The code **fails to provide sufficient guidance**. For example, it does not specify the nature of customary business practices, common courtesies and so on. Employees have no idea about whether they can offer a potential customer a glass of wine, a bottle of wine or a case of wine.

(ii)   The code gives **no information** about the **repercussions** for employees for contravening the code. There is therefore no indication of the seriousness with which the organisation views breaches of the code.

(iii)   The penultimate sentence about 'favours or entertainment, appropriate in our sales programmes' implies a **double standard** and may encourage sales personnel to adopt a position which could damage the good name of the organisation.

(iv)   The unclear nature of the code relating to sales means that, because **behaviour is not actually illegal**, it may be **adopted** because it increases the organisation's short-term profits (despite the fact that it might have longer-term repercussions).

(v)   If **performance measures** are based on **short-term profit**, **employees** may feel **pressurised** into adopting unethical or even illegal behaviour.

Suggested amendments to the code of conduct

Given the above comments there are various amendments which could be made to the code of conduct to increase its acceptability.

(i)   **Ambiguous terms** should be **clarified**.

(ii)   **Penalties** for contravening the code could be **included**.

(iii)   It could be drastically **simplified** and the entire section on business courtesies deleted since the information provided in the remaining section provides an adequate and concise code of conduct.

(iv)   The **code relating** to the conduct of employees working in the **sales** function could be **rewritten** with the intention of making it as **strict** and **clear** as that covering the purchasing function employees (no entertainment, no gifts and so on). There are commercial problems associated with such an approach, however; the market and customers may expect a more liberal attitude.

Such changes would produce an **unambiguous**, **clear** and **concise code of conduct** which will **protect** the **integrity** of the organisation and allow **employees** to be **confident** that their efforts for the organisation will remain within acceptable limits.

8 Controls over cash and cheques

Top tips. In the exam you are more likely to have to relate the knowledge you demonstrate answering this question to a specific scenario, but this answer is nevertheless a very good test of your knowledge of accounting controls. Note that most of the answer is based round the concepts of internal regulations (particularly important for payments), staffing (including standby arrangements), physical controls, recording, and reconciliation.

(a)   **Receipts by post and cash sales**

The main control problem here is to make sure that none of the cash is stolen or 'goes missing'. Internal controls should include the following.

(i)   Safeguards to minimise the risk of someone **stealing** the mail after its receipt but before it has been opened.

(ii)   Wherever possible, **appointing a responsible person**, who is not the cashier, to open or supervise the opening of the mail.

(iii)   Ensuring that cash and cheques received are:

(1)   **Adequately protected** (for instance, by the restrictive crossing of all cheques, money orders and the like, on first handling); and

(2)   **Properly accounted** for (for instance, by the preparation of pre-lists of the cash received for an independent comparison with subsequent accounting records and book entries).

(b)   In establishing an adequate system of control over **cash sales and collections** the following factors should be decided.

(i)   Who is to be **authorised to receive cash** (ie whether it is to be received only by cashiers or may be accepted by sales assistants, travellers, roundsmen or others).

(ii)   How sales and the receipts of cash are to be **evidenced** and what checks may be used to apply some control over such transactions. For instance, serially numbered receipt forms or counterfoils, or cash registers incorporating sealed till rolls, can be used to prove that a sale has been made and that cash has been received into the company, thereby preventing the person who receives the cash from simply pocketing it.

(c)   **Custody and control of money received**

There should be adequate safeguards over any money received right up to the time it is banked. Suitable internal controls might be as follows.

(i)   The **appointment of suitable persons** to be responsible at different stages for the collection and handling of money received, with clearly defined responsibilities.

(ii)   **Preventing cash** from building up in large quantities, by arranging to bank the cash at suitably frequent intervals.

(iii) **Suitable arrangements** for **agreeing cash collections** with **cash and sales records**. The sales department is responsible for filling customer orders, but any cash for those orders comes into the company via the postroom and cashier. The company should ensure that sales records and cash receipts recorded by the cashier are agreed with each other, otherwise it will be difficult to tell whether goods have been paid for, and whether correct cash amounts have been received.

(iv) Arrangements for dealing with, **recording and investigating any cash shortages** or **surpluses**. If the amount of cash banked does not tally with the amount of cash received, or if the amount received does not tally with sales records, then the company should ensure that there is a standard procedure for investigating such discrepancies.

(d) **Recording cash received**

Incoming cash and cheques should be recorded as soon as possible. Means of recording include (as appropriate) receipt forms and counterfoils, cash registers and prelists. Aspects of internal control would be as follows.

(i) Specifying **who is to be responsible** for maintaining records of money received.

(ii) **Limitations on the duties and responsibilities** of the receiving cashier to prevent him from dealing with such matters as other books of account, other funds, securities and negotiable instruments, sales invoices, credit. In other words, can segregation of duties be applied?

(iii) **Standby arrangement decisions** as to who will perform the receiving cashier's functions during his absence at lunch, on holiday or through sickness.

(iv) In what circumstances, if any, are **receipts to be given** and copies of receipts retained; the serial numbering of receipt books and forms; how their issue and use are to be controlled; what arrangements are to be made, and who is to be responsible for checking receipt counterfoils against cash records and against bank paying-in slips.

(e) **Paying cash into the bank**

Cash and cheques received should be banked with the minimum of delay. It is poor security to have cash lying around instead of safely banked, and it is also poor financial management, as money cannot earn interest until it is banked. Adequate internal controls over banking cash receipts will involve rules concerning the following factors.

(i) How **frequently payments** are to be made into the bank.

(ii) Who is to make up the **bank paying-in slips** (preferably this should be done by a person independent of the receiving and recording cashier) and whether there is to be any independent check of paying-in slips against post-lists, receipt counterfoils and cash book entries.

(iii) **Who is to make payments** into the bank (preferably not the person responsible for preparing the paying-in slips).

(iv) **Whether all receipts are to be banked intact**; if not, how disbursements are to be controlled.

(f) **Cash and bank balances**

Questions to be decided in connection with the control of cash balances include the following.

(i) What amounts are to be **retained as cash floats** at cash desks and registers, and whether payments out of cash received are to be permitted.

(ii) What **restrictions are to be imposed on access** to cash registers and offices.

(iii) **Rules regarding** the **size of petty cash floats** to meet expenses.

(iv)   The **frequency with** which floats are to be **checked by** independent officials, that is, by employees or supervisors who do not have anything to do with the running of the cash float. Internal auditors are quite often used for this purpose.

(v)   **What arrangements** are to be made for **safeguarding cash** left on the premises outside business hours.

(vi)   Whether any special arrangements (such as **cash insurance**) are judged desirable having regard to the nature of the business, the sums handled, and the length of time they are kept on the premises.

(g)   **Regular reconciliation of bank accounts with the cash book**

This should be performed by a responsible official and is an essential element of control over bank balances. Considerations involve deciding to whom bank statements should be issued, how frequently reconciliations should be performed and by whom, and what procedures should be followed when carrying out the **reconciliation**.

(h)   **Cheque and cash payments**

The arrangements for controlling payments will depend to a great extent on the **nature of business transacted**, the **volume of payments** involved and the **size of the company**.

(i)   **Cheque payments**

Amongst the internal controls to be established for the system for payments by cheque are the following.

(i)   What procedure is to be adopted for **controlling the supply and issue of cheques** for use, and who is responsible for their safekeeping.

(ii)   Specification of who is to be **responsible for preparing cheques**.

(iii)   **Specification of the documents** to be used as **authorisation** for preparing cheques.

(iv)   The **names, number and status of persons authorised** to sign cheques; limitations to their authority; the minimum number of signatories required for each cheque.

(v)   **Safeguards** to be adopted if cheques are signed mechanically or carry printed signatures.

(vi)   The **extent to which cheques issued should be restrictively crossed**; and the circumstances, if any, in which blank or bearer cheques may be issued.

(vii)   Arrangements for the **prompt despatch of signed cheques** and precautions against interception.

(viii)   The arrangements to ensure that **payments are made** within **discount periods**, if the organisation would benefit from early payment discounts.

(j)   **Cash payments**

Factors to be considered include the following.

(i)   The **names, number and status of persons allowed to authorise cash expenditure**, and the documentation to be presented and preserved as evidence of cash expenditure.

(ii)   Arrangements to ensure that the **vouchers supporting payments** cannot be **presented for payment twice**. (The usual way of preventing this is to stamp the voucher 'paid'.)

(iii)   Whether the **level of an individual payment** should be limited, for example, a company may set the rule that cash payments can be made up to £100, but anything higher has to be paid by cheque and consequently has to go through the procedures governing cheque payments.

(iv)   Rules as to **cash advances to employees** and officials, IOUs and the cashing of cheques.

So far as possible the person responsible for preparing cheques should not himself be a cheque signatory. In turn, cheque signatories should not be responsible for recording payments. (Although, as mentioned earlier, in the circumstances of smaller companies, staff limitations often make it impossible to divide duties in this manner and in such cases considerable responsibility falls on the adequacy of managerial supervision.)

9 Pacific Group

Top tips. Bear in mind that the examiner has done the hard part already. The risks have been identified, you simply have to assess how serious they are. Make sure that you read the question properly and understand the criteria that the examiner gives you to judge whether risks are applicable or not, then apply those criteria to each risk in the question. If you are not sure, decide whether you can say more in support of classifying it as applicable or non-applicable. You will gain the marks for your explanations even if your final assessment of whether risks are applicable or non-applicable differs from our answer.

Examiner's comments. In part (a), the majority of candidates stated whether each of the given risks was applicable or not, but fewer provided a plausible reason for their conclusions. Too many 'sat on the fence' with a loss of easy marks. In part (b) easy marks were earned for controls over data transfer, cash, back-up measures, etc.

(a)   **Applicable risks**

   (i)   **Failure to invest in new developments**

   Applicable risk. The majority of PG's income comes from **advertising** revenue and therefore it is crucial that they keep up to the cutting edge of advertising developments, particularly when their competitors do. This could have a substantial adverse financial impact if advertisers decide to cut advertising in PG in favour of more up to date advertising techniques in competitor publications such as The Deep.

   (ii)   **Unsuitable credit limits**

   Non-applicable risk. As credit granting criteria are **set**, the chances of giving credit to customers who are poor credit risks should be acceptably low.

   (iii)   **Incomplete data transfer (editorial – invoicing departments)**

   Applicable risk. It is crucial to cash flow and business operations that **published adverts are invoiced**. Only two full page adverts and a half page advert would have to be omitted from invoicing before the effect of this risk would be greater than $5,000, and if the system is failing to transfer data, there is no reason to assume that the problem should be limited to so few adverts.

   (iv)   **Rates charged**

   Applicable risk. As seen above, given the prices of adverts, a **problem with a small number of adverts** can have a significant (>$5,000) impact. So, for example, if two full page and three half page adverts were given a 50% discount and the same number were given 'free' for reciprocal advertising, this could have a significant financial impact.

   (v)   **Individual errors**

   Non-applicable risk. PG is likely to have **reasonable controls over production** to ensure that errors in production such as typos, colour problems and such like are likely to be isolated and no individual advertisement has a significant financial effect on PG.

   (vi)   **Misappropriation of cash**

   Applicable risk. Cash received at front desk is **significant** and there appear to be no controls to ensure that cash is secure and passed on to cashiers. This is a big risk to PG as they may lose a large amount of income in this way. Again, it only requires payment for three full page adverts to be misappropriated to have a significant impact.

(vii) **Errors due to unauthorised access**

Non-applicable risk. It is likely that PG has **basic computer system controls** making this risk a low risk.

(viii) **Availability of systems**

Applicable risk. This risk is applicable because if PG do not have **contingency plans** against **systems failure**, (many companies with computerised systems do not) then the financial and operational risks of delay in invoicing and processing advertising orders could be significant in terms of customer dissatisfaction and delayed payments.

(ix) **Incomplete transfer of information to nominal ledgers**

Non-applicable risk. This is **potentially significant** to the **reported results** of the company but should not affect its operational or financial strength.

(x) **Risk of litigation for inappropriate advertising**

Applicable risk. As PG carries a large amount of advertising in its publication this risk is significant. Although PG is likely to have **insurance** for the financial impact of such litigation, the cost in terms of loss of reputation or/and therefore customers could be significant.

(b) **Controls**

(i) **Failure to invest in new developments**

- **Regular review of developments in competitor products** (for example, each edition, or each quarter)

- **Regular review of developments available** so as to be ready to action them if necessary

- **Regular review of actual investment costs** against budget, to see if any budgetary slack could be utilised

(iii) **Incomplete data transfer (editorial – invoicing departments)**

- **Reconciliations of advertisements** invoiced to advertisements appearing in publications

- **Serial numbering of advertisements** and **sequence checking** by invoicers

(iv) **Rates charged**

- **Authorised price list**
- **Authorised discounts list**
- **Comparison of PG's own advertising budget** to actual (to identify uncharged adverts)
- **Monitoring of percentage yield** for advertisements per issue
- **Minimum percentage yield** for advertisements per issue set

(vi) **Misappropriation of cash**

- **Cashiers to supervise post opening**
- **Front desk staff** to **issue pre-numbered duplicate receipts** for cash to couriers
- At least **two people attend cash opening**
- **Prelisting of receipts**

(viii) **Availability of systems**

- **Contingency plan** to be established to receive/process adverts/invoices if system fails
- **Tests** to be run to ensure disaster plans are successful/well known

(x)   **Risk of litigation for inappropriate advertising**

- **Staff training** in Code of Advertising to reduce inappropriate adverts being run
- **Editorial policy on adverts** should be circulated to all staff
- **Report system** including responsible official for all advert queries

10 Print room

> **Top tips.** Some of the points made in (a) are points you'll have discussed in answers to P1 and P2 questions. This reflects the fact that P3 is also part of the performance (management accounting) pillar of the CIMA qualification. However (a) also focuses on the control aspects which are a main theme of this paper. The point about the launch of the magazine is also significant in the context of this exam, as you will have to consider risk and control issues arising as a result of the strategic and business decisions made.
>
> (a) and (b) also go beyond the management accounting aspects and focus on the important human resource elements connected with performance reporting.

(a)   **Flexing for volume increases**

The cost control report compares the costs in the fixed budget, at an activity level of 10,000 copies, with the actual costs of producing 15,000 copies. Even though the print room has exceeded the original fixed budget for costs, measuring performance on this basis is inappropriate for control purposes, because it ignores the fact that some costs will inevitably increase as the **volume of activity increases**. In particular, **material costs and casual labour costs** should be expected to increase with output volume.

The cost control report should **compare the actual costs** of the 15,000 copies with what expenditure should have been at this level of activity. In other words, the fixed budget should be 'flexed', and cost variances calculated by **comparing actual costs with the flexed budget.**

Controllability

A further principle of control reporting is that costs should be **attributed to the person who has control over them**. In the case of the print room, it is not clear who was responsible for the large increase in printing activity over the budget. The print room manager presumably did the work he was instructed to do by other individuals or managers.

Since printing costs should be kept under control, it would probably be appropriate for the local authority to look at how printing decisions are taken. It might be necessary to establish **formal procedures for authorising** printing work. There is a risk, however, that authorisation procedures might become too bureaucratic, and might reduce operational efficiency as a result.

Early launching of magazine

The premature launch date for the new magazine resulted in having to take on a new full time employee one month earlier than planned. This explains the adverse expenditure variance of £700 on labour costs for permanent staff.

Management should **investigate the reasons for the decision to launch the magazine early**, because this would have affected the volume of work performed as well as the labour costs. It is unlikely that the print room manager is responsible for the decision, and it is therefore inappropriate to 'blame' him for the cost.

Allocation of administrative costs

Since the cost control report is not concerned with revenues and profits, it is questionable whether there is any purpose in allocating a share of administrative costs to the print room. The adverse variance of £500 for the period is outside the control of the print room manager, and serves no useful purpose in the report. If anything, it is misleading, since senior executives are likely to assume that all costs in the control report are **under the control of the manager** nominally responsible for the department.

Future reports should not include administrative costs.

Management style

The print room manager was not consulted over the budget, and did not even know that the cost control report was being prepared. In spite of this, the print room manager has been blamed in a strong fashion by a senior executive. This demonstrates a management style that is almost certain to be **de-motivating** for subordinates.

At the very least, the print room manager should have been notified about the control reporting system. More ideally he should have been **involved in the design of the reporting system**, and in particular how control reports should be used to manage the performance of the print room.

Target setting

The senior executive has also decided that any variance above 5% of the budgeted cost is unacceptable. It is not clear how this variance limit has been established, and it would help if the reasons were made clear.

The executive appears to be concerned with total costs only, but it is preferable to look at **expenses in more detail**. For example, during the quarter, material costs were £2,000 more than they should have been, even allowing for the higher level of activity. Given that the expected cost should have been £15,000, the variance seems quite large and is worth investigating. Although it is reasonable to monitor and control costs in the print room, there might be some benefits in **setting other targets**, apart from a cost budget, as a means of improving performance. For example, targets might be set for output per labour hour, or even targets/limits for total hours worked.

Conclusion

The cost control report suggests that the print room is responsible for a large over-spend. In reality, the figures may point to some overspending, but the figures do not provide a useful analysis for control purposes. In particular, a reporting scheme should be devised that attributes costs to the individuals who are responsible for initiating or incurring them, and who are therefore able to exercise some control over them.

(b)   The print room manager will want to avoid criticism in the next quarter. As a result of the pressure to limit spending, there could be several adverse consequences.

    (i)   **Motivation**. The print room manager will probably **lose much of his motivation**, and might tend to 'blame' others whenever extra costs are incurred, whereas a constructive approach to cost control is required.

    (ii)   **Deferral of expenditure.** The print room manager might be **reluctant to take on work**, or might delay starting jobs, in order to avoid or defer expenditure. For example, he might be reluctant to take on casual labour, and blame lack of labour resources for being unable to meet demand.

    (iii)   **Management time**. The **'blame culture'** might make the manager spend excessive time arguing about the budget and control reports. Some organisations give the impression of management activities feeding in on themselves, with some managers feeling that they have to justify their own positions by creating more and more work for other people. The effect is often to divert line managers from their principal responsibilities for managing their teams.

    (iv)   **Goal congruence**. In an attempt to keep costs down, the manager might take decisions that are not in the **best interests of the organisation**. For example, he might switch to using cheaper paper, that might be of a low quality and unsuitable for the items it is used to produce.

11 JIT

Top tips. (a) provides useful revision of the features of JIT. It's quite possible that you'll encounter a business using JIT procedures in the exam so think when you're reading through the answer to (a) about the threats to JIT (supplier relations, untrained staff, machinery problems being amongst them).

(b) links in JIT to the issue of management systems. Again this is a significant feature of this exam; how should controls develop in response to a decision to introduce JIT. Note that the answer includes a discussion of the features that will no longer be relevant. It also broadens out the discussion to include non-financial measures as well as financial, and information systems in general.

(a) **Origins of JIT**

Just-in-time (JIT) has emerged from criticisms of traditional responses to the problems of improving manufacturing capacity and reducing unit costs of production.

Features of JIT

The JIT approach involves a **continuous commitment to the pursuit of excellence** in all phases of manufacturing systems and design. The aims of JIT are to produce the required items, at the required quality and in the required quantities, at the precise time they are required. In particular, JIT aims to achieve the following.

- The elimination of non-value-added activities
- Zero inventory
- Zero defects
- Batch sizes of one
- Zero breakdowns
- A 100% on-time delivery service

Benefits of JIT

There are two aspects to JIT systems, **JIT purchasing and JIT production,** both of which assist in the benefits highlighted by Aggrawal.

(i) **Reduction in inventories**

JIT purchasing seeks to match the usage of materials with the delivery of materials from external suppliers. This means that material inventories can be kept at near-zero levels. For JIT purchasing to be successful, the organisation will need to have confidence that the **supplier will deliver on time** and that the supplier will deliver materials of **100% quality**, that there will be no rejects returns and hence no consequent production delays. The reliability of suppliers is of utmost importance and hence the company must build up close relationships with their suppliers. This can be achieved by doing more business with fewer suppliers and placing long-term orders so that the supplier is assured of sales and can produce to meet the required demand.

(ii) **Increase in labour productivity**

In a JIT production environment, **production processes** must be **shortened and simplified**. Workers must therefore be more **flexible and adaptable**. They should be trained to operate all machines on the line and undertake routine preventative maintenance. It is factors such as these that result in an increase in labour productivity in a JIT environment.

(iii) **Reduction of necessary plant space**

With JIT production, **factory layouts** must change to reduce movement of workers and products. Product and employee movement is a non-value-added activity that needs to be **reduced or eliminated**. Material movements between operations should be minimised by **eliminating space between work stations** and **grouping dissimilar machines** into manufacturing cells on the basis of product groups. **Storage space** should be **reduced** due to the reasons set out in (i) above. **Plant space** should be therefore **kept to a minimum.**

(iv) **Reduction in quality rejection rates**

Production management within a JIT environment seeks to both **eliminate scrap and defective units** during production and **avoid the need for reworking of units**. Defects stop the production line, thus creating rework and possibly resulting in a failure to meet delivery dates. Quality, on the other hand, reduces costs. Quality is assured by **designing products and processes with quality in mind**, **introducing quality awareness programmes** and **checks on output quality**, providing **training** and implementing **vendor quality assurance programmes** to ensure that the correct product is made to the appropriate quality level.

Producing the benefits

Some of the changes necessary to produce such benefits are quite radical and cannot be implemented overnight. The **co-operation of workers** is vital. They must be **trained** and will need many hours of **practice**. **Close relationships with suppliers** cannot be established straight away. They must be **built up over time** as trust between the two parties develops. It is therefore obvious that the benefits cannot be expected to appear within 24 hours but must be developed gradually to allow the full benefits of JIT to materialise.

(b) **Developments required**

The implementation of JIT will necessitate the following developments in an organisation's management information system in general and management accounting system in particular.

(i) **Simplification of accounting system**. There will be no need for an **elaborate cost accounting system of stores requisitions,** materials transfer notes and so on, since inventories will be very low or non-existent. Many material purchases should be capable of being traced direct to cost units.

(ii) **Inventory levels.** A **system of economic batch quantities** for inventory control will **no longer be valid** since products will be manufactured as they are needed and not manufactured for inventory.

(iii) **Non-financial performance measures.** The system will need to be able to provide **information for non-financial performance measures** such as the percentage of quality control rejects and the ratio of machine downtime to productive time and so on.

(iv) **Information systems**. There will be a need for **electronic data interchange** with customers and with suppliers to facilitate the necessary close relationships.

(v) **Cost collection**. **Cost collection procedures** can be **simplified**. Since production only occurs when demand arises, the output will not be held in inventory and accounting entries can be made as the goods are sold.

(vi) **Variance analysis**. **Traditional variance analysis** as a control technique is not compatible with a JIT environment. JIT is based on a series of zeroes, zero material price variance, zero inventory, zero defects. It implies continual flexibility in response to the wishes of the customer.

12 Measuring risk

> **Top tips.** This question includes techniques that you should be familiar with from other papers – remember knowledge of all of these is assumed for this paper. This question also illustrates that there will be no completely numerical questions on this paper; sometimes the written element in the question will be to explain the techniques that you have carried out.

(a) **Financial and non-financial risks**

Financial risk is narrowly defined as the **possibility of changes in returns or cash flows** arising from unexpected changes in financial factors. The main categories of financial risk are credit risk, gearing risk, interest rate risk and currency risk. **Non-financial risk** is then defined as the possibility of **changes in returns or cash flows** arising from unexpected changes in non-financial factors, such as 'business' or 'operational' factors. Non-financial factors arising from business risk would include the possibility of higher or lower revenue than expected, or higher or lower costs, and variations in returns due to unanticipated actions by competitors.

Financial risk can be defined more broadly to mean the possibility that **returns will be higher** or **lower than expected**, due to any factor whose impact can be measured in financial terms.

(b) **Project risk**

There are different ways of measuring and assessing risk in a project. The simplest approach is to take a view of what is the most **likely result or outcome**, and what are the **worst possible and the best possible outcomes**. An investment decision can be taken on the basis of the most likely outcome, but with an appreciation of how much worse or better the result could be. This approach does not have any mathematical aspect at all.

Expected value

An alternative approach is to assess the probability of different outcomes, and to use these probabilities to calculate the expected value of the project return. An expected value is the **average value of all the different outcomes**, **weighted** to reflect their probability of occurrence. If the number of probabilities is fairly small, risk can be assessed in terms of the probability of different outcomes, for example the overall probability that the project will have a negative NPV.

If the number of probabilities is large, the risk can be measured statistically as a standard deviation of the expected return.

Sensitivity analysis

An alternative approach to analysing uncertainty is **sensitivity analysis**. Perhaps the most common form of sensitivity analysis is to ask **'what if' questions**, such as what if costs are 5% higher than estimated, what if revenues are 10% lower, what if the project lasts two years less than expected or what will happen if the cash benefits are deferred by 12 months, and so on. Alternatively, the approach to sensitivity analysis might be to measure by how much each estimate would have to be changed for the worse before the project only just broke even.

(c) Workings

Year 1

Sales units	Probability	Expected value units
50,000	0.8	40,000
70,000	0.2	14,000
		54,000

Year 1

		£
Expected contribution	54,000 × £6	324,000
Fixed costs		150,000
		174,000

Year 2

Units sold in year 1	Units sold in year 2	Contribution £	Probability
50,000	20,000	120,000	(0.8 × 0.4) = 0.32
50,000	40,000	240,000	(0.8 × 0.6) = 0.48
70,000	50,000	300,000	(0.2 × 0.3) = 0.06
70,000	60,000	360,000	(0.2 × 0.7) = 0.14

Year 2 sales units	Contribution £	Probability	EV of continued £
20,000	120,000	0.32	38,400
40,000	240,000	0.48	115,200
50,000	300,000	0.06	18,000
60,000	360,000	0.14	50,400
			222,000
Fixed costs			150,000
EV of profit			72,000

Year	Item	Amount £	Discount factor @ 10%	EV of NPV £
0	Capital outlay	(200,000)	1.000	(200,000)
1	Cash profit	174,000	0.909	158,166
2	Cash profit	72,000	0.826	59,472
	EV of NPV			17,638

(i) The expected net present value of the project is + £17,638.

(ii) The capital cost would need to increase by more than (17,638/200,000) 8.82% before the EV of the project NPV became negative.

(iii) The EV of sales units in Year 2 is (0.32 × 20,000) + (0.48 × 40,000) + (0.06 × 50,000) + (0.14 × 60,000) = 37,000.

EV of sales	Units	EV of continued £	Discount factor @ 10%	PV of EV of continued £
Year 1	54,000	324,000	0.909	294,516
Year 2	37,000	222,000	0.826	183,372
				477,888

Sales volume (and contribution) would need to fall by over (£17,638/£477,888) = 3.7% before the EV of the project NPV became negative.

(iv) An alternative approach to risk assessment would be to calculate the **probability** of a **negative NPV**. For example, there is a 0.32 probability that sales will be 50,000 units in Year 1 (profit £150,000) and just 20,000 units in year 2 (loss £50,000). Given a capital outlay of £200,000 the NPV would be negative if this occurred. If sales are 50,000 units in Year 1 (profit £150,000) and 40,000 units in Year 2 (profit £90,000), the EV of the NPV would be (£150,000 × 0.909) + (90,000 × 0.826) − £200,000 = £10,690, and the project would just about have a positive NPV. The overall probability of a negative NPV, on the basis of the probability estimates, is therefore 0.32 or 32%.

13 Burnett

> **Top tips**. This question indicates the sorts of things you may be asked about interest rate hedging methods. Although you won't be asked for calculations on FRAs and options, you could be asked for comments on numbers like you are in (a). The discussion in (b) and (c) are examples of possible written elements in questions.

(a)   **Forward rate agreements**

A forward rate agreement (FRA) is a **forward contract on an interest rate**, being an agreement with a bank to fix the rate of interest on a notional principal amount (loan or deposit), for an interest period starting at some time in the future. If the interest rate that prevails is less than the FRA rate then the bank will compensate the company for the difference. However if the interest rate that Burnett received is more than the agreed FRA rate the company would have to make a compensation payment to the bank. An FRA has the effect of fixing the future interest rate that Burnett will receive on its future deposit.

By entering into an FRA at an agreed rate now the amount that Burnett will receive on the deposit which is not to be made for three months can be **fixed now** and whatever happens to actual interest rates in the next three months the amount that Burnett will receive will not alter.

Rate to be used

The deposit will be made in three months time for a period of six months. Therefore the appropriate FRA is a 3v9 which means that the deposit will be made in three months time and will be taken off deposit in nine months time. The interest rate on deposits is the lower of the quoted rates so Burnett will receive interest of 7.10% for the six month period.

(b)   **Advantages of exchange-traded interest rate options**

(i)   The **prices are clearly visible** and no negotiation on price is required.

(ii)   The **market place gives quick access** to buyers and sellers.

(iii)   The **options can be sold if not required**, at any time to expiry.

(iv)   **Gains or losses are computed** ('marked to market') on a daily basis.

(v)   Traded options are **normally American-style** (ie they can be exercised at any time). They are more flexible than many OTC options, which are European-style (ie can only be exercised at the maturity date).

The main advantage of OTC options is that they can be **tailored more exactly** to the **needs of the purchaser**, in terms of maturity date, contract size, currency and nature of interest. Contract sizes are larger than on the traded markets and longer times to expiry are available.

(c)   **Influences on option prices**

(i)   The **price of the specific interest-bearing security** which the option gives the right to buy or sell (eg a notional deposit at the LIBOR interest rate), compared with the exercise price for the option. In-the-money options will cost more than out-of-the-money options.

(ii)   The **remaining time** to expiry of the option. The premium varies with time to expiry, and longer-dated options will cost more.

(iii)   The **volatility** in the price of the underlying item. The premium will be higher when the price of the underlying item is more volatile, and subject to large changes up or down in the remaining time to expiry.

(iv)   The **current interest rate** also has some effect on the premium for an option.

Recommendations

Options can seem expensive, but this is because they act like an insurance policy, providing protection against **increased interest costs** but allowing the **purchaser to take advantage of interest rate falls**. OTC option prices are not as transparent as market traded options, but there is a competitive market of banks and other sellers. As a safeguard, **prices can be checked against option pricing models**.

14 Ferry

> **Top tips.** This question follows a standard format for this paper with identification of risks required in part (a) and identification of controls in part (b). The question requires an assessment of **business risk** so launching into the categories of audit risk would not have earned you many marks.
>
> **Examiner's comments**. Part (a) asked candidates to identify risk. Many provided an explanation of the elements of risk. This theory was not required and did not score any marks. When asked to 'identify' candidates should be brief. Many candidates read the information in the question carelessly. For example, they assumed that it was Ferry who suffered a 'lack of public support and government funds.' A lack of understanding of the real world was also evident. It was often stated that the 20 year old boats should be replaced as they were obsolete in spite of the fact that they had recently been refurbished.
>
> A reason for poor marks on part (b) was not attempting it, or jotting down one or two ideas like 'new boats' and 'take out insurance' without adequate explanation.

(a)   **Business risks**

Rights to operate

The exclusive rights to operate are **only effective** for **another 5 ½ years** . Depending on the likelihood of these rights being renegotiated this raises questions about the ongoing viability of the business.

The right to operate may have been granted provided that **certain conditions** are met. If Ferry does not continue to satisfy these terms its operational existence may be called into question.

Future competition

Profitability could be affected by **future competition**. This might be the case if a new bridge is constructed or if the rights were no longer exclusive to Ferry.

Age of the ferries

It is likely that **running costs** will be higher than those for newer ships.

Fuel consumption is likely to be **higher** as the engines will be less efficient. This is of particular concern in periods when **fuel prices are volatile**. Ongoing maintenance is also more likely to be required.

Emission standards

The company will be required to meet the emission standards which come into force in 20X6. If the necessary modifications are not made the company could incur **substantial penalties**.

Custom may be lost due to the potential disruption caused to services during the period in which the modifications are made to the ferries.

Surplus capacity

The ferries are currently only operating at **40% capacity**

2 boats × 40 vehicles × 6 crossing × 365 days = 175,200

70,000/175,200 = 40%

As a high proportion of the cost of each trip is likely to be fixed (ie fuel), consideration needs to be given as to whether the business is **viable** at this level. The company is also likely to be sensitive to any downturn in business (for example, due to general economic conditions).

Franchise arrangements

The **quality of outsourced services** are outside the direct control of Ferry. Ferry may receive complaints and ultimately lose customers if services are poor.

Subsidy

Ferry may **depend on the subsidy** to continue in business. Cash flow problems could arise if the subsidy stopped (ie it may only be awarded for a given period or be dependent on certain quality standards being maintained.)

If sufficient controls are not in place returns may be **submitted late** or may include **inaccurate information**. **Cash flow problems** could result due to late or non-payment.

There is a risk that details on the return might be **deliberately inflated** to increase the payment received.

Health and safety

Ferry may **not be awarded its Safety Management Certificate** if it fails to meet the performance and documentation standards.

Ferry will find it difficult to **find and retain staff** if working conditions do not comply with health and safety regulations.

Litigation

Ferry may be **sued by customers** for personal injury and damage to, or loss of, property. In the case of serious injury or death damages could be substantial.

Serious incident

A catastrophic incident could lead to a **loss of assets** which may threaten the operations in the short and long term.

(b) **Rights to operate**

It is unlikely that the business is in a position to change the situation regarding the period for which the rights have been granted and therefore is a risk that the **business has to accept**. Management should be aware of any **conditions** which will affect the renewal of rights and take steps to ensure that these are complied with.

Relevant staff should be made aware of any **contractual conditions** and their responsibility for ensuring that these are met. Compliance should be **reviewed** and **monitored** by an appropriate level of management.

Future competition

Management should **monitor any plans** which would introduce new competition, for example the building of a new bridge. Management should also consider how it can **maintain its competitive advantage** by ensuring that its service meets the needs of its customers.

Age of the ferries

Running costs should be **adequately budgeted** for and **cash flows monitored** to ensure that these can be met.

Price structures should be **flexible** to allow increased fuel costs to be passed on to the customer.

Forward contracts could be **used to hedge** against the effect of changing oil prices.

Emissions standards

Management should **familiarise** themselves with the **Environmental Protection Regulations**. Funds should be made available and the work scheduled to ensure that the deadline for compliance is met.

Plans should be made to **minimise the inconvenience** to **the customer** eg changes in the schedule should be advertised, the work should not be planned for peak periods in the year.

Surplus capacity

Management need to be aware of the **capacity** required to ensure that revenue at least covers costs (ie breakeven point). This should be **reviewed and monitored** on a continual basis.

Marketing strategies should be used to **encourage bookings and maximise revenues,** for example discounts for regular users and different price structures for peak and off peak travel.

Franchise arrangements

The **performance of other businesses/franchisees should be monitored** by Ferry through the press, observation etc.

Franchise agreements should stipulate **minimum quality standards** and should include **penalties/termination clauses** for consistent unsatisfactory performance.

Subsidy

Management should be aware of the conditions attached to the payment of the subsidy and ensure that **these targets** are met. If the subsidy is available for a limited period plans should be made to ensure that the business can remain viable by a long-term review of revenues and benefits.

Controls such as checking by other staff should be implemented to ensure that **returns are accurate** and completed on time. Checks by **Internal audit** may provide management with added assurance.

Fraudulent completion of returns is likely to be performed with the knowledge of management. The **seriousness of this risk depends** largely on the **integrity** of the individuals involved.

Health and safety

Management should **monitor activities** and the **completion of safety documents**. This function could be performed by internal audit.

Litigation

Liability should be **limited** where possible (eg telling passengers they leave valuables in unattended vehicles at their own risk.)

Staff training should emphasise public safety. Safety drills should be practised regularly.

The company should have adequate public **liability insurance**.

Serious incident

The ships should be **maintained to a high standard** and **regular checks** should **be made to** ensure that safety equipment is in working order eg life boats.

The ships should be **fitted with up to date equipment** to prevent or deal with serious incidents. This equipment should be tested and maintained regularly.

15 OX

Top tips. The forward rate between Singapore dollars and £ needs to be worked out in two stages. A diagram may have been a useful way of seeing what is going on in the money market hedge. You have to start though by working 'backwards;' you want to end up with $715,000 in three months time, so you need to find the present value of that amount.

In (a) (ii) the US dollars is to be used as the hard currency, so don't worry that no forward market exists between the pound and rupiah.

In (b) you need to consider whether to convert from dollars to sterling immediately or in three months time. Don't forget the conclusion.

In (c) the risk of exchange losses has to be balanced against the improved customer relations (and the possibility of exchange gains).

(a)   **Receipts from export sales**

   (i)   **Sales to Singapore**

   The value of the sales at the spot rate is:

   $$250,000 \times \text{Singapore } \$2.862 \times \frac{1}{3.1800} \text{ (W1)} = £225,000$$

   If OX enters into a contract to sell $250,000 \times 2.862 = $ Singapore $715,500, delivery between two and three months,

   Anticipated sterling proceeds = Singapore $715,500 \div 3.1592 = £226,481$

   OX can take out a **forward option contract** to sell **Singapore dollars forward**, for delivery between two and three months. This will hopefully overcome the uncertainty surrounding the timing of the receipt from Singapore. The exchange rate used is the least favourable quoted rate for delivery during the period (in this case the three month rate).

   Alternatively, OX can cover its foreign exchange risk via the **money markets**, as follows.

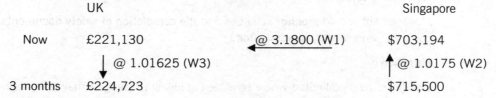

	UK		Singapore
Now	£221,130	@ 3.1800 (W1) ←	$703,194
	↓ @ 1.01625 (W3)		↑ @ 1.0175 (W2)
3 months	£224,723		$715,500

   The Eurosterling deposit will grow to £224,723.

   (ii)   **Sales to Indonesia**

   The value of the sales at the spot rate is $100,000 \times \dfrac{2,246}{2,481} = £90,528$.

   The first alternative is to compute the eventual proceeds using the £ and $ forward market, since payment has been offered in US dollars and no forward market exists in Rupiahs.

   Using the forward market, the contracted receipts from selling US $ 125,000 for delivery in three months are:

   $$\frac{125,000}{1.5105} = £82,754$$

The second alternative is to use the money markets, as follows.

UK		US
Now £81,586	@ 1.4875 →	$121,359
↓ @ 1.01625 (W3)		↑ @ 1.03 (W4)
3 months £82,912		$125,000

Conclusion. The protection should be effected through the foreign exchange market for the sale to Singapore and through the money market for the sale to Indonesia.

(b)

	Rupiahs
Sales value (100,000 × 2,246)	224,600,000
Less 5% discount	(11,230,000)
Discounted sales value	213,370,000

$$\text{Proceeds of sales} = \frac{213,370,000}{1,667.9(\text{W5})} = \$127,927$$

The best US $ deposit rate of interest is 8% pa in a US domestic bank.

The yield after three months is $127,927 × 1.02 = $130,486.

Converted into sterling, using the three month forward market, this is:

$$\frac{\$130,486}{1.5105} = £86,386$$

Alternatively, the US dollar proceeds could be converted immediately into sterling and then invested for three months in eurosterling.

UK		US
Now £86,001	@ 1.4875 →	$127,927
↓ @ 1.01625 (W3)		
3 months £87,399		

Conclusion. The best yield without the offer of immediate payment was £82,912. Both the forward foreign exchange market and the money market yield better returns, with the money market as the better of the alternatives.

Workings

(1) *Cross rates*

	Singapore $ = US$1	US $ = £1	Singapore $ = £1
Spot	2.1378	1.4875	3.1800
1 month forward	2.1132	1.4963	3.1620
2 months forward	2.0964	1.5047	3.1545
3 months forward	2.0915	1.5105	3.1592

(2) *Required Singapore $ borrowings*

The interest rate in Singapore $ is 7% pa or 1.75% for three months.

Thus the maximum borrowing which can be repaid from export sale proceeds is

$$\text{Singapore } \$ \frac{715,500}{1.0175} = 703,194$$

(3) *Euro sterling deposit*

The interest rate for three months is 1.625% (6.5/4)

(4) *Required US $ borrowings*

US $ interest rates (eurodollars) are 12% pa or 3% for three months

(5) *Cross rate*

	US $ = £1	Rupiah = US$1	Rupiah = £1
Spot	1.4875	1667.90	2,481

(c) When a company invoices sales in a currency other than its own, the amount of 'home' currency it will eventually receive is uncertain. There may be an advantage or a disadvantage, depending on changes in the exchange rate over the period between invoicing and receiving payment. With this in mind, invoicing in a foreign currency has the following **advantages**.

(i) The **foreign customer** will **find the deal more attractive** than a similar one in the exporter's currency, since the customer will bear no foreign exchange risk. Making a sale will therefore be that much easier.

(ii) The exporter can **take advantage** of **favourable foreign exchange movements** by selling the exchange receipts forward (for more of the home currency than would be obtained by conversion at the spot rate).

(iii) In some countries, the **importer** may find it **difficult** or even impossible to obtain the foreign exchange necessary to pay in the exporter's currency. The willingness of the exporter to sell in the importer's currency may therefore prevent the sale falling through.

The disadvantages of making export sales in foreign currency are the reverse of the advantages.

(i) The **exporter** (rather than the foreign customer) bears the **foreign exchange risk**.
(ii) If the **exchange movement** is **unfavourable**, the exporter's profit will be reduced.

16 BS

> **Top tips.** This question tests your knowledge of exchange rate hedges using fixed and option forward exchange contracts, and money market hedges. The calculations are reasonably straightforward, but as always with option contracts, you will need to think through carefully the implications of different movements in exchange rates.
>
> Don't forget **netting off** in (a) and make sure you translate the transaction cost at the correct (spot) rate.
>
> In (b) you need to focus on the various elements of risk (what the risks are, what the company intends to do and how the company can cope with them). It's easy to forget the 'simpler methods' of dealing with risk when you have a question about futures and options.
>
> In (c) don't confuse option forward contracts (the **date** of performance is optional, not performance) with option contracts (here the **performance** is optional). Unusually you are told one price to use in the options calculation and you have to select as the other a price above 1.70. We have chosen 1.71 but you could equally have chosen 1.75 or 1.80.

(a) (i) Since both the receipts and payments are expected to occur **on the same date**, BS plc need only hedge the net amount, ie a receipt of $200,000 ($450,000 – $250,000). To hedge this transaction, a three-month forward contract to sell dollars will be required. The rate that will apply for this contract will be $1.6590 – $0.0077 = $1.6513/£.

The **transaction cost** will be paid immediately in US$. BS must therefore **buy dollars now** to cover this at the spot rate of $1.6540.

The net receipt can now be calculated:

	£
Sterling proceeds in 3 months' time: $200,000 ÷ 1.6513	121,117
Transaction costs: $200,000 × 0.2% ÷ 1.6540	(242)
Net receipt	120,875

Hedging using the money market

We need to borrow now to match the receipt we shall obtain.

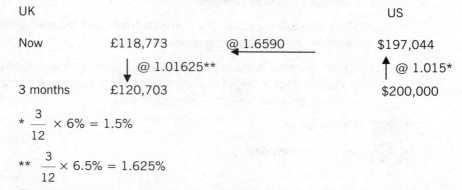

UK

Now   £118,773   @ 1.6590 ◄ $197,044

        ↓ @ 1.01625**   ↑ @ 1.015*

3 months   £120,703 $200,000

US

$$* \quad \frac{3}{12} \times 6\% = 1.5\%$$

$$** \quad \frac{3}{12} \times 6.5\% = 1.625\%$$

The transaction cost will be the same as for the forward market hedge. The net receipt under this method will therefore be £120,703 − £242 = **£120,461**.

The receipts are highest if the **forward market hedge** is used, and this will therefore be the **preferred method**.

(b)   **Factors to consider**

(i)   The **relative costs** of the different options

(ii)   The **ability of the staff** to **manage the techniques**, given that there is not a specialist treasury department

(iii)   The **attitude of the company to risk**

(iv)   The **size of the transaction** in relation to the company's overall operations, and therefore the scale of the risks involved

(v)   The **perceived level of risk** attached to the currencies in question

Alternative options to minimise risk

(i)   **Operating bank accounts in foreign currencies.** This is only an option if the company has regular transactions in the currencies in question.

(ii)   The **use of multilateral netting**. This will only be possible if there are a large number of foreign currency transactions.

(iii)   The company could consider the **use of swaps and option contracts**.

(iv)   The company could consider the **cost and viability** of insisting that more of its contracts are denominated in sterling.

(c)   **Fixed forward exchange contract**

(i)   An immediately **firm and binding contract** (for example, between a bank and its customer)
(ii)   For the **purchase or sale** of a **specified quantity** of a stated foreign currency
(iii)   At a **rate of exchange fixed** at the time the contract is made
(iv)   For **performance at a future time** which is agreed upon when making the contract

Advantages of option contracts

Option contracts are attractive when:

(i) The **date** on which the transaction being hedged will take place is **uncertain**

(ii) There is **uncertainty** about the **likely movement in exchange rates** – the company can take advantage of any favourable movements in exchange rates, while continuing to hedge any unfavourable movements

Main drawbacks to option contracts

(i) They are **more expensive** than **fixed contracts**, and the premium will have to be paid, whether or not the option is exercised

(ii) They are **traded in standard amounts**, and therefore it is difficult to hedge exactly the sum required – in practice, the company will have to carry some of the risk itself, or use two different hedges to cover the transaction fully

Option set up

(a) **Contract date**

June

(b) **Type of option**

Buy £ call option

(c) **Strike price**

$1.70 as current spot rate is greater than other option prices

(d) **Number of contracts**

$$\frac{200,000 \div \$1.70}{£12,500} = 9.41, \text{ say } 9$$

(e) **Premium** $= \dfrac{9 \times 12,500 \times 0.0170}{1.6540}$

$= £1,156$

Closing prices

(a) $1.71
(b) $1.6513

Outcome

(a) **Options market outcome**

	(i)	(ii)
Strike price put (sell at)	1.7000	1.7000
Closing price (buy at)	1.7100	1.6513
Exercise?	Yes	No
Outcome of options position (12,500 × 9)	£112,500	–
Difference in hedge (200,000 – (12,500 × 9 × 1.70))	$8,750	–
Balance on spot market		

	$
Exercise option (12,500 × 9 × 1.70)	191,250
Value of transaction	200,000
Balance	8,750

Translated at spot rate (8,750/1.71) = £5,117

(b) **Net outcome**

	£	£
Spot market outcome translated at closing spot rate 200,000/1.6513	–	121,117
Options position	112,500	–
Difference in hedge at closing rate	5,117	
Premium (added separately as translated at the **opening** spot rate)	(1,156)	(1,156)
	116,461	119,961

Given the **actual movement** in exchange rates that occurred, it is clear that BS's best decision would have been to have used a fixed forward contract rather than an option. However, had the dollar fallen further against sterling, then the option contract would have yielded a greater receipt than the fixed contract.

The key point is that the option contract gives the company the **possibility of benefiting** from unexpected favourable movements in rates, albeit at a higher **premium cost**. The 'correct' choice can only be made once the company has specified the degree of risk that it is willing to accept in this type of situation.

17 Jennie

Top tips. With the forward contract the question indicates you should add the amount (the discount). The rate to use is the unfavourable rate for Jennie. As it's based in Europe and has received $, it wants to buy € with the $ it's received. Hence the rate to use is the **higher** rate, which means it has to spend more $ (1.5912 – 0.0023 = 1.5889) to obtain each € that it wants. We subtract the 0.0023 as the forward rate is quoted at a premium.

For the money market calculation

- You have to **borrow** in the **foreign currency** to match the foreign currency **receipt.** You will pay off the borrowing with the receipt.

- The amount you borrow is less than you will receive (hence the division) because you will obtain interest by **investing** the amount borrowed in your home market.

As you'll be receiving $, you need to buy € futures now, and sell them at the later date when you want to buy € with the $ you receive.

For the futures calculation the date of the contract needs to be **after** the date the transaction is due to be settled. The tick size is 0.01% of the contract size, hence we multiply the contract size by 0.0001. The futures gain has to be translated at the **closing spot rate** as the gain is in $ which is the foreign currency in this transaction.

The key decisions in the options calculation are to choose the right date – again it needs to be **after** the date the transaction is due to be settled. You need to choose the right type of option - here it's a **call** option enabling you to **buy** the **home currency €** that you want using the **foreign currency $** receipt.

The option ensures that you can buy at a reasonable price in the worst possible exchange rate scenario. In some calculations, you may have the information available to be able to calculate which option price to choose. However more often, as you do here, you can choose one as an example (if you're told the closing spot rate, then the example option price you choose will be one where you will exercise the option). Here the option is exercised, because the rate is lower than the spot rate. Remember what we said in Chapter 11; if the foreign currency is quoted at Home currency 1 unit: Foreign currency X units, you have to divide the foreign currency amount (here $5,000,000) by the rate quoted. Dividing by a lower number gives a higher receipt in the home currency of € in this instance.

Because you're using a traded option, there will be a difference between what you're receiving from the customer and the amount covered by the option contract, so you have to calculate the **difference** at the **closing spot rate,** having translated the amount of home currency in the option contracts at the **option strike price.** Remember also that the option premium is translated at the **opening** spot rate.

Hedging using the forward contract

The company should take out a three month forward contract to sell:

$5,000,000 at $1.5912 – $0.0023 = $1.5889

This rate is agreed today for exchange in 3 months, converting to $5,000,000/1.5889 = €3,146,831

Hedging using the money market

We need to borrow now to match the receipt we shall obtain.

	Germany		US
Now	€3,129,764	@ 1.5912 ⟵	$4,980,080
	↓ @ 1.0065**		↑ @ 1.004*
3 months	€3,150,107		$5,000,000

$* \dfrac{3}{12} \times 1.6\% = 0.4\%$

$** \dfrac{3}{12} \times 2.6\% = 0.65\%$

Futures market

 Set up

(a) We shall be buying December contracts as they mature after payment date

(b) Buy € futures

(c) Number of contracts

$$\frac{5,000,000/1.5871}{125,000} = 25.2, \text{ say 25 contracts.}$$

 Closing prices

Closing futures price is 1.5979, closing spot rate is 1.6000

 Outcome

(a) **On futures market**

Opening futures price Buy	1.5871
Closing futures price Sell	1.5979
Movement	0.0108 gain
Gain on futures market	0.0108 × $125,000 × 25 = $33,750 gain

(b) **Net outcome**

	€
Spot market receipt $\left(\dfrac{5,000,000}{1.6000}\right)$	3,125,000
Gain on futures market $\left(\dfrac{33,750}{1.6000}\right)$	21,094
	3,146,094

STEP 1 | **Option set up**

(a)   Contract date

December

(b)   Type of option

Buy call option as buying €

(c)   Strike price

Say 1.5900, as it is closest to the current spot rate.

(d)   Number of contracts

$$\frac{5,000,000 \div 1.5900}{62,500} = 50.3, \text{ say } 50$$

(e)   Premium $= \dfrac{50 \times 62,500 \times 0.0361}{1.5904}$

$= €70,933$

 STEP 2 | **Closing spot rate**

1.6000

 STEP 3 | **Outcome**

(a)   **Options market outcome**

Spot rate	1.6000
Strike price	1.5900
Exercise	Yes

Balance on spot market

	$
Exercise option (62,500 × 50 × 1.5900)	4,968,750
Value of transaction	5,000,000
Balance	31,250

Translated at spot rate (31,250/1.6000) = €19,531

(b)   **Net outcome**

	€
Options market (62,500 × 50)	3,125,000
Balance on spot market	19,531
Option premium	(70,933)
	3,073,598

Conclusion

Hedging with futures appears to offer the best chance of maximising revenues, although the options will be the best choice if exchange rates move significantly.

18 Right

(a) **Swaps**

A swap is an **exchange of cash payment obligations**. Swaps can be used to hedge exposure to exchange rate, interest-rate and other financial risks. Being flexible in the duration of their term, they are often more suitable for longer-term exposure than short-term instruments such as futures, options etc.

The most common types of swap are those of currency and interest rates.

Interest rate swap

An interest rate swap is where one company arranges with a counter party to exchange interest rate payments. For example, a company may be able to raise **fixed-rate finance** at a good rate, but would rather pay floating (variable) rates. It would therefore seek to find another company (usually through an intermediary) that has a good **variable rate deal**, but would prefer to lock into a fixed rate.

Such a swap may also be taking advantage of **market imperfections** – where, for example, the interest-rate risk premium charged in the fixed-rate borrowing market differs from that in the floating rate market for one or both of the parties.

The two companies would then agree to swap interest payments at rates that lead to benefits for both companies in terms of both the payment pattern (Fixed/floating) and the interest rate itself.

Currency swap

Where a company wishes to raise some foreign currency finance, it might find itself at a disadvantage if it is not known in the particular country involved. Its lack of credit status may lead to **higher cost of finance**, or may even deny access to the capital market altogether. To get round this, and also to **hedge against currency risk**, it might identify a counter party (eg a bank) in the foreign country that is prepared to carry out a swap.

This would result in each party **raising finance in its own currency**, **swapping the currency at an agreed rate** (eg spot) with the agreement to exchange back again at a specified future date and rate. A separate agreement would be reached about **interest payments**.

Swaps can be combined with other derivatives such as options ('swaptions' – the option to swap at a later date) which increases their flexibility to the corporate treasurer.

(b) The main risks associated with participating in swaps arise from uncertainties surrounding the underlying commodity (interest/exchange rates), the parties to the contract and the environment within which the swap takes place.

Exchange/interest rate risk

Whilst swaps may be used to 'lock in' interest and exchange rates, and thus avoid unexpected fluctuations in cash flows, there is still the chance that the decision taken was not, with hindsight, the correct one for the company. For example, a company may enter into an interest rate swap, swapping **floating rate interest** for a **fixed rate**, believing that interest rates are about to rise. If, in fact, rates fall, the company may be worse off than if it had not undertaken the swap.

Default of counterparty

As with any contract, there is always a risk that one party will **default on their obligations** under the swap contract. This risk has lessened considerably in recent times, as most swaps are conducted via an intermediary that has a known credit status, such as a bank. This does, however, carry an additional cost. Alternatively, careful credit checking can reduce the risk.

Political risk

If the swap is carried out in an **uncertain political environment**, eg a currency swap involving a currency of a country with political unrest or the possibility of introduction of exchange controls, there is a risk that the swap will be unable to be completed as expected.

(c) **Potential for gains**

Right wants to borrow fixed funds whilst Herbert seeks floating rate finance. Whilst Herbert has absolute advantage in both the **fixed and floating rate markets**, the disequilibrium in differentials mean that savings can be made if a swap is made, rather than each borrowing their desired style directly:

	Right	*Herbert*	
Would pay	6.5%	LIBOR + 0.75%	LIBOR + 7.25%
Could pay	LIBOR + 1%	6%	LIBOR + 7%

This saving needs to be split equally between the two companies, ie 0.125% or £3,750 each.

The swap will consist of Right **borrowing floating rate funds**, receiving **floating rate interest** from Herbert, and paying fixed rate interest to Herbert. The reverse will be true for Herbert. The difference between the inter-company interest paid and received will convert the direct borrowing into indirect borrowing if the desired style, at a saving of 0.125% .

Adjusting the fixed interest payment

$$\text{Swap} = \text{Normal fixed interest payment} - \frac{\text{Total gain}}{2}$$

$$= 6.5 - \frac{0.25}{2}$$

$$= 6.375\%$$

	Right	*Herbert*
Pays interest	(LIBOR + 1%)	(6%)
Pays in swap	(6.375%)	(LIBOR+1%)
Receives in swap	LIBOR +1%	6.375%
Net payment	(6.375%)	(LIBOR + 0.625%)

19 Facilities management

> **Top tips.** The various forms of outsourcing are likely examination topics – particularly the advantages and disadvantages of the outsourcing approach.
>
> 'Alarm bells' should have sounded loudly when reading this scenario, particularly the statement 'The appointment of GDC Ltd was relatively rushed and although an outline contract was agreed, no detailed Service Level Agreement was produced'. Because of this, GDC Ltd is able to provide relatively poor levels of service, yet still meet the terms of the contract.

(a) GDC appears to have met its legal obligations even though the level of service it has provided to DS has been poor. There are a number of reasons for this.

Need for service agreement

DS rushed the appointment of GDC and did not insist on a **detailed Service Level Agreement (SLA)**. The contract does not specify the level of service that GDC will provide.

For example, GDC is obligated to provide 'management information', but there is no detailed definition of what this information will entail, and no deadline for the provision of the information. (eg '...within 5 working days of month-end').

Terms of management

DS handed **complete control** of its IT systems to GDC Ltd. The absence of IT expertise within DS puts it at a **disadvantage** when arguing its case with GDC Ltd.

For example, GDC could spend significant amounts of DS money on sub-standard hardware and software. DC Ltd would **not have the expertise to question** or challenge this purchase, resulting in poor use of DS funds and a poor level of service. However, even when purchasing sub-standard hardware GDC would not have breached the requirement of the contract to 'purchase all hardware and software'.

GDC is also responsible for the writing and maintenance of in-house software. **Unless GDC has a detailed understanding of DS the software written may not be suitable**. As GDC receives a set annual fee, it may be tempted to produce software as quickly and cheaply as possible. As the contract has no mention of software standards, GDC would be meeting its legal obligations.

Length of agreement

Another reason that could be contributing DS receiving poor service is that **the agreement is now two years old**. Changes could have taken place inside DS within the past two years that an outside organisation such as GDC does not understand. The nature of management information required now may be different to that required two years ago.

Service levels could also be suffering because **GDC has no financial incentive to provide a good standard of service.** GDC has the right under the contract to increase the annual fee, above the rate of inflation, without any consultation and with no reference to the satisfaction of DS.

(b)   The courses of action now available to DS relating to the provision of IT services, and the problems involved in each, are outlined below.

(i)   **DS could carry on under the existing agreement**, protecting the knowledge that GDC has built up on the provision of IT services to DS, **but applying 'moral' pressure** (in the form of complaints and meetings with GDC management) to obtain a better level of service.

The main problem with this course of action is that the level of service may not improve at all.

(ii)   DS could terminate the existing contract by giving three months' notice, and **negotiate a new contract with GDC with a well-defined SLA**.

Possible problems include the fact that GDC may not wish to negotiate a new SLA leaving DS with no IT services, or GDC may agree a new SLA but still provide the old shoddy service.

(iii)   DS could terminate the existing contract by giving three months' notice and **look for a new supplier** of all its IT services.

However, this would mean 'starting from scratch'. Even an efficient provider would take time to develop a feel for the requirements at DS, and build up their expertise. There is no guarantee the new service provider would be better than GDC, although a more detailed SLA would help.

(iv)   **DS could establish its own in-house IT team**, probably using a combination of contractors and 'permanent' employees.

The main problems with this option are the time and cost of finding setting up the team and that the team would be 'starting from scratch' and may only receive limited help from GDC during the hand-over.

(v)   Another option would be to include staff with a **good understanding of DS's operations**, but little IS/IT expertise, in a new in-house team (**insourcing**). If these people can be taught IT skills, they should then be able to utilise their business knowledge to ensure relevant IT services are provided.

Problems with this option include finding staff that are suitable and willing to make this dramatic career switch, and replacing any staff who do move to the IT team.

20 Super Retail

> **Top tips.** Requirement (a) of this question is quite general, although the scenario outlines in more detail what should go into your answer. This makes it a tough requirement. It is vital when answering this question, therefore to construct an answer plan, making sure that you include everything in your answer that you should do. Some of the issues you will raise in your answer are quite general issues. The trick to answering this question is not only to include them in your answer, but also to apply them to the relevant facts in the scenario to maximise your marks.
>
> As usual, when approaching a question on risks, bear in mind the components of the risk if that will help you spot the risks in the scenario. Note particularly in this question that the finance director is interested in business risks. Although the section of the question where his requirements are outlined does not specify the type of risk assessment he wants carried out, the fact that he is interested in business risks has been noted earlier in the scenario. In fact, part (a) of this question has nothing to do with audit at all, but rather focuses on business risk assessment and the review of prospective financial information. Do not get confused and start talking about auditing before it is introduced in the question.

(a)   **Report**

To: Finance Director, Super Retail
From: Internal Auditor
Date: December 2006
Subject: Strategy to expand into e-commerce

Terms of reference

This report has been requested in relation to Super Retail's proposed strategy to trade electronically. It covers the following matters:

- Advantages and disadvantages of outsourcing
- Business risk assessment

Outsourcing

(i)   **Advantages**

A key advantage of outsourcing is that it is often **cheaper** to **contract out** a service out than it is to conduct it in-house. It can also significantly help **cost control**, as it results in a predictable cost (the contract price), whereas costs in-house could escalate due to unforeseen events. For similar reasons, outsourcing assists in planning **cash flow**, as the contract terms will make cash flow predictable.

Another advantage is that outsourcing enables the firm to **employ specialists**, whereas, if the service was provided in house, there might be a shallower learning curve.

The terms of the contract with the service provider are likely to **provide indemnity** in the event of problems arising. There would be no such comfort if a service was mishandled in house.

Outsourcing can also provide **speed** of action. In this case, as Super Retail is keen to enter the market quickly (in three months' time), outsourcing the entire operation might be the best way to set up the e-commerce operation, even if in the long-term, Super Retail plans to bring the operations in house.

(ii)   **Disadvantages**

The biggest single disadvantage of outsourcing is that the company **loses direct control** over that aspect of their operations.

The **initial cost** of outsourcing may be **substantial**. The company must also consider whether there will be any impact on the current situation in terms of staff redundancies. In this instance, as the proposed operations would be new, this is unlikely to be the case.

The **outsourcing contract** will have to be **managed** by the company, which could take a disproportionate amount of time.

Business risk analysis

The company is suggesting a **moderate risk strategy** that involves taking essentially the same products to a different market, that is, an electronic market. The strategy of trading electronically raises a number of additional business risks that the directors should consider:

(i)   **Customers**

This form of expansion should in theory open up the company to entirely new customers, that is, ones who do not want to visit the stores and are happy to shop on line. However, the company should be aware of the **risk of losing current customers** to the new system. If in the long run, customers prefer to shop from home, the company might find that they cannot justify the fixed costs of their primary business, that is, retailing from the department stores.

(ii)   **Competition**

Trading electronically will mean that Super Retail **operates against new competitors**. The directors should ensure that they identify who their competitors are and what their strengths and weaknesses are, to ensure that they do not pose a significant risk.

(iii)   **Technology issues**

Moving into e-commerce raises a number of risks in connection with the technology that Super Retail will need to support the expansion. They will face problems connected with **viruses, business interruption** due to crashes or technical difficulties, **potential over-reliance on computer experts** either within or outside of the business. Of course, technical difficulties in connection with the web trading will not affect the core business of trading in the stores, but bad publicity or feeling could.

(iv)   **Personnel**

There may be a need to **engage staff** to operate the new systems, which will represent additional fixed cost. In particular the cost of employing computer experts would be significant.

(v)   **Legislation**

The company should be aware of **additional compliance risks** arising from engaging in e-commerce, particularly in terms of **data protection** and **contractual issues** arising from not dealing face to face with customers.

(vi)   **Fraud**

The fact that Super Retail will not be dealing with these new customers face to face increases the **company's exposure to fraud** through fraudulent payment methods.

Analysis of options

Option 1

Risks attached to Option 1 include the fact that Super Retail will have to take on new employees to run the new operation once it has been set up, and also the problem that the new venture might put **pressure on the current/expanded delivery system**, particularly as it will be difficult to predict the required level of deliveries at the outset.

However, on the positive side, buying in external expertise **reduces the risk of the system being poor quality**, and the terms of the contract should give Super Retail protection against negligence or poor-quality work.

Option 2

Option 2 may **reduce the risk of over or under provision for delivery** discussed under Option 1 above.

However, the **additional cost** of the delivery under this option should be considered. The company proposes to use surface mail, which will in itself represent a significant cost. In addition, the directors must consider whether the use **of surface mail is an appropriate strategy**. Many of the items to be delivered will be substantial, and it may be impossible to have them delivered without using one of surface mail's more specialised delivery services or a courier service. This will substantially **add to the cost** of the strategy.

Option 3

If the entire operation is outsourced, the directors of Super Retail **lose operational control** over the division, and may find it difficult to **enforce quality standards.** However, they **maintain strategic control** and should be able to formulate a contract that contains certain minimum quality standards that must be maintained.

On the positive side, if the operation was outsourced, it would be **more easy to withdraw** it if it proves unpopular. Also, as noted above, outsourcing a new operation like this means that the operation can be **commenced more quickly** and therefore option 3 could be considered as a short or medium term measure, with a view to bringing e-commerce operations in house in the long term.

Option 4

Taking up Option 4 would involve **significant cost at the outset** and although it is not dissimilar to Option 1 in that respect, the cost of buying a family business might be inflated, and would certainly be complicated if the family wanted to be kept on in employment.

There would also be **contractual issues** arising, such as whether the existing delivery contract would be transferable to benefit Super Retail.

It is unlikely that investing in this company would be the ideal strategy for Super Retail, as it might leave them in a situation where they do not have total control over operations, which could impact adversely on the **quality of the product** and therefore **corporate image**.

(b) **Implications of an outsourced division on the internal audit of Super Retail**

Evidence required

The auditors need to obtain **sufficient, appropriate audit evidence** in relation to the division that is managed by a service organisation.

Planning

As part of the planning of the audit, the auditors should determine whether the activities undertaken by the **service organisation** are **relevant** to the audit. In this case, producing revenue and expenditure that shall be reported as part of the financial statements and it impacts significantly on the major business risks that Super Retail faces.

The auditors should assess how the outsourced activity affects the risk of the audit, and also what **procedures** should be carried out in respect of that activity. They should assess whether the **records maintained** at the user entity (Super Retail) are sufficient to obtain sufficient, appropriate evidence, or whether they **are likely to need to obtain information** from the **service organisation** or its **auditors**.

Service agreement

The auditors should **obtain a copy of the service agreement** and ensure that they understand its terms. They should consider how the relevant accounting records are handled and controlled.

21 JS

> **Top tips.** (a) illustrates the variety of issues to look out for in any question involving information risk. An information centre can certainly help alleviate these problems. However, as with other risks, the success of the information centre as a control will depend how certain the strategic direction is, and what feedback has been provided on the current system, for use as the basis for improvements.

(a) **Why information could be incorrect**

(i) **Communication**

JS operates from 10 different sites that cannot communicate with each other, and neither can the various functions within each site. There is therefore little possibility that **discrepancies between overlapping information** in each system will **come to light** in the course of normal day-to-day operations.

(ii) **Piecemeal implementation**

It appears that the systems in use have been built piecemeal over the years and **hardware and software are not compatible** from one system to another. Given that there are certain to be significant overlaps between the data used by functions such as sales, production and inventory control, this situation means that there will be a considerable amount of re-inputting of the same data, inevitably leading to inconsistencies due to inputting errors.

(iii) **Approach to systems development**

Users of different systems in each department have amended the systems. This could mean that data and **files are not being processed** as they are meant to be. Again this will lead to inconsistent and inaccurate information.

(iv) **Systems overload**

Both computerised and manual systems are working **beyond the capacity** that they were designed for. For computerised systems this could result in the systems being **overloaded and crashing frequently.** Unless the operating system and the various applications offer strong protection in the case of a crash, this will result in **some corruption and/or loss of data.** For manual systems it means that **work will be rushed, shortcuts will be taken,** and **matters perceived as non-essential** by tired human information processors will be neglected. Mistakes will be made, procedures will be ignored and information will be incomplete.

(v) **Incorrect decisions**

Within departments it appears that managers follow the correct processes when reaching decisions. Because different departments are basing their decisions on different information, they may come to **different conclusions.** Incorrect pricing and production decisions are specifically mentioned.

(1) **Prices could be wrongly calculated by sales managers** because they have inaccurate information about production costs and inventory availability.

(2) Production departments may manufacture the **wrong type or quantity of products** because they have inaccurate information about sales orders, sales patterns and availability.

(vi) **Co-ordination of decision-making processes**

Nobody in the organisation knows which department's information is the most accurate for a given purpose. What must have been a long-standing problem has only recently come to light and has **taken the company by surprise**. This suggests that there is little **face-to-face liaison** between managers of different departments, which might at least draw attention to the fact that managers have a **different understanding** of the same situation, even if it does not sort out the detail.

(vii) **Manual and computerised systems**

Although the scenario does not give details, the fact that some systems are computerised and others are manual will lead to problems such as **time delays**. Manual processes often take longer than computerised ones, and this will cause problems if computer input depends upon manual processes being completed first. The system will never be fully up-to-date.

(b) **Role of information centre**

An information centre (IC) is a small unit of staff with a good **technical awareness of computer systems**, whose task is to provide a support function to computer users within the organisation.

Need for strategic direction

An information centre alone can do little to address the core problem faced by JS which is that the company has no **corporate-wide IT strategy**. The real needs of the business first need to be recognised by senior management, and there needs to be a commitment to addressing those needs.

Review of current systems

Before an IC can be fully effective, a review is required.

(i) **Examination of systems**

There is a **very clear need to examine the current operation of systems** and find out where errors are occurring. This is probably a job for internal auditors rather than IT systems specialists.

(ii) **Compatibility**

It looks likely that further investment is needed to m**ake data and systems compatible** with each other and to enable them to communicate with each other.

Contribution of information centre

Once current problems are addressed an information centre (IC) could help in the following ways.

(i) **Standards**

The IC can set, and encourage users to conform to, common standards, which will ensure consistency of data and processing and save time.

(1) **Hardware standards** ensure that all of the equipment used in the organisation is compatible and can be put into use in different departments as needed.

(2) **Software standards** ensure that information generated by one department can easily be shared with and worked upon by other departments.

(3) **Programming standards** ensure that applications developed by individuals to help them perform their jobs (for example, word processing macros or spreadsheets for data analysis) follow best practice, are easy to modify, and are replicated to others in the organisation where this is of benefit.

(4) **Data processing standards** ensure that certain conventions such as the format of file names are followed throughout the organisation. This facilitates sharing and storage and retrieval of information by as many users as possible.

(ii) **Applications development**

Part of the current problems are due to the fact that the systems have been subject to **substantial amendments by users.** Many users who develop their own applications have **little or no formal training in programming**; consequently their programs might be extremely crude and virtually incomprehensible.

An IC can help to remedy this situation by providing **technical guidance** to the developers and to encourage comprehensible and documented programs. **Understandable programs** can be maintained or modified more easily by people other than the system developer. Documentation then provides a means of teaching others how the programs work. These efforts can greatly extend the usefulness and life of the programs that are developed.

(iii) **Systems overload**

Problems in this area may be largely due to the fact that the system currently holds **vastly more data** than it needs (several copies of each piece of data) and that much processing simply duplicates processing being done elsewhere. The introduction of compatible systems that can communicate and share data, and of revised procedures may alleviate the problem of lack of capacity without any further input from the IC.

In the future the IC can **develop and maintain good contacts and relationships** with suppliers to ensure that they **fulfil their maintenance obligations** and their **maintenance staff are quickly on site** when needed. It can also monitor growth in system usage, and recommend steps to ensure that extra capacity is available when needed.

(iv) **Problem solving**

An IC usually offers a **Help Desk** to ensure that staff time is spent on their real work rather than on IT problems. The IC will **maintain a record of problems** and identify those that occur most often. If the problem is that users do not know how to use the system, **training** needs to be provided, either in-house or via external courses.

Training software can be **developed or purchased and made available over a network** from a central server. Training applications often contain **analysis software,** drawing attention to trainee progress and common problems, and the availability of such information will enable the IC to identify and address specific training needs more closely.

22 Computer security

> **Top tips.** A good test of your knowledge of a wide range of computer controls. Note that not all threats to the system are deliberate.

The main areas of risk to which a computer system is exposed, and some of the factors which may lead to the exposure are as follows.

(a) **Accidental destruction** or **loss of data** by operator or software error. In addition the possibility of accidental destruction of programs or hardware, particularly the dropping of a disk pack, by an operator, and the consequences thereof, should not be overlooked.

(b) The **acceptance of inaccurate input data** due to inadequate edit or other checks is another frequent cause of loss of data.

(c) A **complete systems failure** can lead to loss of data and may be caused by a failure in the power supply or possibly a failure of the air conditioning or other environmental controls.

(d) **Theft of data** from a **batch processing system** by an operator copying or removing data files, particularly where these are on easily transportable media.

(e) **Theft of data** from an **on line or real time system** by a person obtaining unauthorised access to the system via a remote terminal and either using passwords illegally or alternatively using a 'piggyback system' (in which a valid transmission is intercepted and the final 'logging off' operation stopped in transmission to permit the illegal operator to continue in operation masquerading as the authorised user).

(f) **Theft of software** either by operators copying or removing the program file, and in the latter case possibly demanding a ransom from the rightful owner, or alternatively by programming staff copying and attempting to sell the source documentation, with or without the object program.

(g) **Deliberate destruction of the hardware** has been known to occur, and where adequate protection has not been provided, such acts have also led to the simultaneous destruction of software and data. Similar results may occur as a result of fire or explosion either in the computer room or adjoining premises.

23 Physical threats – contingency plan

Top tips. Hopefully (a) should not have required you to exercise too much imagination. If you can draw on your own organisation's security arrangements, that will be helpful. Often simpler (less technological?) controls will be effective, so that an organisation with a very few well-guarded entrances may well be a lot more secure than one with many entrances, however elaborate the security on each one.

Some interesting issues are discussed in (b). One significant point is that implementation of a contingency plan could itself cause considerable disruption, so the organisation needs to consider how far it can carry on as normal if there are problems. Past experience may be the best guide in assessing the likelihood and consequences of problems. Note also that the answer covers both the key questions about internal control systems; (1) Are they adequate? (2) Are they operating as they should be?

(a) **Potential physical threats**

Threats to SCP's computer centre fall into two distinct areas – **physical threats to the centre** itself and **threats to the software and data on the system**.

Protection against natural and man-made disasters

(i) **Power problems.** The electrical supply should be set up to be **immune** from any **foreseeable interruptions or fluctuations**. This could be done with standby or continuously running generators.

(ii) **Flooding.** The facility should be constructed to be as secure as possible against the **possibility of flooding**, either from internal sources (eg fire control systems) or from external sources (eg leaking roofs, rain, rivers, and so on).

(iii) **Wind damage.** If the facility is in an area which might be susceptible to wind damage, or the building is not sufficiently solidly constructed, then **precautions** should be taken against the possibility of damage from freak wind conditions.

(iv) **Storm and lightning damage.** Both **direct lightning strikes and lightning strikes on** the power grid should be taken into consideration, particularly if the installation is in an area where electrical storms occur. Other storm damage (wind and rain) also needs to be provided for.

(v) **Fire.** Fire is an ever present threat. **Smoking** should be **banned**, and all **electrical and heating apparatus** should be **checked** to ensure that there is no likelihood of its being a source of fire. **Smoke detectors**, **use of low-flammability materials** and **regular fire drills** should all form part of control procedures.

(vi) **Intruders.** Both outsiders and disillusioned staff should be guarded against. Protection could take the form of **security guards**, levels of **physical entry prevention** and **careful adherence to entry checking**.

(vii) **Dust.** For some parts of the system dust can be a major problem. **Access controls** for personnel will aid in preventing dust intrusion, and proper air conditioning, with a system **of sealed/double doors** to important parts of the installation, will manage much of the rest of the problem. Conscientious cleaners will also help limit dust.

Protection against unauthorised physical access

(i) **Restrict the number of entrances**. If the **number of doors** (taking into account safety requirements) is as **low as possible** the number of potential 'weak' access points which could cause a problem is restricted. Emergency exits should be fitted with alarms.

(ii) **Graduated access to different parts of the facility**. Staff and other visitors should only be allowed access to those areas which they **need to visit**. If **different areas** have **different levels of authorisation requirements**, then control becomes more easily implemented.

(iii) **Key card controlled access to the facility**. Using magnetic or electronic key card facilities allows for **sophisticated control on the time and place of access**, as well as more mundane aspects such as preventing double entry of a card before an exit.

(iv) **Time control on access**. Intelligent access control can **limit access to staff to the hours** when they legitimately would need it, and prevent access outside those hours except on override.

(v) **Wearing of ID badges.** Wearing of ID cards with built-in photographs allows both staff and security personnel to maintain a check on people who have access and those who have used the access power. Visitors should also be given badges and asked to wear them.

(vi) **Voice, finger, palm or retina scan and recognition systems** (if the investment warrants it). These systems can be expensive, but prevent card swapping and misuse.

(b) **Contingency plan**

The purpose of a contingency plan is to ensure that when a catastrophe happens, an organisation is **prepared and is able to continue working** in the face of a certain pre-determined level of interruption. Catastrophes may have a wide range of causes. A contingency plan is usually invoked only in the event of a **'major' catastrophe**, typically fire, flooding, failure of the main processor or loss of a power supply.

The organisation needs to establish **how much interruption** could be tolerated in the system, **what the risks of the various types of interruption** are, what the **provisions** are that would have to be **made for those interruptions** and what **costs** would be associated with the failures and with the provision of the responses. Key to any contingency plan is **back-up of data.** However good the alternative hardware facilities, they will be of little use if SCP cannot load up with recent data.

Developing the plan

When a systems administrator sets out to ensure that the issues of security are fully covered, all these factors are taken into account. A team, led by the administrator, may be appointed to investigate the matter.

(i) **Risk assessment.** The team should assess how vulnerable SCP is in principle to any of these problems. It may help to do an estimate of the **likely costs** of any particular threat identified. It is obviously easier to identify the costs of replacing hardware than the costs caused, for example, by a virus infection.

(ii) **Review of previous experience**. The team might review SCP's **past history of security problems** (eg any frauds discovered, and the internal control issues raised by them).

(iii) **Effectiveness of current arrangements**. The team will then assess **how far current security measures** are **sufficient to cope** with the vulnerabilities discovered. This study might be quite a lengthy process, covering detailed technical issues (eg how easy might a hacker find it to enter the network? Are there fireproof cabinets? etc).

(iv) **Implementation of security**. Some analysis will be made of the extent to which the security procedures theoretically in force are in fact being **followed in practice** (eg users might share passwords which they are supposed to keep confidential).

(v) **Additional security measures.** Once some assessment of the risk, both **qualitative and quantitative** has been made, additional security measures may be suggested. These, too, will have to be **costed**, as far as possible, so that the costs of security do not outweigh the anticipated costs of the threats identified.

Standby options

Standby options would include some or all of the following.

(i) **Replacement hardware**. This clearly involves some delay and does not address short-term operational problems.

(ii) **Duplicate sites to which communications links could be switched.** These may be alternative sites already operated by the organisation, as in a **distributed processing environment**, or **operated by a third party**. Third parties may be either companies with which the organisation has some form of 'twinning' arrangement or dedicated companies providing standby services.

(iii) **Duplicate facilities permanently installed.** This is an expensive option, but one which should be considered for a mission-critical system.

24 Outsourcing internal audit

> **Top tips.** The advantages and disadvantages of outsourcing generally is a topical issue. It is certainly therefore a possible exam topic and also links with wider control issues.

Role of internal audit

As highlighted in the question, the role of internal audit has in recent times been extended and highlighted by reports such as the Turnbull report. Internal auditors, once required only to attest that the systems of a business operated as they were supposed to, are now required to be multi-skilled professionals, involved in many aspects of a business, for example:

- Internal controls
- Risk management
- IT strategy and process
- Best Value
- Investigations

This increase in the potential role of the internal auditor has perhaps been behind the trend to outsource the department to the major accountancy firms. Outsourcing can bring **advantages of skills, cost, techniques** and possibly even added protection in the form of **legal liability** being passed to the contractor. However, outsourcing can also bring its problems. The growing popularity of outsourcing suggests that in the main, the disadvantages are outweighed by the advantages.

Advantages of outsourcing internal audit

Procuring skill

An advantage of outsourcing is that the company can procure a **high level of skill** which it might not be able to bring permanently into its business. The reasons for this are various. First, an outsourced internal auditor is likely to be involved in a number of different businesses, and this variety will add to their skills. An in house auditor is not in a position to have such **variety** to call upon, as by his nature, he is tied to the business which employs him. The outsourcing firm is likely also to use the **best techniques** as that is their business.

Another consideration with regard to procuring skill is **cost**. It might be **prohibitively expensive** to buy in the degree of skill required permanently (in the form of an employee), whereas it is **cheaper to hire the skill** for shorter periods of time.

Relationship to the company

There are two elements here. The first is that as outsourced internal auditors are not employed by the company, they bring a degree of **independence** to the task which it is impossible for employees of the company to have. This may enable them to view any issues arising more clearly. It also eliminates the possibility of such issues as internal auditors having difficulty in conducting their task due to **familiarity** and **personal relationships** with other staff.

The second advantage is that as the service has been contracted out, the company has a **degree of legal protection** over the quality of the service. The company is protected against **negligent work**, for example, to the degree that it can be **compensated** for it, which is not the case if the work is carried out by employees.

Relationship to external audit

The firm providing the service may or may not be the firm that provides external audit services to the company. However, it is likely to be a firm that also specialises in external audit and this may produce **synergies** between the work performed. This is firstly because the auditors will be **aware of the work required** for the external audit and may ensure that they undertake work that could be used for the external audit. Secondly, because when conducting their **evaluation of** the **quality** of the work of internal audit, the external auditors are likely to be content to rely more heavily on the work of staff of a reputable firm of accountants than might otherwise be the case.

Cost

Purchasing internal audit services means that the company can **focus** on what they want to gain from internal audit and purchase a focused service. It also means that internal audit may be used on a '**part-time' basis**, for example, two days a week or four weeks a year, rather than having full time employees.

The fact that the service is being bought from a large organisation dedicated to providing auditing services might also mean that the company will benefit from the **economies of scale** which the service provider creates.

Disadvantages of outsourcing internal audit

Procuring skill

The industry the company is in may require that its internal auditor has **specialised** skills. If the audit is outsourced, and the provider does not have the skills which the company first thought, the cost of **changing the service provider** could be high, and the company may have lost staff who did possess the relevant skills.

Relationship to the company

Several negative issues may arise. Firstly the **relationship will be dominated by the contract** between the two parties, which will mean that the contract needs to be drafted carefully in the first place and that **a lack of flexibility** may arise in the long term. It may not be possible, for example, under the contract to drop the current programme and conduct a specific investigation if circumstances which required that arose.

Company employees might feel **threatened by being asked questions** by outsiders, and the internal auditors might find it difficult to carry out their duties effectively or efficiently. Their independence might impose a sometimes **excessive formality**.

Lastly, the audit committee and directors will in practical terms have **less control** over the department than they would have done if the department consisted of employees who were required to obey them. In the event of them being unhappy with the service, they might **only have recourse to legal action** rather than simply changing the internal audit programme. This could prove costly, and have a detrimental effect on future relations.

External audit issues

If the directors of the company wish to use the same audit firm to provide their internal and external audit functions, the audit firm may feel that this would be a threat to their **ethical requirement of independence** as auditors. If the directors then used another firm for either service, this could lead to problems with their accustomed firm.

If the firm determine that no ethical issue arises, it might still appear that the distinction between services is blurred and the **credibility** of the audit report might be affected.

Conclusion

There are significant advantages to the internal audit function being outsourced. However, companies considering such a strategy should be aware of the disadvantages and try to counter them from the outset. For example, the problem discussed above of only having recourse to litigation could be mitigated by **negotiating certain clauses in the contract with the service provider, such** as the right to obtain a second opinion over certain issues, or the right to take problems arising to mediation.

25 Audit and governance

> **Top tips**. Good knowledge of the recommendations of the Turnbull guidance is very important in answering this question. (a) requires knowledge of why the guidance has developed and the problems it is trying to counter, as well as considering the interaction of the audit committee and external audit.

(a)   **Role of external auditors**

The role of the external auditors pre-dates formal systems of corporate governance. By law, the external auditors are **required to make a statement in the annual accounts** as to whether the accounts give a **true and fair view** of the state of affairs of the company as at the date of the statement of financial position and of its profit for the period covered by the accounts.

Limitations on role

In the UK, one of the factors giving rise to the pressure for better corporate governance was concern that some large companies were **not providing fair accounts,** and that profits or asset values were, in some cases, artificially inflated. There was a view that the external auditors were unable to perform their function properly, perhaps because a powerful or unscrupulous chief executive could keep information away from them.

Lack of independence

There have also been criticisms that the external auditors of a company are not always as **independent** as they should be, because they rely on the company not just for their audit fee, but for substantial fees for other consultancy work throughout the year.

Audit committee

Under the UK's Combined Code on corporate governance, large public companies are expected to have an **audit committee of the board of directors**, consisting of non-executive directors. One of the functions of the audit committee should be to maintain an **appropriate relationship with the auditors,** which means that the views of the auditors should be heard by the NEDs. The committee should also establish **formal arrangements** for considering how they should apply the principles for **financial reporting and internal control**, and the requirement to liaise with the external auditors means that the opinions of the auditors on financial reporting and internal controls will be fed into this process. Another function of the audit committee should be to **keep under review the independence and objectivity** of the external auditors, particularly where they perform a large amount of non-audit services for the company.

(b) **Purposes of internal controls**

Internal controls are rules and procedures that are put in place to ensure that **operations are carried out properly, efficiently and effectively**, that the **company's assets** are **safeguarded**, that the **company's internal and external reporting systems** are reliable and that **relevant laws and regulations are complied with**.

Financial controls

Many internal controls are financial controls, such as procedures to ensure that **proper accounting records are kept**, that **financial information** produced by the company is **reliable**, that the company is **not unnecessarily exposed to financial risks**, that **assets** are **safeguarded** and that **fraud is prevented or detected** when it occurs.

Sound system of controls

The Turnbull Report recommended that listed companies are expected to have in place a **robust system of internal control**, which should be reviewed at least annually.

Regular internal control reports to the board should **consider the significant risks** facing the company, the **effectiveness of existing controls** for managing them and whether any **further measures** are **needed** to remedy control weaknesses.

(c) **Role of internal audit**

An internal audit department would be **responsible for monitoring the internal controls** within the company, and for checking that they are **adequate** and **functioning properly.** The department might also be required to **recommend improvements** in the control system where there appear to be weaknesses.

Need for internal audit

The Turnbull Report states that the need for an internal audit department will depend on various factors, such as the **scale, diversity and complexity of the company's operations**, and on the **number of employees**. However, in the absence of an internal audit function, management must have **other monitoring processes** in place to ensure that the system of controls is functioning. The report also states that a company without an internal audit function should **review the need for one** each year.

(d) **Reasons for splitting roles**

The requirement that the positions of chief executive and chairman should not be held by the same person is to prevent too much power within a company falling into the hands of one individual. The Combined Code states that there should be a **clear division at the head of the company**, to ensure a balance of power and authority, and to prevent any one individual having unfettered power over decision-making. The combination of the two roles is increasingly unpopular with shareholders, judged by the recent outcry in the UK over Marks and Spencer, where chief executive Sir Stuart Rose also assumed the role of executive chairman.

Combined Code requirements

Any decision by a company to **combine the roles of chairman and chief executive** should be **publicly justified**.

26 Internal audit effectiveness

> **Top tips**. (a) indicates how questions on internal audit will generally concentrate on the strategic and managerial implications of the function, and you must approach the question accordingly.
>
> In (b) you need to state that internal audit's independence must not suffer as a result of the function being audited. One way of ensuring this is the involvement of the audit committee; the corporate governance reports demonstrate that the audit committee and internal audit should be complementary functions.
>
> In (c) a key element of the process is setting objectives.
>
> The hints given in the question should have meant your answer to (d) was a discussion of the information needed to assess internal audit's performance on a VFM basis. You need to consider costs and resource usage weighed against benefits, as you would for other aspects of the control system. This is probably the toughest part of the question, but if you scored well in the other parts you would not have needed many marks on it. The headers in (d) are the areas that need to be assessed.

REPORT

To: Chairman
From: Finance Director
Date: 20 July 20X4
Subject: Effectiveness of the Internal Audit Department (IAD)

(a) **Objectives of internal audit**

Role of internal audit

Internal audit is an **independent appraisal function** established by the management of an organisation for the **review** of the **internal control system** as a service to the organisation. It objectively examines, evaluates and reports on the adequacy of internal control as a contribution to the **proper, economic, efficient and effective use of resources**. It is an internal control therefore and, like all internal controls, it should be assessed for effectiveness. This appears to be a suitable time for such an investigation.

Review of controls

One aspect of internal audit's work is certainly to **review and report on the adequacy and effectiveness of an organisation's internal controls** The review of controls should cover accounting controls and non-financial controls, controls that ensure compliance with external laws and regulations and internal policies.

Contribution to organisational effectiveness

Internal audit's role should also **contribute** to **overall organisational effectiveness,** by, as the Institute Of Internal Auditors have commented, 'assisting members of the organisation in the effective discharge of their responsibilities…(and furnishing) them with analyses, appraisals, recommendations, counsel and information'. This aspect of internal audit's work will cover recommendations for improvements in the organisation's information systems or its utilisation of resources.

(b) **Who should carry out the assessment?**

Audit committee

The IAD must **maintain** its **independence** from those parts of the organisation which it audits (ie most of the operations of the business). This independence must be maintained when the IAD is itself the subject of the audit for the sake of future IAD audits, and to obtain an objective result in this case. This criteria would exclude me as Finance Director. Other members of the board might be appropriate investigators, but the prime candidate would be a member of the **Audit Committee** (AC) as the IAD acts as almost an executive arm of the committee. A member of the AC with appropriate knowledge and experience would be required.

Another IAD

Alternatives to the AC which we might consider include the **IAD of another company**, which might be approached through contacts of our executive directors. Confidentiality might be an issue here; we would need to make sure that the other company was not a competitor etc.

External audit

Another option would be to use our own **external auditors**. If they were happy with our IAD, then future co-operation between the two sets of auditors might produce a saving in the external audit fee. However, if they were unhappy with the work of our IAD then the external auditors may decide that they need to perform extra audit work in future, and **fees might then rise**.

I do not feel it is appropriate for me to decide who should carry out the investigation of IAD: this is a decision which should be made by the board.

(c) **Detailed work**

Audit objectives

Like any other audit, a management audit involves deciding the **audit objectives** (which managers to audit, what aspects of their work and so on), carrying out an investigation, gathering evidence and reporting the results. The objectives are very important: they must be positive, to encourage co-operation in the IAD staff. The objectives will determine exactly what information is required, but at the least IAD files and reports will be accessed. This will require **explanation and comment** from members of the IAD. Samples will be taken of the IAD's work as it will not be possible to examine all of it.

Collection of information

Information, both written and oral, will also be **collected** from those **outside** the IAD, including the external auditors, the board members of the AC and the operational staff audited by the IAD. In the case of the latter, given the nature of the work, the weight of their evidence will have to be judged according to the level of criticism raised against them by the IAD in the past. In all cases the information collected should be properly recorded, and the documents collected and created should be controlled. This is a sensitive audit, so working papers should remain confidential and kept secure at all times.

(d) **Information required**

Value for money

The audit will seek to determine whether the IAD operates:

(i) **Economically**, producing the appropriate quantity and quality of work at lowest cost
(ii) **Efficiently**, using minimum resources for the quality and quantity of service provided and
(iii) **Effectively**, achieving its set objectives

Comparisons are important for VFM audits. However, it may be difficult to obtain any **industry averages**. Two possible sources are non-executive directors who can gain information on IADs in other companies; and bodies regulating auditing, for example the Institute of Internal Auditors. In addition, **information over time** needs to be collected, again for comparative purposes. Such data should be both quantitative and non-quantitative.

Detailed information

(i) **General set up of the IAD**

This will involve investigating the **structure** of the IAD; what **work** the IAD has been asked to carry out (routine vs specials); **who requests** work to be done; **who receives IA reports**.

(ii) **Resources used by IAD**

The resources used by the IAD should be quantified: **staff**, **equipment** (computers etc), **training**. It should be relatively easy to compare such costs with industry data.

(iii) **Utilisation**

How well is the IAD **utilising** these **resources**? Is training undertaken in slack periods? Are IA staff sitting around the office too much?

(iv) **IA procedures**

The methods and procedures used by IAD to carry out investigations should be examined. Does the IAD use **standardised procedures** and **documentation**? Are **files up to date and well maintained**? Is **staff time recorded accurately and compared to budgets**? Are **audits completed in time and to budget**? Are **review procedures appropriate and effective**?

(v) **Report effectiveness**

The efforts of the IAD must be in vain if the reports **do not reach the appropriate decision-makers**. They in turn must **take action** based on the IAD reports. Assessment is also needed whether, as a result of IAD investigations, **costs** have been **reduced** (including external audit costs).

I hope that this report has provided a good starting point for an assessment of the IAD function and I suggest that you pass it to the Audit Committee with your comments.

Signed: Finance Director

27 Analytical review

> **Top tips.** The examiners have stated that you might be asked to analyse numerical data and this is one area of the syllabus where you might have to, although obviously assessment of accounts comes up in a number of other papers. Remember that you are trying to use analytical review to identify the key risk areas, particularly areas where controls are lacking or not operating, because these are the areas of most interest to the internal auditor.

(a) **Inventory**

Inventory represents a significant proportion of current assets (59%) and the average age of inventory has increased from 74 days in 20X1 to 95 days in 20X2 compared to an industry average of 73 days.

Average age of inventory = (average inventory/cost of sales) × 365

Receivables

Receivables represent a significant proportion of current assets (33.3%) and the average age of customers has increased from 32 days in 20X1 to 37 days in 20X2 compared to an industry average of 30 days.

Average age of receivables = (average receivables/sales) × 365

Non-current assets

Of the net assets employed in the business 52% is invested in non-current assets. (Is the valuation of non-current assets reasonable in view of the need for a loan issue to enable part of the plant to be remodelled?)

Net profit before tax on net assets employed

The percentage return has declined from 17.5% in 20X1 to 16.4% in 20X2 and compares unfavourably with an industry average of 19.5%. It appears that there is a particular problem on profit margins.

Net profit and gross profit before tax on sale

The net profit before tax on sales has marginally increased from 8.3% for 20X1 to 8.5% in 20X2 but compares poorly with an industry average of 11%. The gross profit on sales barely changed, being 31.7% in 20X1 and 31% in 20X2 but the industry average is 34%.

Expenses

There has been a saving on administration expenses but selling expenses are now 11.5% on sales as compared to 9.5% in 20X1.

Other matters

An analysis of current liabilities is required so that this item can be further investigated. The interest cover was 5 times in 20X2 as against 6.7 times in 20X1 whereas the industry average is 8 times.

(b) The areas which cause particular concern are inventory, gross profit on sales, sales expenses, receivables and the proposed loan stock issue.

Inventory

The average age of inventory has shown a marked increase with a result that there are increased holding costs with the greater amount of inventory, loss of capital tied up in inventory, dangers of obsolescence, pilferage and so on. As a consequence the auditors will need to pay particular attention to **obsolete, slow moving and damaged inventory**. They must ensure that inventory is **adequately insured** and they should carefully examine the **system of inventory recording and reporting** to management of inventory movements and levels. They will also require a detailed breakdown between raw materials, work in progress, completed machines, consumables etc. In addition to the normal checks on these figures, questions need to be asked as to the **proportion of spares** held as a service to customers and company policy as to **retention of spares for obsolete machines** including their valuation.

Gross profit on sales

The reason why Patchit is earning less than the industry average could be due to a number of different factors, for example **lower sales** prices, **more costly materials**, poor materials, **higher production costs**, **poor workmanship**, inventory control or valuation problems. The internal auditors should be aware that any of these areas could lead to gross profit reductions and their work should encompass these areas.

Sales expenses

The auditors will require an analysis of this between **fixed salaries**, commission, travelling expenses, entertainment and so on, before they can investigate further. They will be particularly concerned that management are aware of the increases which have been authorised by them. During their routine audit tests they will examine the documentation relating to certain of **the payments** made.

Receivables

The average age of receivables has slightly increased but this is an area which should be tightly controlled as the firm is losing money due to the fact that customers are taking **longer to pay**. There is also a greater danger of **bad debts** being incurred. The auditors must therefore pay particular attention to the adequacy of the provision for doubtful debts and the systems of credit control.

Proposed loan stock issue

Although this is a matter for the directors to decide, the internal auditors' advice may be sought or they may feel that they ought to advise the directors in any case. It has already been pointed out that the **interest cover** is not as good as the industry average and if the further issue is made the cover could in fact be worse. This is particularly the case with an industry which it is stated is unpredictable. Is it wise to have such heavy borrowings in such an industry? There is a possibility that if business deteriorates there could be a strain on liquidity as interest payments must be met. A possible alternative could be a bonus issue by capitalisation of part of the reserves followed by a rights issue to raise the additional cash.

28 Stoy Toys

Top tips. The question asks about risks for shareholders. These include short-term risks to profits, as dividends are a constant proportion of earnings – you need to concentrate on threats to sales. Shareholders will also be concerned with longer-term strategy, as this may influence how popular the shares are if Stoy is listed and hence the capital gains shareholders can achieve.

Directors' remuneration is not only a problem in terms of costs reducing profits; there are agency issues involved. Are the directors running the company in the best interests of the shareholders? The clue to this is in the first paragraph of the question, where the scenario highlights the fact that the majority shareholders are not involved in management.

Clues in (b) are the excessive level of detail, the over-emphasis on budgets and the inability of the system to provide information for director (ie strategic) decision-making. The various techniques discussed can be justified by the information given. Total quality management is clearly very significant because of the production failures and the risks discussed in (a) of sub-standard toys being sold. Many toys will have a limited lifecycle and development is therefore important, so a lifecycle costing approach could be very helpful. Because the market for a lot of toys is price-sensitive target costing can also be justified.

In (c) the UK Higgs report provides the framework of the four major aspects of the non-executive directors' role. However your answer needs to demonstrate how NEDs can make an effective contribution to Stoy. Partly this involves being prepared to disagree with the chief executive! The NEDs must also tackle the issues of concern to shareholders, particularly the remuneration packages. The answer also shows how the committee structure helps NEDs by giving forums to discuss matters away from the executive directors.

(d) represents a selling exercise; you are trying to sell to the board (in particular the chief executive) the benefits of internal audit. You need to get away from work on financial accounting controls and explore internal audit's wider role in reviewing operations. Again a corporate governance report (here the Turnbull report) can be used to provide a useful framework for your answer. Although it isn't specified in the question, you should get a couple of marks for using the memo format.

(a) (i) **Decision to develop new products**

Diversification

Ideally diversifying by producing different toys should be an effective way of managing risks. Producing a wide range of toys should mean that Stoy Toys can **maintain returns** even if individual toys become less popular. However as the company's recent experience indicates, developing new toys can be a high-risk strategy.

Development risk

The main risk of development is that **expenditure is wasted on projects** that have little commercial appeal. There is also a risk that time will be spent on projects that are **not in line with corporate strategy**. Stoy has had limited success in developing new toys in recent years. Shortcomings with Stoy's management accounting information systems may be hindering an effective assessment of research and development, with all the emphasis being on meeting budget, and little assessment of how effective the department has been.

Branding and marketing risk

Stoy's current association with cuddly toys may **undermine the appeal of its new range**, which Stoy is marketing as a contemporary range. Stoy's current **marketing strategy** may also need to be **changed** if it is to appeal to a mass market, as mainstream commercial channels are showing fewer children's programmes. The alternative is advertising on specialist children's channels with smaller audiences and competing against lots of other manufacturers.

Competition risk

Stoy is also at risk from competitors responding to its activities by taking action themselves. Stoy may be vulnerable to a **counter-advertising campaign** by its competitors. Its 'Attitude Girl' package may be seen as **too expensive** by parents and children. It may be **undercut** by competitors selling similar items, separately, thus appearing more affordable. Alternatively Stoy Toys may be vulnerable to '**pirate copies**' being made of Attitude Girls toys. Possibly the legal protection offered to manufacturers in the East Asian People's Republic is insufficient to prevent other manufacturers there copying the designs.

(ii) **Outsourcing**

Supply delivery risk

Although using overseas suppliers will minimise production costs, there may be other costs and drawbacks from doing so. The **guarantees about reliability** may be **dubious**; the supplier may also face problems with **its own country's infrastructure**, for example **loss of electricity**. A lot of annual toy demand takes place in the run-up to Christmas; supplier delays and hence failure to reach the shops in time for this market will have a serious impact on revenues. This particularly applies to new toys due to be launched and marketed at Christmas.

Supply quality risk

Stoy may be less able to monitor quality than it has been if supply is outsourced. Failures in quality that are believed to **put children's health at risk** will have particularly serious consequences. Companies have had to withdraw entire ranges of toys because for example they contained dangerous lead paint, or the wrong mix of ingredients was used and a dangerous substance produced instead.

Reputation risk

Any problems with poor quality or dangerous toys may not only affect demand for those toys, but all other toys Stoy produces, even if there is no cause for concern with some of them. Stoy may also suffer **consumer boycotts** if the supplier is revealed to be using **low-wage labour** to meet its cost targets.

(iii) **Directors' bonus**

Flaws in packages

The fact that directors receive high basic salary increases that bear **little relation to company success** indicates that the packages are flawed. Directors can be rewarded well **without any increase in company performance being required**. The directors' security is further enhanced by the long-term contracts that they have entered; if their employment is terminated early, perhaps for under-performance, Stoy may have to pay **large amounts of compensation**. **Contract lengths** are **much longer** than are allowed by most corporate governance codes.

Short-termism

The limited performance-related remuneration that is in place is not without flaws either. Although it is **consistent with Stoy's strategy** of developing new products, it places excessive emphasis on toy development that will yield **short-term results**. There is no benefit gained from building a portfolio of more toys that will bring long-term returns to Stoy like the Puppy Pups have. There is also **no downside risk** from this element of the package. Directors can pour money into speculative new investments, in the knowledge that they won't be penalised if these are unsuccessful.

Benefits

The benefits in kind that are given to directors again do not appear to be linked with company performance. This could be an example of the **agency problem,** directors rewarding themselves, reducing company profits and not acting in a way that benefits shareholders. **Employees** may also be particularly unhappy with these benefits as not only are they not available to them, but directors are enjoying them at a time when employees feel that their own jobs are under threat of being outsourced.

Reputation risk

Excessive remuneration may also worsen the threat to sales if seen in conjunction with **other reputation risks**, particularly if Stoy is using suppliers that employ sweatshop labour.

(b) **Problems with current situation**

Lack of strategic focus

The focus on cost targets seems to mean that operational management spends excessive time on **relatively unimportant items**. Achieving the target is seen as an end in itself, rather than a means of implementing the right strategy. This may well indicate that the board has **not developed a fully coherent strategy**.

Failure to focus on key issues

The current information trail seems **too focused on production**. There seems to be a lack of awareness of the influence of **design on cost patterns**; the usage of factors of production will be determined by decisions made at this stage. The business also seems **very internally focused**, with little attention paid to customer satisfaction measures, possibly because effective measures of customer satisfaction are non-quantitative.

Possible improvements

Strategic management accounting system

To make decisions effectively the directors require a management accounting system that provides information that **assists strategic decision-making**. This includes information about **competitors**, such as their cost margins and how competitor action has affected the demand for Stoy's toys. Given Stoy's plans to seek new funding through a listing, the board needs information about the consequences of **capacity expansion**. The directors also need strategic computerised systems, such as **executive support** or **strategic enterprise management systems** to aid decision-making.

Different aspects of performance

To counter the chief management accountant's complaint about the focus on operational costs, Stoy should use a management accounting approach that assesses different dimensions of performance. The main advantage of such an approach will be a greater emphasis on measures that indicate customer satisfaction or which assess performance aspects that have most impact on customer satisfaction. These include customer complaints, on-time deliveries and quality control rejects. The balanced scorecard should also have an **innovation and learning** dimension, with measures including the % of revenue earned from new products. This should enable the directors to assess Stoy's capacity to **maintain its competitive position**.

Total quality management

Because of the severe consequences of producing sub-standard products quality management and measurement should be an important part of control systems. **Quality reporting** should not only apply to internal operations, it should also apply to the outsourced suppliers. **Cost reports** should highlight the costs of quality management; the costs incurred to prevent problems and appraise quality and non-conformance costs such as waste and refunds to customers. **The level of customer complaints** would be important non-financial data.

Life cycle costing

Stoy may adopt a life cycle costing approach, which means attributing all costs, **production and non-production**, to products. Life cycle costing is often most helpful when a large percentage of total life cycle costs are incurred at the **start of a product's life cycle**; this applies to Stoy where the development, design and marketing costs will be a significant proportion of total costs. This will enable better understanding of individual product profitability and Stoy's ability to develop new products.

Target costing

Alternatively a target costing approach may be appropriate for Stoy. This will mean estimating what the market is prepared to pay for new toys, again demonstrating the importance of **understanding the customer**. A desired profit is calculated for the range of toys, and analysis made of whether costs can be limited to a level that will generate the desired profit margin. If the target cannot be met, decisions to reduce costs can be made at the design stage, or the product not manufactured at all. If the product is made, appeal to the market will be maintained by reducing costs and hence being able to reduce price.

(c) **Strategy**

As members of a single board, NEDs have responsibility along with executive directors for the **strategic decisions** that the board takes. NEDs should come from a variety of business backgrounds, but should have sufficient experience to contribute effectively. NEDs should not automatically support executive directors; instead they should evaluate, and if necessary challenge, the proposals made by executive directors, using their own experiences to reinforce their contribution.

Performance scrutiny

Once clear strategic objectives have been decided upon, NEDs should monitor whether the **board and senior managers have met these objectives**. This will be particularly important if a greater proportion of director remuneration is dependent on performance. They should represent shareholder interests and seek to ensure that **agency problems do not arise between shareholders and executive directors and managers**.

Risk

NEDs have certain specific tasks, to **scrutinise the reporting of performance** and the **effectiveness of risk management and internal control systems** in countering the risks that the company faces. Governance reports recommend that an audit committee staffed by independent NEDs is particularly important. NEDs should be able to conduct their reviews in this environment away from executive director pressures. Internal and external auditors can report to NEDs and raise concerns with them, and thus the auditors' position will be enhanced as well.

People

Again the governance reports recommend that committees staffed by NEDs, the remuneration and **nomination committees**, are the best way for NEDs to **exercise their influence**. In this environment NEDs can effectively scrutinise and make recommendations about pay and contract issues. Since NEDs' remuneration should ideally be fixed by the company in general meeting, and since they are elected for set terms, they can take an **objective view** of what rewards and contracts are desirable for executives. The nomination committee should review director appointments, also other issues affecting the board such as succession arrangements and the need for the board to have an appropriate mix of skills. This will be particularly important if the company expands and diversifies after its listing.

Listing implications

If Stoy Toys does obtain a listing, then it will be **obliged to appoint non-executive directors** under the corporate governance codes. If non-executive directors are appointed before Stoy is listed, they can have an important input into the strategic decision of whether a listing is appropriate.

(d) **To:** Board
From: Consultant
Date: 29 June 20X8
Subject: Establishment of internal audit function

Turnbull report

The UK Turnbull report lists a number of issues that should be considered when deciding whether to establish an internal audit department that are relevant to Stoy.

Scale and complexity of operations

This has clearly increased recently with **rapid growth** meaning more products and activities, and possibly more that can go wrong. Internal audit review can act as a check on the decision-making processes, that all the **implications of the change in business** have been **fully considered**.

Number of employees

Recent increases in employee numbers are an indication of the need for **development of human resource systems**, which internal audit would wish to evaluate. If the decision was taken to outsource manufacture, although staff numbers might fall, internal audit may still be needed to assess whether systems dealt appropriately with redundancy and related issues.

Changes in organisational systems

Overall control systems will have to develop, and **internal audit** will be an important part of this change. Internal audit may be particularly needed as a check on the development of other parts of the business systems; with rapid growth, there is a danger that information systems for example may not develop in a way that is best for the company.

Changes in key risks

Changes and expansions in products and activities will bring changes in risks. There are the **risks associated with the production and sales of the new products such as the Attitude Girl range**, including production stoppages and distribution difficulties. There may also be **changes in the general risks** that Stoy faces, with possibly the **increased risk of inefficiencies and diseconomies of scale**. Internal audit can **review the adequacy** of the **overall risk management systems for** coping with these changes and carry out work on specific areas of high areas.

Problems with internal control systems

The machine breakdown has highlighted possible problems with **quality standards**. Quality control standards established in the past may now be inadequate anyway, if there has been a significant investment in new machinery.

However the current quality standards have not been followed conscientiously, and this calls into question whether other parts of the control systems are working as effectively as they should be. Internal audit should definitely investigate these systems. If internal audit recommendations can reduce the chances of a breakdown happening in future, clearly this will be a major benefit.

Cost-benefit considerations

Clearly cost-benefit considerations are significant. Fears that internal audit will interfere with operational departments may well be exaggerated, and well-directed internal audit work should **bring benefits**.

The benefits internal audit contributes may not just be finding mistakes. Internal audit's presence may **prevent problems** by deterring potential wrongdoers from carrying out frauds, owing to the probability that internal audit will detect the frauds. Internal audit should also be able to stand back and **report objectively** on the organisation. This will **significantly improve** the **overall environment** in which the business carries on and controls operate.

SPECIMEN EXAM PAPER

580

CIMA – Strategic level
Paper P3
Performance Strategy

Specimen exam paper

You are allowed three hours to answer this question paper.
In the real exam, you are allowed 20 minutes reading time before the examination begins during which you should read the question paper, and if you wish, highlight and/or make notes on the question paper. However, you will **not** be allowed, **under any circumstances**, to open the answer book and start writing or use your calculator during this reading time.
You are strongly advised to carefully read all the question requirements before attempting the question concerned (that is all parts and/or sub-questions).
Answer ALL compulsory questions in Section A.
Answer TWO of the three questions in Section B.

DO NOT OPEN THIS PAPER UNTIL YOUR ARE READY TO START UNDER EXAMINATION CONDITIONS

SECTION A – 50 MARKS

The indicative time for answering this section is 90 minutes

Answer this question

Question 1

Power Utilities

Pre-seen Case Study

Background

Power Utilities (PU) is located in a democratic Asian country. Just over 12 months ago, the former nationalised Electricity Generating Corporation (EGC) was privatised and became PU. EGC was established as a nationalised industry many years ago. Its home government at that time had determined that the provision of the utility services of electricity generation production should be managed by boards that were accountable directly to Government. In theory, nationalised industries should be run efficiently, on behalf of the public, without the need to provide any form of risk related return to the funding providers. In other words, EGC, along with other nationalised industries, was a non-profit making organisation. This, the Government claimed at the time, would enable prices charged to the final consumer to be kept low.

Privatisation of EGC

The Prime Minister first announced three years ago that the Government intended to pursue the privatisation of the nationalised industries within the country. The first priority was to be the privatisation of the power generating utilities and EGC was selected as the first nationalised industry to be privatised. The main purpose of this strategy was to encourage public subscription for share capital. In addition, the Government's intention was that PU should take a full and active part in commercial activities such as raising capital and earning higher revenue by increasing its share of the power generation and supply market by achieving growth either organically or through making acquisitions. This, of course, also meant that PU was exposed to commercial pressures itself, including satisfying the requirements of shareholders and becoming a potential target for take-over. The major shareholder, with a 51% share, would be the Government. However, the Minister of Energy has recently stated that the Government intends to reduce its shareholding in PU over time after the privatisation takes place.

Industry structure

PU operates 12 coal-fired power stations across the country and transmits electricity through an integrated national grid system which it manages and controls. It is organised into three regions, Northern, Eastern and Western. Each region generates electricity which is sold to 10 private sector electricity distribution companies which are PU's customers.

The three PU regions transmit the electricity they generate into the national grid system. A shortage of electricity generation in one region can be made up by taking from the national grid. This is particularly important when there is a national emergency, such as exceptional weather conditions.

The nationalised utility industries, including the former EGC, were set up in a monopolistic position. As such, no other providers of these particular services were permitted to enter the market within the country. Therefore, when EGC was privatised and became PU it remained the sole generator of electricity in the country. The electricity generating facilities, in the form of the 12 coal-fired power stations, were all built over 15 years ago and some date back to before EGC came into being.

The 10 private sector distribution companies are the suppliers of electricity to final users including households and industry within the country, and are not under the management or control of PU. They are completely independent companies owned by shareholders.

The 10 private sector distribution companies serve a variety of users of electricity. Some, such as AB, mainly serve domestic users whereas others, such as DP, only supply electricity to a few industrial clients. In fact, DP has a limited portfolio of industrial customers and 3 major clients, an industrial conglomerate, a local administrative authority and a supermarket chain. DP finds these clients costly to service.

Structure of PU

The structure of PU is that it has a Board of Directors headed by an independent Chairman and a separate Managing Director. The Chairman of PU was nominated by the Government at the time the announcement that EGC was to be privatised was made. His background is that he is a former Chairman of an industrial conglomerate within the country. There was no previous Chairman of EGC which was managed by a Management Board, headed by the Managing Director. The former EGC Managing Director retired on privatisation and a new Managing Director was appointed.

The structure of PU comprises a hierarchy of many levels of management authority. In addition to the Chairman and Managing Director, the Board consists of the Directors of each of the Northern, Eastern and Western regions, a Technical Director, the Company Secretary and the Finance Director. All of these except the Chairman are the Executive Directors of PU. The Government also appointed seven Non Executive Directors to PU's Board. With the exception of the Company Secretary and Finance Director, all the Executive Directors are qualified electrical engineers. The Chairman and Managing Director of PU have worked hard to overcome some of the inertia which was an attitude that some staff had developed within the former EGC. PU is now operating efficiently as a private sector company. There have been many staff changes at a middle management level within the organisation.

Within the structure of PU's headquarters, there are five support functions; engineering, finance (which includes PU's Internal Audit department), corporate treasury, human resource management (HRM) and administration, each with its own chief officers, apart from HRM. Two Senior HRM Officers and Chief Administrative Officer report to the Company Secretary. The Chief Accountant and Corporate Treasurer each report to the Finance Director. These functions, except Internal Audit, are replicated in each region, each with its own regional officers and support staff. Internal Audit is an organisation wide function and is based at PU headquarters.

Regional Directors of EGC

The Regional Directors all studied in the field of electrical engineering at the country's leading university and have worked together for a long time. Although they did not all attend the university at the same time, they have a strong belief in the quality of their education. After graduation from university, each of the Regional Directors started work at EGC in a junior capacity and then subsequently gained professional electrical engineering qualifications. They believe that the experience of working up through the ranks of EGC has enabled them to have a clear understanding of EGC's culture and the technical aspects of the industry as a whole. Each of the Regional Managers has recognised the changed environment that PU now operates within, compared with the former EGC, and they are now working hard to help PU achieve success as a private sector electricity generator. The Regional Directors are well regarded by both the Chairman and Managing Director, both in terms of their technical skill and managerial competence.

Governance of EGC

Previously, the Managing Director of the Management Board of EGC reported to senior civil servants in the Ministry of Energy. There were no shareholders and ownership of the Corporation rested entirely with the Government. That has now changed. The Government holds 51% of the shares in PU and the Board of Directors is responsible to the shareholders but, inevitably, the Chairman has close links directly with the Minister of Energy, who represents the major shareholder.

The Board meetings are held regularly, normally weekly, and are properly conducted with full minutes being taken. In addition, there is a Remuneration Committee, an Audit Committee and an Appointments Committee, all in accordance with best practice. The model which has been used is the Combined Code on Corporate Governance which applies to companies which have full listing status on the London Stock Exchange. Although PU is not listed on the London Stock Exchange, the principles of the Combined Code were considered by the Government to be appropriate to be applied with regard to the corporate governance of the company.

Currently, PU does not have an effective Executive Information System and this has recently been raised at a Board meeting by one of the non-executive directors because he believes this inhibits the function of the Board and consequently is disadvantageous to the governance of PU.

Remuneration of Executive Directors

In order to provide a financial incentive, the Remuneration Committee of PU has agreed that the Executive Directors be entitled to performance related pay, based on a bonus scheme, in addition to their fixed salary and health benefits.

Capital market

PU exists in a country which has a well developed capital market relating both to equity and loan stock funding. There are well established international institutions which are able to provide funds and corporate entities are free to issue their own loan stock in accordance with internationally recognised principles. PU is listed on the country's main stock exchange.

Strategic opportunity

The Board of PU is considering the possibility of vertical integration into electricity supply and has begun preliminary discussion with DP's Chairman with a view to making an offer for DP. PU's Board is attracted by DP's strong reputation for customer service but is aware, through press comment, that DP has received an increase in complaints regarding its service to customers over the last year. When the former EGC was a nationalised business, breakdowns were categorised by the Government as "urgent", when there was a danger to life, and "non-urgent" which was all others. Both the former EGC and DP had a very high success rate in meeting the government's requirements that a service engineer should attend the urgent break-down within 60 minutes. DP's record over this last year in attending urgent breakdowns has deteriorated seriously and if PU takes DP over, this situation would need to improve.

Energy consumption within the country and Government drive for increased efficiency and concern for the environment

Energy consumption has doubled in the country over the last 10 years. As PU continues to use coal-fired power stations, it now consumes most of the coal mined within the country.

The Minister of Energy has indicated to the Chairman of PU that the Government wishes to encourage more efficient methods of energy production. This includes the need to reduce production costs. The Government has limited resources for capital investment in energy production and wishes to be sure that future energy production facilities are more efficient and effective than at present.

The Minister of Energy has also expressed the Government's wish to see a reduction in harmful emissions from the country's power stations. (The term harmful emissions in this context, refers to pollution coming out of electricity generating power stations which damage the environment.)

One of PU's non-executive directors is aware that another Asian country is a market leader in coal gasification which is a fuel technology that could be used to replace coal for power generation. In the coal gasification process, coal is mixed with oxygen and water vapour under pressure, normally underground, and then pumped to the surface where the gas can be used in power stations. The process significantly reduces carbon dioxide emissions although it is not widely used at present and not on any significant commercial scale.

Another alternative to coal fired power stations being actively considered by PU's Board is the construction of a dam to generate hydro-electric power. The Board is mindful of the likely adverse response of the public living and working in the area where the dam would be built.

In response to the Government's wishes, PU has established environmental objectives relating to improved efficiency in energy production and reducing harmful emissions such as greenhouse gases. PU has also established an ethical code. Included within the code are sections relating to recycling and reduction in harmful emissions as well as to terms and conditions of employment.

Introduction of commercial accounting practices at EGC

The first financial statements have been produced for PU for 2008. Extracts from the Statement of Financial Position from this are shown in **Appendix A**. Within these financial statements, some of EGC's loans were "notionally" converted by the Government into ordinary shares. Interest is payable on the Government loans as shown in the statement of financial position. Reserves is a sum which was vested in EGC when it was first nationalised. This represents the initial capital stock valued on a historical cost basis from the former electricity generating organisations which became consolidated into EGC when it was first nationalised.

Being previously a nationalised industry and effectively this being the first "commercially based" financial statements, there are no retained earnings brought forward into 2008.

APPENDIX A

EXTRACTS FROM THE PRO FORMA FINANCIAL STATEMENTS OF THE ELECTRICITY GENERATING CORPORATION

Statement of financial position as at 31 December 2008

	P$ million
ASSETS	
Non-current assets	15,837
Current assets	
Inventories	1,529
Receivables	2,679
Cash and Cash equivalents	133
	4,341
Total assets	20,178
EQUITY AND LIABILITIES	
Equity	
Share capital	5,525
Reserves	1,231
Total equity	6,756
Non-current liabilities	
Government loans	9,560
Current liabilities	
Payables	3,862
Total liabilities	13,422
Total equity and liabilities	20,178

End of Pre-seen Material

Unseen material for Case Study

New investment

Following the privatisation of PU, the board are now considering the investment needed to retain and improve the productive capacity available to the company. Currently, PU operates 12 power stations which were all built over 15 years ago. Life expectancy for coal fired power stations is around 25 to 30 years. This means that all 12 power stations will need replacing within 10 to 15 years. This will be a significant capital cost for PU which will almost certainly have to be financed by borrowing or other forms of external investment.

Although the Asian country PU operates in does have coal reserves to fuel new coal fired power stations, the board are keen to investigate other methods of power generation such as gas, nuclear and more environmentally friendly alternatives such as wind and wave power. If coal fired power stations are built they will have to meet new environmental legislation in the Asian country, as well as global agreements to decrease the amount of Carbon Dioxide emissions from this type of power station. This will mean that the cost per power station will be higher in real terms than when the power stations were first built.

The non-executive directors in PU have recently identified that there is a lack of an effective Executive Information System for the Board. This means that board members cannot either monitor the current management and financial information produced within PU, or appraise new investment projects. One option to replace coal fired power stations is coal gasification. In this process, coal is mixed with oxygen and water vapour under pressure, normally underground, and then pumped to the surface where the gas can be used in power stations or converted into petrol and other similar fuels. The process has the benefit of significantly reducing carbon dioxide emissions although the technology is not widely used at present and not on any significant commercial scale.

One of the non-executive directors is aware that country Zee is a market leader in coal gasification processes. Country Zee is located in Africa; while Zee appears to be financially stable, there is some political unrest caused partly from ethnic divergence and issues of inequitable income distribution. Country Zee appears keen to retain its lead in this technology; at present the technology has only been made available to one other company in another country. The government of country Zee required this company to establish a subsidiary in Zee and manufacture the gasification equipment in Zee prior to export to the other country. This is the only method currently available to obtain the technology. To repeat the process, an initial investment will be required in Zee$, although the government guarantees to purchase the subsidiary at prevailing market prices in Zee after five years. A further requirement was that 80% of the workforce had to be drawn from the population of country Zee.

Environmental information

Legislation in the Asian country requires PU to provide environmental information each year on its activities, with specific reference to emissions of carbon dioxide from its power stations. This environmental information is collated at each power station and then forwarded to PU's head office for inclusion within PU's overall environmental report. Information from each power station is audited on a rotational basis by PU's internal audit department.

This year, power station N3 was part of the rotational audit. The internal audit department discovered significant discrepancies between the published emissions information and actual information obtained from the records maintained in the power station itself. The manager of the power station indicated that emissions were actually higher than expected due to faulty extraction filters fitted to the power station. Although PU's head office was aware of the problem, funds were not made available to rectify this. The matter was reported by the head of internal audit to the Managing Director with the recommendation that the emissions information was amended to show actual emissions.

Required

Working as a consultant to the board of PU:

(a) The board of PU needs to assess methods of power generation in preparation for replacing the existing coal fired power stations. Advise the board how to develop an Information strategy to support this objective. **(12 marks)**

(b) Evaluate the financial and other risks affecting PU if a subsidiary is established in Zee to manufacture coal gasification equipment. **(16 marks)**

(c) (i) PU's internal audit department may be asked to participate in the environmental audit of PU.

Explain the term "environmental audit" and evaluate the attributes that PU's internal audit department should have prior to carrying out this work. **(8 marks)**

(ii) There is a discrepancy in environmental returns from power station N3. Recommend the actions (apart from reporting to the Managing Director) that the internal audit department of PU should undertake regarding this situation. **(8 marks)**

(d) Discuss the extent to which false reporting of environmental information is a source of risk to PU and explain control mechanisms that may be used to avoid false reporting. **(6 marks)**

(Total = 50 marks)

SECTION B

The indicative time for answering this section is 90 minutes

Answer *two* of the three questions – 25 marks each.

Question 2

The Y company produces a range of dairy products such as yoghurts, cream and butter from one factory. The main ingredient for these products is milk, which is obtained from 27 different dairy farms (fields where cows are allowed to graze and produce milk) within a 60 km radius of the factory. Y requires that milk must be delivered within 6 hours of being obtained from the cows and that the farms themselves use "organic" principles (farming without using manmade pesticides, growth hormones etc.). Transportation systems in Y's country are good and milk is rarely delivered late.

Each farm provides a quality certificate on each batch of milk produced confirming adherence to these standards (this is important to Y although customer satisfaction surveys show Y products are sold on taste, not sourcing of ingredients).

In Y's factory, yoghurt is produced in batches. The inputs to each batch such as milk, fruit, *appropriate* bacteria and other ingredients, are recorded in the batch database showing the source of that ingredient, that is the specific farm. During production, Y's quality control department tests each batch for purity (lack of contamination from *harmful* bacteria etc) and acceptable taste, with the results being recorded in the quality control database. Any batches not meeting quality standards are rejected and destroyed. Y's costing systems have maintained a 5% failure rate in production for the last 6 years which is now well in excess of the industry average.

On completion of each batch, the quality control department again undertakes purity control and taste testing. Batches are rejected where standards are not met; a further 2% failure rate is expected at this stage.

Batches of yoghurt etc are packed on Y's premises and then despatched for sale via retail outlets such as supermarkets; Y does not sell direct to the consumer. However, Y has an excellent brand name resulting from innovative advertising and high product quality. Product reviews in magazines and news websites have always been favourable meaning that Y does not need to pay much, if any, attention to customer feedback.

Required

(a)   Evaluate the control systems in Y for the manufacture of yoghurt, recommending improvements to those systems where necessary.   (12 marks)

(b)   Explain the process of risk mapping and construct a risk map for Y. Discuss how risk mapping can be used within the Y organisation.   (13 marks)

(Total = 25 marks)

Question 3

A is a small company based in England. The company had the choice of launching a new product in either England or France but lack of funding meant that it could not do both. The company bases its decisions on Expected Net Present Value (ENPV) and current exchange rates. As a result of this methodology, and the details shown below, it was decided to launch in England (with an ENPV of £28,392) and not France (with an ENPV of £25,560).

England		*France*	
	Probability		*Probability*
Launch Costs		*Launch Costs*	
£145,000	0·1	£190,000	1·0
£120,000	0·9		
Annual Cash Flows		*Annual Cash Flows*	
£65,000	0·4	£90,000	0·5
£42,000	0·4	£70,000	0·2
£24,000	0·2	£30,000	0·3

Required

(a)   Discuss the risks associated with each launch option. Advise how these risks may be managed by the company.   (12 marks)

Company A wishes to raise 3 year £500,000 floating rate finance to fund the product launch and additional capital investments. Company A has a choice between:

Alternative A: floating rate finance at LIBOR + 1·2% or

Alternative B: fixed rate finance at 9·4%, together with an interest rate swap at a fixed annual rate of 8·5% against LIBOR with a swap arrangement fee of 0·5% flat payable up front

Required

(b)   (i)   Discuss the potential benefits and hazards of interest rate swaps as a tool for managing interest rate risk.   (8 marks)

        (ii)   Ignoring the time value of money, calculate the total difference in cost between the two alternative sources of finance available to Company A.   (5 marks)

(Total = 25 marks)

Question 4

X is an organisation involved in making business-to-business sales of industrial products. X employs a sales team of 40 representatives and assigns each a geographic territory that is quite large. Sales representatives search for new business and follow up sales leads to win new business, and maintain contact with the existing customer base.

The sales representatives spend almost all their time travelling to visit clients. The only time when they are not doing this is on one day each month when they are required to attend their regional offices for a sales meeting. Sales representatives incur expenses. They have a mobile telephone, a fully maintained company car and a corporate credit card which can be used to pay for vehicle expenses, accommodation and meals and the cost of entertaining potential and existing clients.

The performance appraisal system for each sales representative is based on the number and value of new clients and existing clients in their territory. All sales representatives are required to submit a weekly report to their regional managers which gives details of the new and existing clients that they have visited during that week. The regional managers do not get involved in the daily routines of sales representatives if they are generating sufficient sales. Consequently, sales representatives have a large amount of freedom.

The Head Office Finance department, to whom regional managers have a reporting relationship, analyses the volume and value of business won by sales representatives and collects details of their expenses which are then reported back monthly to regional managers. At the last meeting of regional managers, the Head Office Finance department highlighted the increase in sales representatives' expenses as a proportion of sales revenue over the last two years and instructed regional managers to improve their control over the work representatives carry out and the expenses they incur.

Required

(a) Explain what an internal control system is, how it relates to the control environment and its likely costs, benefits and limitations. (8 marks)

(b) Discuss the purposes and importance of internal control and risk management to the X company and recommend action that should be taken to overcome any perceived weaknesses identified in internal control and/or risk management systems. (12 marks)

(c) Recommend how substantive analytical procedures could be used in the internal audit of X's sales representatives' expenses. (5 marks)

(Total = 25 marks)

Question 1

Text references. Chapters 1 and 10 on the risk issues, Chapter 13 on information systems, Chapters 15 and 16 on internal audit.

Top tips. The first point to make in (a) has to be the link between information strategy and business strategy, particularly here the choices facing the business. Applying all three elements of the information strategy (systems, technology and management) to PU would earn you the bulk of the marks.

(b) emphasises the importance of what can be one of the overlooked areas of the syllabus. You shouldn't get trapped into thinking that the main international risks are transaction risks that will be hedged using derivatives. Longer-term risks connected with the business's international strategy will often be very important at this level, as here.

(c) may demonstrate the significance of environmental issues in this paper, although in fact more of the marks would be available for discussing internal audit considerations that would apply to any specialist area audited. Similarly (d) is about reporting risks and how to manage them, rather than being about environmental issues. The considerations would equally apply, for example to reporting to a financial services regulator.

Easy marks. There are a few easy marks for explanation of concepts scattered throughout this question.

(a) **Information strategy**

An organisation's information strategy deals with its **information needs**. It ought to support its business strategy. In PU's case, the business strategy revolves around how the coal fired power stations are going to be replaced.

The key information needs to support this strategy will therefore be analysis of the **feasibility, costs and benefits** of the various power generation options, new coal fired stations, gas, nuclear, wind and wave power. The strateg needs to set out how to **obtain and analyse this data**. An information strategy has three elements.

Information systems (IS) strategy

This deals with how the **information needs** will be **satisfied** and what systems will be required. In order to have the information it needs, PU's board needs to consider the following:

- **Employing a management accountant or specialist** in this area to obtain and analyse the data

- **Gathering information from PU's internal accounting systems** on the cost of running the current power stations, as well as any additional costs that will result from the need to comply with new legislation

- **Obtaining data on alternative methods of power generation**, which may involve contacting organisations using these methods, as well as sourcing research papers from the internet or consultants

Information technology (IT) strategy

An IT strategy deals with how the **IS strategy** will be **implemented,** specifically what investment will be made in hardware and software, and what vendor partners will be used.

PU will require the capacity to **store and analyse significant volumes of information**, comparing financial outcomes as well as scenario analysis. Investment in a data warehouse may well be appropriate.

The results of the analysis will ultimately be presented at board level for strategic decision-making, so the systems must be able to generate output in **graphical, summarised format**.

Information management (IM) strategy

The IM strategy deals with **how information will be provided to users** and stored, accessed and controlled.

As noted above, the strategy will need to ensure that the specialists dealing with the information are able to **communicate results** to the board, perhaps delivered as a type of dashboard.

Some of the information will be obtained externally, so **links to information providers** may be needed. However, the stored information will be highly sensitive. **Access** to it thus needs to be **restricted** by use of passwords, physical security etc.

(b) **Currency risks**

As PU will be investing and trading in Zee$, a different currency to its domestic one, it will face several types of currency risk.

Economic risks

Economic risk is the threat to **long-term cash flows and competitiveness** as a result of foreign exchange movements. Because the gasification equipment will be manufactured in Zee, the costs of manufacture will be in Zee$. If the Zee$ appreciates against PU's currency, costs will rise without any corresponding increase in revenue, reducing profits.

In addition, the government of Zee is prepared to buy the subsidiary after five years, but the price will be in Zee$. If the Zee$ has depreciated in those five years, the amount PU receives for the subsidiary will be less.

Translation risks

At the end of a financial year, a company must translate all assets and liabilities into its reporting currency. The risk that foreign exchange movements will **reduce the value of an asset or increase the value of a liability** is translation risk. While it does not affect cash flows, it does affect retained earnings and may affect a company's valuation.

PU will be required to consolidate its Zee subsidiary into its financial statements. If the Zee$ falls during the year, the value of the subsidiary will fall. This may **restrict PU's ability to pay dividends,** or **affect investor attitudes,** making it difficult to raise new finance.

Transaction risks

This is the risk that a transaction entered into at one rate is **settled at a different rate,** leading to a loss.

PU's subsidiary will be exporting the gasification equipment back to the home country. PU will therefore run the risk that exchange movements will mean that it ends up **paying more than it planned.** Conversely, the subsidiary will risk **receiving less than it planned**. This is only a risk for the separate entities, at group level any differences will eliminate on consolidation.

As well as currency risk, PU will face several other risks relating to the subsidiary.

Political risks

This is the risk that **government action** will have an adverse effect on an organisation. Political risk is generally higher for companies operating overseas because they are **less familiar with local politics**. Governments are also often inclined to treat overseas companies worse than domestic ones.

Zee is experiencing political unrest. The unequal income distribution may mean that workers are **more inclined to strike**. In extreme cases, instability could lead to **damage to property and equipment.**

There are risks resulting from the fact that 80% of the workforce must be drawn from the population of Zee. There may not be enough workers with **sufficient skills,** which could limit PU's ability to start production. Perhaps PU will need to pay higher wages to attract the workers, which will raise costs.

A change of government may lead to PU's subsidiary **having to trade on less favourable terms**, or even having its **assets seized.** Zee's government may also **change the tax laws,** resulting in the subsidiary paying more tax, or perhaps making it more difficult or expensive to remit funds back to its parent.

Product risks

Product risks result from the **failure of a product to perform as expected**, or be **attractive to customers**. The coal gasification process is a new technology. There is a risk that it will **not work as specified**, or will cause **unexpected environmental or other damage**. This could lead to PU having to write off its investment or pay damages or rectification costs.

Cultural risks

PU is currently focused on its domestic market and has no experience of operating internationally. It is possible that PU's **culture and management practice** will **not translate well** when it runs a business in Zee.

Trading risk

There are a number of risks resulting from the distances involved and time taken in international trade, such as **goods being lost or stolen in transit**, and **increased credit and liquidity risks** resulting from a longer working capital cycle. As PU is trading with its own subsidiary, the key risk is that the gasification equipment is damaged or stolen during transit from Zee to PU's home country.

(c)   (i)   **Environmental audit**

An environmental audit is an evaluation of how well an organisation is fulfilling its duties as a good corporate citizen in protecting the environment. It includes **reviewing compliance with internal policies and external standards and laws,** as well as ensuring that any **environmental reporting is true, fair and complete**. In PU's case, such an audit will focus on carbon dioxide emissions and PU's reporting requirements.

To carry out this work effectively, PU's internal audit department will need a number of attributes.

Independence

The internal audit function must be independent enough to **produce unbiased reports** and **resist any management pressure** to change or "water down" its findings. This should be safeguarded by **reporting to the audit committee** which, if PU is in line with best practice, will comprise independent non-executive directors.

Skills and knowledge

The staff will need to be **suitably experienced and trained** in how to carry out audits, possibly holding a professional qualification in this area. However, to carry out this assignment, they will also need a **good understanding of environmental issues** and particularly the **requirements of legislation in relation to emissions and reporting.** They will also need a good understanding of the process by which the **information is gathered and reported on** at each power station.

Authority

To carry out an effective audit, the internal auditors will need **sufficient authority to gain access to all relevant staff and records**. They will also need sufficient authority to ensure that any **recommendations** they make, for example improving controls over reporting, are **accepted** rather than ignored.

(ii) **Recommended actions for internal audit**

Report to the audit committee

As well as reporting to the Managing Director, the internal audit function will need to submit a report to the audit committee. The head of internal audit may want to meet with members of the audit committee to ensure that they **understand the issue and discuss appropriate follow-up**.

Review controls and recommend improvements

The internal auditors will want to **review the existing controls over emissions reporting,** for example the procedure for checking and sign-off. As these controls have clearly not been effective, they may want to **recommend improvements**, such as requiring an additional check and sign-off before the reports are submitted to head office.

Review prior year returns

The fact that the information submitted is incorrect will raise suspicions that prior year returns from power station N3 may also have been incorrect. Internal audit may therefore wish to carry out **checks on these returns.**

Review returns from other power stations

Assuming that the controls over reporting are similar across the different power stations, the issues at N3 may also be occurring at other power stations. The internal auditors will therefore wish to **prioritise review of other power stations' returns.** They will probably start with those stations showing better than expected figures, as this may be an indication of errors, even if they are not part of the planned rotational audit.

Planned future review

Internal audit will probably schedule a **follow-up visit** to N3 at a future date, perhaps one year ahead, to check that any **control recommendations** have been **implemented** and **returns** are now **correct.**

(d) False reporting may be a source of risk for a number of reasons.

Reputational damage

If the incorrect reporting becomes public knowledge, PU may gain a reputation for **dishonesty and poor controls**. This may impact on a number of areas of the business including **relationships with suppliers, customers and government**, and ultimately damage profitability.

Financial penalties

The breach of environmental legislation may lead to **fines** being levied, which will lead to further reputational damage as well as a direct financial cost.

Impact on control environment

A high-profile control breach in this area may lead to a general perception within PU that **controls and accurate reporting are unimportant.** The fact that head office seems complicit in this breach will make this risk more serious. This perception could impact on the **general culture and ethos** in PU and therefore undermine control effectiveness throughout the organisation.

Control mechanisms which may help avoid false reporting are as follows.

Internal audit checks

Internal auditors should substantively check reporting, as they do at present. However, rather than audit on a rotational basis, they may use **surprise visits** or focus on those stations with high risk factors, such as a history of error.

Response to errors

Management needs to **respond quickly and decisively to errors**, ensuring that they are corrected and that anyone found to have behaved unethically faces **disciplinary action.** This will send a clear signal about the importance of controls and correct reporting.

Management tone

Management needs to communicate clearly the **importance of following procedures and ethical behaviour**, reinforcing this at every opportunity, and **setting an example** in their own behaviour. The actions of head office in this case are obviously unhelpful.

Question 2

Text references. Chapters 2 and 6.

Top tips. The focus in the scenario is on a process, suggesting very clearly that you ought to think about controls over input, processing and output. The answer looks at areas where controls are non-existent (independent verification of farm certification and obtaining customer feedback), inadequate (clear hints that 5% rejection rate is unacceptably high) and inefficient (testing by Y occurs too late in the process). It's worth noting that lack of use of feedback is an important issue at various points here.

In (b) it's likely that the marks would be split fairly evenly between the description of the process, the risk map for Y and the advantages for Y. Description of one risk in each quarter of the quadrant should have earned you the marks for risk mapping for Y, provided your assessment of risk levels was reasonable. Remember that the more serious risks are likely to be due to strategic factors, factors having a major impact upon demand and major operational failures such as delays in production.

Easy marks. The description of risk mapping is core knowledge.

(a)   **Input**

Farm self-certification

Y relies on farms to certify their adherence to its quality standards. Y does not **attempt** to **verify the accuracy** of the information that farms supply.

In order to ensure that it maintains its name for sourcing organically, Y should **obtain independent evidence** of the accuracy of the certification by farms, either through carrying out testing itself or outsourcing the testing to independent examiners.

Testing before production begins

At the moment 5% of batches are **rejected** after some processing has already taken place. The problems found could have been **picked up before the production process starts**.

Y should begin the **quality testing of milk before processing starts**. This should reduce the failure rate and costs of production, and also make it easier to **trace poor quality milk back to specific suppliers**.

Processing

Lack of use of information

Although information about rejections is **recorded on the quality database**, no further use appears to be made of that information.

The information about failure should be analysed to see if there are any **patterns or common features** in the batches that have been rejected. This information should be compared with information about inputs, to see if any problems can be traced back to specific suppliers.

High rejection rate

The rate of 5% is **high by industry standards** and has **not changed over the last six years**. The cost of this processing is money wasted, and appears to have been tolerated for too long.

Earlier testing and better use of information should bring down the rejection rate. Y should also have a target each year for **continuous improvement, reducing the rate incrementally**, certainly to at **least as low as the industry average.**

Output

Testing of output

Tests on **batch completion** lead to further batches being rejected, this time after they have incurred all the costs of processing.

Again the **reasons for rejection** at this stage should be **carefully analysed.** In particular the results of output testing should be compared with the results of testing during processing, to see why batches that passed during processing were rejected at the completion of the process.

Consumer reaction

At present no attempt is made to **gauge consumer views** on a large-scale basis. Relying on old reviews may mean that Y is **slow to identify customer dissatisfaction** and **longer-term shifts in consumer tastes**.

Y should try to **obtain consumer feedback on a continuous basis,** by surveys or by forums on websites.

(b) **Risk mapping**

Risk mapping involves **organising the results of a risk assessment** by **grouping risks into families** on the basis of the **likelihood or frequency** of the risks materialising and the **severity** of the consequences if they materialise. The risk map can then be used to determine what actions should be taken:

- No action may be taken against risks identified as **low likelihood, low severity**

- Risks that are identified as **high likelihood, low severity** may be **reduced** by control procedures designed to **prevent the risks materialising** or designed to **minimise their consequences** if they do occur

- The organisation may seek to **transfer risks** that are **unlikely to materialise** but will have **severe consequences** if they do, by, for example, insuring them

- The organisation will try to **avoid high likelihood, high severity risks** by, for example, not undertaking the activities that generate these risks

		Severity	
		Low	**High**
Likelihood	**Low**	Lack of availability of milk supplies (diverse supplier base should ensure supplies maintained).	Late delivery of milk, leading to production delays and threats to quality. Customers' taste change, they no longer regard Y's products as tasty and Y fails to identify changes quickly.
	High	Farms do not supply quality certificate with milk – quality relates to adherence to organic principles about which customers care little.	Quality control procedures fail to identify problems and pass output that should fail. Customers may fall ill and Y be liable for fines and a collapse in its reputation. Unscrupulous supplier being discovered using non-organic methods, threatening Y's reputation.

Uses of risk mapping

Identifying all risks that need to be met

Analysing risks in this way emphasises the need to **take some action** in relation to all risks other than low: low risks. The process may identify risks where **insufficient action** has been taken.

Determining priorities

The risk map should help determine the **priorities for tackling risks**, with higher risks being tackled first and more resources being utilised to manage them.

Aiding board review

A risk map is important evidence for the board when it conducts **regular and annual reviews of risk**, as required by corporate governance best practice.

Strategic decision-making

Higher risks will often derive from **key strategic decisions** that the board takes. Risk mapping provides evidence for strategic decision-making, and the balancing of acceptable risk levels versus acceptable returns.

Question 3

Text references. Chapters 1, 8, 9 and 10.

Top tips. (a) is asking specifically for risks that differ between launching in France and England. For each risk, you would probably get 1 mark for identifying it, 1 mark for discussing how to manage it but it is not that easy to generate ideas from the limited details given.

In (b) A wants floating rate interest so has to pay fixed rate interest and then swap. Since you are given the amount of the loan, you need to calculate the total benefit. However the question does tell you the terms of the swap, so you don't need to work those out.

Easy marks. The benefits and drawbacks of interest rate swaps should be eight of the easiest marks in this exam.

(a) **Risks associated with product launch in England**

Launch costs

The **actual net present value** will prove significantly **lower** than the expected net present value if launch costs turn out to be the less likely possibility, £145,000.

A should identify the factors that could cause launch costs to be £145,000 and take steps to **avoid these factors materialising**, for example **tight cost control**.

Data risk

We do not know how the data for annual cash flows was compiled, for example the time period over which the probabilities were forecast. Using a **different time period** as the basis for compiling data may have led to a different decision being taken.

A should consider a range of different scenarios, including using **data predicted over different time periods and different market conditions**.

Strategic 'stop' error

By failing to launch in France, A may be committing a 'stop' error – failing to launch in a country with **better long-term potential**. Not launching in France may prevent A from achieving any more than the limited growth available in the domestic market.

A's board should carefully consider the **available strategic options**, taking into account the portfolio of risks that A faces. This should help identify other, more attractive, overseas investment opportunities that A may have.

Risks associated with product launch in France

Exchange risks

A strengthening of the € would mean that the product launch in France would be worthwhile. However if the **€ weakens against the £,** then launching in France would be the wrong decision.

A can reduce this risk by **obtaining finance in France in euros** to fund the launch of the product. This would **match costs of finance against cash flows from the product**, and thus provide a **hedge against currency movements**.

Finance risk

If A decides to raise funds in France, it may find that the finance it can obtain is **more expensive** than it would have available in England because of its better credit history in England.

A may be able to counter this risk by obtaining funding in England and then arranging a **currency swap**.

Market risks

As A is based in England, it may find it more difficult than anticipated to break into the French market if it lacks experience of it. It may not have contacts and also lack an appreciation of **different taste and cultural conditions**. A may also find it **more difficult to withdraw** from the French market once it has made the commitment to enter the market, since it may jeopardise its future chances of success abroad.

A should **reduce this risk** by **undertaking market research** and **employing French staff as agents**, to advise on the French market and to provide means of establishing sales and distribution networks.

(b) (i) **Benefits of interest rate swaps**

Transaction costs

Transaction costs are **low**, being limited to arrangement fees, and potentially much lower than the costs of terminating one loan and taking out another.

Flexibility

Swaps are **flexible**, since they can be arranged in any size.

Credit ratings

Companies **with different credit ratings** can **borrow in the market** that offers each the best deal and then swap this benefit to reduce the mutual borrowing costs. This is an example of the principle of **comparative advantage**.

Capital restructuring

Swaps allow **capital restructuring** by changing the nature of interest commitments. This is helpful if, for example, a company will find it difficult to raise finance at **favourable fixed rates**.

Risk management

Swaps can be used to **manage interest rate risk** by swapping floating for fixed rate debt if rates are expected to rise.

Hazards of interest rate swaps

Risk of default

The swap is subject to **counterparty risk,** the risk that the other party will default leaving the first company to bear its obligations, unless the contract has been guaranteed through an intermediary.

Interest rate risk

If a company takes on a floating rate commitment, it may be vulnerable to **adverse movements in interest rates**. The commitment to the swap arrangements will also mean that a company committed to a fixed rate payment **cannot take advantage of falls in interest rates**.

Costs of hedging

The company will incur the costs of **managing hedging arrangements**.

(ii) **Alternative A**

Pay interest at LIBOR + 1.2%

Alternative B

Swap

Pays to bank if swap agreed	(9.4%)
Details of swap	
Floating	(LIBOR)
Fixed (W)	8.5%
Net outcome	(LIBOR + 0.9%)

The gain is 0.3% in each of three years, total 0.9%. The 0.5% fee is payable once, therefore net gain = 0.9 % – 0.5% = 0.4%

0.4% × £500,000 = £2,000

Question 4

> **Text references.** Chapter 6 covers the main elements of internal control. Chapters 5 and 7 are also helpful on specific controls.
>
> **Top tips.** This question requires you to think beyond traditional activities. The mark scheme would give scope for different approaches.
>
> **Easy marks.** The definitions of internal control systems and control environment are pretty much straight quotations from auditing standards – however the marks are only easy if you know the definitions.

(a)

> **Top tips.** In (a) there are a lot of different elements that a definition of control can bring out. Make sure you understand how wide systems are. Benefits include improved performance as well as elimination of loss, costs of lost opportunities as well as direct expenditure. Bringing in examples from the scenario could help your answers, although the question requirements don't specify that you should.

Internal control system

The internal control system includes the **policies and procedures** adopted by the directors and management of an entity to assist in achieving their objective of ensuring the **orderly and efficient conduct of its business**.

The internal control system extends beyond those matters that relate directly to the accounting system and should **evolve over time** in response to changing risks. The internal control system consists of two main elements, the **control environment** and **control procedures**. Control procedures include operational controls, communication, reports to management and review.

Control environment

The control environment is the **overall attitude, awareness and actions of directors and management regarding internal controls** and their importance in the entity. The control environment encompasses the **management style**, and **corporate culture and values** shared by all employees. It provides the background against which the various other controls are operated.

Costs

The main costs of the internal control function are the salary costs of staff employed to operate controls, such as **internal audit or compliance staff**. Other costs include **training** and **IT investment**. The costs are also the **lost revenues** as a result of operational staff operating internal controls, such as the managers carrying out expense reviews rather than being employed on profit-making activities. There may also be **intangible costs**, such as authorisation procedures **limiting the organisation's flexibility** to respond to new business.

Benefits

The benefits of internal control are **avoidance of losses** caused by disruption of operations, assets being stolen or losing their value through neglect, also as here **reducing or eliminating unnecessary expenditure** and **improving the utilisation of resources and employee performance**.

Limitations

The main limitations of internal controls are **poor design** leading to controls being set up which are **inadequate or inappropriate**. Controls that depend on the judgement of those operating them are **vulnerable to human error**. Controls may be overridden as a result of **collusion between employees or bypassed by directors or senior managers**. Even a **well-designed control system** will be designed with **'normal' transactions or 'normal' risks** in mind and may not be able to cope with unusual transactions or unexpected occurrences.

(b)

> **Top tips**. (b) is a good example of a question part with more than one verb (discuss and recommend). You can't afford not to register the second verb and fail to recommend controls. Your answer, however, should have covered not just control of expenses but control of sales representatives' time, as the finance department raised the issue of control over work as well as expenses. Some of the controls we recommend are general, some are standard accounting system controls. Some seek to prevent problems by taking away from sales representatives the decisions over expenses, and some seek to identify problems (principally the review by regional managers).

Internal control and risk management systems

The internal control systems in X should ensure that salesman's activities are carried out in accordance with the **policies and procedures operated** by X, and that the key risks that relate to sales representatives' activities, particularly **not following policies or procedures**, are **avoided or reduced.**

Key risks

Sales representatives are an important feature of X's business. Unless X adopts an alternative B2B model, the sales force will have to be maintained. However greater control is needed for the following reasons.

Excessive costs

The risks of excessive costs include claims for **expenses not incurred**, **claims for private expenses** and **claims for excessive expenses**.

Inefficiencies

In pursuit of new customers and hence higher remuneration, sales representatives may try to **spend amounts to woo them** that are **higher than is desirable** given the chances of picking up their business or the volume of business they are likely to generate. There is also a **risk of inefficiencies** in sales representatives' practices, particularly in the distances they travel. They may be able to concentrate on smaller geographic areas each day.

Controls

Recruitment and training

Proper **references** should be obtained, and sales representatives trained in **selling techniques**.

Employment contracts

Sales representatives should have **employment contracts** detailing the behaviour expected and how their performance will be measured. There should be **disciplinary procedures** for employees who transgress.

Expense policies

Formal policies should clarify the **distinctions between business and personal expenditure**, and also what else constitutes **acceptable and unacceptable expenditure**. Policies should include recovery of expenditure charged but used for private purposes such as private motoring.

Targets

Employees should be set **budgetary targets** for expenditure and **variances** between **budgeted and actual expenditure** should be **investigated**.

More regular review of expenses

Regional managers could collect the data themselves, and be required to review expenses more regularly than they have been doing, maybe **weekly or fortnightly**. The difficulty may be that regional manager success is primarily judged by **how much** business their sales representatives have picked up, so **head office review** will continue to be required and regional managers' performance assessment should be considered (see below).

More detailed review of expenses

However regular they are, manager reviews will only be effective if managers undertake a detailed review of expenses and are prepared to take queries up with the sales representatives. Managers should review **records of all expenditure above a certain limit**, and **compare sales representatives' expenses over time and with other sales representatives under** their authority. Expenses should be **clearly related** to **customers**.

Prior authorisation

Proposed expenditure of certain types, particularly **entertainment**, above a certain limit should require prior authorisation by managers, and would have to be justified by sales representatives on the grounds of the business it was expected to generate.

Central control

Certain costs could be limited by taking decisions from sales representatives and having them **dealt with centrally**. **Hotels** for example could be booked by a single employee, who might be able to obtain discounts from hotel chains as well as limiting the hotels sales representatives can use. More generally, there could be a system of web-based expense authorisation, where sales representatives scan in receipts and invoices. They could then be authorised centrally and payment made.

You would also have scored marks if you had discussed the following controls.

Payment means

The risk of **non-existent expenses** would be **reduced by payment on invoice or by credit card settlement** rather than employee reimbursement.

Time spent with customers

Regional managers should review sales representatives' call records to see that an **acceptable volume** of calls has been made, and excessive time has not been spent on certain customers. They should monitor how successful the salesman has been in **turning potential customers into actual customers**.

Customer satisfaction

They should also check with customers to confirm their **satisfaction** with the salesman's efforts.

Performance assessment

A key control may be to change the way sales representatives, and possibly regional management, are assessed. Performance measures should be written into sales representatives' employment contracts, and should cover:

(i) **Targets for sales calls and business generated**, with assessment being made of whether the salesman has been instrumental in winning the business.

(ii) **Comparing the expenses incurred** to generate new clients and keep existing clients with the **volume of business generated**. Depending on how generous the remuneration is, this should reduce the risk that illegitimate expenses will be charged, and will encourage sales representatives not to spend excessive amounts on low volume business.

(c)

> **Top tips.** In (c) the limited number of marks suggests that your discussion needed to concentrate on reasonableness comparisons; from the scenario there is plenty of evidence available for these. A definition of analytical procedures may earn 2 marks but no more, so don't spend too much time on this.

Substantive analytical procedures

Substantive analytical procedures are comparisons of ratios, trends and patterns **over time** and **between different businesses,** for example **departments or people**. They can be used by internal audit at the planning stage, as a means of **highlighting key risk areas**. They can also be used as part of detailed audit testing to spot unusual trends, inconsistencies or areas where fraud may have taken place.

Tests at X

Auditors should examine the level of sales representatives' expenditure and consider whether expenditure levels appear reasonable and are in accordance with the **expectations of the auditors**.

(i)   **Over time**, that there are not wide variations in expenditure and they appear reasonable in relation to sales revenue

(ii)   **In comparison with other sales representatives** reporting to different regional managers. Auditors would expect the levels of certain types of expenditure to be reasonably consistent between different sales representatives

(iii)   **In the light of the sales representatives' circumstances**, for example fuel claims fairly reflecting the area the salesman chooses to travel, also the **car make** and **frequency of visits to clients**

INDEX

Note: **Key terms** and their references are given in **bold**.

Absorption costing, 217
Access control, 413
Accidental damage, 400
Accountability and audit, 60
Accounting measures, 148
Accounting risks, 237
Adaptability culture, 142
Advance fee fraud, 236
Advocacy, 99
Agency theory, 61
Analytical review, 469
Annual review of controls, 476
Anthony, 208
Anti-virus software, 418
Applications portfolio, 375
Arbitrage, 326
Arithmetical and accounting, 164
Armstrong, 144
Attributes of directors, 68
Audit committee, 80, 93, 473
Audit planning, 456
Audit sampling, 466
Audit software, 467
Audit trail, 415
Authentication, 419
Authorisation and approval, 164

Backflush costing, 224
Back-up, 415
Badaracco and Webb, 107
Balanced scorecard, 218, 382
Base currency, 311
Basel committee, 246
Bayes' strategy, 240
Benefits of internal controls, 180
Best value, 442
Bet your company culture, 31
Beta versions, 402
Beyond budgeting, 215
Bid-ask spread (bid-offer spread), 312
Bilateral netting, 320
Black-Scholes model, 277
Blocked funds, 297
Board, 87, 88, 89, 94
Board committees, 95
Board composition, 94
Board meetings, 95
Branson, Richard, 29
British Standard Code of Practice for
   Information Security Management (BS 7799),
   405
BS 7799, 405
Budget centre, 212
Budgetary slack, 213
Budgeting, 211
Business case analysis, 382
Business context, 370

Business continuity planning, 412
Business Process Re-engineering (BPR), 139
Business risk, 7, 457, 460
Business system, 123

Cadbury committee, 59, 64, 473
Call option, 345
Capital expenditure, 198
Caps, 272
Cash flow hedge, 256
Cash flow risk, 235
Cash system, 193
CDs, 416
Centralisation, 135
Centralised, 386
Certainty-equivalent approach, 239
Chain of command, 132
Chairman and Chief Executive, 87, 88, 89
Changeover arrangements, 390
Check digits, 414
CIMA's Ethical Guidelines, 98
CIMA's risk management cycle, 27
Closed loop systems, 128
Closed system, 126
CobiT, 406
COCO framework, 160
Collars, 272
Commitment, 145
Commodity price risk, 10
Commodity risks, 10
Communication with employees, 174
Company code of conduct, 104
Company secretary, 95
Competitive advantage, 301, 371
Competitor risks, 9
Compliance, 145
Compliance audit, 440
Compliance-based approach, 103
Computer Assisted Audit Techniques (CAATs),
   467
Computer fraud, 417
Computer literacy, 401
Computer support department, 410
Computer theft, 416
Confidentiality, 99
Conformance, 30, 64, 67
Consistency culture, 142
Consolidation, 34
Contingency, 411
Contingency plan, 38, 244, 411
Contingency theory, 131
Contract settlement date, 340
Contracts of employment, 147
Contractual inadequacy risks, 14
Control, 127
Control environment, 159, **161**
Control of internal audits, 472

Control procedures, 159, **162**
Control Self-Assessment (CSA), 178
Control systems, 127, 301
Control totals, 414
Controlling, 362
Core businesses, 136
Corporate codes, 102
Corporate culture, 31, 102
Corporate governance, 58, 94
Corporate governance a practical guide, 69
Corporate philosophy, 443
Correct controls, 163
COSO framework, 159
COSO's risk management model, 24
Cost accounting methods, 216
Cost centre, 211
Cost-benefit analysis, 381
Costs of internal controls, 180
Credit risk, 16, 235, 255, 293, **303**
Critical success factors, 374
Cultural control, 142
Cultural risks, 14, 293, 301
Culture, 104, **141**
Currency future, 338
Currency of invoice, 319
Currency option, 344
Currency quotes, 311
Currency risk, 12, 255
Currency swap, 350
Cybernetic control system, 127
Cybernetics, 131

Data, 362
Data capture, 363
Data integrity, 414
Data processing department, 409
Data protection, 403
Database administrator, 384
Deal and Kennedy, 31
Decentralisation, 135
Decentralised, 386
Decision Support System (DSS), 378
Decision-making, 362
Denial of service attack, 403
Departmentation, 134
Derivatives, 254, 263
Detection of fraud, 172
Dial-back security, 419
Digital envelope, 419
Digital signature, 419
Direct changeover, 425
Direct controls, 163
Direct quote, 312
Directors' remuneration, 77
Disaster planning, 410
Disaster recovery plan, 411
Disclosure, 66
Disruption risks, 16
Distribution systems, 301
Diverse businesses, 136
Diversification, 247

Division of responsibilities, 71, 74
Divisionalisation, 137
Documentation, 425
Documenting systems, 461
Double loop feedback, 128
Downside risk, 4
Due care, 99

Earl, 373
Earl's grid, 382
Earl's three leg analysis, 373
E-commerce, 372
Economic risk, 292, **294**
Edscha, 32
EFQM Excellence Model, 219
Elements of systems, 123
E-mail, 419
Embedded audit facilities, 468
Empowerment, 133
Encryption, 418
End-user computing, 410
Enron, 120
Enterprise analysis, 369
Enterprise resource planning s ystem (ERPS), 377
Enterprise risk management, 24
Environment, 125
Environmental audit, 443
Enviromental reporting, 220
Environmental risk, 10
Equity instrument, 253
E-SAC, 407
Ethical conflicts, 99
Ethics, 17, **98**
Event identification, 33
Event risks, 16
Exchange control regulations, 296
Exchange controls, 297
Exchange-traded options, 344
Executive Information System (EIS), 377
Executive Support System (ESS), 377
Expatriate staff, 302
Expectations theory of forward exchange rates, 322
Expected cash flows, 240
Expected values, 239
Expert opinion, 465
Expert system, 378
Exposure of financial assets, 34
Exposure of human assets, 35
Exposure of physical assets, 34
External audit, 42, 445
External auditors, 475
Extranet, 420, 421

Facilities Management (FM), 388
Factory quadrant, 376
Fair value hedge, 256
Familiarity, 99
Feedback, 128
Feedback control, 129

Feedforward control, 130
File conversion, 425
Finance providers' risks, 13
Financial accounting system controls, 165
Financial asset, 253
Financial control, 136
Financial control style, 136
Financial instruments, 254
Financial interests, 108
Financial liability, 253
Financial records and reporting risk, 13
Financial risk, 11
Financing risks, 234
Fire, 400
Firewall, 418
Fisher effect, 317
Flat organisation, 132
Flooding, 400, 410
Floors, 272
Forward contracts, 249
Forward exchange contract, 321
Forward exchange rate, 313
Forward rate agreements (FRAs), 267
Fraud, 168, 401, 417
Fraud and employee malfeasance risks, 16
Fraud and error, 169
Fraud risks, 169, 236
Fraudulent use of the computer system, 401
Full cost accounting, 220
Functional organisation, 136
Functional structure, 136
Fundamental principles, 98
Fundamental risk, 4
Futures, 249

Global credit crunch, 7
Goal theory, 213
Goold and Campbell, 136
Greenbury report, 64

Hackers, 402
Hacking, 402
Hampel report, 63, 64
Handy, 141
Hash totals, 414
HBOS, 6, 31, 44, 60
Health and safety risks, 15
Hedge, 318
Hedge effectiveness, 256
Hedged item, 256
Hedging, 248, 256
Hedging instrument, 256
Help desk, 385
Hierarchy, 132
Higgs report, 64, 72
High risk cultures, 31
Horizontal organisation, 139
Human relations, 213
Human resources, 202, 302
Human resources audit, 202
Human resources management, 144

Human threats, 400

IAS 32 Financial instruments: Presentation and disclosure, 253
IAS 39 Financial instruments: Recognition and measurement, 253
Identity and values guidance, 107
IFRS 7 Financial instruments: Disclosures, 253
IFRS 9 Financial instruments, 257
Import quotas, 296
Inadequate systems risks, 16
Independent person (the auditor), 443
Indirect quote, 312
Inducements, 109
Information, 362
Information as a commodity, 368
Information Centre (IC), 385
Information management, 367
Information Management (IM) strategy, 367, 370
Information requirements of directors, 175
Information society, 368
Information system, 362, 367
Information Systems (IS) strategy, 369
Information systems department, 383
Information technology, 367
Information Technology (IT) strategy, 369
Information Technology Infrastructure Library (ITIL), 383
Information value, 368
Inherent risk, 458
Input controls, 163, 414
Input fraud, 401
Inputs, 124
Insourcing, 392
Integrated Test Facility (ITF), 468
Integrity, 99
Integrity controls, 163, 414
Integrity-based programmes, 104
Interest rate futures, 268
Interest rate option, 271
Interest rate parity, 316
Interest rate risk, 12, 255, **264**
Interest rate swaps, 279
Internal audit, 42, 96, **436**, 444, 474
Internal audit – a guide to good practice for internal auditors and their customers, 438
Internal audit reports, 472
Internal control, 79, 158, 474
Internal Control Evaluation Questionnaires, 461
Internal control frameworks, 159
Internal Control Questionnaires, 461
Internal strategies, 252
International credit risk management, 303
International Fisher effect, 317
Internet, 371, 402, 418
Internet risks, 402
Intimidation, 99
Intranet, 420
Inventory system, 196
Investigation of fraud, 173

Investment appraisal, 218, 244
Investment centre, 211
Investment risk, 13
Investment workstation, 379
Involvement culture, 142
IS/IT Strategy, 370
ISA 315 Identifying and assessing risks, 464
ISA 500 Audit evidence, 463
ISA 520 Analytical procedures, 469
ISACA, 406
ISO 14001, 443
IT strategy, 373

Job evaluation, 145
Judgement of outsiders, 148
Just-in-time (JIT), 221
Just-in-time production, 221
Just-in-time purchasing, 221

Kaizen, **224**
King report, 58, 65, 67, 94
Kingfisher, 266
Knowledge management risk, 15
Knowledge Work Systems (KWS), 379
Knowledge Workers, 379

Lam, James, 43
Laptop, 416
Leads and lags, 320
Lean management accounting, 222
Legal risks, 14, 299, 300
Legal, political and cultural risks, 14
Letters of credit, 303
Life cycle costing, 222
Lightning and electrical storms, 400
Limit checks, 415
Liquidity risk, 16, 234, 255
Lobbying, 121
Local managers, 302
Logistics, 200
Logistics audit, 200
London Stock Exchange, 69
Loop systems, 128
Loss control, 38
Loss reduction, 38
Low risk cultures, 31

Manageable businesses, 136
Management, 164, 371
Management accounting
   historical development, 206
Management accounting function, 224
Management accounting systems, 206
Management audit, 442
Management charges, 298
Management control, 208
Management control information, 209
Management fraud, 236
Management information, 371

Management Information Systems (MIS), 376, **378**
Management of internal audit, 449, 472
Management performance measures, 148
Management review of internal controls, 476
Managerial performance, 148
Market risk, 12, 235, 255
Marketing, 201
Marketing audit, 201
Marks and Spencer, 71
Matching receipts and payments, 319
Mathematical models, 465
Matrix organisation, 137
McFarlan and McKenney, 375
Media, 301
Microsoft, 102
Mintzberg, 131
Mission culture, 142
Money market hedge, 324
Morris, Glynis, 21
Motivation, 144
Multilateral netting, 320
Multi-tier boards, 77

Natural threats, 400
Negative feedback, 129
Negative risks, 4
Netting, 320
Nomination committee, 68
Non-audit services, 93
Non-business risk, 7
Non-executive directors, 74
Non-financial controls, 162
Non-financial measures, 148
Non-tariff barriers, 296
Notebook, 416

OAS, 380
Objectives, 98
Objectives of internal audit, 436
Objectives of systems, 123
Objectivity, 99
OECD Principles of Corporate Governance 2004, 66
Off balance sheet transactions, 93
Office Automation System (OAS), 380
Off-line testing, 424
Open system, 126
Operational audit assignments, 441
Operational audit planning, 457
Operational control, 208
Operational control information, 210
Operational controls, 166
Operational information, 210, 364
Operational planning, 209
Operational risk, **8**
Operations control, 385
Option forward exchange contracts, 322
Option premiums, 350
Options, 250
Organisation, 164

Organisation culture, 141
Organisation for Economic Co-operation and
    Development (OECD), 66
Organisation structure, 134, 212
Organisational information requirements, 373
Organisational risk, 16
Output controls, 164, 415
Output fraud, 401
Outputs, 124
Outsourcing, 140, 388
Over the counter (OTC) options, 344
Ownership and management, 66
Oxfam, 18

PA Consulting Group, 397
Parallel running, 426
Parsons generic strategies for IS, 375
Participation in budgeting, 213
Particular risk, 4
Partner rotation, 93
Passwords, 413
Performance, 30, 64, 67
Performance agreements, 148
Performance management activities., 148
Performance measurement, 210, 362
Performance measures, 217
Performance Practitioners, 299
Performance-related rewards, 149
Personnel, 165
Personnel controls, 408
Phased changeover, 426
Physical, 164
Physical access control, 414, 429
Physical damage, 400
Physical risk, 15
Physical threats, 410
Pilot operation, 426
Planning, 362
Political risk, 14, 235, 293, **295**
Pooling, 266
Poor customer service, 17
Population, 466
Portable, 416
Positive feedback, 129
Post-completion audit, 203
Post-implementation review, 426
Prevent controls, 163
Prevention of fraud, 171
Principles vs rules, 63
Probability distribution, 240
Probity risk, 17
Process culture, 31
Process risk, 8
Processes, 124
Processing controls, 163, 415
Processing fraud, 401
Procurement, 201
Procurement audit, 201
Product risks, 10, 293, 299
Professional behaviour, 98
Professional competence, 99

Profit centre, 211
Program testing, 424
Project team, 422
Property risks, 15
Public interest, 98
Public Oversight Board, 92
Purchases and expenses system, 188
Purchasing power parity, 316
Pure risk, 4
Put option, 345
Pyramid scheme frauds, 237

Quality of control, **458**

Range checks, 415
Ratio analysis, 470
Reasonableness tests, 471
Reference currency, 311
Regression analysis, 243
Relationship between external and internal
    audit, 447
Remuneration, 77, 95
Remuneration committee, 78
Remuneration policy, 89
Reporting on corporate governance, 80
Reporting risks, 13
Reputation risk, 17
Research, 465
Research and development audit, 203
Resource wastage risk, 16
Responsibility accounting, 211
Revenue expenditure, 198
Risk, 4, 41
Risk acceptance, 40
Risk analysis, 33, 240, 457
Risk and return, 5
Risk and uncertainty, 5
Risk appetite, 28
Risk architecture, 27
Risk assessment, 33
Risk aversion, 30
Risk avoidance, 38
Risk categorisation, 18
Risk conditions, 32
Risk culture, 28
Risk diversification, 39
Risk formula, 458
Risk hedging, 39
Risk identification, 32
Risk management, 95, 167, 437
Risk management cycle, 27
Risk management group, 42
Risk manager, 43
Risk map, 36
Risk monitoring, 259
Risk policy statement, 41
Risk pooling, 39
Risk prioritisation, 35
Risk quantification, 34
Risk reduction, 5
Risk retaining, 40

Risk register, 37
Risk reporting, 47, 48
Risk review, 45
Risk sharing, 40, 252
Risk specialists, 43
Risk thermostat, 30
Risk toleration, 30
Risk transfer, 40, 253
Risk-based audits, 440
Risks of fraud, 401
Rockart, 374
Royalty, 298
RSM Robson Rhodes, 69

SAC, 407
Safeguards, 100
Sales system, 186
Sarbanes-Oxley Act, 65, 92
Scenario building, 244
Security, 404, 410
Security policy, 407
Segregation of duties, 164
Self-interest, 99
Self-review, 99
Sensitivity analysis, 238
Service bureaux, 388
Service Level Agreement (SLA), 390
Service Level Contract (SLC), 390
Shared service centre, 386
Shareholders, 81
Single loop control, 128
Smith report, 64
Social audits, 443
Social risks, 10
Social systems, 126
Software piracy, 416
Speculative risk, 4
Spot rate, 310
Stakeholder risks, 10
Stakeholder theory, 62
Stakeholders, 18, 66, 82
Standard costing, 217
Standards for internal audit and ethical
    considerations, 448
Standby hardware facilities, 412
Steering committee, 384, 422
Stewardship theory, 61
Stock Exchange requirements, 90
Strategic analysis, 382
Strategic analysis approach, 369, 374
Strategic audit planning, 456
Strategic control, 136
Strategic control style, 136
**Strategic Enterprise Management Systems
    (SEMS), 377**
Strategic grid, 375
Strategic information, 363
Strategic level information systems, 367, 376
Strategic management accounting, 209
Strategic planning, 136, **208**
Strategic planning information, 209

Strategic planning style, 136
Strategic quadrant, 375
Strategic risk, 7
Strategic scorecard, 69
Strode's College, 42
Subjective measures, 148
Substantive procedures, 463
Subsystems, 125
Sufficient appropriate audit evidence, 463
Sufficient expertise, 108
Supervision, 164
Supply risks, 10
Support centre, 385
Support quadrant, 376
Sustainability, 96
Swap, 251, 350
Swaptions, 283
System, 123
System boundary, 125
System objectives, 123
System testing, 424
Systems audit, 439
Systems Control and Review File (SCARF), 468
Systems development life cycle, 421
Systems development risks, 404
Systems integration, 388, 390
Systems integrity, 400, **414**
Systems risks, 16

Tactical audit planning, 457
Tactical information, 209, 363
Tactical planning, 209
Tactics, 209
Tall and flat organisations, 132
Tall organisation, 132
Target costing, 223
Targets, 123
Tariffs, 296
Tate and Lyle, 266
Technical manual, 425
Technology risks, 14
Teeming and lading, 236
Tendering, 389
Term currency, 311
Test data, 468
Testing plan, 423
Testing strategy, 423
Three Es, 443
Three legs of IS strategy development, 373
Tight and loose HRM, 144
Time share, 388
Total Quality Management (TQM), 221
Tough-guy macho culture, 31
Trade risk, 15
Traded interest rate options, 273
Trading limits, 259
Trading risk, 15, 302
Training, 425
Training and learning, 147
Training staff, 175
Transaction cost economies, 224

Transaction costs, 420
Transaction exposure, 317
Transaction Processing Systems (TPS), 380
Transaction risk, 292
Transactions, 362
Transactions audits, 439
Transfer pricing, 218
Translation risk, 292, **295**
Transparency, 66
Treasury function, 246
Treasury management, 246
Trend and relationship analysis, 471
Turnaround quadrant, 375
Turnbull committee, 64, 79, 158, 178, 436, 476, 478

UK Corporate Governance Code, 87
Upward appraisal, 148
User acceptance testing, 425
User manual, 425
User requirements, 382

User satisfaction surveys, 466

Valuation of options, 277
Value at risk, 240
Value for money, 441
Value for money audit, 441
Value of information, 368
Virgin, 29
Virgin Galactic, 29
Virtual reality systems, 380
Virus, 403, 418

Wages system, 190
Water, 400
Water damage, 410
Whistleblowing, 93, 173
Woolworths, 30
Work hard, play hard culture, 31

Notes

Notes

Notes

Review Form & Free Prize Draw – Paper P3 Performance Strategy (6/10)

All original review forms from the entire BPP range, completed with genuine comments, will be entered into one of two draws on 31 January 2011 and 31 July 2011. The names on the first four forms picked out on each occasion will be sent a cheque for £50.

Name: _____   Address: _____

_____

_____

How have you used this Study Text?
(Tick one box only)

☐ Home study (book only)

☐ On a course: college _____

☐ With 'correspondence' package

☐ Other _____

Why did you decide to purchase this Study Text? *(Tick one box only)*

☐ Have used BPP Texts in the past

☐ Recommendation by friend/colleague

☐ Recommendation by a lecturer at college

☐ Saw information on BPP website

☐ Saw advertising

☐ Other _____

Which BPP products have you used?

Text	☑	Success CD	☐
Kit	☐	i-Pass	☐
Passcard	☐	Interactive Passcard	☐

During the past six months do you recall seeing/receiving any of the following?
(Tick as many boxes as are relevant)

☐ Our advertisement in *Financial Management*

☐ Our advertisement in *Pass*

☐ Our advertisement in *PQ*

☐ Our brochure with a letter through the post

☐ Our website www.bpp.com

Which (if any) aspects of our advertising do you find useful?
(Tick as many boxes as are relevant)

☐ Prices and publication dates of new editions

☐ Information on Text content

☐ Facility to order books off-the-page

☐ None of the above

Your ratings, comments and suggestions would be appreciated on the following areas.

	Very useful	Useful	Not useful
Introductory section	☐	☐	☐
Chapter introductions	☐	☐	☐
Key terms	☐	☐	☐
Quality of explanations	☐	☐	☐
Case studies and other examples	☐	☐	☐
Exam skills and alerts	☐	☐	☐
Questions and answers in each chapter	☐	☐	☐
Fast forwards and chapter roundups	☐	☐	☐
Quick quizzes	☐	☐	☐
Question Bank	☐	☐	☐
Answer Bank	☐	☐	☐
Index	☐	☐	☐

Overall opinion of this Study Text	Excellent ☐	Good ☐	Adeqate ☐	Poor ☐

Do you intend to continue using BPP products?   Yes ☐   No ☐

The BPP Learning Media author of this edition can be e-mailed at: nickweller@bpp.com

Please return this form to: Nick Weller, CIMA Publishing Manager, BPP Learning Media Ltd, FREEPOST, London, W12 8BR

Review Form & Free Prize Draw (continued)

TELL US WHAT YOU THINK

Please note any further comments and suggestions/errors below

Free Prize Draw Rules

1   Closing date for 31 January 2011 draw is 31 December 2010. Closing date for 31 July 2011 draw is 30 June 2011.

2   Restricted to entries with UK and Eire addresses only. BPP Learning Media Ltd employees, their families and business associates are excluded.

3   No purchase necessary. Entry forms are available upon request from BPP Learning Media Ltd. No more than one entry per title, per person. Draw restricted to persons aged 16 and over.

4   Winners will be notified by post and receive their cheques not later than 6 weeks after the relevant draw date.

5   The decision of the promoter in all matters is final and binding. No correspondence will be entered into.